BIOLOGY
The Science of Life

Biology

THE
SCIENCE
OF
LIFE

GENERAL LEARNING PRESS

SCOTT, FORESMAN AND COMPANY

A LEOGRYPH BOOK

SARAH M. PARKER
Project Editor

SHARON RULE
Art Editor

EDMÉE FROMENT
Design

STEVAN A. BARON
Art and Production Director

EILEEN MAX
Production Manager

THE CLARINDA COMPANY
Composition, Aster

KEITH LONG
Cover design, chapter opening art, feature background art

Copyright 1977 SILVER BURDETT COMPANY

Manufactured in the United States of America

Published simultaneously in Canada

Library of Congress Catalog Card Number 76-26813

ISBN 0-382-18280-4

For information write to:

General Learning Press
250 James St., Morristown, N.J. 07960

Contents

Patterns
of
Maintenance
and
Regulation

Patterns of Reproduction and Development

Patterns of Change

CONTENTS   **xi**

Interacting with the Environment

24. RESOURCES AND POLLUTION   505

Biogeochemical Cycles. The water cycle—The carbon cycle—The nitrogen cycle—Phosphorus: a mineral cycle
Pollution. Pests and pesticides—Air pollution—Water pollution—PCBs
Population Ecology. From percentages to people—Populations and pollution
Summary
Review questions

Preface

Every college student and instructor must at one time or another have indulged in a wistful pipe dream. It is the dream of finding the perfect textbook—one that is appealing to the eye and covers the material soundly and with intellectual integrity, but yet manages to be clear and comprehensible. While it would probably be inviting thunderbolts from on high to claim that we have achieved that perfect textbook, this has at least been our aim.

Biology: The Science of Life covers all of the topics normally included in an introductory biology course, plus a few more that instructors can use as they see fit. The style is lively and readable, and difficult subjects such as biochemistry and genetics are explained in clear, step-by-step, logical fashion. Important terms are set in boldface to catch the reader's attention, and new terms are explained as soon as they are introduced.

Summaries and review questions are provided at the end of each chapter, to help students test their understanding of the material—not merely the recall of facts, but the comprehension of what the facts mean. A glossary of important terms appears at the end of the book, along with an annotated list of scholarly and popular readings. In addition, the text is supplemented by more than four hundred illustrations, most in full color, which help to clarify difficult points and also to keep students aware of the fact that biology is not merely a collection of cold abstractions but is tangible, breathing life.

Two features should be especially attractive to the introductory student. Each chapter contains a two-page essay on some animal or plant—ostrich, octopus, bristlecone pine, sperm whale, the world's only known albino gorilla—describing its appearance, habits, special adaptations to its environment, and the things that render it, perhaps, amazing or amusing to a human viewer. There is also, in each chapter, a shorter feature dealing with some current topic related to health, medicine, or agriculture—for example: Is organic farming practical? Can antibiotics be killers? Will an antipregnancy vaccine soon be on the market?

Throughout the preparation of this text, it has been our assumption that biology does not have to be "made interesting" to the student. It *is* interesting by its very nature and by its relevance to pressing questions of individual and social human life. What is needed—and what we have tried to do—is to clear away the barriers and let that fascination come through.

Organization

The book is divided into five major sections, organized around major life functions and the structures that serve them.

Part I: Patterns of Structure and Function. The three chapters in this section deal with the structure and function of cells and with elementary biochemistry—atomic structure, molecular bonding, the principal types of organic compound, and the energy reactions of photosynthesis and cellular respiration. Numerous diagrams help to clarify the various structures and processes, and a foundation is laid for understanding the cellular activities that underlie the larger activities of organisms.

Part II: Patterns of Maintenance and Regulation. In the seven chapters of this section, the principal physiological systems are discussed—digestion, transport, gas exchange, support and locomotion, the various aspects of homeostasis, and hormonal and nervous system regulation. Animals and plants are treated together, to bring out the unity of life across taxonomic divisions. Since the students' particular interest, however, is likely to be in their own species, special attention is given to each system as it appears in humans.

Part III: Patterns of Reproduction and Development. In these four chapters, the outlook widens from the maintenance of individual organisms to the processes by which they reproduce and assure the continuance of their kind. Chapter 11 surveys various past and present theories of the first origin of life—assessing probabilities rather than making final assertions—and then goes on to discuss the basic processes of cellular reproduction through mitosis and meiosis. The following three chapters build on this with an examination of reproduction and the stages of development in plants and animals. Again, human patterns are given particular attention.

Part IV: Patterns of Change. Here the outlook broadens again, from the reproduction of individuals to the means by which characteristics are inherited and species are changed. Classical genetics is discussed first, with numerous diagrams; then the molecular structure of the gene is considered, and how the cell operates to translate coded genetic instructions into working substances and structures needed by the organism. With this cellular and molecular basis established, the next three chapters consider the principles and probable history of population variation and species evolution. Pre-Darwinian theories of evolution are presented objectively, in the contexts that made them seem reasonable and probable to their proponents; Darwinian natural selection is then presented as the theory that at present seems to offer the most satisfactory explanation of the observed facts. The last chapter in the section deals with taxonomy—the reasons for taxonomic classifications and the major phyla according to the Whittaker five-kingdom system.

Part V: Interacting with the Environment. Today we are aware, as perhaps never before since the modern age began, of the dependence of all living creatures on their environment—an environment that includes the fellow members of their own species, the members of other species, and the nonliving world of earth, water, air, and the airless space beyond. These last four chapters, therefore, deal with relationships on this level. Subjects include the means by which animals receive and communicate information, their patterns of individual and social behavior, the ecological interactions by which they fit into their living and nonliving surroundings, and finally the pressing questions of finite resources and human destruction thereof by wastage and pollution.

Acknowledgments

It is impossible to cite by name all the persons whose labors are essential to creating a book of this scope. Appreciation is extended to all those who contributed their talents to various parts of the manuscript, reviewed and criticized chapters, and attended to the thousand details of art and production that make the difference between an inviting and a dreary-looking final product. We would especially like to thank the reviewers who are listed opposite the title page. Their criticisms and suggestions were invaluable to us in the preparation of the final manuscript. They are not, however, responsible for any errors of fact or interpretation that may remain. Special thanks also go to those who are listed on the copyright page and to Karen Judd, Dan Liberatore, Charity Scott, Barbara Tokay, Jeff Cooper, and Debbie Daly.

Structure and Function of Cells

Biology—the science of life. Ever since people first began to be aware of life, they have been fascinated by the puzzles it presents. What makes a rabbit different from a rock? Why do living things die? How does a baby come to exist in a woman's womb? How is the life of a plant different from that of an animal? Sheep and goats can live on grass, so why can't wolves and lions do the same? Do fish breathe? How does a caterpillar become a butterfly? The questions are endless, but finally they are all parts of perhaps two main questions: What is the world, and what is our place in it? The science of biology is an attempt to find some answers to those questions.

Life can be studied at many levels. Its smallest unit is the individual cell, on which we shall focus in these first chapters. Its largest unit, so far as we yet know, is the whole interrelated complex of living beings associated with the planet Earth. In the final two chapters we shall examine some of the relationships of living things and their environment. We shall also note some of the dangers that arise when these relationships are ignored.

Between these levels, there are others. Cells work together in a variety of ways. Living organisms contain many structures and systems, each of which has its characteristic, important function. Individuals interact with other individuals of their own kind—in food-getting, in attack and defense, in play, in reproduction.

Furthermore, there are questions of history—how life began, and how it came to be as it is today. This, too, is the province of the biologist.

The practical applications of biological

knowledge seem to be virtually unlimited. Particularly in medicine and agriculture, dramatic advances have been made in our own time as a result of biological research. "Miracle" wheat and rice, polio vaccine, organ transplants—these are only a few of the achievements. Each achievement raises new questions—questions of what we can do and, increasingly, questions of what we ought to do.

Biology, then, is not only the study of what life is and how it works. It is also the study of how, through understanding and cooperating with natural processes, our own human living can be enriched. In this sense, too, biology at its best is truly the science of life.

THE CELL

It is impossible to credit any one person with the discovery of the cell. The early Greeks had speculated that living matter must be composed of tiny, similar particles of some sort. Scientists and philosophers who came after them kept the idea alive. But no one could do much more than speculate. Such particles, if they existed, were far too small to be seen with the naked eye. Only after microscopes became available, in the seventeenth century, was it possible to look for them.

Many people were looking—not necessarily for cells, but for all the tiny things that could now be seen, and that had never been seen before. The Dutchman Antonie van Leeuwenhoek, beginning in the 1670s, turned up all sorts of interesting objects with his very simple microscope. He observed blood cells, sperm, and an assortment of microscopic organisms, which he called "animalcules." Even earlier, in 1665, Robert Hooke in England cut slices of cork with the knife he used for trimming his quill pens, and examined them under the microscope. In the slices he saw row upon row of tiny, box-like chambers, separated by thin walls. The chambers reminded him of small rooms—like jail cells, or the cells in which monks lived in monasteries. So he called them "cells." (Actually, they were not cells. Rather, they were walls enclosing spaces that had once contained living cells.) At about the same time, a fellow Englishman, Nehemiah Grew, discovered living cells in plants. The Italian Marcello Malpighi, another seventeenth-century observer, found them in animals. By 1759 a German naturalist, C. F. Wolff, felt justified in stating that all organisms are made up of cells as their smallest units.

However, the matter was not settled to everyone's satisfaction, even yet. Many scientists still doubted whether cells were really so important. For that matter, were they really there at all? The microscopes of the time could not show them clearly enough, and it was impossible to be sure. So the controversy went on.

By the nineteenth century, more evidence was in hand. Things were becoming clearer. In 1802 the French investigator Mirbel suggested that plants were:

. . . wholly formed of a continuous cellular membranous tissue. Plants are made up of cells, all parts of which are in continuity and form one and the same membranous tissue.[1]

In 1824 another Frenchman, Dutrochet, concluded from his research that the cell was indeed the basic unit of structure in both plants and animals.

All organic tissues are actually globular cells of exceeding smallness, which appear to be united only by simple adhesive forces; thus all tissues, all animal [and plant] organs, are actually only a cellular tissue variously modified. This uniformity of finer structure proves that organs actually differ among themselves merely in the nature of the substances contained in the . . . cells of which they are composed.[2]

Other scientists were coming to similar conclusions, and making further discoveries. Theodor Schwann and Matthias Schleiden,

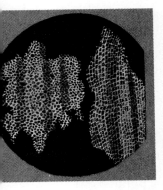

Figure 1-1. Drawing of cork cells by Robert Hooke. In this case Hooke was really seeing the empty spaces which had once contained living cells.

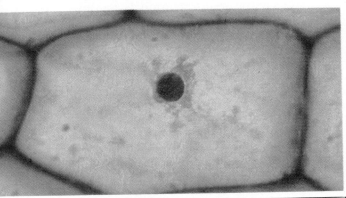

Figure 1-2. A typical plant cell. Note the clearly defined nucleus.

Figure 1-3. Animal cells. These cells from the lining of a dog's trachea possess hair-like cilia, which help to filter the air as it passes toward the dog's lungs.

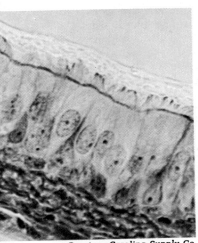

Courtesy Carolina Supply Co.

in the 1830s, are credited with recognizing that the cell was more than a passive structural unit. It was an active, functional unit as well. Things happened in cells that had an influence on what happened in the organisms they were part of. This, of course, made it even more important to understand how the cell was constructed, and what went on inside it.

In 1845 it was discovered that not all cells were packed together with other cells in larger organisms. Some could function on their own. This was shown by the researches of Karl von Siebold, a German biologist, who had been studying microscopic aquatic organisms. He recognized that many of these organisms were single cells, living separately from each other. Von Siebold's discovery extended the cell theory and made it truly universal. Now cells could be regarded as both the building blocks of plants and animals, and also the units common to all forms of microscopic life. The cell could be considered the universal component of all life.

The recognition that some organisms may be single cells suggests something else. Even the simplest organism must perform a number of functions if it is to live. For instance, it must take in nourishment and get rid of wastes. To do this, it often must move around. It must also reproduce itself, if the species is to continue. If a single cell is able to do all these things, this suggests that it has some "machinery" for doing them— some specialized smaller structures inside itself. In fact, such structures—called **organelles**—do exist. When the cell theory was first accepted, it was impossible to see many of them. Microscopes and microscopic techniques were not yet good enough. But today we can see many of the organelles, and much has been learned about what they do and how. The more important organelles will be described later in this chapter.

Where do cells come from?
By the middle of the nineteenth century, cer-

tain statements about cells were generally accepted by biologists. It was agreed that all forms of life are made of cells, and that there are many different types of cell. Now, though, another question was being raised. Where do cells come from?

This was just one part of a much larger question: "Where does life come from?" People had been debating this question for centuries, and the debate has not really ended yet. In the mid-1800s it was at its peak. Did all life have to come from other life? Or did some life originate spontaneously from nonliving matter?

In particular, where did microorganisms come from—those incredibly tiny, single-celled creatures that could be seen only under a microscope? Everyone knew that cats came from other cats, and oak trees from acorns. Yet you seemed to be able to get microorganisms without having other microorganisms to start with. For instance, if you boiled a flask of beef broth long enough, you could kill all the microorganisms in it. But then, if you let the flask stand, you would find in it a whole new crop of microorganisms, very much alive. Where did they come from? How did they get there?

The answers to these questions came primarily from the work of a French chemist, Louis Pasteur (1822–1895). Pasteur had gotten involved with microorganisms when he was asked to discover why wine often "spoiled" and turned to vinegar. In his investigation, he found millions of microorganisms in the "spoiled" wine. He showed that these microorganisms caused the "spoilage." From his research, he developed the process that we now call pasteurization. In this process, the wine is heated to kill the microorganisms, and spoilage is prevented. Pasteur also went one step further, and found the "good" microorganisms that could be added to grape juice to produce wine without getting vinegar.

Such research, of course, brought Pasteur into the thick of the "where does life come from?" debate. He considered the possibilities and set out to find some answers.

First, he put beef broth into flasks and sealed the flasks, so no air could get in or out. Then he boiled the broth long enough to kill any microorganisms it contained, and allowed the flasks to stand for a while. The broth remained clear, implying that it contained no microorganisms. This, said Pasteur, showed that microorganisms could not magically appear where none were present already. They had to get in from outside—probably by being carried on dust particles in the air.

Pasteur's opponents, though, pointed out a weakness in the demonstration. By sealing the flasks, Pasteur had cut off the oxygen supply to the broth. Suppose the broth, or the air, contained an "active principle" that was needed to generate microorganisms. Such an active principle might easily be destroyed by the heat of boiling and the lack of oxygen. Could Pasteur show that this was not what had happened?

Pasteur then designed an experiment that has become a classic. He put some more beef broth in flasks. Then he heated the necks of the flasks and "drew them out" into long, thin, curved shapes, with very small openings. He boiled the broth and let the flasks stand. They were not sealed. The air and any "active principle" in it could get into them and reach the broth. But dust particles could not. They would be trapped in the long, curving necks of the flasks. So if any microorganisms appeared in the broth, they could not have been carried in, but would have to have been produced by spontaneous generation. None did appear. Growth of microorganisms began only when Pasteur tipped the flasks. This allowed some of the broth to come into contact with the dust—and microorganisms—that were trapped in the neck of the flask. Thus Pasteur showed that spontaneous generation did not cause the appearance of microorganisms where none had been before.

Rudolph Virchow, a German scientist who lived at the same time as Pasteur, was also interested in the question of spontaneous generation. Like Pasteur, he was a

Figure 1-4. Pasteur's flasks. With these flasks, which he designed himself, Pasteur helped to disprove the concept of spontaneous generation.

Figure 1-5. Cell division. These two new daughter cells have been formed by fission of a single parent cell.

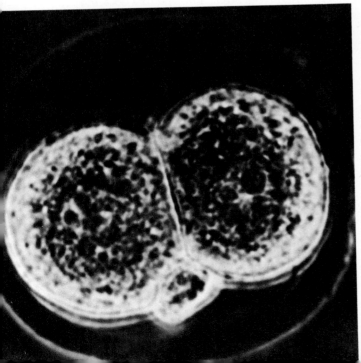

pioneer in cellular research. Pasteur had shown that microorganisms come from other microorganisms. Virchow widened this to the more all-embracing idea that "life comes from life." His concept is honored in biological literature as **Virchow's principle.**

Where a cell arises, there a cell must have been before, even as an animal can come from nothing but an animal, a plant from nothing but a plant. Thus in the whole series of living things there rules an eternal law of continuous development. There is no discontinuity nor can any developed tissue be traced back to anything but a cell.[3]

Usually Virchow's principle is stated, "every cell must come from another cell," or "every cell from a cell."

As usual, the answer to one question led to a new question. If all life comes from life, and every cell from a cell, how do they do it? An answer to this was suggested by the work of Walther Flemming, a younger contemporary of Virchow. He was a German biologist who studied the tissues of rapidly growing salamander larvae. He killed specimens, sliced the tissues very thin, and observed them under the microscope. In examining them, he noticed that many seemed to have been "caught in the act" of producing new cells. How were they doing it?

Basically, cells produce new cells by dividing. One cell divides and becomes two. These two cells grow to a specific size and then divide to become four cells, and so on. Thus, **cell division** is a process of multiplying. In unicellular (one-celled) organisms this results in reproduction. In multicellular (many-celled) organisms it may result in growth of the organism, or in replacement of damaged or worn-out cells.

THE TOOLS OF STUDY

The discoveries about the cell were tied into the development of tools to see with. The chief of these, of course, is the **microscope.** It is easy to forget how much microscopes have improved since Leeuwenhoek first looked at his "animalcules." The microscope used by a first-year biology student today is better than those that were available to research biologists even in the early twentieth century.

Microscopes are needed because the human eye can distinguish only objects that are at least 100 microns in size. (A micron is one one-thousandth of a millimeter, and there are over 25,000 microns in an inch.) Anything smaller than this will look blurred. With an ordinary microscope, called a light microscope, we can distinguish objects as small as 0.2 microns in size. This is the best we can do. Anything smaller than 0.2 microns will look blurred, because 0.2 microns is the smallest wavelength of light our eyes can perceive. But there are many structures smaller than this. Before they could be studied, microscopes had to be developed that used something other than light waves to produce an image.

Another problem in studying cells is that most cells cannot simply be taken from their tissues and put under the microscope. A good deal of preparation is needed first. The tissue must be stained with some sort of dye to make the structures more visible. By the time all this has been done, does the cell still look the same as it did when it was alive? As we shall see, scientists have argued for years about certain structures seen in cells under the microscope. Were such structures really to be found in living cells? Or were they **artifacts**—that is, flaws that were accidentally created when the tissue was prepared for study? Some of these arguments could not be settled until the living tissue itself could be studied. For this, new microscope designs were needed.

Improvements in the light microscope

The light that strikes our eyes can be imagined as a moving beam of many different wavelengths. As it passes through different substances, the beam is **refracted** (bent) at different angles. If it is passed through a glass lens of suitable shape, the bending can be controlled to spread the light over a larger area. If the light has been reflected off an object before entering the lens, the spread-out light will produce an enlarged or magnified image of the object. This is the basic principle behind the microscope.

However, magnification creates some problems. If you have ever looked through an inexpensive magnifying glass, you may have noticed two of them. One is **chromatic aberration.** This is a sort of rainbow fringe of color around objects seen through the glass. It occurs because different wavelengths are refracted at slightly different angles as they pass through the lens. Thus wavelengths of one color may be spread out slightly more than those of another color. If you are trying to study the fine details of an object, chromatic aberration may be a serious inconvenience.

The second problem you may have noticed is **spherical aberration.** This is a distortion of the shape of the image, and is caused by the curvature of the lens. The distortion is usually worst toward the edge of the lens. (If you wear glasses, try looking through the edge of the lens at a long, straight line such as the corner of a wall. Does it look slightly curved?)

Chromatic and spherical aberration were two problems that had to be corrected before microscopes could be developed very far. It was found that two lenses could be combined to act as a single lens. The two could then be made of different kinds of glass. Since each kind refracted the light differently, they could be made to cancel out each other's chromatic aberrations. The curvature of one lens could then be adjusted to correct the spherical aberration caused by the other. With this improvement, much better and higher-powered microscopes could be built.

Two other improvements came about because of the work of Ernst Abbe, a nineteenth-century German physicist. One

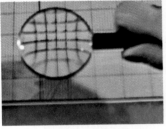

Figure 1-6. Chromatic aberration (top). Note the rainbow effect. Spherical aberration (bottom). The image is distorted so that it appears stretched.

was his development of the **oil-immersion technique.** In the light microscope, the light beam must ordinarily pass through the specimen, then through the air, and finally through the lens. Some of the light rays are always refracted by the molecules in the air. This distorts the image they are carrying. Abbe found that certain oils do not refract light as much as air does. He developed a technique in which a drop of oil is placed between the specimen and the objective lens of the microscope. Since the light does not pass through air between the specimen and the lens, distortion is reduced.

Abbe's other contribution is a device known as the **Abbe condenser.** A microscope must not only be able to magnify objects. It must also be able to make their fine details clear, and to distinguish between separate objects, even when they are extremely close together. That is, it must have a high **resolving power.** Abbe recognized that the resolving power was somehow related to the angle of the light as it passed from the specimen to the lens. In 1873 he devised a practical lens system that could focus the light before it passed through the specimen. With this, the angle of the light, and thus the resolution, could be controlled.

These and other developments greatly improved the microscope image. However, they did not solve the other main problem. It was still not possible to study living tissue. To reduce dependence on stained dead cells, special types of microscope had to be devised. These were the **phase-contrast** and the **polarizing** microscope. In them, the light is directed in a special way that eliminates the need for stains. Hence living cells can be studied. Using these new tools, researchers have been able to confirm in living cells many things that had already been discovered in dead cells.

Electron microscopes

No matter what improvements were made in the light microscope, it could not be used to study objects smaller than a certain size. If an object is smaller than a 0.2-micron light wave, no amount of magnification will resolve it clearly. And many cellular structures are smaller than that. The limitations of the light microscope created a barrier that cell researchers tried for years to overcome.

What finally broke this barrier was the introduction, in the 1950s, of the **electron microscope.** Instead of light, this microscope used beams of electrons. Electron beams have a far shorter wavelength than light. Therefore the electron microscope can resolve much smaller objects. Objects can now be magnified several hundred thousand times.

Of course, our eyes cannot see electron beams. The image must be translated into visible light. Sometimes this is done by projecting the image on a fluorescent or a TV-type screen. Often, though, the beam is used to make a photograph, or **electron micrograph,** which can be kept and studied.

Two types of electron microscope are especially useful to biologists. One is the **transmission electron microscope.** In this, the electron beam passes through the specimen, just as a light beam would. The other is the **scanning electron microscope,** or SEM. This works by means of a very narrow electron beam that scans the surface of the specimen. Moving rapidly back and forth, the electron beam produces an image in much the same way as a TV camera does. Micrographs made with the SEM have a three-dimensional appearance that can be quite exciting. Whole cells and organisms can be viewed in detail in this way, instead of in flat-looking sections. Cells can also be specially frozen and fractured, and the surface of their membranes and organelles studied. Moreover, the resolving power is so great that viruses and even large molecules can be seen. However, living cells cannot yet be studied with either type of electron microscope.

CELL STRUCTURE

Living organisms come in a wide variety of shapes and sizes. Cells are no exception. The yolk of the egg we eat for breakfast is a single giant cell. The human egg cell, on the other hand, is barely visible to the naked eye. Most other cells in our bodies are considerably smaller. Bacteria are smaller yet. The largest bacteria measure only about 5 microns.

As for shape, there is hardly any shape that some unicellular organism does not exhibit. The shapes of cells in multicellular organisms are often rather geometrical, depending on how the cells are arranged in the tissues. Some are flat, some are rectangular "boxes," some are six-sided. Still others might remind you of footballs, baseballs, tree branches, fingers, bar-bells, springs, or toothpicks.

The size and shape of a cell are determined by its function and by what it needs to do to maintain itself. It must be large enough to contain all the necessary organelles (internal structures). But it must be small enough to supply all its parts with nutrients, get rid of its wastes, and generally keep in contact with its environment. An important factor is its **surface-to-volume**

ratio. A cell's surface is its supply line to the environment. It must have enough surface to maintain adequate supply lines for the volume of its interior. As it grows larger, though, its volume increases faster than its surface area. You can see this if you imagine a square box measuring 2 inches each way. Its surface area is 2×2—the area of each side—multiplied by 6—the number of sides. This gives it a surface area of 24 square inches. Its volume is its length times its width times its depth—$2 \times 2 \times 2$, or 8 cubic inches. Thus it has a surface-to-volume ratio of 24 to 8, or 3 to 1. Now imagine a box measuring 4 inches on each side. Its surface area is $4 \times 4 \times 6$, or 96 square inches. Its volume is $4 \times 4 \times 4$, or 64 cubic inches. The surface-to-volume ratio is 96 to 64, or 3 to 2. Therefore, each square inch of surface has to take care of twice as much volume in the larger box, or cell, as in the smaller one. As you can imagine, another such increase in size would be likely to overload the supply lines. So before the volume gets too large, the cell usually divides into two cells of more manageable size.

When nineteenth-century scientists examined the material of which cells are made, they named it **protoplasm.** They meant by this that it was the "first substance," the most basic living matter of all. More recent study has shown that protoplasm is a variable mixture of many substances, dissolved or suspended in water. Molecules of protein, fat, mineral salts, sugars, amino acids, and other materials are all present. Some of them appear to be formed into a wide variety of tiny and important structures, the organelles we have already referred to.

On the basis of structure, we can distinguish two main types of cell. Bacteria and the closely related blue-green algae are **procaryotic** cells. All other cells, including those in our own bodies, are **eucaryotic.** Eucaryotic cells are the more complex kind. They contain many different organelles. In particular, they have a clearly defined region called a nucleus, which is surrounded by its

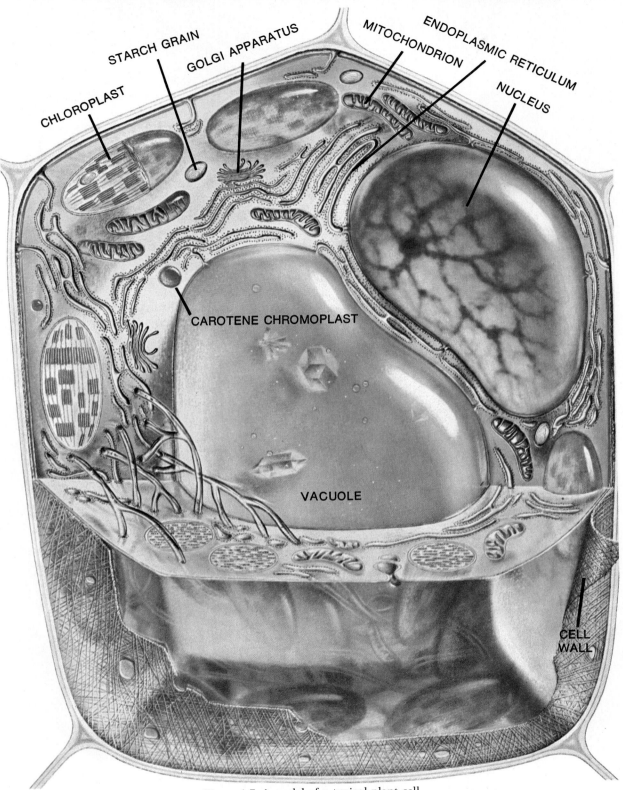

Figure 1-7. A model of a typical plant cell.

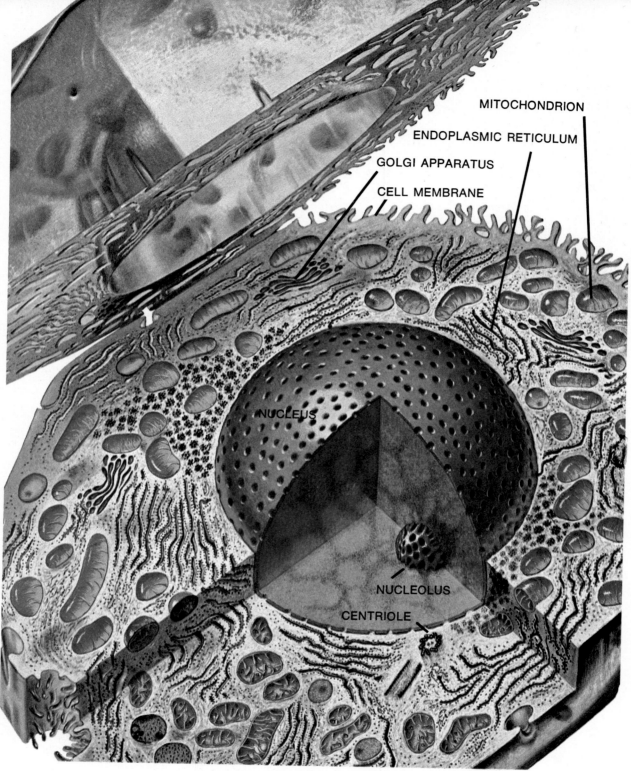

MITOCHONDRION

ENDOPLASMIC RETICULUM

GOLGI APPARATUS

CELL MEMBRANE

NUCLEUS

NUCLEOLUS

CENTRIOLE

Figure 1-8. A model of a typical animal cell.

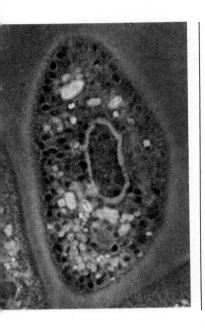

Figure 1-9. Paramecium. The internal structure of this one-celled organism is clearly visible in this phase-contrast photomicrograph.

own membrane and contains the reproductive instructions for the cell. Procaryotic cells have nuclear material, but it is not surrounded by a membrane. Nor do they have as many other organelles. Procaryotic cells are considered to represent a more primitive type of cell. Their simple structure does quite well for the needs of a very small unicellular organism. But multicellular organisms, apparently, need the more elaborate equipment of the eucaryotic cells. Let us see what some of this equipment is.

The nucleus

The **nucleus** was the first organelle to be discovered. It was identified in 1827 by Robert Brown, a botanist who was studying the leaves of orchid plants. Most eucaryotic cells have one nucleus, but some have two or more. The nucleus is important because it contains the genetic information for the cell. Without this information, the cell could not reproduce itself properly. Nor could it maintain all of its structures in good order, or carry on other life processes. The genetic information is coded in a chemical called DNA, which we shall study in more detail in chapter 16. The DNA is arranged on long, thread-like structures. In stained cells, portions of these structures can be seen as **chromatin bodies** under the light microscope. When the cell is dividing, they shorten and thicken, and become easier to see. In this stage they are known as **chromosomes.**

The nucleus also contains a small, round body known as a **nucleolus,** or "little nucleus." The nucleolus manufactures certain important substances that are used outside the nucleus.

We said above that the nucleus is surrounded by its own **membrane.** Through this membrane, some substances pass back and forth between the nucleus and the rest of the cell, which is known as the **cytoplasm.** Single molecules can get through the membrane fairly easily. But some of the substances manufactured inside the nucleus are quite complex. They consist of many molecules that have to stay connected to each other in particular ways. These substances appear to get out of the nucleus by way of special thin places in the membrane, sometimes known as **nuclear pores.**

Endoplasmic reticulum and ribosomes

Outside the nucleus, in the cytoplasm, is an extensive network of membranes called the **endoplasmic reticulum**, or ER. Much remains to be learned about the function of this organelle. However, the number of ER membranes in different cells gives a clue. In cells that make and export many products, the ER is very well developed. It is much less well developed in cells that make and export few products or none. These observations suggest that the ER is probably involved in making and transporting such products.

Some of the production is carried out on tiny, dot-like structures called **ribosomes.** The ribosomes are produced in the nucleolus, and are somehow carried out to the cytoplasm and attached to parts of the ER. ER that has ribosomes attached to it is known as **rough ER.** Rough ER appears to be the protein-producing center of the cell. In particular, it seems to make, or synthesize, many of the special proteins, called enzymes, that are important to the chemical activity of the cell. ER without ribosomes is known as **smooth ER.** This kind seems to synthesize other materials, particularly certain lipids (fat-related substances).

The ER membrane surrounds a narrow space or channel that seems to be used for storage and transport of the materials made by the ER. It may also transport materials manufactured by the nucleus, for the ER has direct connections with the nuclear membrane and the outer cell membrane. There is evidence that materials may be able to move all the way from the nucleus to the outside of the cell through this channel system.

The Golgi apparatus

Some of the material stored by the ER seems to be turned over to another organelle, the **Golgi apparatus,** for transport. The Golgi apparatus is named for Camillo Golgi, who found it in nerve cells in 1898. For many years there was a good deal of controversy about this organelle. Scientists were not sure whether it really existed in living cells. They feared that it might be an artifact, created when cells were prepared for study. But modern electron microscopes have shown that it is a real organelle, and that it has a rather interesting structure.

The Golgi apparatus has been called "a stack of sacs." It is just that—a series of flat, membranous sacs, stacked together in a sort of multilayered sandwich. The sacs contain enzymes or other materials manufactured by the ER. New sacs are formed when small vesicles, or pouches, pinch off from the smooth ER and migrate to one side of the Golgi apparatus. Several vesicles may fuse together and become the newest sac. Meanwhile, the oldest sacs, on the far side of the Golgi apparatus, separate from the stack one after another. They move to the surface of the cell, fuse with the outer cell membrane, and empty their contents into the space outside. When enough Golgi apparatuses are working, a surprising amount of material may be produced. The enzymes that digest our food are produced by ER and delivered to our digestive tracts in this way.

The Golgi apparatus is not merely a transport system, though. While the sac is in the stack, the enzymes it carries are gradually modified. Often they become more concentrated. Sometimes, too, the membranes of the sac manufacture additional, nonprotein substances. These are added to the enzymes and other proteins originally contributed by the ER. Thus, what is eventually delivered to the surface of the cell may be richer or more complex or more refined than what first went into the sac. Finally, when the sac has been emptied, its discarded membranes may be added to the outer membrane of the cell. Nothing that can be used is wasted.

Lysosomes

The **lysosomes** are the cell's way of coping with a potentially dangerous internal problem: destruction of the cell's own cytoplasm. How does this problem arise? Cells can take materials from their environment into their cytoplasm. Single-celled organisms, for example, are constantly feeding on smaller single-celled organisms. They do so by surrounding the food with a "bag" formed from the cell membrane, and then breaking off the bag and letting it move deeper into the cell interior. But how do cells digest these materials? Digestion requires enzymes, and digestive enzymes are powerful. If they are strong enough to digest food, they are also strong enough to digest the cytoplasm of the cell they belong to. How are they prevented from doing so?

The answer, it seems, is, "put the digestive enzymes in a bag, too." That is what a lysosome is—a bag of digestive enzymes. It is probably formed from some of the sacs of the Golgi apparatus, though this is not certain. When a bag of food is brought into the cell from outside, lysosomes attach them-

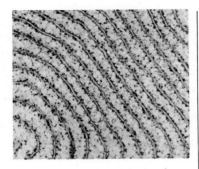

Figure 1-10. Endoplasmic reticulum. The ER appears as a network of canals running through the cytoplasm.

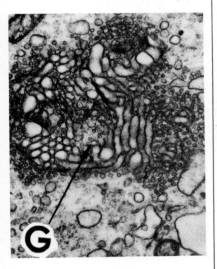

Figure 1-11. Golgi apparatus. Its layers of vesicles give the Golgi apparatus (G) the appearance of a "stack of sacs."

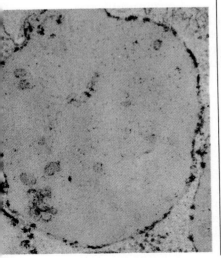

Figure 1-12. Lysosome. This bag of digestive enzymes, from a mouse kidney cell, has been magnified 65,000 times.

selves to it. They empty their enzymes into the food bag, and the food is digested there. The digested materials then pass through the membranes of the bag, into the cytoplasm. The enzymes, however, remain in the bag, where they cannot harm the rest of the cell. Later they are emptied out of the cell.

Sometimes, though, the enzymes and their digestive activity are needed outside the cell. For instance, when the human embryo is being formed, before birth, there is a web of tissue between fingers and toes, like the web of a duck's foot. By the time of birth, this web has disappeared. Apparently it is dissolved by its own ruptured lysosomes, without harm to neighboring areas.

Mitochondria

All the activities that go on in a cell require energy, and the **mitochondria** are the cell's energy factories. Perhaps it would be better to call them energy converters, for they do not manufacture energy. Rather, they put it into a form that the rest of the cell can use. The process by which they do this is rather complicated. It is enough to say, for now, that they take sugars and oxygen delivered from outside the cell, break down the sugar, and use the oxygen to cart away leftover hydrogen in the form of water. The energy from the sugar is repackaged in a new chemical, known as ATP. The ATP is then carried to places in the cell where manufacturing or other activity is going on. It is broken down, and some of the energy stored in it is taken up and used. In chapter 3, we shall examine this energy-conversion process more closely.

Mitochondria, like most of the other organelles we have seen so far, are composed mostly of membranes. (It begins to look, in fact, as though membranes are very important to the cell.) There is an outer membrane envelope, and an inner membrane which is much more extensive. The inner membrane is folded and pleated so that it fits inside the outer one. Each step of the rather lengthy process of ATP synthesis is performed at a particular site on the inner membrane. One could say, thus, that the mitochondrion contains a sort of assembly line. This ensures that all the steps are carried out in proper order. Most cells have many mitochondria. They are particularly numerous at places—such as near the ER—where a great deal of energy-using activity is going on.

Chloroplasts and plastids

The energy that mitochondria convert, and that all organelles use, has to come from somewhere. In the beginning it comes from the sun. Trapping this energy, and storing it in a form that organisms can use, is the function of the **chloroplasts.**

Chloroplasts are a type of organelle found in plants, but not in animals. Each chloroplast has an outer membrane covering, surrounding a protein solution called the **stroma.** Embedded in the stroma are many flattened, sac-like **thylakoids,** which are often arranged in stacks, or **grana.** The thylakoids contain a green pigment called **chlorophyll,** and also yellow and orange pigments. Chlorophyll is able to trap small units of light energy and convert it to chemical energy. The chemical energy is then used to assemble small carbon compounds— sugars—from carbon dioxide and water. These sugars form the basic food of all organisms—both of the plants, and of the animals that eat the plants. Hence, it would be no exaggeration to say that without chlorophyll, life as we know it could not exist.

The process by which chlorophyll traps energy and synthesizes carbon compounds is known as **photosynthesis,** or "putting together with light." It is extremely important, and will be discussed in more detail in chapter 3.

Related to chloroplasts are two other types of organelle that are also found only in plants. **Chromoplasts** contain only yellow, orange, and sometimes red pigments. They give color to many fruits and vegetables, and

to some flowers. **Leucoplasts** are colorless organelles that store food in plants. Oily or starchy fruits and vegetables are rich in leucoplasts. Leucoplasts, chromoplasts, and chloroplasts are known collectively as **plastids.**

Microtubules

Some cells can withstand considerable mechanical force without breaking. This is true in particular of many plant cells and unicellular organisms. How do they do it? In the 1960s, investigators discovered **microtubules**—very small tube-like structures that appear to have several roles in the cell. They are found in parallel bundles in the cytoplasm, often just inside the cell membrane. They are often particularly numerous in cells that can withstand great mechanical force. Apparently they produce new material to thicken and strengthen the cell walls. They also appear to help channel the movement of materials in the cell.

Centrosomes

Near the nucleus in most cells is a special region that functions during cell division. This is called a **centrosome,** and we shall consider its role more fully in chapter 11. In animal cells, but not in most plant cells, the centrosome contains a pair of rod-like **centrioles.** These are composed mainly of microtubules, symmetrically arranged in nine sets of three around a center. In cross-section, a centriole looks strikingly like a pinwheel.

Cilia and flagella

How does a unicellular organism swim? Usually by means of tiny, hair-like appendages called **cilia** or **flagella.** Fundamentally, the two types are the same; they differ only in size and number. Flagella are longer, and a cell will have only one or two of them. Cilia are shorter, and may cover the entire surface of the cell. Not all cells have these

14

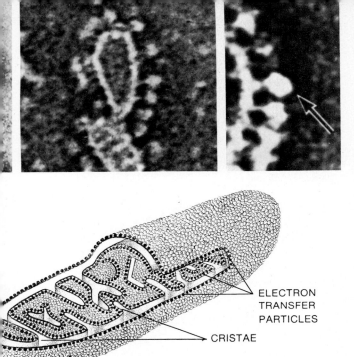

Figure 1-13. Mitochondrion. This micrograph shows the knob-like electron transfer particles on the mitochondrion's cristae. The accompanying model shows these structures more clearly.

ELECTRON
TRANSFER
PARTICLES

CRISTAE

Figure 1-14. Vacuoles. Several large vacuoles have formed in the body of this absorptive cell from a mouse intestine. Other vacuoles are developing between the columnar extensions of the cell's surface.

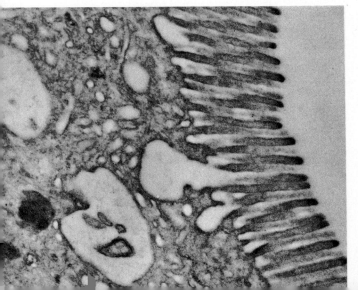

appendages. They are found on cells that need to move freely, and on those that need to move other substances past themselves. A sperm, for instance, swims up the reproductive tract by means of a single flagellum. And the membranes of our respiratory tracts contain cilia that move dust and mucus up toward the nose and mouth, where they can be expelled by coughing or sneezing.

Cilia and flagella, like centrioles, are composed of an arrangement of microtubules. In this case, nine pairs, rather than nine triplets, are arranged around a center. Each cilium or flagellum is attached to the cell by a **basal body,** which is really a centriole. In flagellated cells, the centrioles of the centrosome serve as basal bodies. In ciliated cells, extra centrioles are formed for the purpose.

Vacuoles

Certain membrane-enclosed pockets of fluid in the cytoplasm are known as **vacuoles.** They may be permanent or temporary, and they serve several functions. The "food bag" we mentioned in connection with lysosomes is properly called a **food vacuole.** Food vacuoles are common in unicellular organisms, and in some multicellular organisms. Also found in some unicellular organisms is the **contractile vacuole.** This collects excess water that seeps into the cell, and periodically expels it to the outside.

In mature plant cells, but not in animal cells, there is a large **central vacuole** which may take up most of the space in the cell. It contains cell sap, a solution of sugars, mineral salts, and other substances in water.

Cell walls

Plant cells and many unicellular organisms are surrounded by a stiffening **cell wall.** This is synthesized by the cell itself, and serves for support and protection. The cell walls of plants are composed largely of cellulose fibers. In the thin primary wall of young cells, these fibers form a fairly open network.

15

THE OSTRICH

Suppose you want to make a batch of pancakes to serve about fifty people. Your recipe might run something like this:

5 pounds flour
1 cup baking powder
1 egg

One egg? Well, yes. One egg should do it—that is, if it happens to be an ostrich egg. In fact, you just might have enough of the egg white left over to make a meringue pie.

The size of its egg—about six inches long and three pounds in weight—is only one of the fascinating things about the ostrich. The yolk of that egg, for example, is a single enormous cell, roughly the size of an orange. And the shell of the ostrich egg has several features that more closely resemble fossil reptile eggs than those of modern flying birds.

Ostriches are probably the most familiar of the ratites, or flightless birds. The ratites have a long history, dating back some 135 million years to a huge flightless bird called *Aepyornis*. *Aepyornis*, of course, is long extinct. Unfortunately, so are at least two modern varieties of flightless bird, the dodo and the moa, both victims of human hunters.

For a while, it appeared that ostriches might also become extinct. There was such a great demand for their spectacular plumes and the soft leather made from their hides that the wild ostriches of northern Africa were nearly wiped out by human hunters. Now, however, the birds are raised on ostrich farms, and even the wild ostriches are growing in numbers.

In the savannahs and desert areas of Africa, ostriches live in flocks that may include as many as fifty birds. An adult male ostrich may stand eight feet tall, although more than two-thirds of that height is taken up by its legs and its long, scrawny neck. It resembles nothing so much as a turkey with stilts at one end and a periscope at the other. Both the legs and the long neck have important survival value to the ostrich. If frightened or pursued, this bird can run at a speed of nearly 40 miles per hour. Its long neck and unusually sharp vision allow the ostrich to detect approaching predators a long distance away.

That long neck does have one disadvantage, since it can draw attention to the ostrich. Contrary to popular belief, ostriches do not bury their heads in the sand to escape detection. Instead, they lie on the ground and stretch their necks out flat, a behavioral pattern that can be seen even in very young chicks.

Ostrich courtship differs from that of most other birds, in that the female dominates most of the courtship ritual. She woos the male with a graceful dance that contrasts sharply with her usual awkward gait. More than one female may compete for the attentions of the same male. Eventually, the male ostrich accumulates a harem of several hens.

The hens of an ostrich family lay their eggs in a community nest scratched out of the dirt or sand. The hens sit on the eggs by turns during the daytime, and the male takes his turn at night. But since the large number of eggs in each nest can hardly be covered by one sitting ostrich, this is for purposes of protection rather than incubation. The warmth the eggs must have comes from the dirt or sand surrounding them. The ostrich chicks hatch in about forty days, and are soon able to keep up with a running flock of adult birds.

Ostriches do quite well in captivity, and their curiosity enables them to adjust to a variety of human demands. They can be trained to carry riders or pull carts, although their span of endurance is fairly short. The ostrich, however, can be as bad-tempered and stubborn as a camel. And like the camel, when he gets tired of working for humans he will simply lie down and refuse to go any farther.

The question of why ostriches are flightless presents an evolutionary puzzle. The original assumption was that they had once been able to fly but later lost the ability. However, current research into the biology of ratites seems to indicate that these birds may never have been able to fly at all. For one thing, they do not possess the enormous breastbone that serves to anchor the wing muscles of flying birds. Their feathers are not differentiated into the several types that serve different purposes in flying birds, and the general structure of the feathers is simpler. In fact, it is possible that their feathers have always been used only for insulation.

Whatever their evolutionary history, ostriches manage very well without flight. Their unusually heavy legs have a central toe that is almost like a hoof, and they can use this hoof to deliver a powerful defensive kick. Their running speed is as fast as the air speed of many flying birds, and their sheer size tends to repel most small predators. Ostriches also tend to travel along with herds of grazing animals, which gives them added protection.

And of course, if you want neither the ostrich's plumes nor its leather, there are always those eggs. Want to make an omelette for fifty people? Take two eggs . . .

Older cells may form a secondary wall inside the primary wall. This secondary wall is thicker and denser, and is often reinforced with a substance called lignin. Wood is composed of cells that have died, leaving only their lignified walls. These cells provide mechanical support and serve as tubes through which water flows. The cork of bark, such as Hooke observed, is also composed of the walls of dead cells.

Cell membranes

One part of the cell structure that we have not yet considered is the thin **cell membrane** that surrounds every cell. This membrane cannot be seen with a light microscope, so biologists long disagreed on whether it existed at all. They knew only that certain characteristics of cellular activity could be more reasonably explained if such a membrane were present. When electron microscopes were developed, the membrane could be seen and the issue was settled.

The membrane is the cell's contact with its environment, but it is also its protection against that same environment. The cell needs to take in many substances from outside. But if it simply let them in without discrimination, its own internal organization would be hopelessly upset, and it would quickly die. To prevent this, the membrane must be constructed in a way that lets it be selective in its action. It must be able to admit materials that the cell needs, and keep out those that would be harmful. Sometimes, however, harmful substances do penetrate the membrane, injuring or killing the cell.

As this suggests, the cell membrane is far from being merely a simple, passive envelope. Unlike the cell wall, it performs many functions, and is intricately structured. Traditionally, scientists have regarded the cell membrane as consisting mainly of proteins and phospholipids (fat-related substances). There appear to be two layers of protein molecules, with two layers of lipid molecules sandwiched between

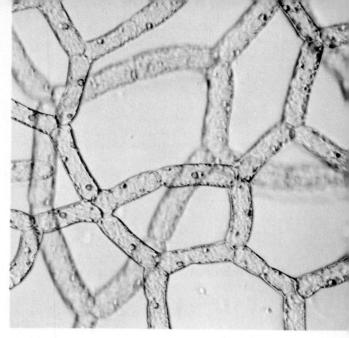

Figure 1-15. Cell walls. Although these green algal cells were magnified only 180 times, their cell walls can be clearly seen as borders surrounding each cell.

them. In some areas, very small microtubules can be seen. These are most common where new membrane is being formed, or where cell wall is being produced outside the membrane. It is also thought that one or both of the protein layers may be missing in some places—like a hole in the bread that lets the sandwich filling show through. Presumably this affects what substances can be transported through the cell membrane passively, by a process called **diffusion.** (This will be described in more detail in chapter 5.) Others get through much faster, or in larger quantity. Evidently there is some system in the membrane that allows **active transport** of these molecules. We have already seen how still larger molecules and particles, such as bits of food, may be carried through in vacuoles made from parts of the membrane itself.

This "unit membrane" concept implies that the membrane is always more or less the same in composition and arrangement. More recent findings, though, seem to

18

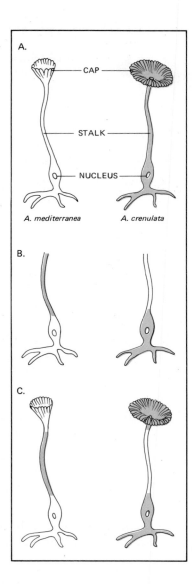

A.

CAP

STALK

NUCLEUS

A. mediterranea   *A. crenulata*

B.

C.

Figure 1-16. Two species of *Acetabularia*. *A. mediterranea* and *A. crenulata* differ in the shape of their caps (A). When the stalk of one species is grafted to the base of the other species (B), the "mixed" individual that results grows a cap that matches its base (C). This illustrates the dominating influence of the nucleus.

suggest that this may not be so. Rather, the membrane may be constantly changing, and it may be made up of many subunits, containing different arrangements of proteins and phospholipids. In any event, much remains to be learned about cell membranes, and about the membranes of the organelles. This is one of the more active areas of cell research today. Thanks to electron microscopes, biologists are able to study these minute and important structures more closely than ever before.

Who's in charge here?
As scientists discovered more and more structures in the cell, they began wondering where the "control center" was. Was it really in the nucleus, as was thought? Or did the cytoplasm also have some active control function? A series of classic experiments suggested some answers.

Acetabularia are a group of small green algae. Like many algae, they are single-celled—but the cells are extraordinarily large. They may be as much as 1 to 3 inches in length. This makes them much easier to work with than many unicellular organisms.

Two species of *Acetabularia* were used for the experiments. Both are shaped rather like miniature mushrooms. Each has a slender stalk with a cap-like structure at one end and root-like branches at the other. The nucleus in each species is in the base. But the two caps are different in appearance. The cap of *A. mediterranea* looks rather like an umbrella that has been blown inside out. *A. crenulata*, on the other hand, has a cap that resembles the arrangement of petals on a daisy.

In one experiment, the base of a *med (mediterranea)* cell, which contained the nucleus, was grafted to the stalk of a *cren (crenulata)* cell whose base and cap had been removed. If the stalk grew a new cap, which type would it be? If it was umbrella-like, this would indicate that the *med* nucleus in the base had controlled its formation. If it was daisy-like, the *cren* stalk must be the controlling factor. The new cap turned out to be umbrella-like.

In a reverse experiment, a *med* stalk was grafted onto a *cren* base and nucleus. A *cren*-type cap was formed. Clearly, the nucleus had the main influence in determining the character of the cap. These experiments, then, suggested that the nucleus was indeed the control center.

However, further experiments showed that the cytoplasm also affects the nucleus. After *Acetabularia* cells mature, the nucleus ordinarily starts to divide and multiply. But if the cap is removed just before the cell reaches maturity, the nucleus does not divide. Apparently some influence from the cytoplasm in the cap is needed for division to occur. In another experiment, a mature cap was grafted onto the stalk and base of an immature cell. The nucleus of the immature cell promptly began to divide—almost two months before division would normally have occurred. This again indicated that some influence from the cytoplasm in the cap was reaching the nucleus.

Evidently, then, neither the nucleus nor the cytoplasm is the sole control center of the cell. In normal development and functioning, each influences the other.

TISSUES, ORGANS, AND SYSTEMS

In the smallest organisms, cells do not work alone. Rather, they are joined together in groups that are specialized for particular functions. These groups are known as tissues, organs, and organ systems.

The cells of a **tissue** are mostly of the same sort, and are all engaged in the same function. Muscle tissue contracts; brain tissue transmits nerve impulses. In each tissue, the cells are bound together by some substance which they themselves secrete. Bone tissue is a good example. Most of what we call bone is a matrix of mineral salts and

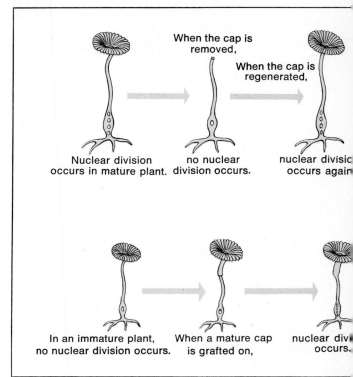

When the cap is removed,

When the cap is regenerated,

Nuclear division occurs in mature plant.

no nuclear division occurs.

nuclear division occurs again

In an immature plant, no nuclear division occurs.

When a mature cap is grafted on,

nuclear division occurs.

Figure 1-17. These experiments with *Acetabularia* indicate that the cytoplasm exerts a regulatory influence on the nucleus.

protein fibers, secreted by the living bone cells. These cells form a network, embedded in this matrix.

Most of the cells that make up the tissues are more or less specialized, as we shall see in later chapters. A muscle cell is quite different from a bone cell. A leaf cell that carries on photosynthesis is different from a root cell that stores food. The difference is not merely one of size and shape. The kind and number of organelles differ as well. Cells that secrete large amounts of enzymes are likely to have many sacs in their Golgi apparatus. Those that use a great deal of energy usually have many mitochondria. And the mature red blood cells of birds and mammals have no nucleus at all.

20

In an **organ,** one or more tissues form a structural and functional unit. The heart is an organ. It includes muscle tissue that contracts, nerve tissue that transmits impulses, connective tissue that binds other elements together, and so on. All the tissues work together in producing a heartbeat.

But not all organs are so clearly active as the heart. Our skin is an organ, made up of

digestion, or internal transportation, or waste disposal.

It will be important to remember, throughout our study, that life is interdependent at all levels. Cells depend on other cells, tissues on other tissues. Organisms can function only if their cells do, and vice versa. A change in the functioning of one organ affects other organs. It is true, of course, that

NEW X-RAY SYSTEM GIVES THREE-DIMENSIONAL VIEWS

A new X-ray device that provides cross-sectional views of the body's internal structures may soon enable physicians to diagnose internal ailments earlier and more accurately than ever before. The new machine, called the body scanner, is currently being tested at the Mayo Clinic and other hospitals throughout the United States.

The new device works in this manner: as the patient lies on the examining table, a ring of scanners rotates in a half-circle around his body. As they rotate, the scanners transmit an ultra-thin beam of X-rays through the body, in the plane of rotation. Thus, the X-rays penetrate the same organs from many different angles. On the other side of the body, opposite the scanners, the X-rays strike sodium iodide crystals, which react by giving off

flashes of light. Measurement of the amount of light shows how much of the X-ray beam was absorbed by the body. This information is fed to a minicomputer, which uses it to construct an image of the entire body plane X-rayed. The image is flashed on a TV-type screen, where it appears as a cross-section view. If cross-sections of several "slices" a centimeter or so apart are shown in rapid sequence, a three-dimensional effect is created.

The current tests are designed to determine the ultimate diagnostic value of the new device. Among the questions to be answered are: can the body scanner distinguish between a benign tumor and a cancerous one? Can it detect the different stages of cancer? Can it locate post-operative complications such as abscesses or hemorrhages? Positive answers to these questions, and others, will mean that another important weapon against disease has been added to the growing arsenal of medical science.

many different tissues. So is the leaf of a plant.

Finally, a number of organs may be linked together in an **organ system.** The human digestive system is an example. It includes the teeth, tongue, esophagus, stomach, small and large intestines, and other organs. An organ system usually performs a major set of functions in an organism. It may carry on

we need to consider structures and processes one at a time. Otherwise we would never be able to see their patterns and understand their working. But we can never expect to find things happening one at a time. Everything is going on at once, and affecting everything else. This can be one of the frustrations of studying biology. But it can also be a part of its fascination.

Table 1-1. Table of equivalent measurements

1 centimeter (cm) = 1/100 meter = 0.4 inch = 10^{-2}m

1 millimeter (mm) = 1/1,000 meter = 1/10 cm = 10^{-3}m

1 micron (μ) = 1/1,000,000 meter = 1/10,000 cm = 10^{-6}m

1 nanometer (nm) = 1,000,000,000 meter = 1/10,000,000 cm = 10^{-9}m

1 angstrom (Å) = 1/10,000,000,000 meter = 1/100,000,000 cm = 10^{-10}m

SUMMARY

The invention of the microscope enabled early scientists to observe cells for the first time. It was finally recognized that cells were active, functional units, the universal components of all life. Pasteur proved that microorganisms came from other microorganisms, and Virchow's principle stated that every cell must come from another cell. Flemming later discovered that cells produce new cells by dividing.

Even with improvements, the light microscope could not be used to observe objects smaller than a certain size. This barrier was finally broken by development of two types of electron microscope. So far, though, living cells can only be studied with the light microscope.

Cells come in a variety of shapes and sizes. But their surface-to-volume ratio is an important factor in allowing them direct contact with their environments. Before the volume of a cell gets too large, it usually divides into two cells of more manageable size.

Bacteria and blue-green algae are procaryotic cells, with few organelles and without a clearly defined nucleus. Eucaryotic cells contain many more organelles and a discrete nucleus surrounded by its own membrane. Procaryotic cells are considered the older and more primitive type.

The nucleus was the first organelle to be discovered. It contains the genetic information which enables the cell to reproduce itself, as well as a small body called the nucleolus which manufactures certain important substances. Substances pass between the nucleus and the cytoplasm of the cell through the nuclear pores.

The endoplasmic reticulum is a network of membranes in the cytoplasm. Rough ER has ribosomes attached to it, and seems to be the protein-manufacturing center of the cell. Smooth ER apparently manufactures other materials, including certain lipids. The channel enclosed by the ER membrane seems to be used for storage and transport of materials made by the ER.

The Golgi apparatus is an organelle often described as a "stack of sacs." The sacs contain enzymes and other materials manufactured by the ER. They migrate to the cell membrane and empty their contents outside of it. The Golgi apparatus also modifies the enzymes it carries by making them more concentrated.

The lysosome is a bag of digestive enzymes. Food from outside is digested within the bag, and then passed through its membranes into the cytoplasm. The enzymes remain in the bag, so that they cannot digest the cytoplasm itself.

Mitochondria are the cell's energy converters. Each mitochondrion contains an assembly line that produces ATP by repackaging the energy released from the breakdown of sugar. Mitochondria are numerous in cells that use a great deal of energy.

Chloroplasts are found only in plants. They contain the pigment chlorophyll, which can trap light energy and convert it to chemical energy by the process of photosynthesis. Chromoplasts contain other pigments, and leucoplasts are colorless organelles that store food. These three organelles are collectively known as plastids.

Centrosomes function during cell division. In animal cells they contain two rod-like centrioles, composed mainly of micro-

PATTERNS OF STRUCTURE
AND FUNCTION

tubules. Unicellular animals swim by means of cilia or flagella, which are also composed of microtubules.

Vacuoles are membrane-enclosed pockets of fluid in the cytoplasm. Food vacuoles are used for digestion. Contractile vacuoles collect and expel excess water from the cell. In plant cells, a large central vacuole contains cell sap.

Every cell is surrounded by a cell membrane. Many substances move through the membrane by diffusion. Plant cells and many unicellular organisms possess a stiffening cell wall which provides support and protection. In plants the cell wall is largely made of cellulose fibers.

Cells may be joined together in specialized tissues, organs, and organ systems. Tissue cells are all engaged in the same function. An organ is a functional unit made up of one or more tissues. And numbers of organs may be linked together to form an organ system.

Review questions

1. Name three early scientists who made microscopic observations of cells.

2. What are organelles?

3. Describe Pasteur's classic experiment that disproved the theory of spontaneous generation.

4. What is Virchow's principle?

5. Name at least two problems that complicate the study of cells.

6. Distinguish between the two types of electron microscope.

7. Explain why surface-to-volume ratio is important in determining the size to which a cell can grow.

8. What are the structural differences between eucaryotic and procaryotic cells?

9. Describe a typical eucaryotic cell, stating whether each structure is found in the nucleus or the cytoplasm.

10. What sort of cells contain well developed ER? What is the probable significance of this?

11. Distinguish between rough ER and smooth ER. What substances does each manufacture?

12. What are the functions of the Golgi apparatus?

13. Explain why a cell does not digest itself when it ingests nutrients.

14. What is the primary activity of a mitochondrion? Which cells are likely to possess the greatest number of mitochondria?

15. Name two organelles that are found only in plants.

16. What is chlorophyll and why is it so important?

17. What are the apparent functions of microtubules?

18. Distinguish between cilia and flagella. What types of cell possess them?

19. Name three types of vacuole and the function of each.

20. What is the function of a cell wall? In what types of cell is it found?

21. Describe the structure of a cell membrane.

22. List two important functions of the cell membrane.

23. What two components of a cell share control of its activities? How was this determined?

24. Distinguish between tissues, organs, and organ systems.

25. Name some possible structural differences among different types of specialized cell.

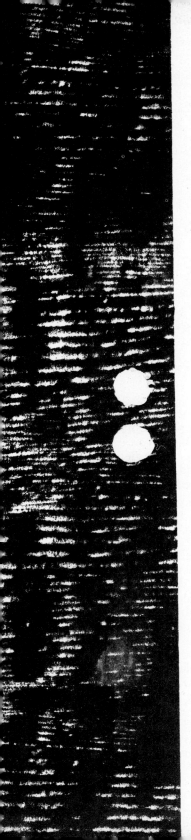

Chemicals of Life

Why study chemistry in a biology course? Many students have asked this, and the answer is simple. All matter, including that which composes living organisms, is made from the same fundamental units. What we call the "processes of life" are really a series of chemical reactions involving combinations of these fundamental units of matter.

To understand these reactions, we must know a little about the structure of matter and the principles of chemical reaction. In this chapter, we will discuss the chemistry fundamentals you will need to know to understand biological functioning.

One hundred and three different types of matter, or **elements,** have been discovered by chemists over the past several hundred years. Of these, 92 elements occur naturally on this planet.

Six of these elements occur very frequently in living organisms. They may therefore be considered essential for life as we know it. These elements are carbon, hydrogen, nitrogen, oxygen, phosphorus, and sulfur.

The composition of the human body is shown in Table 2-1. As you can see, dozens of elements are important to living organisms. We will concentrate on the properties of certain of the essential elements, however. We will also discuss the **compounds,** or combinations, that they form.

Important compounds and classes of compounds that we will mention include water, carbon dioxide, and the organic compounds. In living systems, four groups of organic compounds are particularly abundant. These are carbohydrates, lipids, proteins, and nucleic acids.

UNITS OF MATTER

In chapter 1, we studied the fundamental unit of all living tissue—the cell. Just as the cell may be considered the fundamental unit of the living organism, the **atom** can be considered the fundamental unit of all matter. An atom is the smallest quantity of matter that has all the chemical properties of an element. For instance, we can look at an atom and say, "This is hydrogen," or "This is carbon." But if we take the atom apart, the pieces are not hydrogen or carbon. They are only particles that can be used to make hydrogen, or carbon, or tin, or gold, or any other element.

Just as the cell is composed of different parts with special functions, the atom is also composed of smaller particles with definite characteristics.

Atomic structure

Let us look at the hydrogen atom first, because hydrogen is the simplest element. The hydrogen atom contains one **proton** in its **nucleus.** (Do not confuse this with a cell nucleus.) The proton has a positive electrical charge of +1, so the nucleus of the atom, which always contains protons, is always positively charged. Most of the substance in any atom is contained in the nucleus.

The hydrogen atom also has one **electron** that orbits the nucleus. The electron is a very small particle. It has a negative charge of −1, so that the outer region of an atom, which contains the electrons, is always negatively charged.

One other basic type of particle occurs in the atom. This is the **neutron,** which is found in the nucleus. The neutron has no charge—it is electrically neutral.

The ordinary form of hydrogen has no neutrons. All other types of atom have at least one neutron. Let us look at oxygen, for example. Oxygen has eight protons and eight neutrons in its nucleus. It also has eight electrons orbiting its nucleus. (All

Table 2-1. Atoms in the human body

ATOM	SYMBOL	% of Total BODY ATOMS
Hydrogen	H	63.0
Oxygen	O	23.5
Carbon	C	9.5
Nitrogen	N	1.4
Calcium	Ca	0.31
Phosphorus	P	0.22
Potassium	K	0.057
Sulfur	S	0.049
Sodium	Na	0.041
Chlorine	Cl	0.026
Magnesium	Mg	0.013
Iron	Fe	0.0039
Zinc	Zn	0.00015
Manganese	Mn	0.00002
Copper	Cu	0.00002
Fluorine	F	0.00001
Iodine	I	0.00001
Molybdenum	Mo	0.00001
Cobalt	Co	0.00001

atoms have equal numbers of protons and electrons. But they often have a different number of neutrons.) Oxygen's eight electrons do not all orbit at the same distance from the nucleus. Instead, the electrons are grouped in what are called different **electron shells.**

Electron shells

What is an electron shell, and why is this concept important? Electrons travel in orbits at specific average distances from the nucleus of the atom. They are so small and travel so fast that we cannot pinpoint their exact position at any given moment. All electrons traveling at the same average distance from the nucleus belong to the same electron shell. Some elements with very complicated atomic structures, such as uranium, have as many as seven electron shells.

The first electron shell, the one closest to the atom's nucleus, can contain no more than two electrons. The outermost shell can

PATTERNS OF STRUCTURE
AND FUNCTION

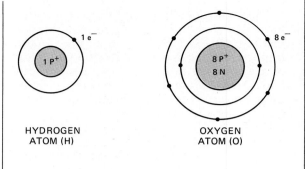

HYDROGEN
ATOM (H)

OXYGEN
ATOM (O)

Figure 2-1. Hydrogen and oxygen atoms, showing the nucleus of protons and neutrons, and the electrons arranged in concentric shells around the nucleus.

contain a maximum of eight electrons. Shells between these two can contain varying numbers—in some cases, as many as 32.

Atoms are most stable—least apt to react with other atoms—when their outer electron shells are complete. For some reason, they "seek" to complete their outer shells, either by transferring electrons to other atoms, or by sharing electrons. The electrons in the outer shell that atoms will transfer or share are called the **valence electrons.**

The concept of electron shells is important, therefore, when we want to understand how certain atoms will combine with certain other atoms.

Combinations of atoms

When atoms transfer or share electrons, a **chemical bond** is formed between the atoms. The combination of atoms joined by a chemical bond is called a **compound.** This differs from a **mixture,** which is composed of molecules of two or more compounds.

Compounds have properties that are quite different from the properties of the atoms that compose them. For example, chlorine, which is one of the elements in the compound sodium chloride (table salt) is a

poisonous gas. However, when a chlorine atom picks up an electron from a sodium atom, forming sodium chloride, it ceases to be poisonous.

Compounds can be formed with more than one type of chemical bond. The kind of chemical bond in a compound is often important in biological functions, so we will look at the different types a little more closely.

CHEMICAL BONDS

As we mentioned above, atoms can form bonds with each other either by sharing their valence electrons or by transferring them. When two atoms share electrons, the bond formed is called a covalent bond. When atoms transfer electrons, they form an ionic bond with each other. Another type of bond, a weak covalent one, is also important in biological systems. This weak bond is called a hydrogen bond. Let us look at the ionic bond first.

Ionic bonds: the give-and-take bonds

As we said earlier, atoms may complete their outer electron shells by transferring electrons. An atom may take on new electrons, or it may give up some of its electrons.

When an atom takes on or gives up electrons, its charge changes. An atom normally possesses an equal number of protons, each with a +1 charge, and electrons, each with a −1 charge. The plus and minus charges balance out, and an atom is electrically **neutral.**

If an atom gives up an electron, however, it is left with more protons than electrons, so it is no longer neutral. Instead, it has a charge of +1. When an atom takes up an electron, it takes up an extra negative charge, and then has a charge of −1. This charge value is called its **valence.**

A charged atom is called an **ion.** The bond formed between two atoms when they transfer electrons is called an **ionic bond.**

Let us look at an example of a compound formed with an ionic bond. Sodium (Na) and chlorine (Cl) transfer electrons to form the compound sodium chloride (NaCl).

A sodium atom has 11 electrons. Two are found in the first electron shell, eight in the second, and one in the third, and outer, shell.

Remember that the outer electron shell may be considered complete if it contains eight electrons. In order for a sodium atom to complete its third shell, it would have to pick up seven electrons. For a number of reasons, an atom is not likely to pick up this many extra electrons. Instead, an atom with less than four electrons in its outermost shell is more likely to give up those electrons. If the sodium atom gives up the one electron in its third shell, it will be left with a complete second shell. The atom will become a positive ion with a valence of $+1$. It is then symbolized as Na^+.

Chlorine (Cl) has 17 electrons. Seven of these electrons are located in its third and outer shell. Thus, the chlorine atom needs to add only one electron to complete its outer shell. When a chlorine atom gains an extra electron, it becomes a chloride ion, a negative ion with a charge of -1. The chloride ion is symbolized as Cl^-.

When sodium and chlorine come together and form sodium chloride, the sodium atom gives up one electron to the chlorine atom, and an ionic bond is formed. Sodium chloride in its solid form, which we know as table salt, exists as a three-dimensional network of chloride and sodium ions.

Ionic compounds ionize
Compounds formed with ionic bonds have another property that is very important in biological functioning. When a compound such as sodium chloride is placed in water, it **ionizes.** That is, the water molecules come between the sodium and chloride ions, and the ions separate. This is what we mean when we say that salt **dissolves** in water. In water, then, sodium chloride exists principally as sodium (Na^+) and chloride (Cl^-) ions.

Since the contents of cells are suspended in a watery medium, most ionic compounds inside cells exist as ions. Ions play many important roles in cells. Materials could not be transported in and out of cells without ions. Muscles could not contract without their presence. We will discuss such functions of ions in later chapters.

Acids and bases: the pH scale
Two kinds of ionic compound are especially important in living systems. These compounds are **acids** and **bases.** Although chemists have more complicated definitions, we may say that any compound which, when it ionizes, increases the number of hydrogen ions (H^+) in a solution is an acid. Any ionic compound that decreases the number of hydrogen ions in a solution is called a base.

Acidity (the concentration of H^+ ions in water) is measured by a system known as the **pH scale.** Any solution with a pH value of less than 7 is called acidic. Any solution with a pH value of more than 7 is called basic or alkaline. Water has a pH of 7. In other words, pure water is neither acidic nor basic, but neutral.

The pH scale is a logarithmic scale. This means that as the H^+ concentration of a solution increases ten times, the pH of that solution decreases only one unit. So a substance with a pH of 5 is ten times as acid as one with a pH of 6.

Why are acids and bases and the pH concept important? Most chemical reactions taking place inside living organisms will occur only within a very narrow range of pH values. For example, the normal pH value of human blood is approximately 7.4. Under ordinary circumstances, if blood pH goes above 7.8 or below 7.0 for more than a few minutes, death will almost surely result.

Covalent bonds: the sharing bonds
When two hydrogen atoms share their electrons, a **covalent bond** is formed between

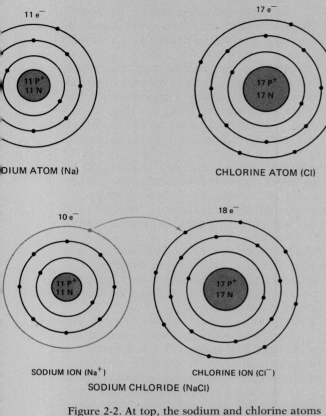

11 e⁻

17 e⁻

11 P⁺
11 N

17 P⁺
17 N

DIUM ATOM (Na)

CHLORINE ATOM (Cl)

10 e⁻

18 e⁻

11 P⁺
11 N

17 P⁺
17 N

SODIUM ION (Na⁺)

CHLORINE ION (Cl⁻)

SODIUM CHLORIDE (NaCl)

Figure 2-2. At top, the sodium and chlorine atoms are separate and uncharged. At bottom, one electron has been transferred from the sodium to the chlorine, resulting in charged ions and an ionic bond between them.

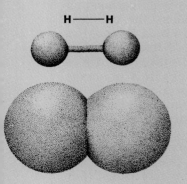

H——H

Figure 2-3. A molecule of hydrogen can be depicted by a formula, a ball-and-stick model, and a space-filling model.

them. Each hydrogen atom shares its one electron with the other, so that both atoms have two electrons in their outer electron shells. That is, each of the shared electrons orbits both nuclei. Both atoms satisfy their tendency to complete their outer shells in this way.

The compound formed when two hydrogen atoms come together is called a hydrogen **molecule** (H_2). A molecule is the smallest identifiable unit of a compound, just as an atom is the smallest unit of an element.

Some atoms can form covalent bonds with more than one other atom at the same time. For example, oxygen has eight electrons, two in its complete first electron shell and six in its second, outer, shell. In order to fill its outer shell, an oxygen atom needs two more electrons (to make a shell of eight electrons). Oxygen atoms often form covalent bonds with two hydrogen atoms, making water (H_2O). Each hydrogen atom shares one electron with the oxygen atom.

Carbon is the most important atom forming covalent bonds. It is a major element in all living organisms. Carbon dioxide (CO_2), the gas used by plants in the process of photosynthesis, is also formed with covalent bonds. The covalent bond is found throughout living tissue and the compounds utilized by living organisms.

Hydrogen bonds

We mentioned earlier that one type of weak chemical bond is extremely important in biological functioning. This is the **hydrogen bond.** It forms between the positive hydrogen atoms and small, highly negative atoms such as oxygen or nitrogen.

When two hydrogen atoms combine with an oxygen atom and form a water molecule, all three atoms do not share their valence electrons equally. The oxygen atom "pulls" the electrons away from the hydrogen atoms more strongly than the hydrogen atoms "pull" electrons away from the oxygen atom. The result of these unequal pulls is that the oxygen side of the water molecule is

29

more negative than the hydrogen side. The hydrogen atoms in the water molecule are almost, but not quite, hydrogen ions or naked protons. This unequal sharing of electrons is what makes the hydrogen bond important. It is really a special type of covalent bond, known as a **polar covalent bond.**

The water molecule is called a **polar molecule** because it has a positive pole (where the hydrogens are located) and a negative pole (where the oxygen is located). The water molecule, with its two poles with opposite charges, is very much like a magnet.

As you know, opposite poles of two magnets will attract each other. In a collection of water molecules, then, the positive pole of one water molecule (the hydrogen pole) is attracted to the negative pole (the oxygen pole) of another water molecule. This attraction between the hydrogen of one water molecule and the oxygen of another water molecule is also a hydrogen bond. The attraction between nearby water molecules causes these molecules to move closer together and gives water some of the special characteristics we will discuss in the next section.

WATER: SOLVENT OF LIFE

Without water, life as we know it would never have happened. Most biologists believe that the first living organisms began their existence in the oceans. All organisms require at least some water to live. Some animals that do not drink it, manufacture it. And all living tissue is composed largely of water—usually 80 to 95 percent.

Structure of water
The properties of any substance—the ways in which it behaves—are determined in part by its structure. Most important in that structure are the kinds of bond that hold the atoms and molecules together, and the ways

those bonds are arranged. The hydrogen bonds that hold water molecules together give to liquid water a number of unusual properties.

For instance, on a calm summer day, you can often see water insects moving over the surface of a pond or lake. These insects actually "walk on water." How do they do it?

Water molecules attract one another quite strongly. This attraction between molecules of the same substance is called **cohesion.** It makes it difficult for an object to break apart the water molecules on the surface of a body of water. That is, it gives the water a high **surface tension.** Water has a higher surface tension than any other liquid except mercury.

When molecules of two different substances are attracted to one another, the process is called **adhesion.** Water adheres very strongly to other substances, as well as cohering to itself.

A property of water which depends on both its cohesive and its adhesive properties is called **capillary action.** This is a tendency to flow through very narrow pores or tubes, even moving upward against gravity. If you dip one corner of a paper towel in water, the water molecules will seep through the pores of the paper until the whole piece is soaked. In a similar way, capillary action allows water to travel through spaces in the soil, reaching the fine root hairs of plants.

Water tends to adhere especially to certain large molecules of living substances. When this happens, more and more water tends to move into the neighborhood of the molecule. For instance, the cellulose molecules in the cells of a seed can hold so much water that the seed itself begins to swell. This type of water intake is known as **imbibition,** or "drinking in." It is an important first step in seed germination.

Again, water is unique among compounds in that it is more dense in liquid than in solid form; that is, the molecules are more tightly packed together in the liquid. Thus, a pint of water is heavier than a pint of ice, because it contains more molecules. If it

30

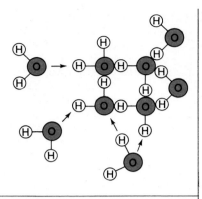

Figure 2-5. Water molecules attract one another. This is the reason for water's cohesive properties.

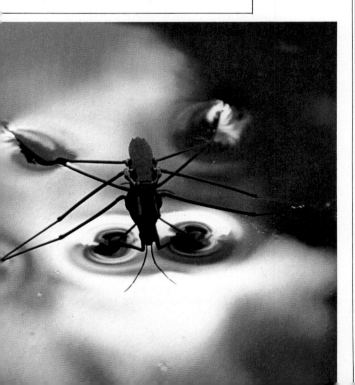

Figure 2-4. Surface tension results partially from the cohesive forces between molecules of water. This tension makes it possible for some insects, such as the water strider, to move over the surface of water.

were the other way around, life as we know it would not exist on most of the earth.

Why is water **density** so important? Remember that life is believed to have begun in the oceans. Because water at freezing temperatures is less dense than water a few degrees warmer, the freezing water rises, and ice forms first at the surface of any body of water. Fish and other organisms can continue to live and function in the unfrozen depths below. But if ice were more dense than liquid water, the ice would sink. Lakes and oceans would gradually become solid blocks of ice from the bottom up, and all the life in them would be destroyed.

Solvent properties

Water is often called the "universal solvent." Water does not really dissolve all substances, but it is an excellent solvent for many different kinds of material.

Most ionic compounds and polar molecules will dissolve in water. Most ionic compounds also ionize in water. However, fats and oils, which are neither ionic nor polar compounds, are not soluble in water. Many of the large molecules in cells are at least partially insoluble in water.

Water's solvent properties are essential to most of the reactions that take place inside living tissue. Since water is a major component of the cell, the ability of water to dissolve so many substances facilitates the reactions that take place inside the cell.

ORGANIC AND INORGANIC COMPOUNDS

Today all chemical compounds are divided into two classes: **organic** and **inorganic**. Organic compounds are all those that contain chains of carbon atoms. There are many different types of organic compound. We will talk about four kinds in this chapter: carbohydrates (sugars, starches, and cellulose), lipids (fats and waxes), proteins (and their basic units, the amino acids), and nucleic acids (DNA and RNA).

Inorganic compounds are those that do not contain carbon chains. Although the structural materials in our bodies (except for water) are largely composed of organic compounds, and although organic compounds supply much of our energy, we still need inorganic compounds as well. We could not live, for instance, without sodium chloride, potassium chloride, the iron compounds, and the calcium compounds.

Remember that all compounds, both organic and inorganic, are formed from inorganic elements. Therefore all compounds obey similar fundamental physical and chemical laws.

Let us look first at some of the elements that form compounds essential to living organisms.

Carbon and the structure of organic compounds

Carbon (C) is found throughout living organisms. Carbon compounds form most of the structural and functional material in any organism. Cell walls in plants, muscles and bone in animals, membranes, and the enzymes produced by cells are all made up of carbon compounds. Carbon compounds are also utilized by living organisms for energy. Why is carbon, an element quite rare in the composition of the planet, so important and so plentiful in living organisms? The structure of the carbon atom gives us part of the answer.

The carbon atom has six protons and six neutrons in its nucleus, and six electrons orbiting the nucleus. Two electrons are found in the atom's first and inner shell, and four electrons in the second and outer shell.

Earlier, we said that this second electron shell is complete when it holds eight electrons. The carbon atom, therefore, needs four electrons to complete its outer shell. Rather than give away or pick up electrons, the atom keeps its outer electrons and shares them in covalent bonds.

One carbon atom can form covalent

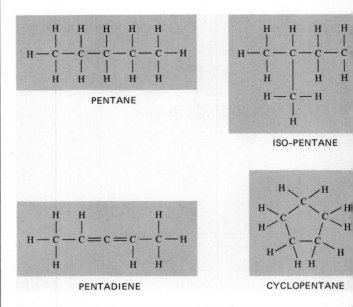

Figure 2-6. Four different carbon compounds. Each compound has five carbons, and each carbon has formed four bonds—yet the resulting structures are very different.

bonds with four hydrogen atoms. Or it can form covalent bonds with other carbon atoms, creating long chains of carbons. A carbon atom can share more than one electron with another atom, forming a **double** or **triple bond.**

The carbon atom is very flexible in the ways it can form compounds, and there are a great many carbon compounds. In fact, the number of carbon compounds has been estimated to be as high as one million.

Why are there so many carbon compounds? First, carbon atoms can form carbon chains of any length. The chains may be branched, or may form ring-like structures. Second, carbon chains of the same length can have different numbers of hydrogen atoms attached to them because of the abil-

32

ity of the carbon atoms to form double and triple bonds. Third, the longer the chain, the more ways the structure of the chain can be arranged. These rearrangements, which contain the same numbers of atoms (both of carbon and of the other elements) but which have different shapes, are called **isomers.**

hydrogen are sometimes called **functional groups.** They carry an ionic charge, and each group reacts, or functions, as though it were a single atom. For instance, the hydroxyl group (OH) has a charge of -1, and can be used in a compound just as any other -1 ion can. Many compounds contain such func-

---

HYPERKINESIS AND FOOD ADDITIVES

Some five million American children suffer from the condition known as hyperkinesis. They are uncontrollably active, impulsive, and sometimes violent. In school, they cannot concentrate long enough to learn, and their behavior usually keeps other children from concentrating, as well. The cause of hyperkinesis is unknown, but the standard treatment consists of regular doses of powerful tranquilizers and amphetamines. No one pretends that this heavy drugging is good for the children. But it has seemed the only way of enabling them to live more or less normally.

A California allergist and pediatrician, though, thinks differently. Dr. Ben Feingold believes that some children are genetically predisposed to hyperkinesis, and that the condition is triggered by eating certain substances. The most important of these substances, he says, are the artificial colors and flavors added to a wide range of foods. Many of the foods popular with children—such as

soft drinks, sugary cereals, candy, and potato chips—are high in these chemical additives. Another trigger, Feingold suspects, is natural rather than artificial. This is an aspirin-related substance that occurs in large concentrations in certain fruits and vegetables.

With this hypothesis in mind, Feingold devised a diet for hyperkinetic children. All foods with artificial additives were barred. So were tomatoes, cucumbers, strawberries, apples, oranges, and other fruits containing the aspirin-related substance. At least 50 percent of the children he treated by this diet seemed to be helped by it, and no longer needed drugs. A problem for parents, though, is that additives in foods are not always listed on the labels. So it is hard to keep children from eating the additives by accident. And a very small amount seems sufficient to bring on an episode of hyperkinesis that may last for days.

After several years of skepticism, the Food and Drug Administration has begun testing Feingold's diet. If his theory is confirmed, it may eventually be possible to pinpoint the exact additives that cause the trouble, and perhaps to discover just how they produce their unwanted effects.

Finally, different atoms or groups of atoms may be substituted for the hydrogens on the carbon chain to produce still different compounds. The atoms that most often substitute for hydrogen are oxygen, nitrogen, phosphorus, and sulfur.

The "groups of atoms" that substitute for

tional groups, and it helps in memorizing formulas if you learn to recognize some of the common ones. For example, all alcohols contain hydroxyl groups, and all amino acids, the building blocks of protein, contain an amino group (NH_2) and a carboxyl group (COOH).

The organic uses of oxygen

Oxygen, as you remember, combines with two hydrogen molecules, forming water (H_2O), a compound essential to all living organisms. Oxygen's ability to attract the electrons of the hydrogen atoms toward itself leads to hydrogen bonding and the unusual properties of water.

Two atoms of oxygen also combine with one carbon atom, forming carbon dioxide (CO_2). Carbon dioxide and water are used by green plants in the making of organic compounds through photosynthesis, which we will discuss in chapter 3.

Animals eat plants and use the materials plants have made by photosynthesis as a source of energy and in growth. The animals and other organisms break down these complex substances and excrete carbon dioxide and water as waste products. Carbon dioxide is thus found at both the beginning and the end of the carbon cycle.

Molecular oxygen (O_2), a gas, is used by most organisms in the energy-yielding processes called oxidations, which we will also discuss in chapter 3.

Oxygen is also an element frequently found in the organic compounds—the carbohydrates, lipids, proteins, and nucleic acids. We will look at these compounds next.

CARBOHYDRATES

Carbohydrates—sugars and starches—are used by living organisms in several ways. Animals use some types of sugar—especially glucose—in energy reactions. Both animals and plants use other types of carbohydrate as energy storehouses. Plant starch is an example of an energy storage carbohydrate. The energy storage compound usually found in animals is glycogen.

Some complex carbohydrates are also used as supporting materials. Cellulose, the carbohydrate found in plant stems, is an example of this type of carbohydrate.

The carbohydrates are made up entirely of carbon, hydrogen, and oxygen. In the simplest carbohydrates these elements are present in 1:2:1 proportions.

One of the most important carbohydrates in the reactions that take place in living organisms is glucose. Glucose is a six-carbon sugar, with six hydrogens and twelve oxygens. Its structure is shown in figure 2-7.

Simple carbohydrates such as glucose are sometimes arranged in the straight-line structure shown in the figure and sometimes in a ring. The ring structures of these simple sugars may be chained together in a reaction that involves removing two hydrogens and an oxygen to form a water molecule. This is how the more complex carbohydrates, such as starch and glycogen, are formed.

Simple sugars

Glucose, the carbohydrate whose structure is shown in figure 2-7, is a **simple sugar,** or **monosaccharide.** Simple sugars have only one ring in their structures.

The simple sugars that contain six carbons—particularly glucose—are very important in many biological reactions. As we shall see in the next chapter, they are used directly in the energy reactions that are absolutely necessary to all living organisms.

There are other six-carbon sugars. Fructose is a six-carbon sugar found in many kinds of fruit. Fructose has the same composition as glucose (six carbons, twelve hydrogens, six oxygens), but its structure differs slightly from the glucose structure. Fructose must be converted into glucose to be used in most chemical reactions occurring in the body.

Disaccharides

Some sugar compounds have two rings bonded together. Sucrose, or table sugar, has one glucose ring and one fructose ring in its structure. When a glucose molecule and a fructose molecule combine, hydrogen and oxygen are broken off and a water molecule

34

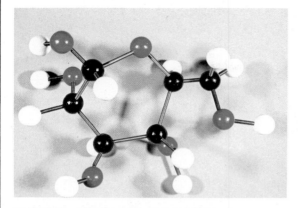

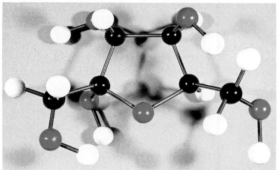

Figure 2-7. Models of two simple monosaccharides, glucose (top) and fructose (bottom). Black represents carbon; white, hydrogen; and red, oxygen.

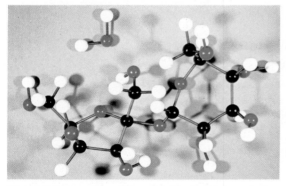

Figure 2-8. Sucrose, a disaccharide, is composed of a glucose and a fructose molecule.

is formed. An oxygen atom of one simple sugar combines with a carbon atom of the other, and a **disaccharide** (two-sugar) molecule is formed.

Disaccharides cannot be used by the body directly. They must first be broken down into simple sugars. The reaction that breaks apart the disaccharide molecule requires the addition of a molecule of water.

Polysaccharides

The chaining together of simple sugar molecules does not have to stop at two sugars. **Polysaccharides** ("many sugars") are complex carbohydrates formed by the chaining together of many simple sugar molecules.

Starch, glycogen, and cellulose are all composed of many glucose units. However, the number and arrangement of glucose units differ in each of these three compounds.

LIPIDS

When we think of fat, we generally regard it as something undesirable, to be dieted away. But the **lipids,** the organic group that includes the fats, perform many functions in the body. Lipids are used for energy storage. They are part of the cell and organelle membranes, where they regulate the flow of materials in and out of the cell or organelle. Some hormones are lipids. Hormones are molecules that stimulate important activities in an organism, such as flowering in plants or speeding up the heartbeat in animals. We will discuss them in some detail in chapter 9.

Fats

Fats are a type of lipid composed of one molecule of glycerol and three fatty acid molecules (see figure 2-9). The fatty acid molecules are chains of carbon atoms with different numbers of attached hydrogens. Notice that these are elements that are also found in carbohydrates. When you eat more carbohydrates than you can use immediately for energy, or store as glycogen, the carbohydrates are converted into fats and stored in your body for later use.

Today many cooking oils and margarine spreads are advertised as being "low in saturated fats and cholesterol." What does this mean, and why are saturated fats supposed to be bad?

A **saturated fat** is one whose fatty acid molecules contain as many hydrogens as can possibly bond to all the carbon atoms. An **unsaturated fat** has double or triple bonds between some of the carbon atoms in the fatty acid chains. When these bonds are broken, more hydrogen can be added to the fatty acid molecules.

If your diet is high in saturated fats, the production of cholesterol, another type of lipid, is increased. Cholesterol is essential for the digestion of some other types of fat, and for synthesizing hormones, but when the body has too much cholesterol, it may be deposited on the walls of the blood vessels. Deposits of cholesterol gradually narrow the blood vessels. This increases your likelihood of developing high blood pressure and having a heart attack.

Phospholipids

In some lipids a phosphoric acid group (a functional group such as we described earlier in the chapter) replaces one of the fatty acid chains. A nitrogen compound is usually attached to the phosphoric acid group. These lipids are called **phospholipids.**

Phospholipids are polar molecules. The part of the phospholipid containing the phosphoric acid group is water-soluble and positively charged. The fatty-acid end of the molecule is not charged, and therefore is not soluble in water.

Phospholipids, as we saw in chapter 1, are components of the cell membrane. The

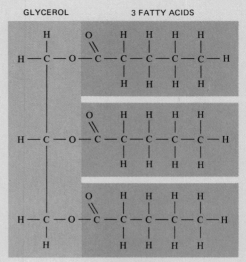

SATURATED FAT

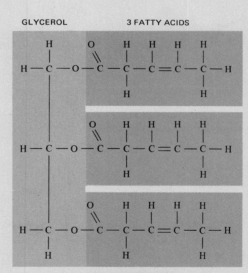

UNSATURATED FAT

Figure 2-9. Saturated and unsaturated fat molecules. In the unsaturated fat, a double bond has formed between two of the carbons in each fatty acid. By reducing this to a single bond, each of the two carbons can be freed to bind to another atom of hydrogen.

PATTERNS OF STRUCTURE
AND FUNCTION

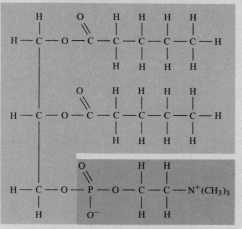

LIPID (GLYCEROL AND FATTY ACIDS)
UNCHARGED; INSOLUBLE

PHOSPHATE-NITROGEN GROUP
CHARGED; SOLUBLE

PHOSPHOLIPID

Figure 2-10. A phospholipid molecule. Note the negative charge on the oxygen at lower left in the phosphate–nitrogen (phosphoric acid) group. This is what gives this end of the molecule its charge and makes it water-soluble.

phospholipid molecules appear to line up in a double layer so that their water-soluble end points outward and their insoluble end points in toward the center of the membrane. This arrangement is very important in all the various activities of the membrane, such as its interactions with materials inside and outside the cell, and the transporting of materials through the membrane itself.

Waxes

Still another group of lipids are the **waxes.** These, like fats, are composed of fatty acid chains linked to a molecule of alcohol. However, the alcohol molecule is larger than glycerol, with more carbons. Also, the fatty acid molecules are nearly always saturated. Waxes are rarely found in cells. Instead, they are secreted by the cells and form a protective outer covering, or sometimes a specialized structure. The waterproof beeswax cells of honeycombs are examples of such structures. Waxy coverings, called cuticles, are secreted by practically every land plant on leaves, young stems, and other surfaces that might be injured by drying. Apples have a cuticle—this is why they can be polished to a high shine. Animals also secrete waxes. We are all familiar with earwax. Another animal wax is lanolin, which is secreted onto the wool of sheep. It is removed when the wool is processed, and forms an important part of some cosmetics and pharmaceuticals.

Steroids

Another class of lipids, called **steroids,** have a very different structure from the other lipids we have mentioned. Instead of chains of fatty acids, they have four interlocking carbon rings, with a variety of side groups attached. Cholesterol is a steroid; so are many hormones and some vitamins. Another is cortisone, widely used to treat asthma, allergies, and other conditions.

THE MOSQUITO

It's a cool, pleasant summer evening. As you sit on the porch of your vacation cabin and watch the sunset over the lake, your mood is tranquil and relaxed. Abruptly the tranquility is broken by an ominous buzzing and the realization that something small and winged has just whisked by your nose. You swat at it. The buzzing fades, but returns quickly. This time you leap up from your chair, pursuing the creature across the porch with waving arms. When it seems to be gone for good, you return to your seat. All is peaceful—until you feel a sudden tiny stab in your arm. Once more you swat, and then scratch the itching welt that is rising rapidly. The ubiquitous mosquito has struck again.

Almost without exception, wherever humans are to be found the mosquito is somewhere nearby. This prolific pest is more than just a biting nuisance. It is also a major carrier of diseases, all of them serious and frequently fatal. Among the more familiar are malaria, yellow fever, and viral encephalitis. Until the relationship between mosquitoes and disease was recognized and methods of mosquito control were devised, large portions of Africa and South America were, for all practical purposes, uninhabitable by humans. Attempts at settlement of these areas were met by hordes of disease-carrying mosquitoes.

But pest that it is, the mosquito is, at least, an interesting pest. It belongs to the order Diptera, which includes a variety of stinging and biting flies as well as many that are useful to humans. There are about 2,000 known species of mosquito, but the one most frequently encountered in the United States is the common house mosquito, *Culex pipiens.* In southern climates *Culex* may be a carrier of viral encephalitis. But in northern parts of the country, especially where routine methods of mosquito control are exercised, this disease is rarely seen.

The life cycle of *Culex,* like that of all mosquitoes, begins in the water. While a few species lay their eggs in cold, flowing streams, *Culex* prefers warmish, stagnant water. The female will choose any location from a rain puddle to a swamp to an old tin can. Resting lightly on the water and supported by its surface tension, she deposits her eggs and then forms them into a floating raft, held together by a sticky, glue-like substance.

The eggs hatch into tiny larvae, often called "wrigglers" because of the way they move. Mosquito larvae are air-breathers, but since they live under water this requires a special adaptation. The wrigglers dangle from the surface of the water by a snorkel-like tube at the rear of their bodies. They receive air through the tube when hanging from the surface, but can close the end of their snorkel when they wish to submerge

completely. This unusual method of breathing has provided an important key to mosquito control. If a film of oil is poured over the surface of the water, the wrigglers' snorkel tubes cannot penetrate the oil, and they quickly suffocate.

The pupal stage that follows is also air-breathing. The pupae are called "tumblers." Unlike most insect pupae, they remain active, turning somersaults as they move through the water. After a period of time that varies with the species and the weather, the adult mosquito emerges from the pupa. It rests briefly on the surface of the water, and then flies away in search of a meal and a mate.

Among mosquitoes, the female of the species is decidedly more deadly than the male. Both males and females feed on plant juices, but in order for her eggs to mature and develop after mating the female must also have blood. At least one blood meal, animal or human, is necessary before egg-laying can begin, and the female may feed on several different hosts in succession. It is during this process of moving from meal to meal that the mosquito transmits disease, injecting contaminated blood from a disease-carrying victim into the body of the next victim she bites.

The mosquito's "bite" is actually a puncture wound made by her long stylet, and its discomfort is not solely due to the piercing of the skin. Before she begins to suck up blood from the puncture, the mosquito first injects the wound with her saliva, which contains a chemical that prevents the blood from clotting. It is this chemical that causes the itching, burning sensation of a mosquito bite, and the swelling of the flesh around the point of puncture.

As many people are aware, mosquitoes seem to be capriciously attracted to some individuals but not to others. Research indicates that the female mosquito is attracted to her victim by its body heat, and that the individual's particular appeal for her is determined by its natural body odors. Most mosquito repellents that are applied to the skin contain an aroma which the insect dislikes. Mosquitoes also prefer to attack people wearing dark-colored clothing rather than those dressed in white or light colors.

With all its unpleasant features, the mosquito still has considerable value to the ecological scheme. Wrigglers and tumblers provide food for many birds, as well as for a variety of water-dwelling animals. The so-called "mosquito fish," a member of the minnow family, is often deliberately imported into waters where a mosquito problem exists. It is harder, though, to find words of praise for the adult mosquito. However, we might note that it can transmit the virus which causes myxomatosis in rabbits, a disease which has been used to control the spread of rabbit populations in England and Australia.

Dubious praise, indeed!

PROTEINS

Proteins are everywhere in living tissue. Yet only in the past few decades have scientists made some progress toward understanding their structure and how they perform in living organisms. Proteins form a large part of many structural tissues. Hair, skin, bone, and teeth are formed largely from proteins. Proteins make it possible for our muscles to move our bones and for our hearts to beat. Enzymes, the biological catalysts which regulate all chemical reactions in the body, are proteins.

Proteins are very large molecules. Like other carbon compounds, they can have many different structures. Although the structure of most proteins is not known, we can describe protein structure in general terms. This is possible because we know how the basic units of the protein, the **amino acids,** are linked together.

Amino acids

Each protein is composed of a long chain of amino acids, just as the polysaccharides are composed of long chains of simple sugars.

What does an amino acid look like? Each amino acid has five essential parts. As you can see in figure 2-11, each amino acid is built around a central carbon atom. A hydrogen atom is always attached to this carbon atom, as are an **amino group** (HNH or H_2N) and a **carboxyl group** (COOH).

These groups and the hydrogen atom provide three of the electrons carbon must share with other atoms to complete its outer electron shell. The fourth electron is provided by what is called an **R group.** "R group" is shorthand for any group of atoms. Each of the 20 different amino acids has a different R group. Three of the simpler amino acids are shown in figure 2-12. The R group is shown attached to the carbon atom from below.

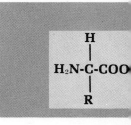

Figure 2-11. The parts of an amino acid are shown here. Attached to the carbon atom in the center are a single hydrogen atom (above), then (reading clockwise) an acid group, an R group, and an amino group.

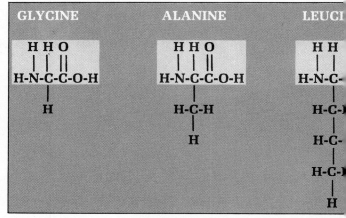

Figure 2-12. These are three of the simplest amino acids. Only the R group differs in each one.

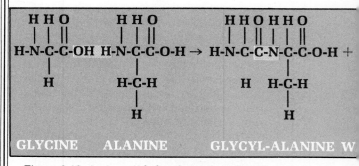

Figure 2-13. Amino acids bond together, forming a molecule of water by dehydration.

40

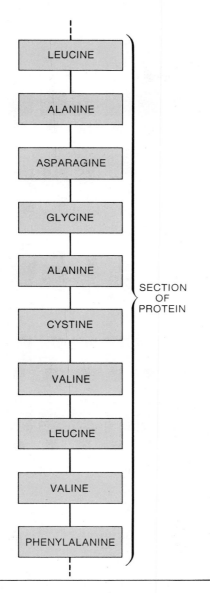

LEUCINE

ALANINE

ASPARAGINE

GLYCINE

ALANINE

CYSTINE

VALINE

LEUCINE

VALINE

PHENYLALANINE

SECTION
OF
PROTEIN

Figure 2-14. Proteins are long chains of amino acids. Their sequence is called the protein's primary structure.

How is a protein constructed from amino acids? The first step is the linking together of amino acids to form an amino acid chain. The amino group (H₂N) of one amino acid links itself to the carboxyl group (COOH) of the next amino acid in the chain. In this reaction **(dehydration)**, a molecule of water is formed, just as when two simple sugar molecules form a disaccharide. Several amino acid chains combine to form the protein molecule.

The order or sequence of the amino acids in the chain is very important in determining how the protein will act. If the amino acid sequence is not correct—sometimes if even one amino acid is out of place—the protein will not function correctly. The sequence of amino acids forming a particular protein is called the **primary structure** of the protein.

However, proteins do not exist as long, straight chains. Each chain usually forms a spiral like the threads of a screw. The spiral is produced by hydrogen bonding between branches of the amino acids on the chain. Occasionally, other shapes are formed instead of spirals. The regular twisting of the amino acid chain is called the **secondary structure** of the protein.

Sometimes, in addition, the amino acid chain will double back on itself, winding around to form a globular protein. This type of twisting is called the **tertiary structure** of the protein. Bonds between sulfur atoms (called disulfide bridges), hydrogen bonds, and other weak interactions between the different R groups hold the tertiary structure in place.

The structure of a protein is important. If the sequence of amino acids in the chain— that is, the primary structure—is changed, this affects the way in which the chain can spiral and twist to form the higher levels of structure. The entire shape of the protein may be different. This, in turn, is likely to change the way in which the protein will attach to other molecules. Therefore it changes the shape of the larger structure being formed, and upsets its functioning.

Sickle-cell anemia: one wrong amino acid

Sickle-cell anemia is an inherited disease involving hemoglobin, the oxygen-carrying protein found in red blood cells. When people with sickle-cell anemia do not get enough oxygen, the hemoglobin in their red blood cells forms long crystals. The hemoglobin crystals change the shape of the red cells so that they look somewhat like sickles, instead of concave. "Sickled" cells are more fragile than normal red blood cells, and they do not carry oxygen as well.

Hemoglobin is a protein composed of four amino acid chains. The chains are arranged around an iron-containing pigment, reddish in color, called heme. (This is what gives red blood cells their color.) The heme pigment combines with oxygen in the blood and carries it to all parts of the body.

Vernon Ingram, an English scientist, studied the structure of the hemoglobin protein. In 1957, he identified the amino acid sequence in the four amino acid chains. He found that the hemoglobin in sickle cells was very slightly different in amino acid composition from that found in normal cells.

There are 547 individual amino acids in the four amino acid chains. In sickle-cell hemoglobin, one amino acid was different. At position six in two of the chains, the amino acid glutamic acid was found in normal hemoglobin. In sickle-cell hemoglobin, however, the amino acid valine was found at this position in one of those chains.

This single substitution in amino acid sequence is the cause of a serious disease. How does the substitution have this effect?

In this case, the problem is not a change in the tertiary structure of the protein, such as we described above. Sickle-cell hemoglobin is basically the same shape as normal hemoglobin. But that substitute valine is on the surface of the molecule, in contact with the surrounding watery environment in the

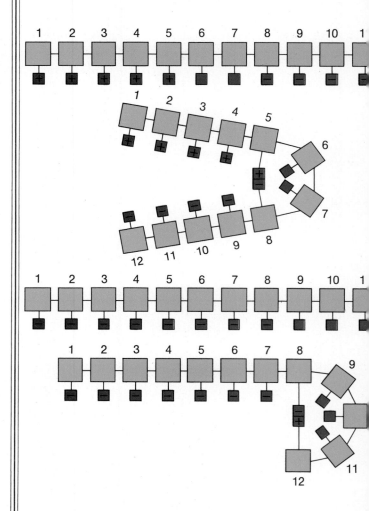

Figure 2-15. A protein chain of amino acids can twist and bend in a variety of ways, because certain amino acids bond with each other. In the top illustration, amino acids 5 and 8 bond with each other, bending this protein chain in half. In the bottom illustration, bonding between amino acids 8 and 12 produces a very different shape. (The pluses and minuses are used here to indicate that only certain amino acids can bond with each other.)

42

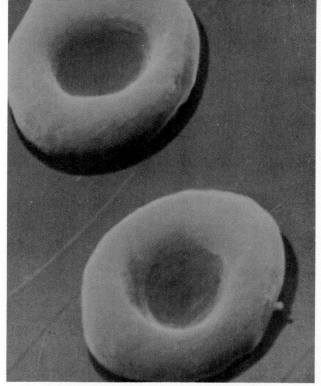

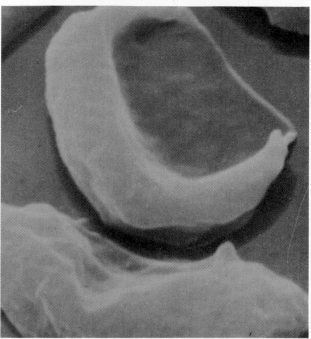

Figure 2-16. Two normal red blood cells are shown in the top picture. The two red blood cells in the bottom picture are "sickled" cells that cannot carry oxygen as efficiently.

cell. Valine, unlike glutamic acid, is relatively non-polar, so it tends to be attracted away from the polar water molecules and toward a non-polar area on a neighboring hemoblogin molecule. This tendency is strongest when oxygen is in short supply. It is this linking up of non-polar areas that produces the long hemoglobin crystals and misshapen, dangerously fragile red cells of sickle-cell anemia.

Enzymes

Before we finish our discussion of proteins, we should mention one particularly important class—the **enzymes.** Enzymes are globular proteins (like hemoglobin). They are usually fairly large.

Enzymes make it possible for biological reactions to occur. They assist in these reactions without being changed themselves. Every time something is built up or taken apart in the cell, enzymes are involved. We shall see in the next chapter how they operate.

NUCLEIC ACIDS

The last class of carbon compounds we will mention are the **nucleic acids.** Nucleic acids are the major components of the hereditary and information-carrying units of the cell.

Nucleic acids are composed of fundamental units called **nucleotides.** Nucleotides are composed of carbon, hydrogen, oxygen, phosphorus, and nitrogen. There are different types of nucleotide—just as there are different types of amino acid. We will discuss nucleotide structure in greater detail in chapter 16.

Each nucleic acid is composed of a specific sequence of nucleotides. The sequence determines the properties of the nucleic acid, just as the sequence of amino acids in the amino acid chain determines the properties of a protein.

SUMMARY

In this chapter we have looked at some fundamental chemistry concepts necessary to understanding of the chemical reactions that take place in living organisms.

Ninety-two elements occur in nature. The smallest unit of matter is the atom. Atoms are composed of still smaller particles called protons (+ charge), neutrons (no charge), and electrons (− charge). Electrons orbit the central nucleus of the atom, which contains protons and usually neutrons. The number of electrons in the outer electron shell of an atom is important in determining the types of compound it will form.

A compound is formed when atoms share or exchange electrons to make a chemical bond. Atoms may form covalent bonds by sharing electrons, or ionic bonds by transferring them. The hydrogen bond is a weak polar covalent bond.

When ionic compounds are placed in water, they ionize to form ions, or charged particles. Two special kinds of ionic compound are the acids (compounds that increase H^+ ions in a solution) and the bases (compounds that decrease H^+ ions in a solution). The acidity of a solution is measured on the pH scale.

The elements most essential to living organisms are carbon, oxygen, hydrogen, phosphorus, sulfur, and nitrogen. Water (H_2O) makes up 80 to 95 percent of living matter. It is an excellent solvent for many substances used by living organisms. Water has unusual properties because of the hydrogen bonding that occurs between its molecules.

Compounds are either organic or inorganic. Organic compounds are those that contain carbon chains. They are very numerous because of the structure of carbon. The four most important classes of organic compounds are carbohydrates, lipids, proteins, and nucleic acids.

Carbohydrates are energy compounds. The simple sugar glucose is used in many reactions that produce and store energy in the body. Disaccharides such as sucrose (table sugar) are formed from two molecules of simple sugar. Polysaccharides (complex carbohydrates) are long chains of simple sugar molecules.

Lipids, the class of compounds that includes fats, are also used for energy storage. Other types of lipid are phospholipids, waxes, and steroids.

Most of the structural material in living organisms is formed of proteins. Proteins are constructed from chains of amino acids, coiled and twisted into specific shapes. The shape of a protein is important in determining whether it functions correctly. Enzymes are a very important class of proteins.

Nucleic acids are compounds that compose DNA and RNA. They are made up of long chains of nucleotides.

Review questions

1. How many elements are currently known? How many of these occur naturally on this planet?

2. Name the six elements necessary to life as we know it.

3. What are the four important groups of organic compounds?

4. Define the term "atom." What do we mean by calling the atom the fundamental unit of matter?

5. Distinguish between protons, electrons, and neutrons. What charge does each carry?

6. What is an electron shell?

7. How is a compound formed?

8. What happens to an atom when it gives up an electron? When it takes up an electron?

9. What is an ionic bond?

10. A sulfur atom has 16 electrons in three shells. Draw a diagram of the arrangement of these electrons in electron shells.

11. When a sulfur atom bonds with another substance, will it tend to pick up or lose electrons? How many? What will its valence be then?

12. What is ionization?

13. A potassium atom has 19 electrons. A chlorine atom has 17. Draw a diagram to illustrate the formation of an ionic compound between these two atoms. Which is the positive ion?

14. Distinguish between acids and bases.

15. What is the importance of pH value to chemical reactions within the body?

16. What is a covalent bond?

17. Why is water (H_2O) called a polar molecule?

18. Distinguish between cohesion and adhesion.

19. What is capillary action?

20. What are the two classes of chemical compounds? Name several examples of each.

21. What properties of the carbon atom make it possible for almost a million hydrocarbon compounds to exist?

22. How is a polysaccharide formed?

23. What would happen if the cell membrane were composed of the water-soluble simple sugar glucose instead of partially insoluble phospholipid molecules?

24. Name the five parts of the amino acid molecule.

25. How does the substitution of one amino acid for another in the amino acid sequence of a protein alter the effectiveness of that protein?

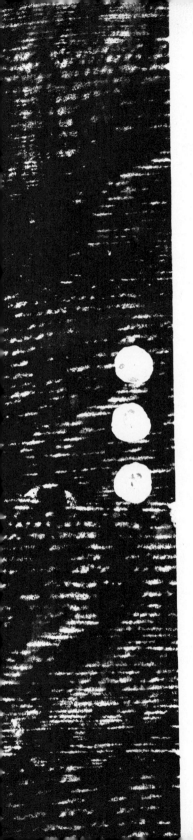

Energy and Organisms

Anything an organism does requires energy. The chemical reactions that take place in cells involve the use or transfer of energy. The very structures that carry on the reactions are themselves "storehouses" of energy, for energy is contained in the bonds that hold them together. How, then, is this energy obtained, stored, and made available for use?

When atoms or molecules come together into compounds or more complex compounds, energy is used in forming the bonds that join them. As long as the bond holds, that energy is, in some way, stored in it. When the bond is broken, the energy is released and becomes available for some other use.

In this chapter we will look at how cells store, release, and transfer chemical energy. For long-term energy storage, most cells use the complex molecules of fats or of polysaccharides, such as starch. However, it appears that most chemical energy used by cells in chemical reactions is made available through the "high-energy" phosphate bonds of compounds called **triphosphates.** The most common of these seems to be adenosine triphosphate, abbreviated as **ATP.**

ATP: ENERGY CURRENCY OF THE CELL

All cells—whether they are found in algae, an oak tree, or your own body—use triphosphates to power most vital chemical reactions. The principal triphosphate, ATP, stores chemical energy in high-energy bonds that attach three phosphate groups to adenosine, a nitrogen-containing compound.

When the bond between the second and third phosphate group is broken, as shown in figure 3-1, a large amount of energy is released. This bond can be imagined as a coiled spring. When the spring is tightly coiled, it contains **potential energy,** energy that is locked in the coil but is not available for use. When the bond is broken, the spring uncoils and the energy is released. This energy, which is now available to do work, is called **kinetic energy.**

Breaking off the last phosphate group from ATP leaves a compound called adenosine diphosphate, or **ADP.** In a simplified way, this reaction can be written:

$$ATP \longrightarrow ADP + phosphate + energy$$

There is another high-energy bond between the first and second phosphate groups in ADP. Sometimes this bond is also broken, leaving adenosine monophosphate, or AMP.

Because ATP is used by all cells as their chief energy carrier, it is often called the "energy currency" of the cell. Most reactions that do any work in the cell require the energy carried in ATP and other triphosphate compounds.

How is ATP made?

The next question is: Where do cells get the ATP they need? Cells do not contain an endless supply of ATP; in fact, they contain very little of it at any one time. Nor do they take it in from the outside. Where does it come from?

The answer is that ATP is formed inside the cells as it is needed, by adding a phosphate group to ADP, a reaction known as **phosphorylation.** This reaction can be written:

$$ADP + phosphate + energy \longrightarrow ATP$$

But for this reaction, energy is required. So we seem to have an endless circle. ATP is needed to provide energy, but energy is needed to manufacture ATP. Where do cells obtain the necessary energy to begin with?

Some cells, called **autotrophic** cells, can

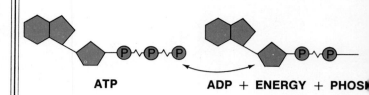

ATP   ADP + ENERGY + PHOSI

Figure 3-1. The structure of adenosine triphosphate (ATP). The bonds between the phosphates are high-energy bonds. A break in the bond between the second and third phosphate group releases a large amount of energy.

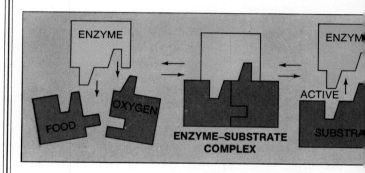

ENZYME   ENZYM

FOOD   OXYGEN   ACTIVE

ENZYME–SUBSTRATE COMPLEX   SUBSTRA

Figure 3-2. The enzyme is a catalyst, combining oxygen and food molecules by forming an enzyme–substrate complex. This process is reversible.

trap energy from sunlight by means of chlorophyll and transform it into the chemical bond energy of ATP. This process is called photosynthesis. The energy stored in the ATP is then used in synthesizing energy-rich carbohydrates from water and carbon dioxide, which are low in energy. In the process, molecules of oxygen are produced. The excess oxygen can then be used by other organisms. Photosynthetic cells are found in many microorganisms—especially the one-celled algae—and in the green parts of plants.

Cells that are not autotrophic can still synthesize ATP from ADP and phosphate. These **heterotrophic** cells obtain the necessary energy by breaking down complex compounds, such as carbohydrates. This process is called **cellular respiration.** (Cellular respiration should not be confused with breathing—a process that is sometimes called respiration.)

Cellular respiration usually involves the use of oxygen and results in the breakdown of complex carbon compounds—which are rich in energy—to carbon dioxide and water, which are energy-poor. Some of the energy released along the way is used in synthesizing ATP.

ENERGY REACTIONS IN THE CELL

If you were to light a match and throw it into a tank of gasoline, what would happen? Probably the gasoline would explode into flames, as it combined with the oxygen in the surrounding air. The flame of the match would provide the initial heat energy necessary to start the reaction of gasoline with oxygen. As the reaction got under way, the bonds of the gasoline molecules would be broken suddenly and violently. The heat generated by the release of energy from the broken bonds would cause the gasoline to burst into flames.

This same type of reaction occurs in the engine of an automobile, but the engine does not go up in flames. Here, the reaction is carefully controlled. Small amounts of gasoline and oxygen are allowed to mix in the presence of a spark generated by a spark plug. Enough heat is generated by their reaction to expand gases in the engine cylinder. The expanding gases move the pistons, thus harnessing chemical energy as mechanical energy.

The reactions that take place in living cells are more like those occurring in the automobile engine than like the explosion in the tank. Cellular reactions are very carefully controlled. If the amount of heat released by reactions in a cell were too great, the cell would be injured or destroyed. Thus, it is important that all cellular reactions take place step by step. Energy and heat must be released at each step in amounts the cell can handle.

Now, though, a new problem arises. Even a step-by-step reaction needs some heat energy to get it started. If the energy is not available, the reaction will not occur, or else it will proceed too slowly to meet the cell's needs. But the amount of heat that would be enough to start a reaction would also be enough to kill the cell. This is where enzymes come in.

Enzymes and catalysis

Enzymes, as we noted in chapter 2, are proteins that assist in, or **catalyze,** chemical reactions in the cells. Basically, they act by lowering the amount of energy needed to start the reaction. Thus, the reaction can take place without dangerous overheating of the cell.

Enzymes are large molecules. The reacting substances in biological reactions are usually smaller molecules. These small molecules, or **reactants,** fit into particular sites on the enzyme molecule. In this way, the different reactants are held close together at these **active sites** until they react with one another. Then the product of the reaction is released. The enzyme itself is not changed, and can continue to catalyze more reactions of the same sort. Such a molecule, which assists in a reaction without itself being changed, is called a **catalyst.**

Enzymes catalyze all the steps in photosynthesis and cellular respiration. Because of this, the reactions can be kept going smoothly—fast enough, but not too fast. The cell can get the products it needs, without burning itself up in the process.

thought, though, that the reactant often plays a more active role in the reactant–enzyme combination. The reactant is thought to "induce" the enzyme to assume the correct shape as it binds to the enzyme. This theory is called the induced fit theory.

Oxidation–reduction reactions
The reactions taking place in cells are like

AND NOW, AN ARTIFICIAL LEAF

We hear a lot about solar energy these days. There is plenty of it around; the problem is, how to tap it? How can the sun's radiation be harnessed to help solve the energy crisis, the food crisis, or whatever other crisis needs solving? Plants, of course, have been tapping the sun's energy for thousands of years, by photosynthesis. Scientists have dreamed of finding out how they do it and putting the knowledge to work.

Now it appears that the dream may be on the way to becoming reality. A group of Illinois scientists have created an "artificial leaf" that actually performs the first step in photosynthesis. The new invention looks more like a grasshopper than like a leaf. It consists of a glass compartment, divided by a plastic membrane. On one side of the membrane is an oxidizing chemical, on the other a re-

ducing chemical. The membrane between them contains chlorophyll.

The artificial leaf operates much as its natural counterpart does. When the chlorophyll is exposed to light, electrons are transferred through the membrane from one side to the other, setting up an electrical charge. In natural leaves, such a charge is believed to start up the process of splitting water molecules, synthesizing carbohydrates, and releasing oxygen.

If the new leaf can be elaborated so that it will do these things, important practical applications are possible. For one thing, the artificial leaf could be used to store electricity for power, just as is now done in batteries. More dramatically, it could synthesize carbohydrates and protein for food—perhaps vastly increasing the world's annual production. Or it could be used to help clean up the environment by turning out fuel in the form of hydrogen, which is non-polluting.

Each enzyme catalyzes only a specific kind of reaction. Some enzymes catalyze only one reaction. Why are enzymes so specific? The answer lies in their structure.

Each enzyme possesses active sites of a particular shape. Only certain reactants fit into these sites. One theory of enzyme action—the lock-and-key hypothesis—compares the enzyme to a lock opened only by a particular key—the reactant. It is now

the one in the automobile engine in another way. Many cellular reactions, including photosynthesis and respiration, are **oxidation-reduction** reactions. The burning of gasoline with oxygen is also an oxidation–reduction reaction.

In this type of reaction, one chemical compound donates an electron to another compound. The compound giving up the electron (the **electron donor**) is said to be

PATTERNS OF STRUCTURE
AND FUNCTION

oxidized, while the compound that takes up the electron (the **electron acceptor**) is said to be **reduced.**

In a sense, there are really two reactions—an energy-releasing one and an energy-using one—with a net transfer of energy from one compound to the other. The compound that is oxidized loses energy, because a bond is broken when the electron is lost. The compound that is reduced gains energy, because a bond is formed. Thus we may speak of oxidation–reduction reactions as **energy-transfer reactions.** In many reactions inside living cells, a compound is oxidized or reduced by the removal or addition of a hydrogen atom. As we have seen, the hydrogen atom consists of a single proton orbited by a single electron. So far as the energy is concerned, all that is important is the electron of the hydrogen atom. However, when a compound is reduced by the addition of hydrogen, both the proton and the electron of the hydrogen atom are transferred to the reduced compound)the electron acceptor).

A compound may also be reduced by the removal of an oxygen atom, or oxidized by the addition of oxygen. (This is how oxidation reactions got their name.) In living cells, however, reduction or oxidation is usually accomplished by the addition or removal of hydrogen.

In the remainder of this chapter we will be studying the energy-transforming reactions—those that result in the creation of ATP—in living cells. All these reactions have several characteristics in common: (1) they take place in a series of small steps; (2) they involve enzymes; (3) they involve oxidation–reduction reactions; (4) in common with most other reactions, they are regulated by the cell's need for their products—that is, when the ATP supply exceeds the demand, oxidation temporarily slows down or stops.

PHOTOSYNTHESIS

First we will look at the process of photosyn-

thesis, the set of reactions on which all living cells, directly or indirectly, depend for energy.

Most photosynthesis occurs in chloroplasts, the chlorophyll-containing organelles of autotrophic cells. Here, ATP is formed from ADP and phosphate groups, and sugars are synthesized from carbon dioxide and water. The overall reaction of photosynthesis may be written:

$$6CO_2 + 12H_2O \xrightarrow[\text{light}]{\text{chlorophyll}}$$
$$6O_2 + C_6H_{12}O_6 + 6H_2O$$

There are two sets of reactions in photosynthesis. One set takes place only in the light; the other set can occur in the dark. However, the dark reactions must utilize the products of the light reactions, so they cannot go on by themselves for very long.

Before we describe the reactions of photosynthesis, we will first consider the unique characteristics of the autotrophic cell that make photosynthesis possible.

Chlorophyll: the light-sensitive pigment

Chlorophyll, the green pigment in autotrophic cells, absorbs some wavelengths of light energy, mostly in the blue–violet and red regions of the spectrum. It appears green because it reflects most green light, rather than absorbing it. There are several slightly different kinds of chlorophyll. These absorb slightly different wavelengths of light and appear as slightly different shades of green. The most common, and most important for photosynthesis, is chlorophyll-*a*.

When light strikes a chlorophyll molecule, the molecule absorbs light energy and transfers it to an electron. The electron is raised to a higher energy level, or "excited." An "excited" electron is unstable and tends to "fall back" to its previous energy level, releasing its extra energy as it does so.

If chlorophyll is isolated in a test tube and stimulated with light, the excited electrons fall back to their original energy levels very quickly. As they do this, they give off the extra energy in the form of visible light, or fluorescence. This phenomenon shows that the electrons of chlorophyll are able to absorb light energy. In the test tube, though, they cannot hold onto the extra energy.

In the cell the electrons do not lose their extra energy as light. Instead, a series of other pigments and electron acceptors take up the excited electrons. Each time electrons are transferred to another acceptor at a lower energy level, some of their extra energy is given up, and is used in reducing some substance.

In chapter 1, we described briefly the structure of chloroplasts. These are the cell organelles in which chlorophyll is usually found. You will recall that the chlorophyll is contained in sac-like thylakoids, and that these are often arranged in stacks called grana. More precisely, the thylakoids contain layers of specialized membranes called **lamellae.** The chlorophyll molecules are built into these lamellae. Also found in the chloroplasts are the enzymes that catalyze the reactions of photosynthesis. The chlorophyll and other pigments are organized into photosynthetic units in the lamellae.

The enzymes for the light and dark reactions of photosynthesis are found in different regions in the chloroplasts. Therefore, it appears that these reactions take place in different parts of the organelle.

The light reactions: photophosphorylation

The light and dark reactions of photosynthesis are an interesting example of the ways in which the basic chemical reactions of life interact and support one another. In the light reactions, light energy is trapped and stored in the high-energy bonds of ATP. Also, in these reactions, water molecules are split and their hydrogen atoms are eventually picked up by hydrogen carrier molecules, while their oxygen diffuses out of the cell and is not used. The ATP and the hydrogen from the carrier molecules are then used in the dark reactions, in which sugars are produced. Without the dark reactions, plants

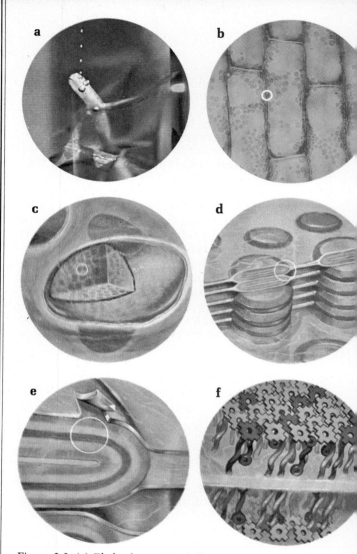

Figure 3-3. (a) *Elodea* leaves give off oxygen bubbles during photosynthesis. (b) Light energy is transformed and oxygen is released by the chloroplast (circled). (c) Magnification of the same area chows the chloroplast more clearly. (d) The grana in chloroplasts contain thin layers of chlorophyll. (e) Each chlorophyll layer contains many bead-shaped photosynthetic units. (f) Chlorophyll molecules (green) are found among other molecules of pigment.

Figure 3-4. Glucose can serve as raw material for all manufacturing processes of the cell. The albino corn plant in the foreground contains no chloroplasts. It was kept alive and growing while fed only glucose.

Figure 3-5. A solution of chlorophyll in alcohol fluoresces when a bright light shines on it.

could not produce carbohydrates. But without the light reactions, they would not have the energy and the hydrogen needed for the dark reactions. How, then, do these reactions work?

The **light reactions** of photosynthesis are unique to autotrophic cells. These reactions, unlike those in any other type of cell, use light energy to produce ATP and to split water molecules into hydrogen and hydroxyl (OH^-) ions. All other energy-transforming reactions, in both autotrophic and heterotrophic cells, require chemical energy, usually in the form of ATP.

The light reactions begin when light strikes chlorophyll molecules in the chloroplast and excites their electrons. The excited electrons do not immediately return to their previous energy level. Instead, they are passed from one chlorophyll molecule to another, and then "lifted" to a chain of molecules called **electron carriers.** Some of these are iron-containing pigments called **cytochromes.**

Because the series of reactions followed by the electrons is regular and consistent, it is often referred to as a "pathway." In the simplest pathway of the light reactions, the excited electrons are passed down the chain of cytochromes until they return to the group of chlorophyll molecules from which they were taken. As they pass down the chain, they lose their "excitement" energy bit by bit. Some of this energy is used in the formation of ATP from ADP and phosphate groups in the cell environment. The rest of the energy is passed off as heat.

This form of light reaction is known as **cyclic photophosphorylation.** It is cyclic because the electrons return to their chlorophyll source and can be reused in the same process. "Phosphorylation" means that phosphate is added to the ADP to form ATP, and "photo" means that this is done by means of light energy.

Cyclic photophosphorylation would be enough to supply the energy for synthesizing carbohydrates. But a supply of hydrogen is also needed. The hydrogen is obtained from water, through the second form of light reaction. In this form, too, light energy is used and ATP is formed, but the excited electrons are not returned to the chlorophyll. Therefore the pathway is known as **noncyclic photophosphorylation.**

In noncyclic photophosphorylation, light energy strikes chlorophyll in a different photosynthetic unit, called **photosystem II.** Here, too, an electron is excited and boosted up to a cytochrome carrier chain. It passes down the chain, giving up energy, and ATP is formed. But when it reaches the bottom of the chain, it does not fall back into the chlorophyll of photosystem II. Instead, it apparently goes to the chlorophyll of the cyclic pathway, known as **photosystem I.**

This gives the cyclic pathway an extra electron, which it must get rid of. So when the chlorophyll is struck by light and the new electron (or another one) is boosted up to the top of the electron carrier chain, it is not passed down the chain. Instead, it is transferred to another electron acceptor—

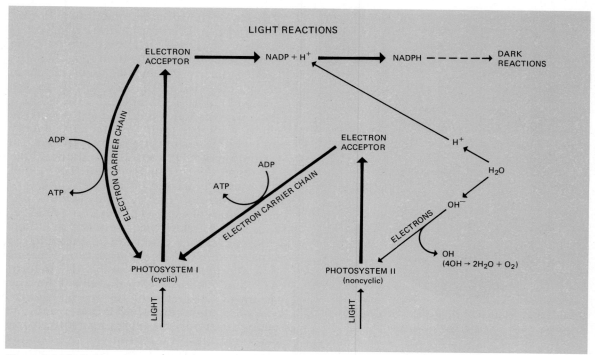

Figure 3-6. The light reactions of photosynthesis. The curved arrows "bouncing off" the main pathways of the reaction indicate that something—in this case ADP— is fed into the reaction and either loses or gains material, contributing to the main reaction as it does so.

often a compound called **NADP** (nicotin-amide adenine dinucleotide phosphate)—and taken out of the cyclic pathway. This restores the proper number of electrons in photosystem I.

In the meantime, the chlorophyll of photosystem II has been left with one electron too few, since its excited electron was not returned to it. To understand how it obtains a new electron, we must recall something that was said in chapter 2. You will recall that water is a polar compound, easily split into hydroxyl ions (OH^-) with one extra electron, and hydrogen ions (H^+), with one electron too few. Since the chlorophyll of photosystem II is missing one electron, it has a positive charge, and acts like a positive ion. This enables it to split the water molecule and attract the negative OH^- ion. The chlorophyll takes the extra electron

from this ion, giving photosystem II a full supply of electrons. The leftover OH groups accumulate, and eventually four of them react with one another, producing two water (H_2O) molecules and one molecule of oxygen (O_2).

But what about that other electron, the one that was taken out of the cycle at the other end of the noncyclic pathway? We left it attached to an electron acceptor. This, of course, gives the acceptor a negative charge. So now the negative acceptor attracts a positive hydrogen ion (H^+) from the water and forms a compound with it—generally NADPH. This is the carrier molecule that will transport hydrogen and contribute it to the dark reactions.

Noncyclic photophosphorylation, then, is like cyclic photophosphorylation in that it produces ATP energy units. But it is unlike

PATTERNS OF STRUCTURE
AND FUNCTION

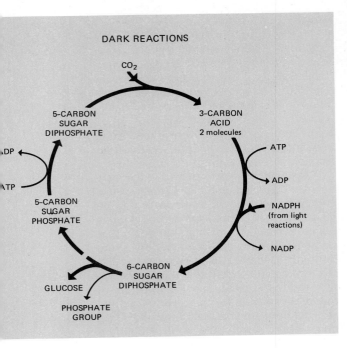

DARK REACTIONS

CO₂

5-CARBON
SUGAR
DIPHOSPHATE

3-CARBON
ACID
2 molecules

ATP

ADP

NADPH
(from light
reactions)

NADP

ADP

ATP

5-CARBON
SUGAR
PHOSPHATE

6-CARBON
SUGAR
DIPHOSPHATE

GLUCOSE

PHOSPHATE
GROUP

Figure 3-7. The dark reactions of photosynthesis: a
simplified presentation omitting some steps.

Figure 3-8. Heterotrophs, such as this moose, cannot
synthesize ATP using energy from the sun. They must
depend on the food provided by autotrophic organisms.

the cyclic pathway in that it also contributes hydrogen for carrier molecules such as NADPH. Both the ATP and the NADPH are now available for the dark reactions.

The dark reactions: carbohydrate synthesis

The **dark reactions,** unlike the light reactions, depend on ATP as an energy supply. In this respect, though not in all, they are like the energy-transformation reactions that take place in heterotrophic cells.

The dark reactions involve many steps. Each step is catalyzed by a separate enzyme and involves oxidation and reduction. In the course of these steps, carbon dioxide (CO_2) is reduced to glucose ($C_6H_{12}O_6$) by the addition of hydrogen atoms from NADPH and other hydrogen-carrying compounds. This reduction involves a complex cycle of reactions. The basic energy for the reactions is provided by the NADPH and the ATP produced during the light reactions. The glucose may then be used by the cell in cellular respiration, or in synthesizing a variety of organic compounds. Usually, glucose molecules are joined together to form a polysaccharide such as starch. Starch, which is very compact and insoluble in water, is kept in the cell as an energy storage compound.

CELLULAR RESPIRATION

Heterotrophic cells cannot synthesize ATP using energy from the sun. Instead, they utilize the chemical bond energy of food—complex compounds such as carbohydrates, proteins, and lipids—in making ATP and doing the work of the cell. The reactions that do this make up the process of cellular respiration. In this section, we will look at several different sets of reactions in this process.

Anaerobic respiration

The first steps in respiration do not require oxygen. Hence, they are called **anaerobic**

55

THE MANDRAKE

Most people have heard of Mandrake the Magician, that comic-strip hero endowed with seemingly supernatural powers. Few of us, however, realize where Mandrake got his name. And yet, mandrakes—certain members of the nightshade family of plants—have formed an important part of medical and magical lore since the dawn of history.

The mandrake probably originated in Persia and spread throughout Europe and Asia along the trade routes. Its deep green leaves grow directly from a long, forked root, and its white, blue, or violet flowers are followed by golden fruit in the summer. It is the root of the mandrake, with its fancied resemblance to the human figure, which has provided the basis for much far-fetched superstition and an equal amount of well-founded medical practice.

Superstitions regarding the mandrake date back to Old Testament times. Ancient Babylonian writings and the Book of Genesis speak of the mandrake as a cure for sterility. The women of the ancient Near East often wore amulets of carved mandrake root to promote passion and fecundity. The Egyptians worshipped the roots as household deities. And in ancient Assyria, pieces of dried mandrake were strung as beads, in the belief that the sight and smell of mandrake protected the wearer from plagues and evil spirits.

The ancient Greeks referred to the mandrake as *Circeium,* in honor of the mythical enchantress Circe, who was skilled in the malevolent use of magical and poisonous plants. However, the Greek physician Hippocrates conducted extensive investigations into its medical uses. He observed that the root could be used to induce perspiration, and recommended an infusion of mandrake in wine for the relief of depression. At the same time, he warned that large doses of the plant could result in delirium and mental distress.

Even the Greeks, however, were not quite able to separate fact from superstition where the mandrake was concerned. Theophrastus, the noted Greek botanist, devised an elaborate ceremony for the gathering of mandrake. This ritual included the drawing of three magic circles around the growing plant with a sword of virgin iron, and anointing the digger with oils as he faced west. Finally, the digger was required to recite a catalogue of the mysteries of love as he dug. (Since practitioners of such magic arts were usually required to remain celibate, at least in theory, it is probable that the recitation was often very short indeed!)

Superstition notwithstanding, the mandrake has been employed effectively throughout the ages to induce semiconscious states in both willing and unwilling subjects. In fact, its genus name, *Mandragora,* is derived from two Sanscrit words which mean "a sleeping substance." Hannibal is said to have left wine spiked with mandrake on a battlefield, to be consumed by his unwitting enemies who were thus drugged into lethargy and later slaughtered. It is related that Julius Caesar escaped from captors by stupefying them with mandrake wine. During the Middle Ages, a mixture of mandrake with certain other herbs was used by physicians to put patients to sleep prior to surgery.

Myths about the mandrake persisted well into the seventeenth century, to the annoyance of the Christian Church. Many twelfth-century Europeans confidently believed that mandrakes grow best under a gallows, that they radiate light at night, that the root should be drenched with a woman's urine or menstrual blood before it is removed from the ground, and that mandrakes shriek when uprooted. The mandrake was thought not only to make men virile and women passionate but to cure every infirmity known to man.

Not surprisingly, many people were willing to pay large sums of money to procure a mandrake root. Since it was most highly regarded when it closely resembled the human figure, a thriving business was built around the carving of mandrakes into human shape—and often, the carving of totally different roots as well, to be sold as mandrakes to the gullible. So-called "hairy mandrakes" were much valued as a defense against demons and witches. In the British Isles, where the plant was rare, some enterprising individuals sold a native root cleverly implanted with sprouted millet grains to resemble a hairy mandrake.

In medieval Germany, magicians used the mandrake to cast their spells. The Church denounced the use of mandrake in such rituals, and attempted to collect and destroy the roots. Still, many beliefs surrounding mandrake-gathering became connected with traditional Church lore. The root was usually gathered on the day consecrated to Saint John the Baptist, and prayers were recited before digging began. After being washed in mothers' milk, the root was placed on the church altar and consecrated by masses in which the name of the Virgin Mary was invoked. Often, the digger was robed in vestments much like those of a priest, and offerings of bread and wine were made to the mandrake.

By the end of the seventeenth century, the legends and ceremonies associated with the mandrake had become so numerous and contradictory that the mythology itself began to erode. The pseudo-science of alchemy was gradually evolving into the science of chemistry, and more people were sufficiently educated to question superstitious beliefs. While mandrake roots were still collected and carved into human shape, few people really accepted their magical properties. The roots became curiosity items, and many of them can still be viewed in museums throughout the world. And yet, in some parts of the East they are still worn as amulets and charms. Even in this modern age, the mandrake has not completely lost its hold on the minds of those who need a sense of magic and mystery in a world of modern technology.

(airless) **respiration.** They occur in the cytoplasm of the cell, require ATP, and are regulated by enzymes.

Respiration usually begins with a carbon-chain compound. Glucose is the basic one. (Proteins and lipids do enter the reactions of respiration. But they are usually converted first to products that enter the respiration cycle at a later step than glucose. Glucose enters at the beginning.)

Glucose is a stable compound with much energy locked into its bonds. Because it is stable, it does not break down into simpler compounds without the addition of energy. The reactions of respiration use enzymes to lower the amount of energy required. But some energy is still needed. This is supplied by ATP from a previous round of the same reactions. Only a small amount of energy is used to start anaerobic respiration. By the time it is finished, a much larger amount of energy will have been released, and more ATP will be formed than has been used. Thus, ATP energy units must be spent to gain energy.

The role of NAD and NADH

In the first series of reactions, the original six-carbon glucose molecule is split into two three-carbon molecules, each with a phosphate group attached. The phosphate group is donated by a molecule of ATP, leaving ADP. Now another set of reactions involving **NAD** (nicotinamide adenine dinucleotide) and ADP occurs. NAD is a hydrogen acceptor, very similar to NADP.

Each three-carbon molecule donates two hydrogen atoms to NAD, yielding two molecules of **NADH.** Meanwhile, it picks up another phosphate group. Donating the hydrogen atoms concentrates energy in the phosphate bonds of the three-carbon compound. In the next series of reactions, these high-energy phosphate groups are transferred to ADP, forming two molecules of ATP.

So far, the respiration of the original six-

Courtesy Carolina Biological Supply Co.

Figure 3-9. Two examples of heterotrophic plants that must obtain their food from the moist soil. Shown below are Indian pipes, a seed plant. The mushrooms above are fungi.

Courtesy Carolina Biological Supply Co.

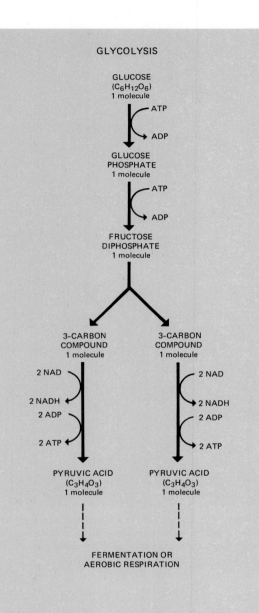

GLYCOLYSIS

GLUCOSE
($C_6H_{12}O_6$)
1 molecule

ATP

ADP

GLUCOSE
PHOSPHATE
1 molecule

ATP

ADP

FRUCTOSE
DIPHOSPHATE
1 molecule

3-CARBON
COMPOUND
1 molecule

3-CARBON
COMPOUND
1 molecule

2 NAD

2 NADH
2 ADP

2 ATP

2 NAD

2 NADH
2 ADP

2 ATP

PYRUVIC ACID
($C_3H_4O_3$)
1 molecule

PYRUVIC ACID
($C_3H_4O_3$)
1 molecule

FERMENTATION OR
AEROBIC RESPIRATION

Figure 3-10. The reactions of glycolysis. Can you trace what happens to all the atoms of the original glucose molecule on the way to the formation of pyruvic acid?

carbon glucose molecule has cost two molecules of ATP and produced four new ones. The three-carbon compound is oxidized to **pyruvic acid.** The whole set of anaerobic reactions that starts with glucose and ends with pyruvic acid is called **glycolysis.**

In the absence of oxygen, the pyruvic acid enters another anaerobic process, called **fermentation.** In this process, in animal cells and in some bacteria and fungi, the pyruvic acid takes two hydrogen atoms from NADH to form lactic acid and NAD. In plant cells and yeasts, pyruvic acid is converted to ethyl alcohol, also by fermentation.

Aerobic respiration

If oxygen is present, pyruvic acid follows another reaction pathway. This pathway is called **aerobic respiration** and, unlike glycolysis, it takes place inside the mitochondria. The NADH molecules that are generated during glycolysis do not donate their hydrogen atoms to pyruvic acid. Instead, the hydrogens ultimately combine with oxygen to produce water.

Like glycolysis, this pathway involves a number of steps. The hydrogen atoms move down an electron-transport chain in the mitochondria, called the **respiratory chain.** Most of the molecules in the chain are cytochromes, iron-containing pigments similar to those we have already mentioned in our discussion of photosynthesis.

As the hydrogens are passed along the chain, they lose energy. Some of the energy is used to manufacture ATP by combining ADP and phosphate. This process is called **oxidative phosphorylation.** For every two NADH molecules that enter the cytochrome chain from glycolysis, four ATP molecules are produced.

The Krebs cycle

While the hydrogens from NADH are moving through the cytochrome chain, the pyruvic acid is following another pathway,

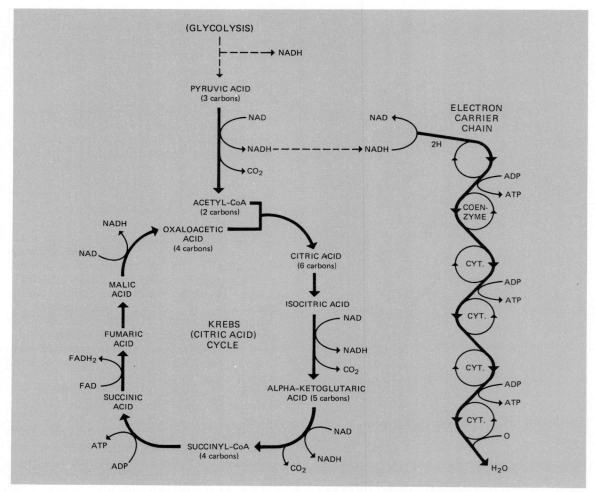

Figure 3-11. Aerobic respiration: the Krebs cycle and the electron carrier chain. This is a simplified presentation, and shows the respiration of only one acetyl-CoA molecule. It is not important to memorize all the steps, or the names of all the intermediate compounds, but you should have an understanding of the general pattern.

PATTERNS OF STRUCTURE
AND FUNCTION

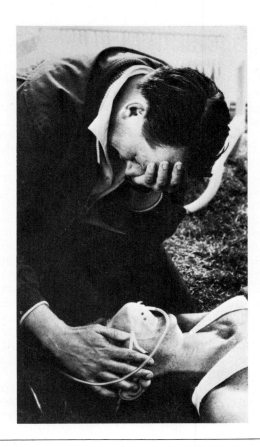

Figure 3-12. The oxygen this runner is receiving after his strenuous exercise helps to erase his oxygen debt more quickly.

which is also part of aerobic respiration. In the presence of oxygen, pyruvic acid also enters the mitochondria. Here it begins a series of reactions known as the **Krebs cycle.** To start the Krebs cycle, pyruvic acid is first converted to a two-carbon compound called **acetyl-CoA,** and CO_2 is released. This reaction produces a molecule of NADH. Unlike the previous NADH molecules, this one is inside the mitochondrion. Therefore, for reasons we will not go into here, it yields three molecules of ATP, instead of two, when it is fed into the cytochrome transport chain.

Acetyl-CoA attaches itself to a four-carbon compound, forming six-carbon **citric acid.** The citric acid then undergoes a series of oxidations. Each is catalyzed by a different enzyme. By means of these oxidations, hydrogens are released and CO_2 is produced. Most of these hydrogens, like the previous ones, attach to NAD and then are fed into the cytochrome transport chain. Eventually, there remains a four-carbon compound like the first. This compound picks up another molecule of acetyl-CoA, and the cycle begins again.

During the Krebs cycle, enough hydrogen atoms are removed from each citric acid molecule to produce twelve ATP molecules. Eleven of these molecules are produced as the hydrogens are passed along the cytochrome electron transport chain. The twelfth is produced within the Krebs cycle itself. Since each glucose molecule yields two molecules of acetyl-CoA, it provides enough material for the Krebs cycle to "go around" twice. Thus, one molecule of glucose yields twenty-four molecules of ATP through the Krebs cycle.

Whereas glycolysis takes place in the cytoplasm of the cell, the Krebs cycle and the reactions of the cytochrome electron-transport chain take place in the mitochondria. Some of the enzymes for these reactions are actually built into the inner membrane of the mitochondrion. The components of the cytochrome chain form clusters on the membrane. Each cluster contains all the cytochromes and other enzymes necessary for the whole chain of reactions. These units are called **respiratory units,** and their number varies with the need of the cell for ATP.

Summing up cellular respiration
How many ATP molecules can be produced during cellular respiration? If we start with one molecule of glucose and go through both anaerobic and aerobic respiration, we will end up with a "profit" of thirty-six ATP molecules. Of the total energy available in

the glucose bonds, about 40 percent has been converted into ATP bond energy, which can be used by the cell. The remainder is passed off as heat.

Two of the thirty-six ATP molecules are produced during glycolysis. Actually, four ATP molecules are formed during these reactions, but two were used to initiate the reactions, so the net gain is only two molecules.

The remaining thirty-four ATP molecules are produced during aerobic respiration. Thirty-two of these are produced via the cytochrome transport system. Aerobic respiration is thus the more efficient of the two types of cellular respiration.

However, anaerobic respiration is not merely a wasteful second-best. Fermentation in yeast, to name only one example, is a commercially important anaerobic process. Anaerobic respiration is also an important emergency system for animals. When you exercise violently, for example, your muscles may exhaust the available supply of oxygen. In this situation, they switch to anaerobic respiration, following the pathway that leads to lactic acid. The lactic acid that accumulates during this anaerobic respiration is what makes you stiff after unaccustomed or very strenuous exercise. When sufficient oxygen is supplied to your muscles once more, the lactic acid is oxidized back to pyruvic acid, erasing the "oxygen debt."

SUMMARY

All chemical reactions within cells involve the use or transfer of energy. The energy is stored in the bonds that join atoms or molecules in compounds. When the bond is broken, the energy is released. Most chemical energy is stored in the phosphate bonds of triphosphate compounds, the commonest of which is ATP. The stored energy is called potential energy; when it is released it becomes kinetic energy.

Cells form the ATP they need by adding a phosphate group to ADP. In autotrophic cells, energy from sunlight is transformed into the chemical bond energy of ATP. This process is called photosynthesis. Heterotrophic cells break down complex compounds to make ATP in the process called cellular respiration. Both reactions occur step by step.

The reactions that produce energy are catalyzed by enzymes. By lowering the amount of energy needed to start the reaction, these catalysts prevent the cell from overheating. Each enzyme catalyzes a specific kind of reaction. According to the lock-and-key hypothesis, each enzyme can receive only a particular reactant. The induced fit theory postulates that the reactant may somehow induce the enzyme to assume the correct shape.

In oxidation–reduction reactions, a compound that gives up an electron becomes oxidized and loses energy. A compound which receives the electron becomes reduced and gains energy. Many such reactions involve the removal or addition of a hydrogen atom.

All cells depend on photosynthesis for energy, either directly or indirectly. Photosynthetic reactions are based on the ability of chlorophyll molecules to absorb and transfer light energy. Photosynthesis is divided into light reactions and dark reactions.

Light reactions occur only in autotrophic cells. They use light energy to produce ATP. The simplest form of light reaction is called cyclic photophosphorylation. In noncyclic photophosphorylation, hydrogen carrier molecules are also produced.

The dark reactions depend on ATP for their energy supply. Using energy from the ATP, they reduce carbon dioxide to glucose through a series of steps. The glucose is then used in forming more ATP through cellular respiration, or in synthesizing other compounds.

Heterotrophic cells synthesize ATP by breaking down complex compounds—carbohydrates, proteins, and lipids. The reactions that do this make up the process of cellular respiration. The first steps of this process are called anaerobic respiration and occur in the cytoplasm of the cell. This series of steps begins with glucose and ends with pyruvic acid.

If oxygen is absent, the pyruvic acid next enters the process of fermentation. In animal cells the pyruvic acid forms lactic acid and NAD. In plant cells and yeasts, it is converted to ethyl alcohol.

If oxygen is present, pyruvic acid follows the pathway of aerobic respiration. Hydrogen atoms are passed along a respiratory chain, and some of the energy they lose is used to manufacture ATP in the process of oxidative phosphorylation. In the meantime, the pyruvic acid begins a series of reactions called the Krebs cycle, by which one molecule of glucose eventually yields 24 molecules of ATP. Whereas glycolysis takes place in the cytoplasm, the Krebs cycle takes place in the mitochondria.

Aerobic respiration is the more efficient type of cellular respiration. For animals, anaerobic respiration serves as an emergency backup system, which takes over during strenuous exercise if the muscles exhaust the available supply of oxygen.

Review questions

1. What are triphosphates? What is their significance to the use and transfer of energy?

2. How does ATP store and release energy?

3. Distinguish between potential energy and kinetic energy.

4. Describe the reaction by which ATP is formed from ADP.

5. What is photosynthesis? In what kind of cell is it performed?

6. How do heterotrophic cells obtain energy? What is this process called?

7. What role do enzymes play in photosynthesis and cellular respiration?

8. What is the induced fit theory?

9. Distinguish between oxidation and reduction. What happens to each compound involved in an oxidation–reduction reaction?

10. What is chlorophyll? Describe its function in photosynthesis.

11. Describe the two types of light reaction. How do they differ?

12. What are the dark reactions? Where do they obtain their energy?

13. How do heterotrophic cells manufacture ATP?

14. Trace the first series of reactions in anaerobic respiration.

15. What are the reactions that involve NAD and ADP?

16. How is pyruvic acid formed?

17. Describe the process of fermentation. Under what circumstances does it take place?

18. What is oxidative phosphorylation?

19. Trace the steps of the Krebs cycle.

20. In what ways does the Krebs cycle differ from glycolysis?

21. During cellular respiration, about how much usable energy is produced? What happens to the remainder?

22. Which type of respiration is more efficient? Why?

23. What are some advantages of anaerobic respiration?

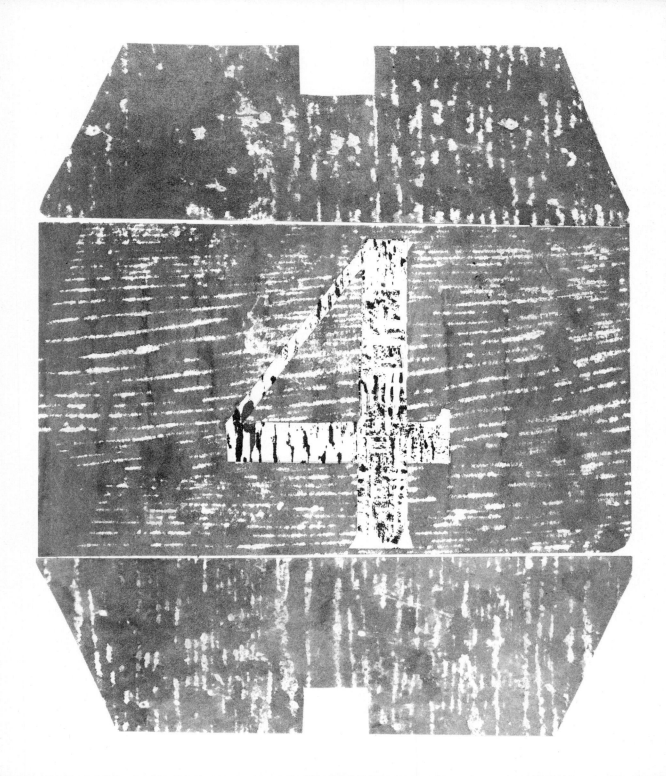

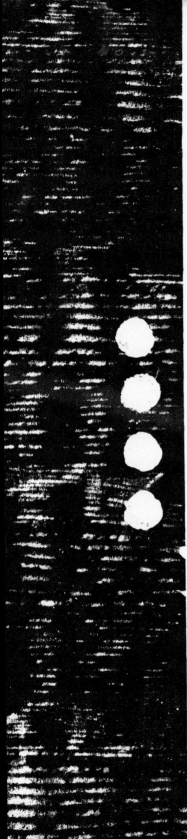

Patterns of Digestion

The chemical reactions of the cell provide the basis for all life. Each organism is put together differently, yet all living cells share common features. Every design reflects a successful approach to the problem of organizing these reactions in a way that meets the needs of an organism to survive in a particular environment.

NUTRITION NEEDS IN DIGESTION

We have already noted that all organisms require energy in order to do work. They also need it to grow and reproduce. And they must maintain themselves, which includes repairing any damage and regulating such vital activities as breathing and heartbeat. To supply these needs, they make use of molecules known as **nutrients.** Nutrients include carbohydrates, fats, proteins, vitamins and minerals, and water. The heterotrophic organisms—both plants and animals—cannot make their own nutrients and therefore must ingest such molecules in the form of food. Organisms that eat only plants are called **herbivores.** Other organisms consume the predigested plant material by eating animals. These are called **carnivores.** Finally, organisms that eat a mixture of plants and animals are called **omnivores.**

Carbohydrates, fats, and proteins are all energy-yielding foods, although they differ in the amount of energy they can yield. This energy is usually expressed in **calories.** A calorie is a measure of heat. Specifically, it is the amount of heat required to raise the temperature of one gram of water 1 degree

C, at a pressure of one atmosphere (the air pressure at sea level). Large *C*alories are commonly used in referring to foods or diets. One large Calorie is equal to 1,000 small calories. Fats are the highest energy source, yielding about nine Calories for every gram consumed. Carbohydrates provide about four Calories for every gram, as do proteins. Carbohydrates are stored for energy by plants, in the form of starch, and by animals, in the form of glycogen. Fats provide energy and are very good insulators, keeping the organism warm in cold weather. In addition, fats insulate some nerve cells.

Proteins are made up of amino acids. Amino acids can be converted into fats or carbohydrates and stored in the body. Thus they provide an energy reserve when sufficient food carbohydrates and fats are not available. More importantly, they supply the material the organism needs to build its own protein molecules. These new molecules may be enzymes, used by the cell in chemical reactions. Or they may be structural materials, needed for forming new cells and repairing damaged ones. Heterotrophs require some twenty amino acids in order to synthesize their own protein. Few heterotrophs, and none of the vertebrates, can make every amino acid from raw materials. Human beings can make twelve of them, either from other amino acids or from nitrogen compounds. The other eight, called essential amino acids, must be gotten in food. All twenty, of course, are essential, but these eight are essential in the form of food protein. Because not every amino acid is available in each source of protein, animals must consume several different protein foods.

Minerals are inorganic substances that assist in growth and repair. Calcium and phosphorus are known for their role in the formation and growth of bones and teeth. Other calcium compounds assist in blood clotting and muscle action. Phosphorus, as we have seen, is necessary for the production of ATP and ADP. Minerals such as potassium, sodium, magnesium, calcium, and chlorine function in activities such as muscle contraction and nerve impulse transmission. Many elements, such as zinc, tin, vanadium, cobalt, and fluorine, are needed in very small, or trace, amounts by the cell membranes. In larger quantities, though, these same minerals can be dangerous poisons.

Some minerals function more indirectly. Iron, for example, forms a large part of the oxygen-carrying hemoglobin in the blood. But in order for iron to be utilized by the blood cells, a minute amount of copper is also needed. In this respect copper works as a catalyst. Indeed, it is likely that many of the minerals found in heterotrophic organisms function as parts of **coenzymes** in catalyzing chemical reactions. The coenzyme is a relatively small molecule that is attached to the end of the large protein part of the enzyme. It is essential in enabling enzymes to catalyze a reaction. All organisms need specific coenzymes for the functioning of certain enzymes that catalyze cellular respiration.

Vitamins also work in the cell as coenzymes, helping to regulate cellular activities. The B vitamins, for example, are part of the chemicals that transfer energy during the breaking down of glucose. Thus they are essential to cellular respiration. Vitamins are large organic molecules which must be synthesized in the body or obtained from food. Plants and some bacteria can make vitamins from simple substances such as glucose and mineral elements. Some animals can make vitamins, but not all those that they require. Insects, for example, cannot synthesize vitamin B, and apes cannot produce vitamin C. Those vitamins that they cannot make themselves must be consumed ready-made. Human beings cannot synthesize any vitamins themselves, so they must get all of their vitamins from outside. Moreover, the human body cannot store every vitamin. Many vitamins are soluble in lipids, and can be stored in fat pockets in the cells. But some vitamins are soluble in water, and thus cannot be stored. These include

PATTERNS OF MAINTENANCE
AND REGULATION

Table 4-1. Vitamins Important in Human Nutrition

Class	Some Natural Sources	Some Results of Deficiency in the Diet
†A	Yellow vegetables (carrots, yams), liver, butter	Eye disorders, night blindness, retarded development, skin dryness
§*B₁ Thiamine	Whole cereals, egg yolk, yeast, pork	Beriberi—digestive upsets, loss of appetite, paralysis, fatigue
§B₂ Riboflavin	Liver, milk, meat	Impaired cellular respiration—retarded growth, eye disorders, loss of hair, nerve degeneration
§*B complex nicotinic acid, biotin, folic acid	Pork, liver, yeast, milk, vegetables, eggs, whole grains, nuts	Pellagra—nervous and mental disorders, skin disorders, diarrhea
§B₆ pyridoxine	Same as B complex	Growth failure, anemia, nerve and skin disorders
§*B₁₂	Liver	Pernicious anemia
§*C	Citrus fruits, tomatoes, cabbage	Scurvy—bleeding gums, painful joints
†*D	Egg yolk, fish oil	Rickets—bowed legs, tooth decay, swollen joints
†E	Lettuce, whole wheat	Sterility in certain animals
†K	Liver, cabbage, kale, tomatoes, spinach	Delayed blood coagulation

*Necessary for life   †Fat soluble   §Water soluble

vitamin C and the B vitamins, which must be replenished regularly.

Biologists learned about the role of vitamins in the body by noticing what happened when they were lacking. The ancient Egyptians used liver to cure eye diseases that are now known to be due to vitamin deficiency. More than 200 years ago the British navy supplied its sailors with limes to keep them well during their long sea voyages. (Hence the name "Limeys.") We know now that vitamin C in the limes was responsible for the good health of the sailors. Without vitamin C they would have come down with the disease called scurvy. Its symptoms, once common among sailors, include swelling of the joints, weakness, and loosening of the teeth. The action of the British navy was the result of practical experience without any real knowledge of the nature of the disease or its cause.

The beginning of real insight into the role of vitamins came in 1886 from a Dutch physician, Christiaan Eijkman. Eijkman was stationed in Java at a prison camp, where he observed the ravages of a disease called beriberi. This disease affects the nervous system, producing weakness and paralysis and eventually death.

At that time beriberi was thought to be caused by a microbe. Dr. Eijkman, however, noticed that chickens that fed exclusively on polished rice from the floor of the prison dining room developed beriberi, just as did the prisoners. By adding rice husks to their diet, Eijkman was able to cure the chickens—and the prisoners. This was proof that for healthy cells an animal's diet must include more than fats, carbohydrates, and proteins. In the case of the beriberi, this extra necessity was eventually found to be the B vitamin thiamine.

Although daily vitamin requirements are hard to establish, it is probable that the amount of each vitamin needed to ensure good health is quite small. If we eat a varied diet of non-processed foods, we should get all we need. This is not to say that all vitamin pills are a waste of money. For one reason or another, some people are not always able to eat a balanced diet. Nor do they always choose to. And modern food processing techniques often reduce the vitamin content. This was the case with the

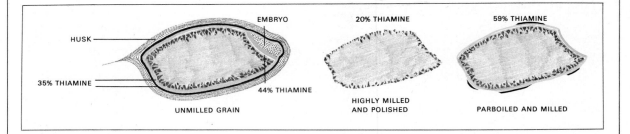

HUSK

EMBRYO

20% THIAMINE

59% THIAMINE

35% THIAMINE

44% THIAMINE

UNMILLED GRAIN

HIGHLY MILLED
AND POLISHED

PARBOILED AND MILLED

Figure 4-1. In rice, most of the thiamine, or vitamin B_1, is contained in the embryo and the covering just beneath the husk. However, these parts spoil easily. To preserve the grains, millers "polish" them, thereby losing about 80 percent of the thiamine. If the rice is parboiled and milled, only about 40 percent is lost.

"polished" rice fed to Java prisoners, which had lost its vitamin B. The same thing happens when hulls of grains are removed in the manufacture of flour. In modern "enriched" flour and other grain products, some of these lost vitamins have been replaced.

Essential as all of these nutrients are, none of them would be of any use to an organism without one final substance, water. Water, as we saw in chapter 2, is an active participant in all hydrolytic reactions and provides a solvent medium for all chemical reactions.

DIGESTION INVOLVES SPECIALIZATION

Nutrient molecules, even when very small, are often too large to pass across the cell membranes. The process by which organisms break down these large molecules, enabling them to be used inside the cell, is known as **digestion.**

For that matter, if large molecules could enter the cytoplasm of the cell, they would kill the cell. The cellular machinery is geared to the use of small subunits of these large molecules. For example, the machinery for protein synthesis is equipped to take individual amino acids and assemble them into proteins. It is not equipped to handle larger protein molecules directly. Similarly, the enzymes of the mitochondria are suited to the task of disassembling small glucose molecules, thereby releasing energy in the form of ATP. They cannot tackle the large polysaccharides, or chains of glucose molecules.

Digestion can take place either outside or inside the cell itself. Digestion that takes place outside the cells, either in the environment or in a specialized cavity, is known as **extracellular digestion.** Digestion within the cell is known as **intracellular digestion.**

Extracellular digestion
Many single-celled organisms digest extracellularly. They secrete enzymes into their environment to break down food molecules. The smaller molecules can then pass through the cell membranes—usually by diffusion. This method is used by the fungi. Surprisingly, a similar technique is also used by the starfish. This creature thrusts its stomach out through its mouth and in between the halves of the clamshell it has pulled open. There the stomach secretes enzymes that partially digest the soft parts of the prey. The material is then drawn into the intestine, where digestion is completed.

Most complex animals also use extracellular digestion. But in these cases the cells release the digestive enzymes into a

PATTERNS OF MAINTENANCE
AND REGULATION

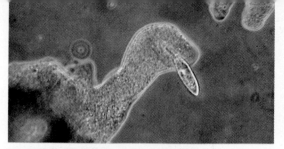

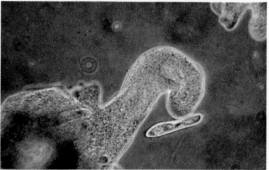

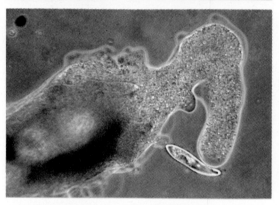

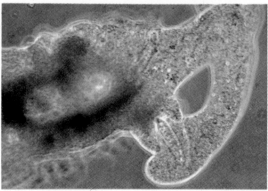

Figure 4-2. This series of pictures shows an amoeba engulfing a particle of food.

specialized organ, such as the stomach or intestine. The result is the same: the food molecules are broken down into smaller subunits for use in the cell. The smaller molecules that result pass through the cell membranes.

Intracellular digestion

The single-celled protozoa may also accomplish digestion inside the cell itself. Strictly speaking, though, this process is not carried on directly in the cytoplasm of the cell. For example, the amoeba completely surrounds a food particle with extensions of its protoplasm known as pseudopods. Figure 4-2 shows how the food particle is finally engulfed by the cell. Notice that the particles are not actually suspended freely in the cytoplasm of the cell, however. Instead, they are "walled off" from the cell's interior, isolated within bubble-like structures called vacuoles. Lysosomes, such as were described in chapter 1, fuse with the vacuole, and their enzymes digest the food. The smaller molecules then diffuse through the membrane of the vacuole and into the cytoplasm.

A somewhat more specialized protozoan, the paramecium, carries on intracellular digestion by means of an **oral groove.** This channel-like structure is lined with constantly moving cilia. The water currents created by the action of the cilia sweep particles into the oral groove, which carries them to one end of the organism. Here they are surrounded by a vacuole, and enzymes are secreted into the vacuole to digest them.

The beginnings of specialization

As single-celled organisms evolved into multicellular ones, they developed increasing degrees of specialization. This enabled them to perform the task of digesting and absorbing large particles of food. The simplest of all multicellular animals are the sponges. These organisms digest food intracellularly in a manner much like that of the paramecium. The difference lies in the fact that cells are specialized to carry out the various functions which in the paramecium were done in a single cell. Specialization in the sponge is structurally very simple. The entire animal is composed of only a few kinds of cell, arranged in two layers.

Figure 4-3 shows a generalized sponge. The cells are arranged in a hollow, vase-like shape. The outer layer consists of closely fitted, flattened epithelial cells. In between are microscopic openings to specialized pore cells. The pores connect the exterior to the hollow interior, which is lined with collar cells. Each collar cell has a flagellum extending into the internal cavity of the animal. The beating of the flagella creates a current of water that enters through the pores and leaves through the opening known as the **osculum** at one end of the sponge. This moving stream of water brings with it a continuous supply of food to the sponge's interior. Minute food particles collect on the collar. From there they move toward the interior of the collar cell, where they are engulfed. In between the layer of flat surface cells and the layer of collar cells are free-moving cells known as **amoebocytes,** unspecialized cells that take on a variety of tasks. They may become pore cells. Or they may become collar cells, engulfing and digesting food particles. At times they remove wastes to the surface of the organism.

Gastrovascular digestion
At a slightly more complex level of organization is the hydra. Digestion in the hydra is carried on both within the cell and in a specialized digestive cavity outside the cell. By means of this cavity the hydra can ingest larger pieces of food than individual cells can manage. The cavity, or gut, also functions as a container where the food can be stored during the initial stages of digestion. Because the mouth is the only opening to the cavity, any indigestible matter must leave the same way it came in. A digestive cavity with only one opening for the passage of

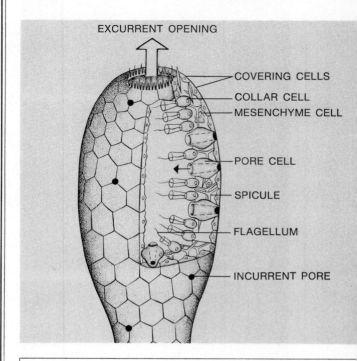

Figure 4-3. A cutaway view of a typical sponge. Food is engulfed and digested by the collar cells.

EXCURRENT OPENING

COVERING CELLS
COLLAR CELL
MESENCHYME CELL
PORE CELL
SPICULE
FLAGELLUM
INCURRENT PORE

Figure 4-4. The sequence at right shows a hydra stinging and t̶ eating another tiny aquatic organism. Digestion will take place the hydra's specialized gastrovascular cav̶

PATTERNS OF MAINTENANCE
AND REGULATION

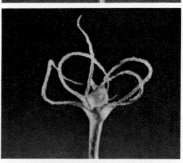

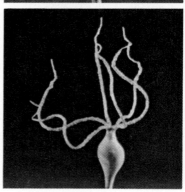

both food and wastes is known as a **gastrovascular cavity.**

The hydra lives in fresh-water ponds and streams, where it feeds on smaller animals within its reach. Sensitive tentacles surrounding its mouth are covered with specialized cells known as **cnidocysts.** Some of these cells inject a paralyzing substance into the prey. Others produce a sticky substance, enabling the tentacles to hold the victims and draw them into the mouth. The mouth leads to the gastrovascular cavity, which is lined with three kinds of specialized cell. Flagellated cells wave their whip-like extensions to move food around within the cavity. Gland cells secrete digestive enzymes when stimulated by the presence of food. In this way, extracellular digestion breaks down the whole animal into smaller food particles, and intracellular digestion begins.

The third group of specialized cells, digestive cells, engage in intracellular digestion. They extend pseudopods and engulf the smaller particles into food vacuoles, in much the same way as the amoeba ingests its prey. There the food is reduced to molecules small enough to diffuse into the rest of the cells.

The complete digestive tract

In contrast to the one-opening gastrovascular cavity, the digestive tract of most animals has two openings, one for incoming food and the other for outgoing wastes. In most animals, food passes through this one-way traffic system only once. Specialized areas of the system perform specialized functions in the process of breaking down and absorbing the food as it passes by.

A familiar small invertebrate with a **complete digestive tract** is the earthworm. Basically, the earthworm's body plan can be described as a "tube within a tube." The outer tube is the worm's body wall, made up of protective skin and body muscles. The inner tube, the digestive tract, consists of several organs. Each organ performs a different function. The lip-like protrusion over the mouth is very useful for shoveling, serving to loosen the soil and its decaying organic matter. This food is then pulled into the mouth by the suction of a muscular organ called the **pharynx.** From the pharynx it goes into a passageway called the **esophagus,** where it is moistened with water. Next it enters the soft, thin-walled storage area called the **crop.** Here a large quantity of food can be stored, providing the worm with a reserve when the pickings are poor.

From the crop the food moves to the **gizzard**—a tough, thick-walled grinding organ. The constant muscular action of the gizzard pulverizes the food as it is rubbed against the sand particles that were swallowed with it. This mechanical breakdown represents an added step in the process of changing large particles to small molecules. By dividing large food particles into smaller ones, it exposes more surface for the enzymes to work on. In this way the gizzard functions much as human teeth do.

The paste-like mass that leaves the gizzard passes into the **intestine.** This long, tubular organ extends almost the full length of the body. It ends in the last segment, at the anus. Gland cells in the intestine secrete digestive enzymes that finish breaking down the food. The small molecules that result are then absorbed into blood vessels that line the inner walls of the intestine. The nutrients are carried in the bloodstream to all the cells of the body. As the worm's intestine is very long, the far end of it is further specialized to reabsorb water. Indigestible food and inorganic soil matter pass out the **anus.**

All the more complex animals, including humans, have a digestive system made up of specialized organs that are similar in function to those of the earthworm. The basic plan is simply a long tube. Almost always there is an enlarged area where food can be stored before it is digested. Birds, like earthworms and grasshoppers, have crops for this purpose; frogs and all mammals have stomachs. Birds also have gizzards for

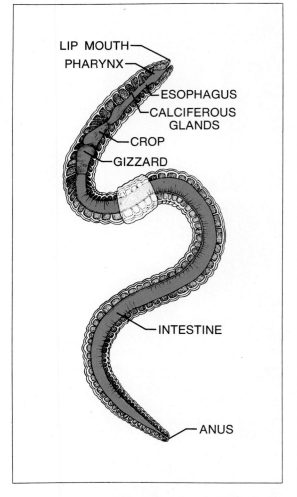

Figure 4-5. The complete digestive tract of the earthworm is made up of several specialized digestive organs. Each organ performs a different digestive function.

mechanical action. In them, therefore, mechanical breakdown occurs after the food has been stored. Animals that have evolved teeth are able to tear or grind the food into smaller pieces before storing it. In all of the higher animals, other organs are specialized for such purposes as enzyme secretion, absorption of small molecules into the bloodstream, and elimination of wastes.

Because a specialized digestive tract al-

PATTERNS OF MAINTENANCE
AND REGULATION

FROG

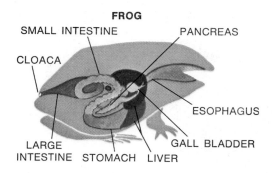

SMALL INTESTINE

PANCREAS

CLOACA

ESOPHAGUS

GALL BLADDER

LARGE
INTESTINE   STOMACH   LIVER

GRASSHOPPER

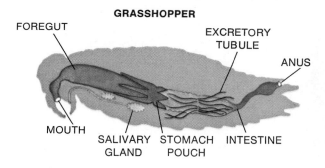

FOREGUT

EXCRETORY
TUBULE

ANUS

MOUTH

SALIVARY   STOMACH   INTESTINE
GLAND   POUCH

BIRD

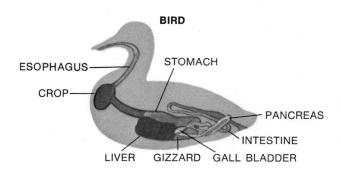

ESOPHAGUS

STOMACH

CROP

PANCREAS

INTESTINE

LIVER   GIZZARD   GALL BLADDER

Figure 4-6. In the more complex animals the digestive system is basically a long tube. Usually there is an enlarged area where food can be stored before it is digested. A variety of organs aid in the digestive process by secreting enzymes and other substances into the digestive tract.

lows multicellular animals to consume large pieces of food, we might assume that all large animals ingest and mechanically grind up such large pieces. But a number of quite large animals continue to feed on very tiny food particles. They simply consume large quantities. These animals, known as **filter feeders,** strain their food out of currents of water taken through specialized body structures. Bivalves, such as clams and mussels, filter huge amounts of water through openings in their ciliated gills, catching the tiny organisms on a mucous lining. Enormous baleen whales snag vast numbers of plankton on the rows of vertical bone-like filter plates just behind the mouth.

THE HUMAN DIGESTIVE SYSTEM

Human digestion begins in the mouth. While the teeth begin to pulverize the food, the tongue moves it around, and mixes it with **saliva.** Saliva is produced in three pairs of salivary glands, connected to the mouth by tubes or ducts. It consists primarily of water, mucus, and two digestive enzymes, **amylase** and **maltase.** Together these enzymes start the process of digesting the starch molecules. Enzymes, as we have seen, act as catalysts in the process of hydrolysis, breaking down molecules by the addition of water. Thus digestion is really a form of hydrolysis. Each digestive enzyme acts on a different substance.

The mucus assists the still bulky mass down the esophagus, the passageway to the stomach. The muscles of the esophagus alternately contract and relax, causing a wave-like motion known as **peristalsis.** The force of the waves causes a ring-shaped muscle at the opening of the stomach to relax, allowing the food to pass through. Once food is past, this **cardiac sphincter** closes again until the next peristaltic wave occurs. Food may remain for three to four hours in the stomach. There it is continuously squeezed and churned, completing mechan-

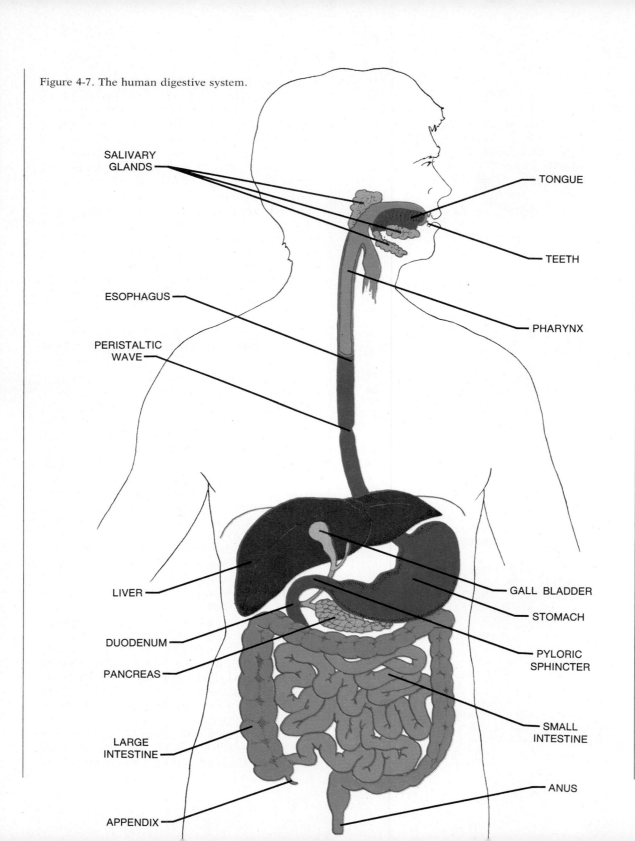

Figure 4-7. The human digestive system.

ical digestion. At the same time, secretions of the stomach, known as **gastric secretions,** begin.

The lining of the stomach is made up of column-shaped epithelial cells coated with a thick mucous cover. Mucus, which protects the stomach from its own juices, is secreted from cells in this lining. Additional

and peptides. In addition to forming pepsin, the hydrochloric acid starts to break up the food. In this way it exposes a much greater surface area to the action of pepsin. The acid also dissolves some of the minerals contained in food. And it destroys many bacteria that enter with the food. Occasionally some of it gets through the cardiac sphincter

---

TOO MUCH OF A GOOD THING?

The current interest in healthful living has its dangers as well as its blessings. One danger is that some people may be poisoning themselves with overdoses of certain vitamins. A statement by a committee of the National Research Council has warned, for instance, that many Americans may be getting more vitamin D than is good for them.

Vitamin D promotes absorption of calcium from the intestine. A lack of this vitamin, therefore, leads to calcium deficiency and—if severe enough—to the bone-deforming disease called rickets. But too much of it works in the opposite way. Too much calcium is absorbed, and the excess may be deposited in the body's soft tissues, causing pain and injury. The kidneys are especially likely to be injured. Symptoms of such damage may include weakness, lack of energy and appetite, and constipation. Even after vitamin D overdose has been stopped, excess calcium may remain in the bloodstream for months.

The Research Council regards 400 international units of vitamin D as a sufficient daily dose for most people. Its statement held that most people get that much in their normal diet, and from sunlight. Egg yolks, salmon, sardines, and tuna are all good natural sources. In addition, nearly all commercially sold milk is fortified with extra vitamin D. Finally, vitamin D is created in our bodies by the action of sunlight on a chemical in the skin. Hence the statement recommended against concentrated vitamin D supplements for most people. In fact, many adults have been advised against drinking vitamin D–fortified milk at all.

Vitamins A and E are other vitamins that can be harmful in large quantities. Like vitamin D, they are fat-soluble and can be stored in the fatty tissues of the body. Vitamin C and the B vitamins, on the other hand, are water-soluble, are not stored in the body, and seem to be safe in almost any reasonable concentration. There is some possibility that the acidity of vitamin C may cause problems in extremely high dosages.

---

gland cells secrete a complex of substances which combine to form gastric juice. One of these is **pepsinogen.** This becomes the gastric enzyme pepsin when it combines with another of the secretions, **hydrochloric acid.** Pepsin is a **proteinase.** It begins the process of protein hydrolysis, breaking large protein molecules into shorter chains of amino acids

into the esophagus. (This is most likely to happen when a person belches.) The acid irritates the membranes of the esophagus, causing the unpleasant sensation known as heartburn.

A rare—and bizarre—opportunity to observe the action of digestive juices was afforded to surgeon William Beaumont early in the nineteenth century. Beaumont tended a gunshot wound in the stomach of a Canadian trapper, Alexis St. Martin. This wound never completely closed, leaving a permanent fistula, or opening, into the stomach. From this Beaumont could take samples of stomach juices before and after meals, and even insert food directly and then withdraw it after various lengths of time. The surgeon performed some 116 experiments on St. Martin. He recorded and published his observations on the effects that hunger, thirst, taste, alcohol, seasonings, and anger had on the stomach.

Human digestion is by no means finished in the stomach. About twenty to thirty minutes after the food enters the stomach, some of it may be sufficiently broken down to pass on to the small intestine for final digestion. Partly digested food enters the intestine through the **pyloric sphincter,** another ring-shaped muscle located at the exit of the stomach. When this muscle relaxes, small spurts of food enter the small intestine.

The first part of the small intestine is about a foot long, and is called the **duodenum.** It is followed by an eight- to ten-foot coiled section known as the **jejunum** and an even longer final section called the **ileum.** It is along the length of the small intestine that chemical digestion is completed.

Two passageways, or **ducts,** supply secretions to the duodenum. One carries secretions of the liver and one carries secretions from the pancreas. Just before reaching the wall of the small intestine they join, and the secretions enter the duodenum together. **Bile** from the liver empties into the duodenum by way of a duct from the **gall bladder,** where it is stored between meals, when the stomach is empty. Bile emulsifies large fat globules. That is, it causes them to separate into many small droplets suspended in water. As a result there is much more surface area on which the intestinal enzymes can act.

The most powerful of the intestinal enzymes come from the pancreas. **Pancreatic**

lipase works on the emulsified fat droplets, breaking them into fatty acids and glycerol. Another enzyme, **pancreatic amylase,** continues the hydrolysis of starch molecules begun by the salivary amylase. Still other pancreatic secretions finish the protein breakdown begun in the stomach by pepsin.

Gland cells in the intestine itself add still more enzymes. Some of these are similar to the protein-digesting enzymes from the pancreas. Others act to break down carbohydrates into simple sugars, or monosaccharides, which can be absorbed by the blood vessels. These enzymes are **maltase, sucrase,** and **lactase.** Together these secretions form the intestinal fluid.

A final secretion from the pancreas, **sodium carbonate,** is a salt, not an enzyme. It neutralizes the powerful acid mixture which empties into the small intestine from the stomach. The stomach enzymes work best in a highly acid environment, but the intestinal ones work best in an alkaline one. Because of this, the intestinal walls do not need to be so well protected as those of the stomach.

Digestion, of course, takes place gradually, through the entire length of the small intestine—over twenty feet. Peristaltic waves move along the intestinal walls, pushing the food down to the end. Digestion is complete when the food molecules have become small enough to be absorbed by the cells of the intestinal walls. These walls are twisted and folded repeatedly, making the total length far longer than the distance from the stomach to the large intestine. Along the folds and bends, small finger-like projections called **villi** project into the interior. Each villus is covered with epithelial cells, which are themselves covered with tiny hair-like projections, called **microvilli.** A single cell may have up to 1,000 microvilli. As a result of these extensions, the surface area of the small intestine is twenty-five times greater than it would be if it were just a smooth, straight tube. Because of this, the tiny nutrient molecules have countless opportunities to be absorbed as they pass

Table 4-2. Substances in the Human Digestive Process

Place of Digestion	Digestive Juice	Material Digested	Enzyme	Product Absorbed
Mouth	Saliva	Starch	Salivary Amylase	None
Stomach	Gastric Juice	Fats and Oils	Lipase	Fatty Acids Glycerol
	Gastric Juice	Proteins	Pepsin	None
Small Intestine	Pancreatic Juice	Starch	Amylopsin	None
	Intestinal Juice	Dextrins Maltose	Maltase	Glucose
	Intestinal Juice	Sucrose	Sucrase	Glucose Fructose
	Intestinal Juice	Lactose	Lactase	Glucose Galactose
	Bile	Fats and Oils	None	None
	Pancreatic Juice	Emulsified Fats and Oils	Steapsin	Fatty Acids Glycerol
	Intestinal Juice	Emulsified Fats and Oils	Lipase	Fatty Acids Glycerol
	Pancreatic Juice	Proteoses Peptones	Trypsin Chymotrypsin	None
	Intestinal Juice	Polypeptides	Carboxypeptidase Erepsin	Amino Acids

along the intestine.

Inside each villus is a network of blood vessels and lymph vessels. The molecules pass through the epithelial cells of the villi by diffusion or by a form of active transport. From there they can enter the tiny capillaries or the lymph vessels. The simple sugars, amino acids, and minerals enter the blood vessels and are carried to the liver, where they are stored. From there, they are distributed through the bloodstream to the body cells, as needed. The liver also receives any bacteria or toxins that have managed to get as far as the bloodstream. These toxins are converted in the liver into less harmful substances and sent out again in the bile. Fatty acids and glycerol enter the lymph vessels of the villi. Eventually they pass into the bloodstream, and travel to the body cells.

All the indigestible matter, some water, and other unabsorbed materials, including the converted toxins from the liver, pass through yet another sphincter into the large intestine, or **colon.** This tube is wider but shorter than the small intestine. It reabsorbs most of the water secreted in the digestive process, as well as some minerals. The action of bacteria that live in the colon begins to decompose the remaining material, which is finally pushed out of the body through the anus.

Around the anus there are two additional sphincter muscles, one inside the

PITCHER PLANTS

No one gives a second thought to the idea of animals eating plants. After all, we figure, that's perfectly natural. But why do so many of us grow squeamish at the thought of plants that eat animals?

The early tales of carnivorous plants, told by travelers to mysterious lands, made for exciting reading. People were delighted to learn about a Brazilian tree that supposedly lured monkeys by its enticing odor and then devoured them, leaving nothing but clean white bones. Fortunately, no such tree is actually known to exist. Despite what we may see in science fiction movies, no known plant eats any creature larger than an insect, or at most a small rodent.

We know that most plants can manufacture their own food, though animals cannot. Why, then, do some plants eat animals as well?

Carnivorous plants contain chlorophyll. They produce flowers and seeds and can survive without trapping insects. However, most of them have poorly developed root systems and grow in bogs in which nitrogen is not readily available from the soil. So the plants obtain nitrogen and other elements essential for growth by trapping and digesting insects.

The pitcher plants are a group of carnivorous plants that catch insects in hollow, pitcher-like structures. One genus, Nepenthes, thrives in the bogs and marshes of tropical Asia. It has figured prominently in folklore and has been credited with powers ranging from causing rain to curing bed-wetting. The drug of forgetfulness given to Telemachus by Helen of Troy, in Homer's *Odyssey,* was called nepenthe. Was it made from this plant? Unlikely, but possible.

The urn-shaped *Nepenthes* pitcher collects not only food but considerable amounts of rainwater as well. It is covered by a projecting lid that serves to prevent flooding and to keep trapped insects from escaping. Despite the lid, a pitcher may accumulate enough water to satisfy the thirst of a passing ape. Occasionally, birds and small rodents are drowned in a pitcher.

Nepenthes plants attract insects by their conspicuous red and purple mottled appearance, and by the sweet-smelling nectar they produce. The mouth of the pitcher is surrounded by a rim of woody tissue that makes it rigid and keeps it open. The upper region of the inner wall is made up of waxy cells. An insect that lands on the inner rim is directed downward by a row of incurved hooks, which make it difficult to climb upward and fly away. Once the victim reaches the waxy inner wall, it slides helplessly down into the fluid below. The neutral liquid secreted by the pitcher tissues turns acid when an insect falls into it. It contains a peptic enzyme that digests the soft parts of the insect's body.

Some small creatures, though, have learned to exploit the pitcher as a source of food or shelter. The fluid serves as a home for certain blue-green algae, nematodes, flies, and butterfly and moth larvae. Some spider and mosquito species have adapted to life in the pitcher to such a degree that they are found nowhere else. It is believed that these organisms have an anti-enzyme that protects them from the peptic enzyme in the pitcher fluid.

Many animals look to *Nepenthes* for food. Some fly larvae feed on insects captured by the plant. A small rodent called *Tarsus spectrum* sometimes perches on the edge of the pitcher, sticks its head into the opening, and scoops out the insects inside. However, the creatures that exploit *Nepenthes* seldom give it any help in return. One species of moth lays its eggs in the pitcher, and the caterpillar that hatches from them feeds on the leaves and destroys the pitcher in which it was born.

Nepenthes is not the only plant that captures insects in a pitcher. Another type, *Sarracenia*, grows in the swamps and marshes of eastern North America. At one time, the root of this plant was believed by certain Canadian Indians to be useful as a medicine against smallpox. For a while, this treatment was popular in Victorian England.

Unlike that of *Nepenthes*, the pitcher of *Sarracenia* is formed from the entire leaf. It stands erect, protected by an upright flap, and kept open by a stiff rim. The rim is surrounded by a flat extended surface, which offers a ramp on which the unsuspecting insect can comfortably rest before crawling into the mouth of the pitcher.

Sarracenia captures its prey much as *Nepenthes* does. Nectar is produced on the lid, rim, and outer surface. Insects slide down the waxy inside wall of the pitcher into a lower region, covered with long bristles that prevent the captive from escaping. At the bottom of the pitcher is a fluid which contains an enzyme that breaks down the digestible parts of the insect's body. This enzyme is not the same as the one in *Nepenthes*.

As with *Nepenthes*, many small animals take advantage of *Sarracenia's* appeal to insects in order to acquire their own meals. One species of spider spins a web over the mouth of the pitcher and captures the insects that come to feed on the plant's nectar. Sometimes birds devour visiting insects, or even split the pitcher open with their beaks to feed on undigested insect matter.

other. These two complete the system of sphincters that separate each specialized section of the human digestive system from the next. The outside muscle can be controlled voluntarily, allowing the individual to control the elimination of wastes, or feces.

Nervous and hormonal regulation

The human digestive process is closely coordinated with the rest of the body processes. This coordination is controlled by both nerves and hormones. Early evidence of the role of nerves in digestion was noted by Dr. Beaumont in his work on St. Martin. He noted that if St. Martin was angry or upset when he ate, the secretion of gastric juice stopped. Later experiments by other scientists showed that if the nerves leading to the stomach are cut, gastric secretion is reduced by about 25 percent.

A more important influence on the secretion of digestive juices is that of hormones. As soon as even a small amount of food enters the stomach, a hormone called **gastrin** is released by the gastric cells. Gastrin, in turn, stimulates the epithelial cells to secrete hydrochloric acid.

The lining of the duodenum, when stimulated by the entrance of food, produces a number of hormones. Each hormone improves the intestinal environment for the digestion and absorption of the food that has just entered. One hormone, for example, stimulates the pancreas to release its enzymes. Another causes contractions of the gall bladder, which then releases the stored bile. And still another hormone stimulates the small intestine to secrete enzymes.

Nerves and hormones often work together. Nervous responses may trigger the release of the hormone epinephrine from the adrenal glands. Epinephrine not only inhibits the secretion of digestive enzymes but also slows down the rate of peristalsis. Hormonal control of digestion thus regulates both enzyme secretion and muscle action in the digestive system itself.

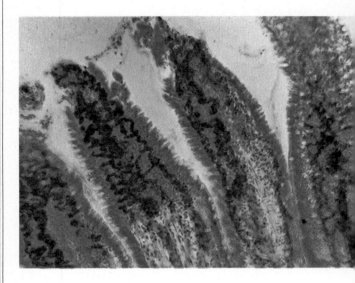

Figure 4-8. Intestinal villi are pictured in the micrograph above. Below is a diagram of the same villi. The cells surrounding each villus function in absorbing simple sugars, amino acids, fatty acids, and glycerol. The sugars and amino acids enter the capillaries and are carried to the liver for storage. The fatty acids and glycerol enter the lymph vessels, from which they pass into the bloodstream and eventually reach the body cells.

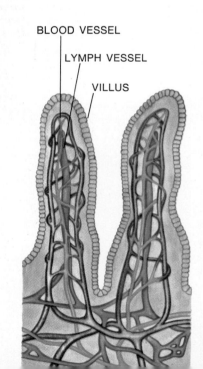

BLOOD VESSEL

LYMPH VESSEL

VILLUS

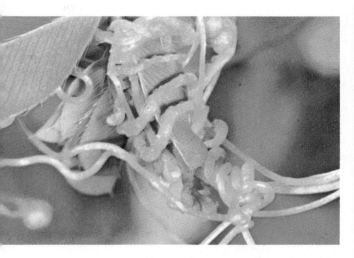

Figure 4-9. Dodder is a plant parasite that is dependent on its host—in this instance, clover—for most of its nutrition.

Figure 4-10. Ripe papaya fruit. The unripened papaya produces a type of proteinase called papain, which has been used for centuries by native islanders of the South Pacific as a natural meat tenderizer. In its processed form, papain forms the basis for the powdered meat tenderizers commonly used in cooking.

DIGESTION IN PLANTS

Plants, like animals, depend upon food to provide energy and build new cells. Most plants can make their own food, by the process of photosynthesis. The only raw materials necessary are water and carbon dioxide. Some minerals, including nitrogen, phosphorus, and potassium, are required for growth, but these inorganic substances can be absorbed directly from the soil. Photosynthesis cannot take place without light. But green plants can store the products of photosynthesis, and use them even when no light is available. Digestion in green plants, therefore, is a matter of converting and using the stored food.

The products of photosynthesis are stored as complex sugars, starches, fats, and proteins. Because they are almost insoluble in water and thus will not be drawn into the chemical processes of the cell, these large molecules can be stored throughout the plant in roots, stems, seeds, and even leaves. Then they can be taken from storage and used as food. Before they can be used in respiration or move from cell to cell, however, they must be able to cross the cell membranes. For this they must be made small and soluble, just as in animals.

Thus the mechanics of digestion in plants are very similar to those that operate in animals. The food, the enzymes that act on the food, and the results of the enzyme actions are similar. There is only one major difference. In most multicellular animals, digestion is extracellular. But in autotrophic plants it is intracellular, and can occur inside any cell in which food is stored.

A few plants, however, do not have chlorophyll and cannot make their own food. Some of these heterotrophic plants are **saprophytes,** which live off dead organic matter such as foodstuffs or dead plants and animals. The rest are **parasites,** which live off other living organisms, known as their hosts. Saprophytes and some parasites digest extracellularly, secreting enzymes that break down the organic substances. Many parasites absorb predigested nutrients into their own cells from the bodies of their hosts.

The conversion of starch to sugar by digestive enzymes in plant cells is very similar to hydrolysis in the mouth. The plant cell secretes amylase and maltase. These enzymes act as catalysts in the conversion of polysaccharide starch molecules to glucose. Glucose, you recall, is the energy-yielding molecule used in cellular respiration. It can be produced in large quantities from stored food as the need arises: for example, in the germination of seeds. Because it easily diffuses and penetrates the cells, it can be transported from one part of the plant to another.

The digestion of fats and oils in plants occurs through the action of the enzyme lipase, just as it does in animals. However, the fatty acids and glycerol that result from this process may not be used directly in respiration but may be converted into sugar first. Experiments have shown that as a seed germinates, the oil in it decreases while the sugar content increases.

Plant proteins are broken into amino acids by specific proteinases. A type of proteinase found in pineapple, bromelin, is easily detected. If fresh pineapple is placed on gelatin, which is a protein food, the gelatin will liquefy as a result of the digestive action of the bromelin. If you eat enough fresh pineapple, you may find the bromelin having a similar effect on your lips.

Another type of proteinase, papain, is produced by the unripe papaya, a tropical fruit. Papain is a natural meat tenderizer. Its digestive action on the connective tissue and muscle fibers makes the meat easier to chew.

SUMMARY

All organisms use nutrients in the production of energy, in growth and repair, and in the maintenance and regulation of body activities. Nutrients include energy-yielding fats, carbohydrates, and proteins, all usable as energy savers or cell-building materials, and a number of different vitamins and minerals. Vitamins and minerals contribute to both growth and repair in their role as coenzymes in the chemical reactions of the cell.

Green plants can make their own nutrients from nitrogen, carbon, and oxygen found in the soil and the atmosphere. Heterotrophic organisms, including all animals, cannot manufacture their own nutrients and must ingest them in the form of food. The way in which this food is broken down into nutrients available to cells is known as digestion.

Digestion can take place either inside the cell (intracellular digestion) or outside of it (extracellular digestion). Many single-celled organisms digest intracellularly, engulfing food particles and surrounding them in a vacuole. Lysosomes, containing enzymes, fuse with the vacuole to form a digestive vacuole. Enzymes then break down the particles for use throughout the cell. Unicellular organisms sometimes digest food particles extracellularly, secreting digestive enzymes directly into the environment to break down food. The smaller food molecules then pass into the organisms by diffusion. Most multicellular animals also digest extracellularly, but their digestive enzymes are usually secreted into an internal digestive cavity.

Multicellularity involves specialization. At a low level of specialization, food particles are simply engulfed by one kind of cell and passed along to all other cells. Food molecules must be small enough to be used in all of these different cells. At a higher level of specialization, larger food particles can first be broken down outside the cells in a specialized cavity known as a gastrovascular cavity, with a single opening through which food is taken in and wastes are eliminated. Then the smaller particles can be engulfed by the cells for intracellular digestion.

A complete digestive tract, with one opening for the intake of food and another for the elimination of wastes, is found in most animals. Cells are organized into tissues and organs that perform different functions at different locations along the tract. The earthworm's digestive tract is similar to those in most animals, with specialized organs for storage, mechanical and chemical digestion, absorption and elimination of wastes.

A system of hormonal and nervous controls coordinates the functions of the digestive system with each other as well as with the other activities of the body.

Plants also carry on digestion. Autotrophic plants synthesize food from basic raw materials and do not usually need to ingest organic nutrients. Digestion therefore consists of breaking down stored food in a cell from large insoluble molecules to smaller soluble ones. The enzymes, the substances they break down, and the end products they produce are similar to those in animals. Nongreen heterotrophic plants are either saprophytes or parasites, and obtain nutrients from the host organisms by means of extracellular digestion or absorption of predigested material.

Review questions

1. Name at least five important nutrients. Which is the most abundant source of energy?

2. Distinguish between herbivores, omnivores, and carnivores.

3. What is a Calorie?

4. What is the importance of protein to the nutrition of heterotrophs? Why?

5. Populations in underdeveloped countries often subsist on a diet almost solely composed of carbohydrates and having a high Calorie content. What might we expect to observe about their physical condition and general health?

6. Name some important minerals and their functions.

7. What are vitamins? Name the two general types of vitamin and give some examples of each.

8. What is digestion? Why is it necessary?

9. Name the two types of digestion.

10. Describe the process of digestion in an amoeba.

11. What is a gastrovascular cavity? What advantages does it confer?

12. Trace the progress of a piece of food as it passes through the digestive tract of an earthworm.

13. What are filter feeders? Name two or more examples.

14. Where does digestion of starches begin? What two enzymes start the process in motion?

15. What is the function of pepsin? Where does it take place?

16. Where is chemical digestion completed?

17. Name the digestive enzymes secreted by the liver and the pancreas. Describe their functions.

18. What symptoms might we expect to see in a person who has had a large part of the stomach surgically removed? A part of the small intestine? A part of the colon?

19. Describe the structure and function of the intestinal villi.

20. In what two ways is the digestive process regulated? Name one or more examples of each type of regulation.

21. What raw materials are necessary to photosynthesis?

22. Where does digestion take place in plants?

23. Distinguish between saprophytes and parasites.

24. In what four forms are the products of photosynthesis stored?

25. What are proteinases?

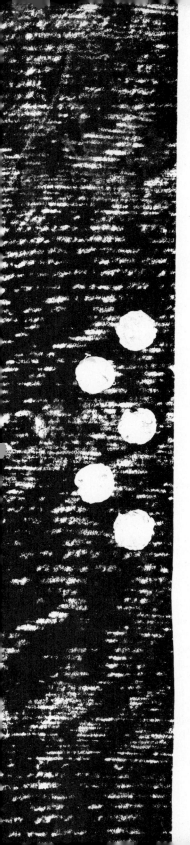

Transport in Plants and Animals

In the last chapter we examined the systems that various organisms use for digestion of nutrients. In the next chapter we will discuss their systems of gas exchange. In this chapter, however, we will concentrate on the body function that makes both digestion and gas exchange possible—the function of **transport.**

In order to carry on their life processes, grow, and divide, cells need access to energy and raw materials. Therefore, they need supplies of food, water, and minerals. Heterotrophic organisms must take in all of these materials from outside. Autotrophic organisms can manufacture their own food, using energy from the sun, but they too need to take in water and minerals. Moreover, these substances must not only be taken into the organism, but must be distributed to all its cells. Finally, all cells must get rid of waste products, or they will soon die.

How are these demands satisfied in organisms that are made up of millions of cells? Obviously, rather elaborate transport systems are needed. In this chapter we will examine some of the basic ones. We will see that in some of the simpler animals, coordinated activity by specialized cells and tissues is enough. But in complex organisms, transport involves coordinated activity by several entire organ systems.

CELLULAR BASIS OF TRANSPORT

The simplest level of transport, without which more elaborate systems would be useless for life, is transport into and out of the cell. Digested nutrient molecules, for example, cannot get out of the intestine and into the bloodstream unless they can pass through the cells of the intestinal wall, and through the walls of the blood vessels. There are several means of transport for such molecules. The simplest, and perhaps the most common, is diffusion.

Diffusion and osmosis

Diffusion is a movement of molecules from one place to another. Molecules and ions of all substances are in constant motion. They can be made to move more rapidly by heating them and so increasing their energy, or to move more slowly by cooling them. But they stop moving only at the temperature known as absolute zero: -273 C.

Not all molecular movement is diffusion. Diffusion occurs when more molecules of a substance move in one direction than in another. That is, it is a net movement of molecules in one direction. It takes place when the molecules of a substance are more concentrated in one place than in a neighboring one. For example, you might put a drop of perfume in one end of a long tube, then close that end and begin sniffing at the other end. Eventually, you would smell the perfume. Some molecules of the perfume would have diffused through the length of the tube to your nose.

When the molecules of a substance are evenly distributed through the available space, diffusion stops. Molecules still move back and forth, but there are equal numbers of them going in all directions. There is no net movement in one direction.

Consider how this works for a single-celled organism—say, one in a pond. The cell is respiring, so it is using up oxygen. As it does so, the concentration of oxygen molecules inside the cell becomes less than that outside. This sets up what is called a **concentration gradient.** Oxygen molecules from outside diffuse into the cell, along the concentration gradient. They continue to do so as long as the inside concentration is lower than that outside. Meantime, the cell

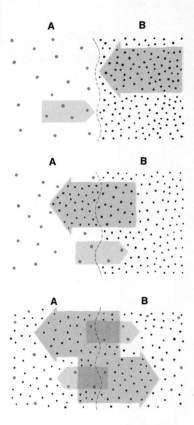

Figure 5-1. The molecules of two gases indicate how diffusion takes place. When the relative percentage of the two gases is the same in each region, diffusion ceases. This means that the net movement of molecules has ceased, even though individual molecules still cross the barrier between the two regions. However, these random movements cancel each other.

is producing carbon dioxide. This is more concentrated inside the cell than outside, so the concentration gradient runs in the opposite direction. The carbon dioxide diffuses out. Thus two substances can diffuse in opposite directions at the same time.

Not only dissolved substances diffuse. Water and other solvents do so also. If pure water is placed on one side of a membrane, and a salt-in-water solution on the other side, water molecules will diffuse from the pure water to the solution, while salt will

PATTERNS OF MAINTENANCE
AND REGULATION

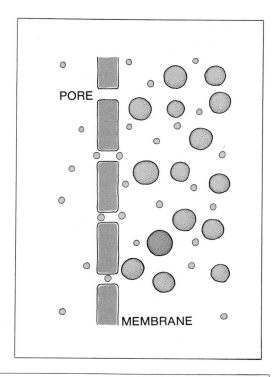

Figure 5-2. The pores in a semipermeable membrane are large enough for some molecules to pass through, but not all.

Such a membrane, through which some substances can pass but others cannot, is said to be **semi-permeable.** The cell membrane is very permeable to water, oxygen, carbon dioxide, and other small inorganic molecules. It is less permeable to simple sugars, such as glucose, and to ions of mineral salts, acids, and bases. It is not permeable to the large molecules of starch, proteins, fats, nucleic acids, and even double sugars (disaccharides) such as sucrose. However, some large molecules are soluble in fats. These seem to penetrate lipid parts of the cell membrane, where protein molecules are absent, and thus cross the membrane without going through the pores.

The semi-permeable character of the membrane is very important to the life of cells. A completely permeable membrane would let many molecules that are essential to life diffuse out. It would also make it impossible to keep a higher concentration of non-water molecules inside the cell than outside. This concentration is needed because it makes for a higher concentration of water molecules outside the cell. Thus water always tends to diffuse into the cell. This keeps the cell inflated, creating what is known as **turgor pressure.** A cell must have turgor pressure in order to function well.

The diffusion of water, or any other solvent, across a semi-permeable membrane is called **osmosis.** This term does not apply to diffusion of dissolved materials such as sugars, salts, or gases.

Since the concentration of water is usually higher outside a cell than inside, there is danger that too much water will diffuse into the cell. This would cause the cell to swell, stretching or even breaking the membrane and killing the cell. In some unicellular organisms, such as *Amoeba* and *Paramecium*, the excess water is collected in contractile vacuoles, which burst at intervals and release the water to the outside again. Bacteria, algae, and plants have a relatively rigid cell wall outside the membrane. This wall restricts swelling and stops the diffusion of water into the cell. Thus high turgor

diffuse from the solution to the pure water. Diffusion will cease when the concentration of both salt and water is the same on both sides of the membrane.

Obviously, molecules cannot diffuse in and out of cells unless they can pass through the cell membrane. We described the cell membrane in chapter 1, as a structure composed of protein and lipid molecules. The membrane apparently has small pores— large enough to allow very small molecules to pass through, but not larger molecules.

TRANSPORT IN PLANTS
AND ANIMALS

pressures can develop in plant cells without breaking the membranes. In fact, turgor pressure helps to support the plant.

Under certain conditions, the concentration of water may be higher inside the cell, causing water to diffuse out. This generally occurs when fresh-water organisms are placed in sea water, or when too much fertilizer is added to the soil in which plants are growing. It causes shrinkage, or **plasmolysis,** of the cells. Cells usually recover from plasmolysis without serious damage if they are quickly returned to a solution with a higher water concentration. But if plasmolysis is prolonged, the cell will die.

Osmotic pressure

The concentration of a solution is determined by the percentage of dissolved molecules, or solutes, in the water. If the solute concentration is high, the water concentration, naturally, is low, and vice versa. If two solutions on opposite sides of a semipermeable membrane have different concentrations, then concentration gradients exist between them, just as between pure water and a solution. When the concentration difference is great, the gradient is said to be steep; when it is slight, the gradient is shallow. The steeper the gradient, the stronger will be the tendency of water to move down it—to diffuse through the membrane from the side with the high water concentration to the side with the low water concentration. We can see this if we start with the two solutions at the same level in the container. Gradually, the level on the side with the higher solute concentration (and lower water concentration) will actually rise above the level on the other side. The tendency of the water to diffuse down the gradient acts as a kind of pressure, pushing the level up. The steeper the gradient, the greater the pressure, and the higher the level can rise on one side in relation to the other.

But the diffusion of water through the membrane gradually makes the two solu-

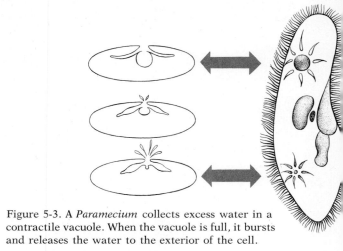

Figure 5-3. A *Paramecium* collects excess water in a contractile vacuole. When the vacuole is full, it bursts and releases the water to the exterior of the cell.

Figure 5-4. A normal and a plasmolyzed plant cell.

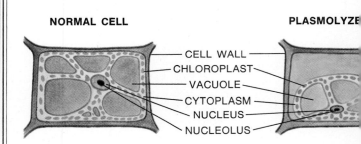

NORMAL CELL　　　　　　　　　　　　　　　**PLASMOLYZE**

CELL WALL
CHLOROPLAST
VACUOLE
CYTOPLASM
NUCLEUS
NUCLEOLUS

Figure 5-5. Measurement of osmotic pressure. Water has diffused from the left-hand chamber into the right-hand chamber along a concentration gradient, raising the level of the solution on the right. As the level rises, increased hydrostatic pressure ("water pressure") causes more water to diffuse in the opposite direction. When the two pressures are equal, the level on each side remains steady. The amount by which the solution level has risen can be translated into a measurement of osmotic pressure.

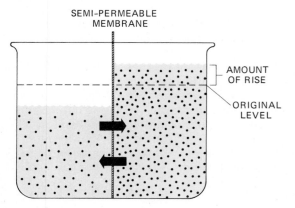

SEMI-PERMEABLE
MEMBRANE

AMOUNT
OF RISE

ORIGINAL
LEVEL

tions more alike in concentration. This lessens the steepness of the gradient, reducing the tendency for water to diffuse across the membrane. In the meantime, the rising level of the solution is exerting pressure in the other direction, also tending to slow the diffusion. When the two tendencies are equal, diffusion stops; there is no more net movement of water across the membrane.

Thus the difference between the old and new levels of the two solutions when diffusion stops can be used as a measurement of the solutions' difference in concentration. This measurement is called the **osmotic pressure** of the solution. Differences in osmotic pressure between the contents of cells, or between a cell and its environment, are important to an organism's functioning.

Flow and active transport

Gases diffuse quickly, but liquids and materials dissolved in them diffuse slowly. Thus, diffusion is an effective means of transport only over short distances, such as between one cell and the next, or between a cell and its immediate environment. For transport over longer distances, flow is more rapid and effective.

Flow is the mass movement of liquids or gases. It is the movement of many molecules as a unit, powered by some outside source of energy, rather than of individual molecules moving under their own energy. Water is made to flow through a pipe by the energy of a pump or of gravity. Air is made to flow in a breeze by the energy of a change in air pressure or of a spinning fan. We might compare diffusion to people walking out of a football stadium after a game gradually scattering to less crowded places, while a few maintenance people move into the stands and onto the field to clean up. Then flow could be compared to people being driven away in buses. The bus is more effective than walking for long-distance travel—for instance, if the fans of the visiting team want to get home that night.

Flow may occur both inside and outside of cells. Inside, the cytoplasm is often kept flowing. Outside, the flowing of water or air constantly changes the substance in contact with an organism. This may be of considerable importance. In still water, the substances that a microorganism is absorbing may become greatly reduced in concentration in the region next to the cell. Likewise, substances diffusing out of the cell may become quite concentrated in the immediate environment. This lessens the concentration gradients of these substances, and slows diffusion. The flow of water or air past the cell helps to keep the concentration gradient high.

In recent years, research has indicated that osmosis may involve flow of water through cell membranes, as well as diffusion. The reason for thinking this is that water seems to enter a cell more rapidly than it could by diffusion alone.

Like flow, **active transport** serves to speed up the passage of molecules across the cell membrane. But it also allows them to travel the "wrong way"—against the concentration gradient, from regions of lower to higher concentration. Thus the ions of some mineral salts usually continue to enter cells even when they are much more concentrated inside the cell than outside. As we noted in chapter 1, active transport may be accomplished by **carrier molecules**, which carry substances through the membrane. However active transport works, it requires energy, which is usually provided by ATP. If a cell is damaged so severely that no more energy is available, the ions that have accumulated in the cell by active transport begin diffusing out.

ANIMAL TRANSPORT SYSTEMS

The cells of most organisms obtain nourishment in similar ways. The movement of a liquid medium transports materials to and from the cells. Depending on the particular organism, this liquid may be either water or blood. Diffusion, flow, or active transport then carries the materials across the cell membranes. Animal transport systems can be divided into two basic categories. The first category is found in the simpler aquatic animals, whose body structure is usually made up of only two cell layers. Familiar examples in this category are sponges, *Hydra*, and jellyfish. The second category is found in all other animals, whose body structures are formed from their basic cell layers. Such animals have more complex transport arrangements.

Transport in simple animals

Simple multicellular animals obtain needed materials by bringing the water that surrounds them into contact with the cells that line their interior body cavities. Eventually, oxygen and nutrients dissolved in the water will reach the interior cells. Wastes from these cells will be carried away by the water as it leaves the animal. This transport system is no more complex than that of a microorganism whose cell surface is completely surrounded by its liquid environment. In fact, these animals have only one transport problem, that of moving the surrounding water so that it will flow in and out of the interior cavity.

The sponge moves water through its cavity by beating the water with the flagella of its collar cells. Water enters the sponge through pores in its body, bringing food and oxygen to the interior cells and removing carbon dioxide and other wastes released from those cells. Each cell of the animal's body is in close contact with the water, and diffusion into and out of the cells can take place very rapidly.

Transport is also relatively simple for *Hydra* and its larger relatives, the jellyfish. Like the sponge, those animals have a body structure consisting essentially of two layers of cells. Digestion takes place within the gastrovascular cavity, or stomach–circulatory cavity, and digested food diffuses through

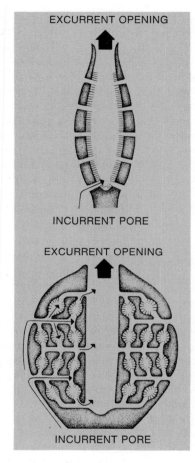

Figure 5-6. Water enters the sponge through pores in its body, nourishing the cells in much the same way as single-celled organisms are nourished. In large sponges (bottom), a system of folds within the sponge retains the water for a considerable period of time.

PATTERNS OF MAINTENANCE
AND REGULATION

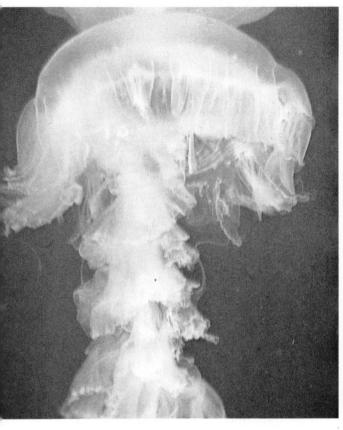

Figure 5-7. The jellyfish digests food within the gastrovascular cavity. Flagellated cells lining the walls of the cavity keep water and dissolved nutrients circulating.

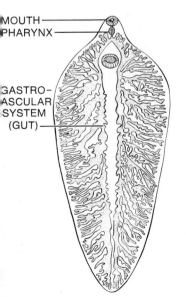

MOUTH

PHARYNX

GASTRO-
VASCULAR
SYSTEM
(GUT)

Figure 5-8. The sheep liver fluke has an intricately branched gastrovascular system.

the inner layer of cells to the outer layer. Some of the cells in the cavity are flagellated. These assist in keeping water and dissolved nutrients circulating in the cavity.

Transport in complex animals

More specific demands are placed upon the transport systems of more complex animals. Since such animals possess more than two layers of cells, it is virtually impossible to circulate water to every cell, even in an aquatic environment. So transport above the cellular level is carried out in other ways.

The sheep liver fluke, a member of the flatworm family, demonstrates one interesting way of doing this. This fluke is a parasite that gets its nourishment from its host, the sheep. The mouth of the fluke opens into a gastrovascular cavity that branches several times, forming a network that extends into all parts of the body. Therefore, in a sense, every cell of the fluke is near the external environment, since the branched gastrovascular cavity allows food to be transported close to every cell. The fluke also possesses a many-branched excretory system, which transports waste material away from the cells.

One difficulty with the system of the sheep liver fluke is that it is not very efficient for oxygen transport. However, this animal leads a relatively sluggish existence as a parasite, and does not require a great deal of oxygen. Some oxygen may be absorbed through the exterior cells, supplementing the small amount that is probably obtained through the gastrovascular cavity.

For larger and more active animals, such a system is insufficient. In these animals transport is largely performed by a special liquid—**blood**—that supplies the internal cells. However, all blood is not alike. Particularly among the invertebrates, it may bear little resemblance to the red liquid we are familiar with, and often its chemical makeup is radically different.

While the primary function of the transport system is the exchange of food, oxygen, and wastes with the cells, it also carries on other activities. For example, the transport system plays a major role in internal heat regulation. When the body is too warm, blood travels close to the surface of the skin where it can be cooled. Under conditions of cold, it is transported deeper within the tissues, where its heat is retained. Until recently it was thought that this occurred only in "warm-blooded" animals—birds and mammals—but it is now known to take place also in "cold-blooded" animals such as amphibians and reptiles.

The transport system also serves a protective function. Through the activities of certain cells, and of antibodies in the blood, disease-causing agents can be destroyed. Tissue damage can be repaired by the action of other specialized cells in the blood and by mechanisms of blood clotting. In this chapter we are not concerned with these additional functions, which will be discussed in chapter 8.

CIRCULATORY SYSTEMS

When we examine the systems by which blood reaches all the cells of an animal, we find two general types, known as open and closed circulatory systems.

Open circulatory systems

The essential feature of the **open circulatory system** is that the blood moves through a body cavity—such as the abdominal cavity—and bathes the cells directly. The open circulatory system is particularly characteristic of insects and other arthropods, although it is also found in some other organisms.

In most insects the blood does not take a major part in oxygen transport. Oxygen enters the animal's body through a separate network of branching tubes that open to the atmosphere on the outside of the animal.

(This type of respiratory system will be discussed in more detail in the next chapter.) Blood in an open circulatory system moves somewhat more slowly than in the average closed system. The slower system is adequate for insects because it does not have to supply the cells with oxygen.

Most mollusks also have an open circulatory system. In many mollusks—the clam, for example—oxygen is transported by the blood. However, because these are sedentary animals, far less active than most insects, their need for oxygen is not great. Transport by the open circulatory system is obviously sufficient for their needs.

We can observe the workings of a typical open circulatory system in the grasshopper. The only true blood vessel is the **aorta.** This vessel runs dorsally—that is, on the upper side of the body—through the thorax, or "chest," and the abdomen. In each segment of the abdomen the aorta is enlarged, forming a simple "heart." From the thorax and abdomen the aorta continues to the head segment, where it ends. Contractions of the hearts force the blood toward the head.

Each enlarged section of the aorta has two slit-like openings called **ostia.** When the "hearts" contract, the ostia close automatically, forcing the blood in the aorta toward the head segment, rather than into the body cavities. As the hearts relax, the ostia open, admitting blood from the body cavities.

The anterior end of the aorta is open, and releases blood into the head of the grasshopper. This "free" blood then trickles down and backward through the cavities of the thorax and abdomen. As it flows, it picks up digested nutrients from the cells of the digestive tract, and collects dissolved waste products released by all the body cells. The wastes are removed from the blood as it flows around a system of hairlike excretory tubules. The action of muscles in the abdomen moves the blood upward to the hearts, where it reenters the aorta through the ostia.

The course traveled by the blood in this open circulatory system is not really as haphazard as it sounds. Walls known as

92

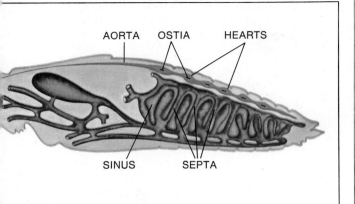

Figure 5-9. The open circulatory system of the grasshopper.

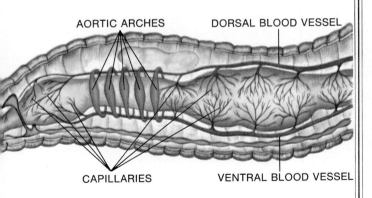

Figure 5-10. The earthworm has a simple closed circulatory system. Only a portion of the extensive network of capillaries is shown here.

septa divide the insect's body cavities into smaller cavities, or **sinuses.** The septa route the blood in a definite backward direction through the sinuses in the thorax and abdomen. Furthermore, although the pumping of the hearts creates very little blood pressure, the blood moves more quickly when the insect is active, aided by contractions of muscles in the thorax and abdomen.

Closed circulatory systems

In a **closed circulatory system,** the blood flows through a well-defined system of vessels with many branches. In the majority of closed systems the blood is responsible for oxygen transport. To supply all the body cells with sufficient oxygen, the blood must move quickly through the blood vessels. A closed circulatory system must therefore have an efficient pumping mechanism, or heart, to set the blood in motion and keep it moving briskly through the body.

All vertebrates possess closed circulatory systems. Simple closed systems are also found in some invertebrates, including the annelid worms. A good example of such a simple closed circulatory system can be seen in the earthworm.

The circulatory system of the earthworm is centered on two main blood vessels. The **dorsal blood vessel** lies just above the digestive tract, and runs the length of the earthworm's body. This vessel contracts rhythmically, forcing the blood toward the anterior end of the animal. Along the lower side of the worm, the **ventral blood vessel** carries the blood in the opposite direction, toward the rear of the body.

At the anterior end, in the region of the esophagus, the dorsal and ventral blood vessels are connected by five pairs of enlarged "hearts," the **aortic arches.** Contractions of the aortic arches help to regulate the pressure of the blood as it flows into the ventral blood vessel. Both the arches and the dorsal vessel have valves that keep the blood from backing up. Like one-way doors, the valves can open only in the direction of the blood

TRANSPORT IN PLANTS
AND ANIMALS

THE ELEPHANT

One of the most imaginative creations in the history of animated film was Dumbo the elephant. How many of us remember laughing at the floppy-eared elephant and his devoted friend and protector, a tiny mouse? Or despairing over the cruel separation of Dumbo and his mother? Or cheering when our hero learned he could fly?

Elephants appeal to people of all ages. Nearly every large circus and zoo features an elephant or two among its main attractions. But a herd of elephants in the wild is a far more impressive spectacle. Visitors to African game preserves quickly learn the wisdom underlying the posted signs: "ELEPHANTS HAVE THE RIGHT OF WAY!"

Elephants come in two basic models, African and Asian. African elephants are generally somewhat taller and heavier. The African bull elephant stands about 11 feet high at the shoulders and weighs as much as seven tons. The Indian bull is about a foot shorter and a ton lighter. In both species, the female weighs one or two tons less than the male.

If you want to transport an elephant, your truck had better have good springs. The ears alone of an African elephant weigh 130 pounds. An adult elephant carries some 6,000 pounds of muscle and a mere 200 pounds of fat on a 3,500-pound skeleton. Its trunk weighs over 250 pounds and its heart some 45 pounds!

The part of the elephant that holds the greatest financial interest is the tusk, a greatly elongated front tooth. The tusks are composed almost entirely of ivory, tipped by smooth enamel caps. They continue to grow throughout the elephant's life, and a single tusk may be over ten feet long and weigh more than 200 pounds. The tusks are used both as weapons for fighting and as tools for gathering food. The female Asian elephant, though, has no tusks.

In addition to the tusks, the elephant has four molar teeth. Even these are huge. Each is about a foot in width and eight pounds in weight. As each group of teeth wears down, it is replaced by four larger ones. This repeats six times. After its final set of teeth wears down, the poor toothless elephant is unable to eat properly, and eventually starves to death. The average elephant lives to about the same age as the average human.

As might be expected, the elephant needs a great deal of food to nourish its massive body. Elephants consume several hundred pounds of plants every day. But the huge teeth and 40-yard digestive tract are so inefficient that the animal digests less than half the food that it eats. Wild elephants spend some 16 hours a day in search of food, traveling great distances to

satisfy their vast appetites.

An elephant also needs a great deal of water. An adult will drink about 50 gallons of water a day, sucking it up in its trunk and squirting it into its throat. The trunk is actually an elongated upper lip and nose. Used mostly for bringing food and water to the mouth, it also serves for caressing a mate, spanking a calf, and taking a refreshing shower or dust bath.

Do elephants lie down when they sleep? It appears that elephants require surprisingly little sleep, but that they do lie down periodically for a two- to four-hour nap. In addition, they occasionally doze lightly on their feet for several minutes at a time. Oddly, their pulse rates seem to increase, rather than decrease, during slumber.

Anyone who has ever seen a Tarzan movie knows that elephants generally travel in large herds. The female elephant is usually more aggressive, and assumes leadership in the herd. Elephants are extremely loyal and will assist each other when wounded or ill. A calf that loses its mother will usually be adopted by another cow. Although elephants are extremely noisy as they crash through a forest, they can get their large selves out of sight very silently in times of danger.

Water presents no serious barrier to elephants. They are excellent swimmers. The trunk can be useful here, too. It is not uncommon for a line of elephants to be observed fording a shallow river by walking along the bottom with their trunks raised above the surface as snorkels.

The old notion that elephants are afraid of mice is, of course, untrue. An elephant does not fear any animal in its native habitat. Still, elephants do not go looking for trouble. Those in India and Burma, for example, are very careful to avoid poisonous snakes, which could bite them in the soft flesh between the toenails.

Elephants are not always good-natured giants, however. Periodically, a gland between the ear and the eye secretes an oily substance onto the lower part of the face. When this happens, the elephant enters a state called "musth" and becomes either extremely excited or morose. An elephant in musth may suddenly turn against a human with whom it has enjoyed a long and close relationship. The reason for this odd phenomenon remains a mystery.

Another time at which an elephant can pose a threat to human life and property is when it becomes intoxicated. Captive elephants seem to have a great fondness for beer and other alcoholic beverages. Elephants in the wild often seek out naturally fermented grains or fruits. Drunken elephants may fight among themselves, trumpet noisily, push down trees, and chase any animal that is foolish enough to get in the way. No one knows, though, whether drunk elephants see pink people.

flow. They thus keep the blood from being forced backward when the dorsal vessel and the aortic arches contract.

The dorsal and ventral blood vessels branch out through the earthworm's body, extending into all the organs and to the skin. Eventually the branches divide still further into a network of very fine vessels called **capillaries.** The capillaries are so numerous that they come into contact with every cell, and their walls are only a single cell thick. Thus, substances can diffuse easily into and out of the capillaries from the body cells.

As it flows through the capillaries, the blood picks up digested nutrients from the intestine. It also receives oxygen from the air at the surface of the skin, and discharges carbon dioxide into the air. As the blood passes by the body cells it supplies them with these nutrients and oxygen. At the same time, carbon dioxide and nitrogenous wastes from the cells enter the blood. Still other capillaries carry the blood past excretory organs, where the nitrogenous wastes diffuse out and are gotten rid of. The capillaries join together, forming progressively larger vessels that return the blood to the dorsal and ventral blood vessels.

In the lower vertebrates we find a more highly developed type of heart, working in conjunction with an extensive system of blood vessels. However, in many of these animals the circulatory arrangements are mechanically less efficient than in birds and mammals. In fish, for example, blood goes directly from the gills to the body, and only afterward returns to the heart. Both gills and body contain capillary beds. This means that the blood must pass through at least two sets of narrow capillaries, each of which slows it down, before it gets a new boost in pressure from the heart. Contractions in the aorta are some help, but the heart must still work very rapidly to keep blood pressure high. Otherwise the blood would not move fast enough through the networks of capillaries.

In amphibians and some reptiles, the heart contains three chambers. Blood goes from the heart to the lungs or gills, comes back to the heart, and then goes out to the rest of the body. This improves the pressure situation, since the blood is re-pressurized by the heart after picking up fresh oxygen. But oxygen-rich blood coming from the gills or lungs can be mixed, in the heart, with oxygen-poor blood returning from the body circulation. Some of this oxygen-poor blood thus may get back into the body circulation without going back first to the gills or lungs. The three-chambered heart, therefore, would seem rather inefficient for oxygen transport. Actually, this may not be as much of a problem as it seems. Reptiles, for instance, have an arrangement of folds in the walls of the lower heart chamber that direct the blood flow so that probably very little mixing takes place. As for amphibians, they take in a good deal of oxygen through the moist membranes of the skin and mouth. So the circulatory system of these animals is quite adequate for the demands that are made on it.

THE HUMAN CIRCULATORY SYSTEM

The human transport system, like that of other mammals, is a closed system. Like any other closed system, it consists essentially of a pumping heart connected to a network of blood vessels, and its functions are supplemented by the activities of other systems. The respiratory system, consisting of the lungs and associated organs, is one of the supplementary systems. It brings in oxygen from the atmosphere, and disposes of carbon dioxide and water. There are also elaborate nervous and gland systems, which help to regulate the distribution of materials by the circulatory system. These other systems will be discussed in later chapters.

Composition of the blood
Within the human body, the actual function of transport is performed by the blood. The

PATTERNS OF MAINTENANCE
AND REGULATION

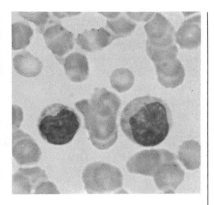

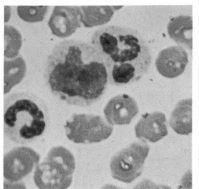

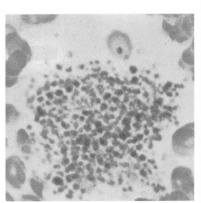

Figure 5-11. The three main groups of formed elements in the blood. At top, the numerous cells without nuclei are the erythrocytes, or red blood cells. The white blood cells are larger and have darkly stained, lobed nuclei. The platelets, shown in the bottom photograph, appear as small, dark particles.

structures of the circulatory system—heart, arteries, veins, and capillaries—are merely an elaborate "plumbing system," which conducts the blood from one part of the body to another. To understand how the blood carries out its primary function of transport, we must first see what it is composed of.

When a sample of blood is spun in a centrifuge for a few minutes, it separates into two general components. A sediment, composed of various types of cells or cell-like bodies, makes up about 45 percent of its volume. These materials are collectively called the **formed elements.** The remainder of the blood, about 55 percent of its volume, is a fairly thick, straw-colored fluid called **plasma.**

By far the most plentiful formed elements are the red blood cells, or **erythrocytes.** It has been estimated that the blood of an adult human contains about 25 trillion of them. The blood of male adults possesses a slightly higher percentage of erythrocytes than the blood of females or children, since one of the male hormones (testosterone) stimulates production of them. A higher percentage is also found in the blood of persons living at high altitudes. We will see the reasons for this when we examine the primary function of erythrocytes.

While the term "red blood cell" is commonly used to describe the erythrocyte, this is not quite an accurate description. Unlike other cells, the mature erythrocyte does not possess a nucleus. Erythrocytes arise from **precursor** ("going-before") cells produced by the red bone marrow, primarily in flat bones such as the skull, pelvis, ribs, and breastbone. (See chapter 7 for a fuller explanation of the role of bone marrow.) These precursors, called **erythroblasts,** possess a nucleus. However, the nucleus is lost when the cell is released into the blood and matures into an erythrocyte. The mature erythrocyte might best be described as a small cell-like structure that carries out limited functions. It is biconcave in shape, like a round cookie with both surfaces dented in the middle.

The primary function of erythrocytes is the transport of oxygen. They derive their red color from an iron-containing pigment called **hemoglobin (Hb)** which can bind to oxygen molecules. The liquid plasma is not a very efficient carrier of oxygen, and the presence of hemoglobin-containing erythrocytes enables the blood to transport more than 50 times as much oxygen as plasma alone could handle. As oxygen-rich erythrocytes pass through the capillaries, the hemoglobin molecules release their oxygen, which then diffuses through the capillary walls and enters the surrounding cells. Hemoglobin also binds to carbon dioxide.

The other important formed elements in the blood are the **leucocytes,** or white blood cells, and the **platelets.** Leucocytes are of at least five different types. All of them contain nuclei and are much larger than the tiny erythrocytes. Unlike the erythrocytes, leucocytes can move, in an amoeba-like fashion. They function mainly for defense. The platelets are much smaller. They form a part of the blood-clotting mechanism which, along with other defense and repair mechanisms, will be discussed in chapter 8.

Plasma, the liquid component of the blood, is about 90 percent water. However, it also contains other substances important to body functions. Among these are the plasma proteins **albumin,** the **globulins,** and **fibrinogen.** As we will see in a later chapter, fibrinogen is important in the blood-clotting process. Plasma proteins in general help to regulate the acidity, water content, osmotic pressure, and viscosity (thickness) of the blood. Globulins also play a role in immunity to foreign substances and disease.

Blood plasma also contains a number of inorganic ions. These include, among others, calcium, sodium, potassium, bicarbonate, and phosphate ions. The inorganic ions are important for osmotic regulation of the internal and external environments of body cells.

Organic nutrients are not exactly part of the blood, but are carried by the plasma. Glucose, sometimes called blood sugar, is one such nutrient. There are also variable amounts of nutrient amino acids and lipids. Plasma is also responsible for transporting carbon dioxide, the various hormones secreted by the body, and the nitrogenous wastes, which include urea, uric acid, and creatinine. Medicinal and other drugs, if they are present, are likewise carried by the plasma.

Because of the very complexity of the blood structure, variations in the makeup of the blood can be a sign that disease is present in the body. Some types of disease represent a failure of a particular function in the blood itself. Other diseases may directly or indirectly cause such a failure. Anemia, for example, may be caused by a variety of illnesses; but no matter what the cause, the net result is that either too few erythrocytes are present or else the erythrocytes contain too little hemoglobin. General fatigue and body weakness are among the symptoms, resulting from an insufficient supply of oxygen in the blood.

The heart and circulation

The more scientists study the heart, the more they are impressed by this organ's enormous capacity for work. The human heart begins its lifetime of labor only a few weeks after conception. Over a normal life-span of 65 to 70 years, it will continue to beat from 70 to 80 times per minute, and will pump a total of nearly 50 million gallons of blood. For sheer durability and consistency of performance, no other organ in the body can match it.

The human heart is a cone-shaped organ about the size of the fist. It is enclosed by a protective sac called the **pericardium,** made up of two membrane layers with a lubricating fluid sandwiched between them. This pericardial fluid helps to prevent friction as the heart beats. The organ itself is divided into three layers. These are the **epicardium** or outer membrane sheath, the middle muscle layer or **myocardium,** and the **endocardium** or inner membrane lining. The force of

PATTERNS OF MAINTENANCE
AND REGULATION

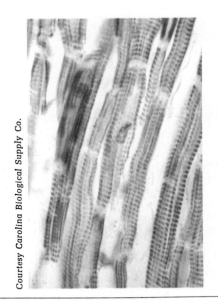

Courtesy Carolina Biological Supply Co.

Figure 5-12. Cardiac muscle has certain structural similarities to skeletal muscle. However, cardiac muscle is not under conscious control of the nervous system. (Courtesy Carolina Biological Supply Co.)

Figure 5-13. The human heart. Numbers indicate the path of blood flow from right atrium to aorta.

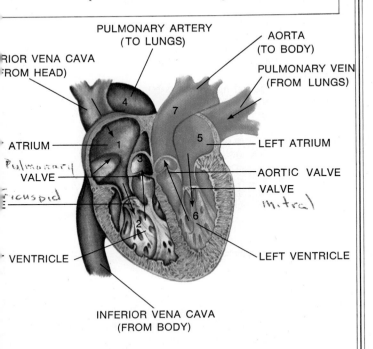

PULMONARY ARTERY
(TO LUNGS)

AORTA
(TO BODY)

PERIOR VENA CAVA
(FROM HEAD)

PULMONARY VEIN
(FROM LUNGS)

ATRIUM

LEFT ATRIUM

Pulmonary
VALVE

AORTIC VALVE

Ticuspid

VALVE

mitral

VENTRICLE

LEFT VENTRICLE

INFERIOR VENA CAVA
(FROM BODY)

the heart's contraction arises from the thick, powerful myocardium.

Cardiac muscle (heart muscle) is involuntary—that is, it is not under conscious control of the nervous system. We will look more closely at the structure of cardiac muscle in chapter 7. For now, we will merely note that the cells of the heart muscle can contract without being stimulated by the nervous system. A heart in which all nerve connections to the rest of the body have been cut—as is necessary when a heart is being transplanted—will continue regular contractions. Even a small piece of cardiac muscle, entirely separated from the heart itself, will still contract rhythmically. Under ordinary circumstances, however, impulses from certain nerves do affect the strength and rate of contractions by the heart.

The pace of the heartbeat is controlled by the activity of two **nodes.** The **sino-atrial** or **S-A** node is located in the right **atrium,** or upper chamber, of the heart. The **atrio-ventricular** or **A-V** node is found in the lower part of the wall, or septum, which separates the right and left atria. Both nodes are small masses of special nervelike muscle tissue, which act as pacemakers by regulating the rate at which the heart beats.

The human heart contains four chambers. As we saw above, the two upper chambers are the atria. The two lower chambers, which are much larger, are the right and left **ventricles.** Essentially, the heart is a double pump; each half of the pump is made up of one atrium and one ventricle, and the two halves are completely separated by a solid longitudinal septum. Both halves of the heart pump at the same time. Each contraction forces blood out of the heart. During each relaxation, blood flows in from the veins and fills both receiving chambers.

The easiest way to understand the circulation of the blood is to follow its path through a single circuit. Blood returning to the heart from the upper and lower parts of the body enters the right atrium through two large collecting veins, the **superior vena cava** and the **inferior vena cava.** The blood then passes through a one-way valve from the right atrium into the right ventricle. It is helped along by a contraction of the atrium.

Contraction of the right ventricle forces the blood out through another one-way

The pulmonary aorta branches almost immediately into the right and left **pulmonary arteries,** one leading to each lung. In the lungs, these arteries subdivide still further, into smaller and smaller branches

---

HEADING OFF A HEART ATTACK

Everyone has heard of heart transplants, but some other types of heart surgery are almost as intriguing. Consider, for instance, the Vineberg procedure for victims of atherosclerosis.

For the person with atherosclerosis—fatty clogging of the arteries—the rules are clear and strict. No smoking, regular exercise, and a sharp cut in the consumption of animal fats. In many patients these steps slow or even halt the formation of new fat deposits, but they do not remove those that are already present. If major arteries, such as the coronary arteries that supply blood to the heart muscle, are already severely blocked, does this mean that a heart attack inevitably lies ahead? It used to, but no more.

The problem with blocked coronary arteries, of course, is that blood—and therefore nutrients and oxygen—is prevented from reaching the strenuously working heart muscle. The shortage of oxygen is the first to be felt, and this shortage may lead to painful attacks of angina pectoris, especially after stress or physical activity. Severe and frequent angina, therefore, is a warning that a myocardial infarction—death of a portion of the heart muscle—may be in the offing. This

is when the Vineberg procedure, perfected by Dr. Arthur Vineberg in the 1950s, may be worth trying.

There are several versions of the Vineberg procedure, but all are founded on the same basic idea. Since the fat-clogged coronary arteries can no longer supply enough blood to the heart, blood must be brought in by another route. To provide such a route, the Vineberg procedure uses one or both of the large internal mammary arteries, which normally supply blood to the chest area. Each artery is implanted into an artificially created tunnel in the wall of the heart. Here the artery actually develops its own new system of arterioles and capillaries, joined with whatever existing vessels are still undamaged. Within about six months, the mammary arteries have completely taken over the job of supplying blood to the heart.

For some reason not yet understood, the mammary arteries are not subject to atherosclerosis, either in their normal location or in the new one. Thus, even though the coronary arteries may eventually become totally blocked, the implanted mammary arteries can be relied on to provide the heart muscle with a sufficient blood supply for an indefinite period. Patients can usually return to full physical activity, free from angina and other frightening symptoms.

---

valve into the **pulmonary aorta,** the large artery that leads to the lungs. Like all arteries, the pulmonary aorta is equipped with a thick layer of circular muscle, and rhythmic pulsations of this muscle aid in pushing the blood forward on its route.

called **arterioles,** which have progressively thinner walls. The branches finally form a network of tiny capillaries surrounding the air sacs in the lungs. Oxygen molecules from air in the lungs diffuse through the capillary walls and bind to hemoglobin molecules in

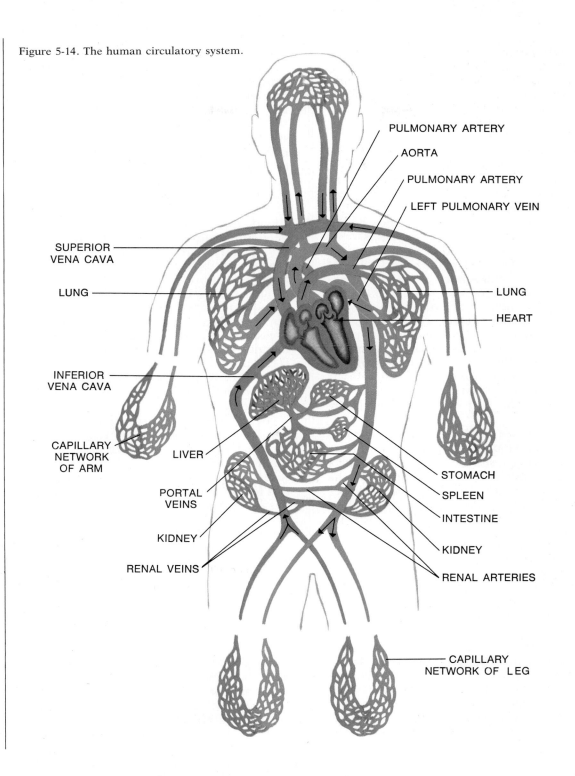

Figure 5-14. The human circulatory system.

PULMONARY ARTERY

AORTA

PULMONARY ARTERY

LEFT PULMONARY VEIN

SUPERIOR VENA CAVA

LUNG

LUNG

HEART

INFERIOR VENA CAVA

CAPILLARY NETWORK OF ARM

LIVER

STOMACH

SPLEEN

PORTAL VEINS

INTESTINE

KIDNEY

KIDNEY

RENAL VEINS

RENAL ARTERIES

CAPILLARY NETWORK OF LEG

the erythrocytes. At the same time, carbon dioxide molecules in the blood diffuse out through the capillary walls into the lungs. The resulting oxygenated blood is bright scarlet, whereas the deoxygenated blood, loaded with carbon dioxide, is a darker shade of red.

Next the capillaries begin to join, coming together like streams flowing into a river. They form slightly larger blood vessels, the **venules,** which in turn join to form **veins.** The veins may be the same size as the arteries, or even larger; however, they do not have the same thick, muscular walls.

The oxygen-rich blood from the lungs returns to the left atrium of the heart by way of several large **pulmonary veins.** It passes through another one-way valve into the left ventricle, which in turn pumps it out through the **systemic aorta,** the largest artery. The systemic aorta is the main pathway to the rest of the body. By the time the blood passes through the various capillary networks of the body, and enters the veins, it is largely deoxygenated. It returns to the right atrium of the heart, thus completing the circuit.

The pressure of the blood as it travels through the veins is much less than in the arteries, for it loses the force of the heart's original contraction as it passes through the narrow capillaries. Particularly in the lower part of the body, the blood moves so sluggishly through the veins that it would tend to flow backward into the capillaries unless this were prevented. Fortunately, there are one-way valves in the veins, and these keep the blood from backing up. Ordinary muscle movement in the body compresses the veins and moves the blood along.

So far we have seen two distinct circulatory patterns. The **pulmonary circulation** is the route of blood from the heart to the lungs and back again. The **systemic circulation** is the main route followed by the blood to the rest of the body. Within the systemic circulation, a number of local circuits supply vital organs. The **portal circuit,** for example, includes the system of veins that collect digested nutrients from the intestine and transport them to the liver for detoxifying, conversion, or temporary storage. Other special circuits supply the kidneys, the pelvic organs, and the head.

Contraction of the ventricles is known as **systole,** and is followed by a period of relaxation called **diastole.** During systole the muscular, elastic walls of the arteries expand as blood is pumped out through them. During diastole, they contract, maintaining blood pressure at a reasonably constant level. **Blood pressure** is stated in terms of the height of a column of mercury. The systolic pressure in an average adult, as measured in the arm, is about 120 mm. of mercury, and the diastolic pressure about 80 mm. This is usually expressed as a fraction, 120/80.

As we might expect, the rate and character of the heartbeat and the level of blood pressure are important guides for doctors in diagnosing heart and circulatory problems. Heart disease is currently the leading cause of death in Western societies, and **hypertension,** or high blood pressure, is a major contributing factor.

Most "heart" diseases actually involve blood vessel changes rather than the heart muscle itself. The heart muscle uses a vast amount of energy in its work, and so it must receive a rich supply of blood. Accordingly, it is fed by its own extensive system of **coronary** veins and arteries. Many so-called "heart attacks" are the result of a **coronary thrombosis,** the blockage of a coronary artery by a blood clot.

The major form of heart attack, however, is usually preceded by a condition known as **atherosclerosis.** The arteries become clogged with a lining of fats deposited by the blood, the most familiar of which is **cholesterol.** The passageway through the artery is narrowed by this accumulated fat, so that the blood flowing through it reaches a dangerously high pressure. Scar tissue and calcium deposits also develop, reducing the artery's elasticity and lessening its ability to cope with high pressure. The amount of nutrients and oxygen the narrowed arteries

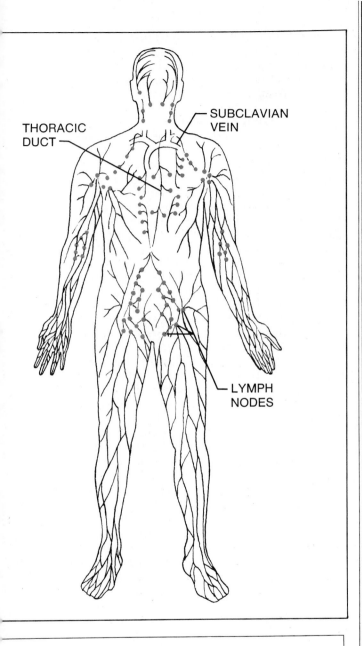

THORACIC
DUCT

SUBCLAVIAN
VEIN

LYMPH
NODES

Figure 5-15. The lymphatic system. Lymph is eventually returned to the bloodstream through a duct that empties into the subclavian vein.

can supply to the heart is greatly decreased. Eventually the artery may become completely blocked, and a part of the central myocardial layer may simply die from lack of nourishment. The result is a **myocardial infarction,** the commonest type of heart attack. The pain of the heart attack is so severe that the nervous system may react by blocking the heart contractions, so that the heart stops functioning entirely. Unless it is quickly restarted by shock, adrenalin, or heart massage, the victim will die. But if the affected portion of muscle is small, or the heart is strong, contractions can continue after the attack. In this case, the surrounding muscle tissue can carry the workload until new blood vessels grow into the area.

Many researchers believe that the increasing incidence of heart disease can largely be blamed on modern patterns of diet and behavior. Smoking has been linked very definitely to heart disease, as well as to lung cancer. A typical Western diet, high in animal or "saturated" fats, is linked to the development of atherosclerosis. And a sedentary way of life has largely eliminated regular exercise patterns that would benefit the heart as well as every other muscle. It has been suggested that the nonsmoker who exercises regularly and eliminates most animal fats from his or her diet is much less likely to suffer from heart and circulatory diseases.

The lymphatic system

From our examination of the circulatory system, we might conclude that the blood always stays inside the closed system of arteries, veins, and capillaries. However, this is not entirely true. Most of the formed elements and a number of large plasma proteins do stay inside the circulatory vessels. But large amounts of the water-soluble part of plasma, and certain of the formed elements, leak out through the capillary walls, passing directly into the extracellular environment. This fluid is called **lymph;** simply defined, it is blood plasma that contains neither blood cells nor platelets. It does, however, contain special lymph cells or **lymphocytes.** The body cells outside the circulatory system are continually bathed and nourished by this fluid.

Since lymph is constantly being leaked into the surrounding tissues, there must be a means of returning it to the main circulatory system. The **lymphatic system** is a separate network of circulatory vessels that includes capillaries and thin-walled veins, but not arteries. Lymph diffuses from the tissues into the lymphatic capillaries, travels through the lymphatic veins, and is then filtered through structures called **lymph nodes** before the lymphatic veins empty it back into the blood.

Like blood, lymph transports certain nutrients. It is particularly important in transport of fats from the small intestine to the bloodstream. But the most important function of the lymphatic system is in defense against disease and repair of damage. We will discuss this function more fully in chapter 8.

TRANSPORT IN VASCULAR PLANTS

The transport system in plants, as in animals, becomes complex only in the major land types. These include the ferns, conifers and their relatives, and flowering plants. Because their transport systems are made up of well-developed conducting vessels, they are called the **vascular plants.**

Vascular plants possess two kinds of specialized conducting tissue, **xylem** and **phloem.** These tissues can be found in all regions of the plant—roots, stems, and leaves. Whether the plant is a huge tree or a fragile herb, the structures and processes involved in transport of materials are basically the same.

Water absorption

Water and essential minerals enter the plant's transport system from the soil. All of the ways by which they do so are not fully understood. However, we know that water passes through the outer cell layers of the root by diffusion and osmosis, traveling either through the cells themselves or through the spaces between. This process is known as **passive absorption.**

When we examine the tip of a young root under magnification, we see that it is covered with **root hairs.** These root hairs are specialized projections from the layer of epidermal cells on the outside of the root. The surface area of the root is increased 5 to 20 times by the additional surface area of the root hairs. The normal water concentration gradient is from the outside to the inside of the root hair. Thus, water diffuses to the interior, as also do dissolved minerals. Root hairs usually function for only a few days, but they are constantly being replaced by new ones nearer the growing tip. Next, the water moves from the root cells and spaces into the xylem, the specialized water-conducting tissue. To do this, it must pass through a sheath of surrounding cells, called the **endoderm.** The endoderm is so constructed that water can pass only through the cells themselves, not through the cell walls or spaces between. This permits some control of what substances pass through. Excess minerals, for example, can be kept out.

When the water reaches the xylem cells, it is virtually pulled upward by the events taking place in the leaves. Water in the leaves evaporates in a process called **transpiration,** which we will discuss in the next chapter. Its place is taken by water moving up the stems, maintaining a continuous column. This creates a water concentration gradient in the root and root hairs.

The transporting cells in the xylem are thick-walled, vertically elongated cells known as **tracheids** or as **vessel cells,** depending on the type of plant. These cells are structurally well suited for transport. They are about 4 mm. long, with openings in their walls that permit water to move in and out. Mature tracheids and vessel cells are nonliv-

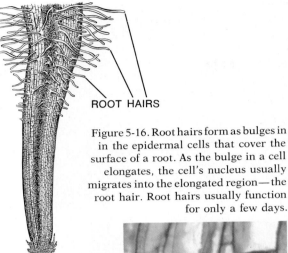

ROOT HAIRS

Figure 5-16. Root hairs form as bulges in in the epidermal cells that cover the surface of a root. As the bulge in a cell elongates, the cell's nucleus usually migrates into the elongated region—the root hair. Root hairs usually function for only a few days.

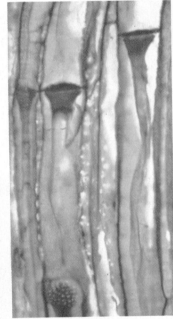

Figure 5-17. Sieve tubes can be seen in this longitudinal section of phloem tissue.

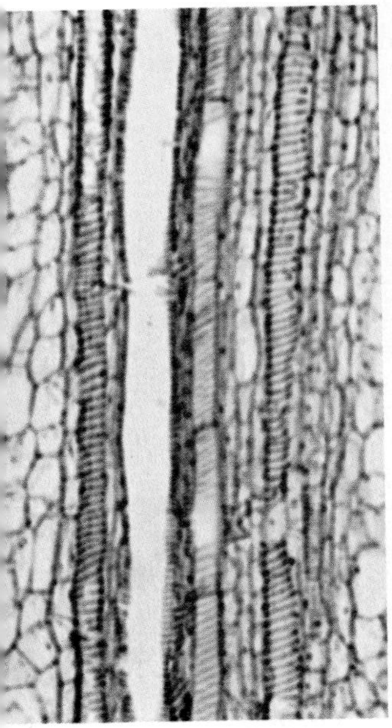

Figure 5-18. A longitudinal section of xylem tissue.

ing, having lost their nucleus and cytoplasm after the cell wall was formed. But they are efficient conducting tubes, through which water and dissolved mineral salts flow upward from the roots.

Phloem is the other conducting tissue. In trees and shrubs, it is just under the bark. Transport through this tissue takes place in the **sieve tubes,** formed by long, living **sieve cells,** or **sieve tube elements,** which are connected end to end. The cells are separated at the ends by **sieve plates,** which are perforated cell walls. The cell membranes covering these openings can allow food to pass, or can block it. At one time it was thought that xylem conducted materials upward through the plant, while phloem conducted materials downward, in a one-way system. It is now known that the phloem conducts nutrients in both directions, although mostly downward.

In addition to conducting water and nutrients, both xylem and phloem provide structural support for plant stems. Phloem contains hard fibers called **sclerenchyma fibers,** and the xylem cells have tough, woody walls.

Structure of woody stems

If we examine a cross-section of a young woody stem, we see that the xylem and phloem form a cylinder around a central **pith.** The elongated cells standing vertically next to one another look much like a bundle of soda straws standing upright in a glass.

When we examine a cross-section from the trunk of an older tree, we see a series of concentric rings. The phloem is a dark, fine-grained layer just beneath the bark. Next as we progress inward, is a single-celled layer, the **vascular cambium,** which produces new xylem and phloem cells.

Next to appear are concentric circles of nonliving xylem, which form the **annual growth rings.** Formation of these rings by the cambium increases the thickness of the stem. Each growth ring is made up of two layers. The inner layer is **spring wood.** It

TRANSPORT IN PLANTS
AND ANIMALS

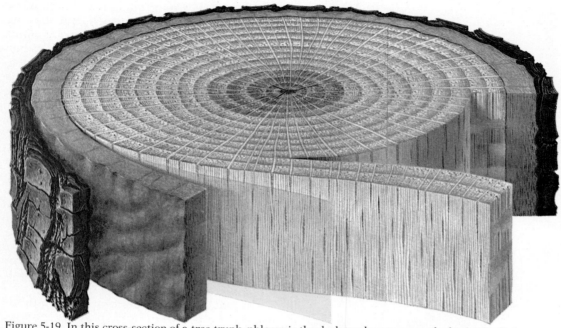

Figure 5-19. In this cross-section of a tree trunk, phloem is the dark tan layer next to the bark. The light tan part is xylem tissue. The tracheid cells that make up the xylem are no longer alive. Their cell walls remain, preserving a tube-like structure through which dissolved materials can move. The yellow-green layer between xylem and phloem is the cambium. It contains living cells that produce the new xylem and phloem cells, thus increasing the girth of the tree.

consists of tracheids or vessel cells containing large, open cavities that can be seen under the microscope. The outer layer is **summer wood,** made up of denser tracheids or vessel cells that give it a darker color. The differences between spring wood and summer wood are caused by variation in cell size, the cells being larger in the moist spring than in the drier summer. The amount of annual rainfall can affect the width of the growth rings. Measurement of the width of these rings can provide an index to past periods of drought or heavy rainfall.

At the core of the trunk is the pith. Food and water are transported across the trunk through the **vascular rays,** bands of cells that extend horizontally from the pith, through the xylem and phloem, and to the outer **cortex.** Both the pith and the cortex serve as storage areas.

The outermost layer is the bark, which includes the stem from the phloem outward. The bark contains the **cork layer,** which prevents water loss and acts as an insulator against extremes of temperature.

Translocation

The movement of materials within a plant is called **translocation.** Translocation can be demonstrated by girdling a tree—that is, removing the phloem layer in a circular section completely around the trunk. The result is twofold. First, the stem above the girdle grows, but the portion below does not. Second, the tree gradually dies from the roots upward. This is because water can still be transported upward through the uncut xylem. But food can no longer move to the roots, since the phloem layer has been removed. Without their food supply, the roots eventually die. This can happen when fun-

106

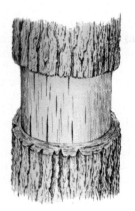

Figure 5-20. Water continues to be transported to the cells above the girdled area, since the xylem is uncut. But since the phloem layer has been removed, food can no longer move to the roots, which will eventually die.

gus infections get under the bark and destroy the phloem. At one time it was believed that the living plant cells pumped materials in the phloem, but this has now been disproved. The final explanation of how movement takes place is still being investigated.

The cohesion theory
The most widely accepted explanation for the upward movement of water in a plant is called the **cohesion theory.** As water evapo-

rates from leaves, the outer leaf cells make up the deficit by absorbing water from the cells nearer the xylem of the veins. Water begins to move from inner to outer cells by osmosis, and is replaced by more water that is "pulled" into the inner cells from the veins. The "pulling" force set up in this way is called **osmotic tension.**

In chapter 2 we saw that water molecules exert a very strong cohesive force on each other. Apparently, osmotic tension on the cohesive water molecules in the xylem is capable of pulling adjacent molecules all the way up the column from the roots, across the living cells of the cortex into the root xylem, and into the roots from the soil by passive absorption. It is probable that this **tension–cohesion pull** is more important to water distribution than the action of osmosis alone. In the spring, however, water movement may be begun by the "push" of water entering the roots from the soil, which is often very moist at this season.

SUMMARY

All organisms need a transport system to enable the cells to receive raw materials and get rid of wastes. In multicellular organisms, this involves movement of a liquid medium, which may be water or blood.

The simplest form of transport is transport into and out of the cell. This transport is based on diffusion, a net movement of molecules in one direction. Two substances can diffuse in opposite directions at the same time. Thus CO_2 can diffuse out of a cell as oxygen diffuses into it. Diffusion of a solvent across a semi-permeable membrane, such as a cell membrane, is called osmosis.

Simple aquatic animals with only two layers of cells, such as sponges, jellyfish, and *Hydra*, transport substances by bringing the water into contact with practically all the cells. Diffusion into and out of the cell layers can take place very quickly.

More complex animals transport only

selected materials to the cells of the internal environment. The sheep liver fluke possesses a gastrovascular system which branches into a network that allows food to reach every individual cell. This system is not efficient for oxygen transport, but the parasitic fluke needs little oxygen.

Larger and more active animals have circulatory systems in which transport is performed by the blood. In an open circulatory system, such as that of arthropods and most mollusks, the blood moves through a body cavity and bathes the tissues directly. In most insects the blood does not perform oxygen transport. The grasshopper has a typical open circulatory system. Its only true blood vessel is the aorta, with heart-like enlargements in each abdominal segment.

In a closed circulatory system blood flows through a well-defined network of vessels. The earthworm's circulatory system is based on two main blood vessels connected by five pairs of aortic arches. These vessels branch out through the entire body, finally forming a network of capillaries. Substances diffuse into and out of the capillaries from the body cells.

Lower vertebrates possess more highly developed hearts with two or three chambers. Birds, mammals, and some reptiles have four-chambered hearts, which are strong pumps in which oxygenated and deoxygenated blood cannot mix. Their circulatory systems transport food, wastes, and oxygen, and also function in heat regulation and defense against disease.

Human blood is composed of plasma and formed elements. The formed elements include erythrocytes, leucocytes, and platelets. Hemoglobin in the erythrocytes gives the blood its red color. The plasma contains plasma proteins, inorganic ions, and a number of nutrients. It also transports carbon dioxide and nitrogenous wastes.

The heart is made up of involuntary cardiac muscle. The rate of heartbeat is controlled by the S-A and A-V nodes. The heart is a double pump, divided into two atria and two ventricles. The right side receives deoxygenated blood from the body and sends it through the lungs; the left side receives oxygenated blood from the lungs and sends it out through the rest of the body. Contraction of the ventricle is called systole. It is followed by a period of relaxation called diastole.

Two major contributory factors in heart disease are hypertension and atherosclerosis. The commonest type of heart attack is myocardial infarction, death of a portion of cardiac muscle.

Lymph is plasma that contains neither blood cells nor platelets, but does contain white cells called lymphocytes. The plasma leaks out through the capillaries into the tissues, where it is picked up by the lymphatic system before being returned to the blood. The lymphatic system transports some nutrients and functions in defense against disease and repair of damage.

Vascular plants possess two types of conducting tissue. Xylem transports water upward, and phloem transports nutrients in both directions. Water enters the roots by the processes of active or passive absorption, and is pulled upward by osmotic tension on its cohesive molecules. The movement of materials within a plant is called translocation.

Review questions

1. Explain why transport is necessary to all types of organism.

2. Explain how oxygen and carbon dioxide are exchanged across a cell membrane. What is this process called?

3. Describe the transport mechanism of *Hydra*. Why can it use such a simple system? Name two other animals which use similar systems.

4. How does the sheep liver fluke transport substances? Why is this system impractical for larger animals?

5. What is the primary function of blood in an open circulatory system?

PATTERNS OF MAINTENANCE AND REGULATION

6. Describe the circulatory system of the grasshopper.

7. List the functions of the blood in a closed circulatory system.

8. Trace the passage of the blood through the circulatory system of the earthworm.

9. What animals possess two- or three-chambered hearts? Describe the circulatory pathways in such animals.

10. In most animals the transport system has additional functions beyond carrying nutrients and oxygen. List some of these.

11. Name the two general components of human blood. About what percentage of each is present in normal blood?

12. Where are erythrocytes produced? How do they differ from other cells?

13. Why is hemoglobin necessary?

14. Name and describe two other formed elements.

15. List six components of blood plasma, and describe the function of each.

16. Polycythemia is a condition in which the blood contains far too many erythrocytes. What symptoms might we expect this condition to cause?

17. Describe the structure of the human heart.

18. Beginning with its entry into the right atrium, trace the path of a drop of blood through the human circulatory system.

19. Name the two principal circulatory patterns in mammals. Name at least two local circuits.

20. List two conditions that frequently contribute to the occurrence of a heart attack. Name at least two behavior patterns that do the same.

21. Extreme hypertension has very damaging effects on the capillaries. In what important body organs might we expect the worst damage to occur? Why?

22. What are the functions of lymph?

23. Name the two specialized conducting tissues in vascular plants, and describe the functions of each.

24. Describe the structure of a typical tree trunk, as seen in cross-section.

25. What is translocation?

26. Describe the cohesion theory.

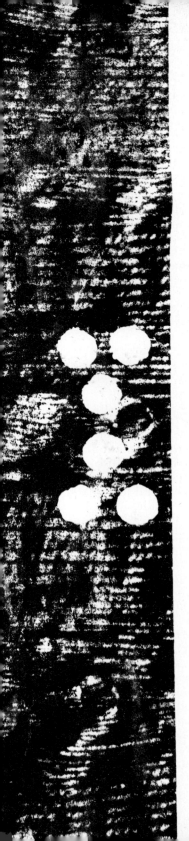

Gas Exchange Systems

In the last chapter we discussed some of the means by which food and oxygen are transported in various organisms. We have seen that a fluid carrier is needed to conduct oxygen to all the cells of the body. This carrier may be air, water, or blood, depending on the organism. In multicellular organisms, gas exchange also depends on a fluid carrier. In this chapter we will discuss the basic structures that enable organisms to obtain oxygen and release carbon dioxide.

Cellular respiration releases energy by the breakdown of certain organic molecules. Energy is released when the chemical bonds of glucose are broken. This energy is usually converted to bond energy in the ATP molecule. In aerobic respiration, oxygen is needed for the release of this energy. Plants use energy in synthesizing fats, proteins, and some other compounds; in cell division and other aspects of growth; and in a variety of other activities. Animals use it in similar activities, and also in muscle contraction and nerve impulses. And both plants and animals form carbon dioxide as a product of cellular respiration. This is gotten rid of as oxygen is taken in.

Organisms such as the sponge and the hydra exchange gases with little difficulty. Every cell of these organisms is either in direct contact with the water in which oxygen is dissolved, or is only one cell removed from it. Oxygen enters and carbon dioxide leaves by diffusion. As we saw earlier, diffusion is a net movement of molecules from one place to another. A substance diffuses from an area where it is in higher concentration to an area where it is in lower concentration. And two different substances may diffuse in opposite directions at the same time.

GAS EXCHANGE IN ANIMALS

Animals use a wide variety of structures in gas exchange. Single-celled organisms exchange gases with the water that surrounds them by diffusion across the cell membrane. In some multicellular animals, such as the earthworm, the entire body surface takes part in gas exchange. Many of the larger aquatic animals, such as fish, have special gas exchange structures called **gills.** A few water organisms have an internal exchange area. Air-breathing animals may have **lungs,** as in the case of mammals, reptiles, birds, and amphibians. Or, like the insects and other land arthropods, they may have what are called **tracheal systems.**

We will examine the major gas exchange mechanisms in detail. Two ideas should be kept in mind as we discuss them. First, no matter what the respiratory structure is, a thin, moist membrane stands between the oxygen-containing medium and the fluid carrier. Second, the moist surface of this membrane must be extensive enough to absorb sufficient oxygen for the needs of the organism.

Gas exchange in structurally simple organisms
For single-celled organisms, gas exchange by diffusion across the cell membranes is a simple process. Once within the cell, the gases are distributed with the aid of a supplementary form of transport. When such unicellular forms are observed under the microscope, their cytoplasm rarely appears motionless. Often it is moving quite rapidly, in a definite pattern of flow. This flow can easily be seen in an active amoeba. In some plant cells, the flow follows more than one current. This movement is known as **cytoplasmic streaming.** It can distribute substances through the cell much more rapidly than diffusion alone.

There is a relation between the surface area of the gas-absorbing membrane and the needs of the animal. The larger and thicker the organism, the smaller the proportion of its cells that are on the surface and thus in direct contact with the air or water outside. If no special gas-exchange surface existed, the organism would not be able to obtain enough oxygen. The sea cucumber is an example of an animal that uses an **invaginated,** or inward-protruding, internal area for gas exchange. The sea cucumber possesses a system of long branched tubes called a **respiratory tree.** These tubes extend through the animal from the open chamber at the end of its digestive tract. Water is drawn into the respiratory tree, and gas exchange takes place over the large membrane area formed by the system of tubes.

The type of structure that carries the respiratory gases into and out of an organism is an adaptation to the environment in which the organism lives. For example, the sea worm *Nereis* swims with paddle-like parapods which extend from the sides of each of its segments. These parapods also function as gills. They contain a capillary system which provides a rich blood supply close to their surfaces. An exchange of gases takes place between these small blood vessels and the surrounding water.

Gas exchange in structurally complex animals
In *Nereis* and more complex animals the gas-exchange system functions in union with a circulatory system. The circulatory system transports oxygen rapidly from the exchange site to the cells. This is important, because if cellular respiration is to release sufficient energy, the exchange of gases between the environment and the cell must occur quickly. In the air to which land organisms are exposed, lungs or similar structures deep inside the body are used in gas exchange. Smaller land animals may have respiratory structures that are similar to those of marine creatures. But we must remember that a moist membrane is essential.

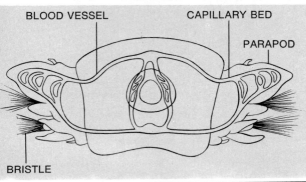

BLOOD VESSEL   CAPILLARY BED

PARAPOD

BRISTLE

Figure 6-1. *Nereis* is an aquatic relative of the earthworm. It swims through the water with paddle-like parapods, which extend from the sides of each segment. The diagram shows a cross-section of a segment, and the structures that allow the parapod to function as a gill for gas exchange.

Figure 6-2. The grasshopper has a many-branched tracheal system, permitting even the tissues deep within its body to come into direct contact with the atmosphere.

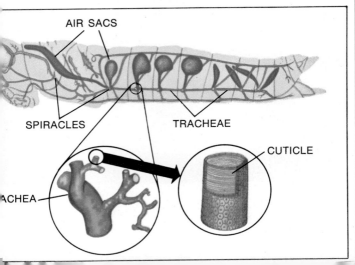

AIR SACS

SPIRACLES   TRACHEAE

CUTICLE

ACHEA

Oxygen can diffuse through a membrane efficiently only if that membrane is moist. This is true in land animals as well as in water dwellers.

The common earthworm is a good example of a "skin breather." The earthworm's skin is thin, and it must be kept moist if gases are to be exchanged through it. Beneath the outer surface of the skin lies an extensive network of capillaries. Oxygen from the air diffuses through the skin and into the capillaries. The oxygen is then carried by the blood to all the cells of the body. Carbon dioxide is picked up from the cells by the blood. It is carried to the surface capillaries, and diffuses out through the skin. Glands in the epidermis, or outer skin layer, of the earthworm secrete mucus that helps prevent the skin from drying. It is further dampened by moisture in the soil where the worm lives. In dry weather, as soil near the surface dries out, earthworms burrow deep into the ground, thus staying moist. When it rains, on the other hand, the earthworm's burrows fill with water, and they must come to the surface to escape drowning. This is why we find them all over sidewalks and paths after a rainstorm.

In insects, such as the grasshopper, air reaches every portion of the body through a system of hollow tubes called **tracheae.** The tracheae contain stiff rings of chitin that prevent them from collapsing. They open to the outside through valves called **spiracles,** which can be seen along the sides of the insect. The spiracles may be opened and closed by means of a special muscle. In some ways they resemble the nasal passages of higher animals, since they are lined with hair-like projections that filter out dust and other foreign particles. Researchers in the field of pest control have found that some of the most effective insecticides are those that clog the spiracles and prevent oxygen intake.

Within the insect's body the tracheae widen into air sacs. These sacs can be compressed like bellows by muscular contractions, forcing air through the narrow, branching tubes beyond. These small tubes are about one micron (0.00004 inch) in diameter. The oxygen diffuses through their walls into the cells. No part of the body is more than a few cells away from one of these air-supply tubes.

The tracheal respiratory mechanism is quite efficient for such small animals as insects. However, it would not serve for a large animal. The tracheae would have to be so long that air could not get through them fast enough. Fortunately for us, this limits the size an insect can achieve. The human race is engaged in a constant battle against insects that carry disease, contaminate food, and destroy property. It is just as well that we do not have to contend with two-foot mosquitoes, cockroaches, or termites!

Lobsters and crabs, like insects, are arthropods, and resemble their land-dwelling relatives in basic structure. However, they have an entirely different system of gas exchange. The lobster, for example, possesses gills, rather than the tracheae and spiracles of the grasshopper.

The gills of the lobster work in union with an open circulatory system. They are delicate, feathery extensions of the body wall. The respiratory cavity contains twenty pairs of gills, covered by a large, protective chitinous shell. The under-surface of this shell is not attached to the lobster's body. Water can thus enter the bottom of the respiratory cavity and circulate up around the gills. The gills themselves are attached to the tops of the legs and the nearby body wall. As the lobster moves its legs, water is stirred up in the respiratory cavity around the gills. The water then moves forward through the cavity, passing out the front of the shell. Small appendages near the mouth paddle the water, keeping it in motion. This flow keeps the gills surrounded by fresh, oxygen-rich water. The same type of respiratory system can be seen in the crayfish, the lobster's fresh-water cousin.

As we mentioned earlier, the lobster possesses an open circulatory system. Before blood returns to the heart it collects in a

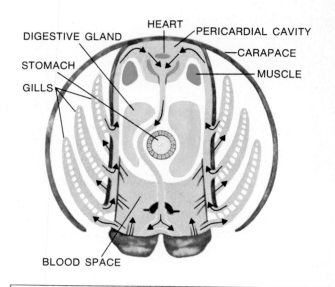

Figure 6-3. This cross section of a lobster shows the relationship of the feather-like gills to the carapace and internal blood supply.

Figure 6-4. The fragile gills of this carp are completely hidden by the protective operculum.

THE STRUCTURE OF GILLS

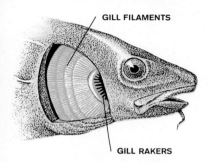

GILL FILAMENTS

GILL RAKERS

Figure 6-5. In this diagram the operculum has been removed to show the gill filaments arranged in over lapping rows. Note the gill rakers, which extend into the cavity behind the fish's mouth.

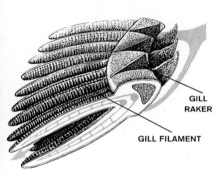

GILL RAKER

GILL FILAMENT

One row of gill filaments is shown here. Water flows in the direction indicated by the arrows—over and between the filaments. The rakers strain out most food particles, which may be swallowed.

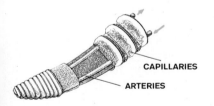

CAPILLARIES

ARTERIES

This diagram shows the flow of blood through a gill filament. Oxygen and carbon dioxide are exchanged in the capillaries. The arteries transport the blood to and from the filament.

special cavity, or **sinus,** and then passes through the gills. When the blood collects in the sinus, it has just come from the body tissues, so it is rich in carbon dioxide. After it loses the carbon dioxide and picks up oxygen in the gills, it is pumped back into the tissues through the heart.

Fish also respire through gills. But the gills of fish are associated with a closed circulatory system. Water enters through the mouth, passes over the gills, and leaves through the openings in the sides of the head. The fragile gills themselves are hidden by a protective gill cover called the **operculum.** Beneath the operculum, the gills are red. This is due to the rich supply of capillaries that bring blood to the surface of the gills. The blood is often separated from the water only by the single cell of the capillary wall and one cell of the gill surface.

Breathing in the fish consists of two steps. During inhalation the gill covers bulge, and the mouth opens, admitting water. The water rushes into the space formed by the bulging. As the fish exhales, the mouth closes and the gill covers flatten, forcing the water out behind them.

There is a set of gills on each side of the head. Each is composed of three parts: (1) a bony arch, (2) a set of tooth-like rakers, and (3) a feathery membrane surface of gill filaments. The gill rakers extend into the cavity behind the fish's mouth. They strain most food particles out of the water before it reaches the filaments. These bits of food may then be swallowed by the fish. The gill filaments are made up of thousands of tiny folds of membrane called **lamellae.** The lamellae greatly increase the surface available for gas exchange. Thus, although only a small part of the fish's body surface is devoted to respiration, the gills provide a high surface-to-volume ratio of gas-exchange area. As water moves across the gills, the oxygen it carries diffuses into the underlying capillaries, and carbon dioxide in the blood diffuses out.

As the water flows in one direction over the surface of the lamellae, the blood in the capillaries flows in the opposite direction.

WALKING CATFISH

It is a rainy night, and you are driving down the Florida highway. Suddenly, you see some small animals crossing the road. Slamming on the brakes, you stare in bewilderment at the creatures hip-hopping across the highway. If you didn't know better, you'd swear they were some kind of catfish! In point of fact, you would be perfectly correct. Today, tens of thousands of walking catfish can be found throughout southern Florida. Where do these improbable creatures come from? Originally a native of southeast Asia, the walking catfish was imported to America by some dealers in tropical fish. One day, one of these dealers discovered that his walking catfish had in fact gone for a walk—after devouring the other exotic fish in his aquarium. The escaped fish reproduced to the point of posing a serious ecological threat to the southeastern United States.

The walking catfish is about a foot long and weighs about one pound. The long body ends in a large head with eight long barbels, or "whiskers," that serve as sense organs in the fish's constant search for food. Because most of the original specimens were albinos, many of the walking catfish found in Florida are pale pink in color. A growing number of the new generation, however, show the normal gray, brown, or black pigmentation of their Asian ancestors.

The walking catfish walks very much like a person crawling along on his elbows. Each of its pectoral (breast or forward) fins has a long, stiff spine, which the fish digs into the ground as it inches its way forward. The fish then arches its back and pulls its thrashing tail forward, moving as much as five feet in a minute on wet ground. Walking catfish may migrate more than a quarter of a mile betweeen lakes or rivers, sometimes traveling together in large groups—much to the surprise of passing humans. Because it needs moisture, the fish generally does its walking at night, preferably in the rain. When necessary, the resourceful fish can

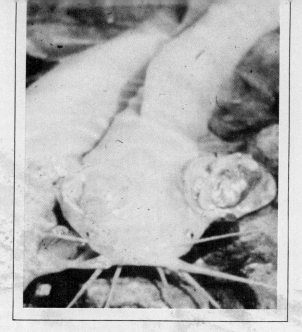

wait out a drought for weeks by burrowing into damp mud until the weather takes a turn for the better.

It is strange to think of a fish that can breathe air, but the walking catfish is adapted to life both on land and in the water. The rear part of each of its gills is modified, forming a lung-like structure with which the fish breathes when it is out of the water. Even in the water, a walking catfish will often surface for a breath of air, especially when it is in a pond with little oxygen. In an emergency, this improbable fish can survive out of the water for up to 24 hours.

Despite its interest as a biological curiosity, the walking catfish is not a welcomed guest in Florida. To the contrary, ecologists view the creature as a serious threat to the ecological balance. A native of Asia, the fish has no natural enemies in the lakes and rivers of the southern United States. It is an aggressive animal with a voracious appetite. Even the deadly piranha retreats from it. Few other fish survive where the catfish arrive in large numbers. Although they are prized among Asians as a food fish, the walking catfish have displaced entire populations of bass and other native food species in America.

The takeover of Florida's waters by the walking catfish gives every indication of continuing in the years to come. Large numbers of native fish die every year during the drought period, when water levels drop significantly and some ponds dry up. But a dried-up pond poses no serious threat to a walking catfish. It simply walks away from the dried-up bed and heads for the nearest lake.

There is a serious possibility that this combative invader will someday spread beyond central Florida. Some biologists predict that it will soon reach Georgia, Alabama, and Tennessee, although cold weather will probably prevent it from moving any further north. So far, efforts to control the population explosion of the rapidly-reproducing walking catfish by poisoning its ponds have succeeded only in killing off other species. After all, how do you kill a fish that simply gets up and walks away? Recruit a vigilante squad of cats?

This **countercurrent flow** permits a much greater oxygen absorption than would be possible if both blood and water flowed in the same direction.

We should note here that although a fish has nostrils, these have nothing to do with respiration. In most fish the nostrils are not even connected with the mouth cavity. They serve only for smelling.

Most amphibians (animals that live both on land and in water) utilize three different respiratory mechanisms. Gills are used mostly at the tadpole stage. Skin and lungs serve for breathing in the adult. We can observe this clearly in the frog, a typical amphibian.

The fertilized frog's egg develops into a small, legless tadpole. The tadpole is a true aquatic organism. It has three pairs of feathery external gills, which extend from the sides of its head. The walls of these gills are so thin that when they are observed through a microscope the capillaries can easily be seen, with the blood cells flowing through them. Exchange of gases takes place through the thin capillary walls.

As the tadpole grows, an operculum develops over the external gills. The gills, now enclosed, become similar to those of a fish. Later, the tadpole develops lungs, from a sac that forms at the back of the throat. As the lungs reach their full development, the gills cease to function and disappear, and two forelegs develop in their place. The animal—no longer a tadpole but a frog— must now come to the surface of the water to breathe air. At the same time, the moist, thin skin also takes over most of the job of gas exchange. The frog becomes essentially a land animal.

Unlike mammals and birds, frogs and other amphibians use **positive-pressure breathing.** This is sometimes called the "gulp-and-swallow" method. Lowering the floor of its closed mouth to create a larger cavity, the frog sucks air through its nostrils. Some gas exchange takes place in the mouth, which has a thin, moist lining well supplied with capillaries. If additional oxy-

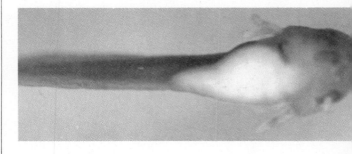

Figure 6-6. Finger-like gills extend from the head of this tadpole. Blood circulating through the gills is clearly visible to the observer.

gen is needed, some of the air from the mouth is forced into the lungs. This is done by closing the nostrils and raising the floor of the mouth. The frog exhales by opening the nostrils and raising the floor of the mouth.

We tend to think of lungs as being characteristic only of reptiles, amphibians, birds, and mammals. However, some species of fish possess air bladders that function as very simple lungs. One such species lives in the Amazon River basin in South America. In late summer the level of the water falls, and the fish may be trapped in a drying puddle. If this happens, the fish encloses itself in a mud cocoon, fills its "lung" with air, and goes into a kind of hibernation. It can survive in this way until the rains come and the river rises once more.

Most modern fish possess a **swim bladder.** This organ enables the fish to remain at any level instead of sinking to the bottom. The swim bladder contains gases. The fish is able to change the volume of gas in the bladder, thus adjusting to changes in water pressure. Many biologists think there may be an evolutionary connection between the swim bladder and the primitive lung, although the bladder now performs an entirely different function.

118

THE HUMAN RESPIRATORY SYSTEM

Birds and mammals, which are warm-blooded, have more complex gas-exchange systems. They use an immense amount of energy in sustaining their stable—and fairly high—body temperature. Accordingly, their oxygen demand is much higher than that of the lower animals. The lungs of birds and mammals have very complex branching channels, providing a far greater proportion of surface area for gas exchange. We can regard the human respiratory system as typical of mammals.

The most ancient written records associated breathing with life. More recently, in the seventeenth century, Robert Boyle demonstrated that animals must have air to live. But its important component, oxygen, was not isolated until the eighteenth century, by Joseph Priestley. Even then, further experimentation was necessary before the importance of oxygen was proved.

It is easy to trace the path of respiratory gases in humans. When a person inhales, air enters through the **nostrils** (or sometimes the mouth). It passes through numerous nasal cavities, where it is warmed and moistened. Many of the cells that line the nasal

Figure 6-7. The human respiratory system. Oxygen enters and carbon dioxide leaves the body through the nasal cavity. After air containing oxygen enters the cavity, it passes through the pharynx, larynx, trachea, and into the bronchus. The bronchus branches into smaller bronchioles which end as alveoli. The sections of an alveolus (right) show that gases must diffuse through two cell layers—the wall of the alveolus and the wall of the capillary.

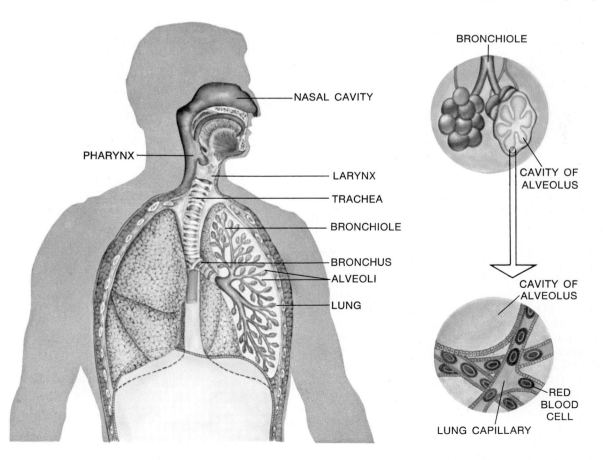

cavities possess cilia, which filter dust particles out of the air. At the same time, receptor cells for the sense of smell respond to any odors present.

Next, the air passes through the **pharynx** and into the **trachea** or windpipe. The walls of the trachea are encircled by bands of cartilage which make it rigid and keep it from collapsing. The topmost part of the trachea

At its lower end the trachea divides into two tubes called the **bronchi.** These, in turn, lead into the two lungs, spongy organs with a rich supply of blood vessels. Each bronchus branches repeatedly into smaller and smaller tubes known as **bronchioles.** This branching is so plant-like in appearance that the system of tubes is often called the "bronchial tree." At the end of each smallest

---

THE DEADLY SNIFF

For some time, scientists have been suggesting that fluorocarbons—the gases used as propellants in aerosol cans—may be eroding the earth's protective ozone layer. But it now appears that aerosol deodorants, paints, and other such substances present an even more immediate danger. It has been established that at least 125 Americans die each year as a result of inhaling fumes from spray cans. Most of the victims are youths who deliberately inhale the chemicals to get "high."

The chief cause of the deaths is the fluorocarbon gases, such as Freon or fluorotrichloromethane. Inhaling large quantities of some of these gases can cause pulmonary edema. The lungs fill up with fluid, preventing the victim from breathing. Furthermore, Freon is the gas used for cooling purposes in refrigerators and freezers. Under certain condi-

tions, its cooling effect works just as well on human respiratory tissues. The lungs and bronchial passages are, in effect, quick-frozen, and the victim dies almost instantly, his heart overwhelmed by the shock.

In view of the growing concern about fluorocarbons, some manufacturers of spray products have begun introducing pump-type cans as alternatives to aerosols.

In addition to the fluorocarbons, certain other ingredients of some spray deodorants may be dangerous. Zirconium, for example, is a metallic element that has been added to some deodorants to keep the skin dry. But a group of scientists found that tiny particles of zirconium could enter the lungs and induce tumor-like growths. These growths can damage the lungs permanently. Furthermore, it has not been shown that zirconium really improves the keep-dry quality of a deodorant.

The Food and Drug Administration is investigating some of the zirconium antiperspirants. Manufacturers in general feel that the danger has not been really proved.

---

is known as the **larynx.** The larynx contains the vocal cords, which vibrate when air passes between them in speaking or singing.

From the larynx the air goes down the **trachea.** The cells that line the trachea also possess cilia. These sweep foreign particles and mucus up into the throat away from the lungs. (When enough mucus accumulates in the throat, coughing occurs.)

bronchiole is a cluster of small air sacs called **alveoli,** which looks rather like a bunch of grapes. Each individual alveolus is surrounded by a dense network of capillaries. It is here that the exchange of gases takes place.

As oxygen diffuses into the capillaries from the alveoli, it passes through two layers of cells. One layer forms the wall of

PATTERNS OF MAINTENANCE
AND REGULATION

Figure 6-8. A model of the hemoglobin molecule.

the alveolus, and the other layer the wall of the capillary. Diffusion occurs because of the difference in oxygen concentration on either side of the double cell layer. The concentration of oxygen is higher in the alveoli than in the blood. This establishes a concentration gradient, along which oxygen moves from the alveoli into the blood. As the blood travels to the rest of the body, a new concentration gradient is established each time it contacts a new cell. If the cell contains less oxygen than the blood, oxygen diffuses into the cell. Since the cells are continuously using up oxygen in their internal respiration, more oxygen can always enter.

In the meantime, the cells are constantly producing carbon dioxide as a by-product of cellular respiration. For carbon dioxide, the concentration gradient runs the other way.

Since blood carried from the lungs contains very little carbon dioxide, the carbon dioxide from the cells diffuses into the blood while oxygen diffuses from the blood into the cells. When the blood saturated with carbon dioxide returns to the alveoli, the carbon dioxide passes out into the air, where the concentration is still lower. This process of diffusion is the basis of gas exchange in all cells and in all oxygen-breathing organisms.

The plasma of the blood is not, by itself, a very efficient carrier of oxygen. In humans and other vertebrates, oxygen is transported in the blood by combining with a pigment called **hemoglobin** in the red blood cells. Hemoglobin gives these cells their characteristic color. It is represented by the symbol **Hb.** When a molecule of hemoglobin combines with a molecule of oxygen, **oxyhemoglobin** is formed:

$$Hb + O_2 \rightarrow HbO_2$$

The greater the concentration of oxygen, the more oxyhemoglobin can be formed. Therefore, much oxyhemoglobin is formed in the lung capillaries, where oxygen is present in great quantity. When the oxygen concentration is low, the oxyhemoglobin releases oxygen:

$$HbO_2 \rightarrow Hb + O_2$$

This release occurs in capillaries near cells that lack oxygen.

Carbon dioxide also requires a transporter in the blood. It diffuses into the blood and combines with water, producing carbonic acid:

$$CO_2 + H_2O \rightarrow H_2CO_3$$

Almost immediately, the carbonic acid dissociates to form hydrogen ions (H^+) and bicarbonate ions (HCO_3^-). Most of the carbon dioxide is transported as bicarbonate ions. A small percentage combines with hemoglobin to form **carboxyhemoglobin:**

$$CO_2 + Hb \rightarrow HbCO_2$$

Another small part is carried as dissolved

CO_2 in the blood plasma. When carbon dioxide diffuses out of the blood plasma in the lungs, the balance between dissolved carbon dioxide and the bicarbonate form is upset, and the reaction is reversed. Carbonic acid forms again, finally breaking down to water and carbon dioxide. This carbon dioxide, too, then diffuses out of the blood.

Breathing

Birds and mammals utilize **negative-pressure breathing.** This involves muscular contractions of two different regions. The human lungs are located in the chest cavity, one on either side of the heart. The right lung has three lobes, the left lung only two. The lungs are protected by the **rib cage.** Below them lies the **diaphragm,** a thin, flat, muscular partition which separates the chest cavity from the abdominal cavity.

Inspiration, or breathing in, is an active process, requiring muscle contraction. Muscles between the ribs move them upward and forward, the diaphragm lowers, the stomach bulges, and the chest expands. The volume of the chest cavity is thus increased. Since this increase reduces the air pressure in the chest to a level below the outside air pressure, air rushes into the lungs, expanding them.

Expiration, or breathing out, on the other hand, is passive. The chest muscles relax, the ribs move down and in, the diaphragm arches upward into its rest position, and the stomach recedes. These movements decrease the volume of the chest cavity. Air pressure in the lungs rises above that of the outside air, and the air in the lungs is forced out.

Normally, the lungs are not completely filled. Nor are they ever completely deflated. Usually only about one-eighth as much air as they can hold is inhaled at each breath. Even in the deep breathing of trained singers and athletes, the air inhaled mixes in the respiratory tract with some of the air left over from previous breaths. This is not a drawback at all. It reduces the oxygen con-

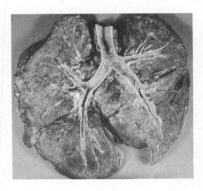

Figure 6-9. The structure of the "bronchial tree" can be clearly seen in this picture of a pair of healthy human lungs.

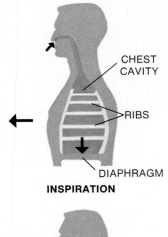

CHEST CAVITY

RIBS

DIAPHRAGM

INSPIRATION

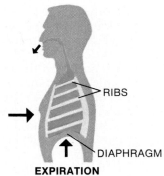

RIBS

DIAPHRAGM

EXPIRATION

Figure 6-10. During inspiration, the rib cage expands and the diaphragm lowers. During expiration, the rib cage compresses the sides of the lungs, while the diaphragm pushes up from below.

PATTERNS OF MAINTENANCE
AND REGULATION

centration of the air reaching the lungs. Air containing too high a concentration of oxygen can actually cause lung irritation.

The lungs and the inner walls of the chest cavity are covered by a smooth, moist membrane called the **pleura.** The pleura has a lubricating effect, which prevents friction between the lungs and the chest wall during breathing. Inflammation or irritation of this lining may cause the very painful symptom called **pleurisy.**

Normal breathing can usually supply more than enough oxygen for proper functioning of the cells. But to take in enough oxygen during intense muscular activity, the lungs must be fully expanded. The rates of respiration and circulation increase, delivering more oxygen to the cells.

If these increased rates are not sufficient to meet the cells' needs, an **oxygen debt** results. That is, the body's demand for energy must be satisfied by a supplementary process in addition to the usual aerobic respiration. To meet this demand, the anaerobic form of respiration called **fermentation** takes place. As you may recall from chapter 3, one kind of fermentation produces lactic acid. Some of the lactic acid is transported to the liver, but most of it accumulates in the muscle cells. This accumulation causes changes that we experience as muscular fatigue. When the fatigue becomes too intense, the individual cannot continue activity and is forced to rest.

After exercise, the energy level of the cells is restored by intake of oxygen. The lactic acid in the muscle is changed back to glycogen. During sports events, it is not unusual to see a player or runner receiving oxygen from a respirator after particularly strenuous or prolonged activity. This helps to repay the oxygen debt more quickly.

It is impossible to hold the breath voluntarily for more than a short period of time. As the level of carbon dioxide in the blood increases while the breath is held, the involuntary control centers in the brain take over and force breathing to resume. But an opposite effect occurs when the carbon dioxide level is deliberately reduced by deep, rapid breathing, or **hyperventilation.** After hyperventilation the breath can be voluntarily held for a longer period of time. Swimmers frequently use this technique to allow them to remain under water longer. However, the process carries a distinct element of danger. As the level of carbon dioxide in the blood drops, so do the heartbeat and the blood pressure. If they fall too low, the result may be a sudden blackout and unconsciousness.

You may have guessed by now that the level of carbon dioxide is actually more important to respiratory regulation than the level of oxygen. Since carbon dioxide increases the acidity of the blood, it must be eliminated to maintain the normal acid–base balance of the blood. If the blood becomes too acid, it cannot take up oxygen as readily as it should. So the reactions of the respiratory centers in the brain are dependent mainly on carbon dioxide levels in the blood.

In addition to the respiratory control center in the brain, small supplementary control centers have been found in the carotid arteries and the aorta. These respond to oxygen rather than carbon dioxide. A shortage of oxygen in the blood causes these centers to send impulses to the respiratory center in the brain. The center reacts by increasing the rate of respiration. It appears that this system is largely reserved for emergency situations rather than routine respiratory functions.

GAS EXCHANGE IN VASCULAR PLANTS

Very simple forms of plant life, like simple animal forms, exchange gases over nearly all of their body surface. But higher plants require a more complicated system, because of their larger size and their tendency to dry out.

In vascular plants, most of the gas exchange is carried on by the green leaves.

Diffusion takes place across the thin, moist cell membranes within the leaves. These membranes provide a very large surface for gas exchange. The leaf itself is generally covered by a relatively impermeable waxy coating called the **cuticle.** But openings in this cuticle called the **stomata** admit air into the interior of the leaf. There the humidity is almost 100 percent, keeping the cell walls and membranes moist and allowing oxygen to diffuse through them into the cells.

The stomata also regulate water loss from the plant. Each stoma is bounded by two **guard cells.** Changes in the shape of these guard cells regulate the opening and closing of the stoma. When much water is present, the guard cells swell because water moving into them forces their walls to expand. The swelling of the guard cells is called **turgor,** literally meaning "swollen with water." As they swell, their central edges pull away from each other, leaving an open space or **stomatal pore.** As the stoma opens, water vapor diffuses through it into the atmosphere. This process is called **transpiration.** Gas exchange in the leaf takes place while the stomata are open, usually during the daytime. When enough water has been lost through transpiration, the guard cells shrink, and the stoma between them closes. This ordinarily occurs in late afternoon of a hot day.

There appears to be a conflict between the conditions required for conserving water and those required for photosynthesis. Since photosynthesis requires both light and carbon dioxide, the stomata must be open for gas exchange during at least part of the day. But while this system seems inefficient because it contributes to water loss, there are two safety factors. First, the humidity inside the leaf stays fairly high even when the stomata are open. This is because water is being constantly drawn up through the stem of the plant and distributed to the leaves. Moreover, if water loss exceeds the level that can be replaced by this method, the leaf cells may begin to wilt, closing the stomata and preventing any more water loss to the plant.

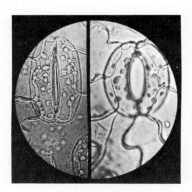

Figure 6-11. Two stomata, one closed (left) and the other open (right). The guard cells of the open stoma are swollen with water, and have pulled away from each other, leaving a stomatal pore.

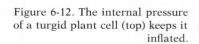

Figure 6-12. The internal pressure of a turgid plant cell (top) keeps it inflated.

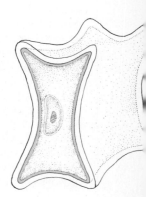

124

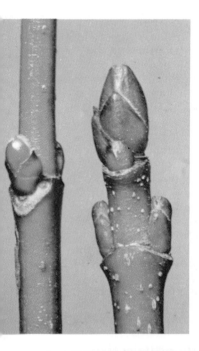

Figure 6-13. These twigs from a red maple tree show a number of white, oval lenticels, through which gases are exchanged.

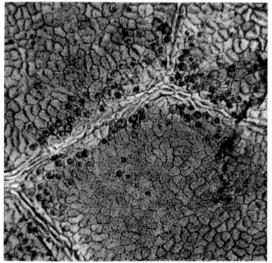

Figure 6-14. A microscopic view of the complex inner structure of a leaf.

Gas exchange in vascular plants is not limited to the leaves. Oxygen also enters through the stems and roots. This allows gas exchange to continue, though at a lower rate, during the winter months when most plants shed their leaves.

The stems and roots of older plants are usually covered by layers of bark, which oxygen cannot penetrate. However, the bark contains groups of loosely joined cells that form pores called **lenticels.** Gas exchange can take place through these pores. Stems without bark have stomata like those on the leaves. Stomata are also present in fruits and in some flower parts.

The roots of higher plants have no stomata. Their root hairs and surface cells are moist enough so that gases can easily diffuse across the cell membranes. However, the soil surrounding the roots must be loosely packed if enough oxygen is to penetrate to the roots. Tightly packed soil containing few air spaces, or soil that has been repeatedly saturated with more water than it can absorb, provides little oxygen. A major purpose behind soil cultivation, such as hoeing and plowing, is to loosen the soil so that oxygen can reach the roots.

SUMMARY

All organisms have gas exchange systems which enable them to obtain oxygen and release carbon dioxide. In simple aquatic animals whose cells are in close contact with their watery environment, gas exchange takes place by diffusion across the cell membrane. This process of diffusion is the basis for gas exchange in cells and in all oxygen-breathing organisms. There are several types of gas exchange system. But no matter what their structure, a moist membrane must stand between the oxygen-containing medium and the fluid carrier, and the membrane surface must be extensive enough to absorb sufficient oxygen for the organism's needs.

In unicellular organisms, gas exchange by diffusion is sufficient. The process may be supplemented by cytoplasmic streaming, which helps to distribute substances more rapidly. In some simple aquatic animals, gas exchange takes place over the surface area of a branched respiratory tree. In others, capillaries close to the body surface allow an exchange of gases with the surrounding water.

In many more complex animals the gas-exchange system is often supplemented by the circulatory system. In the skin-breathing earthworm, oxygen in the air passes through the moist skin and into the capillaries, and is then transported by the blood. In land arthropods such as insects, air reaches every part of the body through a tracheal system, and the circulatory system is not involved. Marine arthropods, such as the lobster, have a system of gills.

The gills of fish are associated with a closed circulatory system, and are covered by a protective operculum. Folded lamellae provide an extensive surface for gas exchange. In amphibians such as the frog, external gills are present during the larval or tadpole stage. These gills are later covered by an operculum like that of a fish. In the adult frog, gas exchange is taken over by lungs and the moist, thin skin. The frog uses positive-pressure breathing.

The human respiratory system is typical of mammals. Inhaled air passes through the nostrils, pharynx, and trachea into the two bronchi. The bronchi subdivide into bronchioles which end in clusters of alveoli, where gas exchange takes place. Oxygen diffuses into the capillaries from the alveoli along a concentration gradient, while carbon dioxide diffuses out.

Blood plasma alone is not a very efficient oxygen carrier. In humans, oxygen is transported in the blood by binding to hemoglobin. Most of the carbon dioxide is transported in the form of bicarbonate ions.

Birds and mammals utilize negative-pressure breathing. Inspiration is an active process which reduces air pressure in the chest and causes air to rush into the lungs. Expiration is a passive process, increasing air pressure in the lungs and forcing the air out.

During intense activity the respiration rate increases. If it still cannot meet the cells' needs, an oxygen debt results, and fermentation supplements the usual aerobic respiration. Fermentation produces an accumulation of lactic acid in the muscle cells, which causes muscle fatigue. The debt is repaid by intake of oxygen after the activity ceases.

Most respiratory regulation is based on the level of carbon dioxide in the blood. Respiration is controlled by a center in the brain. In emergency situations control may be assisted by small centers in the carotid arteries and the aorta, which respond to oxygen rather than carbon dioxide.

In higher plants, most gas exchange takes place by diffusion across the moist cell membranes within green leaves. Air is admitted to the interior through the stomata, whose opening and closing are regulated by guard cells. When a stoma opens, it releases water vapor in a process called transpiration.

Photosynthesis requires both light and carbon dioxide, so the stomata must be open during at least part of the day. Excessive water loss is prevented by two safety factors. First, water is constantly being drawn up into the plant and distributed. Second, if water loss is too great the leaf cells wilt, closing the stomata. Gas exchange also takes place through pores in the stems called lenticels, and through the roots of the plant.

1. Distinguish between cellular respiration and breathing "respiration."

2. List three types of gas exchange system.

3. All gas exchange systems must have two important physical features. What are they?

4. How do unicellular organisms supple-

ment diffusion in performing gas exchanges? What is the value of this?

5. What is a respiratory tree?

6. Explain some of the ways in which an organism's gas exchange system is an adaptation to its environment.

7. In more complex animals, how are the respiratory and circulatory systems related in function?

8. Describe a typical insect tracheal system.

9. Science fiction often uses the theme of invasion by enormous insects. Why is this pure fiction rather than possible fact?

10. How do the respiratory systems of a grasshopper and a lobster resemble each other? How do they differ?

11. Trace the passage of a drop of water through the respiratory system of a typical fish.

12. Describe the three gas exchange mechanisms used by a frog during its life cycle.

13. What is positive-pressure breathing? Name some animals that utilize it.

14. Why do birds and mammals have the greatest demand for oxygen?

15. Trace the path air follows as it is inhaled and exhaled by the human lungs.

16. What two important processes occur in the alveoli? How do they take place?

17. What is the function of hemoglobin?

18. If both carbon monoxide and oxygen are present, hemoglobin will bind to the carbon monoxide. Based on information from this chapter and chapter 5, what symptoms might we expect to see in carbon monoxide poisoning?

19. Describe negative-pressure breathing.

20. What is an oxygen debt? How does the body deal with it?

21. How does oxygen reach the inner membranes of a green leaf?

22. Describe the structure of a stoma.

23. What is transpiration?

24. What safety factors help to prevent water loss during photosynthesis?

25. What are lenticels, and why are they necessary?

Support and Locomotion Systems

If we were to list the functions of the skeletal system, probably the first one on the list would be the function of support. Obviously, a human being without bones would be a rather shapeless jelly-like blob. But two other primary functions of the skeleton become apparent when we consider this human blob. First of all, without a skeleton there would be no protection for vital organs—no hard skull to shield the delicate brain from injury, no bony rib cage to enclose the soft, spongy lungs and vitally important heart, no pelvis to provide a supporting base for the abdominal organs. While the blob might still possess muscles, those muscles would have nothing to pull against. Thus it would be almost incapable of locomotion, though it might manage to flow along in a rippling sort of way.

Keeping in mind these functions of the skeletal system—support, protection, and locomotion—we may find it more useful to identify a skeleton by what it does rather than by what it is. A skeleton is anything that assists in these three important functions. And it is not necessarily made of bone.

TYPES OF SKELETON

At first glance, the skeleton of a common earthworm does not really seem to be a skeleton at all. But the earthworm obviously moves. Its internal organs are protected from the environment, and are supported. Like many other animals, the earthworm has a **hydrostatic skeleton.**

The hydrostatic skeleton is made up of the

129

fluids in the earthworm's body cavity. This fluid resists compression. It can be shifted around in the cavity, but it cannot be squeezed into a space significantly smaller than it normally occupies. It is acted upon by two sets of muscles. These are circular muscles, which encircle the worm's body, and longitudinal muscles, which run lengthwise. The two kinds of muscle are said to be **antagonistic,** because when one kind contracts the other relaxes. The pressure caused by their contraction is transmitted by the body fluid. The entire body of the earthworm is covered by a tough skin or **cuticle,** which adds strength to the contractions.

The earthworm's body is divided into segments, so its hydrostatic skeleton is also segmental. The segments are separated by thin walls called **septa.** Each segment is therefore a closed compartment. It contains its own supply of body fluid and a set of longitudinal and circular muscles. The contraction of the muscles in each segment is independent of the muscles in the other segments.

When the circular muscles contract, they press on the body fluid and force it against the ends of the segmental cavities. The longitudinal muscles relax and are stretched by the pressure of the fluid. This causes the body to become longer and thinner. Tiny bristles called **setae** grip the earth and allow the worm to hold the ground it has gained by extension. The longitudinal muscles then contract, forcing the fluids outward to the sides of the cavities, and the circular muscles relax. The body becomes shorter and thicker, and the posterior end of the worm is drawn forward. The earthworm can pull itself along fairly rapidly by these alternate contractions of longitudinal and circular muscles.

Since the worm is segmented, it is capable of localized movement. That is, one segment can be contracting its longitudinal muscles while another segment is contracting its circular muscles. This system is efficient for digging and burrowing. It ena-

bles the worm to build up a considerable amount of thrust against the soil.

The exoskeleton

The skeleton of marine and land arthropods is easy to recognize, since it is outside their bodies rather than inside. We have already seen an example of such an **exoskeleton** in the lobster, a marine arthropod. In land arthropods the list of examples is endless, covering the entire insect kingdom.

The exoskeleton gives the animal a covering almost like a suit of armor. This hard shell is composed of noncellular chitin, which is secreted by the epidermis. It is made up of substances called amino sugars, and is both strong and flexible. In marine arthropods the exoskeleton is made even tougher by deposits of calcium phosphate and calcium carbonate.

In land arthropods the exoskeleton is much more than a means of protection. It also serves to conserve water, by preventing the soft inner body parts from drying out. Additionally, it gives the body the support needed to move around easily and quickly on land.

The muscles of the arthropod are inside the exoskeleton. The force of their contraction, which in the earthworm was transmitted by the body fluid, is transmitted in the arthropod by the hard outer shell. The exoskeleton is divided by many hinges or joints. At these points the chitin is extremely thin and flexible.

Since the exoskeleton is composed of nonliving material, it does not grow as the animal grows. Instead, it is **molted** or shed periodically, giving the occupant more room. In insects, molting often occurs as the animal passes from one developmental stage to another. We can see a good example of this in the various species of cicada (often popularly called locusts). The newly hatched cicada nymph burrows into the ground. Depending on the species, it remains underground for anywhere from one to nearly seventeen years. The nymph usu-

PATTERNS OF MAINTENANCE
AND REGULATION

Figure 7-1. This cicada has just finished molting, and has left its discarded exoskeleton behind.

ally molts several times as it grows. The last molt takes place after it has finally emerged from its underground shelter. Creeping up the side of a tree, the mature nymph attaches itself tightly to the bark. Its exoskeleton splits down the center of the back, and the adult cicada gradually struggles free of it. The hard, light shell remains attached to the tree. During years when swarms of cicadas are reaching adulthood, the trunks of trees are often covered with thousands of these discarded exoskeletons. The newly emerged adult cicada must remain motionless for a short time, while the soft new exoskeleton hardens on contact with the air.

In marine arthropods, such as the crab, the exoskeleton is molted periodically as the animal grows larger. The soft-shelled crabs which are such a delicacy are not a separate species at all. They are merely ordinary crabs that have just shed their outgrown exoskeletons. Once the old exoskeleton is molted, a number of hours are required for the new one to harden on contact with the water. It is during this very brief period that the crabs are caught and marketed in their soft-shelled state.

Before the new exoskeleton hardens, the arthropod drinks a great deal of water. This causes the animal to swell up, and stretches the skeleton. Once hardening is complete, the animal releases the water and returns to its normal size. Since the hardened exoskeleton cannot shrink, the animal has plenty of room inside for growth before the next molt. By its very weight and the mechanics of its functioning, the exoskeleton appears to limit the size to which an arthropod can grow. Marine arthropods are less limited in this respect. The buoyancy of the water around them helps them to bear the weight of the exoskeleton. In fact, one hears reports of six-foot lobsters and other large arthropods caught in deep offshore waters. On land, though, an arthropod of this size would find its exoskeleton impossibly heavy, and would be almost unable to move.

The endoskeleton

In the vertebrates, or animals with backbones, we find the type of skeleton with which we are most familiar. This is the **endoskeleton,** a framework that is completely internal. The framework is not always made up of bone. In certain marine vertebrates, including the sharks and rays, the skeleton is almost wholly composed of cartilage. But the skeleton of most vertebrates, including humans, contains both bone and cartilage.

Cartilage is one of several kinds of **connective tissue.** It consists of scattered cells embedded in a flexible, noncellular **matrix** which they secrete. There are no blood vessels in cartilage, which is often called "gristle." The cartilage cells apparently obtain their nutrients by diffusion across the matrix from adjoining tissue fluids.

tially supportive material. Much of the external ear is made up of **elastic cartilage,** which tends to spring back to its original shape after being distorted. The vertebrae, or discs, of the spinal column are separated by pads of tougher **fibrous cartilage. Hyaline** ("glassy") **cartilage,** which has a comparatively clear matrix, is found in the trachea,

THE WELL-DRESSED ASTRONAUT

Our natural support and locomotion systems work very well in the environment to which they are adapted—that is, on the surface of the earth. But in radically different surroundings, such as outer space, the systems must be artificially extended. The space suit is an artificial exoskeleton—a miniature world that enables its wearer to live and work in an environment that would ordinarily be lethal.

The basic space suit has six layers, weighs 36 pounds, and costs $400,000. It is airtight and inflated to protect the astronaut from pressure low enough to make the blood boil. This airtight protection, though, also seals in body heat, so water-cooled underwear is worn to prevent the buildup of dangerously high temperatures. Outside the spacecraft, the astronaut must wear yet another garment, a sort of oversuit whose ten layers protect against radiation and any speeding micro-meteorites that may happen along. Topping off the wardrobe is a high-

impact helmet, with visors to shield the eyes from radiation.

A portable life-support system called a biopack extends some of the astronaut's physiological systems. The biopack supplies oxygen for up to four hours. It also controls humidity inside the suit, and eliminates waste carbon dioxide.

Because the suit must be inflated, it becomes unwieldy, hindering the astronaut's mobility. To solve this problem, space-suit tailors (who are really physiologists and engineers) came up with some ingenious designs. They made it easier for the wearer to bend forward by installing a block and tackle between the neck and waist of the suit. To allow free movement of joints, they used special fabric, bellows-like joints, or elaborate combinations of bearings. Some gloves are even equipped with metal fingernails that allow the astronaut to pick up an object as small as a dime (try doing that with ordinary canvas work gloves). One manufacturer claims to have developed a suit that, by means of such refinements, gives its wearer more than 90 percent of the maneuverability of a nude body.

The skeleton of the vertebrate embryo is made up almost entirely of cartilage. Before maturity, much of this is gradually replaced by bone. Some cartilage, however, is permanent. It is retained where both firmness and resiliency are needed.

The human body contains three different types of cartilage, but all of them are essen-

larynx, and nose.

In many respects, the structure of bone resembles that of cartilage. Living bone cells secrete the bone matrix. But this matrix is much harder than the matrix of cartilage, because it contains more mineral matter. It is heavily impregnated with such inorganic compounds as calcium carbonate and cal-

PATTERNS OF MAINTENANCE
AND REGULATION

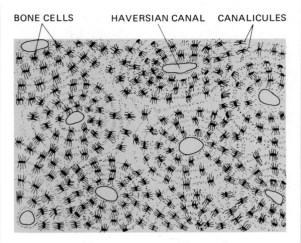

Figure 7-2. Cross-section of a typical long bone.

cium phosphate. Bone is remarkable material in many ways. It is immensely strong, but weighs comparatively little. Its lightness is due to its porous structure and also to the tubular construction of the so-called "long bones."

A cross-section of a typical long bone—for instance, the **femur,** or thighbone—shows that this bone is essentially a hollow cylinder. The middle of the cylinder is filled with yellow **marrow,** which stores fat and plays a part in the production of certain blood cells. The long shaft of the femur is made of relatively solid **compact bone.** The knobby ends are composed of **spongy bone,** which looks much like a section of honeycomb when viewed under the microscope. Red marrow fills the cavities in this part of the bone.

The flat bones of the skeleton include, among others, the ribs and the small bones that compose the skull. Except for the ends of the ribs, the flat bones are made up of compact bone. However, their cavities contain red marrow, which produces some red blood cells.

Bone is made up of small cylindrical units called **Haversian systems.** In each Haver-

sian system, concentric layers of bone matrix encircle a tiny central **Haversian canal.** The Haversian canal contains nerves and minute arteries and veins. Nutrients and other materials can be exchanged between bone cells and the blood vessels of the Haversian canal through **canalicules.** These are tiny channels that penetrate the hard matrix. They are formed by interconnecting, narrow extensions of the bone cells.

Bone is a storage facility for calcium and phosphorus. These elements can be withdrawn from the bone and released into the blood whenever they are needed by the rest of the body. In elderly people so much stored calcium may be withdrawn that the bones become progressively more brittle, and slow to knit if they are broken.

From the standpoint of engineering, the human skeleton is remarkably functional. Its two hundred or so bones range in size all the way from the tiny bones in the inner ear, which are the mechanical basis of hearing, to the largest long bones, which are primarily for support. The tubular construction of the long bones, for example, is a marvelously practical design. Such bones can withstand enormous pressure, yet they are relatively light in weight.

THE STRUCTURE OF THE SKELETON

For purposes of classification, the vertebrate skeleton is usually divided into two components. The **axial skeleton,** along the body's axis, is made up of the **skull,** the **spine** or vertebral column, and the **rib cage.** The ribs, which form the rib cage, are attached in the rear to the vertebrae, and in the front to the **sternum,** or breastbone. Two or more lower pairs of **floating ribs** are attached only to the spine.

The **appendicular skeleton** includes the bones of the limbs or appendages—wings, legs, arms, fins, or flippers. It also includes the bones that join the limbs to the axial skeleton. In the human being these are the **pectoral girdle** and the **pelvic girdle.**

The pectoral girdle is composed of the **scapula,** or shoulder blade, and the **clavicle,** or collarbone. The upper bone of the arm, or **humerus,** attaches to the scapula. The pelvic girdle consists of the **hipbone,** the **sacrum,** and the **coccyx.** The femur attaches to the hipbone at a socket called the **acetabulum.**

The joints

Bones connect with each other at the **joints.** A number of the joints are **immovable.** In such joints only faint seam lines, called **sutures,** indicate that two bones are fused together. The bones of the human skull are connected by such immovable joints. (In newborn infants, some of the skull bones are not completely joined, but are separated by two areas of thin cartilage, called the **fontanelles.** Most of the sutures are also open at this stage. This allows the head of the infant to be slightly compressed as it squeezes through the tight birth canal during delivery.) The bones of the pelvis are also connected by immovable joints. However, in the female the pubic joint is capable of loosening slightly during the days just before childbirth.

Still other joints are **partially movable.** Such joints are found between the small bones of the ankle and wrist. The vertebrae of the spinal column are also separated by partially movable joints. The bones connected by these joints can glide enough to permit some bending or twisting.

But the great majority of bones are connected by **freely movable** joints. These joints are protected by a capsule of hyaline cartilage, which is lined with a **synovial membrane.** The membrane secretes **synovial fluid,** which serves as a lubricant between the bones of the joint. (Synovial membranes and fluid are also found in many partially movable joints.) Tissue strands called **ligaments** tie the bones together at each joint. The ligaments are composed of an extremely tough and fibrous form of connective tis-

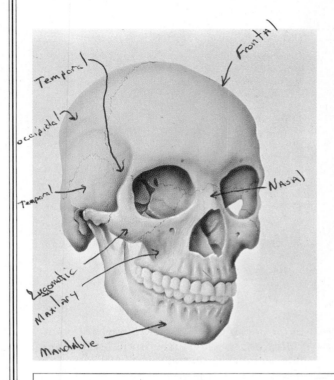

Figure 7-3. The human skull. Although we often think of the skull as being a single large bone, the thin lines indicate sutures between many separate bones.

sue. This connective tissue is elastic, and the combination of joints and ligaments permits a great deal of mobility.

The freely movable joints can be roughly classified as **hinge joints, pivot joints,** and **ball-and-socket joints.** This classification is based on the amount and direction of movement the joint allows.

Hinge joints permit a back-and-forth movement. They control the flexing and extending of the limbs and digits. The joints of the elbow, knee, and fingers are good examples.

Pivot joints allow a turning movement. A pivot joint is found, for example, where the **radius** meets the **ulna** at the elbow. Another such joint, between the first and second vertebrae of the neck, allows the head to turn from side to side.

PATTERNS OF MAINTENANCE
AND REGULATION

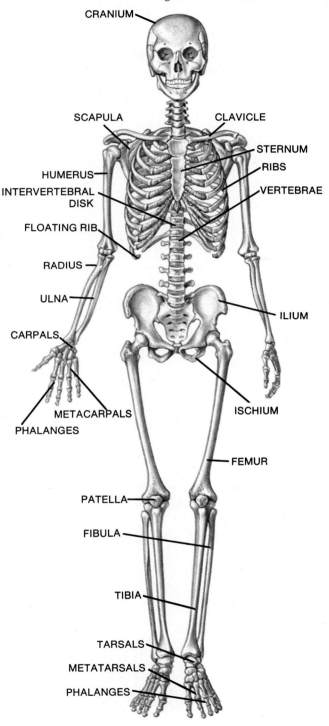

Figure 7-4. The human skeleton.

CRANIUM

SCAPULA

CLAVICLE

STERNUM

RIBS

HUMERUS

INTERVERTEBRAL DISK

VERTEBRAE

FLOATING RIB

RADIUS

ULNA

ILIUM

CARPALS

METACARPALS

ISCHIUM

PHALANGES

FEMUR

PATELLA

FIBULA

TIBIA

TARSALS

METATARSALS

PHALANGES

Ball-and-socket joints permit the greatest range of movement. These joints are found where the femur joins the pelvis and where the humerus joins the scapula. Rotation of the "ball" of the long bone within the "socket" of the pelvic or pectoral girdle allows movement in practically every direction.

THE MUSCLES

Movement of the joints takes place as the result of muscle contraction. When muscles contract they exert a pull. However, no muscle can push. So when a joint is moved in one direction by the contraction of one muscle, it can be moved back to its original position only by the contraction of another muscle. Most of the 600-odd muscles in the human body are arranged in such antagonistic pairs. In some cases two or more muscles may work together to produce a movement in one direction. These muscles are called **cooperating** muscles.

Movement is rarely the result of action by only one pair of muscles. Most movements, however slight, take place by the action of several muscles. Some muscles may provide most of the power for the movement, while others guide it.

In most cases a given muscle is attached to two different bones. One bone serves as a kind of anchor. The contraction of the muscle pulls against the anchor and thus moves the other bone. The **origin** of a muscle is the point at which it attaches to the anchor bone. At its other end, the muscle attaches to the moving bone at the **insertion.** It is possible for a single muscle to have several origins or insertions, either on the same bone or on different bones. The effect produced by the contraction of any given muscle depends largely on the position of its origins and insertions.

Some muscles have their origin on bone and their insertion on other muscles or connective tissue. A few even have their origin and/or insertion on the skin. The facial muscles, which allow us to smile, glare, and otherwise express (or conceal) our feelings, may belong to either of these types. The buccinator muscle, which enables us to smile, has its origin on the maxilla (upper jaw) and its insertion on the skin at the sides of the mouth.

Muscles are attached to the bone or skin by **tendons.** Like the ligaments which connect joints, the tendons are composed of sturdy, fibrous connective tissue. However, they are less elastic than the ligaments.

A complex of muscles, bones, and joints of which some of us become painfully aware is the lower back. "Oh, my aching sacroiliac!" The human spine is shaped in a series of curves. This enables us to move much more flexibly than we could with a perfectly straight back. The curves also absorb much of the shock of two-legged walking. But when muscles are weak, the spine's curves make it very vulnerable to strain. This is especially true at the sacroiliac joint where it attaches to the pelvic girdle. Weak or lazy abdominal muscles allow the abdominal organs to sag forward and down. These organs are attached to the rear body wall and thus, indirectly, to the spine. So, when they sag, their weight pulls on the spine and eventually causes strain. Sooner or later, this may result in damage to the cartilage discs and pressure on the nerves. Even the excruciating back and leg pain known as sciatica can sometimes be traced to this cause.

Types of muscle
Vertebrates possess three different types of muscle tissue. In the human being, about two-thirds of the total body weight is accounted for by muscle.

When we think of muscle we are usually thinking about **skeletal muscle,** the type that is used in voluntary movement. It is also called **voluntary striated muscle.** When viewed through the microscope, skeletal muscle fibers can be seen to be crossed by light and dark bands called **striations.**

136

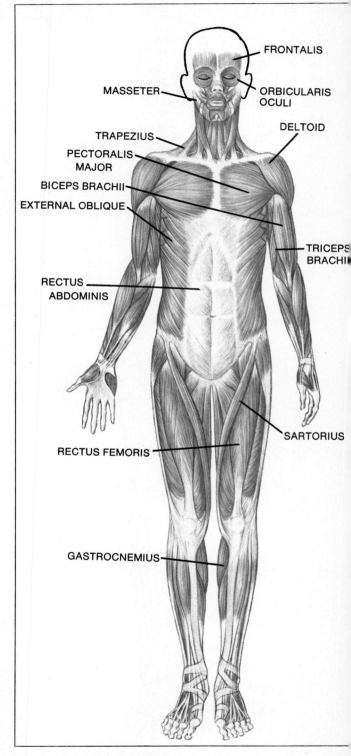

Figure 7-5. Human musculature. Only the most important of the skeletal muscles are shown here.

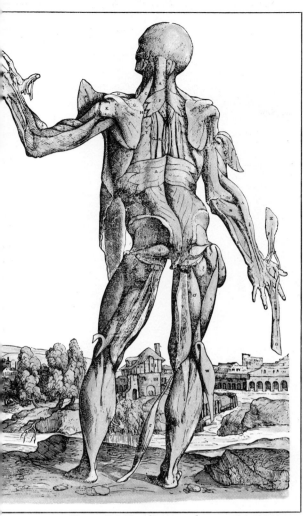

Figure 7-6. Vesalius was the most important anatomist of the sixteenth century. This drawing of the human muscles appeared in his book *De Corporis Humani Fabrica (On the Structure of the Human Body)*, the most accurate book of anatomy that had ever been published at that time. Compare his drawing to figure 7-5.

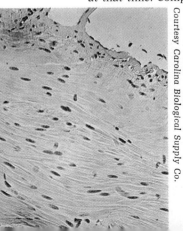

Courtesy Carolina Biological Supply Co.

Figure 7-7. A portion of smooth muscle tissue as seen through a microscope.

Skeletal muscle fibers are long and cylindrical. Each fiber is a single cell, but contains many nuclei. The fibers are grouped together into bundles, bound by tough sheaths of connective tissue. These bundles, in turn, are grouped together to form the muscle itself. Skeletal muscles are under the control of the voluntary or **somatic** nervous system.

Smooth muscle tissue is so named because it does not show the striations seen in skeletal muscle. Smooth muscles are also known as **involuntary** muscles. We seem to have no conscious control over their functioning. Instead, they are controlled by the involuntary or **autonomic** part of the nervous system. Smooth muscle fibers, like those of skeletal muscle, are single cells, but are shaped like fat toothpicks, and each contains only a single nucleus. Instead of forming bundles like those in skeletal muscle, smooth muscle fibers interlace to form sheets. **Multiunit** smooth muscles are found in the walls of blood vessels, in the ducts of various internal organs, and in the uterus. These muscles are stimulated to contract either by nerves or by hormonal action, and they contract very quickly. **Visceral** smooth muscle is found in the walls of the small intestine. It is capable of spontaneous contraction, creating the slow, rhythmic waves of peristaltic movement during digestion.

Cardiac muscle, as its name implies, is found only in the heart. In many ways, cardiac muscle tissues resemble both smooth and skeletal muscle. When they are viewed under the microscope, cardiac muscle cells appear striated like skeletal muscle, but they contain only a single nucleus. Like smooth muscle, cardiac muscle is under the control of the autonomic nervous system. The arrangement of the cardiac muscle fibers is different from either of the other two types. Instead of lying side by side, cardiac fibers are so entangled and interwoven with each other that until recently it was not recognized that they were separate cells. Rather, it was believed that the heart muscle itself was a single cytoplasmic mass with many nuclei.

137

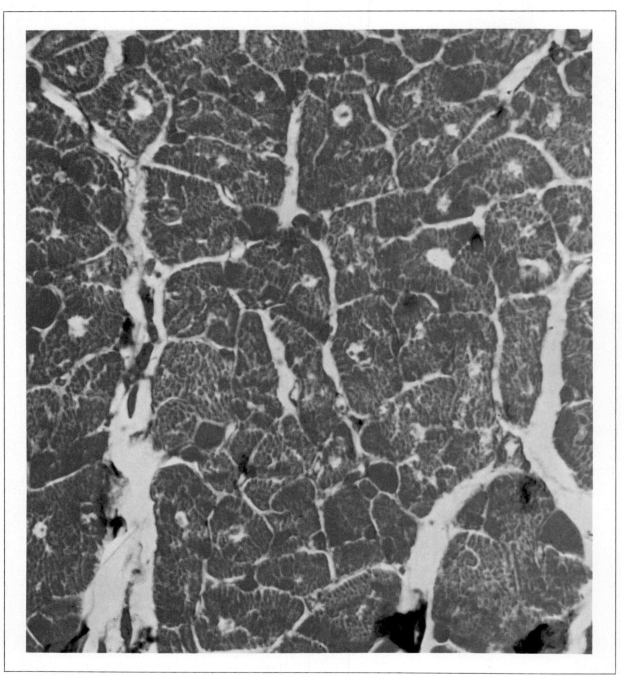

Figure 7-8. A cross-section of cardiac muscle. The cells within the muscle appear as oval shapes, and many capillaries can be seen.

PATTERNS OF MAINTENANCE
AND REGULATION

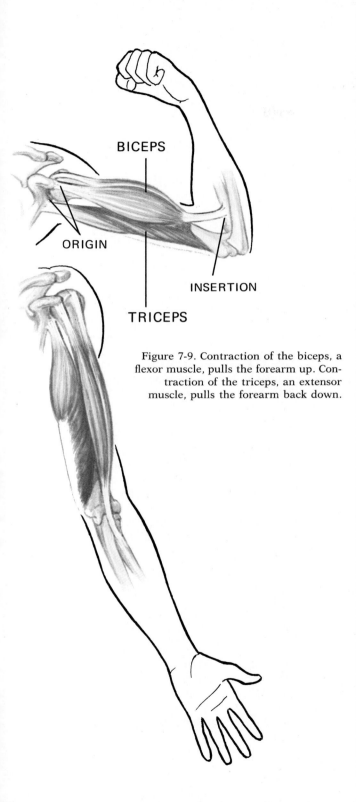

BICEPS

ORIGIN

INSERTION

TRICEPS

Figure 7-9. Contraction of the biceps, a flexor muscle, pulls the forearm up. Contraction of the triceps, an extensor muscle, pulls the forearm back down.

Cardiac muscle differs from skeletal and smooth muscle in a very important way. As you recall from chapter 5, cardiac muscle does not need stimulation by nerve impulses in order to contract. Instead, the muscle itself is inherently rhythmic. If a bit of cardiac muscle tissue is removed from the heart, it will continue to contract and relax spontaneously. And the human heart can continue to beat even when every nerve that leads to it has been severed.

We might note here that muscles of any type are never in a state of complete relaxation. Even during rest or unconsciousness they remain slightly contracted, creating the slight muscle tension called "muscle tone." This tension supports the body generally and maintains posture and body shape. Anyone who has ever lifted both a sleeping pet and a newly dead animal will instantly recognize the difference between the "tone" of resting muscles and the flabbiness of those that have relaxed completely after death.

SKELETAL MUSCLE CONTRACTION

We have already pointed out that muscle contraction is the basis of movement. Muscles can contract in two different ways. In **isotonic** contraction, the muscle shortens as it contracts to move an object. In **isometric** contraction, the muscle tightens and becomes tense and rigid. Its length does not change, even though it is exerting a force. Exercises designed to develop specific muscles were once based exclusively on isotonic muscle contraction, but now the so-called "isometric exercises" are also very popular. In ordinary activity, almost any muscle contraction contains a bit of both elements.

As we have said, most muscles are arranged in antagonistic pairs. As one muscle of the pair contracts and shortens, the other relaxes and lengthens. We can see an example of such antagonistic action in the movement of the human forearm. This movement

GIRAFFES

Two giraffes stand side by side in the African forest. Suddenly, one of them brings its head back and then whips it forward, aiming its horns at the other. The second giraffe steps back and retaliates with a vicious attack to the other animal's knees. The fight continues for a while as the two giraffes butt heads and shove each other with their bodies. Gradually, the hostilities subside, and before long the two antagonists are browsing at the shrubbery as though nothing had happened.

Fights like the one described above are everyday occurrences among male giraffes. Ovbiously, giraffes are not the gentle giants many of us imagine when we think of this distinctive inhabitant of the African bush country. Despite its gawky appearance and quiet demeanor, the giraffe is capable of considerable speed when pursued and, if cornered, can hold its own in a fight.

The giraffe is the tallest of all mammals, sometimes reaching a height of more than 18 feet. Known to the ancient Romans as the "spotted camel," it is easily recognized by its relatively short body and its exceptionally long legs and neck. Two to four horns grow on top of the giraffe's head, and among the males the hair is almost always worn off these as a consequence of constant battles.

The combination of short body and long legs can create some problems in movement. For most four-legged animals, the easiest way to walk or run is by moving one leg at a time on alternate sides. This keeps three legs on the ground a good part of the time, and helps with balance. But it also means that the front leg on each side is reaching backward as the hind leg reaches forward. The giraffe can manage this all right in a short walking stride, but if it tried to run this way, it would probably—quite literally—get all tangled up in its own feet. So it paces instead, moving both left legs together, then both right legs together, shifting its weight from side to side like a human. In a real gallop, the giraffe has still another gait, a fore-and-aft style that has caused some observers to liken it to a long-necked rocking horse. Funny or not, the gallop does the job. At full speed, the giraffe can make about thirty-five miles per hour.

The giraffe's most distinctive feature, of course, is its unusual neck which, despite its great length, contains only seven vertebrae as in most mammals. The neck has many uses. Giraffes are fond of acacia leaves, and they encounter little competition from other animals as they calmly browse on the leaves of tall trees. The animal's great height is also useful in spotting approaching predators long before they can be seen by creatures built closer to the ground.

Neck movement plays a more unusual role in the giraffe's locomotion. The head and neck move back and forth twice during each stride. The forward lunge shifts the animal's center of gravity and aids in the forward motion. The backward movement serves, among other things, to decrease the momentum that might otherwise send the animal toppling forward on its head.

The giraffe's neck is especially useful when sudden danger looms and the animal must go instantly from a standstill to a gallop. Drawing its neck back rapidly, the giraffe shoots it forward, shifting its weight and getting its one-ton body moving in less than a second.

Getting that same body up off the ground is a task for the neck as well. Backward it swings to get a good start, then forward, and the animal rises to its fore-knees. Back and forth again to get the center of gravity forward and pull the hindquarters up. After a momentary pause for stabilization, the giraffe draws its neck back once more to take the weight off its forelegs, and rises to a standing position.

As useful as long legs and a long neck might be for running and for eating leaves, they are not very convenient for drinking at waterholes. A giraffe may solve this problem in either of two ways. Sometimes it will spread its legs slightly and bend its fore-knees until it can reach the water. Alternatively, it may keep its forelegs straight and spread them far apart in a series of jerky motions. In either position, the giraffe is highly vulnerable to the attack of any lion that may be lurking in the tall grass. But with a backward snap of its neck, the giraffe can be upright and ready to fight or run in a single second. Even the giraffe's circulatory system is especially adapted to allow for these rapid changes in head elevation. You've never seen a dizzy giraffe, have you?

is controlled by two basic muscles. The **biceps** is a **flexor** muscle that contracts to pull the forearm up. The **triceps,** on the other hand, is an **extensor** muscle that contracts to pull the forearm back down.

In order to understand the mechanics of muscle contraction, we must examine the structure of the muscle fibers in greater detail. So far, more is understood about skeletal muscle contraction than about smooth muscle. And cardiac muscle presents the greatest number of unanswered questions.

Both skeletal and smooth muscle contract when stimulated by a nerve impulse. Each skeletal muscle cell is innervated by (linked to) only one minute branch of a nerve fiber. A single nerve fiber may have branches innervating several adjoining skeletal muscle cells. The muscle contracts when a nerve impulse reaches it, and relaxes when the impulse ceases. Skeletal muscle contracts very rapidly, and is very responsive to electrical stimuli.

Smooth muscle cells, on the other hand, receive impulses from two different nerve fibers. One fiber is controlled by the sympathetic nervous system and one by the parasympathetic system. (These systems will be discussed in chapter 10.) Impulses from one nerve fiber cause the smooth muscle to contract; impulses from the other fiber cause it to relax. Smooth muscle generally contracts more slowly than skeletal muscle, but it can remain contracted for a longer period of time. It is particularly responsive to chemical stimuli. Thus it can be stimulated by hormones as well as by nerve impulses.

When we examine a single skeletal muscle fiber under a microscope, we can see that it is made up of many smaller fibers. These are known as **myofibrils.** They are separated by cytoplasm that contains many mitochondria. Mitochondria are usually numerous in cells that use a great deal of energy.

The myofibrils, in turn, are made up of cylindrical **sarcomeres.** These are the units which shorten during contraction. Each

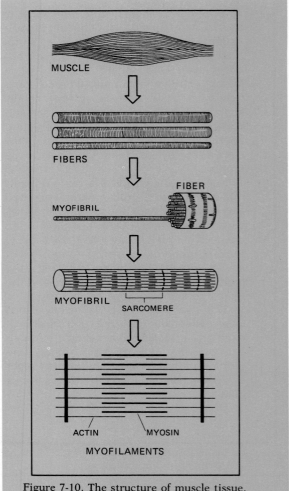

Figure 7-10. The structure of muscle tissue.

PATTERNS OF MAINTENANCE
AND REGULATION

sarcomere is made up of small **myofilaments** of two different proteins. These myofilaments are arranged in a regular pattern which forms the characteristic striations of skeletal muscle.

The two proteins of which the filaments are composed are **myosin** and **actin.** Myosin filaments are thicker, with many projecting points apparently formed by the heads of the myosin molecules. They occupy the middle of the sarcomere. The actin filaments are thinner and shorter, and are at the ends of the sarcomere. In a relaxed muscle, the myosin and actin filaments in a sarcomere barely overlap at their ends. But when the muscle contracts, the two groups of actin filaments slide toward each other between the myosin filaments, almost like coarse-toothed combs meshing with each other. Neither the myosin nor the actin filaments change in length. But as they slide together, the entire sarcomere contracts.

When myosin and actin are extracted from muscle filaments in the laboratory, they can be combined to form **actomyosin** filaments. Actomyosin filaments, in turn, shorten when they are treated with ATP. This leads to the conclusion that these proteins must somehow combine to cause muscle contraction. So when the myosin and actin filaments slide together, they must temporarily connect in some way.

The basis of this connection is not yet fully understood. However, under the electron microscope it appears that cross-bridges form between the two kinds of filament as they slide together. It now appears that these cross-bridges are actually the protruding heads of the myosin molecules within the myosin filaments, and that they bind to special receptor sites on the actin filaments. The resulting actomyosin can then be acted upon by ATP to cause contraction.

But where does the ATP itself come from? Indications are that a single cross-bridge would use up more than 50 molecules of ATP every second, and during strenuous activity the usual process of cellular respiration may

not synthesize it fast enough from glucose. However, muscle tissue contains an abundant supply of **creatine phosphate,** a related compound. This compound can pass a phosphate group on to ADP, which then forms the ATP necessary for contraction.

SUMMARY

The three major functions of any skeletal system are support, protection, and locomotion. Skeletons can be classified as hydrostatic skeletons, exoskeletons, and endoskeletons. The exoskeleton serves the additional function of preventing the organism from becoming dehydrated.

The hydrostatic skeleton is made up of body fluids, which resist compression. They are acted on by circular muscles and longitudinal muscles, which work antagonistically. The force of contractions is transmitted by the body fluid. The hydrostatic skeleton of an earthworm is segmented, and thus the worm is capable of localized movement.

All arthropods possess hard exoskeletons. In land arthropods the exoskeleton is composed of chitin; in marine arthropods it also contains calcium phosphate and calcium carbonate. The muscles are contained inside the exoskeleton, which is divided by many joints. Exoskeletons are molted as the animal grows.

The endoskeleton is a completely internal framework. In most vertebrates it is made up of both bone and cartilage. The embryonic skeleton is almost entirely cartilage, but most of this is gradually replaced by bone. The human body contains elastic, fibrous, and hyaline cartilage.

Bone matrix is harder than that of cartilage because it contains calcium carbonate and calcium phosphate. Bone is immensely strong but comparatively light because of its porous structure. Long bones are essentially hollow cylinders. They are filled with yellow marrow which stores fat and produces certain blood cells. The ends of the long bones, and the flat bones of the skeleton, contain red marrow which manufactures some types of red blood cell. Bone is made up of units called Haversian systems. It stores calcium and phosphorus, which can be released when they are needed by the rest of the body.

The vertebrate skeleton is divided into axial and appendicular components. The axial skeleton is made up of the skull, spine, and rib cage; the appendicular skeleton includes the limbs, pectoral girdle, and pelvic girdle. Bones connect with each other at joints, which may be immovable, partially movable, or freely movable. The joints are connected by tough ligaments. Joints move as the result of muscle contraction. A given muscle is usually attached to two different bones by tendons.

Vertebrates possess three types of muscle tissue. Skeletal muscle is used for voluntary movement, and is controlled by the somatic nervous system. Smooth or involuntary muscle is controlled by the autonomic nervous system. Cardiac muscle, found only in the heart, is controlled by the autonomic nervous system but can contract spontaneously without nerve stimulation.

Muscles can contract isotonically or isometrically. Movement of a joint is controlled by the antagonistic action of flexor and extensor muscles. The movement of skeletal and smooth muscle is stimulated by nerve impulses.

Skeletal muscle fibers are made up of smaller myofibrils. The myofibrils, in turn, are made up of sarcomeres. Each sarcomere contains myofilaments of two different proteins, myosin and actin. When a muscle contracts, actin filaments slide between the myosin filaments, causing the entire sarcomere to shorten.

Myosin and actin combine to form actomyosin filaments, which shorten when they are treated with ATP. Apparently myosin and actin filaments become connected by cross-bridges when they slide together. Muscle contraction requires large amounts of ATP. If this cannot be synthesized fast enough from glucose, creatine phosphate may pass a phosphate group on to ADP, enabling it to form the necessary ATP.

Review questions

1. What are the three primary functions of a skeletal system?

2. Describe the structure of a hydrostatic skeleton.

3. What are antagonistic muscles?

4. The exoskeleton has one primary function not shared by other skeletal systems. What is it?

5. What difference in activity would we expect to see between a hard-shelled crab and a soft-shelled crab? Why?

6. Why are land arthropods usually much smaller than marine arthropods?

7. Name and describe the three types of human cartilage.

8. Babies and young children can withstand constant falls and rough play much better than adults. Why?

9. Compare the matrix of cartilage to that of bone.

10. Name two important functions of bone marrow.

11. Describe the structure of a Haversian system.

12. What are the two main structural divisions of the vertebrate skeleton? What does each include?

13. Name and describe three types of joint. Give an example of each.

14. Distinguish between the structure and function of tendons and ligaments.

15. Explain why poor posture contributes to the development of back problems.

PATTERNS OF MAINTENANCE
AND REGULATION

16. Describe the three main types of muscle tissue and give an example of each.

17. So far, the heart is the only muscle that can be transplanted intact from one body to another. Why is this possible?

18. Distinguish between isotonic and isometric muscle contraction.

19. Define flexor and extensor muscles.

20. In what two ways can smooth muscle be stimulated?

21. Describe the structure of a skeletal muscle fiber.

22. Name the two proteins of which myofilaments are composed.

23. How does ATP function in muscle contraction?

24. What are cross-bridges?

25. Where does muscle tissue get the supply of ATP it needs for contraction?

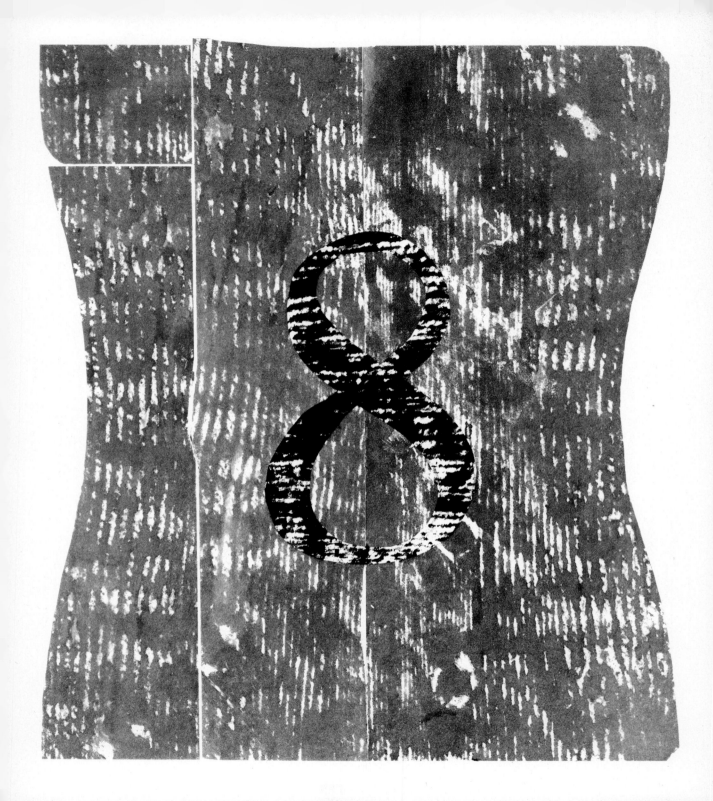

Stability of the Organism

For centuries biologists have been awed, and sometimes even baffled, by the way in which organisms respond internally to stresses in their environment. External responses did not seem mysterious. There was, for instance, nothing unexplainable about a rabbit running away from a coyote. This behavior was an appropriate response to an obvious danger. But inner responses were much harder to account for. Why did the rabbit's heartbeat and rate of blood circulation suddenly speed up in response to the challenge? And why did they slow down, just as automatically, once the threat was removed?

In the middle of the nineteenth century the great French physiologist, Claude Bernard, proposed a new theory. He suggested that these processes kept the organism's internal environment stable in the face of changing conditions in the external environment. Physiologists now consider Bernard's theory to be one of the most important of all biological concepts. The name given to it was **homeostasis,** derived from the Greek *homoios*, meaning "like," and *stasis*, meaning "standing," or "staying." In other words, homeostasis is a steady state. It includes all the processes that preserve the stability of an organism's internal environment.

To maintain a condition of homeostasis, many interacting **homeostatic systems** must function constantly. These systems work according to a delicately adjusted arrangement of checks and balances. In this chapter we will examine the important homeostatic systems that control the internal environments of multicellular animals.

147

INTERNAL TEMPERATURE REGULATION

One of the most important factors in maintenance of a stable internal environment is the adjustment of body temperature. Too cold an internal temperature will slow down the metabolism of the organism by slowing the rate of chemical reactions, and may kill the organism. Too high an internal temperature will speed up the metabolism too much, and kill it also. So every organism has some means of maintaining a body temperature level that will allow it to function normally.

Animals are customarily classified as either "warm-blooded" or "cold-blooded." Newer terminology refers to these forms respectively as **endotherms,** whose internal temperature remains approximately the same no matter what the external environment, and **ectotherms,** whose temperature varies with the temperature of the environment.

Ectotherms

Ectotherms include all animals except birds and mammals. Because their internal body temperature is largely dependent on the temperature of their external environment, land-dwelling ectotherms tend to be excluded from the more extreme climates. Few can survive where the temperature normally remains near or below freezing, or in dry areas with extremely high daytime temperatures and little cooling at night. But in the temperate and tropic zones, they can adjust their behavior to conform to a fairly broad temperature range. Many fish and other aquatic ectotherms, on the other hand, thrive in the cold waters of the Arctic and Antarctic Oceans.

One of the commonest adaptations of ectotherms is confining their activity to the hours of the day when the temperature is moderate. Many lizards in the American desert, for example, become almost completely dormant at night, when the temperature falls near the freezing point. Burying itself in the sand, the lizard leaves only its head exposed. In the morning, heat from the sun strikes the head and warms the blood in a large head cavity or sinus. As this warmed blood circulates, it warms the entire body, and the lizard becomes active. During the desert afternoon, when temperatures may soar above a hundred degrees Fahrenheit, the lizard seeks the shade of a rock or burrows into the sand again for coolness. If no shelter is available, it lies parallel to the rays of the sun, thereby reducing the amount of body surface the sun's direct heat can reach. As the evening chill comes on, the lizard returns to its near-dormant state once more. During the daily cycle, the body temperature of the lizard may vary from around 34°C (93°F) in the sun to barely above 0°C (32°F) at night.

Some ectotherms group together, thus helping to maintain a constant body temperature. Rattlesnakes, for example, may form a tangled ball in a nighttime burrow, sharing body heat. Certain social insects, including honeybees and wasps, keep the hive or nest at a constant temperature by their own activity. If the hive becomes too warm, the insects will sprinkle water inside it, fanning with their wings to evaporate the water and thus cool the air. If the hive becomes too cool, they may cluster over it to keep the heat inside.

During long periods of hot or cold weather, an ectotherm may enter a state of temporary dormancy that can last for days or even weeks. In winter many of these animals **hibernate,** usually retreating to a protected underground burrow of some sort. Their body temperatures fall to near the freezing level, and metabolic activity slows almost to a halt. Respiration drops to only one or two breaths per minute. The heartbeat slows drastically, and the animal draws on fat reserves stored in its body to maintain its vital functions at this greatly reduced level.

Estivation, less common than hibernation, is a dormant period of some animals

PATTERNS OF MAINTENANCE
AND REGULATION

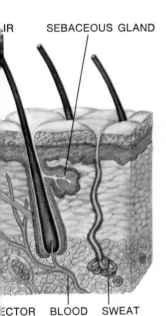

Figure 8-1. The Gila monster, a poisonous lizard of the American desert, has a fat reserve stored in its thick tail. During cold weather it draws on this reserve for nourishment.

SEBACEOUS GLAND

IR

ECTOR
SCLE

BLOOD
VESSEL

SWEAT
GLAND

Figure 8-2. The skin helps to control the body temperature of endotherms. Sweat glands produce surface moisture that cools the body as it evaporates. Contraction and dilation of skin capillaries can control the amount of blood that is carried close to the surface of the skin, thus helping to regulate blood temperature. The erector muscles can raise or lower the hair, fur, or feathers, permitting the animal to control the insulating effect of air trapped next to the skin.

during very hot, dry weather. There is some indication that it is related more to lack of water than to high surrounding temperatures. Frogs and salamanders, for example, may burrow into the mud at the bottom of a pond. Encased in a mud "cocoon," they remain dormant as the sun's heat dries up the pond completely. When the autumn rains refill the pond, the animals return to their normal active state.

Endotherms

Body heat in endotherms is produced by their own cellular respiration. The warm-blooded animal can regulate its body temperature so that it remains nearly the same, no matter what the temperature in the external environment. The temperature-regulating system works by maintaining a balance between heat loss and heat production. The rate of loss or production is controlled by a center located in the hypothalamus, a part of the brain.

The control center in the hypothalamus may bring about heat loss in a variety of ways. As body temperature rises, blood vessels in the skin dilate, bringing more blood to the surface where it can be cooled. Cellular respiration slows down. In animals that possess sweat glands, perspiration is secreted, forming a film of moisture over the skin. As the perspiration evaporates, heat is removed from the body. Most fur-bearing animals, though, possess few sweat glands. They can lose heat by hanging out their tongues and panting. Water evaporates from the tongue and the moist nose, cooling these organs and the blood that flows through them. The air inhaled in panting cools the lungs. Not surprisingly, animals without sweat glands are usually unable to bear extremely high temperatures as well as those that can perspire. Some heat, however, can be lost through the fur.

When the body of an endotherm becomes too cold, the control center in the brain initiates another set of reactions. Blood moves away from the surface into the interior of the body, reducing heat loss. Cellular respiration is speeded up to release more heat. Shivering begins, and generates still more heat. In furred or feathered animals, erector muscles in the skin cause the fur or feathers to stand upright. Pockets of air are thus trapped next to the skin, increasing insulation. "Goose pimples" are the result of a similar reaction in humans.

Behavior patterns also aid in temperature control. On a hot and humid August day, for example, a dog will lie sprawled out and panting in the coolest corner it can find, exposing a maximum portion of its body surface to the circulating air around it. In very cold weather, its response is just the opposite. It curls itself up into a compact ball, reducing the surface-to-volume ratio (see chapter 1) and thus conserving body heat.

Physical characteristics also play an important part in temperature regulation. When we compare some carnivorous animals from the sub-tropic and arctic regions of the world, we can see some obvious differences. Such adaptations can be seen within the same family of animals. The kit fox, for example, is a native of the southwestern desert area of the United States. Its enormous ears present a large amount of surface in which the blood vessels are close to the skin. The blood vessels can dilate or expand, permitting increased blood flow near the surface; this results in cooling of the blood. Its nose has a fairly large, moist surface to allow evaporation of water, and its fur is relatively short. On the other hand, its near cousin, the arctic fox, has small, heavily furred ears that are carried folded back close to the skull. The arctic fox has a proportionately smaller amount of exposed nose surface, and its fur is long and thick.

Endotherms native to areas with cold winters can also hibernate. For most of the larger animals, this is not a true hibernation, since the drop in body temperature may be as little as 8° or 9°C (about 20°F). However, the change is enough to slow the animal's metabolic rate. There is some indi-cation that this form of hibernation is related to sleep, but the nature of the relationship is not yet understood.

Endotherms can adapt to a far wider range of external environmental conditions than the ectotherms can, since they can adjust their own internal environments. We find penguins at the South Pole, parrots in the steamy South American rain forests, caribou above the Arctic Circle, and camels in the hot African deserts.

Humans, of course, can survive in any of these climates. This is largely because they wear clothing or build shelters. It is not surprising that primitive tribes in tropic zones usually wear little clothing, or even none at all. However, the Yahgan tribe of Tierra del Fuego, living where temperatures often fall well below freezing, apparently wore no clothing at all before the arrival of outside settlers. A similar situation has been observed among the aborigines of Australia. It is not fully understood how these people were able to adapt to temperatures that would ordinarily cause a naked human being to die of exposure. Current research suggests that they may have produced unusually large amounts of a thyroid hormone that speeds up cellular respiration and the resulting production of heat. In a recent small-scale study of dolphins, this thyroid hormone was most abundant in members of one species, the Dall porpoise. This is the species most commonly found in far northern waters. So it is possible that the hormone contributes to the dolphin's ability to adapt to the cold.

REGULATION OF FLUID BALANCE

In chapter 5 we discussed the composition of human blood. As we saw, the plasma of the blood contains positively and negatively charged ions and a variety of proteins. These substances are extremely important to regulation of the pH, or acid–base balance, of the blood plasma. The concentration of ions

PATTERNS OF MAINTENANCE
AND REGULATION

Figure 8-3. The chipmunk sleeps for extended periods during the cold winter months. A slight drop in body temperature slows the animal's metabolism, but this is not a true hibernation.

Figure 8-4. This arctic fox is well adapted for existence in a cold climate. Air trapped in its thick fur provides insulation against bitter weather, and its small ears and nose lose very little heat.

Figure 8-5. The small glass catfish is a popular choice for freshwater aquariums. What would happen to this fish if it were placed in a salt-water environment?

in blood plasma also helps determine its osmotic pressure in relation to that of the tissue fluid around the cells. If there is a significant change in ion concentration, the osmotic balance is upset, and serious cell damage can result.

As we saw in chapter 5, the plasma proteins have an important role in regulating the osmotic pressure and viscosity, or thickness, of the blood, and as **buffers** in maintaining a stable pH level in blood plasma. If the plasma is becoming too acid, the plasma proteins bind hydrogen ions, reducing the acidity. Conversely, if the plasma is becoming too alkaline, these hydrogen ions are released.

An important aspect of fluid regulation is the maintenance of a proper salt and water balance in the organism. The body fluids of all organisms contain a variety of salts. But if there is a difference in osmotic concentration between the salts in the body fluid and those in the surrounding medium, some mechanism is needed that will maintain a balance.

Most salt-water fish, for example, are always in danger of dehydration because their external environment—the sea water—is saltier than their own body fluids. There is, therefore, a constant loss of water as it seeps osmotically out of them. The loss is not fatal because they possess specialized cells in their gills that excrete excess salt without losing too much additional water, as would happen if the salt were excreted in the urine. The urine of these fish, in fact, is very scanty.

Fresh-water vertebrates have just the opposite problem. Since their internal environment is saltier than the external one, water is constantly seeping into them. If they had no way of getting rid of the excess water, fresh-water fish would actually drown. Accordingly, they produce enormous amounts of very dilute urine, and absorb through cells in their gills whatever salt is available from the surrounding water.

For land animals, water conservation is a major problem. They are constantly losing water—by evaporation during respiration

PATTERNS OF MAINTENANCE
AND REGULATION

and perspiration, and by elimination. It is replaced by eating and drinking, and some is produced as a by-product of cellular respiration. However, these animals often take in excess salts with their food, so they excrete salts while retaining as much water as possible. We will see that the excretion of salts, and the conservation of water, are bound up with the general problem of removing wastes from the body.

WASTE REMOVAL

Removal of metabolic wastes from the body, or **excretion,** is one of the most important homeostatic mechanisms. Waste materials that are toxic to the organism, as well as excesses of other substances, must be gotten rid of efficiently and quickly. The major substances excreted from the body are carbon dioxide, water, inorganic ions, and nitrogenous wastes.

In single-celled organisms, excretion is hardly a problem. Wastes diffuse directly out of the cell and into the surrounding environment. This is the result both of active transport and of the selective permeability of the organism's cell membrane. Certain protozoa collect wastes and excess water in specialized vacuoles, which then move to the cell membrane and discharge the water outside the organism.

In plants, no organized system for waste removal exists. Nearly all metabolic products in plants can be reused. However, excess gases and dissolved metabolic products diffuse into the surrounding environment, and insoluble compounds are often deposited in old xylem vessels.

Animals dispose of carbon dioxide in a variety of ways. Land animals use lungs, aquatic animals use gills, and some amphibians use their moist skins. Mammals with sweat glands can rid themselves of water and certain soluble impurities through perspiration. Some water is also released from the lungs in the form of vapor during exhalation. But large amounts of water, inorganic ions, and nitrogenous wastes are removed by special filtering devices such as the kidneys.

When proteins are metabolized by an organism, ammonia is produced. Ammonia is the simplest form of nitrogenous waste. It is highly toxic, and must be disposed of as quickly as possible. This presents no problem for most aquatic animals. They excrete the ammonia immediately into the water around them, where it is quickly diluted to a safe level of concentration.

Land animals, however, convert the ammonia into a substance that can be stored in the body for a time. Amphibians and mammals convert it to urea. The difficulty is that urea is highly soluble. Therefore, its excretion necessarily involves the loss of a good deal of water. Birds and reptiles, on the other hand, convert the ammonia into uric acid, which is less soluble. This is excreted with the loss of very little water.

The kidneys

In vertebrates, the **kidneys** are the primary organs of excretion. The human kidneys are bean-shaped organs, located in a well-protected part of the abdominal cavity. They lie against the muscles of the back, and are overhung by the lower ribs. In the front they are shielded by other abdominal organs.

The kidneys perform several important functions. They filter the body fluids, separating waste products from those that should be retained. They reabsorb the products that can be reused, and return them to the blood plasma. They also actively secrete some wastes and toxic substances, adding them to the filtered fluid. And they excrete urine, the end product that carries unusable waste materials out of the body.

Each kidney consists of an outer layer, the **cortex,** and an inner layer, the **medulla.** A large central cavity is called the **renal pelvis.** Blood enters the kidney through a **renal artery** that leads directly from the aorta.

The functional excretory unit of the kidney is the **nephron.** Each kidney contains about a million of these tiny units. The nephron begins with a minute coil of capillaries called the **glomerulus,** surrounded by the cup-shaped **Bowman's capsule.** Fluids diffuse into the cavity of Bowman's capsule from the glomerulus, which receives blood directly from the renal artery.

The diffused fluid, or **filtrate,** next moves into a long, thin, twisting tubule, known as the **proximal convoluted tubule.** Here, reusable substances such as ions and organic material are reabsorbed and returned to the bloodstream, while additional wastes are secreted into the tubule.

The filtrate passes next through the hairpin-shaped **loop of Henle,** where more ions and much water are reabsorbed. Next, in the **distal convoluted tubule,** still more water is removed. More ions are reabsorbed, and some others are added. Most of the reabsorbed material reenters the blood through the blood vessels that surround the tubules.

The remaining fluid, now known as **urine,** moves from the distal tubule into a **collecting tubule.** Still more water is removed here, so that the urine becomes highly concentrated. The collecting tubules empty the urine into the renal pelvis, which in turn joins the **ureter.** The ureter of each kidney serves as a passageway to the **bladder,** where urine is stored until it is voided.

By this process of urine formation, the kidney removes any substance that would upset the normal chemical balance of the blood. Occasionally, for example, it will excrete sugar. However, this occurs only if the level of blood sugar gets too high, as it does in diabetes. In the same fashion, excess acids, bases, or water are also excreted. But essential elements, such as calcium, sodium, potassium, and magnesium, are largely retained.

It should be clear that the kidneys are among the most important organs in the body. Failure of the kidneys to function results in death, unless remedial steps are taken. Today, kidney machines that filter the

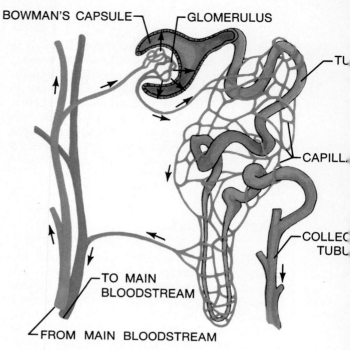

Figure 8-6. Blood enters the glomerulus of the kidney from the renal artery. Much of the fluid portion of the blood diffuses into the capsule. More fluid, along with organic material, ions, and wastes, is removed as the filtrate moves through the tubules and the loop of Henle. The urine which remains becomes more concentrated as it passes through the collecting tubule. After passage through the ureter, the urine is stored in the bladder until it is voided.

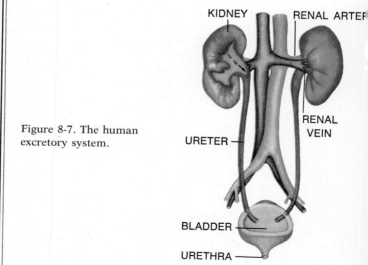

Figure 8-7. The human excretory system.

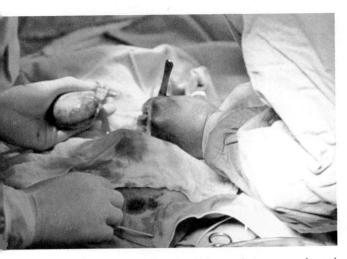

Figure 8-8. This healthy kidney is being transplanted into the body of a patient whose own kidneys have failed. Not all such transplants are successful, but many recipients go on to lead normal lives with the new kidney in place. Note the color of the kidney shown here. Why is it so pale?

blood artificially can often prolong the life of the victim for several years. Kidney transplants are also becoming quite common, although they do not always succeed. Despite such measures, kidney failure due to disease remains one of the leading causes of death in adults.

The liver

While the **liver** does not function in ordinary waste removal, it helps maintain homeostasis by regulating the amounts of certain substances in the blood. One of its most important roles is regulation of blood-sugar levels.

After a meal is eaten, digestion releases large amounts of glucose into the blood. This blood passes from the capillaries of the small intestine into the liver through the **portal vein.** There the liver removes excess glucose. Only enough to meet the body's current demand enters the main circulation. Whatever glucose the liver retains is con-

verted into glycogen, which can be stored. Several hours after eating, the level of glucose in the blood begins to drop. The liver now starts to convert the glycogen back into glucose, and this glucose is released into the bloodstream, maintaining a steady blood-sugar level. If not enough glycogen has been stored to meet the demand, the liver can break down fats to supply the needed glucose. In an emergency, it can also break down proteins, both those in the blood and the structural proteins in the cells.

The liver also performs other functions. It can break down such toxic substances as alcohol and certain other drugs, and detoxify heavy metals such as lead and mercury. It serves as a storehouse for iron and a number of vitamins. Along with the **spleen,** an organ which lies behind the stomach, the liver destroys vast quantities of aging red blood cells as new ones are produced by the bone marrow. And, finally, the liver manufactures a number of the plasma proteins, including albumin, some of the globulins, prothrombin, and fibrinogen. In the following section we will discuss some important roles of plasma proteins in maintaining homeostasis.

THE REPAIR OF DAMAGE

Some of the most important homeostatic mechanisms are those involved in protecting organisms against damage-causing factors in the environment. They include the various mechanisms that go into action when the skin is broken. Among its other functions, the skin is a protective barrier against pathogenic (disease-causing) microorganisms in the external environment. A break in the skin allows these pathogens a point of entry into the body. It also creates a leak from which blood can be lost.

Temporary repair

Blood loss can range from the minor leakage

of a scratch to the huge loss associated with severe injury. Excessive blood loss over a short period of time may lead to **shock.** This dangerous condition is characterized by a drastic lowering of blood pressure, a weak and rapid heartbeat, and a speeding up of respiration rate. Whether the blood loss is minor or excessive, though, the body immediately sets in motion a repair mechanism that is a function of the blood itself.

The initial step is the formation of a **clot** that stops the loss of blood. Blood clotting is an example of a precise chain reaction. It is initiated when a break occurs in the tissues so that some cells are crushed or torn, resulting in jagged surfaces. As blood flows out through the wound, some of the fragile platelets, or **thrombocytes,** are broken on these irregular edges.

Thrombocytes damaged in this way are stimulated to release substances called **thromboplastins.** In the presence of thromboplastins and certain other proteins, an inactive plasma protein called **prothrombin** is converted to its active form, called **thrombin.** Thrombin in turn activates **fibrinogen,** another plasma protein. The fibrinogen, which is ordinarily soluble, changes into **fibrin,** which consists of fine, insoluble threads. The fibrin threads form a net that traps the blood cells, creating a jelly-like clot and stopping the flow of blood.

Despite the fact that normal blood contains these various substances, clotting does not usually occur inside the blood vessels. The clotting reaction must be triggered by contact between the thrombocytes and a jagged surface that ruptures them. However, injury to a blood vessel can leave such roughened surfaces without an actual break, and an internal clot may form. This, in itself, is a protective measure, which strengthens the damaged wall of the blood vessel. Occasionally, though, such an internal clot will continue to grow, or will break loose into the bloodstream. Blockage of a blood vessel by an enlarged clot that remains at its original site is called **thrombosis.** Blockage by a moving clot that has become stuck in a blood

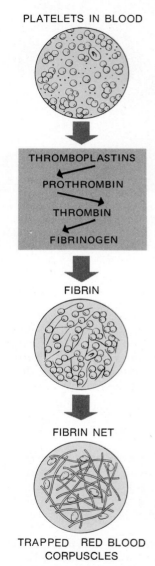

PLATELETS IN BLOOD

THROMBOPLASTINS

PROTHROMBIN

THROMBIN

FIBRINOGEN

FIBRIN

FIBRIN NET

TRAPPED RED BLOOD CORPUSCLES

Figure 8-9. The main steps in the blood-clotting mechanism.

156

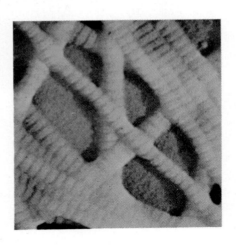

Figure 8-10. This electron micrograph shows a collagen fiber magnified 42,000 times. This protein makes up most of the connective tissue of the body, and plays an important role in repair of tissue damage.

vessel is called **embolism.** Either type of blockage can be fatal, especially if it occurs in a large artery to the brain, the heart, or the lungs.

The blood may fail to clot properly if one or more of the substances needed for the chain reaction is missing. Hemophilia, or "bleeders' disease," is such a condition. When victims of this disease suffer wounds, they need to be given the missing clotting factor immediately. Otherwise they may require massive transfusions to replace blood lost through even a tiny cut or scrape. Even slight bruises can cause crippling hemorrhages into the joints, or fatal bleeding into the abdominal cavity.

One of the fat-soluble vitamins, vitamin K, is also essential to the blood-clotting process. This vitamin is usually synthesized by bacteria in the human digestive tract, and is also obtained by eating green vegetables that contain it. However, deficiencies occasionally occur. Vitamin K is often routinely administered to patients about to undergo surgery, and to women just before childbirth.

Permanent repairs

The blood clot is an excellent device for simple sealing of a wound. However, it is only a temporary form of repair. For permanent repair, other homeostatic mechanisms must be activated. The type of permanent repair the body performs is dependent on the extent and severity of the damage.

In the case of minor cuts and abrasions, repair is usually accomplished by the skin itself. The deeper layers of the skin contain cells that can multiply very rapidly. These cells join together the broken edges of the skin. A few weeks after such a repair, it is almost impossible to see where the damage occurred.

Severe cuts and burns, however, are another matter. Such extensive injuries almost always destroy many of the regenerative skin cells in the damaged area. In these cases, another type of repair is made.

Certain cells of connective tissue, known as **fibroblasts,** synthesize the proteins collagen and elastin. These proteins form a tough, shiny connective fiber called **scar tissue,** which bridges the gap and rejoins the edges of the damaged tissue. However, scar tissue differs in texture, pigmentation, and sensitivity from the normal tissues around it.

Burns present a more difficult problem of repair. A severe burn may damage the deepest layers of the skin, or destroy them completely. The body then loses water rapidly, as lymph and tissue fluids ooze from the surface of the injury. Thus, dehydration is a serious problem in victims of extensive burns, and infection a constant danger. Because the regenerative tissues are damaged or destroyed, healing must frequently be aided by grafting skin from another part of the victim's body onto the site of the burn.

SEA LIONS

"Hey, you guys, hurry up! They're gonna feed the seals!" No visit to the zoo or the circus would be complete without the playful antics of the trained "seal." However, the noisy animal that barks enthusiastically while balancing a ball on its nose is not really a seal at all. In reality, it is a small species of sea lion.

Like all mammals, sea lions are airbreathers. Nevertheless, they spend most of their lives in the ocean and are skilled and graceful swimmers. Two species live off the Pacific coast of North America. The California sea lion is the smaller and more southerly. This is the circus "seal." An adult male may measure over seven feet in length and weigh more than 500 pounds. Females are considerably smaller, with a length of six feet and a weight of 200 pounds.

The larger northern, or Steller, sea lion lives off the Alaskan shore in summer and off the California coast in winter. Bulls may weigh over a ton and reach a length of more than eleven feet. Cows weigh some 750 pounds and are about nine feet long. The northern sea lion is generally not as noisy as the California sea lion, but it can bellow loudly when it wants to make its presence known.

At one time, sea lions were hunted almost to extinction for their hides, meat, and oil. Eskimos even stored the valuable oil in pouches made from the sea lion's stomach. Today, sea lions are protected by law, but many fall prey to their natural enemies, the shark and the killer whale. Sea lions are often disliked and sometimes killed by fishermen who accuse them of eating valuable fish and damaging nets. For the most part, the accusations are untrue. The northern sea lion eats mostly "trash fish," which are of little commercial value. The California sea lion prefers squid. Although sea lions do eat salmon, they also eat lampreys, a snake-like parasitic fish that devours salmon in great numbers. By controlling the lamprey population, the sea lion probably saves more salmon than it eats.

Sea lions come ashore in early summer to give birth and to mate. First to arrive are the bulls, which immediately stake out individual territories along the beach. The cows follow and soon give birth to the single pup that each has been carrying since the previous summer. The newborn pup has about a dozen teeth. Its big blue eyes are open from birth and will turn brown after a few weeks.

The pup is born into a tumultuous world of huge, bellowing adults, and it must mature quickly to avoid being trampled by the teeming mob around it. It can move about within an hour, and can be seen scrambling nimbly among its elders within a few days. It doubles its weight in the first month or two.

The quick weight gain is largely attributable to the extremely rich milk of the sea lion mother. Low in water and high in protein, the milk is almost 50 percent fat, whereas cow's milk is about 4 percent fat. Zookeepers have found it difficult to provide sea lion pups with adequate nourishment in the absence of the mother. At Marineland of the Pacific, an orphaned pup was successfully raised on a diet of whipping cream, liquified mackerel muscle, calcium caseinate, and a multivitamin syrup. Not a very delectable-sounding menu, perhaps, but the pup loved it.

Throw a human infant into the ocean and it would drown. So would a sea lion baby. The only mammals that are known to swim from birth are whales and manatees. Although it will spend most of its twenty-year life in the ocean, the sea lion pup is at first terrified of water. The mother must spend about two months teaching it to swim.

Mating is no quiet affair among the sea lions. Almost immediately after the birth of the pups, the huge bulls begin to wage bloody battles, trying to keep control of their harems of about a dozen cows. Using their long canine teeth as weapons, they fight with great ferocity for possession of the females. Fighting and mating consume so much of the bulls' time and energy during this period that little time is left for sleeping or eating.

At the end of the summer, the sea lions return to the ocean. The bulls, thin and scarred after a busy breeding season, regain their lost weight with several months of active feeding. As the weather grows colder, the huge northern sea lions begin their southward migration, leaving deserted the northern beaches which in warm weather were covered with their massive dark bodies.

The sea lion has to adapt to a considerable range of climate conditions. Its thick blubber and rapid metabolism are assets in the cold northern waters. But the California sea lion ranges as far south as the Galápagos Islands off the coast of South America. How does it adapt to a hot and dry environment?

The most important thing that the sea lion does to stay cool is to sleep in the daytime and take care of business during the cooler night hours. Sea lions in warm climates spend a great deal of time sleeping on the wet sand. Their bodies are designed in such a way that a large surface of the torso comes in contact with the cool ground when the animal lies down. About 10 percent of body heat can be lost in this way. Furthermore, the animal produces nearly 25 percent less heat while it sleeps than it does when awake and active.

Unfortunately, none of the sea lion's cooling mechanisms are highly effective. Ultimately, the animal relies on immersion in the ocean to keep itself cool.

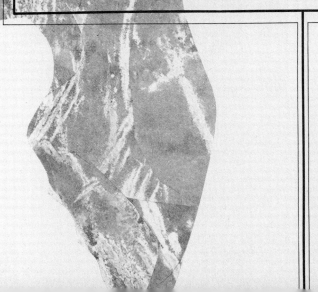

DEFENSES AGAINST DISEASE

When we consider the many microorganisms that cause disease, and the fact that the body is constantly exposed to them, it seems almost a miracle that we are not perpetually ill. These **pathogens** are present in the air we breathe and on the objects we handle daily. They are carried in the saliva of animals that bite—fleas and mosquitoes, rats, dogs, and lions. We ingest pathogens in our food and water. In some cases they are even present in our own body wastes. And yet, for the most part, we stay well. It seems apparent that our body defenses do a very competent job of protecting us against these pathogens.

The human body presents a variety of defenses against entry by pathogens. The skin itself is a formidable barrier. Unless it is broken, most microorganisms cannot penetrate it. The respiratory system provides several other protective mechanisms. Its mucous membranes trap microorganisms together with other foreign particles, and its cilia help to sweep them away. Even our own tears are a protection, since they contain a substance that attacks bacteria. And within our intestinal tract, acid secretions and a host of "friendly" bacteria repel harmful invaders.

Nevertheless, we do become ill occasionally. Most of the diseases we contract are self-limiting. That is, they do not last indefinitely. After we are exposed to them, there is a symptomless period of **incubation** during which they develop. Then symptoms appear, and for awhile we are actively sick. Gradually the symptoms fade, and we start to improve. Finally, after a period of recuperation, we are well again.

This is not to say that a self-limiting disease leaves no after-effects. Scars remain after smallpox, paralysis often follows poliomyelitis, and permanent sight and hearing damage can follow ordinary measles. But the pathogen has gone or become inactive. In this section we will

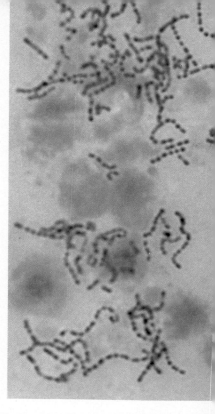

Figure 8-11. *Streptococcus*, seen in this micrograph, is the airborne bacterial pathogen that causes strep throat.

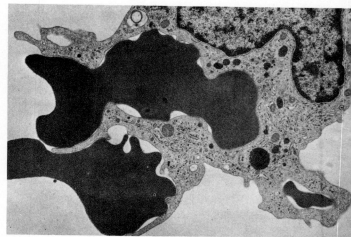

Figure 8-12. Phagocytes surround and ingest bacteria and other foreign particles. Phagocytic cells are found in the bloodstream, in the lymphatic system and in the tissue fluids.

160

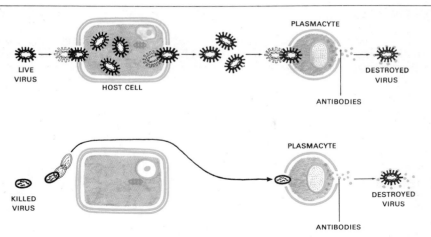

LIVE
VIRUS

HOST CELL

PLASMACYTE

ANTIBODIES

DESTROYED
VIRUS

KILLED
VIRUS

PLASMACYTE

ANTIBODIES

DESTROYED
VIRUS

Figure 8-13. Natural immunization (top) is accomplished when a pathogen, such as a virus, multiplies within the host and begins to attack other cells. Certain lymphocytes are stimulated to produce antibodies that destroy the invader.

In artificial immunization (bottom), a killed or weakened virus is innoculated. This virus cannot infect the host's cells but it does stimulate the lymphocytes to produce antibodies.

examine the ways in which the body fights disease.

Phagocytes: the first line of defense

The term **"phagocyte"** literally means "eating cell"—a very apt description of the phagocyte's activities. Like an amoeba, the phagocyte engulfs and digests food particles. Specifically, it feeds on microorganisms that invade the body, usually at their point of entry. If a break in the skin occurs, for example, the phagocytes flock to the area. There they ingest any invading bacteria present, as well as dead cellular material. The combination of all these materials is what we call pus.

There are several varieties of phagocyte. Among the most important are the **leucocytes,** or white blood cells. These cells are not confined to the bloodstream, but are also found in the tissue fluids.

If an infection begins to spread to other parts of the body, beyond the point of its entrance, other barriers prevent widespread invasion. Microbes that enter the lymph vessels must pass through the **lymph nodes,** which act as filters. Lymph cells called **macrophages** ingest the invading microorganisms as they are caught in the filtering nodes. So-called "swollen glands" are often really lymph nodes that have become filled with pus as the result of filtering out many bacteria. If the bacteria succeed in entering the bloodstream, they must eventually pass through the liver and spleen, where more phagocytic cells destroy them. Because phagocytes attack many different invading microorganisms, they are said to confer **nonspecific immunity.**

Antibodies: the second line of defense

To understand the action of antibodies, we must first understand that the body rejects foreign invaders—whether they are bacteria, viruses, or protozoa—because these organisms are composed of proteins different from the proteins in the body. These microbes, and the waste products of their metabolism, are toxic to the body they have invaded. They upset the body's condition of homeostasis. In fighting them, the body is simply operating to restore homeostasis.

The surfaces of invading microor-

to neutralize the antigens. Antibodies are specific in their action. That is, each antibody deals with a particular type of antigen. The antibody that attacks the measles virus, for instance, is useless against smallpox or diphtheria. For this reason, antibodies are

---

ANTIBIOTICS: MIRACLE DRUGS OR KILLER DRUGS?

A 23-year-old man went to his family doctor with a sore throat. The doctor prescribed an antibiotic called chloramphenicol, to be taken for ten days. Six months later the young man was dead of aplastic anemia, a disease in which the bone marrow is eaten away and replaced by fatty deposits. Yet doctors have known since 1949 that chloramphenicol can cause this deadly anemia—and that it is of no use at all in curing an ordinary sore throat.

This is only one example of the way in which antibiotics and other drugs are being misused in America today. Some experts estimate that 30,000 Americans die every year from the effects of such drugs prescribed by their doctors. And another 300,000 are disabled by such side effects as kidney damage, internal hemorrhaging, and loss of sight.

Antibiotics are truly miracle drugs. They can control a host of bacterial infections. For

this reason, doctors routinely prescribe them for all manner of ailments, from colds to venereal disease. Yet, a recent study shows, most physicians are not sure just what a given antibiotic can do, or what its side effects can be. Of 4,513 American doctors who voluntarily took an examination on the use of antibiotics, half received scores of 68 or lower. The creators of the test estimate that a good physician should score at least 80 percent.

A blue-ribbon panel of physicians and pharmacists noted that the average American probably suffers from an illness requiring antibiotics only once in every five or ten years. Yet it has been estimated that one in four Americans is treated with penicillin at least once a year. Of the 20 to 50 tons of this drug sold annually in this country, fully 90 percent is probably wasted, because it is used for infections on which it has no effect. The conditions for which doctors most commonly prescribe antibiotics are viral sore throats and the common cold—against which present-day antibiotics are absolutely worthless. Intelligent patients are learning to protect themselves when antibiotics are prescribed, by questioning their doctors about the drug's necessity, its purpose, and its side effects, if any.

---

ganisms, and the wastes they excrete, contain proteins called **antigens.** When antigens are present in the body, they stimulate certain lymphocytes to synthesize protein molecules known as **immunoglobulins** or **antibodies.** The sole function of antibodies is

said to confer **specific immunity.**

It is not yet fully understood just how antibodies work. The most widely accepted theory suggests that they are "dove-tailed" to fit closely to the shape of their opposing antigen, rather like a piece of a jigsaw puzzle

PATTERNS OF MAINTENANCE AND REGULATION

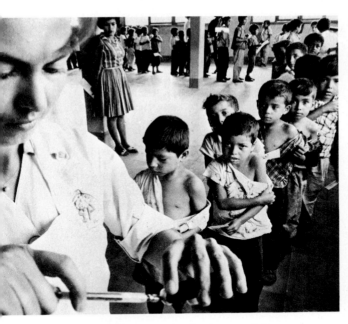

Figure 8-14. Mass vaccination is one of the surest ways to eliminate a disease from the human population.

which is meant to interlock with another specific piece. Presumably the antibody then interlocks with the antigen and binds to it, immobilizing it. It can then be easily ingested by the phagocytes. If the phagocytes can prevent the number of antigens from increasing, homeostasis is maintained. But if the antigens multiply to such numbers that the antibodies cannot cope with all of them, sickness results.

The thymus gland

Until recently, the nature of the **thymus gland** was something of a mystery. Its functions are still not fully understood. The recent discovery that the thymus produces a hormone called **thymosin** definitely classifies it among the endocrine glands, which we will discuss in the next chapter. However, the thymus plays an important role in defense against disease. For example, it has been found that antibody production cannot operate properly unless it is stimulated by thymosin. So a discussion of the thymus fits quite neatly into our consideration of the body's defenses.

The thymus is a double-lobed gland that lies just behind the sternum. It is quite large in children up to the age of puberty, but shrivels up and becomes much smaller in adulthood and old age. During childhood it appears to contain large numbers of multiplying lymphocytes, of a type known as T-cells. The T-cells migrate to other areas of the body, where they may either be killed or reproduce when they encounter antigens. If they reproduce, the daughter cells react with the antigens and inactivate them. They may also secrete substances that enable the nearby macrophages to work more efficiently. Because T-cells are thought to work directly against antigens, and not by producing antibodies, they are said to confer **cell-mediated immunity.** The activity of macrophages and other phagocytes is also cell-mediated immunity.

The lymphocytes that are known to produce antibodies are called B-cells or plasma cells, and are not produced by the thymus gland. They seem to be formed in lymphatic tissues elsewhere in the body.

Occasionally a child is born with the thymus gland either missing or not functional. Children with this defect fail to produce antibodies in response to the presence of antigens. They are highly susceptible to infections of all kinds. Before the era of antibiotics, such children usually died in infancy, since they lacked the natural ability to fight invading pathogens.

The development of immunity

Once the body has reacted to a particular antigen by producing a specific antibody that combats it, a degree of specific immunity, or **immunological memory,** has been developed. In a sense, the body has "learned" how to fight that particular antigen. The next time it appears in the body, "memory cells" may already be present that can produce the specific antibody to neutralize it.

Control of many diseases is based upon the process called **immunization,** which produces specific immunity. A killed or weakened form of an antigen is injected into the body, which reacts by producing antibodies against that antigen. Since an inactive form of the antigen is used, sickness does not occur as the result of the injection, but immunity is produced nonetheless. Routine immunization has nearly wiped out a number of diseases that once had a very high mortality rate, particularly among children—for instance, diphtheria and poliomyelitis. At the time of this writing, widespread immunization against small-pox, once a major scourge, is expected to eradicate the dangerous form of that disease.

Occasionally something goes wrong with the body's mechanisms of immunity, and an individual may produce antibodies against some of his or her own body tissues. These **autoimmune reactions** have been linked to a number of diseases that are difficult to treat and control, including rheumatoid arthritis and rheumatic fever.

SUMMARY

Homeostasis includes the processes which preserve the stability of an organism's internal environment. These processes work according to an arrangement of checks and balances to maintain a steady state. One of the most important factors in homeostasis is adjustment of internal body temperature.

The body temperature of ectotherms is largely dependent on the temperature of their external environment. Land-dwelling ectotherms are thus confined mainly to the temperate and tropic zones. Ectotherms also use behavioral means to adapt to extreme temperatures. They may hibernate during the winter months or estivate during hot, dry periods.

Endotherms produce their own body heat by cellular respiration. The hypothalamus of the brain maintains a balance between heat loss and heat production. Behavior patterns and physical characteristics also assist endotherms in temperature regulation. Some use a form of hibernation less extreme than that of ectotherms.

Regulation of fluid balance is extremely important to homeostasis. Ions contained in the blood plasma regulate its osmotic pressure. The plasma proteins regulate blood viscosity and help maintain a stable pH level.

Fluid regulation also requires proper salt and water balance. Marine fish lose water osmotically, so they have special cells for excreting salt, and their urine is very scanty. Fresh-water fish have the opposite problem, since water flows into them. They have specialized cells for obtaining salt, and produce enormous amounts of dilute urine. Land animals are specialized for excreting salt and retaining water.

Metabolization of proteins produces toxic ammonia. Aquatic animals excrete it directly into the water around them. Birds and reptiles convert ammonia into uric acid, and amphibians and mammals convert it to urea.

In vertebrates the kidneys are the primary excretory organs. They filter body fluids, reabsorb products that can be used again, and excrete urine. Thus they remove substances that might upset the chemical balance of the blood, while retaining essential elements. They are among the most important organs in the body.

The liver helps to maintain homeostasis by regulating blood-sugar levels and breaking down certain toxic substances such as alcohol. It also destroys aging red blood cells. The liver manufactures a number of the plasma proteins.

Repair of damage is important to homeostasis. Blood clotting is a temporary repair mechanism. Permanent repairs depend on the severity of the damage. Minor repairs are accomplished by regeneration of the skin itself. Severe injuries are repaired by the synthesis of scar tissue.

The body has many defenses against pathogens. Phagocytes are the first line of defense, feeding on invading microorganisms. They include leucocytes and macrophages. Antibodies function to neutralize antigens. The thymus gland contains multiplying lymphocytes, which stimulate antibody production.

Specific immunity develops when a body has learned how to fight a particular antigen. Such immunity can be produced by immunization with a killed or weakened antigen. Autoimmune reactions occur when an individual produces antibodies against his or her own body tissues.

Review questions

1. Define the term "homeostasis."

2. Explain why the term "cold-blooded" does not accurately describe an ectotherm.

3. List several behavioral characteristics that help ectotherms adapt to temperature extremes.

4. Distinguish between the type of hibernation seen in ectotherms and that of endotherms.

5. Would a land-dwelling tortoise be expected to hibernate or estivate? A water turtle? Why?

6. List some methods used by endotherms to bring about heat loss and heat production.

7. What difference in normal body temperature would we expect to find between a hummingbird, a cat, and a tree sloth? Why?

8. Many long-haired dogs are clipped for coolness during the summer. Why is this procedure almost useless?

9. List several adaptive physical characteristics of endotherms.

10. Explain why fresh-water fish are in constant danger of drowning, and how they avoid it.

11. What will happen to a marine fish placed in a fresh-water environment? Why?

12. List three important functions of the vertebrate kidney.

13. A person undergoing regular kidney dialysis by an artificial kidney machine no longer urinates. Why?

14. Describe the structure of a nephron.

15. Explain how the liver functions in blood-sugar regulation.

16. Trace the steps which lead to formation of a blood clot.

17. Two men are injured in an auto accident. One suffers such severe leg injuries that both legs must be amputated at the hip. The other suffers third-degree burns covering both legs but does not require amputation. Which man is likely to recover more quickly? Why?

18. List three or more human protective mechanisms against invading pathogens.

19. What is a self-limiting disease?

20. Name two types of phagocyte.

21. Describe the way in which antibodies are believed to function.

22. The thymus is vitally important during childhood but not necessary to the adult. Why?

23. How does immunization produce specific immunity?

24. What is an autoimmune reaction? Give at least one example.

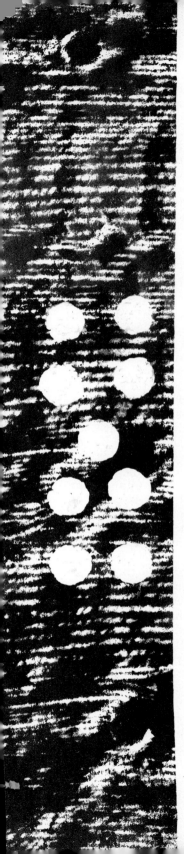

Hormonal Regulation

In previous chapters we have examined the systems used by multicellular organisms for such vital activities as digestion, transport, gas exchange, and locomotion. Even single-celled organisms can perform most of these functions. It is obvious, though, that the more complex the organism, the more it needs some means of coordinating these various systems.

There are two aspects to this problem of coordination. First, communication must be established among the different cells of the individual. Second, there must be some way by which certain cells and organs can influence the functions of others. Two systems are concerned with this internal communication and direction. We will discuss one of these—the nervous system—in the next chapter, although both systems work together in coordinating the body functions of multicellular organisms. In this chapter we will deal with mechanisms of chemical control, which are found even in simple unicellular organisms.

HORMONES IN ANIMALS

A large number of chemical compounds are absolutely necessary to the normal activities of organisms. These include vitamins, enzymes, and hormones. We have already discussed the nature of vitamins and enzymes, as well as the roles they play in chemical control. In multicellular organisms, these substances are regulated, in turn, by **hormones.** Hormones are activator substances, chemical compounds that are

167

secreted by certain tissues directly into the bloodstream.

It appears that certain enzymes may be regulated by the presence or absence of particular hormones. Some hormones may even act as coenzymes. This relationship between hormones and enzymes is still being studied. However, a great deal is known about the source, nature, and many of the actions of hormones.

We can learn much about hormones by studying the problems that occur in the organism when too much or too little of a hormone is present. As in the case of vitamins, an excess or deficiency of a hormone causes an unbalanced state that may be considered a disease. The study of hormone-related diseases very often leads to an understanding of how the hormonal control system functions under normal conditions, and of the specific regulatory effects of particular hormones.

The discovery of hormonal action

Until 1902 it was assumed that the production of digestive enzymes was controlled only by the nervous system. In that year, a number of experiments involving digestive fluids were performed by the English scientists William Bayliss and Ernest Starling. They showed that if the nerves leading from the intestine to the pancreas were severed, pancreatic juices would still flow when food entered the small intestine. This implied that the nerves were not the only means of communication. Perhaps, then, the blood carried some sort of chemical information that controlled the function of the pancreas.

It appeared that the pancreatic flow was stimulated by the presence of food in the small intestine. To prove this, Bayliss and Starling extracted fluid from the cells of the intestinal wall. When this fluid was injected into experimental animals, it caused the pancreatic flow to begin. The intestinal-wall fluid was later discovered to contain a substance that the researchers named "secretin." This was the first hormone to be identified and isolated. (The general name

"hormone" was suggested by Starling; it is derived from the Greek word meaning "to excite.")

The discovery of secretin was followed by isolation of other digestive hormones. Researchers soon realized that hormones must also be involved in the control and regulation of other systems. Since that time a wide variety of hormones and their functions have been identified, and the existence of many others is suspected.

HORMONAL REGULATION IN HUMANS

In multicellular animals, such as humans, hormones may be secreted either by specialized glands or by tissues that also perform other functions. These are called the **endocrine glands** and tissues. The endocrine glands are ductless—that is, they have no ducts through which secretions are carried to definite locations. Instead, their secretions are released into the capillaries, and are carried to the target areas by the bloodstream.

Hormones elicit a very specific response in the cells or tissues they stimulate. Some can stimulate every cell and tissue in the body; others may affect only one particular tissue or organ. Why some cells are sensitive to certain hormones and not to others remains a mystery.

Researchers have suggested three possible hypotheses to explain how a hormone produces a change in a cell or tissue: (1) The hormone may change the permeability of the cell membrane, by combining with some substance in it. (2) The hormone may change the properties of an enzyme in the cell. (3) The hormone may enter the nucleus of the cell and activate certain genes, which then produce new RNA and new proteins.

However they do it, hormones function in two ways. First, they influence cellular activities. Second, they help to coordinate reactions of various organs, enabling the organs to continue working as a team under

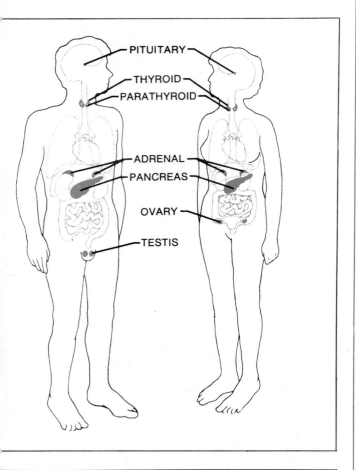

PITUITARY

THYROID
PARATHYROID

ADRENAL
PANCREAS

OVARY

TESTIS

Figure 9-1. These are some of the glands of the endocrine system. Not shown are the pineal, hypothalamus, and thymus. The ovaries and testes illustrated are a part of the reproductive system, which will be discussed in chapter 13.

varying conditions. A hormone may affect several tissues in a variety of ways, or it may affect the same tissue differently, depending on how much of it is present. This ability of a hormone to either stimulate or inhibit is the result of the mechanism known as **negative feedback.**

Simply stated, negative feedback works in this way: A stimulus produces a reaction. Eventually, an end product of that reaction cancels out the stimulus and shuts off the reaction. For instance, a temperature drop in a house may cause a thermostat to turn on the furnace. The temperature will then rise, and will eventually cause the thermostat to turn the furnace off. The hormones released by endocrine glands are like the heat produced by the furnace. When one of them reaches a sufficient level in the bloodstream, it causes the "thermostat"—the gland that began the reaction—to stop producing the hormone.

Negative feedback is an extremely important control mechanism. Without it, a single stimulus could cause an endocrine gland to go on secreting a given hormone even after an adequate level had already been reached. Since only minute amounts of hormones are usually needed, a potentially dangerous imbalance would quickly occur.

The hypothalamus

In the last chapter we discussed the role of the **hypothalamus** in temperature regulation. The hypothalamus is a part of the brain and therefore of the nervous system. But it also has an endocrine function. In fact, it seems to be the key site at which the nervous and endocrine systems interact. Its hormones are secreted in response to nervous stimuli. The hormones then directly or indirectly stimulate other endocrine glands to produce their own hormones. In particular, the hypothalamus produces a number of secretions which stimulate and regulate the production of hormones by the anterior pituitary (see below). There is also some evidence that the hypothalamus directly

Figure 9-2. These rats are litter-mates, born at the same time. The rat on the right, however, has had its pituitary gland surgically removed. The resulting lack of growth hormone has caused this rat to become a pituitary dwarf.

Figure 9-3. An abnormal increase in the secretion of growth hormone after an individual has reached adulthood results in the condition called acromegaly. The hormone does not alter the length of the bones, but causes them to grow in width. The thickening of the bones that results is especially noticeable in the jaw, cheekbones, and skull. These pictures show a man before he developed acromegaly (age 24), at the onset of the acromegalic symptoms (age 29), and as the condition progressed (ages 37 and 42).

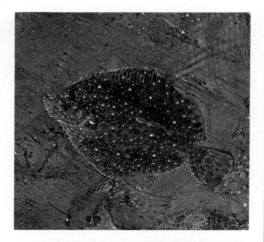

Figure 9-4. Melanocyte-stimulating hormone secreted by the intermediate lobe of the pituitary produces the changes in skin color that allow this flounder to blend in with varying backgrounds.

influences hormone production by the pancreas and another gland, the adrenal medulla.

The pituitary gland

The **pituitary,** or **hypophysis,** is often called the "master gland." Located at the bottom of the brain, just above the roof of the mouth, this gland is about the size and shape of a pea. It is known to release at least fifteen different hormones. The pituitary is divided into the anterior, intermediate, and posterior lobes.

The **anterior pituitary** plays an important part in the regulation of growth, through secretion of the **growth hormone.** This hormone stimulates the organism to retain amino acids. These, of course, are the building blocks of protein. If too little growth hormone is secreted during childhood, the individual becomes a pituitary dwarf, with a very short but normally proportioned body. An overabundance, or hypersecretion, of growth hormone in childhood produces gigantism. The afflicted individual may grow to as much as eight feet in height. Hypersecretion in adulthood causes a condition known as acromegaly. In this, the bones in the jaw, face, and digits begin growing again, causing distorted features and oversized hands and feet.

The anterior pituitary also produces several **trophic hormones.** These are hormones that regulate the action of other endocrine glands. Among them is **thyrotrophic** or **thyroid-stimulating hormone,** abbreviated as **TSH. Adrenocorticotrophic hormone,** or **ACTH,** acts upon the adrenal cortex. At least two **gonadotrophic hormones** influence activity of the sex glands, or gonads. These last, and the glands they act on, will be discussed in more detail when we examine the processes of animal reproduction in chapter 13.

The **intermediate lobe** of the pituitary secretes **melanocyte-stimulating hormone,** or **MSH.** This can produce changes in skin color in many amphibians and fish. The skin

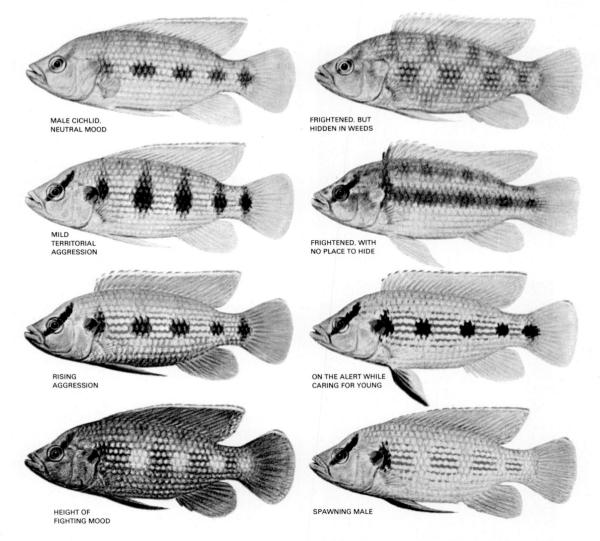

Figure 9-5. The fresh-water cichlid transmits messages by changes in color. These changes result from the expansion and contraction of pigmented cells in its skin, and are controlled by melanocyte-stimulating hormone.

of these animals contains special pigment cells. When light is not present, the pigment cells spread and darken the skin, so that the animal blends in with the dark background. But when the animal moves into a light area, the light-sensitive retina of the eye is stimulated and sends impulses to the pituitary. MSH is then released and prevents the pigment cells from spreading. This keeps the animal light in color, so that it matches its surrounding area and is more likely to be overlooked by any passing predator.

The **posterior pituitary** is structurally a part of the hypothalamus. It stores and secretes two hormones, **vasopressin** and **oxytocin**, which are produced in the hypothalamus. Although these hormones are chemically very similar, their functions are entirely different. Vasopressin is also called the **antidiuretic hormone** or **ADH,** because it regulates the retention or excretion of water by the kidneys. Oxytocin stimulates

PATTERNS OF MAINTENANCE
AND REGULATION

Labels within figure:
MALE CICHLID, NEUTRAL MOOD
FRIGHTENED, BUT HIDDEN IN WEEDS
MILD TERRITORIAL AGGRESSION
FRIGHTENED, WITH NO PLACE TO HIDE
RISING AGGRESSION
ON THE ALERT WHILE CARING FOR YOUNG
HEIGHT OF FIGHTING MOOD
SPAWNING MALE

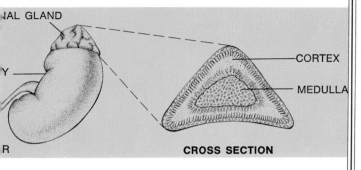

Figure 9-6. Humans possess two adrenal glands, one on top of each kidney. The cross-section shows that each adrenal is really two glands—a cortex and a medulla.

Figure 9-7. Frightened by the photographer's flashbulb, this owl chooses flight over fighting, an indication that its adrenal medulla is secreting a relatively low amount of norepinephrine.

contractions of the uterus, and milk production in the nursing female.

The adrenal glands

In humans the two **adrenal glands** lie on top of the kidneys. Each adrenal is really a combination of two glands with different functions. The central core of the gland is called the **medulla,** and the surrounding outer portion is the **cortex.**

Two important hormones are secreted by the adrenal medulla: **epinephrine** and **norepinephrine,** more familiarly known as **adrenalin** and **noradrenalin.** These hormones are similar in chemical makeup and function. Both take part in preparing the body to meet emergency situations. They stimulate the production of energy and inhibit functions not directly needed during the emergency. When an animal is in a situation that produces sudden fear or anger, these hormones cause the heart to beat faster, thus pumping more blood. The liver is stimulated to release more glucose into the blood. Muscles tense, the pupils of the eyes enlarge, and the blood becomes capable of more rapid clotting. At the same time, there is reduced secretion of saliva and other digestive juices. These changes within the body prepare the animal for "fight or flight." When the level of norepinephrine is relatively high, the animal will probably fight. When it is relatively low, flight is more likely.

Interestingly, the body seems able to get along reasonably well without the adrenal medulla. If it is removed, the nervous system can compensate by producing the same reactions. We are not certain, though, about the long-term effects of such removal.

The adrenal cortex, however, is absolutely necessary for life. If it is destroyed, the organism invariably dies. It is known to produce more than fifty chemical compounds, many of which have hormonal characteristics. The cortical hormones control blood pressure and regulate the concentrations of sodium, potassium, and sugar in the blood. They also determine a number of sexual characteristics. In addition, the cortex enables the kidneys to maintain salt and water balance in the body.

The fight-or-flight situation mentioned above demonstrates the close interrelationship of the endocrine glands. For example, when epinephrine secreted by the adrenal medulla is carried in the blood to the pituitary, the anterior pituitary is stimulated to release ACTH. When the ACTH in the blood reaches the adrenals, the adrenal cortex is stimulated, in turn, to release a group of hormones known as the **adrenal corticosteroids.** One of the most familiar of these hormones is **cortisone.** This hormone group triggers an increase in the breakdown of tissue proteins into amino acids. The amino acids are then carried to the liver and converted into glucose and glycogen, which can be used to meet additional energy requirements.

If the adrenal cortex does not function adequately, the result is a combination of symptoms known as Addison's disease. It is named for Dr. Thomas Addison, who identified it in 1855. Addison observed certain symptoms—including weakness, apathy, chronic low blood pressure, digestive upsets, anemia, and bronzing of the skin—in a number of patients who subsequently died. Autopsies on these patients showed that in almost every case the adrenal cortex had degenerated. He concluded that there must be a causal relationship between the destruction of the cortex and the disease itself. Although Addison reached his conclusion long before the concepts of endocrine glands and hormones were known, it has been confirmed many times since then.

Cushing's disease is a condition that seems to be caused mainly by overproduction of cells in the adrenal cortex. The cortex becomes greatly enlarged, almost like a tumor. The increased number of cells take up so much ACTH that the blood level of this hormone is lowered. This lowering of hormone level stimulates the anterior pituitary to produce abnormal amounts of ACTH. The extra ACTH then causes the enlarged cortex to produce an oversupply of corticosteroids. These result in the symptoms of the disease—obesity, high blood pressure, fluid imbalance, and other disturbances. Removal of the excess cells of the adrenal cortex often corrects the problem, at least partially.

The thyroid gland

The **thyroid** is a paired gland located in the front of the neck, just below the larynx, with one lobe on either side of the windpipe. Normally, it cannot be seen or felt. The thyroid produces the hormones **thyroxin** or **T_4, triiodothyronine** or **T_3,** and **calcitonin.** Both T_3 and T_4 are involved in the regulation of cellular respiration. Calcitonin has no functional relationship to the other two thyroid hormones. It assists in maintenance of a proper calcium concentration in the blood.

Iodine is an integral part of the molecules of thyroxin and triiodothyronine. Thus, the thyroid gland cannot function properly unless iodine is present in the diet. In some regions, such as around the Great Lakes or in Switzerland, iodine is in short supply in the soil and the drinking water. In these places, iodine must be added to the diet, usually through iodized table salt.

Simple iodine deficiency causes an enlargement of the thyroid gland known as goiter. When iodine is lacking and the thyroid cannot produce enough thyroxin, the pituitary secretes increased amounts of thyroid-stimulating hormone. This hormone induces the thyroid cells to multiply. But as long as the iodine deficiency continues, the new cells can produce no more thyroxin than the old cells. Continued deficiency thus causes a progressive enlargement of the goiter, as more and more new cells are added.

Cretinism is a disease of young children, caused by a severe thyroxin deficiency at birth. Cretins develop into dwarfed individuals with a variety of physical defects

PATTERNS OF MAINTENANCE
AND REGULATION

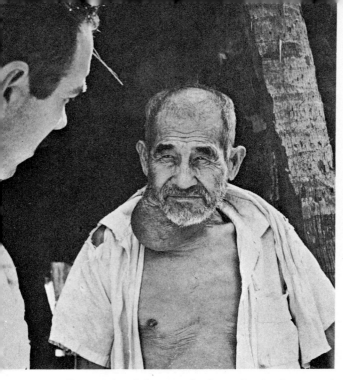

Figure 9-8. A deficiency of iodine in his diet has caused this man's thyroid gland to enlarge into an immense goiter. This disfiguring condition can be surgically corrected, however, and addition of iodine to the diet will usually prevent a recurrence.

Figure 9-9. Extreme thyroxin deficiency has produced the condition of myxedema in this man. Many of the symptoms can be relieved by administration of thyroxin.

Figure 9-10. This child is a cretin as the result of a severe thyroxin deficiency present at birth. Cretinism is becoming uncommon, since identification of the problem soon after birth and prompt administration of the hormone can prevent most of the damage.

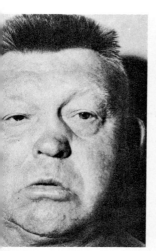

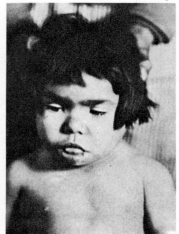

and an intelligence far below normal. If the condition can be identified soon after birth, administration of the hormone can prevent most or all of the damage.

Extreme thyroxin deficiency in adults produces a condition called myxedema, characterized by puffy skin, obesity, lethargy, and general intellectual dullness. Like cretinism, this **hypothyroid** (low-thyroid) abnormality can be relieved by administration of thyroxin.

Hyperthyroidism, an overproduction of thyroxin, causes a sharp increase in the metabolic rate. It produces symptoms just the opposite of hypothyroidism: a rapid pulse, high body temperature, high blood pressure, nervousness, and weight loss. It is often accompanied by exophthalmia, a "pop-eyed" appearance caused by accumulation of fluid in the fatty tissues behind the eyeball. Hyperthyroidism is often difficult to treat, and some of the symptoms may become permanent. Formerly surgery and radiation were used to shrink the thyroid gland, but today drug therapy is more common.

Testing of the **basal metabolic rate,** or **BMR,** is often used to determine if thyroid function is normal. From the amount of oxygen used by the individual during the test, the rate of cellular respiration can be determined. This, in turn, provides a measure of the degree of thyroid activity. The amount of oxygen used is thus an indirect measure of thyroid activity. A more direct test measures the amount of radioactive iodine taken up through the gland. Since the activities of the thyroid depend on iodine, the measure of radioactive iodine absorbed will also be a measure of the activity of the gland.

The parathyroid glands

Humans generally possess four small **parathyroid glands,** two attached to each lobe of the thyroid. The hormone they secrete, called **parathormone,** aids in regulation of calcium and phosphorus concentrations in the blood. Parathormone works

BEYOND THE PILL

As the doctor shows his patient out of the office after a routine examination, he wishes her a pleasant vacation. Then he returns to his desk to complete the notes on her chart. Weight: normal. Blood pressure: normal. Blood chemistry: normal. Vaccines administered: typhoid fever, tetanus, antipregnancy. . . .

An antipregnancy vaccine? Yes, it's coming—probably within ten years. Such a vaccine is already being tested on other primates, such as chimpanzees, and—very cautiously—on human volunteers. All the results are not in yet, and the vaccine may still prove to have unwanted side effects. But there can be no doubt that a safe, reliable vacine against pregnancy is on the way.

Basically, the antipregnancy vaccine will function by tricking the human body into producing antibodies against one of its naturally produced substances. Early attempts to develop such a vaccine were unsuccessful because the antibodies also acted against hormones not connected with pregnancy. But Dr. G. P. Talwar of New Delhi appears to have found a way around this difficulty.

Dr. Talwar's vaccine does not prevent conception, but it interferes with an essential stage of early pregnancy—implantation of the embryo in the wall of the uterus. For about the first five weeks of pregnancy, the embryo produces HCG, a hormone that normally stimulates the ovary to produce another hormone, progesterone. This prevents menstruation, which would displace the newly-implanted embryo. Later, the placenta forms and takes over progesterone production, so HCG is no longer needed. Dr. Talwar's strategy is to prevent the action of HCG.

The HCG molecule contains alpha and beta subunits. Any antibody that attacks the alpha subunit, it was found, also attacks other hormones. So Dr. Talwar found a way to link the beta subunit of HCG—but not the alpha subunit—with a tetanus (lockjaw) vaccine. The body's immune system reacts to the presence of this combination vaccine by producing antibodies to both of its components. By reacting with the beta subunit, the antibodies neutralize the HCG produced by an embryo, and the ovary is not stimulated to produce progesterone. Menstruation occurs as usual, and the embryo, unable to implant, is shed with the menstrual flow.

Studies indicate that the antipregnancy vaccine, like any other, could be renewed by a booster shot. Its effects would also be reversible if pregnancy was desired. The vaccine would be of particular value in controlling population levels of developing nations, where it could easily become a part of existing immunization programs. This method would not require continuous motivation on the part of the woman, who would only have to decide about its use at the time of the original vaccination and whenever a booster shot was due.

---

antagonistically with the calcitonin produced by the thyroid gland. Parathormone stimulates a rise in blood calcium level, but if the increase goes above normal limits, calcitonin acts to decrease it.

In the last chapter we saw that calcium ions must be present in the blood for clotting to occur. They are also needed for correct operation of the muscular and nervous systems. When there is too little blood calcium, the muscle and nerve fibers become extremely irritable. These fibers will then react to even a slight stimulus by producing severe muscle spasms and convulsions. This condition, known as tetany, may lead to death if not corrected by massive doses of

PATTERNS OF MAINTENANCE
AND REGULATION

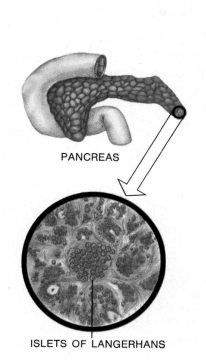

PANCREAS

ISLETS OF LANGERHANS

Figure 9-11. The islets of Langerhans are clusters of specialized cells within the pancreas. They secrete the hormone insulin, which helps to maintain a proper level of glucose in the blood.

calcium. Administration of parathormone can raise the calcium level and prevent the convulsions.

Overproduction of parathormone leads to an excessive level of calcium in the blood. Since this calcium has been drawn from its storage place in the bones, the bones are left soft and pliable, easily bent or broken. This condition is called hyperparathyroidism and is often accompanied by kidney failure.

It is frequently treated by surgical removal of some of the parathyroid tissue.

The pancreas

The **pancreas** lies behind and slightly below the stomach. It functions as both an **exocrine** (duct-possessing) gland and as an endocrine gland. Most of the pancreatic cells secrete digestive enzymes, which collect in tubules that eventually empty into the small intestine. But within the tissues of the pancreas are clusters of cells called the **islets of Langerhans.** These secrete the hormones **insulin, glucagon,** and **gastrin.** Insulin and glucagon work antagonistically to maintain a proper level of glucose in the blood. Insulin lowers the glucose level; glucagon raises it. The function of pancreatic gastrin is not entirely understood. This hormone is also secreted by the mucosa of the stomach, where it stimulates the production of gastric acid. It is possible that pancreatic gastrin works in the same way.

Insufficient production of insulin by the pancreas results in the disease diabetes mellitus (the so-called "sugar diabetes"). In this disease the body cannot utilize the glucose present in the blood. For all practical purposes, the body tissue cells are starving for glucose, while the blood is oversupplied with it. Responding to the tissues' demand for glucose, the liver releases still more of it into the blood, raising the level still higher. At the same time, the kidneys attempt to remove the excess glucose in the blood by filtering it out and excreting it in the urine. Diagnosis of diabetes is confirmed by testing for high glucose levels in both blood and urine.

Until insulin was isolated and its connection with blood glucose levels was recognized, diabetes was invariably fatal, although in older persons its progress was often slow. Like many other scientific breakthroughs, the discovery of insulin was almost purely accidental. Laboratory caretakers noticed that ants were attracted to the urine of experimental animals whose pancreas had been removed. That urine turned out to contain a high level of glucose. Later experiments showed that diabetes could be produced by destroying only the islets of Langerhans. The actual isolation of insulin and its use for control of diabetes were not achieved until twenty years later. In 1932 Dr. F. G. Banting and Dr. C. H. Best received the Nobel Prize for this accomplishment.

Today most diabetics can lead a normal life by taking daily injections of insulin and following a carefully regulated diet. Older persons with the slow-developing form of the disease may be able to control it through diet alone, or by taking a drug called orinase, which helps to lower the blood glucose level. However, questions have arisen about the safety of this drug.

Other endocrine glands

Continued research will probably lead to identification of other endocrine glands and tissues. As we saw in the last chapter, the thymus has only recently been identified as an endocrine gland (by the isolation of its hormone, thymosin).

The **pineal** is a lobe in the forebrain that has now been confirmed as a part of the endocrine system. It secretes the hormone **melatonin,** which lightens the skin and may also affect the action of certain sex hormones. There is evidence to suggest, in fact, that the pineal produces a variety of hormones.

It has recently been shown that the **kidneys** are endocrine glands, as well as excretory organs. They produce the hormones **angiotensin I** and **angiotensin II.** Both of these aid in the regulation of blood pressure, in response to variations in salt and water balance. **Erythropoietin** is another kidney hormone. It increases red blood cell production by stimulating cells in the bone marrow.

Other regulating substances in the body have been either suspected or found, although their sources have not yet been identified. It is practically certain that some of them will turn out to be hormones.

The prostaglandins

Recently an entirely new group of chemical control substances, the **prostaglandins,** has been discovered in mammals. These compounds appear to function in much the same way as hormones. But instead of being produced by specialized endocrine tissues or glands, the prostaglandins are apparently synthesized by virtually all the body tissues. Unlike other regulatory substances in the body, the prostaglandins are fatty acids. It has been suggested that they can inhibit or encourage the action of hormones on the cells.

Prostaglandins may have important medical uses. They are involved in blood clotting, fever, the breakdown of fat cells, hypertension, fertility, reproduction, and other activities. Already they are being used in treatment of high blood pressure, various allergic reactions, and infertility. They are being studied as the possible basis for an absolutely safe and reliable means of contraception.

HORMONAL REGULATION IN INVERTEBRATES

Chemical or hormonal coordination occurs not only in vertebrates but also in invertebrates, such as crustaceans and insects. Our present understanding of hormone function in these organisms is far from complete. However, a good deal has been learned about hormones in arthropods, especially the insects.

Most of the insect hormones thus far identified seem to be concerned with growth and development. In certain insects, though, researchers have also found hormones that control color changes of the epidermis, regulate levels of blood sugar, and control other metabolic functions.

PATTERNS OF MAINTENANCE
AND REGULATION

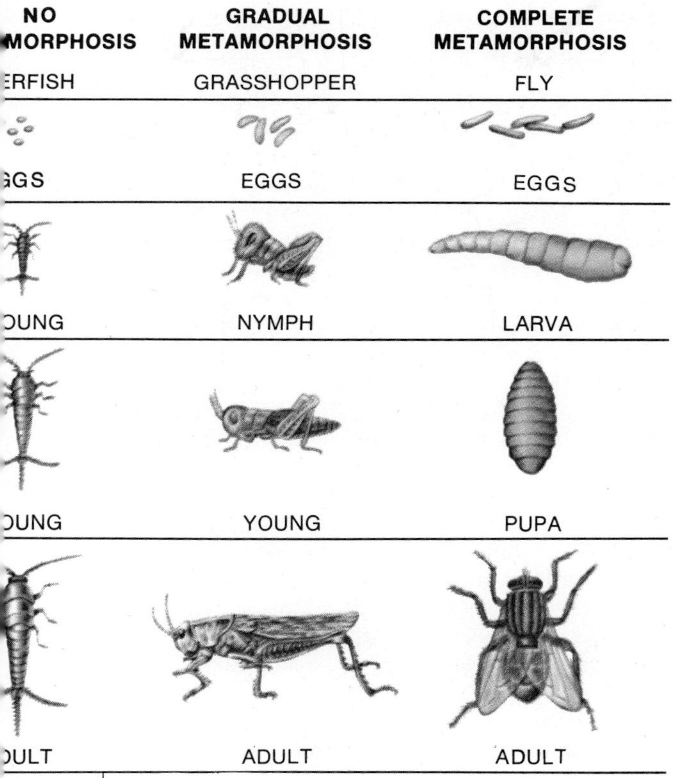

NO METAMORPHOSIS	GRADUAL METAMORPHOSIS	COMPLETE METAMORPHOSIS
SILVERFISH	GRASSHOPPER	FLY
EGGS	EGGS	EGGS
YOUNG	NYMPH	LARVA
YOUNG	YOUNG	PUPA
ADULT	ADULT	ADULT

Figure 9-12. Three patterns of insect development.

There are three general types of life cycle in insects, and hormones play an important part in each of them. The simplest type does not include any **metamorphosis,** or change of form. This type of cycle is seen in several orders of wingless insects, including the familiar silverfish. The eggs of such insects hatch into young that are exactly like adults except for size and maturity. Thereafter, the young grow in size through the molting process we discussed in chapter 7.

A second type of life cycle, known as **gradual metamorphosis,** is found in many common insects such as cockroaches, grasshoppers, and dragonflies. When the young emerge from the egg they are somewhat like miniature adults. However, they have an enlarged head, their wings are undeveloped and they lack reproductive organs. This immature form is called a **nymph.** It molts several times as it grows, emerging from the final molt as a fully developed adult with mature wings and a complete reproductive system.

The third type of insect life cycle, **complete metamorphosis,** is the most complex and by far the most usual. It occurs in flies, moths, beetles, and bees, to list some familiar examples. The insect passes through four stages—egg, larva, pupa, and adult.

The egg hatches into a **larva,** completely different from the adult in structure, habitat, and feeding habits. The crawling caterpillar with a chewing mouth is a larva; its adult form is the winged butterfly with a mouth designed for sucking. This vast difference between larval and adult forms probably has adaptive value. It permits the larva to occupy an environmental niche completely different from that of the adult. Consequently, larvae and adults do not compete.

The larva eats continuously and increases in size. After a number of molts, it changes into a **pupa,** enclosed in either a hard case or a soft cocoon which it usually secretes itself. The pupal phase has often been called

THE MONARCH BUTTERFLY

It is October in Pacific Grove, California, and the trees are brilliant with their autumn colors. But wait a minute! Autumn leaves in southern California? Well, not really. As a matter of fact, the bright black-and-rust color pattern is actually made by the wings of hundreds of thousands of hibernating monarch butterflies. Pacific Grove takes considerable pride in its spectacular winter visitors. It calls itself "Butterfly Town" and levies a large fine on anyone foolish enough to disturb the sleeping insects.

Pacific Grove is not the only American town to welcome the monarch butterfly with the onset of colder weather. Every year, vast numbers of butterflies winter along the warm southern coasts of North America. And every spring, the insects leave to spend the summer in cooler climates. Millions of the fragile-looking creatures take part in this annual voyage across distances often greater than 1,000 miles, with the flocks returning to the same sites year after year. Some of these North American natives have been spotted as far away as Europe and Australia.

About the only thing the monarch seems unable to cross is the Rocky Mountains. Scientists have studied the butterfly's migratory patterns by marking individuals with thin paper tags. They have found that monarchs from the eastern United States and Canada migrate to Florida and the Caribbean, while those on the other side of the Rockies go to southern California and western Mexico. Recently one wintering place for millions of eastern monarchs was discovered in a small mountain grove a few miles north of Mexico City. One tagged butterfly was discovered to have traveled from eastern Canada to Mexico over the course of four months—a distance of nearly 1,900 miles.

For most monarchs, their long migration is a one-way trip. With a life-span of only nine months, few if any butterflies ever live long enough to complete the return trip. It is a tribute to their amazing endurance that the butterflies survive their long journey. For a creature of its size, the monarch flies at astounding speeds—a steady rate of 10 miles an hour and up to 30 miles an hour in spurts.

The migration route of the monarch butterfly is determined in part by the presence of milkweed. The leaves of certain milkweed plants are the monarch larva's only food, and it is on the underside of these leaves that each female lays hundreds of

eggs. After a few days, the eggs hatch and tiny larvae emerge. Over the next two weeks, the larva feeds on the leaves and grows into a full-sized caterpillar. The caterpillar becomes a pupa and eventually emerges from the cocoon as a butterfly. After briefly drying its wings, the newly emerged butterfly immediately takes flight and instinctively joins in the migration.

At one time, the migration of insects was believed to be caused by nothing more complex than changes in wind direction. We now know, however, that the butterfly is as likely to fly against the wind as with it. No one knows why these insects engage in their arduous migration. It is easy enough to understand the trip south in response to cold weather and a shortening day, but how can we explain the insects's return to the north at the end of March? Perhaps the lengthening days have something to do with it.

Another mystery is that of the butterfly's guidance system. How does generation after generation of monarch butterflies follow the same route and arrive at the same destination almost a thousand miles away from where it was born? Some scientists believe that the monarch orients itself according to the position of the sun, much as migratory birds do. Others theorize that the

male monarch leaves a scent-trail in the air that allows subsequent generations to follow the same route and to rest on the same trees year after year. But could any animal, however sharp its senses, follow a year-old odor trail? No one knows.

How does the monarch butterfly avoid being eaten by predators during its long flight? Some milkweeds contain in their milky sap substances known as cardenolides, which are potent heart poisons to certain birds. By feeding on the bitter milkweed sap during its larval stage, the monarch butterfly renders itself highly unpalatable to crows, bluejays, and other would-be predators. A bird that carelessly swallows a monarch will generally vomit it up in a hurry, and be extremely wary of the insect's distinctive scent and coloration in the future.

Unfortunately for the monarch, some predators are unaffected by the poisons. Mice, for instance, apparently regard hibernating monarchs as a choice feast. And the plump little Japanese quail can swallow enough digitalis (another cardenolide) to kill fifty humans, without seeming to suffer any harm. Perhaps the monarchs should redirect their migrations to a mouse-less, quail-less destination. An oil rig in the Gulf of Mexico, perhaps?

a resting state. But during this period of apparent dormancy, an immense number of internal changes are taking place. Many of the animal's tissues break down completely into a formless, soupy mass. This is then reorganized into the adult form, beginning from the **imaginal discs**—bodies that were present but undeveloped in the larva. The adult finally emerges from the pupa to take up an entirely different mode of existence.

Hormones and metamorphosis

The processes of molting and maturation in insects are controlled by three hormones. **Brain hormone,** secreted by cells in the brain, activates glands in the thorax to secrete the molting hormone, **ecdysone.** Ecdysone apparently causes the cells of the epidermis to divide and to develop a new exoskeleton. This is followed by molting of the old exoskeleton.

The third hormone, known as **juvenile hormone,** is secreted by glands near the insect's brain. In gradual metamorphosis, so long as juvenile hormone is present, a nymph will simply become a larger nymph at each molting. It will not become an adult. When the hormone is no longer secreted, the nymph changes to an adult at the next molt. In complete metamorphosis, the absence of juvenile hormone permits the larva to become a pupa.

HORMONAL REGULATION IN PLANTS

Hormones in plants are not produced by separate, specialized organs, as in animals. Most of the known plant hormones are produced by tissues in parts of the plant undergoing active growth. Also, most of them seem to be concerned only with regulation of growth patterns. A number of important plant hormones and their functions have been identified so far.

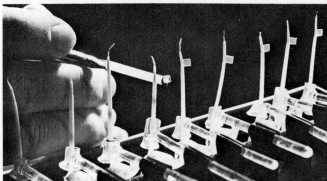

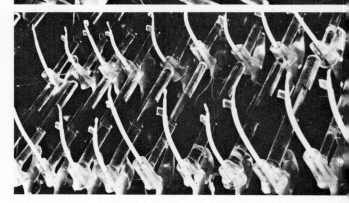

Figure 9-13. The effect of auxin on growth is shown in this sequence of photographs. Tips of oat seedlings are placed on agar blocks (top). The agar blocks are then affixed to one side of the oat seedling stems (middle). In less than two hours, the stems have curved (bottom).

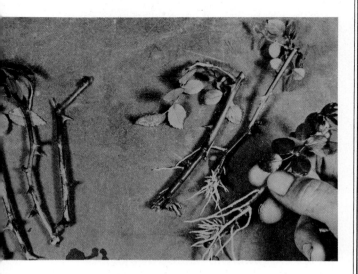

Figure 9-14. The rose cuttings at the right were dipped in a solution of indolebutyric acid, a growth hormone, and then allowed to stand in moist sand for three weeks. The other cuttings were dipped in water only before being allowed to stand for the same length of time.

Auxin

We have all seen that plants bend toward the light, a tendency called **phototropism** (from two Greek words meaning "light" and "turning"). Phototropism results from a more rapid elongation of cells on the shaded side of the plant.

A variety of experiments have shown that this faster growth is caused by a hormone. If the tip of a seedling stem is cut off or covered with foil, the stem will not bend toward the light. This is true even though the part of the stem which would actually bend is below the tip, and may not have been cut off or covered. The obvious conclusion is that bending is controlled by the effect of light on the tip.

A further experiment demonstrates that this control is chemical in nature. If the seedling tip is cut off and a layer of gelatin or agar is placed between the tip and the stem, the stem will still bend below the cut. The controlling factor, then, has passed through the agar, so it must be a chemical. This chemical is **auxin,** a hormone produced by the cells of the growing tip. Light causes auxin to be more concentrated on the shaded side of the stem, and so causes the cells on this side to elongate rapidly.

Another effect of auxin is **geotropism** ("earth-turning"), a plant's response to gravity. If you turn a plant on its side and leave it for a time, its stem will begin to turn upward again, away from the earth. Likewise, its roots will begin to turn downward. In both stem and roots, auxin has become more concentrated in the cells on the lower side, apparently in response to gravity. In the stem, this has the same effect as in phototropism—the cells with a high auxin concentration elongate rapidly, turning the stem's direction of growth away from that side. But in the roots it has the opposite effect, inhibiting cell elongation. Therefore the normal elongation of the unaffected cells turns the root's direction of growth downward. Why this difference? It is known that in many cells, a low concentration of auxin promotes growth, while a high concentration inhibits it. Apparently root cells are more sensitive than stem cells: they are inhibited by a concentration that would stimulate stem cells.

Auxin also controls a variety of other plant movements, such as growth responses to touch, to water, to chemicals, and to electric fields. It influences the enlargement of cells, the beginning of root formation, and the growth of the cambium.

Synthetic auxins

Increasing study of plant hormones has given us considerable knowledge of their chemical structures. As a result, we have been able to develop a variety of related synthetic compounds with effects similar to those of auxin. Along with natural auxin, these synthetics are valuable agricultural tools.

In low concentrations, as we saw above, auxins promote growth, but in higher concentrations they inhibit growth and can be lethal. An important weed killer, 2,4-D, is a substance that in very low concentrations has properties similar to those of natural auxin. For some reason, it is especially effective against non-grasses. Thus it can be used as a broadleaf weed killer in relatively low concentrations, without harming lawns or grain crops.

In some plants, flower formation can be retarded or—very occasionally—induced by auxins. The pineapple, for example, can be brought to flower and produce its fruit weeks early when sprayed with a synthetic auxin. Certain auxins can be used to produce seedless tomatoes, watermelons, and cucumbers. Still others are used to stimulate root growth in cuttings.

The developing seeds in fruit produce auxin, causing the fruit to develop. When the seeds ripen, auxin production ceases and the fruit falls. Commercial growers take advantage of this by using hormones to prevent fruit from falling prematurely, so that it can all be harvested at once.

Apical dominance

When the terminal bud of a plant is removed, the lateral branches begin to grow more profusely. This is why trimming a hedge or "pinching back" a plant encourages bushier growth. The terminal bud produces auxin, which inhibits the growth of lateral branches. This influence is called **apical dominance.** This is another instance in which auxin stimulates growth in some tissues while retarding it in others.

Experiments have demonstrated that the degree of apical dominance determines the type of growth in many plants. In a comparison of two species of aster, one species was shorter and bushier, with many more lateral branches. When the amount of growth hormone produced by each species was measured, the bushier species was found to produce only 75 percent as much auxin as the taller species.

Other plant hormones

In addition to auxin, four other plant hormones are known, and many more are suspected. One of the four is **ethylene,** a hydrocarbon gas that is closely linked with auxin. If slightly more auxin is produced than promotes growth, the plant produces more ethylene. Some botanists believe that it is this ethylene, not the oversupply of auxin, that inhibits growth. The ripening of fruits is caused by the ethylene they produce, and added ethylene will speed ripening.

Another known plant hormone is **gibberellin.** Most dwarf varieties of plants produce much less gibberellin than the tall varieties. If a gibberellin solution is sprayed on the dwarfs they will grow as high as the tall varieties. Adding gibberellin also causes many plants to bloom earlier than they ordinarily would.

Cytokinins are essential for cell division in plants. Thus, along with auxin, they are absolutely necessary for growth. Also, if applied to the petioles of leaves, they will keep the leaves from aging and turning yellow.

Abscissic acid is a hormone that promotes the falling of leaves, or abscission, and inhibits growth. It causes buds to become dormant at the onset of short autumn days, and prevents them from growing in winter.

Photoperiodism

The period of light that plants must receive during a day in order to flower is called the **photoperiod.** Certain species, including chrysanthemums, poinsettias, and potatoes, will flower only if they receive less than a certain critical length of light per day. In natural circumstances, this occurs during the early spring, late summer, or fall. Such

PATTERNS OF MAINTENANCE
AND REGULATION

Figure 9-15. The apple seedling at the left has grown normally. Auxin from the terminal bud has inhibited lateral branch development. The terminal bud was removed from the apple seedling at the right. Without the terminal bud's auxin, lateral branches developed.

Figure 9-16. This common dandelion is an indeterminate plant. Its flowering is apparently unrelated to the amount of daylight it receives.

plants are called "short-day" plants. However, they might better be called "long-night" plants, since experiments demonstrate that the length of uninterrupted darkness is what really determines when they flower. "Long-night" plants can be kept from flowering by extending the light period with artificial illumination, or by interrupting the long dark period with a few minutes of bright light. They can also be forced to flower when nights are short, by keeping them in darkness for the necessary time.

"Long-day" plants, such as beets, clover, and radishes, will flower only when the photoperiod is more than a certain critical length. These "short-night" plants normally flower in the late spring or summer. Certain indeterminate plants, such as beans, tomatoes, and sunflowers, seem to be unaffected by the length of daylight they receive. Their time of flowering is apparently controlled by other factors, such as temperature, moisture, and number of leaves.

It is not completely understood how the length of darkness affects the time of flowering, but a pigment, **phytochrome,** is involved. When the proper photoperiod occurs, changes in the phytochrome set off a complex series of reactions that apparently trigger the production of a hormone, tentatively known as **florigen,** in the leaves. The florigen presumably moves through the phloem to other parts of the plant, and stimulates the production of flowers. The chemical identity of florigen has not yet been determined; it may be different in different plants.

The understanding of photoperiodism is of economic importance, since it enables florists and agriculturalists to force out-of-season flowering. It has also led to investigations regarding the effect of light on animal reproductive activities. Researchers are particularly eager to learn the mechanism that triggers production of the flowering hormone in response to the photoperiod. It may be closely connected to other rhythmic processes that seem to be present in all organisms.

SUMMARY

Multicellular organisms must have a means of coordinating their various systems. Coordination is controlled by the nervous system and the endocrine system. The endocrine glands secrete hormones, activator substances that are released directly into the bloodstream. The study of a hormone often involves observation of the effects when the body contains too little or too much of it. "Secretin" was the first hormone to be isolated and identified, in 1902. Hormones influence cellular activities and coordinate reactions of various organs. A mechanism of negative feedback enables them to either stimulate or inhibit a response.

The hypothalamus of the brain has an endocrine function, since it produces secretions that influence hormone production by the anterior pituitary, or hypophysis. The anterior pituitary produces growth hormone, thyroid-stimulating hormone, adrenocorticotrophic hormone, and at least two gonadotrophic hormones. The intermediate pituitary secretes melanocyte-stimulating hormone. The posterior pituitary, which is a structural part of the hypothalamus, produces vasopressin and oxytocin.

Each adrenal gland consists of the adrenal medulla and the adrenal cortex. The adrenal medulla secretes epinephrine and norepinephrine, which prepare the body to meet fight-or-flight situations. The hormones of the adrenal cortex control blood pressure, regulate blood sodium, potassium, and glucose, and help maintain salt and water balance in the body.

The thyroid produces thyroxin and triiodothyronine, which regulate cellular respiration. Neither can be produced without the presence of iodine. The thyroid also secretes calcitonin, which decreases blood calcium levels. The parathyroid glands produce parathormone, which raises blood calcium and acts antagonistically with calcitonin.

The pancreas secretes insulin, glucagon, and gastrin. Insulin and glucagon work antagonistically to maintain a proper level of blood glucose. The function of gastrin is not yet certain. Insufficient production of insulin results in the disease called diabetes, which can be controlled by daily injections of insulin.

The prostaglandins are a recently discovered group of chemical control substances. They are synthesized by nearly every type of mammalian body tissue. They may inhibit or encourage hormonal action of the cells, and have valuable medical uses.

Insect life cycles are of three types. The simplest does not involve metamorphosis. The two others involve gradual metamorphosis and complete metamorphosis. Metamorphosis is controlled by brain hormone, ecdysone, and juvenile hormone.

Plant hormones are produced mainly in the growing tissues. Auxin controls plant movements such as phototropism and geotropism. Synthetic auxins are valuable agricultural tools. Other plant hormones include ethylene, which stimulates ripening; gibberellin, which stimulates growth; and the cytokinins, which are essential to cell division.

The photoperiod is the amount of daily light (or nightly darkness) which plants must have to flower. Flowering is apparently controlled by a hormone called florigen, but the exact process is not fully understood.

Review questions

1. Define the term "hormone" and describe the two ways in which hormones function.

2. Define negative feedback and describe an example.

3. Using the example from question 2, describe what would happen if negative feedback did not exist.

4. How does the hypothalamus take part in hormonal control?

PATTERNS OF MAINTENANCE AND REGULATION

5. List five endocrine glands and their hormones.

6. Why is the pituitary called the "master gland?"

7. What symptom would appear in both sexes if the posterior pituitary failed to secrete its hormones?

8. Describe the functions of the adrenal medulla.

9. Why can "stage fright" be helpful to a performer?

10. List some functions of the adrenal cortex.

11. What hormones are secreted by the thyroid? What is their function?

12. Explain why hyperthyroidism and hypothyroidism can both be accompanied by enlargement of the thyroid.

13. A doctor observes a patient with abnormally heavy bleeding from a minor cut. He notices that uncontrollable muscle twitching is also present. What hormone deficiency might he suspect?

14. Why are the parathyroids important to homeostasis?

15. What symptoms might appear if the pancreas secreted too little glucagon? Too much insulin?

16. List three theories which might explain how hormones cause changes in cells.

17. What is unusual about the chemical makeup of prostaglandins?

18. List the three types of insect life cycle.

19. What might happen to a caterpillar if its glands failed to secrete ecdysone? If they did not secrete juvenile hormone?

20. Where are plant hormones produced?

21. List several functions of auxin.

22. Name three other plant hormones and their functions.

23. What type of plant might be expected to contain very little abscissic acid?

24. What would happen to a bouquet of blooming flowers placed next to a bowl of ripe apples? What would happen to a green tomato?

25. What is the photoperiod of a plant?

26. In what two ways can out-of-season flowering be stimulated?

Nervous System Regulation

The ability to react to changes in the environment is a basic function of all living things. The cells of all organisms are **irritable**—that is, they are sensitive to stimuli from their surroundings, and can react to these stimuli. Each time an organism receives a stimulus, information about it must be communicated to other parts of the organism so that any necessary adjustments can be made. Maintenance of homeostasis is based on this system of communication and coordination.

In the more complex unicellular organisms, such as *Paramecia*, specialized organelles often assist in communication and coordination. But in multicellular animals, stimulation and reaction to the stimulus may involve thousands of cells. Furthermore, information about a change in the environment may be received by a part of the organism that is far away from some of the parts that must react to the change.

We have already examined, in chapter 9, the hormonal systems that help to integrate cell functions in widely separated parts of the organism. But the action of hormones is usually gradual. Since they are transported through the bloodstream, a certain amount of time must pass before they can reach their targets and take effect. Some hormones, including those involved in the fight-or-flight reactions, can produce a response in a matter of minutes. But minutes are too long if the stimulus is a charging rhinoceros. Obviously, multicellular animals need a speedier means of coordination. The specialized cells, tissues, and organs of the nervous system permit quick perception of changes in the environment and a correspondingly rapid response by the entire organism.

189

Nervous systems, at least in the sense of specialized impulse-conducting systems, exist only in animals. While plants are sensitive to external change and can respond slowly to stimuli, they lack a true nervous system. They are dependent on nutritional and hormonal coordination. Moreover, this coordination is largely concerned with growth and development, rather than with what is usually defined as behavior.

NEURONS: THE BASIC UNIT

The specialized cells that receive stimuli and transmit them are basically the same in all multicellular animals. These nerve cells, or **neurons,** carry on the same vital processes as other cells. However, they cannot reproduce themselves. Most biologists believe that human beings are born with all the neurons that they will have during their entire lifetimes.

The structure of neurons

Like other cells, each neuron contains a nucleus and cytoplasm. One or more projections, or **processes,** extend from the main cell body. Some are branched, and are called **dendrites.** Their function is to receive incoming stimuli or nerve impulses. The **axon,** or nerve fiber, is longer, and is usually unbranched except at the very tip. The branches, or filaments, of the axon often end in rounded **synaptic knobs,** which lie next to the dendrites of another neuron or against a muscle or gland cell. Axons conduct impulses away from the cell body and pass them on.

Axons, except those in the brain and spinal cord, are covered by a single layer of **Schwann cells.** These cells provide nutrients and also a pathway for regeneration of a severed axon. Often the Schwann cells wrap themselves around the axon almost like a rolled bolt of cloth, forming a **myelin sheath** made up of their fatty cell membranes.

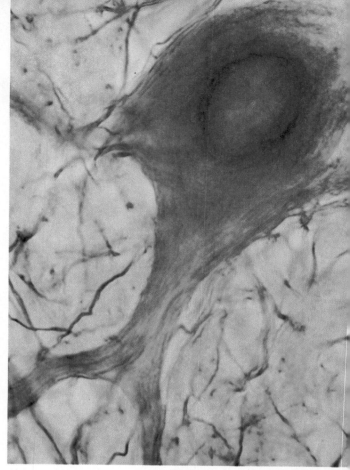

Figure 10-1. The neuron is the basic unit of the nervous system.

Myelin gives the axon a whitish color; in contrast, unmyelinated axons are grey. The myelin sheath acts as an insulator. It prevents impulses from leaping to nearby axons and assists in the conduction of impulses along its own axon.

If a neuron with a Schwann-cell myelin sheath is damaged, it can repair itself if the cell body has not been injured. If its nucleus has been destroyed, the neuron will die, and there will be no new one to replace it. The paralysis that often follows poliomyelitis occurs because the polio virus has attacked and destroyed the nuclei of many neurons.

Axons can be very short or more than several feet in length. One of the longest axons in the human body, that of the **femoral**

PATTERNS OF MAINTENANCE
AND REGULATION

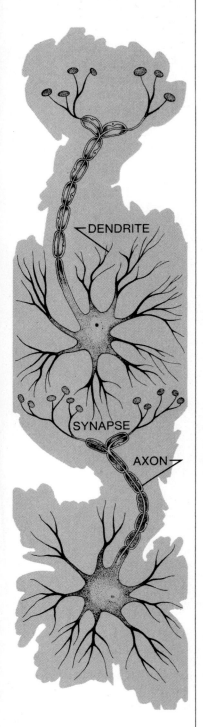

DENDRITE

SYNAPSE

AXON

Figure 10-2. The structure of neurons. Axon and dendrites are branches of the neuron's cytoplasm. An axon can extend out several feet from the main cell body.

nerve, extends from the spinal cord to the big toe. Despite its length, the axon is still microscopically thin. Some animals, such as the squid and certain annelid worms, possess giant axons that are over a millimeter thick and can be seen with the naked eye. Because these axons are so large, they have proved very valuable to laboratory study of nerve function.

A **nerve** (not to be confused with nerve cell) is composed of a group or bundle of axons. In most living organisms, nerves look like tendons or white cords. The thickest human nerve is the **sciatic,** which runs from the lower back into the thigh and may be as much as a half-inch thick.

Surprisingly, most of the cells that make up the nervous system are not neurons at all. Nearly half of the human brain is composed of so-called **neuroglial cells.** The neuroglia are only now beginning to be studied in detail and many of their functions are still uncertain. They form the myelin sheath of axons in the brain and spinal cord, and they may possibly supply nutrients. Schwann cells, too, are now considered a variety of neuroglia. One form of neuroglial cell is phagocytic (see chapter 8) and may act to destroy foreign cells or dead tissue in the event of injury or disease.

The nerve impulse

The method by which the neuron transmits nerve impulses is electrochemical in nature. To understand how the impulse travels, it is necessary to review a few facts about the electrical charges of atoms. As you will recall (chapter 2), neutral atoms have a nucleus containing one or more positively charged protons. The nucleus is balanced by an equal number of negatively charged electrons. Ions are atoms that have lost or gained electrons. They have either a positive charge, when they have lost electrons, or a negative charge, when they have gained electrons. Charged ions tend to return to their neutral state by gaining or losing electrons. The movement of electrons, either from a negatively charged body or to a positively charged body, produces an electric current. In fact, electricity itself may be defined as the movement of electrons.

There is normally a difference in the charge between the inside of a living neuron and the liquid surrounding it. Such a difference in charge is called a **potential.** When it is inactive, or **resting,** the neuron contains a high concentration of potassium ions, and is surrounded by a high concentration of sodium ions. The membrane is more permeable to potassium than to sodium. Therefore, potassium ions tend to diffuse out of the neuron faster, or in greater quantity, than sodium ions diffuse in. Both types of ion have a positive ionic charge, so in effect the neuron is losing positive ions (potassium) faster than it is replacing them (sodium). This may explain why the inside of the neuron has a negative electrical charge, relative to the outside. The cell's potential at this stage is known as the **resting potential.** It is the potential normally carried by an inactive or unstimulated neuron. In this situation—that is, when it has a positive charge on one side and a relatively negative charge on the other—the membrane is said to be **polarized.**

A stimulus upsets the resting condition of the neuron by increasing the permeability of the cell membrane to sodium. When the dendrites are stimulated, the membrane becomes more permeable to the sodium ions outside it. These ions flow in more rapidly, making the charge within the cell more positive. Almost immediately, the membrane returns to its normal permeability for sodium. The net effect is that the membrane's polarity is first neutralized and then reversed. An electrically measurable current is generated, stimulating the next area of the membrane. This portion thus becomes more permeable to sodium ions, and the current travels along the membrane, transmitting the impulse. The minimum strength of stimulus that is needed to begin a nerve impulse is called the **threshold intensity.**

When the polarity of an area of mem-

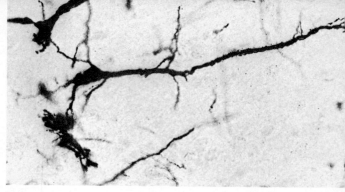

Figure 10-3. A nerve is composed of several neurons. The axon of one neuron and the dendrites of the next are close together at a point called the synapse.

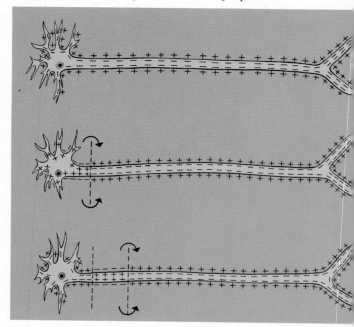

Figure 10-4. The resting neuron (top) is polarized in its environment. Pluses and minuses indicate positive and negative charges. When the dendrites are stimulated (center), the membrane becomes more permeable to the sodium ions. Polarity is first neutralized and then reversed, causing the adjacent area of the membrane also to become permeable to sodium ions (bottom) and thus allowing the impulse to travel along the axon.

brane is completely reversed, that area can no longer respond to a stimulus. No more sodium ions can enter. This period is called the **absolute refractory period,** and lasts for about 0.5 milliseconds. There follows a **relative refractory period** of a few milliseconds, during which the membrane is returning to its normal state. In the first part of this period, the membrane becomes more permeable to potassium, and potassium ions flow out of the cell. Thus the interior of the cell becomes negative—even more negative than it was at its resting potential. Then the membrane returns to its normal permeability for potassium, and the rapid potassium flow ceases. Excess sodium ions are pumped out; potassium ions are pumped back in; and the membrane gradually returns to its resting potential. Moving the sodium ions back across the membrane requires a means of active transport, often called a **sodium pump** or an **ion pump.** That the ion pump is active is shown by the fact that the rate of cellular respiration increases during the relative refractory period. This indicates that additional energy is being used.

During the relative refractory period, the membrane can respond to a stimulus, but the stimulus must be strong enough to overcome the "push" of the sodium ions that are returning to their original place. Since the stimulus must be stronger than when the neuron is resting, we say that the **threshold level** is higher at this stage. The nearer the membrane gets to its normal resting state, the lower the threshold level becomes, and the smaller the stimulus needed to activate it. At the end of the relative refractory period, the membrane is once again in its original polarized state. It can now respond fully to a new stimulus.

These changes can be measured with special electrical equipment, producing a curve on a recording unit called an oscilloscope. The curve is known as an **action potential curve.** Because of this, the nerve impulse itself is sometimes referred to as an action potential.

The amounts of sodium and potassium ions that cross the membrane during a single impulse are very small, not enough to produce a measurable change in the concentrations of these ions. But with many impulses the concentrations would change.

Unless sodium is pumped out of the cell and potassium pumped in, the concentration gradients for these ions would become very slight. A stimulus to the cell would not produce enough change in polarity to transmit an impulse. Thus the role of the active transport system for sodium and potassium is indirect. It does not serve directly to conduct nerve impulses, but it sets up and maintains the gradients that are needed for conducting impulses.

Normally, nerve impulses move in only one direction through the nervous system. An impulse enters the neuron through a dendrite, and leaves by way of the axon. The impulse passes from neuron to neuron at the point where the axon filaments of one neuron lie very close to the dendrite of the next. This point is called the **synapse.** However, the neurons do not actually touch each other at this junction. Somehow, the impulse must jump the **synaptic cleft,** the tiny gap between them.

When a nerve impulse arrives at the synapse, it stimulates the ends of the axon to release a **neurotransmitter chemical.** Several such chemicals have been identified; among the most common are **acetylcholine** and **norepinephrine.** The neurotransmitter serves to transfer the nerve impulse across the synaptic cleft. Only the axon terminals can secrete the chemicals needed for transmission, and only the dendrites are sensitive to it. Once the nerve impulse has crossed the gap, the neurotransmitter chemical is destroyed by an enzyme. The synapse is then ready to receive and transmit a new impulse.

Many neurons may come close to one another at a single synapse, and each carries a separate item of information. Not all these neurons are **excitatory** in their action. That is, not all stimulate the next neuron to transmit an impulse. On the contrary, some are **inhibitory,** interfering with impulse transmission. Depending on the number of neurons of each type that are stimulated, the total number of impulses transmitted in a given time can be modified. This in turn modifies, or modulates, the strength of the response to the stimulus. For instance, it influences whether you swing your arm lazily or punch your neighbor in the jaw. Thus the integrated action of excitatory and inhibitory neurons allows the organism to adjust the strength of its response to the demands of the stimulating situation.

Nerve impulses can travel at speeds of up to 200 miles per hour, depending on the thickness and the degree of insulation of the nerve fibers. In a six-foot man, an impulse

but also by whether or not the axon has a myelin sheath. Myelin is an excellent insulator; therefore sheathed nerve fibers can conduct impulses much faster than those without the sheath. Between the individual Schwann cells are tiny gaps in the myelin sheath, where the axon is not covered. These gaps are called **nodes of Ranvier.** The nerve impulse is delayed very slightly at these nodes; thus it can travel fastest where the nodes are farthest apart, and the segments of myelin are fairly long. Occasionally the

TICKLE YOUR BRAIN TO STOP PAIN?

John Doe was enjoying a quiet evening in front of the TV set. Gradually he became aware that his arthritic hip was starting to ache painfully. He picked up a small book-sized box from beside his chair, held it against his chest, and pressed a button on it. A few minutes later, the arthritis pain vanished. Mr. Doe was comfortable, and would remain so for at least 24 hours.

The box contained nothing more than a few batteries. What Mr. Doe had done was stimulate a certain part of his brain by transmitting an electrical charge into receivers implanted

in his chest. From the receivers, the charge was carried by thin wires running under his skin up to his medial brain stem. This area, located in the middle of the brain, apparently contains a pain-inhibiting chemical with a structure similar to that of morphine. Electrical stimulation of certain parts of the medial brain stem can cause this chemical to act. Little is known of the biochemistry of the substance, save that it is a peptide, a short chain of amino acids.

Neuroscientists are testing 17 other patients who suffer from chronic pain of one sort or another. Like John Doe, they too carry portable battery packs which enable them to relieve pain by electrically tickling their medial brain stems. One patient has used such a device successfully for over two years.

can travel from head to toe in one-fiftieth of a second. Such high speed makes possible almost instantaneous coordination. Interestingly, too, the nerve fibers that transmit touch sensations in humans are thicker, and therefore transmit impulses faster, than those that transmit heat. This is why, when you touch a hot stove, you are aware of touching it a split second before you realize that you are getting burned.

The speed of a nerve impulse is determined not only by the diameter of the axon,

myelin sheath deteriorates, and impulse transmission is slowed. This occurs in a number of degenerative nerve diseases; one of the most familiar is multiple sclerosis.

In vertebrates, most axons outside of the central nervous system (spinal cord and brain) possess a myelin sheath. However, vertebrates do not have the fastest rate of nerve impulse. That distinction belongs to the great squid we mentioned a few pages back. The nerves of the squid are not sheathed; rather, the high speed of their im-

PATTERNS OF MAINTENANCE
AND REGULATION

pulses is due to the enormous size of their axons.

A given neuron will conduct all impulses at one speed, regardless of the strength of the stimulus. Furthermore, every impulse will be equally strong. The neuron will respond to the stimulus either completely or not at all; there is no half measure. The nerve impulse cannot become larger or smaller or change in any other way. Any stimulus—electrical, mechanical, or chemical—that can stimulate a particular neuron will produce an impulse of the same strength, traveling at the same speed. This is known as the **"all-or-none" law** of conduction. Once the threshold intensity has been reached, the strength of the impulse remains the same, no matter how much stronger the stimulus may become. What may change is the **frequency**—how often the neuron produces an impulse in a given period of time. Above the threshold intensity, a stronger stimulus will produce greater frequency, until the limit of the neuron's capacity is reached.

NERVE PATHWAYS

All coordination involving nerves is the result of a response, or reaction, to a stimulus. The simplest type of response is called a **reflex action.** It is an automatic, involuntary response to stimulation of certain specific nerves.

The simplest nerve pathway is the **reflex arc.** In lower animals the reflex arc may involve only two neurons. In higher animals, additional neurons usually take part, and the pathway is therefore more complex. In the most basic form of reflex arc, a **sensory** or **afferent** neuron receives the stimulus from a **receptor.** ("Afferent" comes from the Latin *ad ferre*, "to carry toward.") The receptor may be any sensory organ or another nerve ending. The nerve impulse thus created travels along the axon of the sensory neuron and crosses a synapse to the dendrite of a

motor, or **efferent** neuron (*ex ferre*, "to carry from"). As the impulse continues, it passes down the axon of the motor neuron to an **effector**—a muscle or a gland—where the reaction to the original stimulus takes place. In vertebrates, the synapse between sensory and motor neurons takes place in the brain or spinal cord, which we will discuss later in the chapter.

Reflex arcs are most common in lower animals. However, they are also present in higher animals, including humans. Tickle a dog's belly at a certain spot, for instance, and his automatic response is a scratching motion with one hind leg. This is one familiar example of a reflex arc. Another is the contraction of the muscles around the pupil of the eye in response to bright light. This response is involuntary and uncontrollable; usually the individual is not even aware that it is taking place. In this reflex arc the nerve impulse travels from the eye into a "non-thinking" area of the brain. From there it is relayed to the muscles in the iris, causing them to contract and make the pupil smaller, so that less light enters.

Some reflexes can be suppressed or altered by conscious action. Blinking is an example, although this response cannot be delayed indefinitely. The knee-jerk reflex, which is routinely tested during a physical examination, can also be voluntarily suppressed.

Simple and complex reflex arcs
It is easy to demonstrate a simple reflex arc in the frog. The brain is first destroyed so that no brain control can possibly influence the reaction. This procedure does not kill a cold-blooded animal immediately, although it causes permanent unconsciousness. The neurons can continue to live for several hours. If the skin of the frog's foot is then stimulated by a pinch, the leg will pull upward in response. The stimulus (pinch) causes an impulse that travels to the spinal cord, and the reaction is the contraction of the leg muscles.

The complex reflex arc involves a third type of neuron. This is known as the **connector** or **intermediate** neuron. Intermediate neurons act as connections between sensory and motor neurons, permitting more complicated nerve pathways. They are sometimes called **associative** or **adjustor** neurons because they play an important role in the intricate connections required for thought in the brain.

In a complex nervous system, nerve impulses may pass through a five-part chain, as follows:

1. Receptors: these are usually specialized cells, often located in specialized receptor organs such as the eye and ear.

2. Sensory (afferent) nerve pathways

3. Modulator or relay: this appears to be mainly in either the brain or the spinal cord.

4. Motor (efferent) nerve pathways

5. Effectors: these are usually muscles or glands which perform the response to the original stimulus.

NERVOUS SYSTEMS IN INVERTEBRATES

Unicellular animals possess simple responsive systems that allow them to react to stimuli from their environment. In multicellular animals, the basis of coordination is the receptor–effector mechanism.

The cnidarian nervous system

The basic elements of a nervous system can be found in cnidarians. *Hydra* is a commonly studied cnidarian. Its nervous system has no central or controlling area, but rather forms a generalized **nerve net** throughout the body.

In contrast to the one-way transmission of nerve impulses in higher animals, the neurons and synapses of *Hydra's* nerve net appear to transmit impulses in all directions. For this reason a stimulus at any point of the nerve net can cause the entire animal

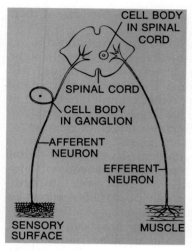

Figure 10-5. This diagram illustrates the simplest type of reflex arc.

Figure 10-6. Contraction of the muscles around the pupils of the eye is an example of a reflex arc. Here the eyes of a great horned owl react to darkness (top) and to sunlight (bottom).

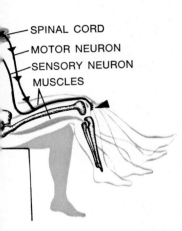

SPINAL CORD
MOTOR NEURON
SENSORY NEURON
MUSCLES

Figure 10-7. A simple reflex arc, such as the one involved in the knee-jerk reflex, allows the fastest possible reaction to stimuli.

Figure 10-8. The nervous system of *Hydra* forms a generalized nerve net through which impulses are transmitted in all directions.

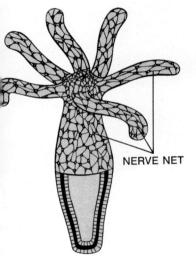

NERVE NET

to respond. Sensory cells in the outer layer of cells receive stimuli from the external environment. Those in the inner layer of cells receive stimuli from the animal's interior cavity. Impulses pass from stimulated sensory neurons to other neurons, and are transmitted throughout the body by means of the nerve net.

The jellyfish, another cnidarian, possesses a slightly more developed nervous system. In many jellyfish, the receptors form well-developed sense organs. Light-sensitive "eyespots" and specialized organs of balance are present. Two **nerve rings**

serve as a primitive control center to which other nerves are linked, allowing a certain amount of coordinated movement. If one of the animal's tentacles is stimulated by the presence of food, all the other tentacles can be brought into action for the capture. Other actions, such as swallowing, also result from interaction of many cells.

True central control, however, is still lacking in cnidarians. These animals are **radially symmetrical**—that is, their body parts are arranged around a central point, rather like the spokes of a wheel arranged around a hub. They have no front or rear. Their uncentralized nerve net allows them to perceive their environment equally well in all directions, and to react to it by movement in any direction.

Bilaterally symmetrical animals, on the other hand, have a definite anterior and posterior end. If the body of one of these organisms is split down the middle, the two halves are more or less mirror images of each other. Humans and all other vertebrates are bilaterally symmetrical. So are many invertebrates. When a bilaterally symmetrical animal moves, it ordinarily travels front end first. Its sense organs tend to be concentrated at this end, allowing it to perceive the environment toward which it is moving. Organisms structured in this way nearly always have some kind of central nervous system.

Development of central control

The first appearance of a true **central nervous system** may be seen in the flatworms, such as *Planaria*. In the anterior end of the flatworm, a concentration of sensory nerves joins with other neurons, forming a two-lobed mass of tissue that functions as a simple brain. The brain acts as a relay station, receiving stimuli—mainly from the head—and passing these stimuli to the rest of the body.

Two ventral **nerve cords** run from the brain to the posterior end of the planarian. The brain and these nerve cords together make up the central nervous system. They are the mechanism that transmits nerve impulses from one end of the animal to the other. From the central nervous system, branches reach out to all parts of the body and carry nerve impulses through the organism. These branches form the **peripheral nervous system.**

The peripheral nervous system permits planarians to behave in a more organized way than the cnidarians. The anterior end, with its primitive brain, relays information to all parts of the animal. But the entire body of the planarian does not respond to all stimuli. The parts can respond individually to stimuli that have been received elsewhere. As a result, the planarian is capable of more complex and varied behavior than the cnidarians. Its central nervous system enables it to organize, classify, and direct a response to the information it receives.

More complex mechanisms of control

In the annelid worms and the arthropods we find a type of nervous system that is typical of many complex organisms. A good example is the common earthworm. The earthworm has a central nervous system that includes the brain and a ventral nerve cord, and a peripheral nervous system that includes main nerves and their branches. Receptor, modulator, and effector neurons are all present. The modulators are located in the ventral nerve cord and the brain.

As in the planarians, most of the sensory areas are located in the anterior end of the earthworm. The nerve cells concentrated in this region form a **ganglion,** a compact mass of neurons that makes up the primitive brain. The earthworm's brain, though, is more complex than that of the planarian, for it must deal with impulses going to and from more structures.

The receptor neurons in the earthworm are varied and sensitive. Its modulator neurons permit a wide variety of connections between receptors and effectors. Most important, nerve impulses travel in only one

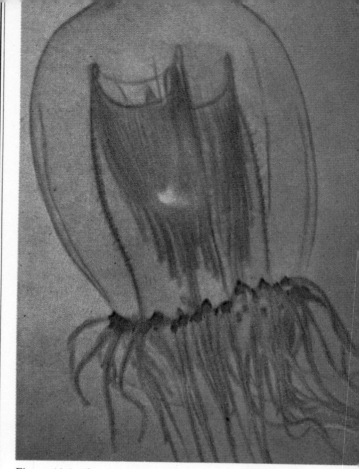

Figure 10-9. This jellyfish resembles an upside-down hydra in structure. Clusters of light-sensitive nerve cells appear as red blotches just above the tentacles.

direction through the system. This, together with the earthworm's more complex muscular system, allows more precise control over responses in different parts of the body.

Other ganglia are found in each of the earthworm's body segments. These **segmental ganglia** are only slightly smaller than the brain itself. They coordinate the nerves that branch off into each segment, and they can operate more or less independently of the brain. This independence is illustrated by the fact that severed pieces of an earthworm will continue to move

The brain of the arthropod is also a ganglion—usually a larger one than that of the annelid worm. Moreover, the arthropod possesses more complex sense organs in its

PATTERNS OF MAINTENANCE
AND REGULATION

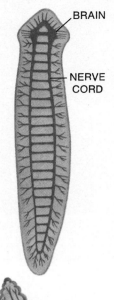

Figure 10-10. The nervous system of *Planaria*.

BRAIN

NERVE CORD

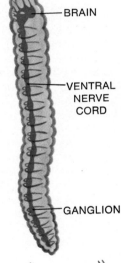

Figure 10-11. The nervous system of an earthworm. Modulator neurons are present in the ventral nerve cord and the brain.

BRAIN

VENTRAL NERVE CORD

GANGLION

Figure 10-12. Each of this scorpion's body segments is largely coordinated by its own segmental ganglion. If you step on the head of a scorpion, watch out for the vicious sting its tail can still deliver!

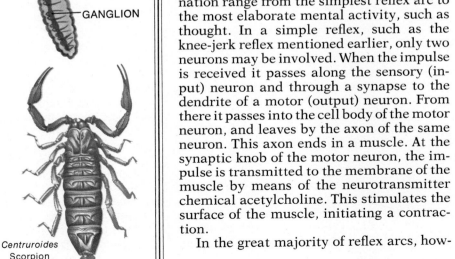

Centruroides Scorpion

head segment, including the compound eye. (Eyes and other receptor organs will be discussed in more detail when we consider communication, in chapter 21.) But other sensory receptors are scattered over the body, relaying information about the external environment to the central nervous system. And the various body segments, each coordinated largely by its own segmental ganglion, continue to behave independently even if the brain has been severed. In the grasshopper, for example, the thorax with its attached legs is capable of walking after it has been separated from the rest of the animal. The male praying mantis frequently mates with the female after first being decapitated by his prospective mate. And a headless honeybee can still deliver a painful sting.

NERVOUS SYSTEMS IN VERTEBRATES

In vertebrates the nervous system is divided into two parts. The central nervous system consists of the brain and the spinal cord, enclosed in a protective covering of bone or cartilage. The peripheral nervous system includes the **autonomic nervous system** and the **somatic (body) nerves.**

Human mechanisms for nervous coordination range from the simplest reflex arc to the most elaborate mental activity, such as thought. In a simple reflex, such as the knee-jerk reflex mentioned earlier, only two neurons may be involved. When the impulse is received it passes along the sensory (input) neuron and through a synapse to the dendrite of a motor (output) neuron. From there it passes into the cell body of the motor neuron, and leaves by the axon of the same neuron. This axon ends in a muscle. At the synaptic knob of the motor neuron, the impulse is transmitted to the membrane of the muscle by means of the neurotransmitter chemical acetylcholine. This stimulates the surface of the muscle, initiating a contraction.

In the great majority of reflex arcs, how-

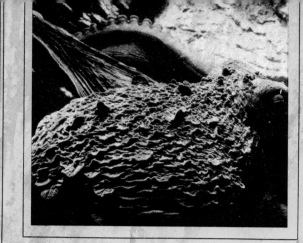

THE OCTOPUS

A moray eel is swimming along in the ocean depths, searching for a meal. Suddenly, its keen sense of smell detects the presence of an octopus. As it snaps hungrily at a black blob which it believes to be its prey, the moray finds itself lost in a cloud of black ink that reeks of octopus. Sensing the presence of its ancient enemy, the octopus has already made its defensive move and escaped, leaving the moray unable to determine which way it went.

Popular ideas about the octopus have always been colored by a variety of myths and misunderstandings. Its very appearance seems alien to us—the pulpy, baglike body, the eight long, sucker-studded arms, the protruding eyes that seem to give us an uncanny glimpse into the workings of an invertebrate brain. And yet, the octopus is an inoffensive creature except to the crabs and small fish it preys on. It is well adapted to its life on the ocean bottom, with keen eyesight that aids in its constant search for food, and the grasping arms and sharp beak that allow it to capture and devour its fast-moving prey with ease.

When threatened, the octopus can employ a number of defenses. Its skin contains a variety of color cells which are under direct control of the nervous system, enabling it to change color rapidly and blend in with its background. The jet of ink it squirts not only clouds the water but temporarily paralyzes the olfactory receptors of an approaching predator. While the octopus usually prefers to crawl along the ocean bottom, it can also propel itself rapidly with its own jet propulsion system, sucking water into its mantle and forcing it out again. Once having escaped, it hides by squeezing its remarkably flexible body into the nearest empty shell or crevice.

Perhaps the octopus' most valuable adaptation for survival is its intelligence. Scientists have studied its learning capabilities in detail, since it readily adapts to life in the laboratory. Comfortably situated in a tank of sea water, provided with a pile of rocks to hide in and a suitable diet, the octopus will spend its days observing the human activity around it with a lively curiosity. Often it will raise its eyes above the surface of the water to get a better view, or reach an inquiring arm toward any object that interests it. Many an unwary scientist standing too close to an octopus tank has been surprised to find the test tube or sandwich he was holding plucked from his hand by this ever-curious cephalopod.

Using food and mild electric shocks as

reward and punishment stimuli, scientists can easily teach an octopus to distinguish between pictured figures of varying shapes and sizes. Its eyes are very much like those of higher vertebrates. The octopus can also distinguish between solid objects by examining them with its suckers, but the differences it can perceive are limited by its physical makeup. The octopus has often been compared to a head with eight independent bodies attached to it, since each of its arms has its own nervous system. There is very little sensory feedback between the arms and the brain, and the octopus depends mainly on localized reflexes for solving day-to-day problems.

Experiments with blinded animals show that the octopus interprets tactile stimuli according to the distortion experienced at each individual sucker. Its perception of size is determined by the effects of the object on each sucker rather than by the extent to which its arm is wrapped around the object. While it can be taught to differentiate between rough and smooth objects, it cannot sense different textural patterns. And although it can be trained to distinguish between a large cylinder and a small one, the octopus cannot feel the difference between a single rod and a thick cylinder made up of many rods bundled together.

Because there is little communication between the brain and the localized nervous systems of its arms, the octopus has no way of knowing where its various arms are in relation to each other. The brain orders the general pattern of movements, but receives little feedback as to how these orders are carried out. The octopus may lift a heavy object, for example, but the extent of muscular effort involved is never communicated to the brain. As a result, it cannot learn to detect difference in weight through practical experience, nor can it be taught any behavioral modification on the basis of sensory feedback.

Experiments with octopuses raise some fascinating questions about the nature of intelligence. The octopus has excellent sensory and muscular abilities, and is a quick learner, but within the limitations imposed by its physical structure. If we define intelligence as the ability to apprehend facts, cope with new situations, and solve problems, then the octopus has certainly taken the capabilities of invertebrate learning as far as humans have taken those of vertebrate learning. The octopus has reached a level of true intelligence different from that of humans, but based upon its own capacities and appropriate to its own distinctive way of life.

ever, a modulator neuron forms a link between sensory and motor neurons. In the human central nervous system, many sensory neurons may synapse with a single modulator neuron. The modulator neuron, in turn, usually synapses with a number of motor neurons. These interconnections make complex nerve coordination possible. For instance, when you touch a hot stove, you do not merely pull your hand away; you also gasp or say "Ouch!" and perhaps thrust the burned finger into your mouth.

The central and peripheral nervous systems

The brain is the most important part of the central nervous system. Because of its great complexity of structure and function, we will discuss the brain in detail in a later section of this chapter. The other part of the central nervous system is the **spinal cord**, contained within a protective column of vertebrae.

Both the brain and the spinal cord are enclosed by three layers of membrane called the **meninges**. These membranes are the **dura mater**, a heavy, protective layer; the **arachnoid**, a middle layer which is nonpermeable; and the **pia mater**, which is heavily supplied with blood vessels. Further protection is given by a surrounding cushion of **cerebro-spinal fluid**, a clear fluid that is similar to lymph but contains almost no cells and little protein.

The spinal cord is shaped like a slightly flattened cylinder. This cylinder is composed of an H-shaped core of **grey matter** and a surrounding layer of **white matter**. The white matter is made up chiefly of myelin-sheathed axons, which are grouped in bundles called **fiber tracts**. These axons conduct impulses through the spinal cord and in and out of it. The grey matter is composed mainly of the cell bodies of modulator neurons.

Thirty-one pairs of nerves are connected to the human spinal cord, entering and emerging through spaces between the vertebrae. Each spinal nerve has a **dorsal root**

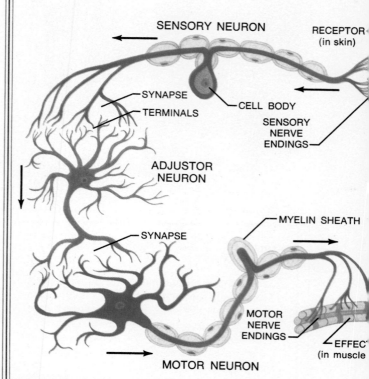

Figure 10-13. Adjustor neurons in the brain or spinal cord act as important links between sensory and motor neurons.

and a **ventral root.** The dorsal root contains sensory axons that conduct impulses into the central nervous system. The ventral root contains motor axons that conduct impulses away from it.

The spinal nerves branch out and form a network that covers nearly all of the body except the head. This network forms most of the peripheral nervous system, the major means of communication between the body and the central nervous system. In humans, the peripheral nervous system also includes twelve pairs of **cranial nerves** which lead from the brain. The cranial nerves communicate with the head and neck. Several also control internal organs below this level.

The autonomic nervous system

The autonomic nerves are a subdivision of

202

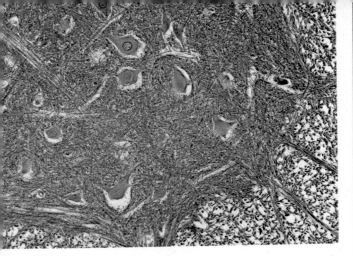

Figure 10-14. A cross-section of the spinal cord.

Figure 10-15. A human spinal cord, shown (above) as it looks in the column of vertebrae. The cord is enclosed within three protective membranes and cushioned by the spinal fluid. A closer view (below) shows the white and grey matter of which the cord is composed. The white matter contains myelin-coated axons. The grey matter is the cell bodies of modulator neurons.

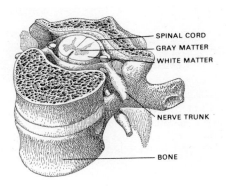

SPINAL CORD
GRAY MATTER
WHITE MATTER

NERVE TRUNK

BONE

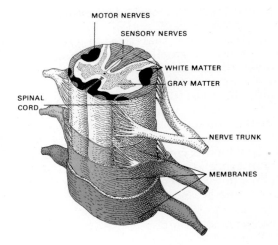

MOTOR NERVES
SENSORY NERVES

WHITE MATTER
GRAY MATTER

SPINAL CORD

NERVE TRUNK

MEMBRANES

the peripheral nervous system. These nerves influence the involuntary, unconscious body activities that maintain homeostasis. They serve internal organs such as the heart, the glands, and the smooth muscles of the digestive tract. In contrast, the somatic nerves— the other part of the peripheral nervous system—are under conscious control and handle voluntary body movements.

The autonomic system is further subdivided into **sympathetic** and **parasympathetic** nerves. These function antagonistically to each other—that is, each type acts to balance the action of the other. Together, they regulate the activities of the vital organs without the conscious control of the organism. Both types are connected to the same organs, but one or the other is dominant at any given time.

Generally speaking, the sympathetic nerves produce excitatory impulses, which can release energy in an emergency. The parasympathetic nerves, on the other hand, tend to conserve energy by inhibitory impulses. For example, the sympathetic nerves would tend to increase the rate of heartbeat, while the parasympathetic nerves would tend to slow it down. In the stomach, sympathetic nerve impulses inhibit the secretion of digestive juices, while parasympathetic impulses promote it. The action of the sympathetic nervous system, therefore, produces responses to a fight-or-flight situation that are nearly identical to those produced by the hormones of the adrenal medulla (chapter 9). However, the sympathetic nervous system produces these responses much more quickly. This lets the animal react fast enough to meet the immediate emergency. The hormonal response, following afterward, organizes the body to keep the reaction going.

THE BRAIN

As we have seen, most neurons are basically the same in structure, and nerve impulses travel similarly in all of them. Moreover, the nerve impulse stimulated by a pinprick is exactly the same, chemically and electrically, as the impulse stimulated by the touch of a feather. Yet these stimuli produce two totally opposite sensations, one of them painful and the other pleasurable. The difference between the sensations lies not in the stimulus, nor only in the receptor that receives it. Rather, the important thing is how the stimulus is interpreted in the brain.

It is true that the various sensory receptors and nerve endings are often specialized for particular sensations, such as heat, cold, and many others. But the way a stimulus is interpreted—the way a body "feels" it—depends upon which area of the brain receives or is stimulated by the impulse. An impulse from the eye is perceived visually because it is transmitted to a visual-perception area of the brain. But if the impulse also travels, by interconnections, to the hearing area, it may stimulate a sensation of sound as well. This may be one reason why seeing a certain thing can sometimes remind you of hearing a piece of music, or some other seemingly unrelated sound.

In vertebrates, the brain is divided into three basic regions: **forebrain, midbrain,** and **hindbrain.** Each region is specialized for particular functions. In the forebrain, the **olfactory bulbs** receive and interpret impulses from the organs of smell. Behind them, two enlarged areas make up the **cerebrum.** Below the cerebrum lie the **thalamus** and the **hypothalamus.** The midbrain contains the **optic lobes,** which interpret impulses from the eyes. Behind the midbrain is the **cerebellum,** the first part of the hindbrain. The hindbrain continues in the **medulla oblongata,** which is joined to the spinal cord.

Much about the way of life of vertebrates can be determined by comparing the size of different regions of their brain. If we examine the brains of a fish, an amphibian, a bird, and a mammal of approximately equal size, we will find that the overall difference in the sizes of their brains is not very great.

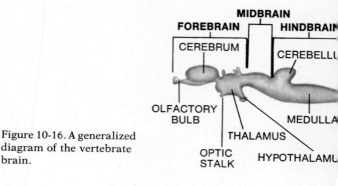

Figure 10-16. A generalized diagram of the vertebrate brain.

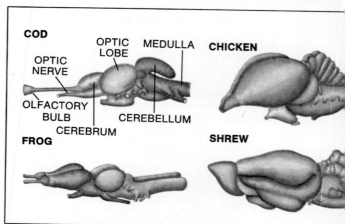

Figure 10-17. The brains of a fish, an amphibian, a bird, and a mammal. The overall difference in the size of the four brains is not great. However, there is a great difference in the relative size of each region.

However, there is a marked difference in the relative size of each region.

In vertebrates that depend greatly on their sense of smell, such as moles and shrews, the olfactory area of the brain is the most pronounced. In birds, on the other hand, the most important sense is sight. Their optic lobes are far more developed than their olfactory bulbs. In the higher vertebrates we see an enlargement of the cerebrum, which is concerned with association and interpretation. And in the primates, including humans, the cerebrum is the largest part of the brain.

PATTERNS OF MAINTENANCE AND REGULATION

The human brain

The human brain possesses the basic characteristics of any vertebrate brain. But it is unique in the high degree to which some of its essential parts are developed. In sheer complexity it does not appear to be matched by any other known structure. Each of its more than 15 billion neurons carries information of only a simple type. Yet this information is sorted out, classified, and interpreted in a constant process of feedback between knowledge already present and knowledge newly acquired. The brain of an individual contains the physical foundation of that individual's memory, reason, thought, and probably most of the attributes of his or her personality. Actually, there is more material available in the human brain than we can hope to use during a normal lifetime. This has led some people to speculate that our life expectancy should be much longer than it is today.

During most of human history, knowledge of the brain's various areas and their functions was largely a matter of guesswork. It was based on the observation of dead brains and injured living brains, but conclusions drawn from these observations were often incorrect. Brain surgery, however, dates back at least to the early Egyptians and Peruvians. Their physicians practiced trepanning—opening up the skull—as a treatment both for injuries and for brain tumors. The mortality rate must have been extremely high. Yet we know that some of these patients survived, since their skulls show an overgrowth of bone where healing took place around the artificial opening.

In the present century, new techniques have enabled researchers to learn more about the brain. Experiments on laboratory animals, along with observations made during surgery on the human brain, have permitted large parts of the brain and their functions to be "mapped" in detail. A vast amount, of course, remains to be learned. However, it is now possible to correct certain conditions caused by brain injury and disease. It is also possible, when certain portions of the brain have been incapacitated, to train other portions to take over their functions.

The hindbrain

The **medulla oblongata** and the **pons** comprise the **brain stem,** the pathway between the spinal cord and the brain itself. The brain stem enters the skull through an opening called the **foramen magnum.**

The medulla transmits nerve impulses between the spinal cord and the brain. In addition, it controls a number of extremely important involuntary functions, including respiration and heartbeat. The human medulla is quite similar to those of other animals—probably more so than any other part of the human brain.

The pons ("bridge") is a bulging area that lies above the medulla. Most of the sensory and motor pathways that pass through the medulla also pass through the pons. It also coordinates a variety of facial movements, including those of chewing and swallowing. In addition, the pons takes part in the transfer of information between the forebrain and the cerebellum.

The **cerebellum** is a roundish structure, about the size of a tennis ball in humans. It is covered with a layer of wrinkled, or convoluted, grey matter over a core of white matter. The cerebellum is the coordinating center for the activities of skeletal muscle. It does not actually initiate muscle movements, but it regulates them through a feedback system which informs it about the progress of each one. An individual with a damaged cerebellum has difficulty performing finely coordinated muscular activities.

The **reticular formation** runs through the medulla oblongata, the midbrain, and into a part of the forebrain. This formation is a network of neurons that receives input from both incoming and outgoing sensory pathways. Part of its role seems to be to provide an "arousal system" for the rest of the brain. That is, when the reticular formation receives a stimulus of sufficient strength from

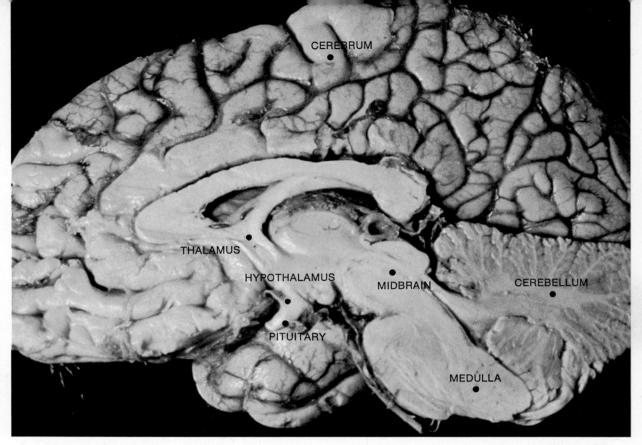

Figure 10-18. The human brain is divided into the same basic parts as the brain of any vertebrate. However, it is vastly more complex. Note the size of the cerebral cortex, which covers the other regions almost entirely.

elsewhere in the body, it activates the brain to respond to that stimulus. Without such activation, the brain will not respond, no matter how strong the stimulus. For instance, if the reticular formation is damaged or its action is suppressed by drugs such as barbiturates, an individual will be unable to wake up.

The reticular formation also seems to classify stimuli according to their importance, screening out those that can safely be ignored. Since the body is constantly being bombarded with stimuli of all sorts, this screening system is important. It prevents the individual from having to respond to all the stimuli at once. Consider, for instance, what would happen if a tightrope walker sixty feet above the ground had to concentrate equally on his performance, the loud

cheers of his audience, and his itching nose!

The midbrain

The midbrain is much larger and more important in lower vertebrates than in mammals. The larger the forebrain of a mammal, the smaller its midbrain will be. In humans, the midbrain functions primarily as a communications link between the forebrain and the hindbrain. As in other animals, however, it continues to aid in the integration of sensory stimuli, particularly those involving the auditory and visual systems.

The forebrain

We saw in chapter 9 that the **hypothalamus,** located in the forebrain, plays an important

PATTERNS OF MAINTENANCE
AND REGULATION

part in homeostasis, since it produces or influences several hormones in the pituitary. Research with laboratory animals, using electrical stimulation of the hypothalamus, has now revealed that this portion of the brain is also the seat of such basic animal drives as hunger, thirst, anger, pleasure, and sexual behavior. Only a small part of the hypothalamus seems to be devoted to each of these functions. Therefore, stimuli only a tiny distance apart can elicit totally different types of behavior. It is apparent that this portion of the brain is a major control center for involuntary body reactions.

The **thalamus** of the forebrain is a receptor and clearing-house for sensory information. The sensation of pain, for example, is registered in the thalamus. In humans, the thalamus shares many of its functions with the **cerebral cortex.** In humans and other primates, the latter is the largest and visually the most obvious part of the brain. It has expanded to cover the other regions almost completely. In the lower vertebrates the cerebral cortex is either very small or completely absent. It is more highly developed in mammals, and reaches its greatest size and complexity of function in the primates.

The cerebral cortex consists of a highly convoluted layer of grey matter over a core of white matter. It contains the sensory centers for the visual, auditory, olfactory, and other receptors. It is the primary site for controlling movement. Apparently it is also the seat of thought and intelligence, including a "memory bank" which compares present experience with a reservoir of stored past experience. The cortex is divided into right and left **hemispheres.** Most nerves from the right side of the body are linked mainly to the left side of the brain, and vice versa. The right hemisphere, therefore, controls voluntary movement for the left side of the body, and the left hemisphere controls the right side. The two hemispheres seem to be structural duplicates of each other. But the majority of individuals (at least in

Western cultures) are "left-brained"; that is, their left hemisphere controls much of their intellectual ability and contains their primary speech centers. Left-brained people are generally right-handed. In left-handed persons, the right hemisphere appears to be dominant.

Mapping of the cerebral cortex has led to some fascinating discoveries. Human memory, for example, is often so faulty that it is rarely thought of as permanent. But experiments with human subjects during brain surgery seem to indicate that a complete memory of a person's life experience is stored in the cerebral cortex. Surgery to remove diseased portions of the cortex is routinely performed under local anesthesia, since the tissues of the brain itself contain no pain receptors. The patient, therefore, remains fully conscious. Electrical stimulation of the cerebral cortex during such surgery causes patients to recall long-forgotten experiences in their entirety. This recall, according to those who have experienced it, is not like normal remembering. It is more like an actual reliving of the particular event. The way in which memory is stored by the cortex is still a matter of debate. Apparently it cannot be performed by the neurons alone. There is some indication that the neuroglial cells may take part in the process. RNA, one of the nucleic acids (to be discussed in chapter 16) may be the molecule associated with memory storage.

Brain waves

During recent years intensive study has been centered on the electrical activities of the human brain. In 1929 Dr. Hans Berger discovered that these activities possess a definite and continuous rhythm. Brain activity can be recorded through electrodes, forming a permanent record called an **electroencephalogram** or **EEG.** Patterns of brain waves indicate states of rest or stimulation, sleeping or waking. They can also be used to determine if brain abnormalities are present and interfering with brain function.

However, each individual has a pattern of brain waves as characteristic as his fingerprints. Thus it is difficult to interpret an EEG, and much study remains to be done.

Recent experiments seem to indicate that the brain can develop and grow with use. Conversely, it appears to atrophy and grow smaller with disuse. There can be little doubt that only a small portion of the brain's potential ability is utilized by the individual. Further investigations are sure to uncover many more intriguing facts about the brain and its functions. Eventually, humans may learn to take fuller advantage of the untapped capacity of this most complex of all structures.

SUMMARY

Maintenance of homeostasis is based on the combined actions of the endocrine system and the nervous system. Nervous systems, which exist only in animals, permit the most rapid response to environmental changes.

The neuron is the basic unit of the nervous system. It possesses dendrites, which receive incoming impulses, and axons, which conduct impulses away from the cell body. Axons are often covered by a layer of Schwann cells, which may form an insulating myelin sheath. A nerve is a bundle of axons.

Nerve impulses are transmitted electrochemically. The resting neuron carries a negative electrical charge, known as the resting potential. A stimulus increases the cell membrane's permeability to sodium so that sodium ions flow into it, reversing the membrane's polarity and generating an electric current. The nerve impulse is transmitted by the current traveling along the membrane. A refractory period follows. During this the membrane first becomes more permeable to potassium, and potassium ions flow out. Then the action of a sodium pump returns the neuron to its resting state.

Nerve impulses are passed from neuron to neuron at the synapse, and are transferred across the synaptic cleft by a neurotransmitter chemical, which may be acetylcholine or norepinephrine. Neurons can be either excitatory or inhibitory in their action, allowing the organism to adjust the strength of its response to stimuli. The speed of a nerve impulse is determined by the size of the axon and by whether or not it has a myelin sheath. A neuron will respond to a stimulus either completely or not at all, following the "all-or-none" law of conduction.

The simplest nerve pathway is the reflex arc; a sensory neuron receives the stimulus from a receptor and transmits it to a motor neuron, which in turn passes it to an effector where the response to the stimulus takes place. A complex reflex arc involves a connector or intermediate neuron, permitting a more complicated nerve pathway.

Simple radially symmetrical animals such as *Hydra* and the jellyfish possess a generalized nerve net with no central controlling area. In the bilaterally symmetrical animals, some sort of control center is present at the anterior end, and the nervous system is divided into central and peripheral components. In the annelid worms and arthropods a ganglion serves as the primitive brain, and each segment of the animal is controlled by smaller ganglia.

In vertebrates the central nervous system consists of the brain and the spinal cord. Both are enclosed by the meninges and a protective covering of bone. The human spinal cord is composed of a core of grey matter and an outer layer of white matter. Thirty-one pairs of spinal nerves and twelve pairs of cranial nerves branch out from the spinal cord and brain to form most of the peripheral nervous system.

The autonomic nervous system contains sympathetic and parasympathetic nerves, which function antagonistically to each other. In general, sympathetic nerves produce excitatory impulses and parasympathetic nerves produce inhibitory impulses. The sympathetic nerves assist in quick response to a fight-or-flight situation.

The brain is the interpreter of stimuli. It is divided into forebrain, midbrain, and hindbrain. The brain stem, which consists of the medulla oblongata and the pons, is the pathway between spinal cord and brain.

The cerebellum in the hindbrain coordinates the activities of skeletal muscle. The reticular formation, running through the medulla, midbrain, and into the forebrain, is a neuron network that classifies stimuli according to their importance.

In humans, the midbrain is primarily a communications link between forebrain and hindbrain. It helps in integration of sensory stimuli involving the auditory and visual systems.

The forebrain contains the hypothalamus, which controls basic animal drives, and the thalamus, which is a receptor and clearing-house for sensory information. In primates, the cerebral cortex covers most of the other regions of the brain. It contains the major sensory centers, controls movement, and appears to be the seat of thought, intelligence, and memory.

Review questions

1. How does nervous system function differ from that of the endocrine system?

2. Describe the structure of a typical neuron.

3. In what important way do neurons differ from other cells?

4. What are Schwann cells?

5. What is the function of the myelin sheath?

6. Distinguish between a nerve and a nerve cell.

7. List some possible functions of the neuroglia.

8. Describe the way by which a neuron transmits a nerve impulse.

9. Name the two common neurotransmitter chemicals.

10. What factors influence the speed at which a nerve impulse travels?

11. Certain diseases cause the deterioration of the myelin sheath. What symptoms might accompany such a condition?

12. Describe a simple reflex arc and give some examples.

13. Trace the five-part path through which nerve impulses can pass in a complex nervous system.

14. Describe a typical nerve net. What is unusual about the way in which it transmits nerve impulses?

15. List some of the important advantages of a central nervous system.

16. What is a ganglion?

17. List the components of the central and peripheral nervous systems.

18. Describe the structure of the spinal cord.

19. Distinguish between the functions of the sympathetic and parasympathetic nerves.

20. Describe the general structure and function of the three parts of the human brain.

21. What is the importance of the reticular formation?

22. List several functions of the hypothalamus.

23. What are some of the recent interesting discoveries about the cerebral cortex? How were these discoveries made?

24. What is an EEG? What is its purpose?

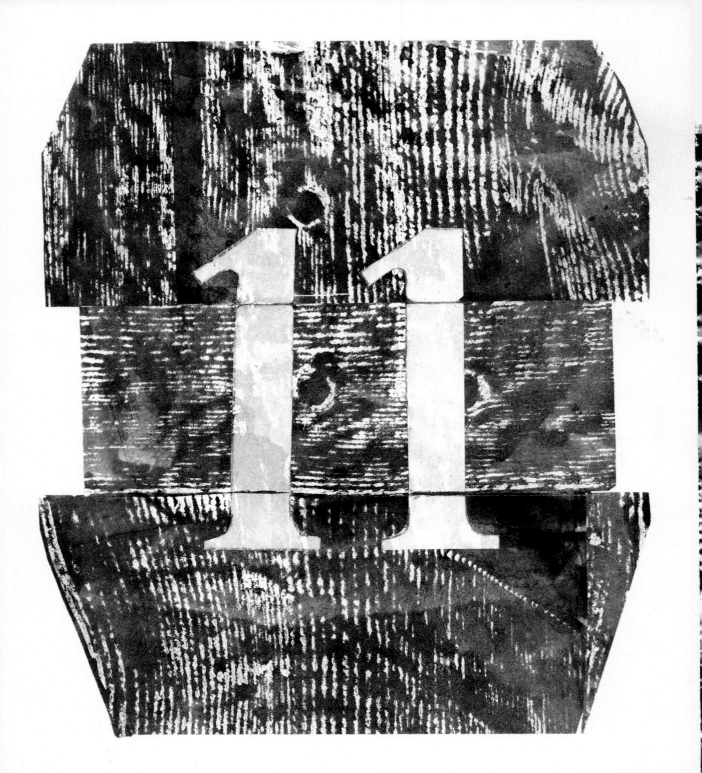

Origin and Reproduction of Life

All matter on earth is made up of relatively few chemical elements. Different kinds of matter contain different selections of elements, arranged in different ways. Some of these arrangements we say are living, and others we say are nonliving. We assume that both follow the same physical laws. Yet most of us feel we can easily tell them apart. Some of us might hesitate to say whether certain things are alive or not, such as the sun, an eye, an atom, or a virus. Yet everyone would agree that plants and animals are alive and that rocks and gases are not. But how do we know the difference? How do we decide that a sheep is alive but that the yarn made from its wool is not? At what point do we distinguish between the life of a cow and the "nonlife" of the football that is made from its skin?

On first sight, nonliving matter seems more stable and durable than living matter. A metal, for example, can be heated and turned into a liquid. The liquid can be cooled and restored to the original solid. Pull a fish out of water, though, and it will die in a few minutes; throw it back and it stays dead. If a tree burns into ash, no force on earth will turn it back into a tree.

Looked at in a different way, nonliving things appear less lasting than living ones. Machines wear out with use. Mountains erode into low hills. And rocks break into pebbles that are ground into dust. On the other hand, while living individuals may die, living organisms as a group have increased and flourished since life itself began. They have become more numerous, more organized, and more complex. Even an individual organism displays increasing complexity and organization over its lifetime.

Starting as a single fertilized cell, the embryo develops organs and tissues. A child increases in size and weight, and becomes an adult.

A machine is built to size. An organism grows to size. A machine, if it breaks down, must be repaired by a mechanic, with parts from outside. An organism can usually make its own repairs. The permanence of living matter, then, is different from the permanence of nonliving matter. Life persists by changing, and by passing on the ability to change. But what, exactly, is life?

THE PROPERTIES OF LIFE

Biology is usually defined as "the study of life." However, biologists will probably never agree on a single definition of "life." One reason is that life cannot be studied in isolation. It cannot be extracted from an organism, as a chemical can be extracted from a solution. Take life away from an organism and you no longer have life to study. There is only a dead body.

Most biologists find the question "What is life?" too general, and therefore unanswerable. They usually rephrase it into more specific questions, such as: How are living things organized? What are they made of? How do they function? They ask these questions in order to determine what properties are common to all living things. And about these there is general agreement.

In noting the development of an embryo into an adult, we have already hinted at one property of living organisms: they are organized into systems. Individual fats, proteins, and carbohydrates are not alive, but they can be organized into a living system by an organism. Furthermore, organisms maintain or change their organization for the proper functioning of the system. In other words, organisms are self-organizing and self-regulating. They are also interacting. They interact with other organisms, and with the physical environment. And systems and organs interact within each individual organism.

But, like machines, organisms do need an outside source of energy for support and maintenance. Through photosynthesis, as we saw in chapter 3, plants change the energy of sunlight into the chemical energy stored in carbon chains. Through respiration, both plants and animals convert the stored energy in food into the energy they need for survival. This ability to transform energy is a second major property of living systems.

A third is reproduction. Reproduction is not essential to the life of the individual organism. A rabbit does not have to reproduce in order to stay alive. But rabbits must reproduce if the rabbit population is to stay alive.

It is true that we now have machines that can duplicate many of these activities. There are machines that can make other machines, and machines that "know" when to adjust their operation to outside conditions. But they cannot do all the things we regard as proper to a living organism. Nor are they usually made of organic substances. Should we say they are alive, or not? Writers and philosophers have been exploring such questions for years.

THE ORIGIN OF LIFE

How life began is a question that has fascinated people for thousands of years. It has always been clear that at least some living organisms were reproduced from other living organisms of the same kinds. But was it certain that this was true for all living organisms? Aristotle, for instance, argued that frogs, fish, mice, and insects were generated from nonliving material, such as filth and moist soil. This is known as the theory of **spontaneous generation.** But Aristotle also believed that the majority of animals were reproduced from similar ones. He called on spontaneous generation to explain only those organisms he could not observe arising from parent organisms.

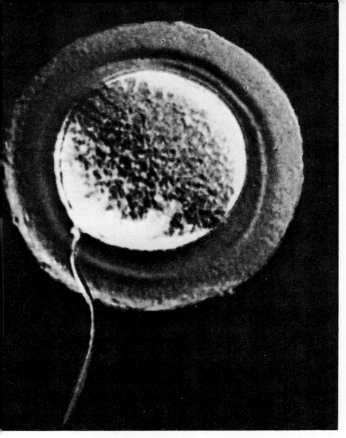

Figure 11-1. Living organisms can reproduce themselves. In this illustration, the tiny sperm cell of the human male is just about to penetrate and fertilize the vastly larger female egg, thus beginning the development of a new individual.

Figure 11-2. These fanciful seventeenth-century woodcuts illustrate the theory of spontaneous generation. Barnacle geese were supposedly hatched from trees (top). Various other organisms were believed to emerge from rotten logs (bottom).

The theory of spontaneous generation went largely unchallenged for the next two thousand years. During the Middle Ages, scholars added cases of their own. "Goose trees," trees that produced geese from leaves under special circumstances, are described in the literature of several centuries. Perhaps the most remarkable "demonstration" of spontaneous generation came from Jean-Baptiste van Helmont, a noted Belgian scientist, who devised a recipe for mice. He claimed that if you took a sweaty shirt, put it in a bin, sprinkled wheat grains over it and came back in twenty-one days, you would find mice created spontaneously from the concoction.

It may seem strange that people could accept such thinking for so long. Obviously, they accepted it mostly on authority. Someone before their time had said it was so, and they believed it. But before we laugh at their mistakes, we might ask whether we are really so different. We accept many things on authority, too. How many of us really know, from our own experience, that the earth goes around the sun? Or that the earth is round? So far, only a few astronauts have actually seen the latter with their own eyes. Like our ancestors, we must depend on "experts" for much of our information. Even the experts must usually depend on other experts for many facts. And some of today's expert information may one day seem as silly as spontaneous generation does now. Scientists rarely find an absolutely final answer to any question. They find the best answer they can, and use it until a better one is discovered.

The theory of biogenesis

By the middle of the seventeenth century, however, at least a few people had grown skeptical about some of the reports of spontaneous generation. Francesco Redi, an Italian physician and poet, was one. Redi claimed that maggots and worms are not generated by dead matter. They arise as offspring from parents, just as any other

APHIDS

It's high noon, and time to move the herd along. Food is getting mighty scarce in these parts. It doesn't take long to round them up, and even though the younger and weaker ones have to be carried, the move is accomplished quickly and easily. The work pays off. Thanks to the new food supply, the herd can be milked much more frequently.

This may sound like a tale out of the old west, but there's a twist. The cowboys aren't people but ants, and the herd isn't cattle but another kind of insect called the aphid. Aphids are sometimes called ant cows because of the unusual relationship between these two species.

The relationship between aphids and certain species of ants is a remarkable example of cooperation between living things. Ants are extremely fond of a sweet, sticky substance called honeydew which the aphid secretes. According to some historians, the manna which was given to the fleeing Hebrews in the Old Testament was probably a large quantity of crystallized honeydew. This substance is still gathered and eaten by some Arabs and Australian aborigines today.

Some ant cowherds stroke their tiny "cattle" with their antennae to stimulate the production of honeydew. The ants eat much of the honeydew immediately and bring some of it back to feed their young. In return, the ants protect the aphids from their natural enemies and move them to better locations when food grows scarce.

The bodies of some aphids have even evolved special structures to allow them to ride on the ant's back. Some species of aphid have grown so dependent on ants as to be virtually helpless without them. Others can fight their own battles. Some have hard outer skeletons; others can kick, jump, or run for self-protection. Still others secrete an oily liquid on the heads of their attackers while emitting an odor that warns other aphids to flee. Aphids that depend on ants for their protection have lost these capabilities and provide an easy meal to any predator that comes along while the ants are away.

Although it may be no bigger than the head of a pin, an aphid has to eat a great deal to meet its nutritional needs. There are very few plant species in the temperate regions which are not fed upon by some species of aphid.

Not surprisingly, aphids are not regarded kindly by the farmers on whose crops they feast. Apple aphids, rose aphids, pea aphids, potato aphids, and corn root aphids are just a few of the many species that live on gardens and food crops. The fact that individuals are so tiny is of little comfort to the farmer. As many as two billion aphids may infest the leaves and shoots on a single acre of land, while another quarter-billion feed on the roots be-

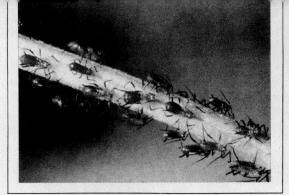

low. Aphids not only stunt plant growth and deform leaves, buds, and flowers but produce plant galls and transmit plant virus diseases as well.

Many aphids feed on only one kind of plant. Unfortunately for farmers, however, most of those that threaten agricultural crops feed on different hosts in different seasons. This allows the insect to take maximum advantage of seasonal changes in its food sources, generally by feeding on grasses in the summer and woody plants in the winter. The bird-cherry—oat aphid, for example, thrives on bird cherry leaves during the winter but switches to oats during the summer months when the level of soluble nitrogen in the bird cherry leaves drops to an unsatisfactory point.

The aphid is well adapted for the extraction of sap from plant cells. It feeds by inserting its sharp mouthpart, called the stylet, into the phloem tissue. Once the sieve tube within a stem or a leaf vein is located, the stylet penetrates the cell and sucks out the sap. Its action is not unlike that of a hypodermic needle. The insect even has an internal pump to help it suck up its food.

The aphid's most dangerous natural enemy is none other than the common ladybug. Aphids are so appealing to the ladybug's palate that one adult or larva can eat as many as 100 aphids in a single day. In the late nineteenth century, several hundred ladybugs from Australia managed to stop a plague of aphids that had threatened to destroy the entire California citrus crop.

Because individual aphids are virtually defenseless against most predators, they depend on rapid reproduction to survive. In summer they reproduce asexually, a fast and efficient method of increasing the population. In autumn they reproduce sexually, producing eggs that survive the winter and hatch to start a new generation in the spring. When reproducing asexually, the female aphid does not lay eggs, as is usual among insects, but rather gives birth to live young. These offspring look much like adults and are born fully active. Most amazing of all, the ovaries of these newly born females already contain developing embryos. So a mother aphid may carry not only the embryo of her daugher but that of her grandson or granddaughter as well.

The aphid's unusual reproductive process allows for tremendously rapid expansion of the population. Aphids require only fourteen days to reach maturity, and some thirty may be born to each mother. Some aphid species produce as many as nine generations over the course of a single year. Under ideal circumstances—that is, in the absence of predators and disease, in a favorable climate, and with unlimited food and space—a single aphid in a single season could generate some 600 billion progeny weighing over 6,000 tons. C'est formidable!

animal does. The dead matter simply serves the parents as a suitable nest to deposit eggs, and as a source of nourishment. To test this belief, he placed meat in two sets of flasks, as shown in figure 11-3. One set was exposed to flies and other insect visitors. The other set was sealed to prevent contamination by insects. Worms appeared in the open flasks, but not in the flasks that were sealed. The use of the sealed flasks as a check, or control, on his results strengthened the case against the theory of spontaneous generation. The alternate theory that Redi argued for held that all life originates from life. It was later called **biogenesis,** meaning "life from life."

But the theory of spontaneous generation was not dead. About the same time as Redi was experimenting, Antonie van Leeuwenhoek published his discovery of microscopic organisms. Most people by then believed that larger organisms did not originate spontaneously. But what else could account for the existence of these microorganisms? For almost two centuries, scientists argued. Some experiments seemed to support biogenesis. Others seemed to indicate that spontaneous generation was the best theory. Pasteur's experiment with beef broth and flasks, described in chapter 1, appeared to settle the question on the side of biogenesis.

The theory of abiogenesis

Instead of putting the spontaneous generation theory to its final rest, however, Pasteur left biologists with another question. How did life begin? Pasteur's experiments had confirmed the principle that every living cell originates from another living cell. If this principle is correct, and we can trace each cell back to its parent cell, and that cell back to its parent cell, and so on, then there must have been an original cell at some time in history. And this one, being the first, could not have arisen from another living cell. Could it somehow have arisen from nonliving matter? Most scientists today believe that it did. Within the past few decades the idea that life on earth originated in nonliv-

ing matter has been revived. There are, however, two major differences between the old theory of spontaneous generation and the new theory, which is called **abiogenesis.** First, it is now clear that, under present conditions, life does not originate from nonliving matter. What advocates of abiogenesis believe is that life could have originated under the different set of conditions which are thought to have existed on earth nearly four billion years ago. Second, the new theory holds that life evolved from nonliving matter not abruptly, but very gradually.

The Oparin hypothesis

In 1936 A. I. Oparin, a noted Russian biochemist, published his *Origin of Life on Earth.* In this he outlined a sequence of events that could have led to the origin and evolution of living organisms. Oparin's hypothesis is based on the set of conditions that he assumed prevailed on the earth at the time these events were occurring. We obviously have no direct evidence of those primitive atmospheric conditions. And since no single set has been agreed upon by all investigators, the hypothesis is still controversial.

Oparin's primitive atmosphere differed drastically from the one we know. Today's atmosphere consists mainly of oxygen and nitrogen. Oparin believed that the primitive atmosphere was made up of inorganic gases like those found on some other planets. These gases include methane, ammonia, water vapor, and hydrogen. With sufficient energy, he said, some of the gases could have broken down and recombined to form organic molecules. These molecules could then have been the building blocks for potential forms of life. The energy required for the initial breakdown of the gases could have been supplied during electrical storms. Such storms are presumed to have been much more frequent during the early stages of the earth's history than they are today. Also, energy from ultraviolet light would have been much more potent in an atmo-

PATTERNS OF REPRODUCTION
AND DEVELOPMENT

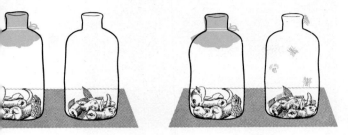

Figure 11-3. Redi's classic experiment helped to disprove the theory of spontaneous generation. He showed that maggots emerged only from eggs that had been laid by flies on decaying meat. When a fine net was used to prevent the flies from landing on the meat, maggots developed on the net but not in the jar.

Figure 11-4. This apparatus was used by Stanley Miller to test Oparin's hypothesis. Methane, ammonia, hydrogen, and water vapor were placed in the spark chamber. From this simple mixture, amino acids condensed in the trap.

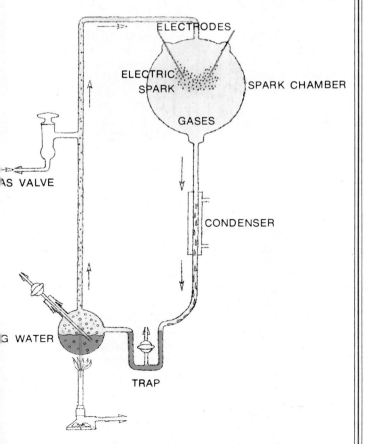

ELECTRODES

ELECTRIC SPARK

SPARK CHAMBER

GASES

AS VALVE

CONDENSER

G WATER

TRAP

sphere that lacked oxygen and ozone. Other possible energy sources include heat from within the earth and radioactive particles in the earth's crust.

Oparin's hypothesis sparked the imagination of many scientists. Among them was Stanley Miller, a young graduate student at the University of Chicago. Inspired by a discussion with Nobel prize winner Harold Urey, in 1953 Miller built an apparatus that was designed to test Oparin's basic theory. This apparatus is shown in figure 11-4.

Miller designed his apparatus to simulate the conditions that might have existed on the primitive earth. He used an electric sparking device to simulate lightning discharges. At the same time, water vapor (supposed to have existed as dense clouds in the primitive atmosphere) was heated and circulated throughout the spark chamber. The chamber contained three other gases thought to have existed then. After passing through the spark chamber, the water vapor was cooled to a liquid. Thus the liquid acted like the rain that would have fallen into the primitive seas during an electrical storm. After continuous operation of the apparatus for a week, analysis of the water revealed a host of organic molecules—including four different amino acids.

Once these results were known, other investigators immediately became interested in the same general type of experiment. Moreover, the Oparin hypothesis began to look more attractive to those who had been skeptical. Other energy sources that were probably present on the primitive earth were tested in various gas mixtures that might have been in the primitive atmosphere. Ultraviolet radiation, for example, was used in experiments that yielded results as dramatic as those obtained by Miller.

Molecules become living cells

Once it was shown that organic molecules could arise from inorganic ones, another question remained. How could the basic organic molecules have become organized into a primitive form of life? Scientists have likened the primitive oceans to a "hot soup" in which great numbers of organic molecules collected on the surface. Such density would allow the molecules to collide accidentally. They might thus combine into more complex substances, such as polypeptides and even nucleic acids. These macromolecules might then have combined to form larger aggregates, or **coacervate droplets.** Such droplets tend to form a definite internal structure, and to carry on chemical reactions that are affected by changes in the structure. They can also join together, or take up particles from outside. Thus they increase in size and become more complex. Biologists assume that the best-organized droplets would grow fastest. Eventually, they would break up. If each fragment possessed essentially the same characteristics as the original, this would be a type of reproduction. Over long periods of time, many such coacervates, containing different chemicals, may have met. They may have fused and broken up, and the particles fused with still other particles. Eventually, these chance combinations of chemicals may have produced the first truly cell-like entity.

It is widely believed that the original cells or cell-like structures were heterotrophic. Unable to synthesize organic molecules for their own nourishment, they would have gotten them directly from the "soup." As time went on, though, they would presumably have used up most of the available supply. Such scarcity would give an advantage to organisms that had become able to use nonorganic sources of energy. These organisms would be able to manufacture at least part of their own organic food out of the abundant supply of simpler, inorganic molecules. In this way, autotrophic organisms may have come into being.

The first autotrophic organisms would probably have been anaerobic. That is, they could not use oxygen in respiration, since the atmosphere of the primitive earth probably contained little or no oxygen. But once some of them began to manufacture their

Figure 11-5. Life in a test tube? Not quite—but amino acids, the building blocks of life, are being created in such laboratory apparatus as the one pictured.

food by photosynthesis, they would begin adding oxygen to the atmosphere. This would make it possible for aerobic (oxygen-using) organisms to evolve. It would also prevent any further production of life by abiogenesis, because the oxygen would break down organic compounds faster than they could be synthesized nonbiologically. Our present atmosphere, rich in oxygen, is one reason why abiogenesis does not occur today.

PATTERNS OF REPRODUCTION
AND DEVELOPMENT

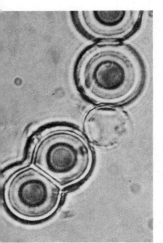

Figure 11-6. Proteinoid microspheres undergo fission, although in a different manner from that of living cells.

Figure 11-7. This salamander larva is similar to the ones Flemming studied when he described mitosis.

Another possible precursor of the living cell is being studied in the laboratories of Sidney Fox at the University of Miami. Fox discovered that when certain mixtures of amino acids were heated, they spontaneously produced short polypeptide chains. Because of their protein-like nature, Fox called these chains **proteinoids.** In later experiments, Fox found that when proteinoids were treated with hot water and then cooled, numerous "microspheres" were

formed. Experiments with the microspheres have yielded some very interesting results. For example, the proteinoids show an enzyme-like activity that breaks down glucose. This is similar to the activities of Oparin's coacervates. In fact, Miller has suggested that the proteinoids may be nearer than the coacervates to the original ancestors of the cell.

CELLULAR REPRODUCTION

Individual cells generally live for only a few days or weeks. Some may live for a few decades. But present dating methods suggest that living organisms have existed for billions of years. What ensures this continuation of life?

Somehow, cells reproduce themselves. And the new cell receives from the parent cell a complete set of information that causes it to become the same sort of cell. The same holds true for whole organisms. Thus elephants have baby elephants and not kittens; horses have foals, not calves; your parents had you, not a turnip, and so on. How does the cell pass on this information?

Mitosis

In the 1880s the German biologist Walther Flemming described the process of cellular division, by which cells arise from other cells. Working with the stained tissues of salamander larvae, Flemming saw that the nucleus of the cell contained a mass of thin, thread-like fibers. He named this material **chromatin** (from the Greek *chroma*, meaning "color") because it was easily stained with certain dyes. He also observed that during cell division, the nucleus goes through a series of changes and divides in two. Flemming called this process of nuclear division **mitosis** (from the Greek *mitos*, meaning "thread"). After the nucleus divides, the cytoplasm also divides. The result of the division of a parent cell is the creation of two identical daughter cells.

As Flemming noted, the division of the cell proceeded in an orderly way. It is not enough for the cell simply to split in two. It must divide in such a way that each daughter cell receives an exact copy of the hereditary instructions that existed in the parent. The parent cell makes a duplicate of the instructions in the nucleus before it divides. (Similarly, a chef would not simply rip a recipe in two so that two cooks could prepare the same dish. He would make a duplicate and give one copy to each cook.)

The early observers of mitosis noted that a cell generally doubled in size before it divided. The daughter cells usually grew no larger than the original parent cell. However, in more recent years scientists have learned that many cells divide without first doubling in size. Some, in fact, get smaller with each new generation. Apparently, then, growth is not the only preparation for cell division.

Although the cell cycle is a continuous process, it has several stages. Depending on how they are counted, there are either four or five phases. Four of them compose mitosis, and can easily be observed with a microscope. The fifth, which we will consider first, is the stage in which the cell spends all its time when it is not dividing.

Interphase. This was originally thought of as a time when the cell was "at rest." We now know that it is a period of great activity. During interphase, the cell performs all its normal functions. It also carries on activities that are needed before division can take place. At this time, the chromosomes are duplicated. Chromosomes, you recall, are the thread-like bodies that make up the mass of chromatin Flemming observed, although they cannot be individually distinguished during interphase. The two new chromosomes formed from each old one remain attached to one another, and are called **chromatids.**

During interphase in animal cells, the organelle called the centriole also reproduces itself. These centrioles will be the principal organizers of the **mitotic apparatus** on

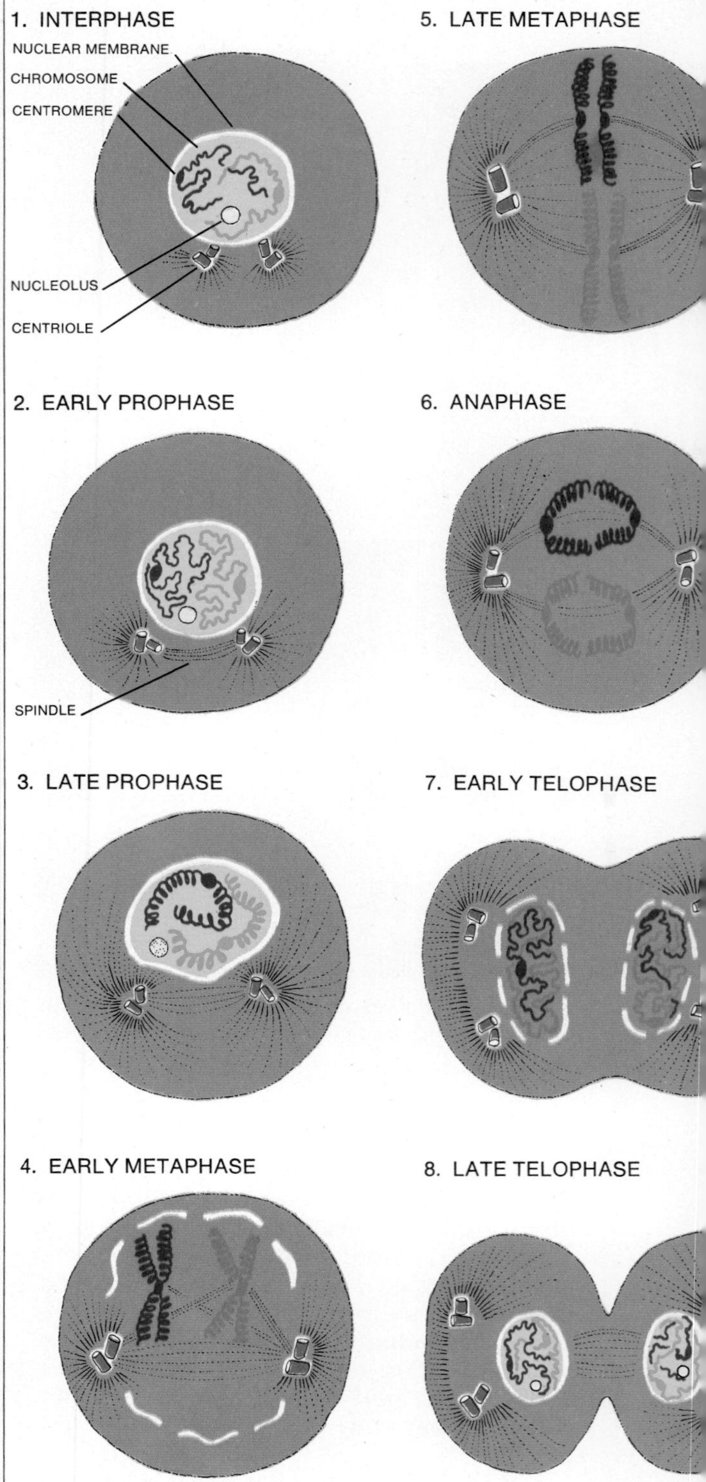

Figure 11-8. The phases of mitosis in a typical animal cell.

Figure 11-9. Micrographs of mitosis taking place in whitefish cells.

Courtesy General Biological Supply House, Inc., Chicago

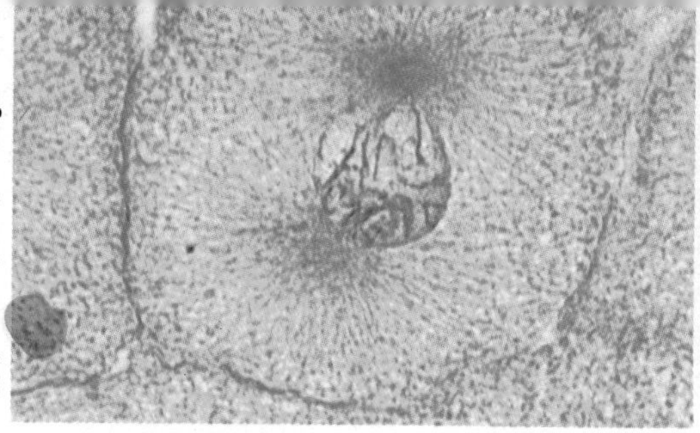

Early Prophase

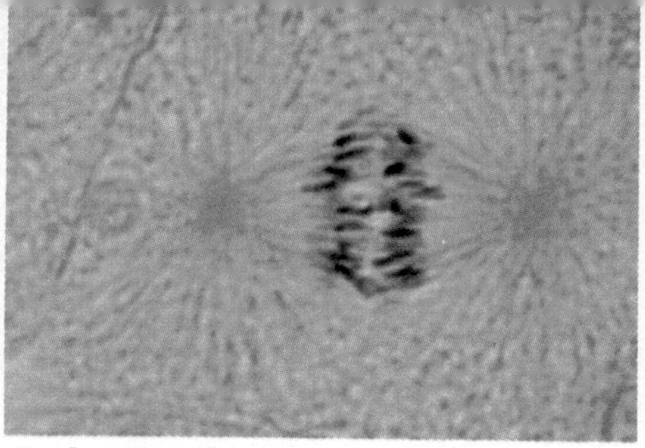

Early Anaphase

Courtesy General Biological Supply House, Inc., Chicago

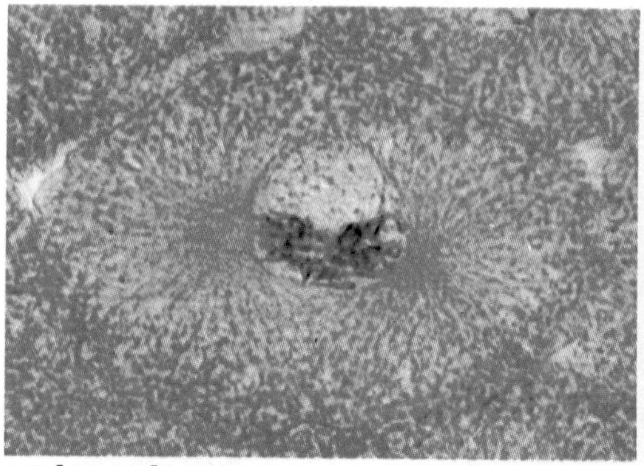

Mid-Prophase

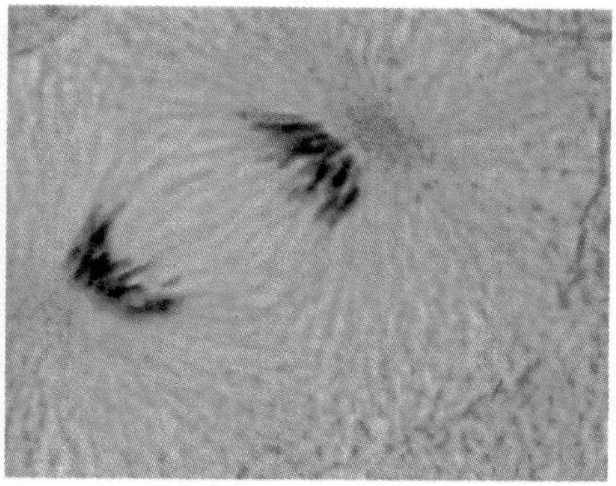

Late Anaphase

Courtesy General Biological Supply House, Inc., Chicago

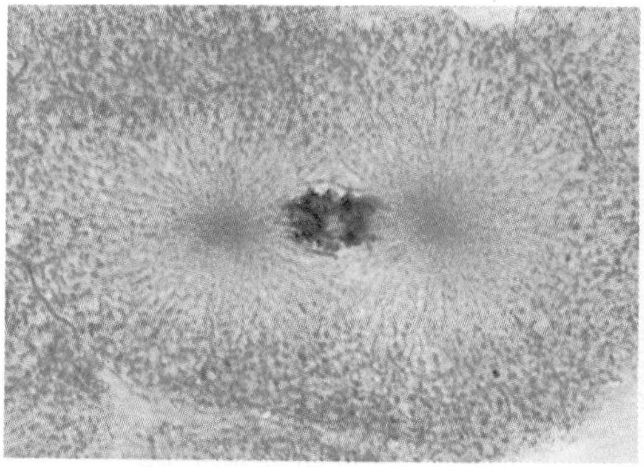

Late Prophase

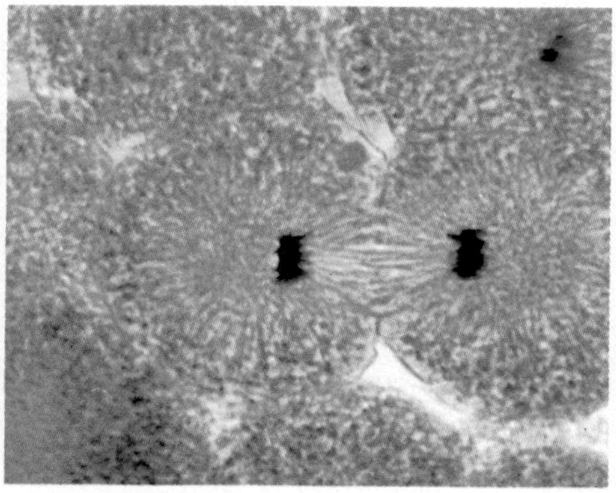

Telophase

Courtesy General Biological Supply House, Inc., Chicago

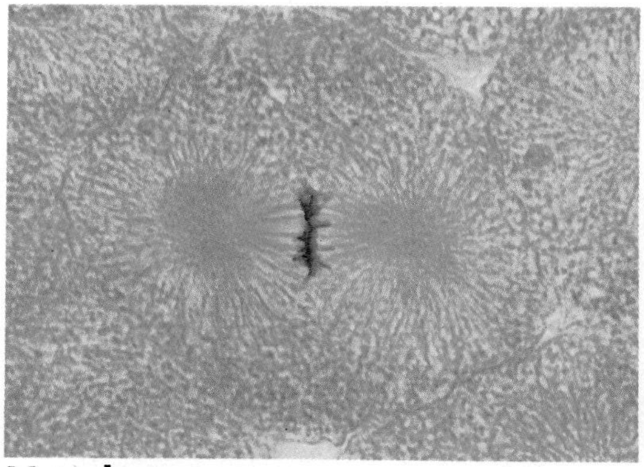

Metaphase

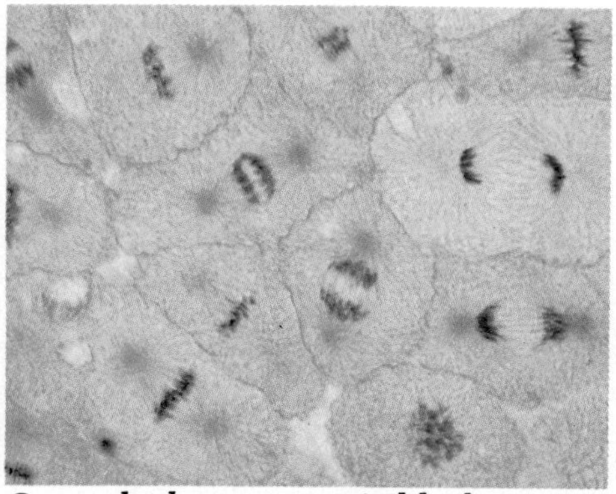

Several phases are visible here.

which the events of mitosis will take place. Centrioles apparently do not occur in most plant cells.

Prophase. This is the first observable from repeated coiling. It allows each chromosome to become disentangled from others, and so eventually makes correct division easier.

BACTERIAL TEST FOR DANGEROUS CHEMICALS

Some 25,000 synthetic chemicals appear in thousands of products regularly sold in the United States. Hundreds of new chemicals are placed on the market each year. How do we know whether any of them are potentially harmful to humans? Too often we do not. In the past, the only tests that could provide such information were so expensive and time-consuming that often they simply were not performed.

Now, it appears, a fast, relatively inexpensive procedure has been devised by a California biochemist. Some initial findings of the new method are rather sobering. They indicate, for instance, that most hair dyes contain mutagens—substances that alter the genetic material in the cells. Since hair-dye chemicals are known to be absorbed into the body of the user, there is a possibility that they may reach the sex organs, damage the eggs or sperm, and lead to the birth of defective children. There is also the fear that any mutagenic chemical may turn out to be carcinogenic—cancer-causing—as well. In fact, most hair-dye chemicals are closely related to known carcinogens. And some 20 million Americans are regular users of hair dye.

The new test uses a type of bacteria, *Salmonella typhimurium,* whose genes have been altered so that it needs the amino acid histidine in order to grow. The modified *Salmonella* are placed on a culture medium of agar, together with spots of the chemical being tested, but without added histidine. In these conditions, the bacteria should not be able to grow. The dish is incubated at 37° C for two days. If colonies of bacteria are then found growing around the chemical shots, only one conclusion can be drawn. The chemicals have caused the genes to mutate, enabling the bacteria to produce their own histidine. This does not in itself mean that the chemical will cause cancer. But it does mean that it should be tested further.

So far, the reliability of the new test seems fairly well demonstrated. Tested on 139 chemicals already known to be carcinogenic, it detected no fewer than 113 of them. Of 59 substances believed to be noncarcinogenic, the test found only 6 to be mutagens.

Older microbial tests for such chemicals can take as long as three years and cost upwards of $100,000 for each chemical tested. The new procedure takes two days and costs $600 to $1500. Thus it can more easily be used to screen large numbers of chemicals, separating those that are probably harmless from those that had better be looked at very carefully before they are put on the market.

---

stage in mitosis. During this stage the chromosomes become visible in the nucleus, changing from very long, thin threads into much shorter, thicker structures. Investigators think that this thickening results

If centrioles are present, they begin migrating to opposite sides of the cell, forming two "poles." Later a delicate mass of filaments, called the **spindle,** forms from one pole to the other. The spindle also forms in

222

plant cells, but without the migrating centrioles.

The chromatids, which are visible during prophase, are held together by a **centromere.** The centromere now becomes attached to the spindle fibers. At the time the spindle is developing, the nuclear membrane and nucleolus disappear.

Metaphase. The mitotic apparatus—consisting of centrioles, chromosomes (1 chromosome = 2 chromatids), and spindle fibers—is complete by the time of metaphase. After the spindle fibers become attached to the centromeres, they begin to "push" or "pull" the chromosomes toward the middle of the cell. Eventually the chromosomes become aligned along one plane, usually referred to as the **equatorial** plane. When all the chromosomes are lined up, the centromeres split and push away from each other, separating the chromatids.

Anaphase. Once the chromatids have separated, the spindle filaments pull them toward opposite poles (one of each pair toward each pole). During this stage, the chromatids often assume a V or J shape, depending on the position of the centromere. Each chromosome looks like a short piece of string being dragged through water by a thread. By the end of anaphase, each of the two identical sets of chromosomes has clustered around one of the poles.

Telophase. When the chromosomes have reached their poles, the final stage of cell division begins. The cytoplasm begins to divide, a process called **cytokinesis.** In animal cells, cytokinesis begins with the appearance of a **furrow,** or groove, in the cell membrane. In plant cells, it begins with the development of a **division plate** in the cell wall and membrane. The furrow or plate continues to grow until the cell divides into two daughter cells. As the cell is dividing, telophase is going on in the nucleus. The chromosomes uncoil into their earlier thread-like shape. The spindle disappears. The nuclear membrane and nucleolus reappear. When mitosis is complete, the two new daughter cells are said to be in interphase.

How long does mitosis take? Anywhere from thirty minutes to almost a day. It varies from cell to cell, although it is fairly constant for cells of the same kind. During most of the division cycle—60 to 95 percent of it—the cell is in interphase. Prophase usually takes longer than telophase; metaphase and anaphase are the briefest stages of all.

Most plant and animal cells undergo mitosis for growth and development. Even when an organism stops growing, some cells continue to divide, replacing old or damaged cells. But some specialized cells, such as mature nerve and muscle cells, do not undergo mitosis at all. If these are damaged or die, they are not replaced. It is not yet understood what determines whether cells will divide or not, but many scientists are actively investigating this problem. Discovery of the mechanism that controls cell division would be very useful in understanding abnormalities such as cancer. These abnormalities are characterized by uncontrollable division of cells.

Asexual reproduction

Some organisms reproduce by mitosis. Such **asexual reproduction** is common among protozoans and single-celled algae. But it is found also among multicellular organisms, especially plants. Suppose you wanted a grove of willow trees to grow in your backyard. All you have to do is find one willow tree and the space for the others. Simply by cutting branches from the tree and placing them in moist soil, you can raise several new trees. The willow tree illustrates a very common type of asexual reproduction called **vegetative reproduction.** The essential feature of vegetative reproduction is that it does not need special reproductive cells. Instead, some part is cut from an organism's body, and can develop into another organism. Usually, the term "vegetative reproduction" is used to describe the asexual reproduction of multicellular organisms.

Vegetative reproduction occurs in some animals, but is more common in plants.

Gardeners make extensive use of it. Bulbs of onions and tulips are used to produce new adults. Carrots and potatoes are cut up and planted to produce more carrots and potatoes. Strawberry "shoots," or "runners," are cut off and planted to produce more plants.

Vegetative reproduction also occurs among some invertebrates, many of which are found in the sea. In fresh water, the hydra serves as a good illustration. At certain times of year, hydras can be seen with "buds" growing on their bodies. The buds are actually young hydras. They will eventually separate from the larger individual and become independent organisms.

A rather extreme example of vegetative reproduction was accomplished a few years ago in the laboratory of Dr. F. C. Steward at Cornell University. Dr. Steward was interested in learning what mechanisms cause stem and root cells of plants to change their structure and function. He placed small pieces of carrot tissue in a medium containing nutrients and hormones. The carrot tissue was made of food-storage cells, not reproductive cells, but in the nutrient–hormone mix the cells began to multiply. Eventually the mass of tissue developed into an adult carrot. Later Dr. Steward isolated single cells from the same tissue. Using the same technique, he was able to grow adult plants. This was dramatic proof that all cells contain the necessary information to form a new organism.

Regeneration is a special form of vegetative reproduction—the regrowth of missing parts. When a starfish is broken into several pieces, each piece may regenerate whatever is needed to produce a new individual. The fresh-water flatworm *Planaria* can do the same thing.

Most animals cannot regenerate complete new organisms. They can merely regenerate certain parts—new tissues and new organs. A salamander, for example, can regenerate a new leg, but the leg cannot regenerate a new salamander. A lizard can regenerate a new tail, but again, the tail

Figure 11-10. These carrot plants were grown from single carrot cells that had been placed in a suitable medium in a flask.

Figure 11-11. Vegetative reproduction occurs not only in plants but in some animals as well. The bud growing on this hydra is nearly ready to separate from its parent and become an independent organism.

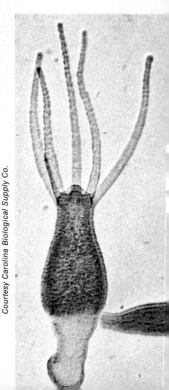

Figure 11-12. This fence lizard has escaped from the badger by leaving its tail behind. The lizard will soon begin to regenerate a new tail.

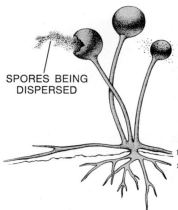

SPORES BEING
DISPERSED

Figure 11-13. The black bread mold reproduces asexually by spores. When the spore case ruptures, the released spores will drift through the air. Those that settle into a favorable environment will produce new molds.

cannot regenerate a new lizard. Human beings have very little regenerative ability. Very few of our tissues can be regenerated when damaged. (The liver is a striking exception.) So far, only plant tissue has been induced to develop into a new organism when placed in a favorable environment. But many biologists think that we may find out how to grow human tissue in the same manner (at least to some degree).

Many organisms produce specialized cells called **spores** that can develop into complete organisms. An excellent example is the common black bread mold. This organism has a specialized organ that produces many hundreds of spores. Eventually this structure ruptures, and the microscopic spores drift through the air. These spores will produce new molds if they settle into favorable environments. Many spores maintain their capacity to produce new individuals for quite a long time.

The ability to reproduce by spores is advantageous to a population. Most spores have specialized "coats" and can often withstand severe environmental conditions. In this way, whole populations of spore-producing organisms may survive adverse periods. Furthermore, the spores are usually light, so wide dispersal by wind is almost guaranteed. Finally, each adult produces thousands of spores. Thus, under certain conditions, the population can multiply very quickly.

Sexual reproduction

In asexual reproduction, each offspring arises from a single parent. It inherits all the characteristics of that parent. Hence vegetative reproduction is useful if we want to preserve these characteristics—for instance, if we want to reproduce a seedless orange.

But many organisms reproduce sexually. That is, cells from each of two parents fuse, forming the first cell of a new organism. In this way, the offspring is likely to inherit some of the characteristics of each parent.

The cells contributed by the parents—the sperm and the egg—are known as **gametes.** The fertilized cell that results is called a **zygote.** The zygote then undergoes repeated mitosis, to provide enough cells for the development of a new individual.

The somatic, or body, cells of sexually reproducing organisms have two sets of chromosomes in their nuclei. One set was contributed by the gamete of each parent. Cells with two sets of chromosomes are called **diploid** cells, and are said to contain a $2n$ number of chromosomes. For example, the diploid cells of a housefly have two sets of 6 chromosomes, or 12 chromosomes altogether. Each chromosome in one set has a similar, or **homologous,** chromosome in the other. Homologous chromosomes are similar in size and shape. They contain hereditary information about the same characteristics—for example, eye color. But because they were contributed by different parents, the information may not be the same. One chromosome may call for blue eyes, while its homologous mate calls for brown eyes.

The formation of gametes requires a special form of cell division, known as **meiosis.** During meiosis the number of chromosomes is halved, producing **haploid** (also called monoploid) cells with an n number of chromosomes. Human somatic cells are diploid and contain 46 chromosomes; human gametes are haploid cells containing 23 chromosomes. (For this reason, meiosis is often called "reduction division.") Each gamete contains only one of the chromosomes from each homologous pair. The fusion of two gametes during fertilization restores the diploid $(2n)$ number of chromosomes.

Within any sexually reproducing population, there are usually two types of gamete. The gamete produced by the male parent is called a **sperm.** The gamete produced by the female parent is called an **egg.** The sperm is usually capable of movement, by means of one or more flagella that propel it through a liquid environment toward the egg. The egg is usually larger than the sperm and is incapable of independent movement.

Sperm and eggs are sometimes produced by the same individual. Such individuals are called **hermaphrodites.** The earthworm is a hermaphrodite. Other animals have separate sexes, and produce male gametes in one organism and female gametes in another.

Meiosis

In many respects, the events of meiosis are similar to those of mitosis. They are even

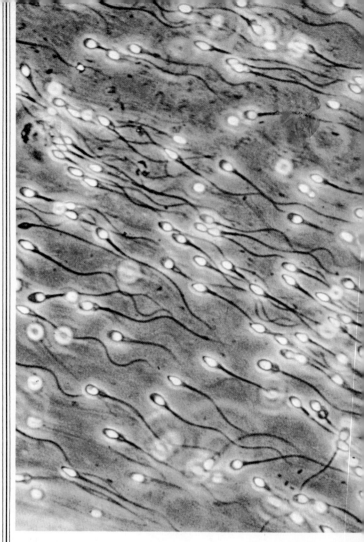

Figure 11-14. Human sperm swimming toward an egg. Only one of these sperm will actually fertilize the egg.

Figure 11-15. Earthworms are hermaphroditic—each individual possesses both male and female reproductive organs. Earthworms may come together and cross-fertilize each other, as shown here.

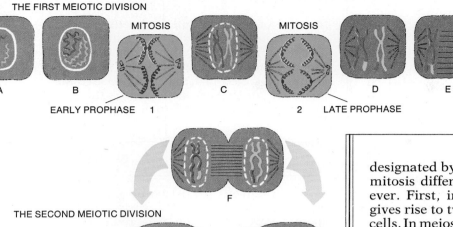

MITOSIS   MITOSIS

A   B   C   D   E

EARLY PROPHASE   1   2   LATE PROPHASE

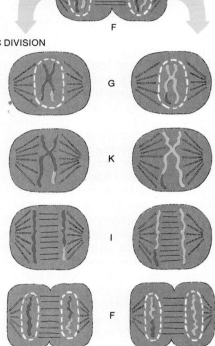

THE SECOND MEIOTIC DIVISION

F

G

K

I

F

Figure 11-16. The stages of meiosis.

designated by the same names. Meiosis and mitosis differ in two major respects, however. First, in mitosis one diploid parent gives rise to two identical, diploid daughter cells. In meiosis one diploid parent cell gives rise to four different, haploid daughter cells. Second, meiosis involves two successive cell divisions; mitosis involves only one.

The first meiotic division consists of six stages, because prophase is broken into three periods.

Early prophase I. The chromosomes condense and become visible.

Middle prophase I. The chromosomes can now be seen to consist of two chromatids joined by a centromere.

Late prophase I. Each doubled chromosome moves next to its homologue, and they line up side by side. This pairing up of homologous chromosomes is called **synapsis,** and it occurs only in meiosis. The arrangement of the four chromatids is called a **tetrad.** The chromosomes are so close to each other that they intertwine, and sections of the inner chromatids may be exchanged. This process of **crossing-over** is shown in figure 11-16 by the overlapping of different-colored sections of the chromosomes. Crossing-over is exceedingly important. It enables the **genes,** which store the hereditary information in the chromosomes, to be recombined in the homologues. Also, during this stage of prophase, filaments of the spindle mechanism become attached to the centromeres. The nuclear membrane and nucleolus disappear.

After prophase, the stages are the same as in mitosis, but the events are slightly different.

Metaphase I. The centromeres of the homologous pair do not line up on an equatorial plane. Instead, they seem to push away from each other. They attach to the spindle so that each centromere, with its pair of chromatids, is pointing toward an opposite pole. This positioning of the chromosomes will enable half of them to be placed in each daughter cell.

Anaphase I. The homologous pairs migrate toward the opposite poles. The chromatids of each chromosome do not separate, however, as they did in mitosis. Instead, they remain joined by their centromere.

Telophase I. Ordinarily, the cell divides at telophase. The two nuclei re-form. The daughter nuclei are not identical, as in mitosis. Each contains two chromatids from one chromosome of each old homologous pair, but nothing from the other (except what may have been exchanged by crossing-over).

The nuclei or cells resulting from the first meiotic division soon divide again. How soon depends on the organism. The second meiotic division is necessary so that the chromatids can be separated from each other. It is similar to mitosis, except that the chromosomes do not replicate. There is no need for them to do so, because each chromosome already consists of two chromatids as a result of the first division.

Prophase II. The nuclei formed by the first division are haploid. That is, they contain only one *(n)* set of chromosomes. During prophase, the nuclear membrane disappears and the spindle begins to form.

Metaphase II. The chromosomes migrate to the equatorial plane. Again, the centromeres attach to the spindle fibers.

Anaphase II. The centromeres divide, the chromatids separate, and the spindle fibers appear to pull the chromatids (now individual chromosomes) toward the poles.

Telophase II. Nuclear and cell division is completed.

The net result of meiosis is the production of four haploid *(n)* cells from one diploid *(2n)* cell, each with one set of chromosomes. In the case of the male, all four cells usually become sperm, functioning as gametes. In many species, though, the female does not produce four eggs. Often one of the four cells is larger and has much more cytoplasm than the other three. This larger cell is the one that will function as a female gamete.

SUMMARY

Living organisms persist because they can reproduce themselves. The early belief in spontaneous generation was replaced by Redi's theory of biogenesis. Pasteur's experiments later proved that microorganisms arise from other microorganisms.

The theory of abiogenesis is similar in some ways to that of spontaneous generation. It proposes that living matter may originally have been generated from nonliving matter, under conditions which are supposed to have existed on the primitive earth. Laboratory tests have tended to support Oparin's theory that organic molecules could have been synthesized from inorganic gases under such conditions, through energy from electrical storms or ultraviolet light.

Scientists are attempting to explain how organic molecules might have given rise to living cells. A variety of organic molecules can be synthesized in devices which duplicate probable conditions on the primitive earth. But this is still a long way from the creation of living cells from nonliving matter.

Cells arise from other cells through the process of cell division. During interphase, the chromosomes replicate. During mitosis, each daughter nucleus receives an identical copy of the original cell's chromosomes, which contain the hereditary information for new cells. Division of the cytoplasm completes the division of the cell.

The somatic cells of sexually reproducing organisms usually have two sets of chromosomes, one received from each parent. These are called diploid cells. The diploid number of chromosomes is preserved through mitosis from generation to generation.

Asexual reproduction results in new individuals with the same genetic material as the parent. In vegetative reproduction, new organisms grow from somatic cells of the parent. Regeneration is a form whereby an individual can replace missing body parts, such as limbs. A few organisms can reproduce by regeneration. Finally, reproduction can occur by production of specialized organs containing spores. These organs rupture, scattering the spores in the environment.

Mitosis results in new cells that are identical to the old ones. This is necessary for proper growth and development of the organism. In sexually reproducing organisms, a second process of cell division, called meiosis, occurs. Meiosis in animals produces reproductive cells called gametes, each containing only half the number of chromosomes present in the somatic cells of the parent. Gametes are therefore haploid cells.

The first meiotic division results in two nuclei, each containing a haploid number of chromosomes. If crossing-over occurs during synapsis, these chromosomes may be slightly different from the original parent chromosomes. Each chromosome is made up of two chromatids.

The second meiotic division results in four nuclei. Each contains a haploid number of chromosomes, each consisting of a single chromatid. When one gamete fuses with another gamete from the opposite sex, they form a diploid cell called a zygote, from which the new individual will develop. The zygote contains a complete diploid set of chromosomes.

Review questions

1. Describe some of the important differences between living and nonliving matter.

2. List three properties of living organisms. Why is each necessary?

3. Contrast the theory of spontaneous generation with the theory of abiogenesis.

4. What is Oparin's hypothesis?

5. Describe Miller's experiment which tested the Oparin hypothesis. What was its result?

6. What are coacervate droplets? How might they have given rise to the first living cells?

7. What probable type were the first cells? Why?

8. Why would the appearance of autotrophic cells prevent further abiogenesis?

9. What are proteinoids? What is their significance?

10. What is chromatin composed of?

11. What important process takes place during interphase?

12. Describe the events of prophase.

13. What structures are included in the mitotic apparatus?

14. During what stage of mitosis does actual cell division occur? What is the sequence of events?

15. Name and describe three varieties of asexual reproduction.

16. What is the significance of Steward's carrot experiments for medical science?

17. What are the advantages to survival of sexual reproduction? Of asexual reproduction?

18. Distinguish between diploid and haploid cells.

19. How is a zygote formed? What is its purpose?

20. In what ways does meiosis differ from mitosis?

21. What is crossing-over and when does it occur? Why is it important?

22. Why is a second meiotic division necessary?

24. What is the end result of meiosis?

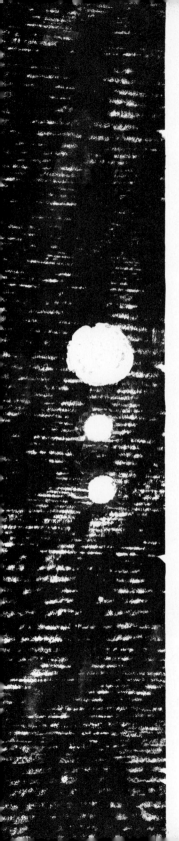

Reproduction and Development in Plants

In the last chapter, we studied the events that take place when a cell divides. Mitosis ordinarily results in two cells that are essentially just like the parent cell. For single-celled organisms, mitosis may be a perfectly adequate way of reproduction. But for multicellular plants and animals, it would be rather unhandy. Imagine a world in which all living things reproduced by mitosis. In a maple tree, for instance, every cell would replicate—in the trunk, in the leaves, in the roots. Then all the cells would somehow be sorted out and assembled into two new trees. It may have happened in science fiction, but it is obviously not the way things are done on this planet.

Instead, as we know, most multicellular organisms have special organs that produce gametes by meiosis. These are the sexual organs. Male and female gametes come together and form a **zygote.** This single fertilized cell is the beginning of an entire new organism. Over a period of days, weeks, or months, it will change enormously. It will divide innumerable times until it contains thousands or millions of cells. At the same time, the new cells will change and specialize. Groups of them will become organized into tissues and organs. The mature organism that will eventually result will be the direct descendant of the original one-celled zygote. Yet it will resemble it not at all.

Development, then, is best understood as the sequence of programmed changes that take place in an organism from zygote to

Figure 12-1. The fragrance and beauty of these flowers have a value that is not entirely esthetic. They are an important part of the plant's sexuality, serving to attract the insects that are needed for pollination.

death. It includes growth and specialization. It also includes the changes that put an end to growth and that eventually cause the organism to deteriorate and die.

When we consider reproduction and development in plants, we are likely to be struck by one key fact. This is that dry land is not an easy environment for plants. Most marine plants have a very simple structure, and reproduce merely by releasing their gametes into the water. They are supported and held up by the water, and all their cells are bathed in it. Land plants lack these conveniences. So, if they are to survive, they need a more complex structure. They need a specialized surface that will protect them

PATTERNS OF REPRODUCTION
AND DEVELOPMENT

Figure 12-2. Ferns, some of them very large, dominated the earth during the Devonian and Carboniferous periods. Sections of the landscape probably looked a great deal like this picture.

from drying out. They need an internal transport system and some kind of supporting "skeleton." Also, they need reproductive organs that do more than produce and release gametes. There must be some way for the gametes to come together without a limitless supply of water to swim in. And the embryo plant must be kept moist and protected until it, in turn, develops its own specialized structures.

The land plants of today are generally classified in two main groups. One is the **bryophytes,** which include the mosses and liverworts. The other is the **tracheophytes** or vascular plants. These include the ferns and all of the seed plants. The two groups differ significantly in their patterns of reproduction and development.

SEEDLESS LAND PLANTS

Fossil evidence indicates that the seed plants have not always dominated our landscape. Four hundred million years ago, extensive forests of ferns and horsetails grew over the land. Mosses and other small plants carpeted the forest floors. Why do these plants no longer dominate the natural landscape today?

The life cycle of a moss
Mosses are widely dispersed over the earth.

Like all the bryophytes, they lack the vascular system that is found in tracheophytes. As a result, they are limited to places where moisture is readily available. They are also limited in height and thickness. All of their cells must be close to the water and nutrients in the environment. Moreover, as we shall see, they cannot reproduce sexually without the presence of water.

Mosses usually grow in moist, shaded places, often in a velvety green clump or carpet. This is actually a tightly packed mass of individual plants. At most times of the year, the body of the individual moss looks like a green, bristly stem. The "bristles" are small, leaf-like structures that carry on photosynthesis. Sometimes, especially during late spring, a long, thin, naked stalk grows up from the moss plant. The stalk has a large, somewhat cup-shaped tip. It appears to be an extension of the individual from which it grows. But it is in fact another stage, growing much as a parasite might on the plant below it.

Gametophyte generation. These two different stages in the life cycle of a moss result from two phases of reproduction. The moss plant that one normally sees, consisting of stem-like and leaf-like structures, represents the gamete-producing generation. Biologists call it the **gametophyte.** In some species, one gametophyte individual may produce both male and female gametes. Generally, however, the sexes are separate. Some individuals produce only egg cells and others only sperm cells. In mosses, the gametes are produced in structures at the top of the gametophyte plant. The female organ, called the **archegonium,** is a flask-like projection. The male organ, or **antheridium,** is club-shaped. Within these organs, the developing gametes are protected from injury and from drying out.

At this point we encounter a key difference between bryophytes and most tracheophytes. In the moss plant's reproductive cycle the sperm must swim through water to reach the egg. Raindrops, dew—even spray from waterfalls—wetting the plant's surface may be enough. But liquid water there must be.

Sporophyte generation. After the egg is fertilized, the zygote remains inside the archegonium. There it begins to divide mitotically, and develops into the naked stalk we described above. The stalk contains some chlorophyll, so it can photosynthesize for a short time. But it keeps its base firmly embedded in the gametophyte, from which it receives its water and nutrients. This new individual contains a diploid $(2n)$ number of chromosomes—one set from the sperm and one set from the egg. When it matures, however, it will produce spores with a haploid (n) number of chromosomes. Because it produces these spores, it is known as the **sporophyte.**

The spores result from meiotic cell division within the **sporangium,** the enlarged region at the tip of the sporophyte. When these haploid spores are ripe, thousands of them burst from the sporangium and are released into the air. They may then be widely scattered by the wind. Each spore has a thick protective coating which allows it to survive adverse conditions, such as cold or dry air, for months. The spore is the first cell of the haploid gametophyte generation. If a spore lands in a favorable environment, it may begin to divide and produce branching, thread-like filaments. The filamentous growth in turn will produce rhizoid cells, like tiny root hairs, that grow into the soil, and stem-like growths that carry on photo-

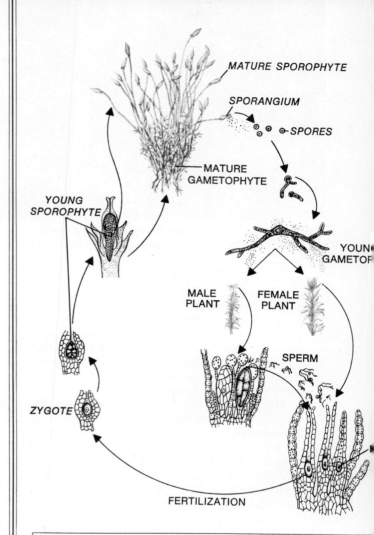

Figure 12-3. The life cycle of a moss.

synthesis. (Remember that these are not true roots or stems, because they lack a vascular system.) The stem-like growths will eventually produce gametes, and so the cycle repeats itself.

The reproductive pattern in which a gametophyte generation alternates with a sporophyte generation is called **alternation of generations.** Note that in the moss the gametophyte—what we think of as "the" moss plant—is larger and more dominant.

234

Figure 12-4. A cluster of moss gametophytes can be seen at the bottom of this photograph. The long, slender stalks are mature sporophytes, with enlarged sporangia at their ends.

In the fern, this dominance pattern is reversed.

The life cycle of a fern

Ferns have a well-organized vascular system and are therefore able to transport water and minerals to a much greater height than the mosses. But ferns, like mosses, can reproduce sexually only in a moist environment.

Alternation of generations occurs in the life cycle of the fern. What we normally call a fern is the diploid sporophyte. The individu-als of the gametophyte generation are so small and unlike the sporophyte that at first they were not even identified with it. Differences in size between the two generations are usually extreme. In a few species, the sporophyte may grow to as much as 30 feet. The gametophyte it produces may grow flat on the ground, smaller than a dime. Yet, despite its small size, the gametophyte is a separate individual. It is capable of photosynthesis, and therefore it can live independently of the sporophyte.

The major stages in the fern's reproductive cycle are outlined in figure 12-5. Spores are produced by meiosis in sporangia on the undersides of the sporophyte leaves. (Groups of sporangia form the familiar black or brown spots on the fern fronds.) These haploid spores are released at certain times of the year. If they land in a favorable environment, they will germinate. As in the moss, a filamentous growth appears first. This soon develops into the **prothallus,** a small, heart-shaped gametophyte fern. The prothallus is seldom more than an inch wide, and is usually only one cell thick. As the prothallus matures, reproductive organs develop on its underside. The archegonia produce eggs, and the antheridia produce sperm. Sperm and egg fuse in the archegonium, producing a diploid zygote and the beginning of the new sporophyte generation.

Again as in the moss, the sperm can reach the egg only by swimming through water. Since the gametophyte grows flat on the ground, the union of egg and sperm presents no problem—provided the environment is moist. This is the key limitation that has kept the ferns from competing with the seed plants on most of the earth's land surface.

Reproductive adaptations

Certain features are common to the reproductive cycles of all plants. Most plants reproduce sexually. Some algae do so through the fusion of two identical gametes. Other algae, as well as the rest of the plant king-

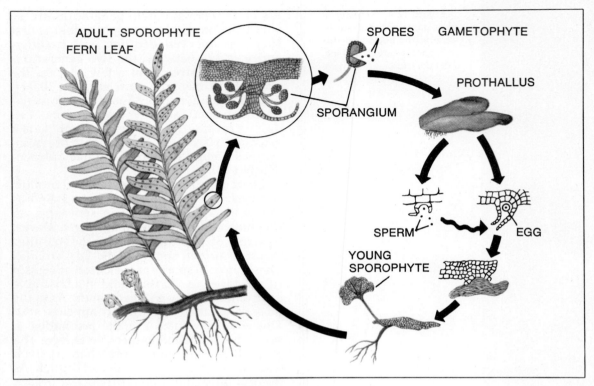

Figure 12-5. The life cycle of a fern.

dom, reproduce through the fusion of two different gametes (egg and sperm). Most sperm are motile, but the egg is usually large and stationary. The egg contains stored food which will be used during the early development of the zygote.

Plants that live mostly away from water have features that protect their reproductive cells from drying out in the air and from injury on land. The archegonium shelters the eggs, and the antheridium protects the sperm. In addition, the young embryo sporophyte remains inside the archegonium. Spores remain in the sporangia until mature. They also develop a thick outer coating which protects them from drying once they are released from the sporangia. The protection of spores, sperm, and egg is a characteristic of nearly all land plants.

Finally, alternation of generations is found in all green land plants. We noted that in the moss, the gametophyte is the dominant generation. But plants that are less protected by water do best if they are more resistant to drying. The sporophyte seems to be better adapted in this respect. In most higher plants, therefore, the sporophyte generation is dominant. The gametophyte is very small and completely dependent on the sporophyte.

PATTERNS OF REPRODUCTION IN SEED PLANTS

Seed plants fall into two major classes. One group, the **gymnosperms,** are apparently older and are simpler in their method of reproduction. Most gymnosperms produce

PATTERNS OF REPRODUCTION
AND DEVELOPMENT

Figure 12-6. The jack pine is a typical gymnosperm. Its seeds are produced in cones.

seeds in cones and are often called **conifers.** The second major class of seed plants, the **angiosperms,** has more species and is more widely distributed. Its members are commonly called **flowering plants.** All the grasses and herbs and most of the shrubs and broad-leaved trees in our environment are flowering plants. In this chapter, we shall emphasize the reproductive mechanisms of the larger and more common of the two classes—the flowering plants. First, however, we shall outline briefly the major stages in the gymnosperm reproductive cycle.

Gymnosperms
The term *gymnosperm* comes from the Greek words for "naked seed." In this group of plants, seeds develop in a rather exposed position. Among the conifers, seeds are borne on the hard reproductive leaves, or **scales,** of the **cones.**

A typical conifer is the pine. The pine we see is the sporophyte, and bears cones of two kinds. The soft male **pollen cone** produces spores that develop into pollen grains, or male gametophytes. The hard female **seed cone** produces spores that develop into female gametophytes.

The seed cone is larger than the pollen cone. Through meiosis, each of the two sporangia on a seed-cone scale produces four haploid spores. One spore from each survives. Through repeated mitotic division, the spore develops into the young female gametophyte. The female gametophyte then develops archegonia in which it will bear the eggs.

The fern gametophyte was an independent plant. But the pine gametophyte always remains attached to the seed-cone scale. Thus it is sheltered and protected by the sporophyte. This in turn means greater protection for the eggs or zygotes in its archegonia.

The haploid spores of the pollen cone develop into thick-walled pollen grains. When they are mature, the pollen grains are released into the air. A few may land on a seed-cone scale, to which the female gametophyte is still attached. The pollen grain develops into the tiny male gametophyte. This grows down through the protective tissues around the female gametophyte and releases two sperm. One sperm unites with the egg of the female gametophyte. (Note that here, no liquid water is required for the sperm to reach the egg.) The resulting diploid zygote is nourished from the stored food of the egg while it develops into an embryonic pine. A tough seed coat develops around the embryo. Finally the seed drops off the cone, and germinates if conditions are favorable.

Angiosperms
The **flower,** the reproductive site of flowering plants, has two major differences from

the cone of the gymnosperms. One is that the flower often helps to attract animals, which in turn help to pollinate the plant. A second difference is that the flower provides additional protective layers around the seed. In fact, the term *angiosperm* comes from the two Greek words meaning "covered seed."

An idealized flower is shown in figure 12-7. The **sepals**, or **calyx**, and **petals**, or **corolla**, are usually the most conspicuous parts of the flower. Both are modified leaves with specialized roles. The sepals are the outer structures of the flower and are usually green and leaf-like. They serve mainly to protect the inner parts of the bud. The generally more colorful petals may attract birds or insects to the flower. Flowers that rely on wind for pollination are often not as brightly colored, and they may lack petals altogether.

The **stamen** is the male reproductive organ of the flower. Most flowers have several stamens. Each consists of a long **filament** topped by a sac-like container of pollen, called the **anther.** Through meiosis, the sporangia of the developing anther produce a number of haploid spores. The nucleus of each haploid spore then undergoes mitosis, but the cell itself does not divide. The result is a single cell with two haploid nuclei. This cell is the male gametophyte, or **pollen grain.** When the anther matures, it splits open and releases the pollen.

The **pistil,** composed of one or more **carpels,** is the female reproductive organ. It consists of three basic structures. The lower portion of the pistil is the **ovary.** The egg is fertilized and will develop into an embryo inside the ovary. Above the ovary, a slender **style** ends in an enlarged, often sticky, area called the **stigma. Pollination** occurs when pollen from a stamen lands on the stigma.

Most flowers are like the one just described. They are called **perfect flowers** because they bear both male and female reproductive structures. Other plant species have **imperfect flowers,** which bear only one or the other. Pollination may appear to be a simple matter in a perfect flower but more

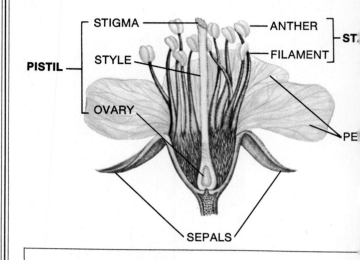

Figure 12-7. This perfect flower possesses both male and female reproductive structures.

Figure 12-8. This close-up of an amaryllis shows six stamens clustered just to the right of the three-pronged stigma.

PATTERNS OF REPRODUCTION
AND DEVELOPMENT

Figure 12-9. This flower receives pollen from a flower previously visited by the bee. Such cross-pollination produces seeds containing hereditary information from both parent plants.

difficult when the male and female organs are in separate flowers. Actually, though, the stamens and pistils are often so arranged that **self-pollination** is unlikely, even among the perfect flowers.

For one thing, in wind-pollinated plants, the anthers usually mature before the stigma. By the time the stigma is ready to receive pollen, the flower's own pollen has already been blown away. In animal-pollinated plants, the pollinator usually brushes against the stigma first and the anther afterward. Thus the stigma receives pollen only from the flower that the insect visited previously.

The chief value of this **cross-pollination** is that it reshuffles the chromosomes among plants in a species. A seed produced by cross-pollination contains hereditary information from both parent plants. It will grow into a plant that is not exactly like either one.

Self-pollination, of course, does not generally have this advantage. But if cross-pollination does not occur, some of the flower's own pollen may land on its stigma and fertilize it. (Pollination is complete when a pollen grain of the right kind has been transferred to the stigma of a flower. Fertilization is the actual fusion of gametes.)

A pollen grain germinates when it lands on a moist stigma. During **germination,** the protective covering around the cell ruptures, and a slender extension of the cell begins to emerge. This extension is called the **pollen tube.** (See figure 12-10.) The pollen tube begins to grow, and digests its way down through the style to the ovary.

Recall that the pollen grain at first contains two nuclei. One of the nuclei migrates to the tip of the pollen tube. It is called the **tube nucleus.** The other nucleus, called the **generative nucleus,** divides into two **sperm nuclei,** or male gametes. These sperm nuclei travel through the cytoplasm of the pollen tube. Thus the pollen tube serves the same function as the water through which the sperm cells of mosses and ferns must swim. The pollen tube grows down until it reaches one of the **ovules** (there may be only one) in the ovary.

The ovules are sporangia inside the ovary. Through meiosis each ovule produces four haploid spores, one of which survives. This spore then undergoes mitotic division, usually producing eight haploid nuclei. These make up the female gametophyte. Three of them will usually be fertilized by the two sperm in the pollen tube. One of the three is an **egg cell.** The other two are known as the **polar nuclei,** and are joined in a single diploid cell before fertilization.

After reaching the interior of the ovule, the tip of the pollen tube ruptures, and the two sperm flow out. One fuses with the egg cell, forming a diploid zygote that subsequently develops into the embryo sporophyte. The other sperm unites with the polar nuclei, forming a **triploid** ($3n$) cell with three sets of chromosomes. This cell produces the **endosperm,** a tissue that is not part of the embryo but may provide food for it. This **double fertilization** does not occur in the gymnosperms or in any other class of plants.

Plants that pollinate—gymnosperms as well as angiosperms—are not dependent on external water for reproduction. The pollen grain can be carried by wind or animals for many miles. Its outer coating protects it until it reaches the female reproductive organ, and the pollen tube provides a way for the sperm to reach the egg.

You may have noticed that, in the angiosperms, the male and female gametophytes are greatly reduced in comparison with those in the plants we discussed earlier. The male gametophyte—the pollen grain—is a single cell with three nuclei. The female gametophyte consists of only a few cells inside the ovule. Both male and female gametophytes are no longer independent individuals, but rely completely on the sporophyte.

As the ovules grow inside the ovary, they develop into **seeds.** The seed is actually the matured ovule, and usually consists of embryo, endosperm, and protective coverings called **seed coats.** In some species the endosperm tissue develops around the embryo. In other species, such as the bean, the food in the endosperm is absorbed by the cotyledons, or "seed leaves," before the seed is mature.

The walls of the ovule begin to harden and develop into the seed coats. These are usually not permeable to water and air, so they prevent the seed from obtaining materials necessary for growth. While in this "sealed-off" condition, the seed seems to slow down or greatly reduce all physiological activity.

Figure 12-10. Within the ovule, one sperm nucleus combines with two haploid egg nuclei (upper) to form a triploid cell. This cell will divide and become the endosperm. The other sperm nucleus (lower) unites with another of the egg nuclei to form a zygote that will develop into a new plant.

POLLEN GRAIN — STIGMA
— STYLE
OVARY
POLLEN TUBE — OVULE

TWO NUCLEI ONE SPERM NUCLEUS FORM ENDOSPERM NUCLEUS

EGG AND ONE SPERM NUCLEUS FORM ZYGOTE

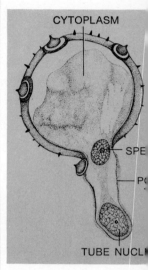

Figure 12-11. This diagram of a germinating pollen grain shows the tube nucleus and one of the two sperm nuclei growing down through the pollen tube. The sperm nuclei arise from the generative nucleus.

CYTOPLASM

SPE

P

TUBE NUCL

This suspended state is called **seed dormancy.**

The **fruit** is the matured ovary, to which other tissues from the flower may be attached. Apples and peaches are fruits, but so are cucumbers, tomatoes, bean and pea "pods," dandelion "seeds," acorns, cockleburs, and many other common products of plants that are not so readily recognized as fruits. Fruit develops only in the angiosperms.

PATTERNS OF REPRODUCTION AND DEVELOPMENT

Figure 12-12. Seeds may be dispersed in a variety of ways. The seeds of the milkweed may be carried by air or by water. The winged fruit of the box elder may spin far from the tree. The cocklebur's barbs hook into any fibers that touch them— whether the fur of an animal or the threads in your clothing.

The fruit may serve a number of functions. One obvious function is the protection of the seed or seeds enclosed in it. Nuts such as the acorn or walnut are excellent examples of such fruits. The fruit may also serve in the dispersal of the seed. The cocklebur with its sharp hooks, the dandelion fruit with its "parachute," and the box elder with its "wings" are some examples of fruits that greatly aid in the dispersal of the seeds they contain. Animals that eat the fruit and later eliminate the seeds also help. Some seeds, such as peaches, cannot germinate unless they have passed through an animal's digestive system. The digestive juices loosen the "cement" that holds the seed coat together.

THE NATURE OF DEVELOPMENT

So far in our discussion we have used the term "development" rather loosely. However, the biologist uses the term more precisely to mean the changes and processes that lead to the formation of an adult organism. "Development" may also refer to changes at levels of organization below that of the whole organism. For example, the biologist might be concerned with **cellular development** or with **tissue development**.

When does the formation of the adult organism start? When does it end? In the higher plants and animals, which normally reproduce sexually, biologists usually think of development as starting immediately upon fertilization, with the zygote and its double set of chromosomes. However, there is no precise ending point in development, no exact moment when one can say that an organism is an adult. We have only a general idea of when a higher plant or animal reaches adulthood. Sexual maturity is one measure used to separate adults from juveniles. When an organism is able to produce gametes, it is often considered to be an adult.

Yet development, unlike growth, does not usually stop when the adult stage is reached.

Adult animals continue to produce new cells and tissues to replace some old or injured ones. Furthermore, plants, unlike most animals, grow in size as long as they are alive. Usually plant development is considered at an end only when the plant ceases to grow and produce new tissue—that is, when it dies.

the same time. For example, consider an egg that has just been fertilized.

Cellular enlargement. Upon fertilization, the nuclei of the sperm and egg combine, forming a single nucleus with a double set of chromosomes. The intracellular and extracellular environments interact with the hereditary information in the chromo-

---

HIGH-PROTEIN CORN

Plant scientists at the International Corn and Wheat Improvement Center (CIMMYT) in Mexico have developed a new type of corn that promises to help improve the diet of the world's hungry. The new strain contains more protein than milk, and the protein is of a higher quality than that in beef. Because of the appearance of its kernels, the new corn is known as opaque-2.

Opaque-2 differs from ordinary corn in its amino acid content. Ordinary corn is poor in two amino acids, lysine and tryptophan. As a result, barely half of its total protein can be used by the human body. Opaque-2, by contrast, is high in lysine and tryptophan. Consequently, almost 90 percent of its protein is usable by humans.

Despite its nutritional value, the new corn is not finding easy acceptance among farmers. It weighs slightly less than ordinary corn, so growers who must sell their corn by weight tend to reject it. And its soft, floury

kernel and white color make it unattractive to people who expect corn to be hard and yellow. The soft kernels are also more vulnerable to pests and disease.

Efforts are being made to correct these defects. By crossing opaque-2 with other corn, researchers have created varieties that are attractively hard and yellow, but that still have the high protein content of opaque-2. They have also developed varieties suited to different climate conditions. The next problem seems to lie in preventing accidental cross-pollination. If a small farmer plants the new corn near a neighbor's plot of ordinary corn, the two types will probably cross-pollinate. The valuable characteristics of the new corn will then be weakened. If the farmer saves some of each year's crop for seed, the situation will get worse each year that cross-pollination occurs. Eventually the "new" corn will be very little different from the old. So it seems that the next step lies not with plant breeders, but with educators, economists, and even governments. The new corn must be widely adopted in some particular region, if its full value is to be gained.

Processes of development

The biologist thinks of development as consisting of four main processes. These are never considered isolated events occurring independently of each other. Development is a smoothly coordinated process during which all four events may be occurring at

somes. The new cell becomes literally a hubbub of activity. Chemical-bond energy is transformed and new molecules are synthesized. At this stage, and at subsequent stages of development, more new molecules are produced than are broken down. The result is an increase in size, or cellular enlargement. Such enlargement implies

PATTERNS OF REPRODUCTION
AND DEVELOPMENT

growth and is a key event in development.

Cellular division. Development must include events other than increase in size. Otherwise an adult organism would simply be one huge cell. Within a short time after fertilization, the zygote begins to divide into two cells by mitosis. The two cells then divide in the same manner, producing four cells; these divide, producing eight cells; and the process continues. This process of cellular division is the second major event in the development of an individual organism.

Suppose that cellular division has continued for some time. What would be the result? Would we see an adult organism? If cellular enlargement and cellular division were the only two processes of development, we would see only a large mass of identical cells. But this mass would hardly constitute an adult organism. Clearly some further process is required.

Cellular differentiation. After cellular division has proceeded for a time, certain cells begin to differentiate. They begin to assume specific forms and to carry on specialized activities. Different kinds of cell appear— for example, guard cells, epidermal cells, and tracheid cells. This third process is called cellular differentiation.

Cells differentiate, or specialize, when hereditary information coded in the chromosomes responds to changes in the cytoplasm or the environment of the cell. What causes this information to be translated at the proper time and in the proper sequence for development to proceed as a coordinated process is still being studied.

Supracellular differentiation. But even cellular differentiation is not enough. The combined events of cellular enlargement, cellular division, and cellular differentiation would result simply in a large mass of specialized cells. In such a multicellular mass the specialized cells would be functioning only as individual cells, not as a unit in a team of tissues, organs, and systems. Still another process is needed.

The fourth characteristic process of development may be called supracellular differentiation. This is a catchall term that refers to the way differentiated cells are organized into tissues, how tissues are organized into organs, how organs are organized into systems, and finally, how systems are organized into individuals. **Morphogenesis** is another term applied to this stage in development.

DEVELOPMENT IN SEED PLANTS

Since development begins with fertilization and the formation of the zygote, plant development is well under way before the seed is even mature. You will recall that the seed usually consists of three main, well-defined parts: the young embryo, the endosperm, and the seed coats. Thus, although the seed is often thought of as a reproductive structure, it is actually more of a specialized container in which the process of development can be temporarily halted. The seed protects the embryo plant, and is the form in which new plants are dispersed. In addition, the stored food the seed contains can be used for energy and raw materials once the embryo germinates and resumes its active development.

Breaking dormancy

Seed dormancy may last for several months or even years, but can be broken by suitable environmental conditions. Many seeds are like those of the apple and the peach. Before they resume development, they must be exposed to extended periods of near-freezing temperatures, alternating with exposures to higher temperatures. This mechanism is of great survival value. Winter is often interrupted by sudden periods of warm weather. If dormancy were to break during the first warm period, the young plant would be unprotected during the next cold spell and would die.

Light may also be responsible for breaking dormancy in some species. Experiments have demonstrated that light in the red portion of the spectrum is especially effective. It was discovered that orange-red light may start a sequence of events that breaks the dormant stage. But, surprisingly, it was also discovered that later exposure to a deeper red light could reverse this effect and thereby inhibit the action caused by the orange-red light.

Biologists do not yet fully understand how the specific mechanisms behind the breaking of dormancy operate. The seed coat may sometimes serve as a simple physical barrier. In this case, the barrier can be broken by physical means, such as water, rough soil, or fire. On the other hand, certain chemicals in the seed may react to conditions in the environment, such as changes in light or temperature, and so cause dormancy to break.

Germination

The period of development from the breaking of dormancy to the stage at which the young plant is independently manufacturing its own food is known as **germination.** Before germination, the seed is practically dehydrated. Germination begins when it starts to imbibe a great deal of water from its surroundings. This softens the seed coat and stimulates an increase in the embryo's metabolism. The cells of the embryo start to divide rapidly again, causing it to grow and finally to break out of the seed.

The plant embryo has already undergone considerable differentiation, both cellular and supracellular, by the time the seed germinates. Four main regions can be identified on the young plant, as shown in figure 12-14. The largest are one or two **cotyledons,** commonly called "seed leaves." The function of the cotyledon is to digest the food in the endosperm. The embryo then uses this food during its early growth.

The cotyledons are attached to the main part of the embryo, which forms a sort of axis. This axis is differentiated into three distinct regions. The portion above the at-

Figure 12-13. The ovary of a flowering plant matures into the fruit that surrounds the developing seeds. As the fruit grows, the flower dies.

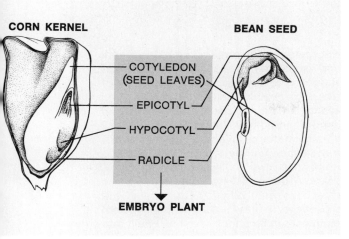

CORN KERNEL

BEAN SEED

COTYLEDON
(SEED LEAVES)

EPICOTYL

HYPOCOTYL

RADICLE

EMBRYO PLANT

Figure 12-14. The embryo plant in a bean seed and in a corn kernel.

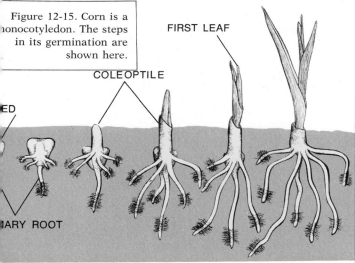

Figure 12-15. Corn is a monocotyledon. The steps in its germination are shown here.

FIRST LEAF

COLEOPTILE

ED

ARY ROOT

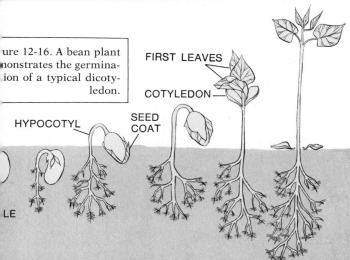

ure 12-16. A bean plant nonstrates the germination of a typical dicotyledon.

FIRST LEAVES

COTYLEDON

HYPOCOTYL

SEED COAT

LE

tachment of the cotyledon(s) is the **epicotyl.** This region normally elongates and develops into the stem of the plant. The lowest portion of the axis is the **radicle,** which elongates and develops into the primary root and root system of the plant. The stem-like region between the radicle and the epicotyl is the **hypocotyl.** The hypocotyl may elongate during the period of germination. It will become part of either the stem or the root of the plant.

Those plants whose seeds have one cotyledon are called **monocotyledons,** or **monocots.** Those with two cotyledons are called **dicotyledons,** or **dicots.** Corn is a good illustration of the pattern of germination in monocots. The first visible signs of germination are the rupturing of the seed coat and fruit and the emergence of the radicle, or primary root. As the root elongates, it develops secondary roots and **root hairs.** These begin absorbing water from the environment, and also serve to anchor the plant in the soil. Next, the epicotyl elongates and the young stem appears. In corn, the stem and young leaves are enclosed by a cylindrical sheath (unique to grasses) called the **coleoptile.** The first leaf soon emerges from inside the coleoptile. The single cotyledon, however, remains inside the seed. It continues to nourish the young plant until photosynthesis is well begun.

The ordinary garden bean illustrates the germination pattern of a typical dicot. The radicle emerges and grows downward, developing a system of root hairs as in the corn plant. In dicots such as the bean, the hypocotyl forms an arch underground. The arch breaks through the surface of the soil, and then straightens in response to light. As it does so, it pulls the cotyledons and epicotyl with it. In some cases, the cotyledons may photosynthesize, functioning temporarily as green leaves on the young plant. After the true leaves have developed, the cotyledons wither and fall off the stem. In other dicots, such as peas, only the epicotyl emerges, and the hypocotyl and cotyledons remain under the surface of the soil.

245

THE BRISTLECONE PINE

What is the oldest living thing? If you guessed the giant California redwoods, you are wrong. Although the world's tallest trees may live to be two or three thousand years old, they are mere saplings compared to a lesser-known tree. This most ancient of all living organisms is the bristlecone pine.

There are bristlecone pines alive today that were already ancient trees when Aristotle was teaching and Alexander the Great was conquering Asia Minor. At the age of 50 years, the bristlecone pine is comparable to a sapling of another species. Today, the average age of living bristlecone pines is 1,000 years, but several are well over 4,000 years old. The oldest living tree, nicknamed Methuselah, is over 4,600 years old.

The bristlecone pine is considerably less imposing in appearance than the redwood. At most, these trees reach a height of 60 feet and a girth of less than 40 feet. Most are much smaller. Unlike the redwoods, bristlecone pines tend to be gnarled and knotted. Yet the bristlecone pine has proved extremely valuable to scientists and historians.

As everyone knows, a tree produces one ring for each year of its growth. By studying tree rings, scientists can tell a great deal about the climate of the years through which the tree has lived. For example, thick rings might mean a year of plentiful rainfall and sunshine, while thin rings might suggest a cold, dry season. The analysis of tree rings can also be used to date historic events. This is the basis of the science of dendrochronology (literally "tree-time"). Weather patterns for a series of years create a corresponding pattern of thick and thin rings that form a "signature" for those years. A piece of wood with that pattern must have come from a tree that was alive in those years. If the wood is part of an ancient temple, then it cannot have been built into the temple before that time.

Unfortunately, tree-ring dating is of little direct value in parts of the world where timber is rare and was consequently never used much as a building material. Thus, it appeared that dendrochronology would be useless in studying the ancient civilizations of Syria, Palestine, Egypt, and Persia. The best tool for dating ancient archaeological finds seemed to be radiocarbon dating. In this method, a date is established by measuring the amount of radioactive carbon in organic materials. The problem was that radiocarbon dating was suspected of being highly inaccurate beyond certain fairly recent times.

The great age of the bristlecone pine—discovered in the 1950s—turned out to hold the key to a solution of this problem. Living trees now provided a dendrochro-

nology reaching back over 4,000 years. And ancient, dead trees carried the story even further. Using eroded stumps and dead wood that has been found lying on the ground in the bristlecone forest, dendrochronologists have built up a chronology that covers a period of over 8,000 years— well into the period of the ancient civilizations.

At last, a basis for correcting radiocarbon dating had been found. The carbon-14 content of the wood in any tree-ring is assumed to be the same as that of any substance which lived anywhere in the world at the time the ring was formed. By cross-checking the carbon-14 content of a piece of charcoal from a prehistoric Chinese village or a scrap of papyrus from ancient Egypt with that of the wood of a bristlecone pine from the same era, scientists can pinpoint the age of archaeological and geological finds with astounding accuracy.

How have these trees managed to live for so long? Bristlecone pines grow only in mountainous regions of six southwestern American states. Most of the largest and oldest are found in the White Mountains of northeastern California. Generally, the oldest and healthiest trees seem to thrive under the harshest ecological conditions, where there is little competition from other vegetation. The average annual precipitation in the White Mountains is only 12 to 13 inches, and most of it falls as snow. In summer, the air is as dry as anywhere in the world.

The bristlecone pine even dies slowly. When parts of the green crown are destroyed by wind, fire, or drought, the bark and xylem tissue on that side gradually die as well. Because the remaining part of the crown has less tissue to supply with food through photosynthesis, the entire tree does not starve. Often, a narrow strip of living bark will survive on a large dead trunk. Pine Alpha—the first tree discovered to be over 4,000 years old—is four feet in diameter but has only a ten-inch-wide strip of living bark.

The dense and resinous wood of the bristlecone pine renders the tree highly resistant to the effects of insects, fungi, and bacteria. Because dry air keeps the tree from rotting, dead bristlecone pines may remain upright for hundreds of years until their roots decay or erode.

Today, the greatest threat to the bristlecone pine's survival is the curiosity of human visitors. Methuselah is intentionally unmarked to protect it from souvenir hunters, and visitors to the White Mountains are prohibited from collecting potentially valuable bits of wood that they may find on the ground. Properly protected, these scientifically and esthetically invaluable trees will prosper and continue to help reveal aspects of the ancient past to many more generations of mankind.

The mechanics of development

We have so far described the development of the young plant as it can be seen by the naked eye. However, most of the activity of development takes place at the cellular level. Not all the cells in the plant are active in development. At any given moment, most of them have finished their development, assumed more or less their final form, and are engaged in their own specialized tasks. But there are a few regions in which development continues. The main regions occur close to the tips of roots and stems, and are known as **apical meristems.** Other meristematic regions in many species are the layers of cambium between the xylem and the phloem, and just under the corky outer bark of trees.

The **meristematic cells** found in these regions are undifferentiated and seem to be able to divide indefinitely. They produce large numbers of other cells which grow, differentiate, and organize themselves into the various specialized tissues of the plant.

The principal event of development in a meristematic region is cell division, which simply multiplies the number of cells. In the apical meristem of the root, the region nearest the tip undergoes the most extensive cell division. At the very end of the root tip is a **root cap,** whose cells protect the elongating root from injury. The outer cells of the root cap are sloughed off as the root grows through the soil, and newer cells take their places.

Just behind the meristematic region is a region of cell elongation. The cells in this region increase not in number, but in size. They enlarge considerably, becoming four to ten times as long as the meristematic cells. It is this process of cell elongation that pushes the root tip through the soil.

Next is a region of cell differentiation. In the root, the cells in this area differentiate into three layers. The outermost layer will mature into the epidermis. Root hairs grow out of this layer and absorb water and mineral salts from the soil. The middle layer will develop into the endodermis and the cortex.

Figure 12-17. This figure shows the apical meristem of a coleus plant. The cells that are actively dividing are located in the central meristematic zone. Below this zone, the older cells are elongating and will differentiate into various types of tissue as they mature.

Figure 12-18. The meristematic tissues of roots are at the tip, above the root cap. Just as in stems, the most rapid growth in roots occurs in the meristematic region and just behind it.

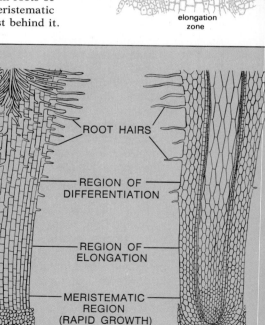

ROOT HAIRS

REGION OF DIFFERENTIATION

REGION OF ELONGATION

MERISTEMATIC REGION (RAPID GROWTH)

ROOT CAP

248

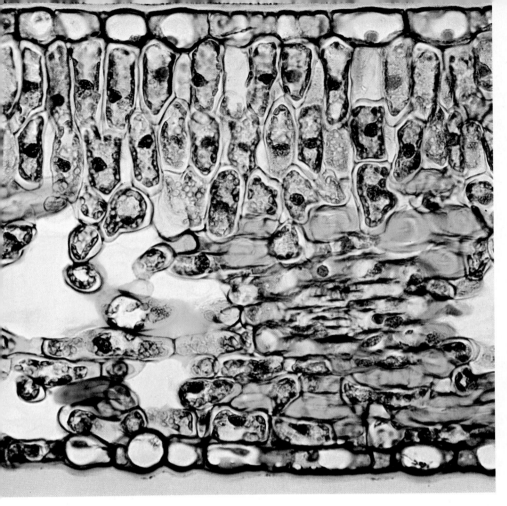

Figure 12-19. This cross-section of a leaf, as viewed through a microscope, shows several different types of cell.

The cells of the innermost layer will differentiate into the xylem, phloem, and cambium. (If you have forgotten the roles of these tissues, refer back to chapters 5 and 6.) Biologists do not yet know why the actively dividing cells of the meristem, which appear to be similar, assume these diverse forms and specialized functions.

The growing region of the stem is also organized into three zones of cellular development. As in the roots, growth results primarily from the elongation of cells produced in the apical meristem. In the zone of differentiation, the outermost layer will develop into the epidermis. The internal cells will form the xylem and phloem, the cortex, and the pith.

The stem must also produce the leaves and branches of the plant. The pattern of development in the apical meristem of the stem is therefore somewhat different from that in the root. As the stem grows, the apical meristem produces, at intervals, small knobs of meristematic tissue called **leaf primordia.** These will give rise to new leaves. In the **axils,** or angles between leaves and stems, **bud primordia** develop. Later, branches may develop from these.

All of the growth and differentiation of tissues produced by the apical meristems is called **primary growth.** It includes not only increase in length and the formation of leaves and buds, but the formation of the original xylem and phloem and of the reproductive structures, such as flowers. Most monocots and some dicots are capable only of primary growth. But dicots that have a vascular cambium between the xylem and the phloem can also produce **secondary growth.** Such plants add layers of new xylem each year. Thus they gradually increase the thickness of stems and roots. The old xylem gradually fills with deposits of waste products and waterproofing materials, and hardens into wood. New phloem is also produced by the cambium. However, this does not add much thickness to the plant, because the old phloem is crushed by the growth of the new xylem and phloem.

Secondary growth is what makes trees possible. Almost all trees are dicots or gymnosperms, because monocots lack a vascular cambium and so are incapable of secondary growth. However, palms, joshua trees, and a few other tree species are monocots.

SUMMARY

Most multicellular organisms reproduce sexually, by means of gametes. Fusion of the gametes results in a zygote, the beginning of a new organism. As it grows, its cells will change, specialize, and organize into tissues and organs. This sequence of programmed changes from zygote to death is called development.

Land plants are classified in two main groups: bryophytes and tracheophytes. They require a more complex structure than marine plants, because of their drier environment. Their reproductive structures must enable the gametes to meet and fuse, and must protect the developing embryo.

Non-seed-bearing plants—bryophytes and ferns—depend on external water to complete their reproductive cycles. The sperm must swim through water to fertilize the egg. Mosses are confined to moist environments also because they lack conducting tissues. Their height is limited by the speed with which water and dissolved substances can diffuse through their cells.

Both mosses and ferns show alternation of generations in their life cycles. In mosses, the gametophyte generation is dominant. In ferns and other tracheophytes, the sporophyte generation is dominant.

Gymnosperms and angiosperms are the two major classes of seed plant. The conifers are the best-known gymnosperms. Their reproductive pattern is essentially the same as that of the angiosperms. But the gymnosperms' seeds are borne more exposed, on the surface of the cone scales.

The flower, the reproductive site of flowering plants, differs in two major ways from the cone of the conifers. Its petals may help to attract animal pollinators, and it protects the seed more completely, inside an ovary.

Pollination must precede fertilization. Some perfect flowers, which produce both male and female gametes, may self-pollinate by transferring pollen from a stamen to a stigma of the same plant. Other perfect flowers, and imperfect flowers (which produce only one type of gamete), cross-pollinate by means of wind or animal carriers of the pollen. Cross-pollination tends to be favored in nature.

A pollen grain germinates when it lands on a moist stigma. A pollen tube emerges from it and digests its way down through the style to the ovules. The generative nucleus divides into two sperm nuclei. One fertilizes the egg cell. The other fuses with the polar nuclei and develops into the endosperm. Plants that pollinate are not dependent on external water for reproduction.

After fertilization, development begins. A seed is formed, consisting of embryo, seed coats, and often endosperm. The mature ovary becomes a fruit. The seed coats protect the embryo, and the fruit may aid in its dispersal. During seed dormancy, development is temporarily arrested.

There are four main processes in development. Cellular enlargement occurs when more molecules are synthesized than are broken down. Cells in a developing embryo also undergo rapid cellular division. Cellular differentiation results in specialized cells with specific functions in the organism. Supracellular differentiation is the organization of cells into tissues, organs, and systems.

The breaking of dormancy and onset of germination may be triggered by changes in the external environment. Alternating periods of temperature change and exposure to light are often involved. Once the seed coats are made more permeable, germination begins with the emergence of the radicle.

Growth within the developing plant is limited to certain regions. Near the tips of stems and roots are the apical meristems, where rapid cellular division occurs. Just behind the apical meristem is a region of cellular elongation, and behind this a third zone of cellular differentiation. The apical meristems are responsible for the plant's growth in length. Meristematic tissue also gives rise to leaves, buds, reproductive structures, and primary xylem and phloem. All of this is called primary growth. The cambium is responsible for secondary growth and increase in thickness. Monocots and some dicots are capable only of primary growth.

Review questions

1. What are the two main groups of land plants? What does each include?

2. How do the reproductive cycles of mosses and ferns restrict them to moist environments? Which generation imposes this restriction?

3. What is a sporangium?

4. What is alternation of generations? Give an example in the life cycle of a plant discussed in this chapter.

5. List some reproductive adaptations of plants.

6. How do the two major classes of seed plant differ from each other? Give an example of each.

7. Distinguish between a pollen cone and a seed cone.

8. Sketch a perfect flower and label its parts.

9. Distinguish between self-pollination and cross-pollination. Why don't imperfect flowers self-pollinate?

10. What is the chief value of cross-pollination?

11. What is the function of the pollen tube in reproduction? Why is it important to land plants?

12. What are the major events in the fertilization of a flower? What is meant by double fertilization?

13. What are the major events in the formation of a seed?

14. Describe the structure of a typical seed.

15. What is seed dormancy? Why is it advantageous for some plants to produce seeds that require alternating periods of warm weather and cold weather before they germinate?

16. What is a fruit? What function does it serve?

17. Describe the four major stages of development.

18. List several differences between animal development and plant development.

19. Name some factors which may break seed dormancy.

20. What is the beginning step in germination?

21. What function is served by cotyledons and endosperm?

22. Contrast the germination of a monocot with that of a dicot.

23. What are meristematic cells? Where are they found?

24. In what parts of the plant does growth in length take place? What three types of change occur in cells as the plant grows?

25. Where does growth in width occur? Are all plants capable of this sort of growth? If not, why not?

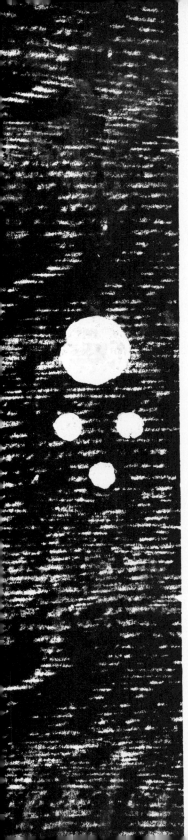

Animal Reproduction

Many forms of life get along very well without sex. Millions of years ago, cells in the primitive seas managed to keep going simply by dividing in two. One-celled plants and animals continue to reproduce in this way, although some can also reproduce sexually. Reproduction of multicellular organisms is somewhat more complicated. Still, there are ways it can be done without sex. But organisms that reproduce in this way lack variety in their populations: each offspring is identical to its parent (except for mutations—see chapter 16). Sex is what makes variety possible. Sexual reproduction thus seems to offer a genetic advantage to the species that have it. In this chapter, we will examine both sexual and asexual patterns of reproduction in the animal kingdom.

ASEXUAL REPRODUCTION

Asexual reproduction occurs when a single individual produces one or more new individuals. We discussed a few methods of asexual reproduction among animals in chapter 11. **Budding** was observed in hydras; it is also found among sponges. A starfish can **regenerate** a missing part, and a part can sometimes regenerate a "missing" starfish. Starfish generally reproduce sexually, however. Regeneration occurs only in case of accident.

Fission

Many single-celled organisms reproduce by dividing in two. This is called **binary fission.**

The amoeba, for example, first duplicates the genetic information in its nucleus by mitosis (chapter 11), then splits in two. A paramecium may also reproduce in this way, but can reproduce sexually if it meets another paramecium.

Fission is a little more complicated among multicellular organisms. It is nevertheless found in a number of invertebrate groups. Many flatworms may separate into two halves, and each half will grow into a whole worm.

Some animals alternate between sexual and asexual methods of reproduction. Many of these animals are parasitic. The liver fluke described in chapter 5, for example, reproduces sexually, producing larvae. The larvae in turn reproduce asexually. By this means, they can increase their number several hundredfold. Like other internal parasites, liver flukes must find very specific hosts. Their ability to produce so many offspring by combining sexual and asexual methods of reproduction increases the chances that some will survive to invade the next host.

Among vertebrates, the adults never reproduce asexually. But the formation of identical twins can be considered a sort of asexual reproduction. In this case, an embryo reproduces itself. A zygote will normally undergo mitosis and multiply its cells after fertilization. But occasionally these cells will separate, leading to the formation of two individuals. Among mammals, there is evidence that the split occurs after several mitotic divisions have already produced a multicellular embryo. These two cells (or groups of cells) then develop normally. The result is "identical" twins—produced by the asexual reproduction of the embryo. Since the genetic information of the zygote is fully present in all the cells of the embryo, the genetic characteristics of one half will be found in the other. Thus, identical twins must always be of the same sex.

Parthenogenesis

Sometimes eggs can develop into adults

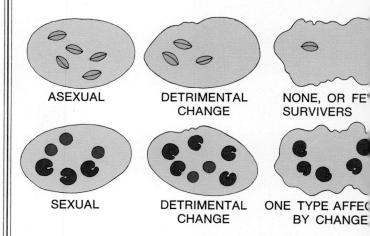

ASEXUAL DETRIMENTAL CHANGE NONE, OR FE SURVIVERS

SEXUAL DETRIMENTAL CHANGE ONE TYPE AFFE BY CHANGE

Figure 13-1. In an asexually reproducing population, a change that is bad for one is usually bad for all. Why are there more organisms living after a detrimental change in sexual populations than after a detrimental change in asexual ones?

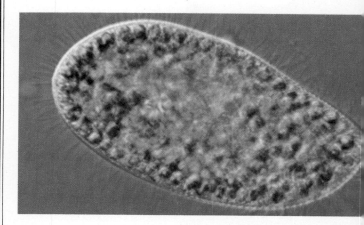

Figure 13-2. Paramecium is a single-celled organism capable of reproducing both sexually and asexually.

without ever having been fertilized. This sort of asexual (or monosexual) reproduction is called **parthenogenesis.** A certain species of desert lizard consists only of females. These lizards lay eggs which, unfertilized, develop into adult females. Laboratory experiments with the eggs of rabbits, frogs, and turkeys have resulted in a very

PATTERNS OF REPRODUCTION
AND DEVELOPMENT

few cases of parthenogenetic development. When pricked with a needle or bathed in certain chemicals, these unfertilized eggs will occasionally develop into normal-seeming adults.

Parthenogenesis is not uncommon among some arthropod species, such as honeybees, water fleas, aphids, and wasps. In spring and summer, female water fleas lay diploid eggs that develop, unfertilized, into female adults. In the fall, however, they lay some eggs that develop into male fleas. The males then fertilize a few haploid eggs laid by the females. These fertilized eggs remain dormant until spring, and then the parthenogenetic female generation begins anew. Honeybees, too, usually alternate a parthenogenetic generation with a sexually produced one.

USE OF ALTERNATIVE METHODS

Except for many one-celled organisms, most animals that can reproduce asexually can—and generally do—reproduce sexually as well. Slow or nonmoving animals must rely mainly on themselves for reproduction. If they happen to meet up with another member of the species, however, most of them are capable of sexual reproduction. Such occasional sexual reproduction seems to make these species hardier. Some isolated animals, such as the desert lizard, must reproduce asexually because they are so few and far between that they would rarely have a chance to mate. But many other species, such as aphids, that can reproduce parthenogenetically rely on sexual reproduction to survive cold, drought, or an otherwise unfavorable environment. Furthermore, as we have seen, sexual reproduction reshuffles the characteristics within a population. And this appears to increase the chances that the species will survive adversity.

Life cycle of Obelia
Obelia is another animal that reproduces asexually as well as sexually. There are two distinct diploid stages in *Obelia*, which correspond to these methods of reproduction.

Obelia is a marine relative of *Hydra*, but its body structure and life cycle are more complex. *Obelia* forms a sessile (stationary) colony, with many similar parts that behave somewhat as individuals. Small, branching colonies of *Obelia* can be found attached to rocks and other objects in shallow marine waters. The individuals in a colony look like "stems," from which several branches may extend. These branches are called **polyps.** *Obelia* may reproduce asexually by budding. Buds grow out of the main stems and develop into polyps. By budding, *Obelia* increases the total population in its colony.

There are two different kinds of polyp in an *Obelia* colony. One is the **feeding polyp,** which closely resembles the individual hydra, with a mouth surrounded by waving tentacles. The other kind is an asexual **reproductive polyp.** It lacks tentacles and serves only to produce the mobile sexual stage of *Obelia*.

Inside the vase-like body of the reproductive polyp there are small, round buds in various stages of asexual development. When they are mature, these buds will separate from the interior and be released into the surrounding water. Once separated, these small buds are called **medusae,** and they resemble tiny jellyfish. The *Obelia* medusae exist independently, stinging and capturing small organisms with their tentacles. This stage is therefore important for spreading the *Obelia* population to new places.

The medusae are diploid, and are responsible for the sexual reproductive phase of *Obelia's* life cycle. Some medusae are male and produce sperm; others are female and produce eggs. The sperm and eggs are haploid cells, produced by meiosis. Medusae gather in groups and release their gametes into the water. Fertilization takes place in the water, outside the animal. A great many gametes are produced, increasing the probability that sperm and egg cells will meet.

If fertilization does occur, the diploid zygote divides repeatedly, becoming a hollow ball of cells only one layer thick. Eventually, after continued cell division, some of the cells are forced into the hollow of the ball. This larval stage thus has two layers of cells. Cilia form on the outer layer, and the larva—now called a **planula**—can swim freely for a short time. It swims to the bottom and settles on a rock or some other solid object. There it becomes a single polyp and develops a main stem at its base. The stem begins budding, and the buds develop into more stems and polyps. Thus a new sessile *Obelia* colony is formed, and the life cycle is completed.

SEXUAL REPRODUCTION

Compared to sexual reproduction, asexual reproduction is easier, surer, and more convenient for an organism such as *Obelia*. Sexual reproduction appears more risky and more difficult. Besides the need for special reproductive structures, there are two other problems to be overcome. The first is that the sperm may never find the eggs. The second problem is faced by the developing zygote. The free-swimming planula is at the mercy of the winds and currents. It may become prey to larger animals in the ocean. When it swims to the bottom, it must land on the right sort of surface, or it will not continue development. As with all organisms, relatively few of the gametes produced are ever fertilized, and even fewer zygotes survive to become adults. The necessity of bringing the gametes together and the vulnerability of the developing zygote are two problems faced by all sexually reproducing animals. The adaptation of animals on land can in large measure be traced through the means they have acquired to solve these problems.

Vertebrate patterns
Fish may be nearly as extravagant as *Obelia*

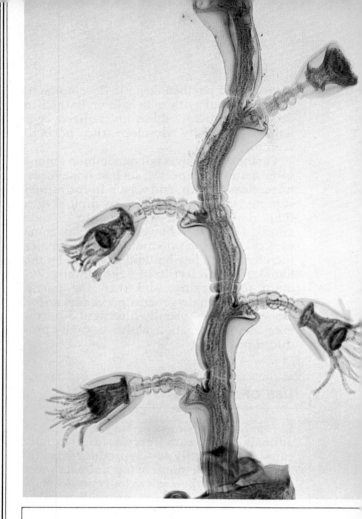

Figure 13-3. A colony of *Obelia*.

in the production of gametes. A female cod, for example, may lay millions of eggs during a single breeding season. Unlike *Obelia*, however, many fish have developed mating behaviors that increase the chances of fertilization. Many species return each year to spawning grounds, so it is more likely that the mature males and females will meet and release their gametes at the same time and in the same place. The well-known migration of the salmon is an example. In addition, some fish, such as the salmon, cover their fertilized eggs with gravel or mud to protect the developing young. Some may even guard the eggs. Most fish, however,

PATTERNS OF REPRODUCTION
AND DEVELOPMENT

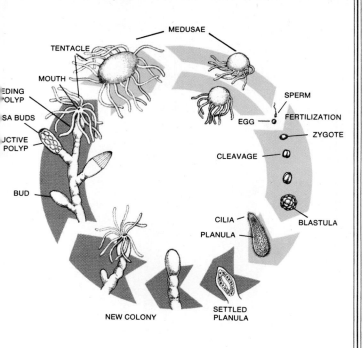

Figure 13-4. The life cycle of *Obelia*.

Figure 13-5. The reproductive system of the male frog.

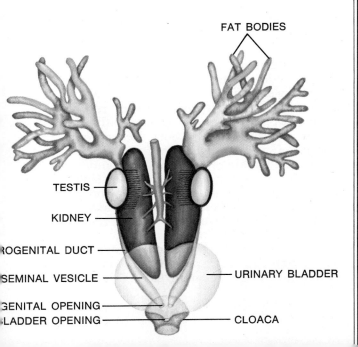

simply abandon their eggs. The fertilized eggs of most ocean food fishes are lighter than water. They float on the surface, exposed to currents, winds, and larger animals. The vast majority will become food for other creatures.

So long as animals stay in the oceans and lakes, sperm can be released and eggs can be fertilized in the open water. On land, however, animals face two additional problems: providing a fluid environment for the sperm, and preventing the egg from drying out. The amphibians seem to represent an intermediate situation. They live a good part of the time on land, but they depend on a watery environment for reproduction and early development.

Frogs are common amphibians. Externally, male and female frogs look almost alike, but internally, they differ greatly. There are two small, rounded **testes** in the abdominal cavity of the male. (See Figure 13-5.) Often they are partially covered with yellow, finger-like fat bodies. The testes are the primary reproductive organs of the male. Each testis contains hundreds of coiled tubes in which sperm are formed. At the time of breeding, millions of mature sperm pass into the tubules of the kidneys, which lie just under the testes. From there they are ejected into the water through the **cloaca,** the same pathway as is used for excretion.

The female reproductive system takes up far more space than the male one. (See Figure 13-6.) The key structures are the two **ovaries.** After each breeding season, the ovaries begin to produce the next year's eggs. As with the sperm, the egg develops a haploid nucleus through meiosis.

The eggs are stored in the ovary during the winter. Then, usually during late spring, they are detached from the ovary and are released inside the abdominal cavity. This release of eggs is called **ovulation.** The female's abdominal cavity is lined with ciliated cells, which "herd" the eggs into the openings of two long, coiled tubes called **oviducts.** As they move through the

257

oviducts, the eggs mature and become ready for fertilization. They also become coated with several layers of a jelly-like substance. This will swell and become firm shortly after the eggs are released into the water and fertilized.

The frogs leave less to chance in the fertilization of eggs than do *Obelia* or most fish. During the breeding season, the male frogs gather on the shores of ponds and croak furiously to attract females. The female, responding, jumps through the group of waiting males. As she does so, the males try to jump on top of her. If one succeeds, he clasps her with his front legs, and will not let her go until both have released their gametes. The male rides along piggyback-style until the female has chosen a spot to lay the eggs. The jelly-like coating, though not firm when just released, causes the eggs to cluster together near the surface of the pond. The male releases millions of sperm over the eggs while they are being laid. This mating behavior, which brings the parents so close together, increases the chances that the gametes will meet and fuse. About an hour after fertilization, each egg expands and the jelly becomes firm, thus protecting the embryo from mechanical injury and from some predators.

Internal fertilization

External fertilization (fertilization outside the mother's body) is possible only among animals that reproduce in water. Sperm must be able to swim to the egg; the fertilized egg must be kept moist if it is to develop. Land animals do not have a watery environment, so they fertilize the egg inside the female parent.

The male has **seminal fluids** that keep the sperm alive and swimming. In some species, the male also has a copulatory organ—a **penis,** in most mammals. This serves to place the sperm well inside the female's body. In others, including many bird and reptile species, the parents simply place their cloacae side by side to transfer sperm.

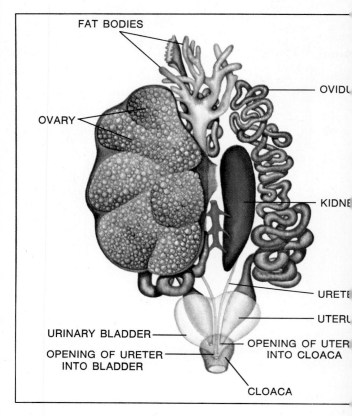

Figure 13-6. The reproductive system of the female frog. One of the ovaries has been omitted to show the position of the kidneys.

The internally fertilized egg can develop either inside or outside the mother's body. If it is to develop outside, it must be protected by a relatively waterproof shell to prevent drying out. Most reptiles lay eggs with protective shells. Some also bury their eggs in "nests" of sand or vegetation. Once her eggs are laid, a female reptile usually abandons them. Birds also lay eggs with shells. However, birds usually guard their eggs and incubate them with their own bodies' warmth.

If the egg is to develop internally, it does not need a shell. The mother's body will provide the needed moisture and protection. This is the case with most mammals. Animals whose eggs are fertilized and develop

258

Figure 13-7. Frog eggs are fertilized externally. As the female releases her eggs, the male riding on her back releases his sperm.

within the female are called **viviparous** ("live-bearing").

Internal fertilization has certain obvious advantages over external fertilization. Sperm deposited inside the female reproductive system have a much greater chance of fertilizing an egg. Because fertilization is more likely, fewer female gametes need to be produced. Internal fertilization is often combined with internal development, so the embryo is further protected. The production of fewer female gametes tends to be correlated with an increase in the care parents give their offspring. If parents protect their young, both before and after birth, then more offspring are likely to survive. Thus

fewer fertilized eggs are needed to ensure that one offspring will survive to adulthood and reproduce.

Mammalian reproduction

The term "mammal" alludes to one important adaptation among this group of animals: **mammary glands** furnish nourishment—milk—to the newborn young. Another mammalian characteristic has already been discussed—internal development. Certain nonmammals ("guppies," for example) also develop within the mother's body, but there is a difference. In the nonmammalian pattern, development occurs within a yolk-filled egg that remains inside the mother's body. In most mammals, however, the embryo develops a direct attachment, the placenta, through which nourishment is provided by the mother. The placenta enables the developing mammal to obtain nourishment for a longer period of time than is the case in a nonmammalian egg. In addition, waste products, instead of accumulating in the egg, are disposed of through the placenta and excreted by the mother's own excretory system.

A few mammals demonstrate two other patterns of reproduction that are considered more primitive than that of the placental mammals. The duck-billed platypus is an example of a **monotreme.** The platypus appears to represent an early stage in the evolution of mammals from reptiles. In several respects it still reproduces much as the reptiles do. The female platypus develops a yolk-filled egg, which she retains inside her body for a while and then lays in a nest. As in reptiles, the young are nourished by the yolk of the egg. After hatching, though, they feed on milk that oozes out of the mother's mammary glands and onto the surrounding hair.

The **marsupial** reproductive pattern is somewhere between those of the platypus and the placental mammals. The kangaroo and opossum are two well-known examples. In the marsupial, a placenta attaches the

embryo to the mother for a short time. During that time development begins. But long before the embryo is mature, it crawls out of the mother's uterus and up into a pouch on her abdomen. There it attaches to one of several mammary glands and continues its development.

HUMAN REPRODUCTION

It has been said that the hen is simply the egg's way of making another egg. By the same token, perhaps we could say that a human is a gamete's way of making more gametes. In that case, human gametes have a fairly slow method of reproducing themselves. Infancy, childhood, and puberty can be seen as simply a long, slow progression toward the preparation and final production of these single sex cells. Let us see where and how human gametes are made and fertilized.

The male reproductive system

The testes are the primary reproductive organs in the male. They produce both sperm and **androgens,** the so-called male hormones. The testes are held in a thin sac of skin called the **scrotum.** The internal temperature of humans is too high for sperm to live for very long inside the abdominal cavity, so they must be produced and kept in these outside sacs, where it is cooler.

Inside the testes there are many coiled **seminiferous tubules. Spermatogenesis**

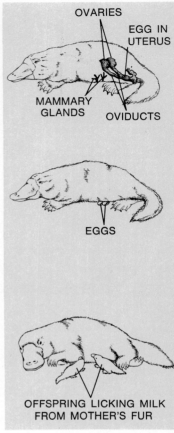

Figure 13-8. The platypus, one of the two known monotremes, combines features of reptilian and mammalian reproduction. Fertilization is internal, but the female lays eggs, and the newly-hatched young are fed milk from the female's mammary glands.

Figure 13-9. The reproductive process in a platypus.

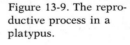

Figure 13-10. Opossum embryos are born after only eight days of gestation. Only a few of each litter manage to creep into the mother's pouch, where they attach firmly to her nipples and continue their development.

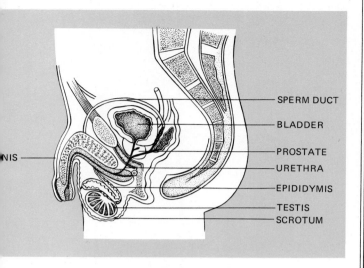

Figure 13-11. The reproductive system of the human male.

(sperm formation) takes place in these tubules, resulting in several hundred billion sperm during the normal lifetime of the male. Human sperm take about two and a half months to mature. They begin as **spermatocytes,** which are diploid cells produced by the lining of the tubules. Spermatocytes undergo meiosis to produce haploid **spermatids.** The spermatids then reshape themselves into **spermatozoa,** as mature sperm are called. Spermatozoa consist mostly of a haploid nucleus, some cytoplasm, and a long, whip-like tail, but these are enough to fertilize an egg. Cells in all these stages of development can be found in the adult human male at any one time. Sperm are produced continuously and without impairment from puberty until death, although somewhat fewer may be produced as the male gets older. About 300 million to 400

million sperm are released during an average ejaculation; a minimum of 100 million seems to be required for fertilization to occur.

Before they are released, sperm are stored and further conditioned for a few weeks in the **epididymis.** The epididymis lies over each testis and is connected to a thicker tube, the **vas deferens.** The two vasa deferentia join, forming the **ejaculatory duct.** Also opening into the ejaculatory duct is the **seminal vesicle.** The ejaculatory duct in turn empties into the **urethra,** which runs the length of the penis. During sexual activity, contractions move the sperm through the vas deferens into the ejaculatory duct. Fluid from the seminal vesicle is added. This fluid neutralizes the acidity of the urine and makes the urethra safe for the passage of semen. At orgasm, more fluid is contributed by the **prostate gland,** through a duct that opens at the meeting point of ejaculatory duct and urethra. The lower end of the ejaculatory duct opens, and the sperm and seminal fluid are forcefully carried down the urethra and out the penis.

Semen is the name for the combination of sperm and seminal fluid. Both urine and semen are expelled through the urethra, although not at the same time. Before orgasm, a gland at the base of the penis secretes a fluid that helps to lubricate the passages of the penis and the female reproductive tract, making it easier for the sperm to pass through.

The penis consists primarily of spongy **erectile tissues.** During sexual stimulation, a sphincter muscle at the base of the penis blocks the flow of blood, causing the penis to grow hard and erect. The penis must be erect in order to enter the female reproductive tract. Some mammals, though not humans, have penis bones that aid in keeping the penis erect.

The female reproductive system

More demands are placed upon the female reproductive system and, not surprisingly, it is more complex than that of the male. Like the male system, the female system produces haploid gametes (eggs) and hormones that regulate their production. In addition, however, the female system houses and nourishes the developing fetus for about nine months. It also produces milk that nourishes the infant after birth.

The primary reproductive organs in the female are the two ovaries. The ovaries are walnut-sized and lie on either side of the lower abdominal cavity, toward the back. Each ovary may produce several hundred thousand immature eggs. Only about 400 of them, though, will mature and be released during her lifetime. All of the cells that will become a female's eggs are in the ovaries at the time of birth. They remain dormant until they are released, usually one at a time, between **puberty** (generally ages 11–15) and **menopause** (generally ages 40–50). Menopause signals the end of ovulation (egg release) and therefore of **fertility** (the ability to conceive a child). Because her eggs have been with her since her birth, an 18-year-old woman releases 18-year-old **ova** (as mature eggs are called). Some biologists believe that the eggs may become injured or weakened with age. This may explain why older women seem to be more likely to produce abnormal offspring than are younger women.

Partially surrounding each ovary are the funnel-like openings of the oviducts, called **Fallopian tubes** in humans. The egg is released from the ovary, is swept into the Fallopian tube by beating cilia on fingerlike projections at the end of the tube, and then moves slowly toward the uterus. A sperm is most apt to fertilize an egg in the upper part of the Fallopian tube. The resulting zygote will begin to develop as it moves down the tube. Eventually it will attach itself to the wall of the uterus, and pregnancy begins. If the egg is not fertilized, it will disintegrate and be discarded.

Unlike that of the male, the genital opening of the human female (the **vagina**) serves as a passageway only for the reproductive

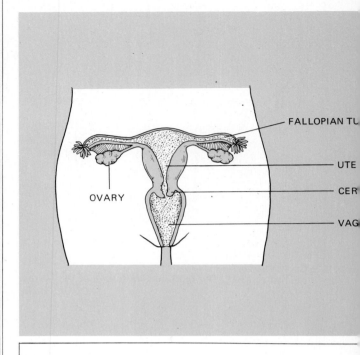

Figure 13-12. The reproductive system of the human female.

Figure 13-13. This human ovum has not yet been fertilized.

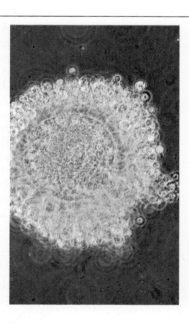

PATTERNS OF REPRODUCTION
AND DEVELOPMENT

tract, not for urine. Above the urethral opening, through which the urine passes, is a small projection called the **clitoris.** The clitoris corresponds anatomically to the penis in the male. Like the penis, it is made up of erectile tissue, and is extremely sensitive to sexual stimulation. Two pairs of fleshy tissues called the **labia** cover these structures. Above the clitoris, over the pubic bone, is a mound of fatty tissue known as the **mons veneris** ("mount of Venus"). The labia, the clitoris, and the mons veneris together comprise the external female genitalia, known as the **vulva.**

The human egg is about the size of the dot over an "i". The original **oöcytes** (immature eggs) that a girl is born with are much smaller than the mature ova.

The oöcyte is diploid, but it undergoes meiosis before becoming a mature ovum. The first meiotic division takes place before ovulation, producing two cells. One cell, the **polar body,** is smaller and will disintegrate. The second meiotic division occurs at the time of fertilization and again produces two unequal cells: the large ovum and another small polar body, which disintegrates. Strictly speaking, the unfertilized egg is an oöcyte, and the mature ovum is produced only after the sperm has penetrated it. Often, however, the unfertilized egg is called an ovum.

In the initial stages of ovulation, the oöcyte matures in a fluid-filled capsule near the surface of the ovary, called a **follicle.** The follicle grows around the oöcyte as it matures. Slowly it migrates to the edge of the ovary nearest the Fallopian tube. At the time of ovulation, it ruptures, releasing the oöcyte. The oöcyte must meet a sperm within 10 to 15 hours to ensure normal fertilization. Usually only one egg is released at a time. However, any eggs that are released may be fertilized. So if more than one egg is released, multiple births may result. These infants are called fraternal twins (or triplets or quadruplets, as the case may be).

If sperm are deposited in the vagina of the female during a short period just before or after ovulation, there is a chance that fertilization will occur. Although millions of sperm are normally deposited, the odds against any one sperm reaching the egg are phenomenally high. Swimming with their whiplike tails, the sperm travel about 1.5 millimeters per minute. They take perhaps two to three hours to reach the upper regions of the Fallopian tube. Muscular contractions of the uterus may help them along. Most sperm die before getting far into the uterus. More get lost in the wrong Fallopian tube or die while swimming up the right one. Only a few hundred will survive and reach the egg. Sperm may stay alive for three or four days, but most of them are capable of fertilizing an egg for only about 24 to 48 hours. On reaching the egg, all the sperm release an enzyme that softens the outer covering of the egg. Fertilization occurs when a single sperm penetrates the egg. Once its head fuses with the egg membrane, the tail drops off. The nucleus migrates toward the egg's nucleus and fuses with it. After that, the egg membrane is modified to form a **fertilization membrane.** This usually prevents all other sperm from entering the egg.

The menstrual cycle

If fertilization does not occur, the female reproductive system usually undergoes a regular sequence of changes known as the **menstrual cycle.** This cycle ordinarily takes about 28 to 30 days, although it varies from woman to woman, and sometimes from month to month.

Hormones from both the brain and the ovaries control the menstrual cycle. Their interrelationships are complicated, but important to an understanding of how the widely used birth-control pills work. The hormones are also responsible for the female secondary sex characteristics. These include breasts, increased fat deposits around the hips and abdomen, and pubic hair.

The hypothalamus in the brain begins the cycle. On the first day of the cycle, this gland begins to secrete a releasing factor. This is

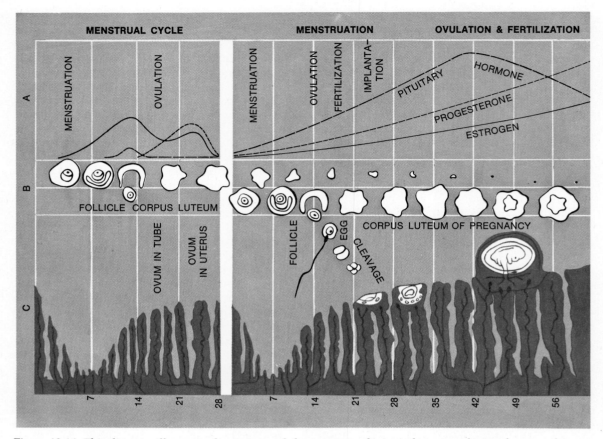

Figure 13-14. This diagram illustrates the timing and the sequence of events that occur during the normal menstrual cycle (left) and during the first weeks of pregnancy (right).

carried through the blood and stimulates the pituitary (hypophysis) to release a hormone that, in turn, stimulates follicle growth. This hormone is called **follicle-stimulating hormone,** or **FSH.** As the follicle grows, it produces another hormone, **estrogen.** The increasing amounts of estrogen gradually cause the hypothalamus to switch to production of a different releasing factor. This causes the pituitary to slow its production of FSH and to start producing **luteinizing hormone (LH).** Because FSH production has slowed, other follicles do not mature. The original follicle, though, keeps growing. The estrogen produced by the developing

follicle also causes the uterine lining to thicken. Meanwhile, large amounts of LH, together with FSH, trigger ovulation about halfway through the cycle. After releasing its egg, the ruptured follicle heals and becomes the **corpus luteum** ("yellow body") which gives the luteinizing hormone its name. The corpus luteum continues to secrete a small amount of estrogen. But it begins to produce greater amounts of another hormone, called **progesterone.** Progesterone inhibits the production of LH and further stimulates the lining of the uterus. This lining develops into a thick, spongy layer, richly supplied with blood and tissue fluid.

PATTERNS OF REPRODUCTION
AND DEVELOPMENT

In this condition, the uterine lining, or **endometrium,** is well prepared to receive a developing embryo, in case conception has occurred.

If a fertilized egg is implanted in (becomes attached to) the endometrium, estrogen and progesterone continue to be produced. The high levels of these hormones during pregnancy help to maintain the uterine lining and therefore the pregnancy. They also suppress the production of FSH and estrogen are now declining, more FSH starts to be produced by the pituitary gland. This hormone begins to stimulate the growth of another follicle, and the cycle repeats itself.

The common birth-control pill contains small amounts of artificial estrogen and progesterone. As we have seen, these hormones suppress the release of FSH and LH from the pituitary gland. By preventing the growth of a follicle, they prevent ovulation,

---

DOCTORING THE UNBORN

Each year, thousands of pregnant women who fear that their fetuses may be abnormal are tested by a process called amniocentesis. In this technique, a small amount of fluid is withdrawn from the amniotic sac around the fetus. The fluid is then tested for evidence of certain defects. Generally, if the fetus proves to be abnormal, the mother has only two options. She may have an abortion, or she may carry the fetus to term and hope the baby can be helped to live a relatively normal life.

Now, pediatricians have reported the successful treatment of a fetal abnormality before birth. Amniocentesis of a Boston woman showed that her fetus suffered from a disorder known as methylmalonic acidemia. Infants with this disease show a high concentration of acids in the body, retarded physical development, and frequent vomiting. The immediate cause of the condition is a deficiency of vitamin B_{12}, which is needed in the breakdown of amino acids.

In hope of reversing the condition, physicians fed the mother huge doses of vitamin B_{12}. Later tests on her urine samples showed that the accumulation of methylmalonic acid had stopped. When the baby was born, its blood and urine were found to contain large amounts of vitamin B_{12}, and its methylmalonic acid level was only slightly above normal. At the time of the report, the baby was nearing its second birthday and developing normally.

---

and LH. As a result, other follicles are not stimulated to grow, and ovulation does not occur during pregnancy.

If implantation does not occur, the corpus luteum degenerates. This cuts off the production of progesterone. Partly as a result, the uterine wall begins to contract and thereby expels the endometrium. The discharge of the endometrium is commonly called the **menstrual period;** it usually lasts three to five days. And since progesterone and thus no egg is released. In a sense, then, the effects of the pill simulate pregnancy. One kind of birth-control pill is taken for three weeks and produces a build-up of the endometrium. Then no pills are taken for about a week. The resulting decline in the hormone levels causes the endometrium to degenerate and be expelled. Thus the woman will have a menstrual period, although she never ovulated. A newer pill is being developed which would prevent implantation rather than interfere with ovulation.

REGULATION OF HUMAN REPRODUCTION

Until recently, most societies encouraged their members to reproduce. Governments saw strength in numbers. Many religions did not permit their followers to interfere with the way of God or nature by controlling their fertility. In agricultural societies, children were welcomed additions to the family labor force. Parents had children to ensure their own security in old age. Yet despite all this, birth control has been practiced by many individuals in most cultures throughout history. And recent changes in living conditions and in attitudes have made birth control more socially acceptable in many parts of the world. Children are less of an economic necessity in industrialized societies. There is increasing alarm over the pressures caused by uncontrolled population growth. Parents with rising standards of living wish to support their children at higher levels, so they limit their numbers. Such factors have helped to make birth-control measures more acceptable and more available. As a result, birth rates in many developed countries have been declining over the last several decades.

Behavioral regulation
Continence is the surest method of birth control, although not a very popular one. Rather than avoid sexual intercourse completely, many couples have tried to avoid the release of sperm into the vagina. This method, called **withdrawal,** is probably the oldest and still the most widely practiced of all birth-control measures. It requires the man to remove his penis from the woman's vagina before he ejaculates. The effectiveness of this method depends on the man's self-control. Furthermore, some semen may leak from the penis before ejaculation, or may be released on the outside of the woman's genitals, and thus still find its way through her reproductive tract, causing pregnancy. Although it is effective in about 80 percent of cases, withdrawal may be physically and psychologically unsatisfying to both partners.

Some couples may decide to avoid intercourse at the time of greatest fertility in the woman's menstrual cycle. This so-called **rhythm method** requires the woman to know when she is likely to ovulate. For this, she must keep a careful record of daily body temperatures and monthly periods. Fertilization is most likely to occur within 15 hours after the egg's release and up to four days after the sperms' release. It is therefore especially "unsafe" to have intercourse up to four days before and up to 15 hours after ovulation. Because most women's cycles vary from month to month, it is often difficult to determine just when ovulation has occurred. Thus to be "safe," a woman must add several extra days to each end of the "unsafe" period allowed for ovulation. If she is quite irregular, she may have to avoid intercourse for nearly half of her cycle. There is also some evidence that ovulation can be induced by stress, outside the normal cycle. This, of course, would render the rhythm method considerably less useful. In fact, the method is only about 50 to 75 percent effective. However, it does not interfere with the act of intercourse itself, and may be preferred on religious grounds.

Chemical regulation
We have already seen how the popular oral contraceptives work to prevent ovulation by altering a woman's estrogen and progesterone levels. The **birth-control pill** has many advantages. It does not interrupt intercourse, it allows intercourse at any time, and it is nearly 100 percent effective when taken as directed. Nevertheless, it has certain drawbacks. There may be undesirable side effects, caused primarily by its estrogen

concentration. These can include nausea, weight gain, darkening of skin, accumulation of water in the tissues, and headaches. Some research has suggested a relationship between the pill and cancer of the uterus, though this has not been proven. It does seem clear, though, that pill users may face a greater danger of blood clotting. The pill affects the delicate hormone balances in the body, and all of its effects will probably not be known until after years of use by millions of women. Interestingly, birth-control pills for men have been developed. But they were never marketed, precisely because they were thought to cause bad side effects.

Fertilization may be prevented by killing sperm before they can reach the uterus. **Spermicides** come in foams, jellies, and creams that can be inserted into the vagina before intercourse. Used in this way, they are about 70 to 80 percent effective. Used as a douche to wash out the vagina after intercourse, however, spermicides are not a reliable method of birth control. Sperm can be carried up the cervical canal into the uterus in a matter of minutes or even seconds, before a douche can be used.

Mechanical regulation

Most birth-control devices must be used by women, but the **condom** is for men. It is a thin synthetic or rubber sheath, designed originally to prevent the spread of venereal diseases. It has since become a popular, inexpensive, and readily available method of birth control. The condom is unrolled onto the erect penis and prevents sperm from entering the vagina after ejaculation. Some users complain that it dulls the sensations in the penis and that it requires an unwelcome interruption of intercourse. If used properly, it is almost always effective.

The **diaphragm** is a rubber cap that is placed over the cervix to prevent sperm from entering the uterus and Fallopian tubes. Its coiled wire rim keeps the diaphragm in place, although it should be checked periodically to ensure that the fit is tight. A spermicidal jelly or cream is usually spread around the rim and inside the cap before insertion (making the combination over 90 percent effective). The diaphragm must be left in place for at least six hours after intercourse. Before the pill was developed, the diaphragm was the most popular female contraceptive. However, some women find it unpleasant to use. They say that the forethought it requires takes away from the spontaneity and pleasure of intercourse. Also, in a few women, it tends to be forced out of position during orgasm.

As the name implies, the **intrauterine device (IUD)** is inserted directly into the uterus, where it may be kept indefinitely. The IUD is a small metal or plastic object (bow, spiral, sheath, coil, or ring) with a string attached which serves as an indication to the wearer that the device is still in place. Although it is over 95 percent effective, scientists do not know just how it works. Many believe that it somehow prevents the egg from being implanted in the uterine lining. The IUD is fairly cheap and does not require any more attention once it has been inserted by a doctor. However, it may cause heavy uterine bleeding, cramps, and sometimes severe uterine infections. It can also be accidentally expelled without the user's noticing.

Abortion

Abortion is the removal of a fetus from the uterus. An abortion that happens spontaneously is often called a **miscarriage.** A surgical abortion, if needed, is usually best performed within the first three months of pregnancy. The fetus is removed either by scraping the uterine wall or by sucking out the uterine lining with a small pump. At a later stage, saline injections can be used to induce labor, which expels the fetus. Abortion is totally effective as a means of birth control. However, in many parts of the world it is illegal or strictly forbidden by religious institutions. Even if performed legally and hygienically by a trained sur-

THE PRAYING MANTIS

"Female bites off mate's head and then devours him!" A headline from a sensationalist tabloid? No, just an example of routine cannibalism in the everyday world of the praying mantis.

This strange insect, found all over the world, has been associated with many myths and legends. Its name—"mantis" means "diviner" in Greek—derives from its habit of swaying gently back and forth, its head raised and its front legs extended as if in prayer. But not all people believe in the piety of the praying mantis. One superstition holds that swallowing a mantis is fatal to a horse. In fact, one of its nicknames is "mule killer."

The voracious appetitie of the praying mantis makes it one of humanity's best friends, since it devours huge numbers of insect pests. Mantises are protected by law in most communities, and many people purchase mantis eggs to protect their gardens against harmful insects. From the standpoint of the pests, the mantis is anything but a friend. And, as we will see, a male mantis in search of a mate might well approach his intended lady with mixed emotions.

The praying mantis is well designed for its predatory lifestyle. Although it has well-developed wings, it rarely flies, preferring to rest on a twig or fence-post and wait calmly for a future meal to approach. Its long, stick-like body is topped by a head that has large compound eyes as well as three smaller eyes. Unlike most other insects, the mantis can turn its head at least 180 degrees in either direction. Extremely sensitive to movement, it may stalk a moving insect several feet away while ignoring a motionless one that is almost within its grasp.

Strangely enough, other insects seem to accept the presence of a deadly mantis with no show of fear or suspicion. Crickets, grasshoppers, and butterflies make no attempt to escape, but seem to accept their fate meekly as the hungry mantis advances toward them. With its powerful spiny forelegs, the mantis seizes its prey and begins to tear it apart with its strong jaws. Praying mantises may display a surprising degree of individuality in their eating habits. Some cause instant death by biting their prey's cervical ganglion. Others start by biting off the head, a wing, or a leg. Still others eat only the inner organs of the abdomen and leave the outer shell completely intact.

The praying mantis is cannibalistic almost from birth. Newly hatched nymphs, still wingless, prey upon small insects but

will devour each other if no more suitable meal is available. For the adult male mantis, the mating season presents a life-or-death problem, particularly since the female is considerably larger than he is. Her appetite is undiminished by considerations of kinship or self-perpetuation, and the male must exercise extreme caution if he is to avoid being gobbled up immediately.

Attracted from a distance of up to several hundred feet by an alluring scent the female mantis secretes, the male may take hours to sneak up on her unnoticed. Once within eyeshot of his intended, he freezes in an attempt to avoid detection. When he is sure she is paying him no attention, he creeps closer, very slowly and cautiously. Finally he leaps onto her back, grasping her with his forelegs as he tries to assume the proper mating position.

If the male mantis misses his grasp, or if he is too slow, it will probably be his last attempt. The lady will attack, bite off his head, and proceed to make a meal of him. It would seem that this behavior does very little to preserve the species, but nature, as always, is full of surprises. In the majority of cases, the decapitated male will struggle away, mount the female, and proceed with his intended business. This guillotining, in fact, stimulates extremely strong reflex actions by the abdominal ganglia which con-

trol the male's sex organs. Having lost his head for love, the male praying mantis is more likely to mate successfully than if he had remained in one piece. The female, in the meantime, remains coldly indifferent to his supreme sacrifice, and will probably continue to munch away at the front end of the male while the rear end is otherwise occupied.

If the male mantis somehow survives the mating, he must be as cautious in his getaway as he was in his approach. Sometimes he will wait motionless for hours until an opportune moment for escape arrives. However, more often he shows little concern for continued survival, and will allow his mate to devour him without any sign of resistance.

Cannibalism of this sort would hardly be suitable for higher animals, but for the praying mantis it seems to serve as an adaptation for survival. The female needs much time and strength to lay the hundreds of eggs that she carries in her abdomen, and live food is often scarce during the mating season. Once mating has taken place, the male mantis is more valuable to her as an item on the menu than as a future breeder. By providing his mate with a much-needed meal, the male praying mantis makes a sacrifice for future generations that would seem to us to be far beyond the call of duty.

geon, an abortion may be complicated by excessive bleeding or infection. Illegal and unprofessional abortions are even more apt to have serious or fatal complications.

Sterilization

Sterilization is as effective as abortion or total abstinence as a means of birth control. A **vasectomy** is performed on men and is simple enough for a doctor to do in his office. The vas deferens leading from each testis is cut, a small piece is taken out, and the ends are tied off. A **tubal ligation** is performed on women, and involves a similar cutting and tying off of the Fallopian tubes. Neither procedure should affect sexual behavior. Sperm and eggs continue to be produced, but simply are never available for fertilization. They are usually reabsorbed by the body. Men can continue to have erections and ejaculations of semen (minus the sperm); women still have their menstrual cycles. Sterilization is nearly always permanent.

SEXUALLY TRANSMITTED DISEASES

Venereal disease is the general name for diseases that are transmitted by sexual contact. **Syphilis** and **gonorrhea** are the two most important ones, but there are many others. At present, some fourteen major venereal diseases are being transmitted among the population. Venereal diseases are second only to the common cold in number of reported cases in the United States. They exceed the number of reported cases of strep throat, scarlet fever, measles, mumps, hepatitis, and tuberculosis combined. And it is estimated that the unreported cases of venereal disease far outnumber the reported ones. It is fair to say that there is a worldwide epidemic of venereal disease among young adults.

One reason for the problem is that disease organisms change. New strains of both syphilis and gonorrhea have developed, which are more difficult to kill than the old ones. In addition, some diseases that are usually transmitted in other ways can come to be transmitted by sexual contact. Among these are hepatitis viruses and some strains of the common herpes-type viruses. In the new environment of the reproductive tract, such disease organisms may develop new, drug-resistant forms. So, while syphilis and gonorrhea are usually easy to cure in their early stages, the same may not be true of some of the other venereal infections.

Syphilis

Syphilis is caused by corkscrew-shaped bacteria (spirochetes). These bacteria thrive in the moist mucous membranes that line the cavities of the genitals, anus, and mouth. Because they depend on warmth as well as moisture, they are very rarely transmitted by towels, toilet seats, bathtubs, and the like. Syphilis appears in three stages. **Primary syphilis** can develop ten days to three months (but usually about three weeks) after sexual contact. The first symptom is a **chancre.** This is a small, blisterlike sore that appears where the bacteria entered the body, usually in the genital area. The lymph nodes in the area may also swell. The chancre is usually painless, and women may not notice it at all.

The chancre disappears after one to five weeks. Its disappearance may lead the individual to think he or she is cured. But the disease has only just begun to spread throughout the body, via the bloodstream. The infected person has now entered the stage of **secondary syphilis.** Usually about two months after the chancre disappears, a rash develops on the skin. Each sore of the rash is caused by swarms of spirochetes. This rash will also disappear spontaneously, without treatment. Far from being cured, however, the individual goes into a period of **latent syphilis.** The disease may remain hidden for years or even a lifetime.

Once it becomes latent, syphilis is not likely to be transmitted by sexual contact.

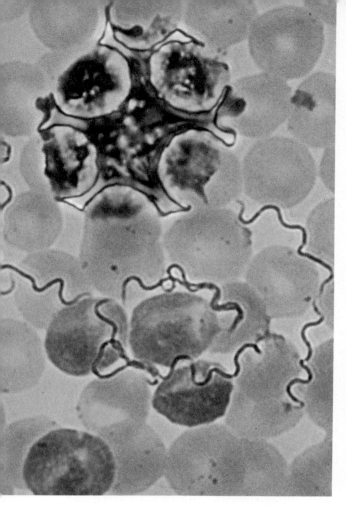

Figure 13-15. Syphilis, caused by this tiny spirochete, has been a widespread venereal disease since the fifteenth century. No mention of it has been found in earlier writings. Some scientists believe that the syphilis spirochete is a mutated form of a previously harmless bacterium.

However, a mother in this stage can infect her unborn child during the first four months of pregnancy. Latent syphilis can be detected by blood tests called **Wasserman tests.** Such tests are usually required before marriage to prevent **congenital syphilis**— syphilis of the newborn.

In about one out of every four cases, the disease reappears in the terrifying form called **tertiary syphilis.** In this, the syphilis bacteria eventually attack the brain, caus-

ing insanity. They may attack the spinal cord, causing paralysis, or the optic nerve, causing blindness. The liver, heart, and circulatory system may also be damaged.

Syphilis can usually be completely cured by penicillin and other antibiotics. However, having the disease and being cured of it does not grant immunity. A person may acquire syphilis again after any sexual contact with an infected person.

Gonorrhea

Gonorrhea is more common than syphilis. It is caused by small, round bacteria (gonococci) that thrive in the same environment as the syphilis bacteria. The first sign of the infection usually appears within a few days after sexual contact. An infected male experiences sharp pain when urinating. He may also discharge pus from his penis. In the female, the bacteria infect the cervix, causing a similar discharge of pus from the vagina. Ordinarily, women do not know they are infected, for they usually experience no pain or other symptoms until after much damage has been done. It is estimated that close to a million female carriers in the United States are spreading the epidemic unknowingly. Women must often rely on their male partners, whose symptoms are much more obvious, to learn of the infection.

Untreated gonorrhea can result in serious complications. If the infection is allowed to spread through the male reproductive tract, it may cause sterility. It may spread to other parts of the body and cause damage. In the female reproductive tract, it may scar the Fallopian tubes. Such scarring is a major cause of infertility among American women. If it spreads beyond the woman's reproductive tract, gonorrhea may cause such serious complications as blood poisoning, inflammation of the pelvic area or kidneys, or rheumatoid heart disease. Like syphilis, gonorrhea in most cases can be fully cured with penicillin. If it is treated early, no permanent damage results.

As in syphilis, a cure does not protect against future infection. Another problem is that some strains of the gonococcus can become dormant and survive in a treated male. They may remain for a long time in the prostate gland and seminal vesicle. In this dormant state, they may be transmitted to a female partner. There, if they find a suitable environment, they may be reactivated and become virulent again. The female, now actively infected, may then retransmit the disease to her "cured" male partner.

SUMMARY

There are several forms of asexual reproduction in the animal kingdom. These include binary fission, parthenogenesis, and budding. *Obelia* reproduces asexually by external budding, and sexually by independent medusae which produce haploid gametes. These gametes fuse, beginning a new diploid organism.

Sexually reproducing animals are faced with two problems. First, gametes must be brought together. Second, the vulnerable developing zygote needs protection to survive. Many female gametes must be produced to offset a low probability that any one zygote will survive if unprotected. Generally, neither fish nor amphibians protect their fertilized eggs. These animals therefore produce a great abundance of female gametes.

Among land animals, reptiles and birds fertilize their eggs internally and surround them with protective shells. Mammals also fertilize their eggs internally, and their offspring usually develop inside the mother's body. Such protection increases the chances for survival, so mammals need to produce and fertilize fewer eggs than do lower animals.

The duck-billed platypus is a monotreme. Though a mammal, it lays its eggs outside the mother's body. Marsupials, such as the opossum, are intermediate between monotremes and placental mammals. A marsupial fetus will crawl out of the mother's vagina at a very early stage, entering a pouch on her body where it continues development.

In humans, the male reproductive system manufactures and dispenses sperm, as well as the androgens that regulate spermatogenesis and secondary sex characteristics. The more complex reproductive system of the female produces the eggs, houses and nourishes the embryo, and furnishes milk for the infant after it is born. It also produces hormones that regulate the process.

One egg is usually released each month. If it is not fertilized, a fairly regular sequence of events called the menstrual cycle follows. The pituitary gland releases FSH, which stimulates a follicle to grow. The follicle releases estrogen, which starts the buildup of the endometrium. Ovulation is stimulated by the release of LH. The ruptured follicle becomes the corpus luteum and begins to release progesterone, which further stimulates the uterine lining. If there is no fertilization, progesterone declines. The expulsion of the endometrium, which follows, is called the menstrual period. Ovulation occurs about midway during the cycle, at which time fertilization may take place. One popular birth-control pill alters levels of estrogen and progesterone in the bloodstream, simulating pregnancy and preventing ovulation.

There are many ways to control human fertility. Withdrawal requires the man to withdraw his penis from the woman's vagina before ejaculation. The rhythm method requires careful calculation of the time of ovulation, and abstention from intercourse for several days before and a half day after ovulation. The condom (for males) and the diaphragm (for females) are mechanical barriers between sperm and egg, often used with spermicides to increase their effectiveness. The intrauterine device (IUD) is believed to make the uterine lining unreceptive to implantation by a fertilized egg. Abortion is not a contraceptive, but is a means of removing the fetus long before

PATTERNS OF REPRODUCTION
AND DEVELOPMENT

birth. Sterilization is usually a permanent method of birth control.

Venereal diseases are transmitted by sexual contact. The two most common types are syphilis and gonorrhea, both of which are caused by bacteria. Untreated syphilis can cause insanity, paralysis, and/or blindness. Gonorrhea in the male is evident as a discharge of pus from the penis and pain during urination. The female experiences some discharge but often does not know she is infected until the latter stages of the disease. Both syphilis and gonorrhea can be cured with antibiotics, but the cure does not protect against future reinfection.

Review questions

1. List three methods of asexual reproduction among animals. Name examples of animals that employ them.

2. Describe sexual and asexual reproduction in *Obelia*.

3. What special problems does sexual reproduction pose for animals? Name some ways in which animals have solved these problems.

4. List some of the reproductive adaptations found in land animals. Why are these adaptations useful?

5. Describe the reproductive process of the frog.

6. What are some advantages of internal fertilization?

7. What are the distinctive characteristics of mammalian reproduction?

8. What are the functions of the placenta?

9. How do monotremes and marsupials differ from placental mammals? Name two examples of each.

10. Describe the path of the sperm through the male reproductive tract.

11. What functions do androgens serve?

12. What are the primary reproductive organs of the female?

13. What is an oöcyte? How does it give rise to a mature ovum?

14. What is the effect of estrogen and progesterone on the lining of the uterus? What glands produce these hormones?

15. What is the difference between identical and fraternal twins?

16. Very rarely, identical triplets or quintuplets may be born. What observations can be made about their conception and early development?

17. How does one kind of oral contraceptive work?

18. List a number of reasons for the growing sentiment in favor of population control. Why is birth control often unpopular in underdeveloped countries?

19. Why can the rhythm method of birth control be unreliable?

20. Why can it be advantageous to use spermicides along with mechanical contraceptive devices such as the condom or the diaphragm?

21. Describe the most common methods of sterilization for both sexes.

22. What are the symptoms of the three stages of syphilis? Can a person who has been cured of syphilis be reinfected?

23. Why are blood tests required before marriage?

24. What are the symptoms of gonorrhea in the male? In the female?

25. What are the effects of allowing gonorrhea to go untreated?

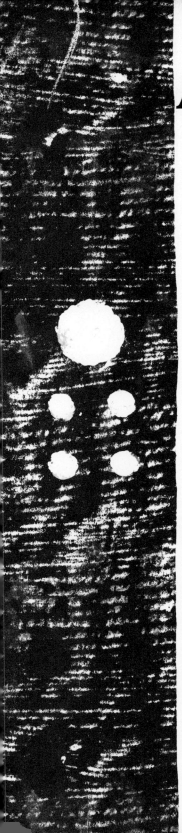

Animal Development

The development of an animal is an astounding spectacle. Watching it is like watching a house build itself out of a single brick. Every sexually reproducing animal begins as a single cell, which may give rise to billions or even trillions of cells. And the original cell produces not just more cells, but cells of different kinds, which will team up in just the right way to make an animal. It is as if our hypothetical brick were able to make not only more bricks out of itself, but also glass windows to put in the walls, and wooden shingles to put on the roof.

The single-celled zygote at the beginning of its development is a very different sort of creature from the multicellular animal at the end. The developing embryo, for example, is not just bigger than the original zygote. It is different in almost every way. It looks and behaves differently; it is more complex and more organized. Except for the kind and number of its chromosomes, the human zygote bears only a slight resemblance to a human embryo. And this, in turn, is a long way from the final human being. In fact, many animals in their early embryonic stages bear more resemblance to embryos of other species than to the adults that they eventually become.

Considering the tremendous number of changes a developing animal undergoes from embryo to adult, one begins to wonder how it ever does so without making some mistakes. More often than not, the fertilized egg eventually develops into an adult with all its pieces in the right places. Almost all of us have eyebrows and toes. Moreover, our eyebrows are over our eyes and our toes are on our feet—and never the other way around. To get a particular shape (a nose, say) at a particular place (in the middle of the face, and nowhere else) requires an incredible integration of developmental processes. In addition, the processes must all take place in the proper order. A heart must be ready to pump blood as soon as there are definite blood vessels to pump it through. The brain must be formed early, so that it can coordinate the responses of other regions. The processes of development are amazingly well synchronized. Although they proceed at different rates in different parts of the animal, they all finish on time. How does that one original fertilized cell "know" how to coordinate all these developmental processes to produce a complete human being?

The truth is, the zygote doesn't "know." However, certain specifications for future development are already present in the genes of the chromosomes. Copies of these specifications are passed on to all the cells of the developing embryo through repeated mitotic divisions. When the time comes for some cells to become brain cells and others to become muscle cells, the cells involved will be in position to respond properly to the stimuli. The new cells thus produced in one part of the embryo show different properties from new cells in other parts. Interaction between cells of different sorts continues to produce more specialization. Gradually the distinction between groups of cells becomes clearer and more fixed. Thus the tissues and organs of the embryo develop. Each stage is founded on the previous one, and is itself the foundation for the next.

DEVELOPMENT IN THE FROG

We can now return to the frog eggs of chapter 13, which we left after they had been fertilized. The eggs are black and white. The white portion, slightly less than half of the egg, is primarily **yolk.** This will serve as a ready source of food for the developing embryo. When the eggs are released into the water, they are not positioned in any particular way. Some have the black part up, some the white. In about an hour after fer-

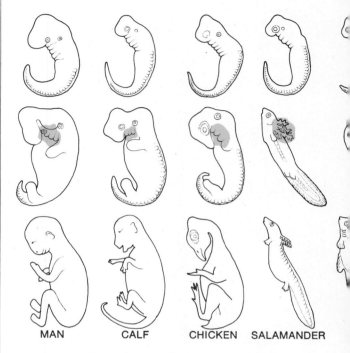

MAN   CALF   CHICKEN   SALAMANDER

Figure 14-1. All vertebrate embryos appear remarkably similar during the very early stages of development. Note that even those that will be air-breathers possess gill ridges at first.

Figure 14-2. Have these frog eggs been fertilized?

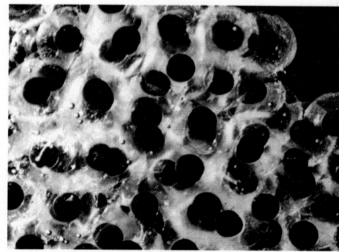

Courtesy Carolina Biological Supply Company

PATTERNS OF REPRODUCTION AND DEVELOPMENT

Figure 14-3. The two-cell stage. (Courtesy Carolina Biological Supply Company)

 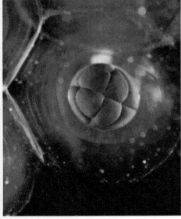

Figure 14-4. During the four- and eight-cell stages (left and center), the cells of this frog embryo are fairly uniform in size. By the time the 32-cell stage is reached (right), their sizes have become quite irregular, and it becomes difficult to distinguish each individual cell. (Courtesy Carolina Biological Supply Company)

tilization, all of the eggs that have the white part up will slowly roll over, so that only the black part can be seen from above. In this position they absorb the sun's heat rapidly, and this may help maintain an even temperature during development. Also, predators looking down into the water will be less likely to notice the eggs. They will see only the dark side, which blends with the bottom of the pond. Predators looking up at the eggs from underneath will see the light side, which blends with the daylight.

An area called the **grey crescent** develops in the cytoplasm between the black and white portions of the fertilized egg. The grey crescent appears before the egg begins to divide. Although it is in the cytoplasm rather than the nucleus, it is essential for the proper development of the embryo. Thus development is controlled by interaction between the cytoplasm and the nucleus, just as in the *Acetabularia* experiments described in chapter 1.

About two and a half hours after fertilization, a furrow begins to appear across the top of the egg. Slowly it deepens and encircles the egg, as the single cell divides mitotically into two. About an hour later, another furrow appears at right angles to the first. It too deepens, and the two cells divide into four. Subsequent cell divisions produce eight cells, then 16, then 32, then 64, and so on. Thus, within a few hours after fertilization, repeated mitotic divisions have greatly increased the number of cells. But they have also greatly reduced the size of each individual cell. At this point, the embryo— —though it is now composed of thousands of cells—is not significantly larger than the original zygote.

Cell division occurs at different rates in the black and white portions of the embryo. The cells in the black part, known as the **animal hemisphere,** divide more quickly than those in the yolk-containing white part, which is known as the **vegetal hemisphere.** As a result, the cells in the vegetal hemisphere are fewer and larger than those in the animal hemisphere.

About twelve hours after fertilization, the embryo still looks round and egg-like. A slightly bumpy surface is the only external sign that it is now composed of a vast number of cells. But a cross-section of the embryo will show a large cavity in the animal hemisphere. The cavity is called a **blastocoel,** and the embryo in this stage is called a **blastula.**

By about twenty hours after fertilization, the cells in the animal hemisphere are dividing so fast that they cannot stay in place in their own hemisphere. Some begin to grow over the surface of the vegetal hemisphere, forming an expanding sheath. The most active growing point is on the side of the hemisphere nearest the grey crescent. Here the dividing cells form a small mound, known as the **dorsal lip.** Gradually the sheath covers the entire hemisphere, like a sack being pulled over a ball. Eventually only a small opening remains, called the **blastopore.**

Meanwhile, the new cells produced by division on the underside of the growing lip form a new inner layer around a new cavity. This cavity is the **archenteron.** As the archenteron develops, the blastocoel grows smaller and eventually disappears. At this stage the embryo is known as a **gastrula.** It has changed from a round to an oblong shape. What was the animal hemisphere is now the anterior end, where the head will eventually form.

The outer layer of cells in the gastrula is called the **ectoderm.** The inner layer of cells which line the archenteron is called the **endoderm.** Between them, a third layer, called the **mesoderm,** now begins to form. Within the mesoderm, still another cavity will eventually form. This is the **coelom,** which will become the internal body cavity of the organism. All the internal organs of the chest and abdomen will grow into the coelom.

The parts of the gastrula provide the basis for the organization of the individual. The archenteron will eventually lengthen and develop into the digestive tube. The blasto-

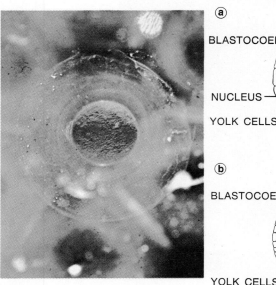
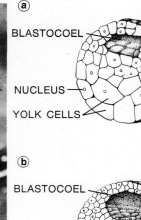

Figure 14-5. This embryo has reached the blastula stage (left). The diagrams (right) show the development of the blastocoel. (Courtesy Carolina Biological Supply Company)

pore will become the anus. The three layers of cells will differentiate and form distinct tissues, which will later be organized into organs and organ systems. The epidermis (outer layer), the brain, and the spinal cord will eventually develop from cells in the ectoderm. The cells of the mesoderm will form most of the tissues in the muscles, bones, circulatory system, and other internal organs. The endoderm will form the inner lining for the digestive and respiratory systems. Because these three layers give rise to tissues, organs, and organ systems, they are called the three **germ layers.**

After gastrulation is complete, **neurulation** begins. This sets the pattern for the entire nervous system. About 40 hours after fertilization, the embryo elongates further, forming the permanent head–tail axis of the future tadpole. Small ridges appear along the axis on the dorsal (back) surface of the embryo, arising out of the ectoderm. These enlarge and grow closer together. When the embryo is about 56 hours old, the ridges will

PATTERNS OF REPRODUCTION
AND DEVELOPMENT

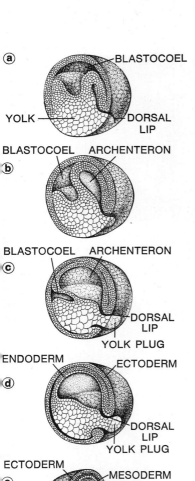

(a) BLASTOCOEL
YOLK — DORSAL LIP

(b) BLASTOCOEL ARCHENTERON

(c) BLASTOCOEL ARCHENTERON
DORSAL LIP
YOLK PLUG

(d) ENDODERM ECTODERM
DORSAL LIP
YOLK PLUG

(e) ECTODERM MESODERM
ENDODERM
DORSAL LIP
YOLK PLUG

Figure 14-6. During gastrulation, cells along one side move down and inward, forming the dorsal lip (a) and resulting in a new cavity, the archenteron (b). As the archenteron develops, the blastocoel becomes smaller and some of the yolk pushes out to form the yolk plug (c). Two layers of cells are recognizable, the endoderm and the ectoderm (d). Later the mesoderm develops (e). In the photograph, yolk plugs are seen as white caps on the gastrulas. (Courtesy Carolina Biological Supply Company)

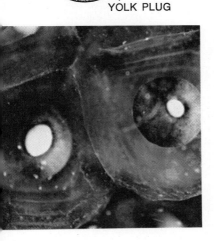

have grown together and fused into the **neural tube.** This is the beginning of the brain and spinal cord. At this time a narrowing in the embryo will distinguish the head from the remainder of the body.

The embryo begins to move after about 76 hours, thrashing its body in jerky, back-and-forth movements. Its heart is active by now and can be seen to pulsate in the lower "neck" region.

After about five days, finger-like gills begin to grow from each side of the head. With a microscope, one can easily see the red blood cells rolling and tumbling through the gills, where they pick up oxygen destined for cells buried in the interior of the animal. During the following two days, a gill cover will grow over each gill. With the appearance of the gill covers, the development of the tadpole is considered to be complete.

To sum up, then, we can see three main stages in the early development of the embryo. First, there is a period of rapid cell division in which the cells do not grow or differentiate very much from one another. This is the period of blastulation. Then comes a stage during which the cells are being differentiated into the three basic germ layers, and the first permanent body cavity, the archenteron, is being formed. This is gastrulation. Finally, during neurulation, the germ layers begin to differentiate further, into specialized organs and tissues. From now on, differentiation will continue, accompanied by growth, until the embryo is mature and ready to function on its own.

EMBRYONIC INDUCTION AND THE NATURE OF DEVELOPMENT

It is easy to say that differentiation occurs. But how? Why does some ectoderm produce brain tissue, while other ectoderm produces epidermis? Why does some mesoderm form soft muscles and other mesoderm hard bones? Differentiation seems to happen, in part, because of where the cells are in the

ANIMAL
DEVELOPMENT

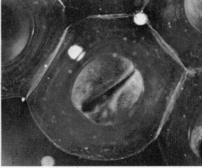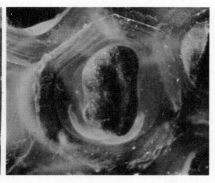

Figure 14-7. Neural ridges are just beginning to rise on the dorsal surface of the embryo (left). These develop into the neural folds (center), which then fuse to form the neural tube (right), the beginning of the brain and spinal cord.

embryo. But it also seems to be influenced by what other cells are nearby. This influence is known as the process of **embryonic induction.**

The cells that make up the ectoderm, endoderm, and mesoderm are originally undifferentiated. Once they have differentiated into skin, muscles, nerves, and so on, their course of development is fixed. Henceforth, they will function only in their specialized roles. Before differentiation, however, they can be transplanted to different parts of the embryo and can take on a different role from the one they would have assumed had they been left where they were.

Hans Spemann, a Nobel-prize-winning German embryologist, demonstrated this in a series of classic experiments in the 1920s and 1930s. Early in his career, Spemann devised ways to conduct surgery on tiny salamander embryos, which are similar to frog embryos in their development. In one experiment, he removed a patch of ectoderm from the top of a developing gastrula and placed it in a solution. If left in place, those ectodermal cells would have differentiated into part of the embryo's neural tube. The cells stayed alive in the solution, but did not differentiate. Moreover, the embryo, which also lived and developed, did not form a complete neural tube.

In another set of experiments, Spemann again removed a patch of cells that normally would have differentiated into the neural

SALAMANDER EMBRYO

REMOVED

Figure 14-8. When Spemann removed the mesoderm from under the portion of ectoderm that normally forms neural ridges, no ectodermal differentiation occurred.

NO NEURAL RIDGES

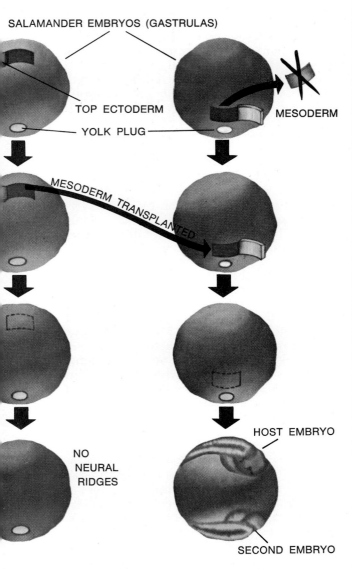

SALAMANDER EMBRYOS (GASTRULAS)

TOP ECTODERM

YOLK PLUG

MESODERM

MESODERM TRANSPLANTED

NO NEURAL RIDGES

HOST EMBRYO

SECOND EMBRYO

Figure 14-9. Spemann transplanted top mesoderm from one gastrula to the belly of another. The host embryo then developed two sets of neural ridges.

tube. This time he also removed, from the bottom of another gastrula, a patch of cells that would normally have developed into epidermis. He exchanged these two patches, grafting each to the place where the other had been cut out. If he transplanted the patches very early in gastrulation, the cells switched their normal courses of development. The would-have-been epidermal cells developed into neural tube, and the would-have-been neural patch developed into epidermis. However, if the transplants were done later in gastrulation, the grafted cells kept on with their original course of development. The epidermal patch that was transplanted to the neural region developed into epidermis. The neural patch that was placed in the epidermal region formed a neural tube.

Spemann knew that the mesoderm was formed later than the ectoderm during gastrulation. Because the transplanted cells could change their courses of development early in gastrulation but not later, he hypothesized that the mesoderm might somehow be inducing the ectoderm to differentiate. To test this idea, he cut a flap of top ectoderm, folded it back, and removed an underlying patch of mesoderm. He then replaced the flap of ectoderm and waited to see whether the neural ridges would form. They did not. The ectoderm healed but never did differentiate into nervous tissue. This experiment strongly suggested that the mesoderm was necessary to induce the differentiation of the ectoderm.

Spemann decided to see what effect a patch of top mesoderm would have on ectodermal cells that would normally become epidermis. In its normal position, this mesoderm would induce its ectoderm to become nervous tissue. From the belly of one embryo, Spemann cut away a flap of would-be mesoderm. From a second embryo, he removed a patch of top mesoderm. He grafted this onto the belly of the first in place of the mesoderm which he had removed. He then folded the flap of ectoderm back in place and waited for further developments. The embryo developed two neural tubes. One was in the normal location, and one was on the belly, where he had transplanted the top mesoderm. These experiments clearly showed that some factor from the mesoderm induced the differentiation of the cells in the ectoderm.

Spemann's experiments help to point up several major characteristics of animal development. First, development shows increasing complexity. Out of simpler and basically similar groups of cells, there arise more complex and dissimilar tissues. At the beginning of development, you will recall, the original cell produces two cells that are fundamentally alike. Repeated divisions result in different cells in the animal and vegetal hemispheres. Out of these cells arise three distinct layers of cells. At the beginning, the cells of these layers are undifferentiated. But they set a pattern that eventually results in all the different tissues, organs, and organ systems in the animal.

Second, many things influence the stages of differentiation. It cannot be only the nuclei of cells that direct their differentiation, for each cell carries an identical set of genetic instructions in its nucleus. At first, differences in the cytoplasm of cells are the main cause of differences in their structure and function. As we saw in the frog, even in the original zygote the cytoplasm was not uniform. One part was light, another was dark, and a grey crescent partly divided the two. As more cells are produced, their position in the embryo starts increasingly to affect their development. As we saw in Spemann's experiments, certain cells can induce differentiation in neighboring cells. Thus, interactions between cells are a second cause of differentiation in the developing embryo. It is now known that selective differences in types of the nucleic acid RNA (see chapter 16) are involved also.

A third characteristic of development is the gradual restriction in the cells' potential to differentiate in various directions. Spemann showed that an ectodermal cell may change its normal course before it has reached a certain point in development, but not after. There is no turning back after differentiation. Once an ectodermal cell has become an epidermal cell, it cannot later become a nerve cell. Before it differentiated, though, it had the potential of becoming either.

HUMAN DEVELOPMENT

In its very early stages, the developing human embryo looks much like other vertebrate embryos. It, too, begins as a single cell, out of which will arise a fully differentiated adult. Its cells undergo similar mitotic divisions. Three comparable germ layers form, and set the pattern for differentiation into tissues, organs, and systems. In fact, two or three weeks after fertilization it is hard to tell a human embryo from that of a fish, a chicken, or a rabbit. The principles, or controlling mechanisms, behind all vertebrate development are essentially the same. It is the specific pattern which varies from species to species. We will use our own human pattern to illustrate mammalian development.

Fertilization to implantation

The earliest stages of development in the human embryo are fairly similar to those in the frog, although they occur more slowly. But an important difference soon appears. The frog egg is deposited in the water, and the embryo develops entirely outside the bodies of its parents. In humans and other mammals, the embryo develops inside the uterus of its mother. It gets its oxygen, nutrients, and other supplies from the mother, by way of a supply line known as the **umbilical cord.** Because it has this supply line, it can stay in the mother's body for many months. Thus it can develop much further before birth than the tiny tadpole can before hatching. So, at an early stage in development, the embryo must form the umbilical cord and related organs, setting up this essential connection with its mother's tissues.

The first cleavage of the human egg takes place about 36 hours after fertilization. The second takes place after about 60 hours, the third after 72 hours. These cleavages result in a solid cluster of cells. Cell division continues as this ball of cells moves down the Fallopian tube, and a blastocoel begins to develop inside it. By the time it reaches the uterus (about three days after fertilization), it has become a hollow sphere of cells known as the **blastocyst.** This corresponds to the blastula of the frog embryo. While the blastocyst floats in the uterus for the next three days, some of its cells gather on one side. The fetus will eventually develop out of this thicker hemisphere of the blastocyst. At first, there are only two layers of cells in this inner mass—the ectoderm and the endoderm. The mesoderm forms later. As in the frog, the ectoderm gives rise to the nervous system and skin; the endoderm to the digestive and respiratory tracts; and the mesoderm to the muscles, bones, blood, heart, and other internal organs.

The other hemisphere of the blastocyst consists of a single layer of cells. This is known as the **trophoblast.** The trophoblast is responsible for **implantation,** or the attachment of the embryo to the lining of the uterus, about seven to nine days after fertilization. Probably by means of some enzyme, the trophoblast literally dissolves its way through the thick inner lining of the uterus and becomes embedded in it. Then the trophoblast begins to develop two membranes around the embryo: the inner **amnion** and the outer **chorion.** The amnion will contain a fluid secreted by the embryo, which will cushion the embryo during its months of development. Nourishment passes directly through the chorion until the placenta is developed.

The **placenta** begins to form from the trophoblast at the time of implantation, and continues to develop through most of the pregnancy. It is made up partly from the chorion, partly from the uterine lining. After about five weeks, the umbilical cord will have developed, attaching the embryo to the placenta. The placenta serves many purposes. Early in pregnancy it keeps the developing individual firmly attached to the wall of the uterus. Throughout pregnancy it functions in respiration, nutrition, circulation, and excretion. The mother's blood does not actually mix with that of the embryo. But in the placenta, blood vessels from the two circulatory systems—the mother's and the embryo's—lie very close together. So oxygen and nutrients can diffuse out of the mother's capillaries and into those of the embryo. Once in the embryo's blood, the oxygen and nutrients are carried through the umbilical cord and into the developing body. Waste products travel the same route in reverse. They diffuse into the mother's blood and are eliminated through her excretory system. Thus the placenta is important as an exchange site between mother and embryo.

The first trimester

Doctors usually divide the period of pregnancy into three trimesters, or periods of three months each. During the first trimester, all of the main systems of the body are begun. In the later trimesters they develop further, while the embryo (now known as a **fetus**) grows in size. At last the baby can safely leave the uterus and begin independent life.

During the first weeks of development, things seem to be changing dramatically almost every hour. Once the embryo has been implanted, its rate of growth speeds up tremendously. For a few days it doubles in size almost every day. By the end of the second week, it has become a gastrula, and the three germ layers have differentiated. A bulge now appears in the ectoderm, forming the so-called **primitive streak.** This defines the line along which the neural tube will soon appear.

During the third and fourth weeks, the differentiation of the nervous system domi-

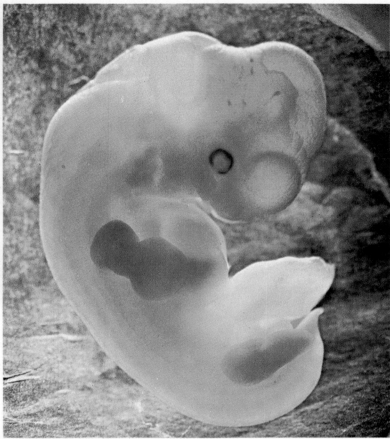

Figure 14-10. A twenty-four-day-old human embryo is the length of this letter "f." It is developing eyes, spinal cord, lungs, stomach, liver, kidneys, and intestines. The heart has already begun to beat.

At five weeks, the embryo is 1/3 inch long. Eyes, arms, and legs are now developing. The pointed tail will disappear into the body as the embryo develops. The larger projection is the severed end of the umbilical cord.

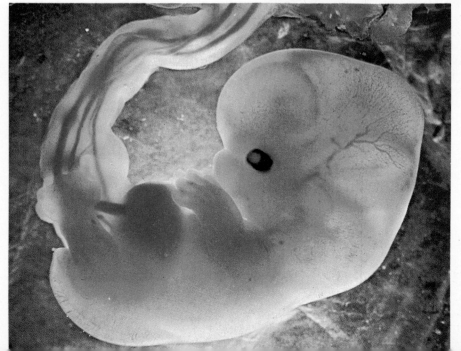

At six and one-half weeks, all internal organs are developing. The embryo has a mouth, lips, and buds for twenty milk teeth. Oxygen and nutrients reach the embryo's body through a vein in the umbilical cord. Two arteries carry wastes to the placenta, where they diffuse into the mother's blood.

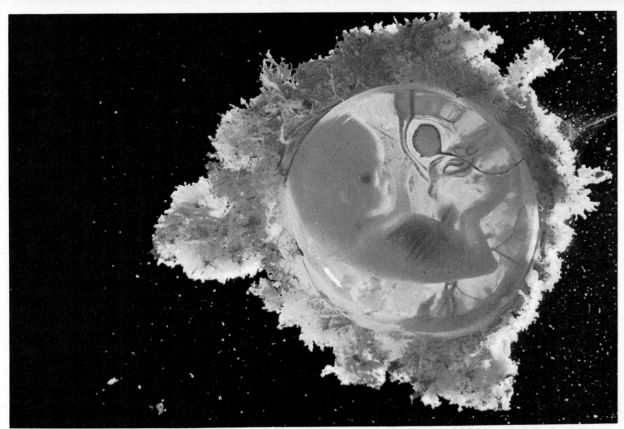

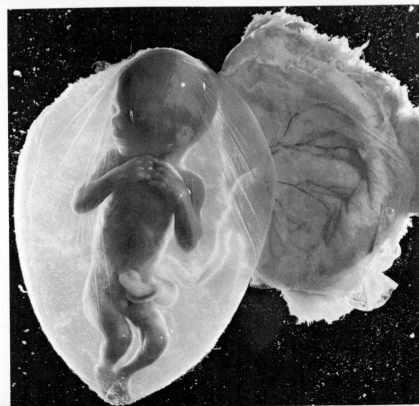

Figure 14-11. After eight weeks, when the bones begin to form, the developing human is called a fetus. This fetus is eleven weeks old and about 2¼ inches long. Cushioned and protected by amniotic fluid, it floats within the amniotic sac, which is surrounded by the spongy placenta. The nervous and muscular systems are now beginning to mature.

By the eighteenth week, the fetus is about 6 inches long and is very active. It may change position frequently, suck its thumb, or double up its fist and punch its mother. From this stage on, most of its development will be growth in overall size.

nates development. The neural tube forms along the primitive streak, and lays the foundation for the brain, spinal cord, and eyes. The foundations for the muscles and skeleton are also laid down at this time, along the line of the neural tube. The gut, or primitive digestive tract, has developed by the end of the first month.

In the second month, arms and legs develop, complete with fingers and toes. The legs develop slightly later than the arms—a pattern that holds true even after birth. The face begins to look more face-like. Eyes, ears, nose, mouth, jaws, tongue, and even gums for the future teeth can all be seen. The gut differentiates into a variety of internal organs. The different regions of the brain begin to form, and nerve connections are established between the brain and the sense organs. The skeleton, which at first was made up entirely of cartilage, begins to develop bone. The lungs appear, though they will not be needed until after birth. If the embryo is a male, the penis begins to develop. If it is a female, the vulva will not appear until the third month.

The heart and circulatory system are functionally complete by the end of the second month—the first of the body's systems to become so. If we think about it, it is logical for them to be first. The developing infant will not need to digest food or breathe air until after birth. But it needs to be able to circulate nutrients and oxygen to its tissues much sooner than that. Without a circulatory system, these needed substances would have to diffuse through the embryo's tissues from the surface. For a multicellular organism, this would be a slow, inefficient process. The embryo would never be able to grow more than a few cells thick. So the heart is formed and begins to beat before the end of the fourth week—even while the blood vessels are still taking shape.

By the end of the fifth week, the foundations for all of the body's major systems have been laid down, though the embryo is still less than a quarter of an inch long. By the end of the eighth week, most of the organs of these systems have begun to differentiate. Now about an inch in length and less than an ounce in weight, the eight-week-old fetus is almost fully formed. Its next seven months will be devoted primarily to growth and the refinement of these structures. Because of the tremendous number of changes occurring at this time, the first two months are the most critical period of development. Drugs, infection, radiation, and other external influences will have a much greater effect during these two months than they will at any later time in pregnancy. (A few years ago, many fetuses were severely damaged by a new tranquilizer, Thalidomide, that was taken by their mothers early in pregnancy. The babies were born alive but deformed, many of them with arms or legs missing.) If the embryo is healthy and normal at the end of its first trimester of life, it has an excellent chance of surviving to be born.

The second trimester

The second trimester is a period of rapid growth and increasing activity. A three-month-old fetus is about two inches long and has plenty of room in the uterus to swim, kick, stretch, and turn. Its movements are not well coordinated, however. By the end of the fourth month, the brain has developed enough to control muscle responses. By the end of the fifth month, the fetus can grasp with its hands. The movements of an 18-week-old fetus are strong enough for the mother to notice.

As the fetus grows, it takes up more space. The uterus expands to make room for it. By the end of six months, the fetus is 12 to 14 inches long and weighs about one and a half pounds. Increasingly, it will respond to both sound and touch. By the end of the fifth month, the mother can waken the fetus by tapping or pressing her abdomen. A loud noise may also disturb the fetus. By the end of the sixth month, the mother can readily detect its squirms and shifts in position. Often the fetus has developed regular patterns of sleep and activity by this stage.

PATTERNS OF REPRODUCTION AND DEVELOPMENT

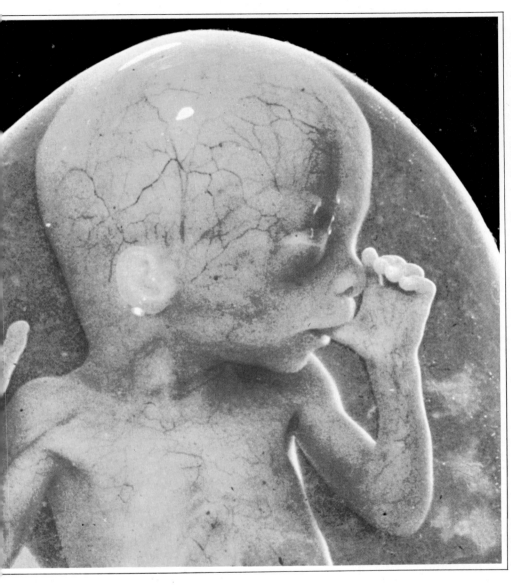

Figure 14-12. Thumb-sucking by this eighteen-week-old fetus develops the muscles that will enable it to nurse after birth.

The face becomes recognizable during the second trimester, and may even show family resemblances. The eyelids, though, remain shut until the end of the sixth month. By the end of the fourth month, the fetus can swallow. It drinks, and can digest some of the amniotic fluid, as well as release urine into it. If the fetus inhales some of the fluid, the lungs will expand and contract, imitating breathing movements and exercising muscles that will be needed immediately after birth.

Other structural details appear at this time. Fingernails and toenails begin to grow. Buds develop in the jaws for the temporary baby teeth that will emerge after birth. The eyelashes and eyebrows appear. Hair starts to grow on the head by the sixth month.

The bones begin to harden significantly during the second trimester. The bone marrow starts to produce blood cells, which until now were produced by the liver and spleen. Muscles in the neck and back develop to support the head. The body becomes more erect. The heart is pumping 25

perature and a sufficient fat layer to keep it warm, the fetus could not survive.

The third trimester

The human **gestation period**, or normal period of embryonic development, averages about 266 days after fertilization. Most babies are born within one or two weeks of this date. The longer the fetus stays in the

COFFEE, ASPIRIN, AND PREGNANCY

It has been known for some time that a pregnant woman who uses large quantities of alcohol or tobacco may be harming her fetus. Now, evidence suggests that perhaps she had better hold down her consumption of aspirin and coffee as well.

In a study of the effects of caffeine on 550 expectant mothers, researchers found that pregnant women who drink six or more cups of coffee per day appear to increase the risk of miscarriage. Among women in the group who reported drinking seven or more cups of coffee per day, 13 out of 14 miscarried. A control group of non-coffee-drinkers had a significantly lower miscarriage rate.

Caffeine cannot be screened out by the

placenta, so it gets into the fetus' bloodstream. The fetus, in turn, is unable to break it down. Caffeine's effects on the cells include genetic and other damage. In fact, they are not unlike the effects of harmful radiation.

Another study suggests that aspirin may also be responsible for fetal injury or death. Two Australian biologists studied 144 pregnant women who used from 2 to 12 aspirin daily during pregnancy. The incidence of several types of complication among these women was higher than among non-aspirin-users. The complications included anemia, hemorrhage, prolonged gestation, difficult delivery, and infant mortality.

The results of both these studies, as the researchers stress, are only preliminary. Further testing is needed. Also, neither aspirin nor caffeine should be seen as the sole cause of miscarriages. Other factors are undoubtedly involved.

quarts of blood a day at the beginning of this trimester, and beats about twice as fast as the mother's.

Although it may look as if it could survive on its own, the six-month-old fetus could not live outside its mother. Neither the digestive tract nor the lungs are sufficiently formed. The fetus must continue to get oxygen and nutrients from the mother, via the placenta. Moreover, the fetus has just formed sweat glands by the fifth month, and they will not open until the seventh month. Without sweat glands to help regulate its body tem-

uterus, the better are its chances of survival: 10 percent at seven months, 70 percent at eight months, and 99 percent at nine months.

The fetus gains five to six pounds during its last three months. Some of the gain is fat. This smooths out the very wrinkled skin that covered the six-month-old fetus. It will also serve both as insulation to help regulate the baby's temperature after birth, and as protection from the violent contractions of the uterus during birth. The growing fetus becomes increasingly cramped inside the

PATTERNS OF REPRODUCTION AND DEVELOPMENT

uterus. It cannot shift position as easily as it did during the second trimester.

The nervous system, particularly the brain, is greatly refined during the third trimester. Specific regions in the brain for sight, speech, hearing, walking, memory, and so on begin to be established during the seventh month. The eight-month-old fetus can be taught to respond to specific stimuli. A fetus can perceive light. It can hear, smell, taste, and feel. Many neural pathways in the brain are firmly established by the end of the seventh month. Since intelligence and personality are in large part founded in the nervous system, this implies that they are determined to a great extent by this time. However, the entire network of nerves is not yet complete, even at birth. Many other connections among nerve cells in the brain will be made after birth as a result of learning and experience. Whether or not these additional brain connections are made depends heavily on the amount of stimulation the young child receives from the environment.

The mother's diet—very important throughout pregnancy—is particularly so during the third trimester. The fetus needs large amounts of some nutrients, and if it does not get them its development will be hindered. Nitrogen, calcium, and iron are especially needed at this time. In particular, poor nutrition at this stage can seriously interfere with brain development.

Birth

By the end of the ninth month, the fetus is ready to be born. It has stopped growing for the last two or three weeks. Now its body usually rotates, so that the head points downward. The birth process begins with slow, rhythmic contractions of the uterus. This stage is called **labor,** and ordinarily lasts for seven to eighteen hours. The contractions eventually break the amnion and release its fluid—a well-known signal that the baby is on its way.

During the early contractions of the uterus, the cervix and vagina dilate (expand) and form an enlarged **birth canal.** The contractions grow stronger and more frequent, teaming up with contractions of the abdominal muscles to push the baby through the birth canal. Passage through the canal is called delivery, and may take up to two hours.

The baby usually emerges from the birth canal headfirst. The bones in the head are still soft, and can be molded slightly to squeeze through the canal. The rest of the body follows more easily, with a little help. Occasionally the baby may start to come out feet-first or rump-first, which can complicate delivery. If necessary, the baby may be removed surgically through the abdomen. This procedure is called **Caesarian section.**

The umbilical cord is cut and tied immediately after delivery. Now that it is no longer needed, it will soon dry up and drop off, leaving the **navel** or "belly button" where it was attached. The placenta is expelled naturally within minutes after birth. (This is why it is traditionally known as the afterbirth.)

The squeeze through the birth canal helps to expel amniotic fluid from the baby's lungs. With its first cry, the baby takes its first breath. Now, at last, it is a true air-breathing animal, ready to live in the outside world.

During pregnancy, the milk-producing tissues in the mother's breasts develop considerably. This development is stimulated mainly by a hormone from the pituitary gland. Actual milk production, however, does not begin right after birth. For the first few hours or days the infant receives instead a yellowish fluid known as **colostrum.** The colostrum is low in calories but fairly high in proteins, minerals, and antibodies. (The infant depends on antibodies provided by its mother for some time after birth, until it can begin building its own immune system.) Once milk production begins, it will continue for many months if the infant is breast-fed. However, if the breasts are not regularly emptied of their milk, milk production stops after a few days, and the tissues shrink.

THE KOALA

"Oh, Bear, I *do* love you!" said Christopher Robin, and his words have been echoed by millions of other children. Bears—from Winnie-the-Pooh to the three encountered by Goldilocks—have been an important part of children's stories and play for many years. But the most beloved bear in the nursery, the one who shares the child's bed, his joys and his sorrows, is Teddy Bear, named after Teddy Roosevelt—and Teddy is not really a bear at all. His prototype, in fact, is the unusual Australian marsupial called the koala.

Biologically speaking, the koala is a one-of-a-kind creature with a family all to itself, although it resembles two other marsupials, the wombat and the ring-tailed possum. No one knows very much about the koala's biological ancestry, although it has been extensively studied since European settlers in Australia first encountered it late in the eighteenth century. Observing these furry little animals in the treetops, the Europeans called them bears—and from the unscientific viewpoint, the koala does look like a cuddly, fuzzy bear cub.

The name "bear" stuck, even though further study showed that the koala was totally unrelated to black bears, grizzly bears, polar bears, or bears of any other kind. But the name "koala" was adopted as well, derived from an aboriginal word that means "no-drink." The Australian aborigines had noticed that under normal conditions the koala does not drink water, obtaining all the moisture it needs from leaves and dew.

Along with its lack of interest in water, the koala displays another distinctive dietary trait. Its arboreal habitat provides it with both bed and board, since it eats nothing but the leaves of certain eucalyptus trees. Furthermore, it is highly selective even about these, preferring the leaves of five species that have a high oil content. And carrying this pickiness one step farther, a koala from one forest may be addicted to leaves that are completely ignored by a koala from another forest.

For a long time, scientists wondered why koalas were so choosy about their food. Eventually, they found that the koala's favorite tree, the manna eucalyptus, periodically synthesizes poisonous prussic acid in certain of its leaves. Wild koalas avoid the leaves that contain this chemical. But until this was discovered, well-meaning zookeepers often gave captive koalas a dubious choice between starving and being poisoned.

An adult koala, about 30 inches long and weighing about 35 pounds, will eat two or three pounds of foliage daily. It becomes so impregnated with oil from the leaves that it smells very much like a eucalyptus cough drop. The leaves also provide chemicals that are important to the koala's health. Cineol, for example, lowers blood pressure and body temperature while inducing muscular relaxation. The smaller koalas of warm northern Australia therefore prefer leaves containing cineol, while the larger koalas of the cool south prefer leaves containing phellandren, a chemical that raises the body temperature.

Koalas mate during early autumn, and their period of gestation is about a month. Like other marsupial babies, the newborn koala is less than an inch long, hardly more than an embryo in its development. But it is born with relatively strong forelimbs, which enable it to climb laboriously from the mother's vagina to the security of her pouch. Once there, it nurses for about six months until it is well-furred and several inches long. Then it is gradually weaned. Resting comfortably in the pouch, which opens downward and toward the rear, the koala cub laps pre-digested foliage from the mother's anus. After two more months in the pouch, it emerges and begins to eat an adult diet.

The koala is relatively slow-growing, reaching sexual maturity at the late age of three or four years. During its first year the cub rides along on the mother's back, often

until it is nearly as large as she is. Gradually it becomes more independent, venturing off on its own in search of food. By the time he reaches maturity, a vigorous young male koala will have acquired a harem of several carefully guarded breeding partners, and be all set for adult responsibilities.

Of course, the koala needs special adaptations to make effective use of its limited food source. It is equipped with cheek pouches and an extra-long appendix that helps in the digestion of eucalyptus leaves. As a further aid to digestion, it will often lick up earth and gravel while eating. But this anatomical system, with all of its specializations, often renders the koala susceptible to a wide variety of kidney ailments and intestinal parasites.

Despite its lack of a prehensile tail—or any tail at all for that matter—the koala is well adapted to its life in the trees. The first and second of its strong, sharp-nailed fingers are opposable to the other three, and serve as double thumbs for grasping branches. It also has an opposable thumb on each hind paw. But in spite of its climbing prowess, the koala is slow-moving, and

easily trapped by the forest fires that occasionally sweep through groves of the highly flammable eucalyptus trees.

Until recently, it appeared that humans might exterminate the harmless koala. Koalas have few natural enemies, and so are not easily frightened by people. Millions of them were slaughtered for sport and for their soft, durable fur. Epidemics at the turn of the century further decimated their numbers; but finally Australia enacted protective legislation. Exportation of koalas was banned, and attempts were made to resettle them in the forests where they had once flourished.

Today the koala is thriving and multiplying rapidly. In fact, the eastern coastal cities of Australia find themselves having to put up road signs warning of "koala crossings." Suburban dwellers, hearing plaintive child-like cries in their back yards, rush out to find that they have been "invaded" by entire furry families of koalas. The lovable koala seems to have found a protected niche at last, where it can be admired and enjoyed by the humans with whom it shares the continent of Australia.

Development after birth

Embryonic development includes both differentiation and growth. These two developmental processes must be finely synchronized. All the major body systems must function properly while the tissues and organs are differentiating and the body is growing in size. It is about as complicated as trying to turn a motorcycle gradually into a Cadillac, while driving the steadily changing vehicle smoothly down the highway at 50 miles per hour.

Development after birth is dominated by **growth.** Unlike plants, most animals do not grow larger throughout life. New cells may continue to replace old cells. But when there is no longer an overall increase in the number of cells, growth stops. If an animal lives long enough, it may even suffer an overall decrease in the number of its cells, and so shrink in size. We see this sometimes in old people.

Not all animals replace their cells. In the adult insect, for example, most cells are never replaced. And in many other animals, not all the cells are replaced. In vertebrates, some cells, such as those of the blood and skin, die and are replaced at a fairly steady rate throughout life. Others, such as nerve and muscle cells, are never replaced, even if injured or destroyed (though, as we saw in chapter 10, parts of some nerve cells can regenerate after injury).

The rates of growth in different parts of the animal's body vary. This changes the animal's proportions at different stages of life. The head of the human fetus and young child seem very large compared to the rest of the body. The legs, which develop more slowly, are relatively small at birth. By adolescence, the head has reached adult size, and the arms and legs make a fast spurt to catch up. Since the trunk grows more slowly, for a while the adolescent may seem to be "all arms and legs." These changing growth rates are referred to as **differential growth.**

The length of the growing period varies

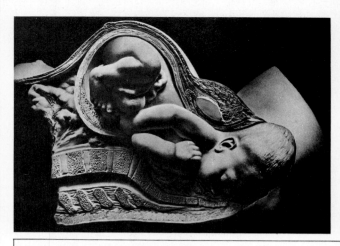

Figure 14-13. This model shows the "head-first" presentation in the normal birth process. Once the head has emerged the rest of the body quickly follows, aided by contractions of the uterus.

among animals. Growth rates may also differ, even among members of the same species. In general, though, most animals follow a similar pattern. There is a burst of growth immediately after birth, followed by a period of slow growth. Then there is a period of more rapid growth until sexual maturity. Finally, there is a period when growth slows down or stops. There are, of course, deviations from this pattern. Insects, which have a confining external skeleton, grow very rapidly after each molt. But they grow hardly at all after each new skeleton has fully formed and hardened.

As in plants, growth in animals is controlled by hormones. However, when an animal reaches sexual maturity, it is believed to secrete other hormones that put a stop to growth.

AGING AND DEATH

As they get older, most animals begin to show signs of aging, or **senescence.** They slow down; their organs wear out; their systems start functioning poorly. All multicellular animals die, though generally not of "old age." Rather, the deterioration that ac-

PATTERNS OF REPRODUCTION
AND DEVELOPMENT

companies aging makes them more susceptible to disease, infection, accident, and predators. These are usually the actual causes of death in an aging animal.

Not all animals seem to age. The bones of many fish and reptiles continue to grow, though rather slowly, until death. As they get older, these animals do not seem to malfunction as badly as those that stopped growing at some time in their lives. Also, not all parts of an aging animal seem to deteriorate. Organs whose cells are continuously renewed (such as the pancreas and liver) do not seem to age much, if at all.

Aging is generally associated with death of the animal's cells. Yet, as we have seen, some cell death is a normal part of growth and development. Blood and skin cells continually die. But they are continually replaced by new cells. It is the death of cells that cannot be replaced—such as nerve and muscle cells—that characterizes aging. The parts of the body whose cells do not continue to divide are the parts that age most quickly.

No one knows what causes aging. However, scientists have pointed out possible contributing factors. Some emphasize genetic inheritance. Certain genes are thought to direct deterioration, just as others direct development. That is, at a certain point in life, these genes naturally cause deterioration, no matter how healthy the individual may be. This may be why each animal has a definite potential lifespan, characteristic of its species. Fruit flies may live for up to fifteen days, frogs as long as twenty years. But they very rarely live much longer. And, although medical science has increased the average life expectancy of individual humans, it has not changed the potential lifespan of the human species. The latter remains about 70 to 80 years, as it has been for centuries (though there are small, rather isolated groups among which a lifespan of 100 years or more seems to be common).

Changes in the levels of sex hormones seem to be related to the aging process. After menopause, for example, estrogen and progesterone levels in women are greatly reduced. These chemical changes seem to be associated with some of the structural symptoms of aging, such as the drying and wrinkling of skin. The lowering of the estrogen level seems also to make women more vulnerable to atherosclerosis (chapter 5).

There are also some factors built into the overall development of an animal which result in its aging. In a sense, one could say that living is itself the cause of aging. For example, wastes tend to accumulate in cells as they grow older. These wastes are poisonous, and contribute to cell malfunctioning. Perhaps this is why tissues and organs whose cells are not replaced tend to function more poorly as they get older. Deterioration of one part of the body puts a strain on other parts, causing them to age as well.

Growth, too, seems somewhat to affect the aging process. Animals that grow to sexual maturity quickly also tend to age quickly. Scientists have been able to lengthen the lives of laboratory mice by slowing down their growth rates.

Also, the external environment may be a prime factor in aging. Radiation, for example, can cause cells to mutate. If abnormal mutated cells accumulate through an animal's lifetime, its tissues and organs may not function efficiently. Again, a strain is put on other body systems, and they deteriorate.

Sooner or later, aging results in death. An animal dies when all its metabolic activities have stopped. Usually, when one vital organ stops working for any reason, the effect spreads quickly through the body, causing death.

The stopping of the heart has traditionally been considered the sign of death in humans. Without a pumping heart, the rest of the cells cannot receive the food and oxygen they need to live. The cells of the nervous system are the first to die. If it receives no oxygen, the brain will be irreversibly damaged within a few minutes. Other cells, such as skin cells, die more slowly, but all die eventually.

Until recently, therefore, if the heart stopped, this was an adequate sign of death.

However, we are now able to keep a person's blood circulating, even when the heart has ceased to function. With such help, a person can sometimes recover and return to normal life after a heart stoppage. But what of the person whose brain has been irreparably damaged, and whose heart and lungs therefore will never function again? Even such people can now be kept "alive" for long periods with the help of mechanical pumps and respirators. The use of such machines has raised some important moral and legal questions. For instance, is it murder to "pull the plug" of a machine that is supporting such a person? Is the person "alive" if there is no chance that he or she can ever function again independently—or even recover consciousness? There is a trend toward redefining death as the failure of the brain to exhibit activity above a certain minimal level. If the brain and nervous system cannot function above this level, a person cannot control any bodily process. Should he or she then be regarded as dead, even if the cells can still be kept alive by extraordinary means?

SUMMARY

Sexually reproducing animals develop from a single cell. Development proceeds in a series of stages, during which complex structures are formed from simpler ones. In the frog, repeated mitotic divisions produce the hollow blastula. In the next stage a gastrula is formed, consisting of ectoderm, endoderm, and mesoderm. All adult structures will arise from these three cell layers in the embryo. Neurulation begins when gastrulation is complete. The neural tube develops, laying the foundation for the nervous system.

Spemann demonstrated that the underlying mesoderm is responsible for the differentiation of the ectoderm of the gastrula. The process by which one tissue induces another tissue to differentiate is called embryonic induction.

Two principal factors influence development: interactions between the cytoplasm and nucleus of each cell, and interactions among cells. As development continues, a cell becomes increasingly restricted in its potential to differentiate. Once it has been committed to a specific course of development, it normally cannot reverse its direction.

The early human embryo resembles other vertebrate embryos, and develops according to the same general principles. By the time it reaches the uterus, the fertilized egg has developed into a blastocyst. Some cells, which will develop into the fetus, have gathered at one end of the blastocyst. Its outer edge is the trophoblast, which is responsible for implantation of the embryo.

The placenta begins to develop upon implantation. It anchors the embryo to the uterine wall and provides nutrition to the embryo via the umbilical cord. The placenta also functions in respiration, circulation, and excretion.

The differentiation of the nervous system dominates development during the first month of pregnancy. The foundations of the other major systems are laid down by the end of the first five weeks, and their organs have begun to differentiate by the end of the second month.

During the second trimester the fetus grows considerably and becomes increasingly active, although the brain is not yet able to coordinate its movements very well. Structural refinement of face, neck, hands and feet are evident, and the body becomes more erect as muscles and bones form along the spinal column.

During the third trimester the fetus gains more weight. Its nervous system becomes increasingly refined, and it can use all of its senses. By the end of nine months it is ready to be born. Birth begins with labor, during which the cervix and vagina increase in diameter, allowing passage of the baby out of the mother's body. The placenta is expelled a few minutes after birth.

Before milk production begins, the nursing baby receives colostrum. This fluid is high in proteins and antibodies, which will give the baby some immunity until it can develop its own immune system.

Postembryonic development in animals is dominated by growth, an overall increase in the number of cells. It may occur at different rates in different parts of the body.

Most animals age as they get older. Aging is generally associated with the death of cells that are never replaced. Organs with a steady turnover of cells do not seem to age. Those whose cells cease to divide are the parts of the body that age most rapidly.

Death occurs when all metabolic activity stops. Now that medical technology can keep the organs alive even when brain activity has ceased, it has been suggested that death should be defined as the stopping of all brain activity.

Review questions

1. Describe the fertilized frog egg. How do its different regions help to protect it from predators?

2. Why might students observing a frog blastula for the first time want to call it an "egg"?

3. What brings about the beginning of gastrulation? What cavity is formed during gastrulation? What will it eventually become?

4. What are the three germ layers of the gastrula? To what body systems do they eventually give rise?

5. What is the importance of the coelom?

6. What is the principal event of neurulation?

7. Why did Spemann suspect that the mesoderm induced the ectoderm of the gastrula to differentiate? How did he demonstrate it?

8. What is embryonic induction?

9. Explain why cells become increasingly committed to a specific course of development as differentiation proceeds.

10. It is often said that the developing embryo retraces the evolution of life on earth. Explain the possible basis for this statement.

11. What events take place between conception and implantation?

12. The human blastocyst consists of an inner mass of cells and a trophoblast. What will each develop into?

13. How does the placenta work? What functions does it serve?

14. Why are the first two months of pregnancy the most critical in embryonic development?

15. Why is it necessary for the heart and circulatory system to become functional so early?

16. Explain why most miscarriages occur during the first trimester of pregnancy.

17. Why is the six-month-old fetus not ready to survive on its own?

18. What function is served by the layer of fat gained during the third trimester?

19. Why is a headfirst exit through the birth canal the best orientation of the baby's body? What would be the disadvantages of other possible orientations?

20. What is colostrum? What are its advantages to the newborn?

21. How does growth in animals differ from growth in plants?

22. Not all animals seem to age, nor do all parts of an aging animal seem to age. Can you relate this to the phenomena of cell division and cell death?

23. What are some of the factors that cause aging? Why can we say that aging and death are all a part of the life process?

24. Why may stopping of the heart no longer be an adequate determiner of death in humans? Why is brain death perhaps a better one?

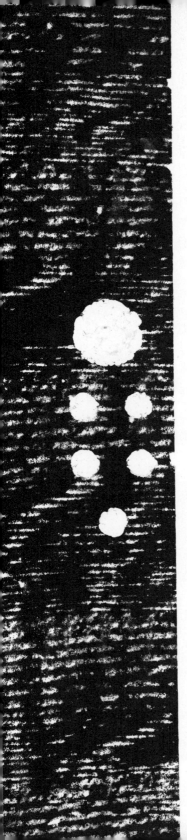

Heredity and New Individuals

So far we have simply been describing the results of sexual reproduction. Now it is time to begin explaining them. Any complete explanation must include the role of the genes. As you know, each parent contributes one set of genes to the offspring through the gametes. The unique combination of characteristics in each individual results from the actions of his or her unique combination of genes. It is impossible to observe gene action directly. However, we can observe it indirectly, by studying some of the characteristics that result from it.

The science of heredity, or **genetics,** began with such a study of the outward signs of gene action. Interestingly, the man who is now considered the "father of genetics" had never heard of genes or chromosomes. Nor did he realize the role of the cell's nucleus in transmitting hereditary information. This man was Gregor Johann Mendel, a monk living in the mid-1800s in what is now Czechoslovakia. All he began with, in his investigations into heredity, were some simple mathematics, a keen interest in plants, and a good deal of curiosity and patience. He ended with the first major discoveries of this new science. It is appropriate that we begin our study where he did.

THE INVESTIGATIONS OF GREGOR MENDEL

Like other plant breeders before him, Mendel had observed that flowers of several different kinds could be produced by crossbreeding a few strains. In the course of

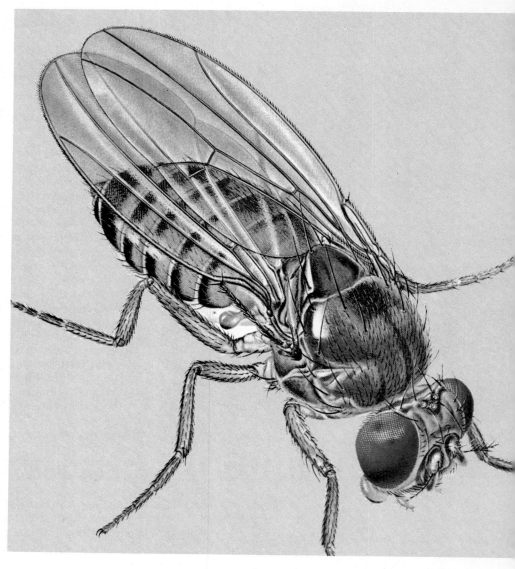

Figure 15-1. *Drosophila melanogaster* seems like too big a name for this tiny fruit fly. But despite its small size, the fruit fly has made an enormous contribution to the study of heredity.

various experiments, he found that he could get regular and predictable results in the offspring of certain parent plants. Mendel could find no satisfactory explanation for such patterns in the scientific literature of his time, so he decided to investigate them himself.

Mendel decided to crossbreed varieties of plants that differed in certain traits, concentrating on one trait at a time. By carefully observing and recording the results of the crossbreedings, he hoped he could see how such a single trait was passed down from generation to generation. He thought that such an approach would show the pattern of inheritance for these traits.

Mendel's experiments

After some preliminary experiments, Mendel chose the garden pea for use in his investigations. His choice was an excellent one for

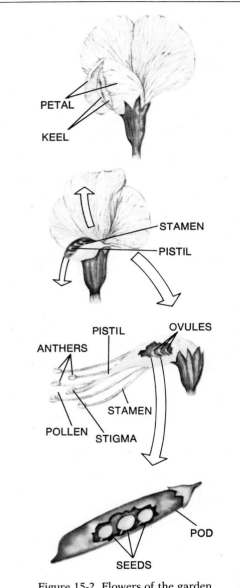

PETAL

KEEL

STAMEN

PISTIL

PISTIL

OVULES

ANTHERS

STAMEN

POLLEN

STIGMA

POD

SEEDS

Figure 15-2. Flowers of the garden pea have a keel that surrounds the stamens and pistil. Cross-pollination occurs when insects land on the keel, forcing it downward. For his experiments in artificial cross-pollination, Mendel had to remove the stamens before they ripened.

several reasons. At that time, the garden pea came in 34 varieties, all readily available. It is also an easy plant to cultivate. In addition, the flower of the pea is structured so that it is normally self-pollinating. However, it can easily be cross-pollinated by hand, and it can be protected from accidental cross-pollination. This last characteristic is very important. In order to be sure of detecting true inheritance patterns in the offspring, Mendel had to be able to control fertilization in the parent plants.

Mendel chose seven different traits for study. These traits appeared in distinctly contrasting forms in plants of different varieties. One variety, for example, always produced yellow seeds, while another always produced green seeds. One variety produced seeds that, when dried, were round and smooth. Another had seeds that were wrinkled when dried. Before he started his experiments, he allowed each variety to self-pollinate for several generations. This was to make sure that they always bred "true"—that is, that the same trait appeared in every generation. Mendel then began a seven-year series of carefully executed experiments.

The first year he crossed plants having contrasting traits. For example, in crosses between round-seed and wrinkled-seed varieties, he removed the stamens from the flowers of the round variety before the pollen matured. Later he transferred pollen from stamens of the wrinkled variety to the mature stigmas of the round variety. With other plants, he reversed the process, transferring pollen from the round variety to the stigmas of the wrinkled variety.

When the pods were mature, Mendel broke them open. He discovered only round seeds in both the round and wrinkled varieties. The wrinkled trait seemed to have disappeared. Mendel obtained similar results from the other crosses. In the cross between the yellow-seed variety and the green-seed variety, for instance, both varieties produced only yellow seeds.

The offspring that result from a cross between two "pure"-breeding plants are called the **first filial generation**, or **F₁ generation.** Mendel named those traits that appeared in the F₁ generation **dominant traits.** He called those that seemed to be lost in the F₁ generation **recessive traits.**

Mendel carefully sorted all the seeds and planted them the next spring. He allowed each plant to fertilize itself. Then, when he opened the pods of plants grown from the F₁ yellow seeds, he found both yellow and green seeds. Likewise, in the plants grown from round F₁ seeds, Mendel discovered both round and wrinkled seeds. The recessive traits—the green or wrinkled appearances—had not been lost. They had been "hidden" for a generation.

As he counted the thousands of seeds in this second, or **F₂ generation,** Mendel began to see a numerical relationship between the dominant and recessive traits. There were, for example, just about three round seeds for every wrinkled seed. There were also about three yellow seeds for every green seed, and so on. In other words, Mendel found a 3:1 ratio between the dominant and recessive traits. To be sure, it was not exactly 3:1; yet it was close. More important, it was consistent. Mendel had indeed found a pattern, but he did not know how to explain it.

He then planted many of the seeds from the F₂ generation, letting the resulting plants fertilize themselves. The wrinkled seeds of the F₂ generation produced only offspring whose seeds were also wrinkled. When he replanted the wrinkled seeds of the F₃ generation, the offspring again bore only wrinkled seeds. In fact, the recessive traits in all his plants continued to breed "true" through successive generations. But when the seeds of the plants showing the dominant trait were planted, the results were not as clear-cut. For example, some of the F₂ round seeds grew into plants that produced both round and wrinkled seeds in the same 3:1 ratio; others grew into plants that produced only round seeds. As a group, the plants of the F₂ generation with dominant traits did not breed "true."

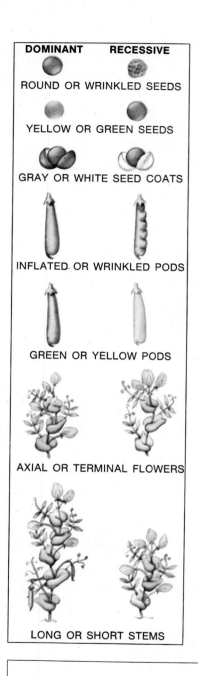

DOMINANT   RECESSIVE

ROUND OR WRINKLED SEEDS

YELLOW OR GREEN SEEDS

GRAY OR WHITE SEED COATS

INFLATED OR WRINKLED PODS

GREEN OR YELLOW PODS

AXIAL OR TERMINAL FLOWERS

LONG OR SHORT STEMS

Figure 15-3. These are some of the characteristics that were studied by Mendel.

Table 15-1. Mendel's results with two generations of garden peas.

Traits Selected For Cross	F₁ Plants	F₁ Self-pollination	F₂ Plants	Actual F₂ Ratio
● X ◉	●	● X ●	5,474 round seeds 1,850 wrinkled seeds 7,324 Total	2.96:1
○ X ●	●	● X ○	6,022 yellow seeds 2,001 green seeds 8,023 Total	3.01:1
◑ X ◐	◐	◐ X ◑	705 gray seed coats 224 white seed coats 929 Total	3.15:1
⬓ X ⬓	⬓	⬓ X ⬓	882 inflated pods 224 wrinkled pods 1,106 Total	2.95:1
⬓ X ⬓	⬓	⬓ X ⬓	428 green pods 152 yellow pods 580 Total	2.82:1
✿ X ✿	✿	✿ X ✿	651 axial flowers 207 terminal flowers 858 Total	3.14:1
✿ X ✿	✿	✿ X ✿	787 long stems 277 short stems 1,064 Total	2.84:1

Mendel's analysis: the principle of segregation

In order to make his record-keeping easier, Mendel began to use symbols for the traits he was studying. He used a capital letter of the alphabet for the dominant trait and the same letter in lower case for the opposite, or recessive, trait. Thus, the round variety was symbolized with an *R*, and the wrinkled variety with an *r*.

What puzzled Mendel was that both round *(R)* and wrinkled *(r)* seeds were sometimes produced in the second generation from a round *(R)* seed of the first generation. He calculated that this could occur only if some of the F₁ round seeds carried two dif- ferent "factors" for seed shape—that is, if they carried factors for both round and wrinkled shapes. If two factors were involved in seed shape, two factors were probably also involved in seed color, in stem length, and so on. Therefore, Mendel reasoned, all seeds carried two factors for each trait. The round seeds could thus be described not simply as *R*, but as either *RR* or *Rr*. The wrinkled seeds could be described as *rr*. Since the presence of a dominant *R* would mask the presence of a recessive *r*, an *Rr* seed would be round. But it would still contain the separate *r* factor, which could be passed on to the seeds of later generations.

Mendel believed that these hereditary factors always appeared in pairs. He also thought that the male and female parts of a plant each contributed one factor to the pair. Mendel further noticed that there was no "blending" of traits during a crossbreeding. There were no greenish-yellow seeds, for example; seeds were either all-green or all-yellow. He therefore assumed that the hereditary factors never blended. Each was passed as a unit from generation to generation. Mendel's assumption that each pair of hereditary factors separated in the parents, and that factors from both parents were recombined (but not blended) in the offspring, is now known as the **principle of segregation.**

We can now return to the original crossbreeding experiments, using Mendel's symbols. It will be easier to keep track of our results if we plot them on a sort of checkerboard. This checkerboard is known as a Punnett square, after the British geneticist R. C. Punnett who devised it. A Punnett square is made by listing the hereditary factors that could be present in each parent's gametes. As you can see in figure 15-4, the male gametes (sperm) are shown along one edge of the square, and the female gametes (eggs) along another edge. The boxes are then filled in with all the gamete combinations that could occur in the offspring.

For instance, take a cross between a purebreeding round-seed variety *(RR)* and a purebreeding wrinkled-seed variety *(rr)*. This cross is symbolized as:

$$RR \times rr$$

The factors are separated when gametes are produced. Each gamete thus contains one factor. Assuming the *RR* parent is the male, each sperm will contain one *R*. If the *rr* parent is the female, each egg will contain one *r*. Furthermore, each of the two sperm has an equal chance of fusing with either of the two eggs. We can symbolize the results of the cross as follows:

Figure 15-4. The results of a cross between round-seed and wrinkled-seed garden peas. The F_1 generation are all round.

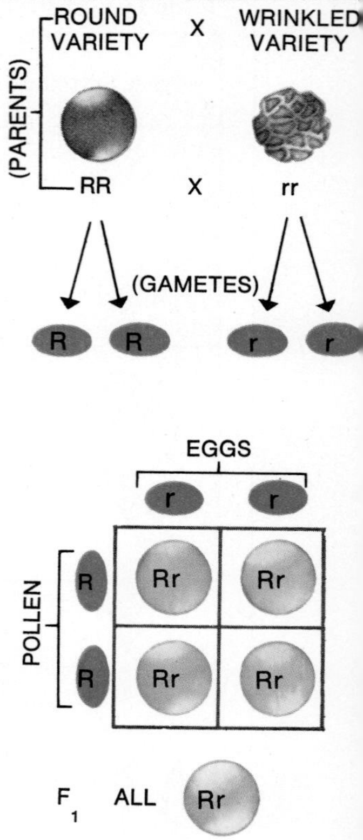

Figure 15-5. The results of a cross between round-seed garden peas of the F_1 generation.

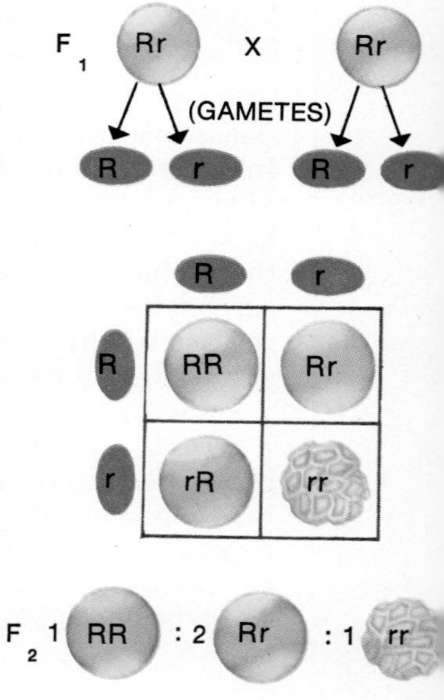

PATTERNS OF CHANGE

	If		Then
sperm		egg	seed
no. 1 *(R)*	×	no. 1 *(r)*	= *Rr* (round)
no. 1 *(R)*	×	no. 2 *(r)*	= *Rr* (round)
no. 2 *(R)*	×	no. 1 *(r)*	= *Rr* (round)
no. 2 *(R)*	×	no. 2 *(r)*	= *Rr* (round)

All possibilities have an equal chance of occurring. Since all possibilities have the same outcome *(Rr)*, all the offspring will have round seeds.

All the individuals produced by this cross make up the F_1 generation. Now, what happens when plants grown from these individuals are allowed to self-pollinate? We can symbolize the self-pollination of the F_1 individual as follows:

$$Rr \times Rr$$

Again, each gamete will contain only one factor, and again there are four possible combinations of gametes in the F_2 generation:

	If		Then
sperm		egg	seed
no. 1 *(R)*	×	no. 1 *(R)*	= *RR* (round)
no. 1 *(R)*	×	no. 2 *(r)*	= *Rr* (round)
no. 2 *(r)*	×	no. 1 *(R)*	= *rR* (round)
no. 2 *(r)*	×	no. 2 *(r)*	= *rr* (wrinkled)

All four possibilities again have an equal chance of occurring. Two of the outcomes are identical (*rR* has exactly the same effects as *Rr*). So there are really only three possible ways the factors could combine: *RR*, *Rr*, and *rr*. These appear in the ratio 1*RR* to 2*Rr* to 1*rr*, or simply 1:2:1. In appearance, though, there are only two possible outcomes: round or wrinkled. Since *R* is the dominant trait, *RR* and *Rr* seeds will both be round. Only *rr* seeds will be wrinkled. The visible effects occur in the ratio of 3 round to 1 wrinkled, or 3:1. Note how this analysis correlates with the data Mendel obtained from his experiments. Mendel found only round seeds in his F_1 generation, and both round and wrinkled seeds in about a 3:1 ratio in his F_2 generation.

Today we call Mendel's factors **genes,** and we refer to the genetic make-up of an individual as its **genotype.** The appearance of an individual is called its **phenotype.** Thus, the phenotypes in our example appeared in a ratio 3:1, the genotypes in a ratio 1:2:1.

Each member of a pair of genes is called an **allele.** *R* and *r* are said to be alleles of each other. Organisms whose alleles for a certain trait are the same are called **homozygous.** *RR* and *rr* are homozygous genotypes. Homozygous plants are **purebred;** that is, they will breed true when crossed with each other. Individuals whose alleles for a given trait are not the same are called **heterozygous.** *Rr* is a heterozygous genotype. An individual that is heterozygous for any trait is called a **hybrid,** and, as we have seen, it will not breed true.

Testing the hypothesis: the testcross
In devising a test for his hypothesis, Mendel established a pattern of testing that has often been used since. It is called a **testcross,** and is performed by mating two individuals. One of these is a known homozygous recessive (such as *rr*); the other's genotype is unknown. The test is to determine the unknown genotype. It may be either heterozygous (such as *Rr*) or homozygous *(RR),* but it is not apparent from the phenotype (round).

Mendel still had some of the seeds produced during his first experiments. He planned a cross between the F_1 round seeds and the original wrinkled seeds he knew to breed true. He hypothesized that the round seeds had a genotype of *Rr*, and the wrinkled seeds of *rr*. In this case, the cross would be symbolized as:

$$Rr \times rr$$

If his hypothesis were correct, he could predict the ratio between the round and wrinkled seeds resulting from this cross:

Sperm   Egg

R × r = Rr (round seeds)
R × r = Rr (round seeds)
r × r = rr (wrinkled seeds)
r × r = rr (wrinkled seeds)

All possibilities are equally likely. Therefore, half of the seeds resulting from such a cross are expected to have a genotype of Rr, and should be round. The other half of the seeds are expected to have a genotype of rr. These seeds should be wrinkled. Thus, crossing a heterozygous with a homozygous recessive individual produces both a genotype and a phenotype ratio of 1:1. Mendel performed the testcross, and harvested 106 round seeds and 101 wrinkled seeds. His result was very close to the one predicted.

On the other hand, suppose the unknown had been homozygous dominant *(RR)* instead of heterozygous? What would be the expected genotypic and phenotypic ratios of the offspring?

Dihybrid cross: principle of independent assortment
Up to this point, Mendel had been dealing only with single pairs of traits. He had not concerned himself with whether his round seeds were green or yellow, or with whether his yellow seeds were wrinkled or smooth. But was there a relationship between traits? Were wrinkled seeds just as likely to be yellow as green, or were they more likely to be one or the other? How did the various factors work together? He set out to find the answer.

By crossbreeding, Mendel produced plants that bred true for two traits. Some plants would produce round–yellow seeds through successive generations, for example, and others would produce wrinkled–green seeds. Because of this, Mendel hypothesized that the factors (genes) in each pair were identical for each trait. Thus, the genotype for the round–yellow seed should be *RRYY*, and for the wrinkled–green seed *rryy*.

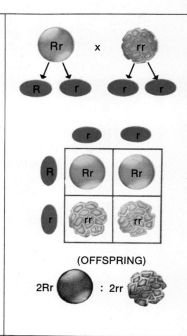

Figure 15-6. The results of a testcross between a heterozygous and a homozygous individual.

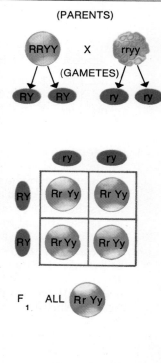

Figure 15-7. There is only one possible result in this cross between two homozygous varieties. The dihybrid individuals of the F₁ generation are heterozygous for two traits.

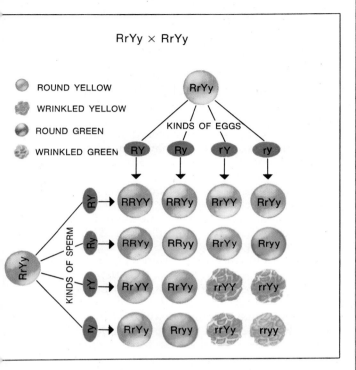

RrYy × RrYy

ROUND YELLOW
WRINKLED YELLOW
ROUND GREEN
WRINKLED GREEN

KINDS OF EGGS

RrYy

RY   Ry   rY   ry

KINDS OF SPERM

RY → RRYY RRYy RrYY RrYy

Ry → RRYy RRyy RrYy Rryy

rY → RrYY RrYy rrYY rrYy

ry → RrYy Rryy rrYy rryy

Figure 15-8. The results from this dihybrid cross illustrate the principle of independent assortment.

What would happen if the two homozygous varieties were crossed, as shown in figure 15–7? How many combinations would be found in the resulting seeds? There is only one possibility if each parent contributes one allele of each pair. All the resulting individuals will have a genotype of *RrYy*. Therefore, all the F₁ seeds should have a phenotype of round–yellow. When Mendel made the cross, the F₁ seeds were as he had predicted—all were round and yellow.

These F₁ seeds were heterozygous, or hybrid, for two traits. Such individuals are called **dihybrids.** Now, what would happen if the F₁ seeds, the dihybrids, were planted and the plants were allowed to fertilize themselves? Theoretically, it seems there are two possible outcomes. The alleles for

seed shape and seed color could stay together from the first generation to the second. Thus *R* would stay with *Y*, and *r* with *y*. This would mean that only round–yellow seeds and wrinkled–green seeds would be produced in the F₂ generation, in the ratio 3:1.

On the other hand, the alleles could distribute themselves independently. If this were the case, wrinkled–yellow seeds and round–green seeds might be produced in addition to the round–yellow and wrinkled–green seeds. Sixteen combinations are then possible. Out of these 16, 9 seeds should be round–yellow, 3 should be wrinkled–yellow, 3 round–green, and 1 wrinkled–green. In other words, if the hypothesis is correct, the overall phenotype ratio of the F₂ generation should be 9:3:3:1. Mendel performed this experiment and obtained a total of 556 seeds:

315 round–yellow
101 wrinkled–yellow
108 round–green
32 wrinkled–green

The results were very close to the predicted ratio 9:3:3:1.

The results from this dihybrid cross do not negate Mendel's earlier results. On the contrary, they support them. The round seeds and wrinkled seeds still appear in the same 3:1 ratio (423 round:133 wrinkled). The ratio of yellow seeds to green seeds is also still 3:1 (416 yellow:140 green). New combinations of traits were created from the dihybrid cross because the alleles for seed shape and those for seed color were separated (assorted) and distributed independently of each other during the production of gametes. The concept that one pair of alleles can be assorted independently of another pair of alleles is now known as the **principle of independent assortment.**

After Mendel

Mendel published the results of his experiments in 1865. However, his work went largely unnoticed, and was forgotten for the next 35 years. Part of the reason for this neglect is that Mendel, not a well-known scientist of his time, published his results in a small and relatively unknown natural history journal.

More importantly, perhaps, his findings seemed preposterous to some of the leading scientists of the time. Most scientists then believed that the traits in the offspring were always a blend of the traits of the parents. These scientists tended to choose more complex traits to observe for their studies of heredity. Their results were correspondingly less simple and clear-cut than Mendel's. Therefore, they may have felt that inheritance was too complex a process to be explained by Mendel's simple pairs of factors. Moreover, most of them did not have Mendel's ability to combine mathematics with biology.

Mendel died in 1884 without ever realizing that his work would be the foundation for a completely new branch of biology. Interestingly, his work was to be rediscovered simultaneously by three different botanists working independently in 1900.

GENES AND THE CHROMOSOME THEORY

Research time was not being wasted during those 35 years while Mendel's work lay unnoticed. The microscope was steadily being improved, which led to advances in the field of cytology (the study of cells). You may recall from chapter 1 that Flemming discovered chromosomes in the nuclei of cells in the 1880s. By the beginning of the twentieth century, scientists could clearly identify many structures in the cell's cytoplasm and nucleus. They also observed many activities taking place within cells. One thing they had not yet found in the cell, however, was Mendel's hereditary "factors," by then called genes. Some people thought genes did not exist at all but were rather a metaphor for some unexplained process going on inside the cell. Others thought genes actually existed, but did not know where. In 1902, Walter S. Sutton provided the first major clue to this problem.

Sutton was a graduate student in cytology at Columbia University, investigating mitosis and meiosis. He was struck by certain parallels between his observations and Mendel's recently rediscovered findings. First, the chromosomes pair up during meiosis. Mendel's factors also came in pairs. Second, by the end of meiosis, each gamete contains one chromosome from each pair of homologous chromosomes. Mendel said that each parent contributes one factor from each pair of factors to the offspring. Third, the fusion of gametes restores the diploid number of chromosomes. Mendel's factors were recombined into pairs in the offspring. Finally, each pair of chromosomes lines up and separates independently of other pairs of chromosomes during meiosis. This corresponds to Mendel's principle of independent assortment. Sutton therefore proposed that Mendel's factors (genes) were located on the chromosomes. Sutton's work laid the foundation for what was later called the **chromosome theory.**

Experiments with *Drosophilia*

Mendel's garden pea was a good experimental choice for someone investigating hereditary mechanisms. It had one serious drawback, however. It had only one generation of offspring each year, so that several years were needed before the investigator could collect meaningful data. Human errors and the hazards of nature could easily wipe out years of careful data collecting. (Mendel might have been influenced to give up his work with peas because a serious beetle infestation ruined many of his plants.)

The followers of Mendel needed a new experimental organism. They needed one that reproduced and developed rapidly and could be reared with little effort. They found one. *Drosophila melanogaster* is its scientific name (meaning literally "black-bellied dew-

PATTERNS OF CHANGE

Figure 15-9. *Drosophila* has a number of characteristics that make it ideal for genetic experiments. Are any of these noticeable in the picture?

Figure 15-10. *Drosophila* has four pairs of chromosomes. These are giant chromosomes from cells in its salivary glands.

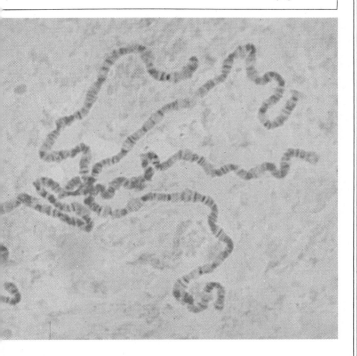

lover"). More commonly, it is called a fruit fly, because it is often found around ripe fruit.

Drosophila offered several advantages to experimenters. It is very small, and thousands can be reared in a few small bottles. It requires no special care or food—just some ripe fruit. One sex hatches earlier than the other, so it is easy to keep them apart until matings are planned. A new generation can be produced about every two weeks. Eventually, scientists discovered one particular characteristic that made *Drosophila* ideal for modern genetic studies. Certain cells in the salivary glands of the fruit fly have chromosomes almost 200 times larger than the chromosomes in other cells. These "giant" chromosomes were an important asset. They provided a clearly observable physical structure on which gene locations could be identified.

The outstanding pioneer of *Drosophila* genetics was Thomas Hunt Morgan, also originally at Columbia University. While examining his fruit flies one day, he noticed a male with white eyes. The normal eye color of the fly is bright red. Morgan crossed the white-eyed male with several red-eyed females. Three of the 1,240 F_1 offspring had white eyes. But if the red-eyed phenotype is dominant, and if the gene causing it is distributed in accordance with Mendel's laws, one would expect all the F_1 offspring to have red eyes. Morgan then crossed the red-eyed males and females of the F_1 generation, expecting an approximate 3:1 ratio (red-eye to white-eye). He obtained 3,470 red-eyed flies and 782 white-eyed flies from these crosses. This was roughly within the range of what he had expected—except for one thing. There were no white-eyed females; all 782 white-eyed flies were male. This seemed to contradict Mendel's principle of independent assortment. How could it be explained?

Sex chromosomes

Morgan performed other crosses and confirmed that certain phenotypes were associated with the sex of individuals. With Sutton's hypothesis in mind, he wondered whether there was a difference between the chromosomes in the male and those in the female. In fact, investigators had already found a difference.

There are four pairs of chromosomes in the cells of *Drosophila*. In the female, all four pairs contain homologous chromosomes. However, in the male, only three pairs have homologous chromosomes. In the fourth pair, the chromosomes are dissimilar. One, called the **X chromosome**, resembles one chromosome in one of the pairs in the female. The other, called the **Y chromosome**, has a hook on one end. The X and Y chromosomes are referred to as **sex chromosomes** because they are always associated with the sex of the individual. All other chromosomes are called **autosomes.**

Morgan's experiment, coupled with the discovery of sex chromosomes, opened up several avenues for investigation. For example, it was discovered that male gametes normally contain either an X or a Y chromosome. Female gametes normally contain an X chromosome, never a Y chromosome. A normal zygote either has an XX pair of chromosomes and becomes a female, or it has an XY pair of chromosomes and becomes a male. Investigators subsequently discovered similar pairs of sex chromosomes in most other animals, including humans. This discovery strongly supported the chromosome theory.

To explain the absence of white-eyed females, Morgan hypothesized that the gene for eye color was located only on the X chromosome, and that there was no allele for eye color on the Y chromosome. Furthermore, he reasoned that the gene for white eyes was recessive. If we let X and Y represent the sex chromosomes, R the allele for red eyes, and r the allele for white eyes, we can symbolize Morgan's initial cross as follows:

Red-eyed female		White-eyed male
$X^R X^R$	$\times$	$X^r Y$

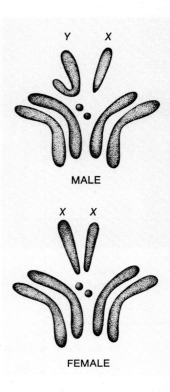

Figure 15-11. The chromosomes in male and female *Drosophila* are illustrated here.

MALE

FEMALE

Figure 15-12. Pairing of chromosomes results in a 50–50 chance of either male or female offspring.

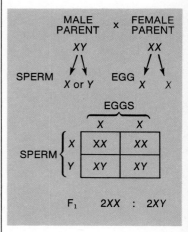

PATTERNS OF CHANGE

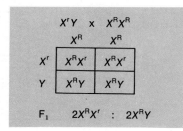

$X^rY \times X^RX^R$

	X^R	X^R
X^r	X^RX^r	X^RX^r
Y	X^RY	X^RY

F_1 $2X^RX^r$: $2X^RY$

Figure 15-13. The results of a cross between a white-eyed male and a homozygous red-eyed female. Why are all of the F_1 generation red-eyed?

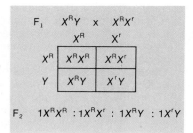

F_1 $X^RY \times X^RX^r$

	X^R	X^r
X^R	X^RX^R	X^RX^r
Y	X^RY	X^rY

F_2 $1X^RX^R : 1X^RX^r : 1X^RY : 1X^rY$

Figure 15-14. A cross between a male and a female of the F_1 generation.

Note that the recessive allele is the only one in the male, since there is no comparable allele on the Y chromosome. Therefore, this recessive gene expresses itself as though it were a dominant gene. We get the following results in the F_1 generation:

Egg		Sperm	
X^R	$\times$	X^r	= X^RX^r (red-eyed female)
X^R	$\times$	X^r	= X^RX^r (red-eyed female)
X^R	$\times$	Y	= X^RY (red-eyed male)
X^R	$\times$	Y	= X^RY (red-eyed male)

Thus, two genotypes can occur in the F_1 generation: X^RX^r and X^RY. There are also two phenotypes: red-eyed female and red-eyed male. In a cross between a female and a male of the F_1 generation:

Red-eyed female   Red-eyed male
X^RX^r $\times$ X^RY

four possible genotypes and three possible phenotypes can result:

Egg		Sperm	
X^R	$\times$	X^R	= X^RX^R (red-eyed female)
X^r	$\times$	X^R	= X^RX^r (red-eyed female)
X^R	$\times$	Y	= X^RY (red-eyed male)
X^r	$\times$	Y	= X^rY (white-eyed male)

Note that there is a 3:1 ratio between the red-eyed and white-eyed phenotypes. This agrees in general with Morgan's results. Note also that there are no white-eyed females in the F_2 generation. White-eyed females were eventually produced from white-eyed males (X^rY) and heterozygous red-eyed females (X^RX^r). Can you work out a Punnett square for this cross?

Linkage

Morgan performed a number of crosses that confirmed his hypothesis that the gene for eye color was located on the X chromosome. (Among them was the cross resulting in the white-eyed females.) Apparently, this gene and those that determined sex were on the same chromosome. Such genes have since been named **sex-linked genes,** or **X-linked genes.** Many sex-linked genes have been discovered in humans, and several will be discussed later in the chapter.

The discovery of sex-linked genes was another major finding that helped to substantiate the chromosome theory. The nature of genes was not yet known, but they could be described as regions on a chromosome. The chromosome, in effect, was a string of many hundreds or thousands of different alleles. Alleles on a single chromosome would tend to stay together in crosses; that is, they would tend to remain linked. The traits in Mendel's peas assorted independently, which implies that their alleles were unlinked. Linkage was first recognized for an allele on a sex chromosome, but it occurs for alleles on other chromosomes as well. Geneticists, in fact, often find it useful to refer to a chromosome as a **linkage group.**

Since, as we saw in chapter 11, different chromosomes do assort independently at

another important result of studies on the fruit fly.

Crossing-over
Morgan performed other experiments on

THE MARIJUANA MUDDLE

Pot, grass, tea, Mary Jane. Whatever you want to call it, marijuana is currently the center of a lively debate among experts and other people alike. On the one hand, some researchers have produced data which seem to show that this hemp product causes brain damage, lowers the production of testosterone (the male sex hormone), retards fetal development, produces birth defects, adversely affects cell metabolism, damages the liver, and lessens the user's ability to handle complex situations.

On the opposite side of the fence, scientists have come up with evidence that, in many instances, wholly or partially contradicts the above findings. In other cases, researchers have pointed out that some of the tests that produced those findings were performed on lab animals, and that the results are not necessarily applicable to humans. These researchers also feel that, in recreational use, marijuana has fewer damaging effects than alcohol.

Caught between these two points of view are the many users of marijuana, who point to its pleasurable effects. Indeed, many of the

pro-pot group say it is downright good for you. Which side is right? At present, no one can say for sure.

Consider, for example, the fifth annual report to Congress on marijuana and health, prepared by the Department of Health, Education, and Welfare. This study seems to indicate that marijuana is neither villain nor panacea. However, the report does state that certain areas of marijuana research warrant further investigation.

One of these concerns possible medical uses for the weed. Until it was outlawed in 1937, marijuana was often prescribed for asthmatics, since it relaxes the constriction of the bronchial tubes which occurs during asthma attacks. The use of marijuana has also been shown to decrease the eye pressure responsible for glaucoma. Similarly, it has been found useful for control of nausea and vomiting in cancer patients undergoing certain kinds of chemotherapy.

So—is marijuana safe or not? The HEW report does not seem sure about any of the plant's good or bad effects. It states, for example, that marijuana should be taken for the benefits it confers, and avoided for the adverse effects it may have. Which, of course, puts us back where we were at the beginning—right in the middle of a muddle.

---

meiosis, we might expect that alleles on different chromosomes would always remain unlinked, and those on the same chromosome would always remain linked. Yet we now know that this is not so. The explanation for this apparent contradiction was

Drosophila, observing it for such traits as body color and wing shape. The genes for body color and wing shape are normally linked in *Drosophila,* and one would expect it to show only two phenotypes for these traits: (1) gray bodies and long wings, which are dominant traits, and (2) black bodies and short wings, which are recessive traits. However, Morgan found that some of his flies had recombined these traits. A few had gray bodies and short wings. A few others had black bodies and long wings. The appearance of these flies could be explained only if their genes had "jumped" from one chromosome to another, breaking the normal link. But how? Why did these genes not remain in their expected linkage groups?

You may have already figured out the answer if you remembered our discussion of synapsis in chapter 11. During this stage of meiosis, the four chromatids of each pair of homologous chromosomes are lined up at the equator. The ends of the inner two chromatids may break off and be exchanged between the two chromosomes. You recall that this process is known as **crossing-over** and results in the exchange of genes between homologous chromosomes. In this way, linked alleles may separate and be distributed on different chromosomes, so that new linkages are created. Crossing-over accounts for the apparent "jumping" of genes from one chromosome to another, and thus for the recombination of traits in the phenotypes. In effect, it "reshuffles" the genes into new combinations, and thus increases variability among the genotypes of a species. Without crossing-over, the linkage groups would limit the amount of variation within a population.

Morgan assumed that the number of genes on one chromosome must be the same as the number of genes on the homologous chromosome. Furthermore, the spacing between the genes along the two chromosomes must be precisely the same. Otherwise, when chromatid sections were exchanged, the chromosomes might end up with a different number of genes than they started with. And this did not seem to be the case in the flies he observed. In their phenotypes, the fruit flies always showed an exact exchange of traits. There was never an increase in some flies and a decrease in others.

If the genes are lined up at regular and fixed points, or **loci,** along the chromosomes, it might be possible to locate them. Morgan had noticed that some traits were recombined more often than were other traits. He assumed, therefore, that the genes for these traits were exchanged during crossing-over more often than were other genes. It was suggested that these frequently-exchanged genes must be farther apart on the chromosome than the seldom-exchanged ones. For instance, if two genes are at opposite ends of the chromosome, a break anywhere on the chromosome will separate them and allow an exchange. But if they are next to each other, they cannot be separated unless a break occurs exactly in the spot between them. Therefore, the traits that recombine more often must correspond to genes that are further apart on the chromosomes. This suggestion created a new interest among geneticists in **chromosome mapping.** By recording the relative frequencies of different trait recombinations, scientists can plot the relative distances between genes on a chromosome.

Incomplete dominance

In Mendel's experiments with the garden pea, the traits he studied were either dominant or recessive. In many cases, however, some traits of the parents appear blended in the offspring. Such an offspring has a phenotype intermediate between those of the two parents. Often, this means that one allele in a pair is not completely dominant over the other allele. This is called **incomplete dominance** or **partial dominance.**

An example of incomplete dominance is the pattern of color inheritance in shorthorn cattle. When homozygous red bulls are crossed with homozygous white cows, the offspring are neither red nor white. They have red hairs and white hairs on their bodies, giving them an overall roan color. Such a cross is symbolized as follows:

$$\text{Red bull} \qquad \text{White cow}$$
$$RR \qquad \times \qquad R'R'$$

(Because white is not recessive, it is indicated by R' instead of by r.) You know by now that all the offspring of this generation will be RR'. This genotype is expressed as a roan color. When a male and female of the F₁ generation are crossed:

$$\begin{array}{ccc} \text{Roan bull} & & \text{Roan cow} \\ RR' & \times & RR' \end{array}$$

the resulting offspring will be:

$$\begin{array}{l} R \times R = RR \quad \text{(red)} \\ R \times R' = RR' \quad \text{(roan)} \\ R' \times R = R'R \quad \text{(roan)} \\ R' \times R' = R'R' \quad \text{(white)} \end{array}$$

The genotypic ratio is a normal Mendelian 1:2:1. But in this case, the phenotypic ratio matches it.

Multiple alleles

Mendel assumed that there were only two possible factors (or alleles) for a given trait. He was correct in the sense that only two alleles for a given trait are normally present in one individual. But there may be more than two alleles for a given trait in the genetic pool of a population. In other words, there may be **multiple alleles.**

The alleles for coat color in domestic rabbits are a good example of multiple alleles. There are four pairs of these alleles, which can be represented genotypically as CC, $C^{ch}C^{ch}$, C^hC^h, and cc. These produce the following coat colors, respectively: normal, chinchilla, Himalayan, and albino. Human blood type is another characteristic for which there are multiple alleles.

Changes in chromosomes

Changes in chromosomes are caused by a variety of factors. They occur at random, usually during cell division. Crossing-over is one change that we have already considered. In animals, though not always in plants, most other chromosomal changes are for the worse, as far as the individual is concerned. Some can be lethal. That is, they will kill the

Figure 15-15. The four coat colors of rabbits. From the top the rabbits are a wild type, an albino, a chinchilla, and a Himalayan.

$C\ C$

$c\ c$

$C^{ch}\ C^{ch}$

$c^h\ c^h$

individual if they are expressed in the phenotype.

Certain abnormalities affect the structure of chromosomes and can be seen under a microscope. Sometimes pieces from two nonhomologous chromosomes may be exchanged. Such an occurrence is called a **translocation.** Occasionally a piece of one chromosome breaks away completely and is lost. Such a **deletion** of genetic material results in one chromosome that is shorter than its homologous one. When the homologous chromosomes pair up during meiosis, their alleles will not match. The effect of a dele-

PATTERNS OF CHANGE

tion or translocation on an individual's phenotype depends on how many genes, and which ones, were lost or abnormally recombined. Another structural abnormality occurs when part of a chromosome gets turned upside down. The chromosome still has the same number of alleles after such an **inversion,** but they are now in a different order. Again, this may pose a problem in the matching up of alleles during meiosis.

Other abnormalities involve changes in chromosome number. Occasionally, a pair of chromatids fail to separate during meiosis, and both migrate to one pole. This failure is called **nondisjunction.** The result is an extra chromosome in one of the cells produced from the cell division, and one chromosome too few in the other cell. Nondisjunction of sex chromosomes sometimes occurs in humans during gamete formation. When this happens, one gamete has two sex chromosomes, while another has none. For example, nondisjunction may produce an egg or sperm with no sex chromosomes. If a zygote is formed by such a gamete, its genotype will be either XO or YO (O indicates the absence of a chromosome). Most YO zygotes fail to develop altogether. The XO zygote will develop, albeit abnormally. The resulting female is said to have Turner's syndrome. She will not mature sexually and may be mentally retarded.

If an egg ends up with two X chromosomes from nondisjunction and then fuses with a normal gamete, the genotype of the resulting zygote will be either XXX or XXY. The presence of an extra chromosome along with a normal pair of chromosomes is called **trisomy.** The XXX combination often produces an apparently normal female, but the XXY combination develops into a male with Klinefelter's syndrome. A male with this genotype will never fully develop sexually. He may also show some female secondary sex characteristics, such as breasts.

Sometimes a sperm is produced with two Y chromosomes. If such a sperm fertilizes a normal egg, the resulting zygote has a genotype of XYY and will develop into an apparently normal male. These males are often taller than average, though, and may exhibit especially aggressive behavior.

Nondisjunction can occur among autosomes as well as among sex chromosomes. A kind of mental retardation known as **Down's syndrome** results from an extra chromosome belonging to the 21st pair of homologous chromosomes in humans. With an extra chromosome, an individual has an extra set of alleles that may affect his phenotype in a variety of ways. Down's syndrome is characterized by abnormalities of the face, heart, skin, neck, feet, and sex organs, as well as by mental retardation. An extra fold of skin around the eyes produces an effect that gave the syndrome the popular but misleading name of "mongolism."

HUMAN GENETICS

Geneticists cannot study the human population with the same methods they use to study nonhuman populations. They cannot perform controlled breeding experiments among humans, for example, as they can among fruit flies. Thus, many human geneticists depend on family histories for their data. In doing so, they must often rely on the memories and observations of unskilled observers.

Other problems include the time it takes to produce new generations and the usually small number of offspring in each generation. With an average generation time of from 20 to 25 years, seldom does any one investigator have the opportunity to observe at first hand more than three generations.

Other problems arise because inheritance of many traits in humans is not as simple as in the garden pea studied by Mendel. Mendel probably chose the traits he did because they had a rather simple pattern of inheritance. The seeds were either smooth or wrinkled, yellow or green; no intermediate types were seen. Such clearly contrasting traits are called **discontinuous traits.** In

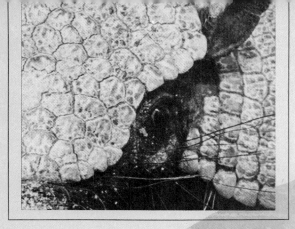

THE ARMADILLO

Driving along a side road in the Florida twilight, the tourist from New England catches sight of an animal by the roadside. A dog, or perhaps a large cat. But the shambling gait is unfamiliar. A small pig, maybe? The driver slows as he approaches the animal. It scuttles fearfully into the underbrush, but not before the tourist has had a good but baffling glimpse of something that resembles a pig wearing a suit of armor. The New Englander has just seen his first armadillo.

Named "little armored one" by early Spanish explorers, the armadillo has a valid claim to being one of America's oldest inhabitants. Millions of years ago a predecessor, a heavily armored creature the size of a modern rhinoceros, roamed the western continent. Now the smaller nine-banded armadillo inhabits southern portions of the United States and much of South and Central America.

There are some twenty species of armadillo, ranging from five inches to five feet in length. The nine-banded armadillo, about thirty inches long, is the only variety found in the United States. Like other armadillos, it is covered by a form-fitting, hinged exoskeleton of bony plates. This suit of armor provides excellent protection against predators; only the ears, throat, and underparts are not covered.

The armadillo is constantly threatened by coyotes, dogs, and other carnivores, and even by humans, who value the "poor man's pig" for its pork-like taste when barbequed. But clumsy-looking though it may be, the armadillo can move surprisingly fast. It can usually outrun a man and outmaneuver a faster animal. If pursued, it may hide in a tangled thicket and quickly dig itself into the ground. Arching its back, it uses its armored plates to wedge itself tightly into the soil. If it is cornered and forced to fight, the armadillo relies on its sharp claws and the offensive odor it emits to repel attackers.

Male and female armadillos look and behave almost exactly alike, their sexual characteristics distinguishable only to another armadillo. And at first glance the armadillo has a definitely reptilian look. But despite its misleading appearance, this odd creature is really a mammal. The nine-banded armadillo mates in midsummer, and the young are born in early spring. This species almost invariably produces a litter of identical quadruplets, arising from two divisions of a single fertilized egg. They are all of the same sex, and are exactly alike in their scale markings and other physical features. Babies are born with their eyes open, and appear to be miniature versions of their mother. They are well-developed in every respect except for their soft armor, which will gradually harden as they mature. The young can walk within a few hours after

birth, and join their mother in foraging for food even before they are weaned.

The armadillo lives almost exclusively on a diet of insects. While it is especially fond of ants, including their eggs and larvae, it also enjoys scorpions, tarantulas, and grasshoppers. Occasionally it will supplement this diet with fungi or wild berries, and it sometimes succeeds in capturing a careless toad or lizard. The belief that armadillos raid henhouses in search of eggs is largely unfounded. But groups of armadillos may sometimes damage crops while they are rooting about in search of food.

Adult armadillos usually live alone or in pairs, but often band together on a foraging expedition. The foraging armadillo travels rapidly, pushing its pig-like snout into leaves and loose soil in search of food as it goes. Occasionally it may pause to sit up on its hind legs and tail as it examines a plant or sniffs the air for the scent of danger. On locating a buried insect or grub, it swiftly digs a hole with its front claws, grunting softly as it works. With remarkable speed, the armadillo can sweep up dozens of ants, eggs, and larvae with a single swipe of its long, sticky tongue.

Water is no obstacle to the armadillo's progress, for the animal swims easily. Relaxing and breathing deeply, it can swallow enough air to inflate its intestinal tract and achieve buoyancy despite the weight of its armor. When crossing short waterways it may simply walk along the bottom, coming up for air along the way whenever necessary.

The nine-banded armadillo usually digs a branching burrow underground, loosening the soil with its forefeet and pointed snout. When a small pile of dirt has accumulated, it balances on forefeet and tail and kicks the dirt backward with its hind feet. In this laborious way it eventually digs a tunnel as much as 25 feet in length. Each branch of the tunnel is lined with grass, leaves, and weeds to serve as a nest. Abandoned armadillo burrows often provide a comfortable shelter for rabbits, skunks, or other small animals.

During the last hundred years the nine-banded armadillo has gradually spread north and east from its original habitat in the lower valley of the Río Grande. However, it is not likely to spread any further. Since it neither stores food nor hibernates, it cannot survive where food is not available all year round. In colder climates, the armadillo's surface prey are killed off in the winter, and even its well-developed claws cannot dig into frozen ground to unearth buried insects. In an extended period of cold, it would probably freeze or starve to death. Its true home is in the warm lands of South and Central America, where the Mayan Indians once believed that the great black-headed vulture did not die of old age but rather was metamorphosed into an armadillo.

Mendel's cases, each trait was determined by only two possible alleles at a single gene location, or **locus.** In many cases, however, discontinuous traits are determined by multiple alleles at a single locus. For example, in the human ABO blood group system, there are three possible alleles and four possible blood types. Here the analysis is more complicated than when there are only two alleles, but the patterns of inheritance follow Mendel's laws.

A different problem arises for **continuous traits.** These include many physical traits in human beings, such as skin color, hair color, and height. Instead of a few very different types, there is a continuous range of types, each one varying only slightly from the next, all the way from very light to very dark, or from very tall to very short. Such continuous traits appear to be **polygenic**—that is, they are determined by alleles at a number of different gene loci. The expression of the trait depends on how the different alleles at the different loci interact. Except where each of the genes can be identified and studied separately, continuous traits are not easily studied by the Mendelian kind of analysis.

Human blood groups

There are four well-known blood groups among the human population, expressed phenotypically as A, B, AB, and O. These blood groups are discontinuous traits, and can be analyzed by Mendelian principles. They have therefore been useful in studying the distribution of genotypes in different human populations.

The ABO blood groups were of great interest to medical scientists for several years before geneticists became interested in them. The blood groups were first discovered in 1900 by Karl Landsteiner, an Austrian physician. Landsteiner wanted to devise a method for matching human blood so that it could be transferred between individuals without causing ill effects.

Blood transfusions had been performed

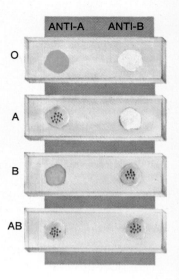

Figure 15-16. The four possible results of ABO blood typing are shown here. On each slide, anti-A serum (dyed blue) and anti-B serum (dyed yellow) are each mixed with a drop of blood. Group O blood is indicated when no clumping occurs. The blood group is A when anti-A causes clumping, and B when anti-B causes clumping. When both groups of serum cause clumping, the blood group is AB.

for many years prior to Landsteiner's discovery, but they were always risky. Sometimes there were no complications. At other times the red blood cells in the donor's blood clumped together soon after they mixed with the blood of the patient. When this happened, the red blood cells clogged the capillaries, and the patient died. Landsteiner devised a technique of premixing the blood of the patient and the plasma of the potential donor in a test tube. In this way clumping could be observed ahead of time, and unsafe donors could be detected.

Scientists now understand the probable mechanisms behind the clumping. It occurs when certain naturally occurring antibodies in the patient's blood plasma react with certain antigens in the donor's blood cells. Human red blood cells contain on their surfaces one, both, or neither of two different antigens, A and B. The blood groups are named according to these antigens. If the red blood cells carry the A antigen, the blood is said to be group A. Group A blood plasma usually contains anti-B antibodies. If the red

Table 15-2. Possible donors and recipients for human blood groups.

DONOR	RECIPIENT			
	A	**B**	**AB**	**O**
A	A→A Antigen not foreign— no antibody reaction	A→B Antigen foreign— antibodies produce clumping	A→AB Antigen not foreign—no antibody reaction	A→O Antigen foreign— antibodies produce clumping
B	B→A Antigen foreign— antibodies produce clumping	B→B Antigen not foreign— no antibody reaction	B→AB Antigen not foreign—no antibody reaction	B→O Antigen foreign— antibodies produce clumping
AB	AB→A Antigen foreign— antibodies produce clumping	AB→B Antigen foreign— antibodies produce clumping	AB→AB Antigen not foreign—no antibody reaction	AB→O Antigen foreign— antibodies produce clumping
O	O→A No antigen No antibody reaction	O→B No antigen No antibody reaction	O→AB No antigen No antibody reaction	O→O No antigen No antibody reaction
SUMMARY	A group-A recipient can receive blood groups A and O.	A group-B recipient can receive blood groups B and O.	A group-AB recipient can receive blood of any group.	A group-O recipient can receive only group O blood.

blood cells carry the B antigen, the blood is group B. Group B blood plasma usually contains anti-A antibodies. If the red blood cells carry both the A and B antigens, the blood is group AB and contains no antibodies. (Any antibodies present would attack the A and/or the B antigens on the red blood cells.) If the red blood cells do not carry either of the two antigens, the blood is group O, and contains both anti-A and anti-B antibodies. (See table 15-2 and figure 15-16.)

A person cannot safely receive blood that contains an antigen his antibodies will attack. For example, a person in blood group A cannot receive blood from a donor in group B or AB. Individuals having group O blood are often called universal donors, because their blood usually has no antigens that could be attacked by antibodies in the recipient's blood. Individuals having group AB blood are often called universal recipients. Their blood usually has no antibodies that could react against antigens in the donor's blood. However, there are minor exceptions to these rules. Therefore blood samples are usually cross-matched before a patient is actually given a transfusion.

In 1925 a hypothesis was developed to explain the hereditary transmission of the genes that control the development of the A and B antigens. This hypothesis is basically unchanged today. Three alleles are involved: two are dominant and one is recessive. A situation in which two alleles are dominant is called **co-dominance.** Both dominant alleles may be expressed simultaneously in the phenotype, hence the existence of the AB blood group. An individual may have any two of the three possible alleles, which we may symbolize as follows:

I^A—dominant allele for A antigen
I^B—dominant allele for B antigen
i —recessive allele for no antigen

The hereditary distribution of these alleles follows the basic Mendelian pattern. Table 15-3 shows the possible genotypes and the blood groups that result.

We can propose a hypothetical cross between two different genotypes to illustrate the patterns of inheritance that can result:

Mother is homozygous A   Father is O
$I^A I^A$ × ii

The resulting offspring would all be $I^A i$, or group A. If the mother's genotype were heterozygous for group A $(I^A i)$, the following offspring would result:

Mother   Father
$I^A i$ × ii
Egg   Sperm
I^A × i = $I^A i$ (Group A)
I^A × i = $I^A i$ (Group A)
i × i = ii (Group O)
i × i = ii (Group O)

In this case, the offspring have equal chances of belonging to either blood group A or blood group O.

Blood group tests are sometimes used to help determine a child's parentage. If the mother is group A and the child is group O, could a group B man be the father? Could a group AB man?

The Rh factor

Landsteiner's discovery of the ABO blood groups set off investigations that resulted in the discoveries of many other inheritable blood factors. The most important of these factors was found in 1940 during a joint investigation by Landsteiner and A. S. Weiner. While experimenting with the blood of the rhesus monkey, they discovered another antigen that caused the production of antibodies in human blood.

Later it was discovered that this antigen, the Rh factor, is present in the red blood cells of about 85 percent of the white population of the United States. Individuals with the Rh antigen are said to be Rh-positive; those without it are said to be Rh-negative.

Table 15-3. Possible genotypes and blood groups for antigens.

GENOTYPE	TYPE OF ANTIGEN ON RED BLOOD CELLS	BLOOD G
$T^A T^A$ or $T^A t^O$	A antigen	Group
$T^B T^B$ or $T^B t^O$	B antigen	Group
$T^A T^B$	A and B antigens	Group
$t^O t^O$	Neither antigen	Group

A single, dominant gene, symbolized Rh, is responsible for the development of the Rh antigen. Its recessive allele rh has no such effect. Therefore, an individual with the genotype $RhRh$ or $Rhrh$ will have the antigen; one with the genotype $rhrh$ will not. Since Landsteiner's and Weiner's discovery, several closely related Rh antigens have been discovered.

When the red blood cells of an Rh-positive donor are combined with the blood of an Rh-negative recipient, the clumping reaction does not always occur, as it does when incompatible ABO groups are mixed. The antibodies that can react against the A and B antigens are already present in the human blood. This is not the case with the antibodies that react against the Rh antigen. It takes time and a variable quantity of the Rh antigen to stimulate the production of Rh antibodies. The first transfusion between an Rh-positive donor and an Rh-negative recipient may not cause the clumping effect. Repeated transfusions, however, can create such a problem.

Rh incompatibility may occur between a pregnant Rh-negative woman and her own Rh-positive fetus. Although the mother's blood and the fetus's blood do not ordinarily mix, a break in the placental blood vessels may allow red blood cells of the fetus to invade the mother's blood. The Rh antigen in the mother's blood then stimulates the production of antibodies in her blood. These

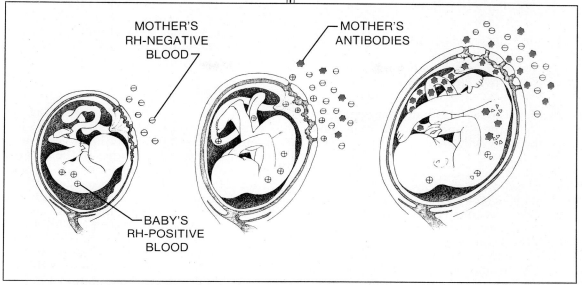

MOTHER'S
RH-NEGATIVE
BLOOD

MOTHER'S
ANTIBODIES

BABY'S
RH-POSITIVE
BLOOD

Figure 15-17. Rh incompatibility may result when the mother is Rh-negative and her baby is Rh-positive (left). Normally the mother's blood does not mix with that of the fetus, but this may occasionally happen if a break in the placental blood vessels allows fetal red blood cells to invade the mother's blood (center). The mother's blood will then produce antibodies to the Rh factor. These antibodies can pass through the placenta and enter the baby's bloodstream (right). Clumping or destruction of the fetal red blood cells may result in jaundice of the newborn, known as fetal erythroblastosis.

antibodies may diffuse back into the blood of the fetus, causing the fetus's own red blood cells to clump or rupture. Usually the condition can be remedied by completely replacing the baby's blood right after birth, thus preventing what in past years was a fatal condition.

Quite often, unless she has received a transfusion of Rh-positive blood, an Rh-negative mother will give birth to her first Rh-positive child without complications. This is because she may not have received enough fetal blood cells to stimulate much antibody formation before the child is born. But during birth she is very likely to receive many of these Rh-positive cells, which will sensitize her, making her more likely to produce antibodies early in her next pregnancy with an Rh-positive child. Therefore she is usually given an injection of Rh antibody shortly after the birth. The antibody destroys any Rh-positive fetal cells in her

bloodstream before she becomes sensitized. This reduces the danger that her own cells will react destructively against those of her next Rh-positive child.

It is now common practice to determine the father's Rh-type if his pregnant wife is found to be Rh-negative. If the father is also Rh-negative, he would have to have the genotype *rhrh*. Thus there is no likelihood that the developing fetus will have Rh-positive blood. But if the father is Rh-positive *(Rhrh* or *RhRh)*, the following genotypes result:

Father	Mother
Rhrh ×	*rhrh*

Rh	×	*rh*	= *Rhrh* (positive)
Rh	×	*rh*	= *Rhrh* (positive)
rh	×	*rh*	= *rhrh* (negative)
rh	×	*rh*	= *rhrh* (negative)

Father   Mother
RhRh × *rhrh*

Rhrh (positive)
is the only
possible result
from this cross

In the first cross, the baby has a 50–50 chance of being Rh-positive. In the second cross, the baby will always be Rh-positive.

Sex-linked genes in humans

Sex linkage occurs in humans, as it does in *Drosophila*. Also, as in *Drosophila*, there are many more genes on the X chromosome than on the Y chromosome. Thus, for many traits, the female will have two alleles (one on each X chromosome), while the male has only one (one on the X chromosome, none on the Y). Even if an X-linked allele is recessive, it will always appear in the phenotype of a male who carries it. A recessive sex-linked allele will not always be expressed in the female, however. This is because her other X chromosome may carry the dominant allele, which masks the recessive allele. For the recessive trait to appear in her phenotype, the female must carry two recessive alleles. For this reason, males show recessive sex-linked traits more often than do females.

Hemophilia is a famous example of a recessive sex-linked trait. Colorblindness is another good example. The genes for color vision are located on the X chromosomes. The dominant allele produces normal color vision; recessive alleles produce defective color vision. A woman may carry both dominant and recessive alleles, one on each X chromosome. This heterozygous woman, called a carrier, has normal color vision. Any sons she may have will have a 50–50 chance of inheriting the recessive allele. Since the father contributes only a Y chromosome (without a color-vision allele) to his son, the son will be colorblind if he inherits the recessive allele on the X chromosome from his mother. The son cannot inherit a recessive allele from his father, so it does not matter whether the father is colorblind or not. However, the daughters of a carrier mother and a colorblind father can be colorblind. Why?

The gene pool

Geneticists usually refer to all the genes in a population as the population's **gene pool**. This idea is useful in studies of the number and kinds of harmful alleles within a population. Harmful alleles are considered those that produce undesirable traits in individuals. Examples are alleles that cause certain kinds of muscular dystrophy, diabetes, heart disease, and nervous system disorders. Many of these are rare recessive alleles that are distributed throughout the population, mostly in the heterozygous state. Therefore, most individuals who carry these harmful recessive alleles are not aware of them. It is only when two of the recessive alleles come together in the genotype of an individual that the undesirable trait appears.

One of the results of studying harmful alleles has been the confirmation of an old folk belief that marriage within families is "bad." Numerous studies have shown that undesirable traits are much more frequent in children who result from such marriages. Why should this be true? The explanation lies in the fact that most such undesirable traits are the result of two recessive alleles coming together in one individual. The persons of a family can carry one of these recessive alleles and never be affected by it. If these persons marry out of their family, they are less likely to encounter another person who is also carrying the same recessive allele. Therefore their offspring will be normal. But if two members of the same family marry (for example, first cousins), it is much more likely that both are carrying the recessive allele. If they are, the chances are then 1 in 4 that their offspring will receive both recessive alleles—and the undesirable trait.

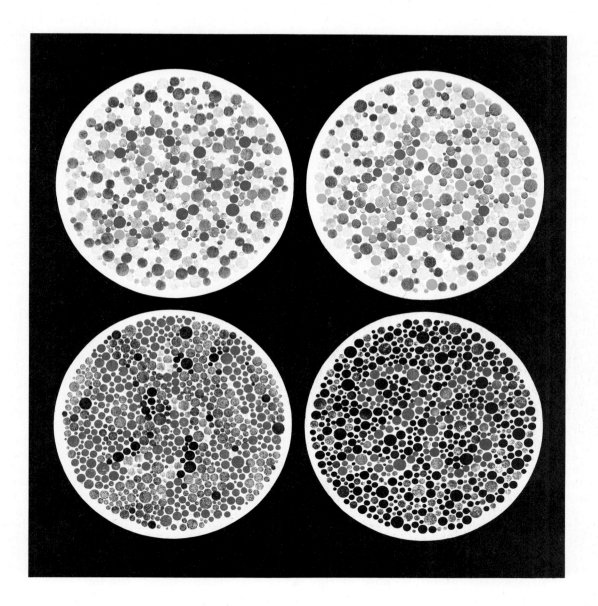

Figure 15-18. Color-blindness is a recessive sex-linked trait. Look at the accompanying picture. If your color perception is normal, you will see a 29 in the top left circle, a 45 in the top right circle, nothing in the bottom left circle, and a 26 in the bottom right circle. If you are red-blind, you see only the 6 in the bottom right circle; if green-blind, only the 2. If you can perceive neither green nor red, you will see a 70 in the top left circle, a 5 in the bottom left circle, and nothing in the other two circles. The person who is totally color-blind can see no figures in any of the circles.

SUMMARY

Gregor Mendel is rightly called "the father of genetics." In cross-breeding experiments with the garden pea he studied seven pairs of contrasting traits. In his first cross, between two purebreeding parents, the F_1 generation all showed the dominant trait. A cross between two F_1 individuals produced offspring with the dominant and recessive traits in a consistent 3:1 ratio. Mendel reasoned that each trait resulted from two separate factors: one dominant and one recessive. He further theorized that pairs of these factors were separated and assorted independently in the parents, and were recombined in the offspring.

Today these factors are called genes, and each gene in a pair of genes is called an allele. In a homozygous individual, both alleles in the pair are identical; in a heterozygous individual, they are different. The appearance of an individual is known as its phenotype, while its genetic make-up is its genotype. A testcross uses an individual with a known homozygous recessive trait to determine the unknown genotype of an individual showing a dominant trait.

Mendel's work remained obscure for 16 years after his death, but researchers continued to study cell structure and activity. Two years after the rediscovery of Mendel's work, Sutton proposed that genes were located on the chromosomes in the cell's nucleus. His suggestion formed the foundation for the chromosome theory.

Researchers found that *Drosophila melanogaster* was an ideal organism for genetic studies, especially useful because of the giant chromosomes in its salivary gland cells. Morgan observed *Drosophila* for eye color, body color, wing shape, and other traits. His discovery of sex-linked traits helped to confirm the chromosome theory. *Drosophila* and most other animals have two sex chromosomes: an X chromosome and a Y chromosome. All other chromosomes are called autosomes. Hundreds or thousands of genes must be on the chromosomes, to account for the thousands of traits in an individual. All the genes on a chromosome form a linkage group.

When sections of homologous chromosomes are exchanged during crossing-over, the normal linkage groups are broken. This helps to explain the variability of genotypes and phenotypes in a population. The relative frequencies of crossing-over can also be used to map the relative distances between genes on a chromosome.

Mendel's principle of independent assortment was modified by the discovery of linked genes. This principle applies only to pairs of genes on different chromosomes, not to linked genes. Mendel's principles were also extended with the discovery of incomplete dominance and multiple alleles.

Translocation, deletion, and inversion are structural abnormalities involving recombination or complete loss of genetic material. Each can cause changes in the structure or number of chromosomes. Nondisjunction results in a change in the number of chromosomes in a cell. Nondisjunction during the formation of gametes may result in abnormalities of the offspring produced from an affected gamete.

Human populations cannot be studied with the same methods as nonhuman populations. Moreover, most human traits are not as simple as those studied in experimental organisms. Many human traits are continuous; those that are discontinuous are often produced by multiple alleles. The latter, such as the ABO blood system, can be studied by Mendelian principles. However, continuous traits such as hair color, which are polygenic, usually cannot.

Human geneticists often study the overall distribution of genes in the gene pool of a population, to locate individuals with harmful recessive genes. Recessive genes causing severe disorders are most commonly found among members of the same family. Marriage between two carriers has a good chance of resulting in afflicted offspring.

Review questions

1. Why was the garden pea well suited for Mendel's experiments? Why was *Drosophila* a better choice for modern genetic studies?

2. Distinguish between dominant and recessive traits.

3. What is the principle of segregation?

4. In a hypothetical plant, blue flowers are dominant over purple flowers. If the two varieties are crossed, what will be the phenotype and genotype of the F_1 generation? Of the F_2 generation? (Use B and b for the alleles.)

5. Using the same plant, suppose also that long stems are dominant over short stems (alleles L and l). In a dihybrid cross (between plants that are heterozygous for both stem length and flower color), what will be the genotype and phenotype ratios?

6. What is a hybrid? What is its distinguishing reproductive characteristic?

7. What is a testcross?

8. A plant breeder has both blue-flowered and purple-flowered individuals of the plant in question 4. How can he find out which, if any, of the blue-flowered individuals are homozygous?

9. What is the principle of independent assortment?

10. What are autosomes?

11. How do sex-linked genes support the chromosome theory?

12. Sex-linked recessive genes are carried by both females and males. Why are they not expressed as often in human females as they are in human males?

13. What is chromosome mapping? How is it performed?

14. What is incomplete dominance?

15. Why could a breeder never establish a pure-breeding strain of roan cattle?

16. Give some examples of characteristics for which there are multiple alleles.

17. List some factors that can cause changes in chromosomes.

18. Why is it harder to study heredity in humans than in peas and fruit flies?

19. What is the difference between continuous and discontinuous traits?

20. Two babies are accidentally switched at the hospital. If the parents—the Joneses and the Smiths—and the babies have the following blood types, which baby belongs to which parents? How do you know?

Mrs. Jones	A	Baby 1	B
Mr. Jones	A	Baby 2	O
Mrs. Smith	AB		
Mr. Smith	A		

21. What is co-dominance?

22. What is the significance of the Rh factor during pregnancy?

23. What would be the possible genotypes of a baby born to an Rh-positive father and an Rh-negative mother?

24. List several conditions which can be caused by harmful genes within a gene pool.

25. Persons with hemophilia usually die before they reach reproductive age. How does this help to explain why females are usually carriers rather than victims of the recessive allele?

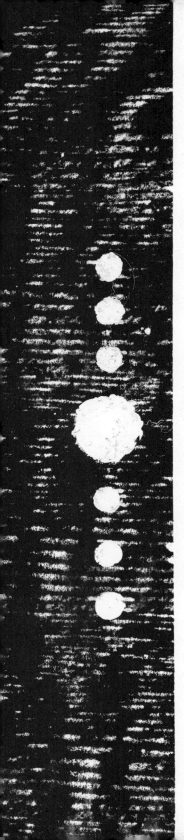

Master Molecules

Much of the work that established the patterns of inheritance was undertaken by scientists who had no idea of the way heredity actually worked. They knew that some unit of inheritance was passed from cell to cell during the process of reproduction. Because microscopic studies had shown the chromosomes dividing during cell reproduction, it seemed likely that the hereditary units, or genes, were part of the chromosomes. But it was hard to imagine how the genes exerted their influence. It seemed incredible enough that the two sets of chromosomes in a single fertilized egg could contain enough information to maintain the process of development through which the egg becomes an embryo. But it seemed literally impossible that they could also contain all the information for the activities of every cell of the organism's body through its entire life span.

In the early twentieth century, biochemists began to determine the structure of many organic chemicals. Impressed by the complexity of the molecules they were examining, they theorized that perhaps chemical structure was the key to the riddle of inheritance. Some component of the chromosomes might have the hereditary information built into its chemical structure. If so, which chemical component was it, and how was the information translated into action?

THE DISCOVERY OF DNA

One of the first significant steps in answering these questions came in 1941. Two U.S. scientists, George Beadle and Edward Tatum, announced a discovery that eventually won them a Nobel prize. Following up clues in the earlier work of a British physician, Sir Archibald Garrod, they found that

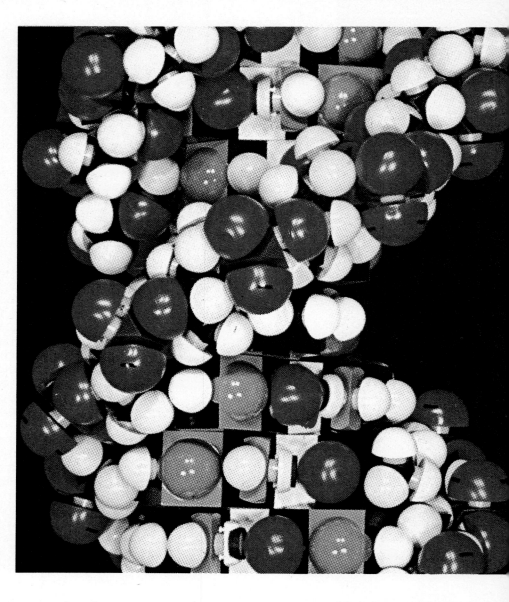

Figure 16-1. The model shown depicts a section of the DNA molecule, with its characteristic double helix shape.

genes and enzymes have a specific relationship with each other. Their experiments were done on the pink bread mold called *Neurospora*. They bombarded the mold cells with X-rays, which damaged the genes. They then observed the growth and reproduction patterns of the X-rayed cells. After many nutrition and breeding experiments, they found that for every damaged gene, the mold failed to produce one specific enzyme.

Their work later became known as the **one-gene–one-enzyme hypothesis.**

The next piece of the puzzle had actually been discovered earlier, in 1928. The English bacteriologist Fred Griffith reported very peculiar results from some of his experiments. His fellow workers were distinctly skeptical. Later, though, they repeated his experiments and got the same results.

Griffith was working with two strains of a

326

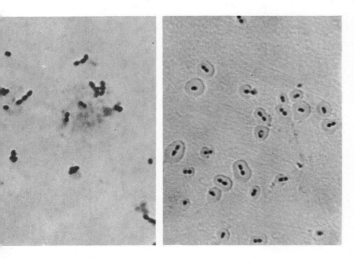

Figure 16-2. The R (left) and S (right) strains of *pneumococcus.*

bacterium called *pneumococcus.* One strain, when grown on a suitable medium, produced small colonies with a rough-looking surface. This strain was called the *R* strain. The other strain of *pneumococcus* was grown on the same medium. It produced colonies that had a smooth surface, and was called the *S* strain. Under the microscope, the two strains look markedly different. The *R*-strain cells look like ordinary bacterial cells. The *S*-strain cells have a thick, slimy coat, or capsule, surrounding the cell. If encapsulated cells (the *S*-strain cells) are injected into an animal such as a mouse, they will cause pneumonia. This disease can kill the animal. When *R*-strain cells (those without capsules) are injected into similar animals, pneumonia does not occur.

Griffith had been doing experiments on mice. He had injected them with *R*-strain and *S*-strain *pneumococcus* and had obtained the expected results. The *S*-strain *pneumococcus* caused pneumonia and the *R*-strain did not. One day he injected a mixture of strains into his mice. It was an unusual mixture of live *R*-strain bacteria (which do not cause pneumonia) with dead bacteria of the *S*-strain (which, when alive, cause pneumonia). Presumably, neither

element in this mixture could harm the mice. But something did, for—to Griffith's surprise—the mice developed pneumonia. Griffith got an even greater surprise when he examined the blood from the diseased mice. Great numbers of live *S*-strain bacteria were there. They were supposed to have been dead. Could he have made a mistake and accidentally injected some live *S*-strain cells? On the chance that this might have happened, he carefully repeated the experiment, and got the same results. He therefore concluded that something had passed from the dead *S* cells to the live *R* cells and caused them to start growing capsules. The *R* cells that were transformed into *S* cells continued thereafter to grow the capsule. The **transformed bacteria,** as they were later called, had their heredity permanently changed.

It is easy to understand why Griffith's colleagues were amazed by his findings. It was as surprising as if he had announced that a baby with brown eyes could "catch" blue eyes by taking a bath with her blue-eyed mother.

Eventually, Oswald Avery and his associates, Colin MacLeod and Maclyn McCarty, of The Rockefeller Institute, solved the mystery of the transformed bacteria. In a series of painstaking experiments, they chemically separated all the components of the *S*-strain bacteria. Then they tested all these different components on *R*-strain bacteria. After many disappointments and frustrations, one of their extracts succeeded. It changed the heredity of the *R*-strain cells and caused them to produce capsules. At the time, the extract was called "preparation 44." Later the chemical in "preparation 44" was identified as **deoxyribonucleic acid—DNA.**

STRUCTURES OF HEREDITY

Nine years after Avery and his associates announced that DNA was the substance that

R cells, without capsules, do not cause pneumonia when injected into mice.

S cells, with slime capsules, cause pneumonia and death when injected into mice.

Heat-killed S cells do not cause pneumonia.

Heat-killed S cells mixed with cells without capsules cause pneumonia.

The extract from heat-killed S cells when mixed with living R cells produces living S cells. This mixture also causes pneumonia.

Figure 16-3

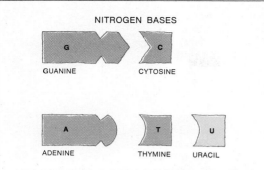

NITROGEN BASES

GUANINE   CYTOSINE

ADENINE   THYMINE   URACIL

Figure 16-4. These symbols will be used in illustrations concerned with DNA and RNA.

BASE PAIRING

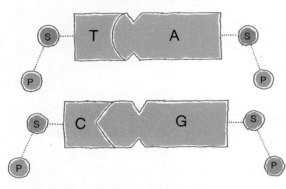

Figure 16-5. Base pairing in the DNA molecule. Adenine always pairs with thymine, and guanine always pairs with cytosine.

transformed bacteria, the world's scientists read another announcement. This was published in the English journal *Nature* on April 25, 1953. Written by James Watson and Francis Crick, it said:

We wish to suggest a structure for . . . deoxyribonucleic acid (DNA). This structure has novel features which are of considerable biological interest.[1]

The structure that Watson and Crick proposed for the DNA molecule was soon verified by the world's scientists. Watson and Crick, along with Maurice Wilkins, who supplied them with data for their studies,

were later awarded Nobel prizes for their discovery. Their work turned out to be one more demonstration of the principle we hinted at in the introduction to this chapter—a principle that underlies the whole science of biology. That principle can be stated in three words: **structure determines function.** When Watson and Crick finally built their model of DNA and carefully studied it, its unique role in the cell became apparent.

The structure of DNA

There are three unique characteristics of the DNA molecule. The first is its shape. DNA is a double helix. This means that it has a structure somewhat like a spiral staircase. If one straightens out the double-helix model of DNA, it looks much like a ladder. The sides of the ladder are made up of alternating sugar and phosphate groups. The rungs are made up of units called **nitrogen bases.** There are four different nitrogen bases in the DNA molecule: **adenine, thymine, guanine,** and **cytosine.** In any given DNA molecule, there are equal numbers of adenine and thymine bases, and equal numbers of guanine and cytosine bases.

If you study the model in figure 16-5, you can see the second unique characteristic of the DNA molecule. The model shows how the bases are arranged in the rungs of the ladder. They are paired according to the **base-pairing rule.** The rule was discovered by Watson and Crick while they were trying to build a model of DNA. They found that adenine bases seemed to pair only with thymine bases, and guanine bases seemed to pair only with cytosine bases.

Between the two bases in each rung is the third unique characteristic of the DNA molecule. The A–T (adenine–thymine) and G–C (guanine–cytosine) pairs are linked together by hydrogen bonds. These bonds are only about one-twentieth as strong as the bonds that hold the rest of the molecule together. This makes a "weak spot" in each rung and therefore down the middle of each molecule. The weak spot turned out to be important for the replication, or copying, of DNA.

When a cell divides by mitosis, as described in chapter 11, and two daughter cells are produced, all of the genes in the parent cell must be replicated. This means that exact copies of the genes have to be made and distributed to each of the daughter cells. Prior to 1953 it was a great mystery how molecules, such as those that make up genes, were replicated in a living organism.

The task did not seem so difficult after a model of DNA was constructed and studied. Because every rung of the DNA molecule has a weak spot in the middle, the whole molecule can be separated into two parts, much like a zipper, as shown in figure 16-8. In fact, we can say that the molecule "unzips." Thus the ends of the nitrogen bases in the rungs are exposed. To understand what happens next, picture the two DNA halves surrounded by a supply of the four different nitrogen bases. Where will the nitrogen bases attach themselves? For example, what base will attach to an exposed thymine base? What base will attach to an exposed guanine base? The base-pair rule will always insure that new A–T and G–C pairs will form along the whole length of each half-molecule. And the sequence in the two molecules that result will be the same as in the original one. That is how DNA is replicated.

As for the sides of the ladder, they are formed very easily. Each nitrogen base is attached to a sugar and a phosphate group. So when the nitrogen bases attach themselves to the rungs, their sugar–phosphate groups line up and are linked together by the action of an enzyme, DNA polymerase.

But this still does not answer the question that goes back to Beadle and Tatum's discovery in 1941. How can one gene be responsible for the existence of one enzyme?

One cannot find the answer simply by looking at a model of DNA. However, Watson and Crick did see how the DNA molecule might have information that could be

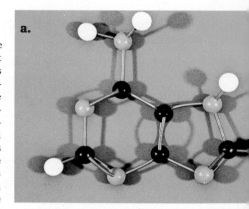

Figure 16-6. These models represent the nitrogen bases of DNA. Red represents oxygen, white represents hydrogen, black represents carbon, and yellow represents nitrogen. Notice that all the bonds between carbon and oxygen are double bonds. The bases are *a.* adenine, *b.* cytosine, *c.* thymine, and *d.* guanine.

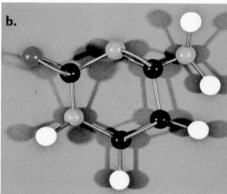

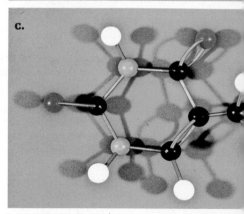

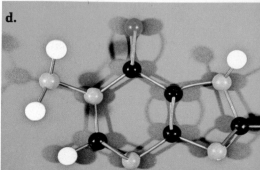

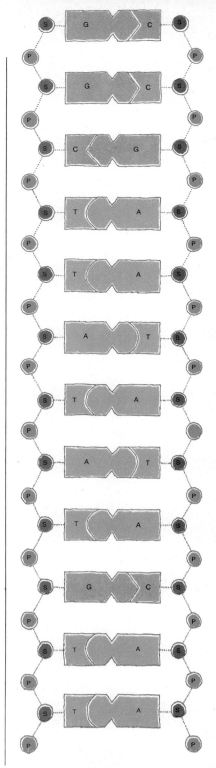

Figure 16-7. A section of a DNA molecule without the helical twist. In this "untwisted" illustration the pairing of bases can be seen more clearly.

copied. They saw that the sequence of base-pairs in the DNA molecule could be a code, and that this code might specify the structure of proteins. Specifically they saw that the code, or sequence of base-pairs, could be a way of organizing the sequence of the amino acids that make up proteins.

There was one major problem, however. DNA is confined to the nucleus of cells (with some minor exceptions) and proteins are found primarily in the cytoplasm. Therefore, proteins could not be manufactured directly by DNA molecules. The factory would be in one location and the products in another.

RNA: carrying the message

DNA is not the only nucleic acid in the cell. The other is **ribonucleic acid** or **RNA.** In fact, three kinds of RNA have now been found in cells. RNA differs structurally from DNA in only a few ways, but the differences are important.

First, RNA is not a double helix. Usually it is like one-half of a DNA molecule, a long chain made up of repeating subunits of phosphate, sugar, and a nitrogen base.

The second difference between RNA and DNA is in the sugar. The sugar in RNA is **ribose,** whereas the sugar in DNA is **deoxyribose.**

The third difference is in the nitrogen bases. Like DNA, RNA also has four nitrogen bases. Three of them—adenine, cytosine and guanine—are the same as those found in DNA. However, the fourth nitrogen base in RNA is **uracil.** Uracil takes the place of thymine, which is in DNA. Like thymine, uracil will bond only to adenine to form a base-pair.

DNA contains a code, which is like a master set of instructions for building all of an organism's proteins. But DNA is in the nucleus and proteins are built in the cytoplasm. Therefore the information from the DNA is carried from the nucleus to the cytoplasm by a "go-between" or messenger. The messenger is one of the three kinds of RNA

331

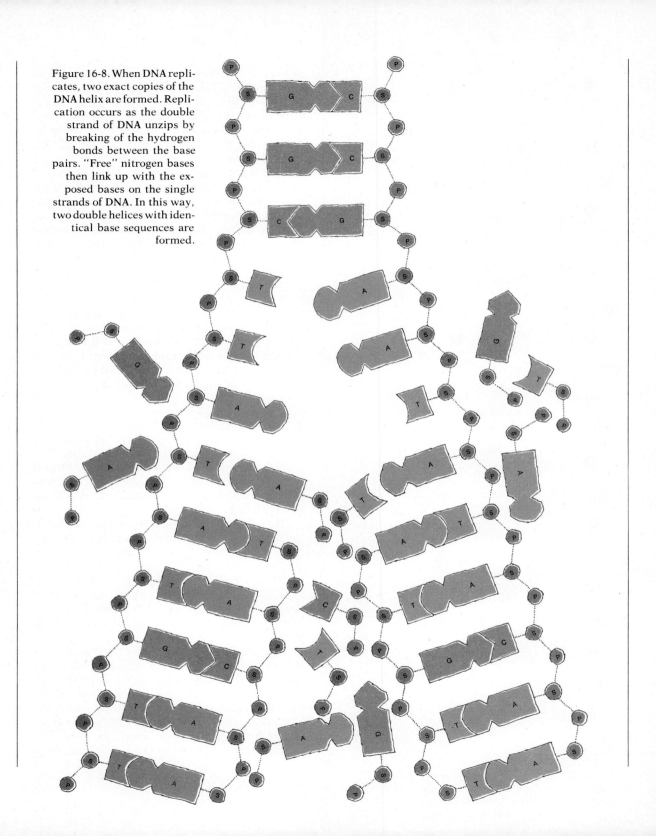

Figure 16-8. When DNA replicates, two exact copies of the DNA helix are formed. Replication occurs as the double strand of DNA unzips by breaking of the hydrogen bonds between the base pairs. "Free" nitrogen bases then link up with the exposed bases on the single strands of DNA. In this way, two double helices with identical base sequences are formed.

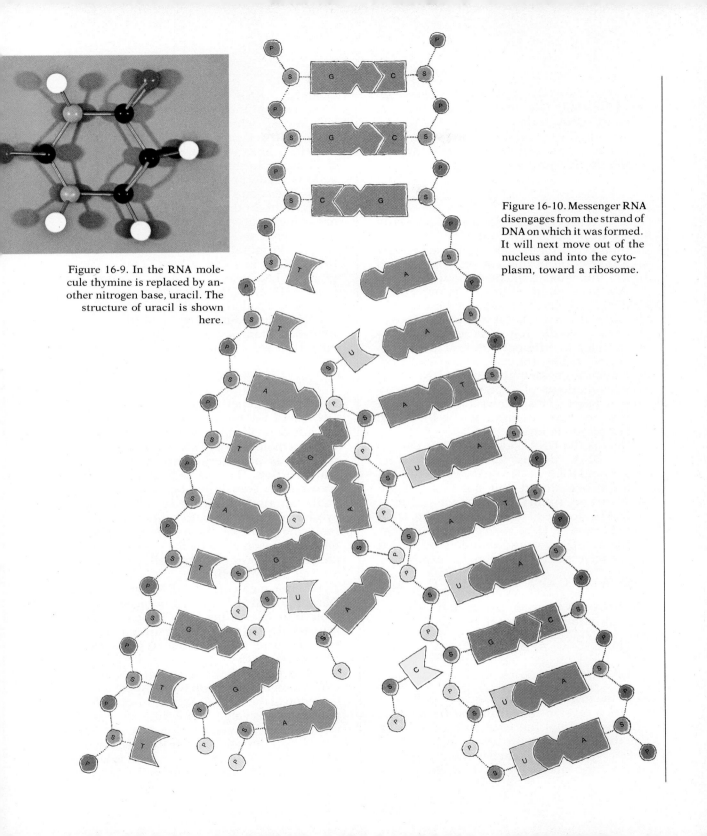

Figure 16-9. In the RNA molecule thymine is replaced by another nitrogen base, uracil. The structure of uracil is shown here.

Figure 16-10. Messenger RNA disengages from the strand of DNA on which it was formed. It will next move out of the nucleus and into the cytoplasm, toward a ribosome.

found in the cell, and is called **messenger RNA (mRNA).** The mRNA copies the code from the DNA. It then travels out of the nucleus, into the cytoplasm. In the cytoplasm, the code on the mRNA is used in the construction of a protein.

The genetic code

Twenty different amino acids are normally found in proteins. The only way DNA can contain a code for all these amino acids is by some variation in the sequence of nitrogen bases. But what sequence? How many nitrogen bases are used to specify one amino acid? If a sequence of two bases were used in the code, there would only be enough possible code "words" (or variations of the sequence) for 16 different amino acids. Therefore, even before the code was discovered, researchers guessed that each DNA code word is made up of a sequence of three nitrogen bases. This allows for 64 possible code words, more than enough for the 20 different amino acids.

How is the DNA code copied? At certain times, DNA "unzips" along a part of its length, and RNA bases join the exposed DNA bases of one strand, but not those of the other strand. In this way, a single strand of mRNA is formed, which copies the DNA code in reverse. Here is an example of what happens: a DNA strand that is to be copied might have the following bases exposed:

DNA—C C G A A T A T A C A A

The DNA–RNA base sequence that would be formed is the following (U = uracil):

```
DNA   C  C  G  A  A  T  A  T  A  C  A  A
      |  |  |  |  |  |  |  |  |  |  |  |
RNA   G  G  C  U  U  A  U  A  U  G  U  U
```

After the mRNA is formed, it "peels off" and carries a reverse code from the DNA to the cytoplasm. Then the DNA strands go back together (see figure 16-10).

Once the mRNA reaches the cytoplasm, its message must be translated. Suppose a strand of mRNA with the above sequence of bases were in the cytoplasm of a cell. From this strand, which amino acids would be assembled and in what order? Now that researchers have worked out all of the code, the answer to that question is simple. The code is made up of mRNA triplets, or **codons.** The codon is like a code word for an amino acid. In the strand of mRNA that we are using as an example there are four codons. They are G G C, U U A, U A U, and G U U. From table 16-1 you can determine that G G C is a codon for the amino acid glycine. Likewise, U U A is a codon for leucine, U A U is a codon for tyrosine, and G U U is a codon for valine. Therefore, this mRNA strand directs the assembly of the following chain of amino acids: glycine–leucine–tyrosine–valine.

Protein synthesis

How is the genetic code in a molecule of DNA used for protein synthesis? We have already described the first step—the formation of a molecule of mRNA using one strand of DNA as a pattern. This step is called **transcription.** The second step is called **translation.** Translation takes place when a chain of amino acids, called a **polypeptide,** is synthesized from the information coded in a molecule of mRNA. Translation takes place on the ribosomes, which we described in chapter 1. These cell organelles serve as a kind of assembly line.

When a molecule of mRNA arrives at a ribosome, it attaches to a **binding site.** Then molecules of another kind of RNA, called **transfer RNA (tRNA),** bring amino acids to the strand of mRNA. Each type of tRNA transports a different amino acid. Also, each of these types of tRNA contains a triplet **anti-codon** that pairs up with a specific triplet codon of the mRNA. For instance, a tRNA molecule carrying a molecule of glycine would have the anti-codon C C G. This would pair up with the mRNA codon for glycine, G G C. A tRNA molecule carrying leucine would have the anti-codon A A U,

Table 6-1. The Genetic Code

FIRST POSITION		SECOND POSITION				THIRD POSITION
		U	C	A	G	
U		Phenylalanine	Serine	Tyrosine	Cysteine	U
		Phenylalanine	Serine	Tyrosine	Cysteine	C
		Leucine	Serine			A
		Leucine	Serine		Tryptophan	G
C		Leucine	Proline	Histidine	Arginine	U
		Leucine	Proline	Histidine	Arginine	C
		Leucine	Proline	Glutamine	Arginine	A
		Leucine	Proline	Glutamine	Arginine	G
A		Isoleucine	Threonine	Asparagine	Serine	U
		Isoleucine	Threonine	Asparagine	Serine	C
		Isoleucine	Threonine	Lysine	Arginine	A
		Methionine	Threonine	Lysine	Arginine	
G		Valine	Alanine	Aspartic Acid	Glycine	U
		Valine	Alanine	Aspartic Acid	Glycine	C
		Valine	Alanine	Glutamic Acid	Glycine	A
		Valine	Alanine	Glutamic Acid	Glycine	G

This table allows one to find the amino acid specified by any codon in the genetic code. For example, to find the amino acid for the codon UGG, look under First Position for U; then go across to G under Second Position. Of the three choices under G, select the amino acid opposite G under Third Position. Answer: tryptophan. Other examples: CAC: histidine, AAA: lysine, GUG: valine.

and so on. In this way the message contained in the structure of mRNA is "read." As the tRNA anti-codons align with the mRNA codons, the amino acids attached to the tRNA automatically fit into the right sequence to synthesize a specific polypeptide. A protein consists of one or more of these polypeptide chains.

As soon as the amino acids are in place and have formed a chemical bond that holds them together, the tRNA breaks away from the mRNA and thus is free to transport another molecule of amino acid to another site along the strand of mRNA.

Although biologists by now understand many of the steps in protein synthesis, there is still much to be learned. One of the remaining mysteries is the role of the third kind of RNA, **ribosomal RNA (rRNA)**. This type of RNA seems to be important to the structure of the ribosome, and therefore cell biologists suspect that it is also important to the process of protein synthesis. It appears to be involved in providing binding sites for mRNA. But its exact role in the process is not known.

REGULATION OF GENE ACTIVITY

Up to this point, we have used the term "gene" in a rather vague way, meaning some unit of heredity. Now we can give a molecular definition of this term. A **gene** is a nitrogen base sequence in DNA that codes for one polypeptide chain. A protein may be made up of one or more such chains. Most enzymes

SNOWFLAKE, THE ALBINO GORILLA

It is a foggy October morning in Rio Muni, a Spanish province in equatorial Africa. A local farmer tending his banana grove spots a gorilla ripping a banana stem apart with powerful hands. The farmer reaches for his shotgun and fires at the creature that endangers his livelihood. Only then does he see a small animal clinging to the long black hair of its dead mother. That small animal is a white baby gorilla—the only white gorilla known to science.

The farmer cared for the orphaned gorilla for four days before turning him over to an interested naturalist in Río Muni's capital. Judged to be about two years old, the young ape weighed in at just under 20 pounds. For several weeks the naturalist and his wife worked with him, feeding him on bananas, sugar cane, cookies, and milk. At the end of a month, the young gorilla was playful and affectionate in the company of people he knew. He was then shipped to the Barcelona zoo, where he immediately won the nickname "Copito de Nieve," or Little Snowflake.

Word of Snowflake's existence spread rapidly. Scientists from Tulane University's Primate Research Center flew to Spain to study him, and determined that he was normal in every respect but one. Snowflake is an albino, lacking normal pigmentation in his white hair, pale skin, and blue eyes.

The word "albino" derives from the Latin *albus,* or "white." Albinism occurs in many animal species, including all the races of humans. Early explorers in the New World discovered native populations with albinos numbering as many as one out of every 140 people. Erroneously, they concluded that some light-skinned European race had interbred with the natives at an earlier date. Albinos were prominent in the museum of living human oddities maintained by Montezuma, emperor of the Aztecs.

Today, albinism is recognized as an inherited genetic defect in which there is partial or complete absence of melanin pigment formation. Melanin serves to protect the skin from ultraviolet radiation, and its absence is connected with an increased incidence of skin cancer. Skin cancer is rare among the dark-skinned races, and most common among albinos.

Different types of albinism are caused by different gene defects. Melanin formation depends upon the presence of the enzyme tyrosinase. Lack of this enzyme, or biochemical errors in the subsequent steps which lead to formation of the pigment, may all be factors in albinism. Most albino humans have a slight amount of pigmentation. Pigmentation may be absent from eyes, skin, and hair, from the eyes alone, or only from parts of the skin and hair. In Snowflake's case, the blue eyes suggest that at least a certain amount of melanin is present.

Some forms of albinism are accompanied by other genetic flaws. Among these are bleeding problems, sensitivity to aspirin-like drugs, and mental retardation. Albinism is often accompanied by crossed eyes. The resulting poor vision is correctable in humans, but would represent a serious threat to survival for a wild animal.

The myth that albinos can see in the dark is untrue. However, their unpigmented eyes are sensitive and may lead them to prefer dim light. For this reason albinos were known as "moon children" among one tribe of Central American Indians. In animals with frontally located eyes, some of the nerve tracts from each eye cross and go to the opposite side of the brain. But the majority of the fibers do not cross, and it is these fibers that are largely responsible for binocular vision and depth perception. In albinos, most of the fibers cross, and this abnormality adds a number of other vision problems to their problem of light sensitivity.

Not all animals are equally prone to albinism. Albino squirrels and catfish, for example, are quite common. Because the catfish feeds on the dark river bottom, poor eyesight is not a serious disadvantage. Albino gorillas, on the other hand, were completely unknown until the discovery of Snowflake.

In order to compare Snowflake to a normally pigmented gorilla, the Barcelona zoo obtained for him a companion, Muni, a black male of about the same size and age. The two young gorillas responded well to captivity and to each other. Thanks to excellent dietary and medical care, they are far healthier than most wild gorillas. Ultimately, Snowflake is expected to live more than 30 years and reach a weight of over 500 pounds.

Comparisons between Snowflake and Muni indicate that the albino gorilla is completely normal except for his color and his slightly deficient daylight vision. He has also displayed a healthy interest in the opposite sex. Now a little over ten years old, he has fathered two offspring by a black female. Both were black, but scientists hope that some day Snowflake will give rise to a strain of white gorillas that can be studied in hopes of filling the gaps in our understanding of albinism.

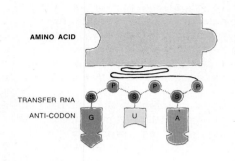

AMINO ACID

TRANSFER RNA
ANTI-CODON

MESSENGER RNA

Figure 16-11. A tRNA anticodon with its amino acid is attaching to its appropriate mRNA (right). As it attaches, its amino acid will link to the one next to it. Once the amino acids link together, their RNA separates from them (left).

are made up of more than one chain. Hence Beadle and Tatum's hypothesis of one-gene–one-enzyme was not exactly correct. One gene generally does not code for a whole enzyme. Usually two, three, four or more genes code for one enzyme or enzyme system.

As we have seen, genes are present on chromosomal DNA in a cell's nucleus during the entire life of the cell. But not all of the information built into these genes is used all of the time. So we are faced with another mystery. How does the gene "know" when to produce RNA for the synthesis of a particular protein? What initiates protein synthesis? What causes it to stop?

One hypothesis to answer these questions was worked out by François Jacob and Jacques Monod, and incorporated into a model called the **operon model.** This model suggests that DNA contains coded information representing three kinds of genes: struc-

tural genes, operator genes, and (in some cells) regulator genes. The **structural gene** contains codes for polypeptides that will be of structural importance in the cell or organism. For instance, a structural gene might contain a code for a polypeptide in an enzyme. Or it might contain a code for a polypeptide in hemoglobin, or for a polypeptide that forms part of the protein in hair.

The **operator gene** contains coded information that also results in a polypeptide. However, this polypeptide will not become part of a structure. Instead, it will influence one or more structural genes, affecting when and how they operate. When it is "switched on" (that is, when it is synthesizing its polypeptide), it seems to initiate transcription of the DNA code in its associated structural genes. When it is "switched off," transcription apparently cannot take place. Therefore no mRNA is formed, and the polypeptides specified by the structural genes cannot be synthesized. An operator gene and all the structural genes it controls form a unit called an **operon.**

What determines whether the operator gene is switched on or off? Apparently a combination of influences from the chromosome and the cytoplasm is involved. Jacob

pressor substance from the cytoplasm. In other cases, the repressor could be inactivated by an **inducer substance,** also from the cytoplasm. If an inducer was present, or if a corepressor was missing, the operator gene remained switched on, and the structural genes functioned.

All this seems very complicated, but one

PUTTING DNA ON THE ASSEMBLY LINE

The speed with which biological science has moved ahead in recent years is almost frightening. Less than twenty-five years ago, Watson and Crick first deciphered the structure of the DNA molecule. Now, instead of merely analyzing what goes into genes, scientists have begun manufacturing them. Some yeast and bacterial genes were synthesized as long ago as the early 1970s. So was part of a mammal gene—one that directs the production of rabbit hemoglobin. Now this same rabbit gene has been synthesized in its complete form by Harvard biologists.

Considering the small size and intricate complexity of a gene, this synthesis is quite a feat. The researchers first purified a length of messenger RNA taken from one of the rabbit's cells. They placed the mRNA in a concentrated bath of nucleotides—the nitrogen bases of DNA, with their attached sugar-and-phosphate groups—and added an enzyme known as reverse transcriptase. The

enzyme reversed the usual DNA-to-mRNA process, and a strand of DNA was assembled according to the code in the mRNA. This provided one-half of the gene. Then, with the aid of another enzyme, the second strand of DNA was built onto a tiny hairpin curve that had been formed at the tip of the first one. Finally, still a third enzyme was used to snip the two strands apart at the bend in the hairpin, and the scientists had a complete, working gene.

If other mammal genes can be synthesized in the same way, there may be valuable applications. For one thing, any number of copies of a single gene could be made for study. Dozens or hundreds of laboratories could do coordinated studies of a single defective gene—one associated with some birth defect or fatal disease, for instance. With such a pooling of research, we might make far speedier progress toward the conquest of such genetic ills as hemophilia or muscular dystrophy. Another possible application is the synthesis of healthy genes to replace defective ones. Of course, it's a long way from duplicating one gene in a laboratory to replacing defective genes in a living human embryo, but—who knows?

and Monod found that the action of the operator gene was prevented by certain **repressor substances.** These were constantly being synthesized by the third type of gene, the **regulator gene.** Why, then, was the operator gene not constantly switched off? In some cases, the repressor substance did not act unless it combined with a **core-**

point is perhaps the most important to remember. This is that some influence from the cytoplasm helps to regulate the activity of the genes. Sometimes, when enough of a substance (such as an enzyme) has been synthesized to meet the cell's current needs, that substance itself will act as a corepressor and stop further synthesis for the time be-

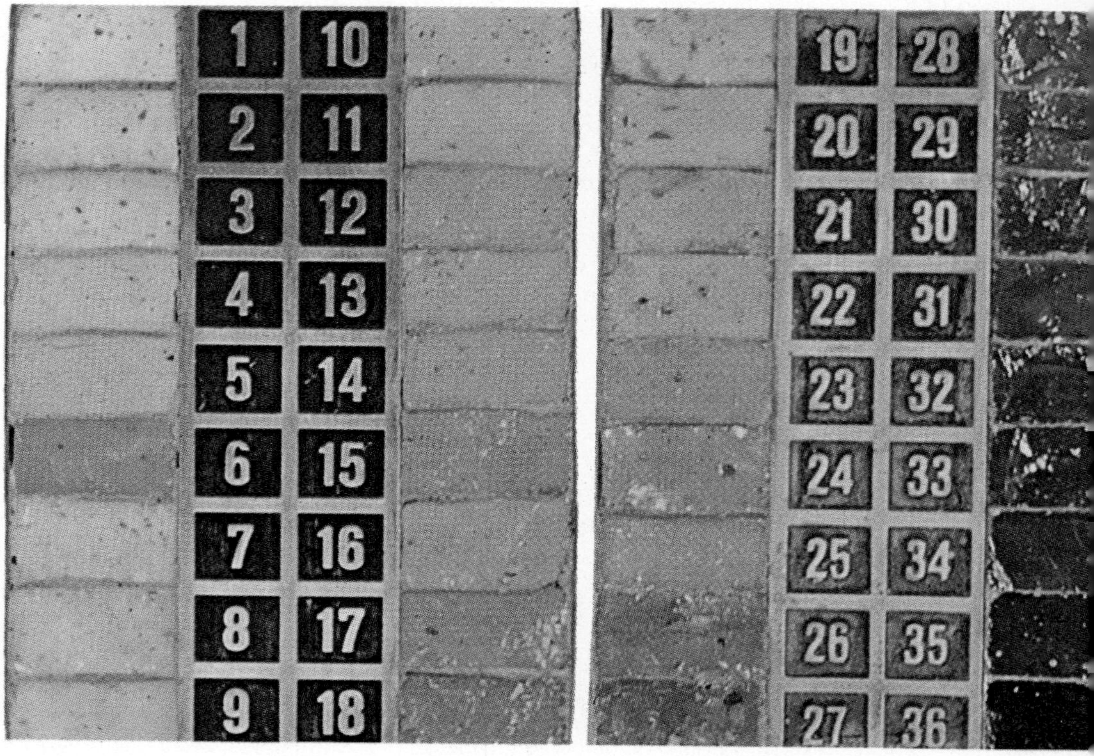

Figure 16-12. Human skin color is an example of a continuous trait. These ceramic tiles illustrate 36 shades of skin color, ranging from white to black. Each shade results from a particular combination of genes.

ing. Sometimes a hormone, secreted by a gland in response to a stimulus from another organ, may serve as an inducer or a corepressor. The result is that the genes are permitted to be active only when the organism needs the substances that are specified in their codon sequences. Otherwise they are shut off.

Jacob and Monod worked with bacteria, which are procaryotic cells. Regulation of gene activity is somewhat different in eucaryotic cells, but it appears to follow a similar sequence of influences. (Refer back to chapter 1 if you need to review the characteristics of procaryotic and eucaryotic cells.) One major difference is that in eucaryotic cells the repressors do not seem to be synthesized by regulator genes. Rather, they are themselves structural parts of the chromosome. However, just as in procaryotic cells, outside influences play a significant part in regulation.

Inherited and environmental factors

We have seen that, at the moment of conception, each new individual inherits a DNA code that allows the synthesis of certain proteins. In humans, a single chromosome may contain the genetic code for hundreds of proteins. For the individual, the presence (or absence) of these proteins determines skin, hair, and eye color; sex and secondary sex characteristics; the tendency to be fat or thin; susceptibility to many diseases, such as diabetes, heart disease, and perhaps cancer; and countless other characteristics. Some findings suggest that it may even play a role in personality characteristics, such as aggressiveness or artistic talent.

However, we must be careful not to overstate the importance of DNA. The genetic code is frequently likened to a blueprint; and anyone who has ever watched a construction job knows that the final result may differ in many ways from the blueprint. The availability of building materials, the skill of the workers, the personal taste of the owner—all of these factors may lead to changes.

Much the same thing happens when the

PATTERNS OF CHANGE

blueprint in the genetic code is finally expressed in the phenotypic characteristics of the individual. The influences of the environment may permit the full expression of some traits, while partially repressing others. A familiar example is an individual's height. Wilt Chamberlain inherited genes that gave him the potential of growing to a height of 7 feet. But it was only through a long series of interactions with the environment that he actually turned out to be that tall. If his mother had not eaten properly when she was pregnant; if he had suffered from malnutrition in his childhood; if he had been seriously ill during his growing years—any of these environmental factors could have robbed basketball of one of its tallest stars.

Much the same pattern is found in the expression of all other inherited characteristics. Extreme examples of the role of environment can be seen in many children born with birth defects, such as incomplete arms or legs, or a hole in the wall of the heart. Such defects were not necessarily built into the genetic code of the baby. They may have been caused by accidents that happened during the process of development. Each time the cells of an embryo divide, there is a chance for the biochemical environment to exert some influence on the process of protein synthesis in the new cells. In particular, the process of cell specialization is vulnerable to such influence. You will recall from chapter 14 that this is the process through which the embryo develops cells of different kinds and eventually different organs. Proper cell specialization depends on a complicated feedback system between the DNA in the cell nucleus, the cytoplasm, and the biochemical environment of the cell. As we saw in Spemann's salamander embryos, if cells are moved from one place on the embryo to another during very early development, they will develop like the others in their new location. Even after cells are completely differentiated, their growth can be affected by environmental factors.

The action of operator genes explains how the feedback between the DNA pattern and environmental influences takes place. For example, in a nutritious environment, a cell might synthesize and accumulate large numbers of key biochemical molecules. The molecules might function as inducers, inactivating a repressor substance that is inhibiting the replication of DNA. With the repressor inactivated, the process of mitosis begins. Through this complicated feedback system, the ability of the environment to sustain more cells would lead to the formation of new cells.

Thus, all processes of differentiation, growth, maintenance, and repair involve a constant interplay of the forces of heredity and environment. DNA does not "control" the cell. It merely provides an inherited range of possibilities. The actual expression of these possibilities depends on the cell's response to environmental factors.

GENETIC ENGINEERING

A baby born in America today has a one-in-18 chance of inheriting a genetic disease. Can our knowledge of the biochemical mechanisms of inheritance be used to combat these problems? Many scientists think the answer is yes. The main question under investigation today is how this can be done and what the potential dangers might be.

In theory, the "cure" for genetic disease is quite simple. For example, a person could be permanently cured of sickle-cell anemia if just one base sequence of his DNA were changed in the cells that produce hemoglobin. If a properly coded section of DNA—one that coded for glutamic acid rather than valine—were substituted for the existing section, the cure could be effected.

The presumed tools for such a procedure are now being investigated. They involve enzymes and viruses. Recent research has isolated a class of enzymes capable of cutting the DNA molecule very precisely into small segments containing only a few genes.

These enzymes could be used in the laboratory to isolate the gene, or combination of genes, that an individual needs. Other research has confirmed the ability of viruses to pick up DNA from one organism and transport it to another. So the needed genes could presumably be introduced into the viruses, which could then be injected into the patient. Such treatment has in fact already been tried. Three sisters in Germany were suffering from a rare genetic disease that produces an excess of arginine (an amino acid) in the blood. They received injections of a virus carrying the gene for an enzyme that could degrade this amino acid. The treatments did cause a reduction in the blood level of arginine. However, the reduction was only temporary. The disease was not cured.

Research to invent and refine the techniques of this sort of treatment, which is called **genetic engineering,** is under way in laboratories all over the world. At the University of Wisconsin, researchers have altered eleven different genes of the fruit fly. In Australia, enzyme-deficient kangaroos are being treated with viruses carrying the needed gene segments. Many scientists think that it is only a matter of time until the technology exists to treat genetic disease in human beings.

Yet the prospect of such treatment raises almost as many problems as it solves. One is the problem of side effects. As one researcher put it, "The treatment might be worse than the disease. Gene therapy might cure galactosemia [an enzyme deficiency related to a single gene] but give you cancer." Other scientists worry about the casual use of viruses. A physician participating in research on transport viruses said, "I noticed that everybody was pipetting the virus by mouth [sucking it up into a tube to transfer it elsewhere], with no precautions at all. It disturbed me. These things were viruses and nobody seemed to know or care very much what they might do in humans or other hosts." Another problem area is the social consequence of publicly labeling some people as genetically defective. The memory of Hitler's campaign to glorify the "master race" of Aryans makes clear the sort of harm such labeling could possibly bring.

Because of the problems associated with genetic research, some people have suggested that it be called to a halt. But even if the political problems of negotiating such a halt could be solved, most scientists seem to be against it. Their philosophy is that true solutions will come through learning more, not through trying to bury the knowledge we already have.

SUMMARY

For a long time scientists were uncertain how hereditary information was passed from cell to cell during the process of cell replication. Advances in biochemistry indicated that this information might have a chemical basis. However, the particular chemical component involved remained in doubt.

Then, in 1941, Beadle and Tatum performed a series of experiments with *Neurospora*. Their work led to the one-gene–one-enzyme hypothesis. The next part of the puzzle had been discovered earlier by Griffith. Working with two strains of *pneumococcus*, he discovered that dead encapsulated cells could pass hereditary information to live cells which originally had no capsules, causing the live cells to begin growing capsules of their own. The component which actually carried the information—later identified as DNA—was finally isolated by Avery, MacLeod, and McCarty.

The actual structure of DNA was discovered in 1953 by Watson and Crick. Their model of the DNA molecule further demonstrated the principle that structure determines function. The DNA molecule is a double helix. Its sides are made up of alternating sugar and phosphate groups; the rungs are made from four nitrogen bases— adenine, thymine, guanine, and cytosine.

The nitrogen bases are paired according to the base-pairing rule, and the pairs are linked by weak hydrogen bonds that allow the molecule to unzip when a cell divides. Each unzipped half of the molecule then acquires the correct bases and sugar–phosphate groups to build a new half.

Watson and Crick saw that the base-pair sequence might be a code specifying chains of amino acids that make up proteins. The messenger that carried information from the DNA in the cell nucleus to the protein-manufacturing centers in the cytoplasm was found to be messenger RNA (mRNA). Each DNA code word for amino acids is made up of a sequence of three nitrogen bases called a codon. When DNA unzips along a part of its length, RNA bases join the exposed DNA bases of one strand, forming a strand of mRNA whose structure copies the code in a process called transcription. The mRNA then peels away from the DNA and carries a reverse code to the cytoplasm, where it is translated and a polypeptide is synthesized from the information coded in the mRNA.

A gene is a nitrogen-base sequence in DNA that codes for one polypeptide chain. Usually several genes code for one enzyme or enzyme system. The operon model suggests that DNA includes structural, operator, and regulator genes. An operator gene and the structural genes it controls form an operon. The operon may be induced to function, or prevented from functioning, by the presence or absence of repressor, corepressor, and inducer substances, some of them in the cytoplasm.

A single chromosome may contain the code for hundreds of proteins. But the code provides only a blueprint for inherited characteristics. Environmental factors play an important part in the way the genetic code is finally expressed. Regulator genes allow a process of feedback between the DNA blueprint and environmental influences.

Genetic engineering may provide a key to the treatment of genetic disease. It may be possible to substitute a properly coded base sequence of DNA for one that is incorrectly coded. However, experiments with such techniques will have to be conducted very cautiously in order to avoid possible side effects.

Review questions

1. Describe the experiment that led to the one-gene–one-enzyme hypothesis

2. Describe Griffith's experiment with *pneumococcus*. What was its significance?

3. What are the nitrogen bases in the DNA molecule? In the RNA molecule?

4. How does the base-pairing rule work?

5. Why is the weak bond between base pairs so important to cell replication?

6. Describe the structural differences between RNA and DNA.

7. How is information carried by DNA transferred from the nucleus of a cell to the cytoplasm?

8. Explain the workings of the genetic code. How does mRNA copy the DNA code?

9. What is a codon?

10. How does translation take place?

11. What is one possible function of rRNA?

12. In molecular terms, what is a gene?

13. Distinguish between structural genes and operator genes.

14. What is an operon? How do regulator genes affect it?

15. Explain why the genetic code is most important in terms of its potential rather than in its ultimate results.

16. How does feedback take place between the DNA blueprint and environmental influences?

17. Describe the potential role of viruses and enzymes in genetic engineering.

18. What problems, both social and medical, are likely to accompany future genetic research?

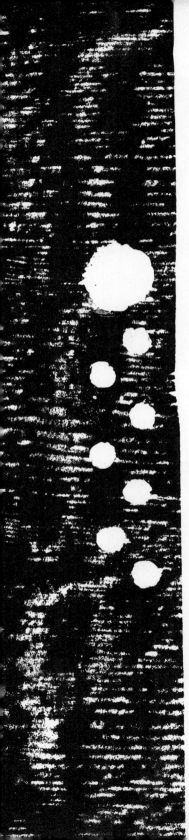

Genetic Variation in Populations

In the last two chapters, we have looked at the ways in which hereditary characteristics are passed from one generation to the next. But another question now suggests itself. What we have studied about heredity tells us how characteristics are transmitted and preserved. The genotypic ratios of Mendel's peas stayed more or less the same from one generation to the next. But we know that this is not always the case. Humans today are very different from their probable ancestors a million or so years ago. And who, seeing the wild, wolf-like dog that shared some cave man's fireside, could have predicted the variety of prancing, yelping, tail-wagging creatures to be found at a modern dog show?

How did these changes come about? There must have been a considerable change in the genotype, for a shaggy, strong-jawed, wolf-like primitive dog to give rise to a tiny, bat-eared Mexican hairless. Were new genes added, or old ones lost? Were the genes changed? If so, how? And are these changes still going on?

The factors that appear to be most important in determining and directing such changes in a population operate on several levels. One level is purely genetic; the others involve behavioral and environmental influences on genetics. We shall consider the genetic factors in this chapter, and the others in the two chapters that follow.

SOME TERMS AND CONCEPTS

Before we can understand what causes

change in the genetic characteristics of a population, we need to define some terms. The first of these is the term "population" itself. In the sense in which we use the word here, a **population** is a community of individuals that sexually interbreed with one another, or may do so. A population may consist of two individuals or of millions. It may be isolated, or it may be mingled with other populations. Human beings on an island are a population if there is no reason why any sexually mature female on the island should not mate with any male. On the other hand, if, for some reason, people on the north side of the island never breed with people on the south side, there are two human populations on the island.

Second, as we noted in chapter 15, the sum total of all the genes in a population is called the population's **gene pool.** This pool is the supply from which genes will be drawn for the next generation.

Finally, the percentages of the various alleles of a gene in a population are called the **gene frequencies** of the population. (See chapter 15 if you need to review "allele.") Suppose a gene has two alleles, M and m. Suppose that in a population of a hundred individuals, ten have the genotype MM, sixteen the genotype mm, and seventy-four the genotype Mm. Since each individual has two genes, there is a gene pool of 200. What are the frequencies of the two alleles? We can figure it out as shown in table 17–1. The frequency of allele M in this population is .47, or 47 percent. The frequency of allele m is .53, or 53 percent. Together, the frequencies add up to 100 percent, or 1.0. Similarly, the frequencies of all alleles of a particular gene in a particular population will always add up to 100 percent. We shall see shortly why it is useful to be able to calculate gene frequencies.

The Hardy–Weinberg principle

In Mendel's experiments, dominant and recessive traits always appeared in a ratio of about 3:1. There were three green peas to

Figure 17-1. The *Kaibab* and *Abert* squirrels probably evolved from a single parent stock. However, because of geographical separation, they became two distinct species.

Table 17-1. Allele Frequencies Within a Gene Pool of 200

Individuals and Genotype	*M* Alleles	*m* Alleles
10 *MM*	20 (10 × 2)	
74 *Mm*	74	74
16 *mm*		32 (16 × 2)
Total number of alleles:	94	106
Percentage of gene pool:	47	53

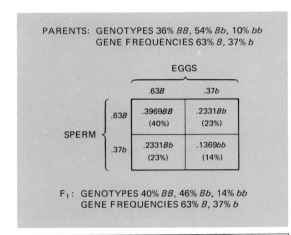

PARENTS: GENOTYPES 36% *BB*, 54% *Bb*, 10% *bb*
GENE FREQUENCIES 63% *B*, 37% *b*

EGGS

SPERM		.63*B*	.37*b*
	.63*B*	.3969*BB* (40%)	.2331*Bb* (23%)
	.37*b*	.2331*Bb* (23%)	.1369*bb* (14%)

F₁: GENOTYPES 40% *BB*, 46% *Bb*, 14% *bb*
GENE FREQUENCIES 63% *B*, 37% *b*

Figure 17-2. Punnett square showing percentages of genotypes.

one yellow, three smooth to one wrinkled, and so on. In the early twentieth century, after Mendel's work was rediscovered, many researchers thought that if Mendel was right, the same ratios between dominant and recessive traits should be found in natural populations. However, this did not happen. Had Mendel been wrong? In 1908 two researchers—G. H. Hardy in England and W. Weinberg in Germany—devised a mathematical theorem that threw some light on the problem, and that has come to be called the **Hardy–Weinberg principle.** It showed that the frequency of a trait in a population did not depend on whether the allele for it was dominant or recessive. The frequency of a trait, and of the alleles that determined it, could be maintained at almost any level in a population, so long as certain conditions were fulfilled.

Let us see how this works out. Take a hypothetical population of 100 individuals, containing the allelic pair *Bb*. Suppose that in the first generation of the population, the genotypes are: 36 *BB*, 54 *Bb*, 10 *bb*. Knowing this, we can calculate the gene frequencies as .63 (63%) *B* and .37 (37%) *b*. Ninety percent of the individuals (36 + 54) will show the dominant *B* trait. We can show by means of a Punnett square what percentage of the offspring will have each of the three genotypes. The percentages are close to, but not quite the same as, those in the parent generation: about 40% *BB*, 46% *Bb*, and 14% *bb*.

Now, if we calculate the gene frequencies in this new generation, what do we find? They are .63 *B*, .37 *b*—just as in the first generation. If we were to work out another Punnett square for the third generation, we would find that the genotype distribution would remain the same as in the second generation. So would the gene frequency. The *Bb* trait, whatever it is, has reached an equilibrium, or balance, in this population. It will stay at about this frequency until something happens to upset the balance. In each generation, about 86 percent of the individuals (40 + 46) will show the dominant trait, and about 14 percent will show the recessive. This is a ratio of about 6:1, instead of Mendel's ratio of 3:1.

This finding can be expressed in an equation, which is known as the **Hardy–Weinberg equation:**

$$p^2 + 2\ pq + q^2 = 1$$

The equation is simply another way of indicating what we did with the gene frequencies in our Punnett square. The letter p represents the gene frequency of our *B* allele (.63) and q represents the frequency of the *b* allele (.37). The p^2 represents the percentage of BB genotypes, q^2 the percentage of bb's, and 2 pq the percentage of Bb's. The same equation can be used to predict the percentages of different genotypes for any population, if the gene frequencies are known.

But, if gene frequencies and genotypic ratios tend to remain balanced and unchanging, how can populations ever vary? Remember that we said this balance is possible only under certain conditions. They are:

1. All mating within the population must be completely random.

2. The population must be large enough so that chance fluctuations will not affect the overall percentages.

3. All genotypes must be equally viable—that is, equally fitted to survive and reproduce.

4. There must be no mutation, which would produce new genes or new arrangements of genes on the chromosomes.

5. There must be no migration—outsiders must not be added to the population, and members of the population must not move out of it.

The first three conditions ensure that each allele in the population's gene pool will have an equal chance of being passed on, and an equal chance of being combined with each other allele. The fourth and fifth ensure that new genes will not be added to the gene pool, nor existing ones taken away. In fact, of course, these conditions (except for the second) are almost never fulfilled. A female robin, for instance, does not mate randomly, with any male she happens to find. She chooses the one with the reddest breast, the greatest vigor, the most acceptable song, the finest nesting site. Thus that male's genotype for these characteristics is more "fit" than that of a less desirable male. His alleles will be passed on in greater numbers, and will have more influence on the gene frequencies of the next generation. Some of the other males may not mate at all, so their

Figure 17-3. Truly random mating rarely occurs. This drab female scarlet tanager has chosen her mate partly on the basis of his brilliant coloring.

alleles will be lost. Gradually, over several generations, the frequencies of the one set of alleles will increase, and the frequencies of the other set will decrease. Variation will have taken place.

SOURCES OF VARIATION

We can see, then, that variation occurs through changes in a population's gene pool. This may mean changes in the frequencies of genes that are already present. Or it may mean the introduction of entirely new genes, or the loss of old ones. New genes or gene combinations may be brought into the population by immigrants from other populations. But they may also arise within the population itself, through mutation.

Mutation
Genetic mutation can be of two kinds. One is **point mutation,** a change in the gene itself. In point mutation, the sequence of nitrogen bases in a DNA molecule is changed. This

changes the "message" of the genetic code in that molecule. The DNA is now coded for the production of a different polypeptide. Depending on the importance of this polypeptide, and the position of the changed amino acid, the change may have a major effect on the organism, or a minor effect, or no apparent effect at all.

A point mutation is important for population change only to the extent that the mutated allele becomes part of the gene pool. If the mutation makes the individual better suited to its environment and situation, then the individual has a better chance of surviving and bearing offspring. Thus there is a good chance that the changed allele will be passed on. On the other hand, if the mutation is disadvantageous, the individual is less likely to survive and bear offspring, and the mutation is less likely to be passed on. Finally, if the mutation is neither advantageous nor disadvantageous, it has about as much chance of being passed on as any other allele.

It was once thought that point mutations occurred only rarely, and that when they did they always had a considerable effect on the individual. If this were true, they would be quite important. But it is now thought that just the contrary is true. Point mutations seem to be very common, and most of them have very little effect. In a way, this is hardly surprising. A complex organism has a vast number of genes—human beings appear to have about 100,000. Changes in most of these genes affect only tiny details of enzyme structure, and have little effect on the organism's functioning. For instance, the structure of enzymes varies quite widely among human beings, but only a few of the variants are known to be harmful. So the majority of point mutations are probably

---

EATING UP THE OIL SPILLS

A biologist at General Electric, using the techniques of genetic engineering, has created bacteria with a ravenous appetite for petroleum. It has been known for some years that certain bacteria can digest some of the hydrocarbon compounds in petroleum. But the new microbe combines the petroleum-eating abilities of four different kinds of *Pseudomonas* bacteria into what its inventor has dubbed "the multiplasmid super bug."

The "super bug" can gobble up about two-thirds of the hydrocarbons in petroleum. And it can do it much faster than other organisms. Moreover, there is an added bonus. After digesting the oil, the bug leaves a residue of carbon dioxide, protein, and water, which can be used by other organisms.

How are the separate microbial strains combined into one super bacteria? In the bacterial cells there are small structures known as plasmids. These are not chromosomes, but they control genetic traits, including the ability to digest hydrocarbons. The designer of the super bug "mated" bacterial strains until he managed to get all four types of plasmid into a single strain. The job was complicated when two of the plasmids proved incompatible—unable to live in the same cell. He solved that problem by fusing them into a single large plasmid. The result is a sort of "modular microbe," which by itself digests more hydrocarbons than the four separate strains working independently. Researchers estimate that it will take about three to five years of further development before the super bug will be available in sufficient quantity for use against oil spills.

---

not very important. They may be passed on, or they may not. Only a few seem to have much effect on the population's adaptation to its environment.

Of greater importance, it appears today, are **chromosomal mutations.** These are rearrangements of parts of chromosomes, such as we considered in chapter 15—translocation, inversion, and so on. In the past it was thought that these mutations were usually harmful, because only the harmful ones were observed. Sometimes these harmful mutations are so severe that the individual dies before reaching maturity, or is unable to mate successfully. But now it is being learned that most such chromosomal mutations are harmless, or even adaptively useful in their effects. For instance, in an inversion, a structural gene affecting the formation of hair might end up next to a different regulator gene than before. As a result, the cells might produce longer hair. The longer-haired individual would then seem to be better adapted than other members of the population for surviving an unusually cold winter.

Mutations of genes or chromosomes may occur in any cell, but in sexually reproducing organisms they can be passed on to the offspring only if they occur in the reproductive cells. Those that occur in other cells may affect the individual, but the changed alleles do not become part of the gene pool of the population.

Migration

Mutation is the only way in which new alleles, or new arrangements of alleles on the chromosomes, can be created. However, some alleles may be found in one population and not in another of the same species. If some individuals migrate from the first population to the second, they may carry those alleles with them, and introduce them into the second population's gene pool. How much this will influence the gene frequencies of the second population depends partly on the number of migrants. As we can see from the Hardy–Weinberg principle, a gene carried by only one or two migrants is not likely to become very common in the popu-

These two tortoises are from different islands in the Galápagos chain. The one at the left is from Hood Island; the one at the right is from Santa Cruz Island. Only the color and shape of their shells are different. What are some of the characteristics these two turtles have in common? Both turtles evolved from the same ancestor. How might you explain their differences?

lation, unless it gives its possessors great advantages. But a gene introduced by a large number of migrants may spread quite widely.

Recombination

Once new alleles enter the population—by mutation or migration—they must be distributed if they are to produce a significant percentage of variation. For distribution, sexual reproduction has certain advantages. Because it involves combining alleles of both parents, it can result in a wide variety of genotypes. This increases the chance that the new allele may form part of a particularly favorable genotype and thus be more widely distributed. For instance, an individual might receive a long-hair allele from one parent, and from the other an allele enabling him to get more energy than usual from a given amount of food. This individual would be better adapted for cold, hungry winters than either parent. Sexual recombination, then, is as important as mutation or migration in changing the genetic combinations and phenotypic character of a population. In fact, most of the study of evolution is really a study of the various influences that affect the process of recombination.

Influences on recombination

Even without mutation or migration, certain factors can affect the recombination of alleles, so that certain alleles are reproduced more often than others, and are therefore maintained at a higher level in the population. Thus the population gradually varies toward a higher percentage of the traits determined by those alleles. Recall the first three conditions that we listed as necessary for gene frequencies to stay in equilibrium. The first was that all mating within the population must be completely random, so that every allele has an equal chance of being paired with every other allele. As we noted with regard to the robin, random mat-

ing simply does not happen in most populations, especially animal populations.

The second condition was that the population must be large enough to cancel out the effects of chance fluctuations, or **genetic drift.** Of the five conditions, this one is the most likely to be fulfilled. But occasionally a population—perhaps on an island—is very small, and is cut off from contact with other populations of the same species. This means that its gene pool is derived entirely from the original founders of the population. There may have been very few founders— perhaps only a single pair. If their genotypes happened to be unusual in some respect, the unusual characteristic may become common in the small population, even though it may remain very rare in the larger population outside. Thus most people on the island might be red-haired, while brown or blond hair might be more common among the mainland people to whom they are related. This is known as **founder effect.** It is a change in gene frequencies that occurs not because one allele is more useful than another, but because only certain alleles happen to be available when the population is begun.

The third condition for equilibrium was that all the genotypes must be equally viable—equally able to survive and reproduce. In fact, in every population there are some harmful alleles, which may reduce the survival potential of the individuals that possess them. Such alleles range all the way from those that do very little harm, to those that kill the individual before it reaches maturity—sometimes even before birth.

If an allele is so lethal that the possessor dies before being able to reproduce, how can such an allele remain in the population? It would seem doomed to disappear within the first generation after its appearance. Actually, this is what will happen if it is a dominant allele. In this case, any individual that has the lethal allele on even one chromosome will show the harmful trait and will die. But suppose the allele is recessive? Then the trait will show up only in homozygous

SNOW GEESE/ BLUE GEESE

It is a summer day in northern Canada. Thousands of geese dot the wind-ruffled waters of Baffin Bay. Some are the pure white birds known as lesser snow geese; others are the darker-colored blue geese. Are these two different species, sharing rather than competing for a single ecological niche? Not really. Despite their strong difference in color, the lesser snow goose and the blue goose are actually genetic variations within the same species.

The discovery that these seemingly quite different birds belonged to the same species solved a mystery which had baffled ornithologists for many years. Every fall, great numbers of blue geese appear along the coast of Louisiana. Here they spend the winter before returning to the Canadian Arctic in the spring. But for years no one could find the blue goose's northern breeding ground. The entire species simply seemed to vanish every spring.

Painstakingly, ornithologists searched an area of some 30,000 miles from Hudson Bay to Greenland. They finally located nesting colonies of blue geese on two islands in Hudson Bay. But, to the scientists' surprise, the blue geese were nesting with lesser snow geese, birds which were supposedly members of a different species.

Among the flock were some apparent hybrids, which suggested that the blue goose and the lesser snow goose were more closely related than anyone had suspected. Furthermore, continued observation revealed that about half of the mated pairs were "mixed marriages" between blue geese and snow geese. If both colors did in fact belong to the same species, a much higher percentage of these mixed matings would normally be expected. On the other hand, if they were of different species the percentage should have been far lower.

After studying the breeding biology of blue geese and lesser snow geese for several summers, the scientists finally determined that both birds did indeed belong to a single species. The blue goose was merely a genetically-determined color variation of the lesser snow goose. But this raised another question: since the birds belonged to the same species, why was there such a comparatively low percentage of mixed matings between white and dark plumage types?

The answer became apparent when it was seen that the geese showed a strong mating preference for birds of their own coloration. Apparently the goslings grew

up to favor mates of the same color as their parents, and only those goslings that resulted from a mixed mating were likely to contract a "mixed marriage" themselves. A long-term study to test this theory involved the raising of blue, white, and pink-dyed goslings with blue, white, and pink-dyed foster parents. It was found that the goslings tended to associate with adults of the same color as their foster parents—including those whose foster parents were pink! Their color preference, apparently, was a learned behavior rather than an inherited one.

The colors of both plumage types serve as protective camouflage for the geese during their breeding season. Although both blue and white birds nest in the same geographical region, the white birds normally begin nesting earlier in the season than the blue ones. Their white coloration helps to protect them from predators during this early period, while snow is still on the ground. The blue birds, on the other hand, are camouflaged appropriately for their later nesting on muddy ground. This staggering of nesting activity minimizes breeding losses while making maximum use of the short northern breeding season.

In most of the arctic breeding colonies, one plumage type is predominant. But geese from widely separated colonies may pair off during their winter visit to Louisiana, later returning to the female's colony to nest. This outbreeding preserves genetic "communication lines" among geographically distant colonies of geese.

Each of the arctic breeding colonies has its own autumn migration pattern. The Baffin Island colony, mostly blue geese, flies directly to Louisiana with only a brief stopover in James Bay, Canada. The Southampton Island colony, mostly white geese, makes several stopovers in southern Canada and the Dakotas. On these stopovers the lesser snow goose is an easy target for hunters. The past half-century of milder arctic climate, which favors the breeding of blue geese, combined with human intervention in the form of goose hunters, has resulted in a significant decline in the population of lesser snow geese.

Other human activities may have an even greater impact on the behavioral and genetic pattern of the geese. Oil, mining, and hydroelectric projects in their arctic nesting regions may eventually have major effects on migration routes and timing. Only time will allow us to see just how much human interference will affect natural selection in shaping the genetic future of the geese of Hudson Bay.

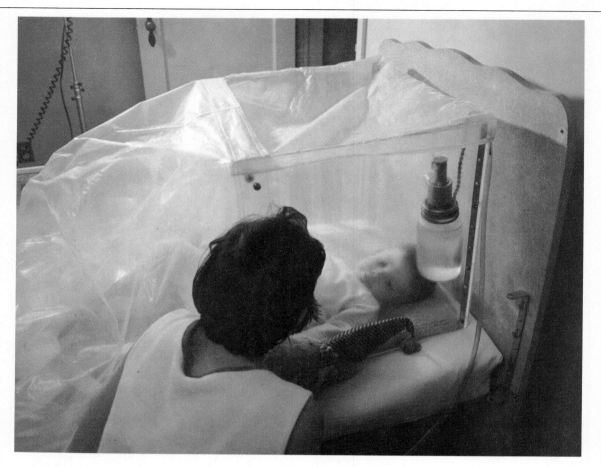

Figure 17-5. This child was born with cystic fibrosis, which he inherited by receiving a recessive allele from each of his heterozygous parents. This disease causes the cells lining the lungs to produce an abnormally thick and sticky mucous secretion. By breathing a special mist, which softens the mucous and prevents infection, the boy continues to live. Without such treatment, the disease would prove fatal.

individuals, which have the allele on both chromosomes. In heterozygous individuals, who have it on only one chromosome, the trait will not appear. These individuals will be normally healthy—or perhaps only slightly affected—and the hidden allele will be passed on. It will remain in the population indefinitely. The allele for the disease called cystic fibrosis is of this sort.

PRESERVATION OF GENES IN A POPULATION

Since there are always adaptive pressures favoring one allele over another, why are unfavorable alleles, such as the one for hemophilia that we discussed in chapter 15, not eliminated from a population, or at least

354

considerably reduced in frequency? Sometimes they are, but not as often as we might think.

For one thing, a particular allele may not always be unfavorable. The population may occupy a wide variety of environments, and some genotypes may be better adapted to one environment, some to another. So long as the possessors of different genotypes can interbreed, all the alleles involved are likely to be preserved in the population.

Or the environment may change. As a hypothetical example, a series of rainy years might be followed by a series of dry ones, and then the rainy weather might return. Alleles that were favored and increased during the wet period might decrease in frequency during the dry time, as their possessors reproduced less successfully. But it ordinarily takes many generations to breed an allele out of a population entirely. Thus, there would probably still be some individuals carrying the wet-favored alleles when rainy weather returned. Then these alleles would again be advantageous, and their frequency in the population would tend to increase.

Finally, the heterozygous individual may have an adaptive advantage over either homozygote. This state of affairs is known as **heterozygote superiority,** or **heterosis.** It is particularly common when neither allele is dominant, so that the heterozygote shows a trait that is intermediate between the two homozygotes. The intermediate trait may be more useful for survival in an environment that varies periodically, as many environments do. Heterozygote superiority results in a situation known as **balanced polymorphism**—the maintenance of a balance between two or more phenotypes in the population.

A particularly interesting sort of heterozygote superiority involves alleles that are seriously harmful or even lethal in the homozygous state. For example, several inherited blood disorders are fairly common among peoples native to the Mediterranean countries, Africa, and certain other parts of the world. These disorders include sickle-cell anemia, thalassemia (Cooley's anemia), and favism, a condition in which serious illness or death is produced by eating the common European broad bean, or fava bean, or by inhaling its pollen. People who are homozygous for these traits generally die in childhood. But those who are heterozygous are only mildly afflicted by the disease, and they appear to have an unusually high resistance to malaria. Since malaria is common in the parts of the world where these diseases are native, the heterozygotes have a clear advantage. So they survive and reproduce with greater frequency than either homozygote group. The disease-allele homozygotes have the blood diseases and die young, and the normal-allele homozygotes are more likely to have malaria, which lowers their reproductive potential, especially by making the males less potent or even sterile.

In that case, why do homozygotes not disappear from the population entirely? Would not a population consisting entirely of heterozygotes be most adaptive of all? It might—but it would be a genetic impossibility. When heterozygotes interbreed, they produce homozygotes as well as heterozygotes, so a balanced polymorphism results.

SUMMARY

Factors that determine genotypic changes in a population may be genetic, behavioral, or environmental. In genetic terms, a population is a community of individuals who are interbreeding with one another or have the potential to do so. The gene pool is the sum total of all the genes present within a given population.

The gene frequencies of a population are the percentages of the various alleles of a gene that are present within the population. These percentages will always add up to 100. The percentages of gene frequencies can be determined by use of a Punnett square or by the Hardy–Weinberg equation.

The Hardy–Weinberg principle states that the frequency of the alleles that determine a particular trait can be maintained at almost any level in a population so long as the following conditions are fulfilled: 1. completely random mating within the population; 2. population large enough so that chance fluctuations will not affect the overall percentages; 3. all genotypes equally viable; 4. no mutation; 5. no migration. In actual practice, only the second of these conditions is usually fulfilled.

Variation occurs through changes in a population's gene pool, either by mutation or by migration. Genetic mutation may be either point mutation or chromosomal mutation. Point mutation involves a change in the sequences of nitrogen bases within a DNA molecule, thus changing the genetic message. Chromosomal mutation involves rearrangement of portions of the chromosomes by such means as translocation or inversion.

Migration involves the introduction of new genes into the gene pool of one population by migrants from another. The greater the number of migrants who introduce the new gene, the more widely it may spread through the population.

Once a new allele enters a population, sexual reproduction helps to distribute it, producing a variety of genotypes by combining the alleles of both parents. This recombination may be influenced by several factors that cause certain alleles to be maintained at a higher level than others. First, completely random mating rarely occurs in most populations. Second, a completely isolated population must derive its gene pool solely from its original founders. Third, every population possesses some harmful alleles that reduce the viability of certain genotypes.

If a lethal allele is dominant, it will disappear from the population within the first generation after its appearance. If it is recessive, the trait it causes will show up only in homozygous individuals. However, it can still be possessed and passed on by heterozygous individuals and thus will remain in the population indefinitely.

Unfavorable alleles may remain in a population because they have some favorable aspects under certain conditions. Heterozygote superiority occurs when the heterozygous individual has an adaptive advantage over both homozygotes. It results in balanced polymorphism, the maintenance of a balance between two or more phenotypes within a population. Although the heterozygotes may be the most adaptive, homozygotes continue in a population because interbreeding of heterozygotes must inevitably produce a certain percentage of homozygotes.

Review questions

1. In genetic terms, what is a population?

2. List several factors that are important in determining changes in a population.

3. What is a gene pool?

4. Explain the Hardy–Weinberg principle.

5. Using the alleles M and m, tell what each part of the Hardy–Weinberg equation expresses.

6. List the conditions necessary to maintain an unchanging balance of gene frequencies and genotypic ratios in a population.

7. Given the conditions above, describe some of the ways by which population variation might occur.

8. Distinguish between gene mutation and chromosomal mutation. Which of these is more important, and why?

9. What is recombination? Explain how sexual reproduction is important to it.

10. Recalling the conditions listed in question 6, what factors may cause certain alleles to be maintained at a higher level in the population?

11. What is founder effect?

12. Explain how a lethal allele can continue to exist in a population after the first generation.

13. What is heterozygote superiority? What are some of its advantages? Give a hypothetical example.

14. What is balanced polymorphism? What causes it?

15. Give an example of heterozygote superiority involving a lethal allele. What are the advantages to the heterozygotes? What are the disadvantages to the lethal-allele homozygotes and the normal-allele homozygotes?

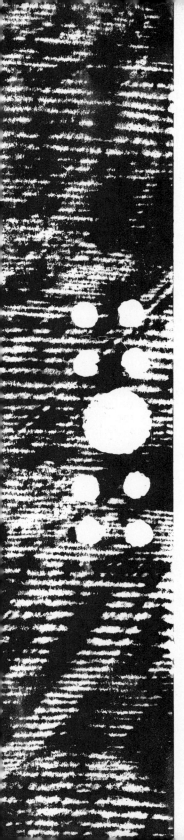

Evolution: The Theory of Natural Selection

We have talked about some of the ways in which genetic variation takes place in a population. The evidence for such variation is all around us. For example, growers and breeders have often been able to induce significant changes in domestic plant and animal populations, such as dogs. Most authorities believe that the modern dog is a direct descendant of the wolf, and that the dog was first domesticated more than ten thousand years ago. Since then, we have succeeded in developing a remarkably diverse group of breeds. All modern dogs are considered to belong to the same species, yet breeds of dogs come in a wonderful assortment of sizes, shapes, colors, and temperaments. Compare the toy poodle with a Saint Bernard!

These variations in breeds of dogs over a period of time are called evolutionary changes. **Evolution** can occur naturally, or it can be induced by humans. In either case, it involves changes in the genetic make-up of a population through time. The fact that evolution has occurred (and is still occurring) seems to most scientists to be well supported by observable evidence.

EVIDENCE FOR EVOLUTION

When most organisms die, their bodies are broken down by decomposers into a few basic chemicals. Nothing is left to show that the organisms ever existed. Sometimes, however, an organism, a part of its body, or some trace such as a footprint, is accidentally preserved. The remains of organisms from earlier periods are called **fossils.**

Some organisms and parts of organisms have had a better chance of being preserved than others. When marine animals die, for example, their bodies settle into the mud at the bottom of the sea. Here there are relatively few decomposer organisms. In addition, such body structures as bones, teeth, shells, and scales are very resistant to decomposition. In time, if there is sufficient pressure, the mud hardens into layers of rock, protecting any remains that are still intact. When these rocks are lifted up from the sea—through volcanic eruption, for example—the enclosed remains are protected. The rock continues to protect them on land from wind and water erosion. Except for the minerals that have seeped in and replaced the soft tissues, the fossil is likely to be much in the same form as the original organism.

Fossils provide direct evidence of many of the kinds of life that have existed on earth.

They do not have to include the whole organism in order to be useful. The length and shape of a single leg bone may provide a good basis for estimating the size and general appearance of the animal. The size and shape of muscles can also be estimated by studying the impressions on the bone where the muscles were attached.

The diameter and internal nature of the bone may shed further light on the size and weight of the animal. How the limb bones fit together and the kind of joints they make help to suggest the animal's posture and way of movement. When such information is combined with that obtained from other portions of the body, such as teeth, vertebrae, and skull, a fairly complete picture of the animal can be constructed. If there are other animal and plant fossils nearby, it is often possible to piece together a fairly full picture of the community in which the animal may have lived.

The study of the history of life through the examination of fossils is called **paleontology.** Paleontologists reconstruct this history through two methods. The first method is

Figure 18-1. Artificial selection by dog breeders has resulted in the development of such remarkably dissimilar breeds as the Pekingese on the left and the Saint Bernard on the right.

Figure 18-2. These trilobites lived in the ocean many millions of years ago. Their fossil remains show their body structure in perfect detail.

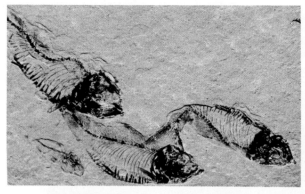

Figure 18-3. The structures of the fish at top and the fern leaves at bottom have been permanently preserved by fossilization.

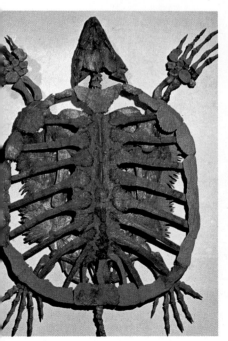

Figure 18-4. Paleontologists have been able to fit together the bones of this extinct marine turtle. From this skeleton they have determined the turtle's size, general appearance, muscle structure, and manner of movement. Some members of this species may have reached a length of 18 feet.

based on the fact that most fossils are found in layers, or **strata,** of sedimentary rock. Generally paleontologists assume that the fossils in the lowest layers represent the oldest forms of life, and that those in each layer above represent more recent forms. But this does not indicate how old or young each form is. So paleontologists use **radioactive dating** (see table 18–1), to determine the approximate age of a fossil. The overall sequence—the arrangement of fossils in time—is known as the **fossil record.**

Hundreds of thousands of fossils have been classified and incorporated into the fossil record—not only animal remains but also plant structures and microscopic organisms. Continued inquiry will undoubtedly yield more. Still, the fossil record is, and always will be, incomplete. A complete fossil record would include a representative specimen from every population that has ever inhabited the earth. However, a great many of the populations that are assumed to have existed did not survive decay and destruction—for example, many soft-bodied invertebrate animals.

Up until now we have stressed the importance of a species' adaptation to its ever-changing environment. Genetic variability within a population, we said, helps to ensure its survival. But from the fossil record we can see that more species appear to be extinct than are living. Why did they not survive? Most often, the environment seems to have changed so greatly or so fast—for instance, in climate—that the species' gene pool did not contain enough variations to enable it to survive.

Industrial melanism

Some changes in populations occur so quickly that we have been able to record them within the past century. Such changes provide evidence of the interaction between environmental change and the genetic variants that already exist in the population.

A good example is the change that has occurred in the peppered moth population

Figure 18-5. The ginkgo tree is a "living fossil" which has survived in unchanged form since the Paleozoic era. Because it is resistant to polluted air and depleted soil, it is popular in city surroundings.

Figure 18-6. A close-up view of the ginkgo's fern-like leaves.

Figure 18-7. Two other types of fossilization are shown here. The beetle (left) is embedded in amber. The dinosaur bones (right) have been petrified.

ATING OCESS	MATERIAL TESTED	POTENTIAL RANGE: YEARS	HALF-LIFE: YEARS
on-14	Wood, Charcoal, Shell	70,000	5,730
actinium-231	Deep Sea Sediment	120,000	32,000
ium-230	Deep Sea Sediment, Coral, Shell	400,000	75,000
ium-234	Coral	1,000,000	250,000
rine-36	Igneous and Volcanic Rocks	500,000	300,000
llium-10	Deep Sea Sediment	8,000,000	2,000,000
m-4	Coral, Shell	—	4.5 billion
sium-40 n-40	Volcanic Ash, Lava	—	1.3 billion

Table 18-1. Sometimes atoms of the same element may contain different numbers of neutrons from one another. Atoms such as these are called *isotopes*, and some elements may have as many as 20 isotopes. Certain isotopes, such as the eight listed at left, are radioactive; that is, they emit nuclear particles and so disintegrate into other elements.

Each radioactive isotope has its own fixed rate of decay, called the isotope's *half-life*. The half-life is the time required for one half of the atoms in a given sample to disintegrate, or decay. Thus, if one knows an isotope's half-life, the age of a specimen can be determined by measuring how much of the isotope is left.

The isotopes listed are used for dating purposes. The table shows the materials to which these isotopes are applied, their potential time ranges, and their characteristic half-lives.

EVOLUTION: THE THEORY
OF NATURAL SELECTION

since 1850. This species of moth, *Biston betularia*, lives in England, which underwent extensive and rapid industrialization during the nineteenth century. Before 1850, most of these moths were white with dark spots scattered over their wings—hence the name "peppered." In the 1850s black specimens, once rare, were beginning to be found more often by collectors.

As England industrialized, soot spread everywhere. It landed on the trees used by these moths as resting places, and it killed the lichens growing on the bark. The lichens had provided good camouflage for the moths. With the soot, however, trees that had been originally grey or light-colored became almost black. And as the trees changed color, so did the moth population, to judge by specimens collected over a period of time. Today, the vast majority of these moths in industrial areas are dark. How this probably occurred should become clear before the end of this chapter. Such a change in pigmentation caused by industrial pollution is called **industrial melanism.**

Chemical resistance

Less visible but more rapid changes have been observed in certain populations within the past twenty-five years. Like industrial melanism, these changes have been induced by the human-made environment. They have usually been observed in large populations that reproduce very quickly and are therefore capable of producing many generations in a short time. A good example is the bacterial species *Staphylococcus aureus*, commonly called staph. Before 1945 these bacteria were considered mild infective agents. When introduced into open wounds, they usually caused local infections, such as pimples and boils, which were controlled by the body's own defense mechanisms.

After 1945, various antibiotics were used to control such infections more quickly and effectively. However, within ten years, doctors were reporting resistant strains of "hospital staph" that were not destroyed by antibiotic treatment. By 1960 hospital personnel across the country were alarmed at the increased number and severity of staph infections. People who underwent surgery and who were accidentally exposed to hospital staph often developed serious postoperative infections. Although the control measures have been improved, people are still contracting such infections. The new and more resistant populations of staph present a threat that was almost nonexistent a few years ago.

Support from other research

The changes we have noted in some contemporary species—peppered moths and *Staphylococcus*—prove that evolution can occur. And scientists have interpreted the fossil record as showing that it has occurred throughout the history of life on earth. They believe that all today's species have evolved from species that lived in earlier eras, and that those species evolved from even earlier forms of life.

Strictly speaking, fossils do not prove that such an evolution of life occurred. It is possible, after all, that each species rep-

Figure 18-8. Carbon-14 dating has revealed that these ears of corn (left to right) date back to 5000 B.C., 3500 B.C., A.D. 200, A.D. 700, and A.D. 1500. Can you give some possible explanations for the progressively larger size of the ears?

Figure 18-9. The tuatara, found only in New Zealand, has remained virtually unchanged since the time that dinosaurs roamed the earth.

Figure 18-10. A peppered moth, *Biston betularia*, and its black form, *carbonaria*, at rest on the soot-covered trunk of an oak tree near Birmingham (left). The same two varieties of moth are shown at rest on a lichen-covered tree in an unpolluted countryside (right).

Figure 18-11. *Staphylococcus* has been grown on blood agar in this petri dish. The white disc of penicillin has prevented the colonies of bacteria from growing in the circular area around it. But some new strains of *Staphylococcus* which are resistant to the growth-inhibiting effect of penicillin are now appearing in many hospitals.

resented in the fossil record was originally created in just that form and did not change into another species. However, most scientists find evolution a more satisfactory explanation. Furthermore, indirect evidence from other fields is also used to support the theory of evolutionary descent. Most of this evidence is based on similarities among apparently dissimilar forms of life.

Similarities of embryonic development are considered good evidence for evolution. Embryologists have long noted that the development of the embryos of most animals follows one basic pattern, such as we described in chapter 14. In closely related animals, the similarities continue through later stages of development. We noted that, in its earliest stages, the human embryo looks more like other animal embryos than it does like the human adult. Moreover, it resembles a reptile embryo for longer than it resembles an amphibian embryo.

Similar structures among animal embryos are believed to have been inherited from a common ancestor. For instance, all vertebrate embryos develop structures called pharyngeal pouches. In fish, most of these pouches later become gills; in land vertebrates they become, instead, the lungs and certain other structures. Only in the embryos can it be seen that all these structures have a common source.

Related to the evidence from embryology is evidence from comparative anatomy, which is the comparison of structural similarities and differences. A common specialty in this field of biology is the comparative study of different vertebrates. Figure 18-12 shows similarities in the forelimbs of humans and four other mammals. Not only do the structures look similar; they also develop from similar structures in the embryo. Such similarities are called **homologies.** Less precise but just as definite homologies can be found in the forelimbs of other mammals, birds, reptiles, amphibians, and fish. Homologous structures are seen as evidence that the different organisms possessing them have evolved from common ancestors.

Homologies can also be observed in other body structures of animals believed to be closely related. The degree of similarity between such animals remains about the same regardless of the organ that is compared. This consistent pattern of homologies between organisms thought to be related is considered very convincing evidence in support of historical evolution.

THE HISTORY OF EVOLUTIONARY THEORY

Scientists of the eighteenth and nineteenth centuries had much of the information that we now regard as evidence for evolution. Comparative anatomists and embryologists had noted the similarities among different species. Paleontologists had found fossils of species no longer on earth, as well as fossils of species that closely resembled living ones. But most scientists of the time did not use this evidence to support a theory of evolution. Why not?

One reason is that the evidence was not as complete then as it is today. The fossil record in particular had enormous gaps, which made it difficult for scientists to interpret the available fossils. Furthermore, their interpretation of the fossil record conflicted with their theology. The idea that life in its modern forms had evolved from earlier forms of life seemed to contradict Biblical accounts of the creation of life. According to the Bible, the earth and all of its species had been created within a week's time. Hence, modern species must be exactly the same as those of the original creation. Moreover, this creation was thought to have occurred about six thousand years ago, which left hardly enough time for all the modern species to have evolved. Most early scientists tried to make the evidence for evolution conform to this theory of "special creation."

Geological change

Geology was one of the first branches of science slowly to turn away from the popular doctrines. Geologists felt that a single "special creation" could not account for the many layers of sediment found in the earth's surface. To account for these layers, some scientists proposed a series of "special creations." At several different times, they said, the earth had undergone violent upheavals. Each catastrophe destroyed all life existing at the time and altered the earth's surface. Life was then created anew. This was one of several theories known as **catastrophism.** It accounted both for the different sedimentary strata and for the different kinds of fossil life found in them, as well as for their creation in a short six thousand years.

James Hutton, an eighteenth-century geologist, had already suggested that six thousand years was simply not enough time for these geological transformations. Rejecting catastrophism, he proposed that certain natural geological forces at work today were the same ones that caused the geological changes in the past. He held that just as the forces of erosion by wind and water, earthquakes, and volcanoes cause changes in the present surface of the earth, so did they transform it long ago. Hutton's theory is called **uniformitarianism.** In essence, it

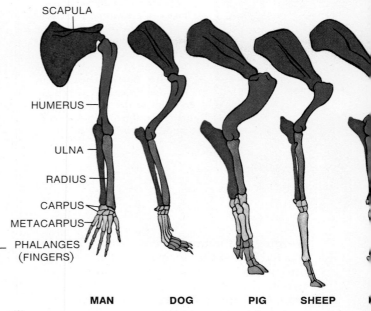

Figure 18-12. Homologies in the forelimbs of these mammals are an indication that they may all have evolved from a common ancestor.

maintains that the natural laws governing the earth have been the same, or uniform, throughout its history. Therefore very long periods of time are needed for major changes to occur. This theory was not popular, however, and was generally ignored.

In the late eighteenth and the early nineteenth centuries, the famous French paleontologist Georges Cuvier proposed a type of catastrophism that depended on natural causes, not divine intervention. Cuvier's investigations further seemed to support a biological theory, known as **progressionism,** that in many ways made use of the geological theory of catastrophism. Cuvier had observed that fossil species found in one stratum were often absent in the one above it. Furthermore, the upper, more recent strata often contained more complex forms of life than did the older, lower strata. With each catastrophe, apparently, higher forms of life were created.

PATTERNS OF CHANGE

Table 18-2. Geologic and evolutionary timetable.

ERA	PERIOD	YEARS AGO DURATION (In millions of years)		PLANT LIFE	ANIMAL LIFE
CENOZOIC	Quaternary	2	2	Decline of woody plants; rise of herbs	Appearance of man
	Tertiary	60	58	Modernization of flowering plants; development of modern forests	Rapid development of higher mammals and birds
MESOZOIC	Cretaceous	130	70	Rise of flowering plants to dominance; decline of conifers	Rise of primitive mammals; first modern birds; dinosaurs become extinct
	Jurassic	175	45	First angiosperms; conifers dominant	First birds, flying reptiles; dinosaurs abundant; first mammals
	Triassic	225	50	Conifers dominant; seed ferns disappear	First dinosaurs
PALEOZOIC	Permian	275	50	Decline of club mosses and horsetails	Mammal-like reptiles; rise of modern insects
	Carboniferous	350	75	Extensive coal formation; club mosses and horsetails dominant	First reptiles; insects common
	Devonian	410	60	Land plants become well established; first conifers	First amphibians; sharks abundant; sea lilies
	Silurian	430	20	Algae dominant; first definite evidence of land plants	First air-breathing animals; first insects
	Ordovician	500	70	Probably first appearance of land plants; marine algae abundant	First fishes
	Cambrian	600	100	Marine algae	Invertebrates abundant; trilobites dominant
PRECAMBRIAN		2,700	2,100	Primitive aquatic plants: algae; fungi	Marine invertebrates; protozoans
AZOIC		?	?	No direct evidence of life	No direct evidence of life

These observations could reasonably be interpreted as evidence that a divine creator was directing the progression of life to a more perfect state, rather than as signs of gradual evolution.

vived Hutton's uniformitarianism and his belief that vast amounts of time were needed for natural geological forces to transform the surface of the earth into its present-day appearance. Lyell set forth his ideas and ob-

---

UPDATING THE DINOSAUR

A dinosaur is a cold-blooded, scaly prehistoric reptile, now completely extinct. Dinosaurs were stupid, clumsy, and an evolutionary dead end, unable to survive because of their inability to adapt to the changing climate of the primitive earth.

A dinosaur is a warm-blooded animal, often furred or feathered, which is now represented on earth by the birds. Many dinosaurs were agile and fairly intelligent, but the larger varieties died out because they were too competitive with each other for a diminishing habitat.

The above may sound contradictory, but it is a fair description of the current state of scientific theory about dinosaurs. Until recently, biologists believed that dinosaurs were very similar to modern reptiles. It was thought that they became extinct because of changes in climate and decreasing availability of suitable food.

But some biologists are now disputing this theory. For one thing, studies of fossil remains show that many dinosaur bones were like those of warm-blooded animals. They had a rich blood supply, and lacked the growth rings characteristic of the bones of ectotherms. And how about that scaly armor all dinosaurs were supposed to have? Fossil remains of a flying dinosaur called *Sordus*

pilosus suggest that this bat-like creature had a heavy coat of either fur or fur-like feathers—and such insulation is typical of warm-blooded animals.

Then there is *Archaeopteryx,* usually called the first true bird because its fossilized remains display well-developed feathers on the tail and front limbs. When we compare its skeleton to those of several small dinosaurs that ran on their hind legs, we find that the skeletons are almost identical. So the latest opinion is that *Archaeopteryx* could not fly; it was a running dinosaur, whose feathers served for insulation. Probably it was quite speedy, easily able to catch the more sluggish reptilian forms it preyed on. Such fast movement is tied in with the high metabolic rate of warm-blooded animals, and many fossilized dinosaur footprints show a length of stride that indicates they could move very quickly.

Of course, it is probable that many dinosaurs were cold-blooded, and also that a variety of transitional stages existed between endothermic and ectothermic forms. In fact, if any one conclusion can be reached on the basis of the current evidence, it is that we still have a lot to learn about dinosaurs. Still, the next time you feed your parakeet or indulge in a chicken dinner, keep in mind that very possibly you are sharing your modern world with the relatives of the prehistoric "terrible lizards."

On the other side of the geological debate stood Sir Charles Lyell, a lawyer and amateur paleontologist. Lyell opposed catastrophism, rejecting the possibility of even naturally-caused catastrophes. He re-

servations in a three-volume work entitled *Principles of Geology,* published between 1830 and 1833. Ironically, the catastrophists accepted his theory, while evolutionists and theologians rejected it.

PATTERNS OF CHANGE

Figure 18-13. Lamarck believed that the giraffe's long neck was an acquired characteristic that was then passed on to its offspring.

Lyell rejected progressionism as an explanation of the more complex forms of life in the higher strata. Like catastrophism, progressionism seemed to rely too much on the supernatural for Lyell. Interestingly, Lyell also rejected evolution. For a long time he maintained that there was too little evidence from the fossil record and from comparative anatomy to conclude that plants and animals had evolved over time. More important, Lyell was skeptical of a theory until he could explain it. Whereas he knew of natural forces that might cause gradual geological change, he did not know of forces that could account for biological change.

Biological change

One of Lyell's great accomplishments was to present clearly the evidence that the earth might be much older than had been sup-

posed. This provided the timespan that was needed if evolution was to be regarded as even a reasonable possibility. But it was still necessary to deal with the prevailing idea that species were fixed, that they had never changed since their creation. This idea also had the support of religious doctrine. All forms of life were believed to be ordered on a Great Chain of Being. At the bottom were the "lowest" forms—worms, insects, and so on. Above were "higher" forms—fish, reptiles, mammals, and eventually humans. Each form was considered immutable and unchanging.

The eighteenth-century French naturalist Jean-Baptiste de Lamarck had partially accepted the Great Chain of Being theory. He believed that life formed a series of stages leading toward humanity, its highest form. However, he did not believe that each species was held in a fixed position in this series. He thought species improved over time, moving up the chain—in other words, that they evolved. Moreover, he proposed a mechanism to show how evolution had occurred.

Lamarck saw life as being in constant interaction with its physical environment. As the environment changed, organisms were forced to change their behavior in order to survive. To make these behavior changes possible, changes were also needed in bodily structures. Certain organs improved with greater use; other organs were reduced with disuse. These structural changes were passed on to the young.

Lamarck used the giraffe to illustrate this theory. He reasoned that the present-day giraffe was descended from a shorter-necked ancestor. He also reasoned that some influence from the environment, such as prolonged drought, caused these ancestors to begin feeding upon the leaves of trees, rather than upon the grasses and shrubs on the ground. As the giraffes continuously stretched to reach normally inaccessible food, they were forced to develop slightly longer necks. Lamarck believed that this need for a longer neck created a force that altered the development of the embryo, producing longer necks in the offspring. Therefore, the modern giraffe has evolved through numerous generations of (1) having to stretch to reach higher leaves, (2) having to acquire slightly longer necks, thus (3) causing the development of longer necks in their offspring.

Lamarck's hypothesis is now generally referred to as the **inheritance of acquired characteristics.** Lamarck himself did not favor this name for his theory; rather, it was popularized by Erasmus Darwin, the grandfather of Charles Darwin.

On its face, the theory seems reasonable enough. Without the knowledge of genetics that Mendel's work later made possible, it must have seemed even more reasonable. Today, however, we know that an acquired characteristic does not by itself make a change in the genes, and the genes are what determine inheritance. So the "acquired characteristics" theory was wrong.

DARWIN AND THE BEAGLE

In his youth, Charles Darwin showed little promise as a biologist. He was only a fair student, preferring to spend his time in more appealing outdoor activities. By the time he was sixteen he was a disappointment to his father, a successful physician.

Darwin's father enrolled him in medical school, but he much preferred to observe plants and animals, a study that was then known as natural history. Realizing that Darwin's interest was not in medicine, his father suggested the ministry as a respectable alternative. Acquiescing again to his father's wishes, Darwin spent three years at Cambridge, only to conclude that the time was "wasted as far as the academic studies were concerned." Then during the summer of his third year at the university, two of his professors gave him an opportunity that changed his life and the future of biology.

They recommended him for a position

Figure 18-14. This is an artist's rendition of H.M.S. *Beagle*. Here it is seen anchored in the Straits of Magellan, where it took on supplies for the journey ahead.

Figure 18-15. These iguanas are well suited for survival in the harsh environment of the Galápagos Islands.

as companion to the captain of the H.M.S. *Beagle.* The *Beagle* was to set sail that autumn for an around-the-world tour, to engage in explorations for the Royal Navy. Realizing that the journey would be long, Captain Fitzroy wanted a gentleman of proper social standing to keep him company, to share his meals and conversation. Darwin was of course a gentleman, and as a companion, he could pursue his interests as a naturalist, so he eagerly accepted the offer. Later on, as it happened, the official naturalist left the ship, so Darwin took over his functions without pay.

The *Beagle* sailed on December 27, 1831, and Darwin was not to return for five years. The ship sailed southward to the Cape Verde Islands and from there to South America, for three and one-half years of exploration. Darwin's notebooks from this period reveal his remarkable enthusiasm for collecting specimens and his care in noting what he saw. He sent many of his specimens back to England in order to study them further upon his return.

At first, Darwin was particularly interested in the geology of the new lands he visited. He had taken along the first volume of *Principles of Geology* and eagerly found confirmation of many of Lyell's geological theories. He was also especially struck by the patterns of distribution of plant and animal life on the mainland of South America and on the coastal islands. Darwin had left England a firm believer in the fixity of species, but as he tried to interpret what he saw now, he began to question that belief.

The Galápagos Islands offered Darwin an excellent field of study. These islands are of comparatively recent volcanic origin, having been formed during the Miocene period, 20 to 25 million years ago. Their harsh environment is drastically different from that of the nearby fertile mainland. What plants and animals should Darwin have found on these islands? As he understood the scientific theory of the time, there were two possibilities. If they had migrated from the mainland, the island species would be exactly like the mainland species. If, on the other hand, they had been specially created after the last catastrophe to fit their bleak, desert-like environment, the island species would be completely different from those on the lush mainland, but like those in other harsh, volcanic areas of the world.

Darwin's findings completely contradicted this theory. The island species were not exactly the same as the species on the mainland, but they were very similar. This discovery led Darwin to study the species of other islands. He found that island species are almost always similar to the species on the nearest mainland, yet not exactly the same.

Darwin saw the same sort of relationship between living species and extinct fossil species. If the extinct species had been created separately, there would be no reason for them to resemble those now alive. But if the fossils were ancient members of the same species, there should be no difference between them, according to the theory of the fixity of species. Darwin observed that many of the living species were similar to but not exactly like the extinct species.

One day Darwin was talking to an official of the islands. The man happened to mention that he could tell from which island a tortoise had been collected simply by looking at it. The separate islands of the Galápagos chain are relatively close to each other. So why, Darwin wondered, would each island have its own species of tortoise? Darwin also observed that species of birds, insects, and plants also differed slightly from island to island. Since the environment of all the islands was practically the same, why should different species be specially created for each one?

Perhaps, then, the different species were not independently created? Perhaps the South American species had once migrated to the Galápagos Islands. There they had gradually evolved in different directions as they adapted to life on the islands.

Darwin had the beginnings of a theory of evolution, but he was not satisfied with it.

THE WILD MUSTANG

A band of mares stand quietly to one side as two stallions confront each other. The males press their foreheads together and stare at each other, their tails arched high. After a long moment, one of them backs off, leaving possession of the indifferent harem to the other. If neither had yielded, one of the two might have died in the shrieking, kicking, biting, life-and-death battle in which the wild mustang willingly engages in order to retain possession of his band.

Where did the wild mustang come from? Like all modern horses, it is believed to have evolved from *Eohippus,* a small creature that appeared in the American west some 50 million years ago, before the continents of Europe and North America began to drift apart. The modern horse emerged in America as *Eohippus* was becoming extinct in the now distant continent of Europe. Then, some 8,000 years ago, horses vanished from the Americas—first from the north and later from the south. Many of them may have been driven out of North America by the climate changes that accompanied the advance of the last great glacier. Human hunters and other predators, too, may have contributed to their extinction. In the last analysis, though, we really do not know why they disappeared.

In any event, the species was saved from extinction, because some of its members had earlier migrated into Asia and Europe, presumably across the land bridge that once joined Alaska and Siberia. It was not until a few hundred years ago that the Spanish conquistadors reintroduced the horse to the land of its ancestors.

Without doubt, the Spanish had the finest horses in the world in the sixteenth century. The ancestry of the Spanish horse included both the sturdy European animals bred to carry medieval knights in armor and the small, swift, highly intelligent beasts favored by the Moors and Arabs. The Spanish brought great numbers of horses to the New World, and only the toughest survived the long, hard voyage across the Atlantic Ocean. It was the breeding of the best of the Spanish stallions and brood mares which resulted in the development of the wild mustangs that were later to populate the western plains.

It is not difficult to imagine what effect the sight of mounted Spaniards had on native Americans who had never before seen a European or a horse. The Spaniards did not hesitate to exploit both the Indians' fear and their own military superiority. However, it did not take the Indians long to discover that they could improve the odds by stealing horses from the invaders. They quickly learned to ride bareback and to use the animal as a shield in battle. Horse-stealing became a prized skill among some Plains Indians; one tribe even boasted that they permitted the Spanish to stay only because they provided a fresh supply of horses.

The horse radically altered the lifestyle of the American Indians and soon assumed a prominent role in their rituals and mythology. Because the Indians were inexperienced as herdsmen and relied on stealing to acquire horses, they allowed many animals to escape. These subsequently formed wild bands, and became so numerous that some northern tribes were familiar with horses generations before ever seeing a European.

Most wild horses today are relatively small. Forced off the grassy plains by humans, the mustang has proved able to survive in the desert and mountains where food is scarce. The toughness and intelligence that helped mustangs survive also made them excellent cow ponies when cattle ranching began on the western lands. Yet, ironically, it was the cattlemen who were largely responsible for chasing the mustang off the grasslands. The ranchers believed, mistakenly, that the wild horses were a threat to the cattle's food supply. In fact, unlike cattle, the horse does not digest grass seeds. By preserving and protecting these seeds in its manure, the horse actually helps to reseed the land and replenish its own food supply.

The social unit of the wild mustang generally comprises a single stallion and his harem. The stallion guards his mares carefully, running behind them to set the pace and to prevent desertion. In time of emergency, he may urge them to greater speed by "snaking"—stretching his neck and weaving his head back and forth. If a mare fails to get the message, he makes his point by pushing and biting. Normally a peaceful vegetarian, a male mustang will fight to the death to retain possession of its mares. Occasionally, a number of stallion-dominated bands will temporarily unite under the leadership of a single stallion.

A mare is permitted to leave the band only briefly when giving birth. A male colt is permitted to run with its mother's band for about two years before it is driven off. Sometimes several adolescents will band together temporarily before acquiring harems of their own.

The stallion needs constant vigilance to protect the band from danger. Wolves, mountain lions, bears, and humans find it next to impossible to sneak up on the ever-watchful sentinel. But his guardianship allows small room for tenderness. In time of danger, a stallion may break a faltering colt's neck to prevent its mother from dallying behind and endangering the welfare of the band.

The wild mustang has been protected only since 1971. Numbering in the millions only a century ago, the mustang today is represented by some 1,600 individuals scattered across eleven western states. There is hope, though, that the days of hunting mustangs for dogfood with high-powered rifles fired from airplanes are over. By an act of Congress, the wild horse has finally been recognized as a "living symbol of the historic and pioneer spirit of the West."

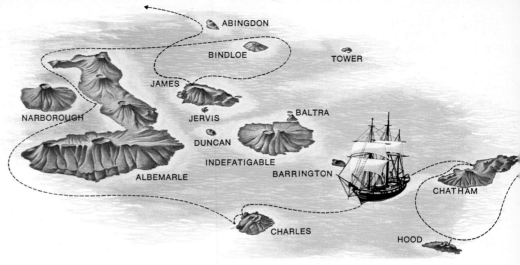

Figure 18-16. This sketch shows the path of the *Beagle* through the Galapágos Islands, as well as their volcanic nature.

NATURAL SELECTION

Searching for a clue, Darwin began to study plant and animal breeding. He knew that breeders had been able to change domestic populations, gradually, over the centuries. He took particular note of pigeons. Pigeon fanciers had developed numerous and fantastic varieties of these birds. Studying them, Darwin concluded that the differences among the varieties were so great that they should be called separate species. Yet all appeared to be descended from a single ancestral species. How did the breeders create these new breeds?

In practice, the answer was obvious. If a breeder wants to produce fine race horses, he selects from a group a few that can run faster than others and breeds them. If he wants to produce a variety of wheat that will grow in cold regions, he selects seed from the hardiest plants in his field. In short, plant and animal breeders change domestic populations by selecting and breeding individuals with the characteristics they want to preserve.

Darwin concluded that selection was also

He could not explain how the various species had evolved. When he returned to England, Darwin continued to seek the mechanism behind evolution.

a factor in the evolution of natural species. But how did it operate? What was the "breeder" that selected individuals with favorable characteristics in the wild? By chance, Darwin read Thomas Malthus's popular *Essay on the Principle of Population*, which provided the clue. Malthus argued that a population increases at a much greater rate than its food supply. Thus its members compete with each other for limited supplies of food and other resources. Malthus called this competition a "struggle for existence." In the struggle, he said, many fewer creatures will survive to carry on the species than were produced in the first place. In Malthus's book, Darwin at once found his natural "breeder":

In October 1838, that is fifteen months after I had begun my systematic enquiry, I happened to read for amusement Malthus on Population and being well prepared to appreciate the struggle for existence that everywhere goes on from long-continued observation of the habits of animals and plants, it at once struck me that under these circumstances favorable variations would tend to be preserved and unfavorable ones to be destroyed. The result of this would be the formation of new species.[1]

After reading Malthus, Darwin saw that only certain individuals within a population survive and produce offspring. It seemed probable that these would be individuals with favorable characteristics for surviving

374

Figure 18-17. The rock pigeon pictured at bottom right is the ancestor of the other four types, which were developed by pigeon fanciers for exhibition.

in a particular environment. Individuals less favorably endowed for that environment would be less likely to survive and to leave offspring. Here, then, was a natural system of selection that was identical in principle to that of the plant and animal breeders. In each case a selected group of individuals was "allowed" to produce offspring. In domestic populations, humans do the selecting. In natural populations, natural events do the selecting by "allow-ing" only the best-adapted to survive and reproduce. The effect of this **natural selection** would be to produce offspring well adapted to their environment.

Darwin might have explained giraffe evolution like this: The giraffe population would tend to increase faster than its food supply. Suppose its original food supply was the leaves on low-hanging branches. There would be some giraffes with slightly longer necks who could also reach the leaves on slightly higher branches. As the low branches became depleted, the shorter-necked giraffes would be undernourished. Having better nutrition, the longer-necked giraffes would be more likely to leave offspring. The offspring in turn would tend to inherit this favorable characteristic, and some might even have slightly longer necks than their parents. They would thus be better adapted to their environment, more likely to survive and produce offspring, and so on.

The changes in the proportions of light and dark forms in the peppered moth population, discussed at the beginning of this chapter, can also be explained by natural selection. Remembering that many birds feed on moths, can you suggest how the changes came about? Similarly, how about the drug-resistant staph?

Acceptance of Darwin's theory

It was almost two years to the day after the *Beagle* had docked in England that Darwin finished reading Malthus's book and thereafter conceived the idea of natural selection. That was October 3, 1838. But it was nearly four years after that, June, 1842, before Darwin put his idea down on paper. This penciled, 25-page abstract was enlarged during the summer of 1844 into a manuscript of 230 pages. However, neither of these statements of his theory was published. He showed them only to a botanist friend, Joseph Hooker. Darwin then turned his attention to the study and classification of barnacles.

In 1856, at the urging of three friends—Lyell, Hooker, and Thomas Huxley—Darwin began to prepare his theory for publication. During the summer of 1858, he received a paper from an English naturalist working in southeast Asia. The paper gave Darwin a tremendous shock, for in it Alfred Russel Wallace had outlined a theory of natural selection that was exactly the same as Darwin's own. Darwin had spent most of twenty years in collecting evidence that

Figure 18-18. This fine Merino ram is the product of artificial selection, achieved by interbreeding over many generations of sheep.

would support his theory. But here was a fellow scientist with the same idea in a form that was ready to be published.

Darwin asked for advice from Hooker and Lyell, the latter of whom was just beginning to accept his friend's theory of evolution. They advised him to prepare a joint paper with Wallace. This paper would include part of his 1844 essay and an 1857 letter to the American botanist Asa Gray in which he outlined his theory, along with Wallace's paper. The joint paper was published later in the summer of 1858, and thus both scientists were credited with the theory.

The joint publication barely caused a stir in the scientific community. But the publication one year later of Darwin's *On the Origin of Species*, in which he presented both his theory and his evidence, started a storm. The first edition was sold out on the day it was published. Darwin had cast doubt on special creation and denied the fixity of species. In later publications he went on to suggest the possibility that humans were descended from an ape-like ancestor. Lyell, Hooker, and Huxley, by their active championship of Darwin's theories, further inflamed the already furious controversy.

There were weaknesses in Darwin's theory, which his antagonists soon discovered. Actually, Darwin himself had already pointed out and discussed many of these weaknesses. One was his admittedly poor understanding of heredity. Since Mendel's paper had not been published yet, Darwin could not have known anything certain about genetic processes. Without this, he could not explain how specific traits are passed on from parent to offspring. Still, Darwin's theory of evolution by natural selection has proved to be one of the greatest hypotheses of modern biology, and it forms the basis of the theory accepted by most scientists today.

ADAPTATION AND SELECTION

In later editions of the *Origin of Species*, Darwin adopted the phrase "survival of the fittest" to explain his theory of natural selection. According to Darwin, the "fittest" organisms were the winners in the "struggle for existence." His choice of words was perhaps unfortunate, for it has led to considerable misinterpretation of his theory. While Darwin was careful to note that "struggle" did not necessarily mean physical combat, later proponents were not. Physical aggression is only one kind of competition for survival. Darwin stressed that flowers in a field or trees in a forest may also be said to "struggle" for available water, soil, and sunlight. These less conspicuous forms of competition have at least as great an impact in determining the survivors.

The "fittest" members of a species have commonly been supposed to be the strongest or toughest. Again, this narrow interpretation is misleading. While strength may play a role in determining which members survive and leave offspring, it is rarely the most important factor. For example, no matter how strong a mule may be, most mules are sterile and cannot reproduce. Among the peppered moths, body color is the crucial factor in determining which individuals survive and therefore reproduce.

The fitness of an individual is therefore

Figure 18-19. The wild rose on the left is strikingly different from its descendant, the American Beauty rose at right which has been developed through artificial selection.

measured by its reproductive capacity. Certain individuals in a population are more likely to reproduce, or produce more offspring than others. Usually these are the individuals best adapted to their environments, and they tend to pass on their favorable characteristics to their offspring. These offspring in turn are better endowed to survive in their environment; they live longer than the less well-endowed individuals, produce more offspring, and so on. This difference in the rates of reproduction between the better-adapted and the more poorly-adapted members of a species is referred to as **differential reproduction.**

Differential reproduction is the determining factor in evolution. The best-adapted individuals contribute the most genes (in the form of the most offspring) to the genetic pool, thus gradually changing the genetic proportions of the population. And, as we have said, evolution is change in the genetic make-up of a population through time.

In modern evolutionary theory, natural selection is thus considered not the "survival of the fittest" but the differential reproduction of individuals. It is this differential reproduction that constitutes the adaptation of species to their environments. Natural selection can work in several ways, depending on the environment. In a relatively stable environment, it tends to eliminate individuals with unfavorable genetic variations, and to conserve the characteristics already present in the population as a whole. This process is called **stabilizing selection.**

In a changing or unstable environment, differential reproduction will tend to produce, over the generations, a population that is better adapted to the changed environment. If the environment continues to change in the same direction—to become colder or dryer, for instance—the characteristics of the population may go on changing in that direction also. When natural selection works in this way, it is known as **directional selection.** The increased resistance of houseflies and other pests to DDT is

an instance of directional selection in response to the increased presence of DDT in the flies' environment.

SUMMARY

Genetic variation that takes place over a period of time is called evolutionary change; it can be human-induced or can occur naturally. Fossil remains provide direct evidence of life forms that no longer exist on earth. The study of the history of life through the examination of these fossils is called paleontology. Such history is reconstructed through radioactive dating of fossils or through the assumption that the older a form of life is, the deeper in rock strata its fossil remains will be found. The arrangement of fossils in time is known as the fossil record.

A change in pigment caused by industrial pollution is called industrial melanism. A good example is seen in the peppered moth population in England. This evolutionary change, which has occurred since 1850, has increased the frequency of a dark-pigmented variation of the peppered moth. This dark moth is well camouflaged when it rests on tree trunks darkened by accumulations of industrial soot. A similar quick evolutionary change has occurred in several species of bacteria since the introduction of antibiotics in the 1940s. Within ten years, antibiotic-resistant strains of bacteria evolved which are proving very difficult to control.

Most modern scientists believe that all modern species have evolved from earlier species, which in turn evolved from primitive forms of life. Indirect evidence for this is provided by studies of comparative embryology and anatomy. These studies reveal a variety of homologies which indicate that many seemingly unrelated modern species have evolved from common ancestors.

The theory of evolution was slow to be accepted because early scientific evidence for it was far from complete. Furthermore, the theory conflicted with popular religious beliefs. Geology was the first science to move toward acceptance of evolution, although such theories as catastrophism, uniformitarianism, and progressionism often obscured the basic concept.

Lyell, who accepted the Great Chain of Being theory, nevertheless made a major contribution by presenting evidence that the earth was much older than had been supposed. Lamarck also accepted the Great Chain of Being theory, but believed that species evolved over time and moved up the chain. The mechanism he proposed to explain how evolution had occurred is called the inheritance of acquired characteristics. Modern knowledge of genetics has proved this theory wrong.

Darwin's theory of evolution, conceived during his voyage to the Galápagos Islands, was based on "survival of the fittest" in the natural struggle for survival. He saw that there was a natural system of selection in which only the best-adapted individuals were "allowed" to survive and reproduce. This natural selection then produced offspring well adapted to their environment. Darwin's theory of natural selection was flawed by his lack of understanding of genetic processes, but it still forms the basis of the accepted modern theory of evolution.

The modern theory of adaptation and selection states that the fitness of an individual is measured by its reproductive capacity. Differential reproduction is the difference in reproductive rate between the better-adapted and the more poorly adapted members of a species. It is the determining factor in evolution. Over time, it will tend to produce a population better adapted to a changing or unstable environment.

Review questions

1. What is evolutionary change? What influences can bring it about?

2. What relatively direct evidence do we have for evolution?

3. In what ways might a single fossilized bone provide clues to the structure and habits of the animal it came from?

4. Why must the fossil record always remain incomplete? What types of animal are likely to be missing or poorly represented?

5. Describe the evolutionary change that has taken place in the peppered moth. What is such a change called?

6. Explain why the medical use of antibiotics has proved to be a mixed blessing. What are the implications for the future?

7. How do comparative anatomy and embryology provide further evidence for evolution?

8. List several reasons why the theory of evolution was slow to be accepted after its introduction.

9. What is the theory of special creation? How did early scientists apply it to geological findings?

10. Distinguish between uniformitarianism and progressionism.

11. What was the Great Chain of Being theory?

12. Describe Lamarck's theory of evolution. What is his hypothesis called?

13. On what observed evidence did Darwin first begin to formulate his theory of evolution?

14. Describe Darwin's theory of natural selection. Give a hypothetical example of how this process might work.

15. What important weakness was present in Darwin's theory?

16. Give an example of how "survival of the fittest" might affect a plant species; an animal species.

17. What is the measurement of an individual's fitness for survival?

18. What is differential reproduction? What are its long-term effects on a population?

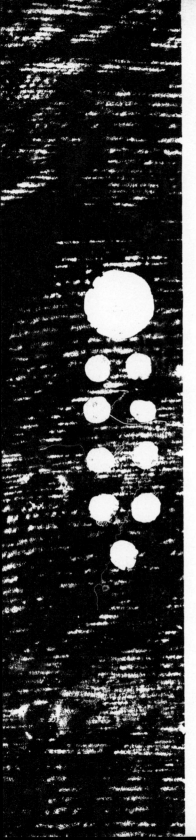

Origin of Species

At the height of the controversy over Darwin's theory of evolution through natural selection, it was considered very amusing to draw a cartoon showing Darwin's head on a monkey's body, or to ask his supporters, "Are you descended from an ape on your father's or your mother's side?" Such banter was fun, but it settled no issues. Actually, the theory of evolution does not hold that humans are descended from any present-day form of ape or monkey. Rather, it claims that monkeys, apes, and humans are all descended from some common ancestor. Moreover, that ancestor was only one of various mammals that are believed to have been descendants, in turn, of a still earlier common ancestor. Ultimately, most scientists think, every mammal, living or extinct, can be traced back to a single ancestral species, itself an offshoot of the reptiles. This poses a new question. How can we explain the evolution of these many species out of one?

Darwin's theory gives us a clue, but not a complete answer. Darwin showed, fairly convincingly, that populations of animals or plants can change through differential reproduction in response to environmental pressures. But this alone does not explain why the offspring of one species should become so different that we can regard them as two or three or a dozen species.

Our study of genetic variation in populations, in chapter 17, suggests that once two populations are separated, they are likely to evolve in slightly different directions. This is because of the many different factors that can influence gene frequencies and the transmission of genes from one generation to the next. An important mutation may occur in the first population but not in the second. Individuals from a third population may migrate into the first population con-

Figure 19-1. Some of these beetles bear little resemblance to one another, and others look very much alike despite minor differences. All of them are probably descended from a common ancestral species. While none of the beetles shown are known to interbreed under natural conditions, it is possible that some of them might be able to interbreed under artificial conditions. Can you suggest some possible circumstances in which such interbreeding might occur?

tributing new alleles to its gene pool, but may not migrate into the second population. Over many generations, these factors could give rise to two recognizably different populations. Would these two populations be different species? And what would explain the separation into two populations in the first place? Let us begin with the first question.

WHAT IS A SPECIES?

"Species" comes from a Latin word used in the Vulgate translation of the Bible to express what the King James version trans-

lates into English as "kind." The plants and animals were commanded to produce offspring "after their kind"—according to their species. So, in Darwin's day, a species was regarded as a group of organisms that looked alike and could produce offspring together.

The definition seemed reasonable, but it contained a hidden pitfall. This was the assumption that any organisms that could interbreed would also look alike. Actually, for the vast majority of organisms, scientists simply did not know whether this was true or not. Scientists had been naming and classifying organisms for centuries, but they had done it mainly on the basis of looks and

382

structure. Often, though not always, they did have evidence that similar organisms bred with each other. But they almost never had evidence that could prove that there was no interbreeding between dissimilar organisms. Could such-and-such a red-spotted beetle breed with such-and-such a red-and-yellow-spotted beetle? They assumed it could not, but they seldom performed breeding experiments to make sure. The assumption made sense, so long as species were thought to be specially created, fixed, and unchanging. If each species of beetle had always been as it now was, there would be no reason for dissimilar beetles to interbreed.

Even after the theory of evolution was generally accepted, in the early twentieth century, most scientists still felt that similar appearance and interbreeding went together. Their reasoning now was based on genetics. They thought that as a species evolved into a form that was well adapted to a particular environment, it gradually lost all of its gene alleles except those that were most suitable in that environment. Only one allele would be left for each site on the chromosomes—for a specific coat color, eye color, or claw length. All members of the species would be homozygous for that allele, unless they happened to carry a rare mutation. So, of course, there would be almost no chance for variation within the species.

However, as we could guess from the Hardy–Weinberg principle explained in chapter 17, alleles are not that easy to get rid of in a population. And the 1930s brought experimental proof of this. Theodosius Dobzhansky, studying a California species of *Drosophila*, discovered that the natural wild populations of this fly showed signs of a great deal of genetic variability. Evidently the gene pool contained many alleles, not one, for most sites on the chromosomes. This finding had several important implications. One was that a scientist could no longer take for granted that two different-looking organisms belonged to different species. A fly with long wings and a fly with stubby wings

might be different forms of the same species. In special circumstances there might even be a whole population composed mostly of stubby-winged flies, which could interbreed with another population composed mostly of long-winged flies. However different the two populations might look, they would form a single species.

Today, therefore, scientists increasingly prefer to define a species as a group of populations that potentially or actually interbreed among themselves. Similarity of appearance may offer a clue, but the criterion is the ability to interbreed and produce fertile offspring.

Such a reproductive definition of species is simple enough in principle, but it runs into problems in practice. For one thing, we are still using many species classifications that were set up under the older definition. In many cases, scientists still do not know whether these "species" are really unable to interbreed with one another—that is, whether they are truly separate species in the reproductive sense. For instance, suppose a botanist finds three types of oak tree, with recognizably different leaves, in a single forest. His books tell him that they are different species. But are they? Can each be fertilized only by pollen from its own type of tree, or will pollen from one of the other types do as well? The botanist can easily find out by cross-pollinating the flowers and planting the resultant acorns. Or he may discover obvious examples of natural cross-breeding. But the forest contains hundreds of other groups of plants, animals, fungi, and microorganisms. Each group may or may not be a distinct species. It could take a lifetime just to identify them all, let alone to check out whether they are true species or not.

Again, suppose two lizard populations live on opposite sides of a river. Members of one population are dark brown with many small white blotches; members of the other population are lighter brown with a white underside. Since neither population can cross the river, they have no opportunity to interbreed. Are they separate species? Or, if they are brought together, will they mate and produce fertile offspring? If they do not, is it because they cannot, or because they have not learned to recognize each other as potential mates? Long and painstaking study may be needed to find out.

All of this may seem like a mere matter of definition, and not very important. It is certainly true that whether or not we are right in calling something a species, this does not change the evolutionary processes by which new species are formed. But mistakes in our classification of species may interfere with our learning what those evolutionary processes are. In the following sections we shall look at several examples and explanations of species-forming, or **speciation.** It is important to remember that a good deal of our knowledge about speciation is based on what we think must have happened in the past in order to produce what we think are species today. We may eventually find that some of the "species" are not really separate species after all. If so, we may have to rethink some of our ideas about speciation. However, let us look at the main outlines as they are currently understood.

GEOGRAPHICAL ISOLATION: FINCHES ON COCOS ISLAND

Four hundred miles north of the Galápagos and about three hundred miles southeast of the Central America mainland lies Cocos Island, a rugged, isolated dot of volcanically formed land. Among its inhabitants are a population of finches, small birds about the size of sparrows. Most finches are seed-eaters, but the finches on this island are tree-dwelling insect-eaters, with narrow, pointed beaks that can probe into cracks and crevices for food. The original founders of the population must have come from elsewhere—perhaps blown from the mainland by the westerly trade winds. Most biologists are inclined to think that these

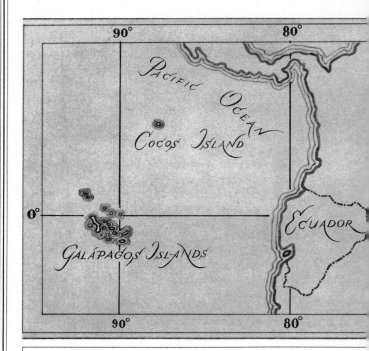

Figure 19-2. Cocos Island and the Galápagos Islands lie off the western coast of South America. Comparison of the island birds has provided biologists with a plausible explanation of how new species may arise.

Figure 19-3. The ground finch has a large, blunt beak that is especially suited to cracking seeds. It is possible that finches like this one were the original founders of the Cocos Island population.

384

Figure 19-4. The heavily forested Andes Mountains on the northwest coast of South America illustrate a lush and hospitable environment. Compare this environment with that shown in Figure 19-5.

Figure 19-5. James Island is one of the Galapágos Islands, volcanic in origin and largely covered with basaltic lava. What possible adaptations might finches from the South American forests have to make in order to survive in such an inhospitable environment?

founders were ground-dwelling seed-eaters, with short, thick, beaks. If so, how can the present population be explained?

Our understanding of genetics and natural selection suggests the following scenario: The original population had the genetic potential for many variations, but the variations had not been expressed under the competitive pressures of mainland living. On the island, there was a plentiful supply of food and living sites, and few competitors. Therefore the finch population expanded, and genetic variations were expressed. Some individuals had variations that allowed them to make use of other food—insects, fruit, nectar—as well as seeds. These individuals may have tended to mate with others like themselves, thus establishing a tendency toward specialized seed-eating, insect-eating, and other varieties. This process of "spreading out" from one variety into several varieties, each adapted to a different aspect of the environment, is called **adaptive radiation.** So long as there was plenty of food and nest space, all the varieties could thrive and produce offspring. Eventually, though, the population probably began to outrun the total food supply. When this happened, the selective advantage would go to individuals that could utilize the widest variety of foods. Even better would be the ability to utilize a food source that the other finches could not use. Very likely the insect-eaters, with their somewhat longer, thinner beaks, had such an advantage, for they could reach insects where the others could not. Thus they were better nourished than the others, left relatively more offspring, and eventually became the sole type of finch on the island.

Several selective forces can be seen at work here. If our scenario is correct, adaptive radiation resulted in a number of somewhat specialized varieties. Then competition for food set up a situation in which one of the varieties had a reproductive advantage over the others. But the potential for all these variations existed in the gene pool of the original finches on the island. So it must have existed also in the mainland population from which they supposedly came. Why, then, did not insect-eating varieties become established on the mainland? The answer seems to be that, on the mainland, other bird species gave the finches too much competition for insects as a food source. In a few small places, insect-eating might have been able to flourish, but the finches in these places continued to interbreed with the rest of the seed-eating population. Before a fully specialized insect-eating variety could evolve, there had to be a break in the exchange of genes—the **gene flow**—between birds living where insect-eating was an advantage and birds living where it was not. The geographic isolation of Cocos Island allowed for such a break. That is, it formed an **isolating mechanism.** It kept mainland finches and island finches from interbreeding. Therefore the Cocos Island finch population, living in an environment very different from that of the mainland, evolved in a different direction. By the time the insect-eaters became the only variety on the island, they probably constituted a new species.

ISOLATING MECHANISMS: FINCHES ON THE GALÁPAGOS ISLANDS

The Galápagos Islands—that archipelago that so stimulated Darwin's interest—have finches, too. Like those of Cocos Island, they are generally thought to have originated from ground-dwelling, seed-eating immigrants. But whereas Cocos Island still has only a single species, the Galápagos—if the usual classifications are correct—have thirteen. Furthermore, as many as ten of these species can be found on a single island. Adaptive radiation would explain the birds' increase in variety, enabling them to take advantage of many food sources, just as they probably did on Cocos Island. But what are the isolating mechanisms that could split this radiated population into so many sepa-

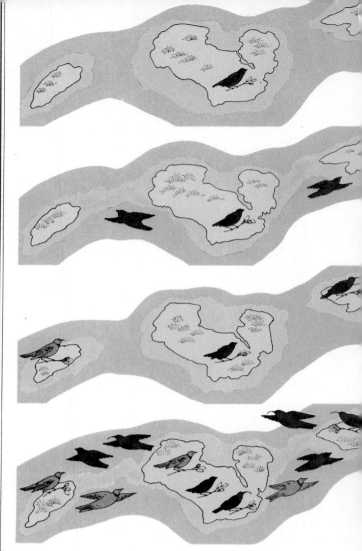

Figure 19-6. A theoretical explanation of how the Galápagos Island finches may have differentiated into separate species. At first, the isolating mechanism was geographic separation (top). Birds migrated to separate islands (second from top). In time, new species arose on the separate islands (third from top). Then when various species came in contact again (bottom), the inability to interbreed became the isolating mechanism.

Figure 19-7. The Galapágos Island finches are readily distinguishable from one another by the shapes of their beaks. Beside each head, the d of the particular type of finch is shown.

INSECT EATER

WARBLER FINCH

IMARILY INSECT EATERS PLUS SOME PLANTS

ECTIVOROUS
FINCH

MEDIUM INSECTIVOROUS
TREE FINCH

SMALL INSECTIVOROUS
TREE FINCH

TOOL-USING
FINCH

MANGROVE
FINCH

PRIMARILY PLANT EATERS PLUS SOME INSECTS

LARGE GROUND
FINCH

MEDIUM GROUND
FINCH

SMALL GROUND
FINCH

P-BEAKED
UND FINCH

CACTUS GROUND
FINCH

LARGE CACTUS
GROUND FINCH

PLANT EATER

VEGETARIAN
TREE FINCH

rate species—and then keep them separate, even on a single island in the group?

Geographic isolation seems likely to have been the first mechanism. The individual islands of the Galápagos are near enough together that individuals can fly from one to another, but far enough apart that land birds such as finches are not likely to do so very often. Probably some members of the original finch population migrated to each of several islands. There they established separate breeding populations. Once this happened, there was little or no gene flow between the islands, and it was possible for the populations to vary in different directions. Some islands may have had slight environmental differences that favored variations already existing in the gene pool. Also, different mutations may have occurred in the various populations. Because each breeding population was small, an advantageous variation or mutation could be distributed widely through the population in relatively few generations. Other mutations, neither advantageous nor harmful, might become established through the chance fluctuations of genetic drift, as described in chapter 17. Thus, on one island, there might evolve a tree-dwelling finch that fed on both seeds and insects. On another island there might be a ground-dwelling seed-eater rather larger than the original immigrants. On still a third, there might develop a smaller ground-dwelling seed-eater, and so on. In addition to size, dwelling-place or habitat, and food source, these varieties might differ in other ways—color, song, the materials they used for nesting, the ways they courted a mate.

After a century or so, a few small, greenish tree-dwelling insect-eaters from one island might migrate to another island. This one might be occupied by large, black, ground-dwelling seed-eaters. What would happen? To begin with, the two groups probably would not interbreed. Their difference in size would make mating difficult. Also, they would probably not recognize each other as potential mates. A tree-dwelling female would be genetically programmed to respond to the courtship of a tree-dwelling male. The size, color, song, and nest site of a ground-dwelling male would not arouse her interest. So there would now be two quite separate breeding populations of finches on a single island. Even though they would now be in close contact, their different colors, sizes, habitats, and behavioral patterns would serve as isolating mechanisms, just as

tree-dwelling species might become strictly insect-eaters. In the meantime, they would probably be undergoing other phenotypic changes as well. Some of these might be a result of founder effect, through their small group of ancestors from the other island. So, after another century or so, the tree-dwellers on this island might be recognizably different from their relatives still living on the other island. Suppose now that some of

MESSAGES FROM OLD BONES

How old is the human species? The answer to that question has been steadily pushed back in recent years. Particularly revealing have been a number of finds in East Africa. In 1972, at East Rudolph in Kenya, Richard Leakey found hominid (human-like) fossils 2.8 million years old. In 1974, in north central Ethiopia, D. Carl Johanson discovered remains that are thought to date back over 3 million years. And more recent discoveries by Mary Leakey, at Laetolil in Tanzania, have been dated to 3.35–3.75 years ago.

What sort of people were these hominids? Many of the remains, as usually happens, consist of jaws and lower teeth. These are similar in size to those of modern humans. For this reason, they are thought to belong to the

genus *Homo*, rather than to more ape-like forms found in the same areas. *Homo*, of course, is our own branch of the primates. Mary Leakey does not speculate on the life-style of the Laetolil individuals. But Johanson, speaking of the Ethiopian hominids, suggests that the small jaw size may tell us important things about their behavior. He feels that they may well have been eating meat, walking upright, and using tools and weapons. If so, they developed these behaviors a good deal earlier than anthropologists once thought possible.

The finding of these older and older remains may change our understanding of human evolution. Did it begin much earlier than has been thought? Or did it proceed much faster? For that matter, did it occur at all? The answers to these questions, in turn, may give us some new insights into how evolution proceeds in general.

geographical separation had done before. In effect, they would now be considered two species.

Probably things would not stop here. The tree-dwelling immigrants would be in competition with the ground-dwellers for seeds, but not for insects. If the seed supply began to run short, natural selection would probably favor insect-eating over insect-and-seed-eating in this population. Thus the

them returned to that island. What might be expected to happen? How many species might there now be on the two islands? By such processes as these, most biologists think, the thirteen finch species on the Galápagos Islands arose.

Isolating mechanisms and environmental niches
We have cited several sorts of isolating

mechanism that may have played a part in the speciation of the Galápagos finches. Let us look at these mechanisms a bit more closely.

Organisms, as we already know, are closely tied to the environment they live in. This environment includes both living and nonliving elements. Each species in a particular habitat serves certain functions in relation to the other species living there. The sum total of these functions is called its **niche.** (We shall consider niches in somewhat more detail in chapter 23.) The species feeds on some organisms and is fed on by others. It lives in burrows or holes or nests, is active by daylight or at night, breeds at certain seasons. In all these activities it affects and is affected by other organisms. Many different species may coexist in a single geographic environment, but only if they have different niches. For instance, two closely related species of flour beetle often compete for the same food. However, one species flourishes best in hot, humid conditions and the other in cooler, drier conditions. Consequently, the two species most successfully reproduce in different parts of the storage bin, and competition between them is reduced.

When two populations compete for the same niche, the process of natural selection will tend to increase the percentage of any variations that reduce the competition and allow the populations to occupy different niches. The evolution from seed-and-insect-eating to strict insect-eating in our hypothetical finch species is an example. The only way these variations can be maintained and increased in the population is through differential mating. If individuals with the useful variation mate with each other, their offspring will be likely to have the variation also. If they mate with individuals that lack the variation, fewer of the offspring will have it. Consequently, any differences that encourage such differential mating will also be favored. This is thought to be one of the bases for the establishment of isolating mechanisms.

The isolating mechanisms in our finch population included differences of habitat (tree versus ground), color, size, and behavior (kinds of food, song, courtship activities). In other species, different times of breeding may create a seasonal isolation. Two weeds in a field may look very much alike, but we may find that one flowers in spring and one in early summer. As far as reproduction of each type is concerned, the other type might just as well not exist.

In the finches, the size difference might not be enough in itself to interfere with mating, but in some species it definitely does. Imagine a tiger trying to mate with a house cat. Such a structural difference, which prevents or strongly discourages individuals from copulating, is a mechanical isolating mechanism.

Isolation by postmating mechanisms

All the isolating mechanisms we have identified so far are **premating** mechanisms. They prevent or discourage the act of mating, and thus effectively divide populations into separate species. But suppose that somehow, despite these barriers, individuals of two closely related species manage to mate with each other. Will they produce offspring? If they do, what will the offspring be like?

Occasionally such a mating does produce offspring, called **hybrids,** that combine the traits of both parent species. Now and then these hybrids are healthy and fertile, but more often they are not. Sometimes the egg and sperm cannot combine and form a zygote, or the embryo is abnormal and dies before birth. Sometimes hybrids are born and reach maturity, but are sterile. This condition is known as **hybrid sterility.** A mule, for example, is the offspring of a mare and a male donkey, and is usually sterile.

In other cases, the hybrids may be fertile and produce offspring, but genetic flaws show up in later generations, producing **hybrid breakdown.** All of these conditions are known, collectively, as **postmating**

THE SPERM WHALE

"Thar she blows!"

None of the seamen glances up at the lookout. Each man knows his job, one which may cost him his life. Oarsmen and harpooners take their positions as the boats are lowered into the sea. There is excitement and fear in every heart as they prepare to engage in a life-or-death struggle with a sperm whale.

Today, whaling is not the incredibly dangerous adventure that Melville immortalized in *Moby Dick*. Modern technological developments have radically altered the business of killing whales in the twentieth century. But the very success of modern whaling may ultimately result in the extinction of the sperm whale and the end of the industry.

The sperm whale is the largest of the toothed whales, with males reaching a length of about 60 feet and females about 30 feet. It is easily distinguished from other whales by the huge fat-filled forehead that makes up the entire front third of its body. Found in every ocean, sperm whales are especially common around the equator, where squid—their favorite food—are most abundant.

The fossil record provides few clues to the whale's ancestry. The most widely accepted theory presumes that it evolved from a small terrestrial mammal which may have lived in estuaries, feeding on crustaceans or small fish. Gradually, the mammal may have adapted to deeper water, using its tail for propulsion and its forelimbs for balance and steering. The useless hind legs eventually disappeared, and the five fingers fused into a paddle-like flipper.

Many other changes would have had to occur before the animal became fully adapted to aquatic living. It acquired a streamlined shape that could overcome water resistance. The outer ear was reduced to a tiny hole, and hair was abandoned in favor of a foot-thick layer of oil-impregnated blubber for insulation. The whale became not a new kind of fish but a mammal adapted for ocean living.

A second theory suggests that no such terrestrial ancestor ever existed. Instead, the whale developed from a line of mammals that were aquatic from the beginning. Since the fossil record is so scanty, neither of these theories is likely to be conclusively proven in the near future, and the whale's ancestral origins will remain a mystery.

Like all mammals, whales must breathe, but they can hold their breath for very long periods of time. The sperm whale surfaces to breathe every 30 to 60 minutes, spouting out a high-arching plume of air and water vapor through a blowhole on top of the head. Its respiratory system is much more efficient than that of land mammals. Each breath replaces nearly four-fifths of the air in its lungs, and it can utilize at least 13 percent of the oxygen in the air, as compared to only 5 percent utilized by land mammals.

How does the sperm whale navigate and find food in the dark ocean depths? This is where the animal's fat-filled head comes in handy. As it swims, the whale emits sharp clicking sounds. Scientists believe that the forehead is used much like a sonar screen, to locate objects in the whale's vicinity as echoes are bounced off them.

That head full of fat is largely responsible for the sperm whale's near extinction at the hands of humans. The head contains oil and spermaceti, a waxy substance from which the animal gets its name. The head of a large male may contain as much as five tons of spermaceti. Whalers in the old days used to cut a hole in the head of a killed whale and bail out the oil in buckets. Whale oil was highly valued and used in ointments, cosmetic creams, candles, and fuel for heat and light. The waxy spermaceti is still an important ingredient of automobile lubricants, candles, and lipstick.

The sperm whale was also once hunted as the source of ambergris, a brown, waxy substance produced in its intestine as a response to irritation caused by indigestible portions of swallowed squids. Used as a fixative in the manufacture of perfume, ambergris was once literally worth its weight in gold. Until it was discovered in the sperm whale's intestines in the middle of the eighteenth century, ambergris had always been found washed ashore, its origin unknown. The largest lump of ambergris found to date was over six feet long and weighed almost half a ton.

Although the meat of the sperm whale is a potentially valuable source of protein, it was once discarded by whalers. Today, it is eaten in Japan, Britain, Germany, and Norway. But most whale meat is purchased by European pet owners to feed their cats and dogs, and by American fur ranchers to feed their foxes and minks.

There is no need for the sperm whale to be hunted today. Adequate substitutes, if not perfect ones, are available for the manufacture of all products for which whale oil was once used. And yet, the killing of sperm whales is currently at its all-time peak. The International Whaling Commission has fixed a minimum length for sperm whales that may be killed, but since it lacks the power to enforce its rulings many whalers continue to slaughter sperm whales with no apparent concern for survival of the species. Unless strict international controls are exercised, the whaling industry will destroy itself as it methodically destroys the entire whale population.

isolating mechanisms. They occur, apparently, because the genes or chromosomes of the two parent species are incompatible in one degree or another.

Postmating mechanisms are valuable as "backup" insurance against the breakdown of species differences. But how do they come about? Premating mechanisms are favored by natural selection, through the favorable or unfavorable offspring they produce. But postmating mechanisms produce no offspring—or none that are of value for future reproduction—so they cannot be selected. Probably such mechanisms arise through mutations that occur in one or other of the parent species, after these species have already been separated by premating mechanisms.

Unless a postmating isolating mechanism develops, there remains the chance, however slight, that the two species might re-evolve into one. That is, if brought together under suitable conditions, they might adjust to one another's differences and began to interbreed. But once a postmating barrier exists, the species are permanently and irrevocably separate.

Polyploidy

A special type of postmating isolating mechanism is of particular interest to plant biologists. This is **polyploidy,** the possession of extra haploid sets of chromosomes. (See chapter 11 if you have forgotten about haploid and diploid chromosome numbers.) Polyploidy apparently occurs when meiosis is somehow disrupted in one of the parent organisms, producing a gamete with an extra set of chromosomes. In animals, a polyploid zygote usually dies. In plants, though, it often results in a plant that is larger and more vigorous than either parent. The polyploid plant is not fertile with ordinary diploid plants. However, it is fertile with other polyploids of the same sort, such as can be produced by vegetative reproduction of the original polyploid. Gardeners take advantage of this to produce some of the hybrid giant strains that take prizes at flower shows and agricultural fairs.

ALLOPATRIC AND SYMPATRIC SPECIATION

When speciation is thought to have taken place in the way we suggested for the Galápagos finches, it is called **allopatric speciation.** That is, the crucial events that made the species unlikely (or unable) to interbreed with each other took place while the populations were geographically separated. The differences between them were originally selected in response to separate environmental pressures, or may even have developed by chance. Only later, if and when the populations were brought into contact again, did these differences have any value as isolating mechanisms.

Species that now occupy different geographic areas, and thus have no opportunity to interbreed, are called **allopatric species.** Like our imaginary lizards early in the chapter, these are the organisms that give biologists headaches over classification. Are they species or not? Can they interbreed or not? Interestingly, human encroachment on natural breeding areas of birds is producing evidence that at least some allopatric "species" are not separate species at all. Some birds, forced into closer contact with each other, have begun interbreeding naturally and producing viable, fertile hybrids. So the classifications are being revised to describe these several "species" as variants of one species.

Some biologists believe that speciation can also occur without a period of geographic isolation. Such a process is known as **sympatric speciation.** This may occur when competition for a single ecological niche favors a certain amount of specialization, such as we suggested for the Cocos Island finches. For instance, suppose there is a population of insect-eaters that usually catch insects in flight, and that the popula-

Figure 19-8. These research biologists have produced a hybrid tobacco plant by fusing genetic cells from two different species. This method makes it potentially possible to cross-fertilize widely divergent species at the cellular level. Possible applications of this technique include the development of entirely new crops and the improvement of existing organisms.

Figure 19-9. Micromanipulators enable investigators to perform microsurgery on individual cells. Such techniques may have been used to produce the hybrid tobacco plant in figure 19-8. Here the nucleus of a cell is being transferred to an adjacent cell.

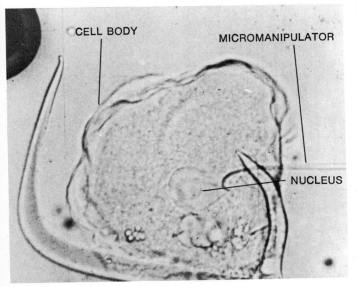

CELL BODY

MICROMANIPULATOR

NUCLEUS

tion is in danger of outgrowing its food supply. Some of the birds may be able, also, to pick insects from tree bark. Therefore these birds will probably come to spend much of their feeding time in trees, where they can feed with less competition from the other birds. Here they may tend to meet more potential mates of their own sort, and fewer of the other sort. Thus the competition has favored a specialization (picking insects from tree bark) and the specialization has favored the development of separate breeding groups. Once the separate breeding groups are established, the specialization is likely to continue, and true isolating mechanisms may eventually appear. Sympatric as well as allopatric speciation may have played a role in the formation of the Galápagos finch species.

SUBSPECIES, RACES, BREEDS

What do we call two populations that are recognizably different and occupy different geographical regions, but will interbreed if brought together? Such groups are known as **subspecies** or **races.** Thus, eastern and western white pine, though they are usually considered separate species, may in fact be subspecies of a single species.

Subspecies may, and presumably do, occur as stages in the evolution of separate species. However, it would be a mistake to think that every subspecies is such a stage. It would be even more of a mistake to think of them as existing in order to become separate species. As we have seen, between allopatric populations there is no way for natural selection to reinforce isolating mechanisms as such. Therefore there is no particular selective reason for isolating mechanisms to develop. Two allopatric subspecies might remain clearly different, yet able to interbreed, for an indefinite length of time. If isolating mechanisms do develop, they do so purely by chance.

A special case of subdivision within

393

species occurs when humans take a hand in the selection. Artificial selection to suit human purposes results in **breeds** or **varieties** of animals and plants—Holstein, Guernsey, and Black Angus cattle, or iceberg, Boston, and oakleaf lettuce. Many of these breeds and varieties would not remain distinct under purely natural conditions, because they have no true isolating mechanisms. A Black Angus bull will mate with any cow he comes across, whatever breed she happens to belong to. Furthermore, the calf she produces will probably be fertile. Yet these breeds and varieties are as genetically distinct as any natural subspecies.

Dogs are the classic example. Any visiting biologist from Mars, surveying a beagle, a German Shepherd, a Doberman, and a Pekingese, would conclude that they represented four separate species. Furthermore, a paleontologist would say that they were descended from four different wolf-like ancestors. If we had found these breeds in the fossil record, we would surely have classified them as separate species. Yet all of them, and all the rest of the more than one hundred recognized dog breeds, are considered members of a single species, *Canis familiaris*. Virtually all of them can mate with one another. Furthermore, unless the breeds of the mating pair are drastically different in size or body build, the offspring will usually be healthy and fertile. Likewise, members of nearly all the breeds can recognize each other as potential mates—as anyone knows who has watched the gathering of the canine clan whenever a neighborhood bitch is in heat.

To add to the confusion, some animals that are not classified as *Canis familiaris* can interbreed with dogs. Among them are the coyote, *Canis latrans;* the grey wolf, *Canis lupus;* and the Texan red wolf, *Canis rufus.* The Eskimos, incidentally, have long known this, and have taken advantage of it to keep their line of sled dogs strong. Since Alaskan huskies form a small population, they tend to become inbred and lose some of their

vigor after a few generations. So, from time to time, the Eskimo will take a female husky in heat and tether her away from the compound, out of reach of the male dogs. Usually a male wolf will scent the female and approach. Since she looks more or less like a wolf, snarls like a wolf, and smells like a wolf, he will recognize her as a mate and proceed accordingly. In due course the pups, vigorous with the infusion of new genes from the *Canis lupus* gene pool, will arrive to swell the local husky population. They will be as much *Canis lupus* as *Canis familiaris*, but everyone will consider them dogs, not wolves.

On the other hand, the wolf would probably not recognize a female chihuahua as a potential mate. He might be attracted by her scent, but on seeing her he might have trouble deciding whether to mate with her or eat her. If they did mate, the gametes would be unlikely to unite successfully; even if zygotes were formed, the pups would probably be born dead or defective. In this case, therefore, reproductive isolation exists. Yet indirectly, through mating across half a dozen breeds of gradually increasing size, genes from the chihuahua gene pool could eventually be mingled with those from the wolf gene pool.

As we can see, therefore, when organisms useful to humans are involved, the species classifications become even more confused than in the case of wild populations. However, the confusion can at least serve to keep us aware of the structure of assumptions on which our understanding of speciation is built. Perhaps next week someone will find evidence that those thirteen species of Galápagos finches had somehow gotten themselves differentiated before they ever left the mainland, without benefit of geographical isolation. Or perhaps it will turn out that they are not species at all, and sometimes successfully interbreed. Then a whole new set of explanations would be needed, and there could be a hue and cry as furious as that which arose over Darwin's *Origin of Species.*

Figure 19-10. The small strawberries shown here are wild field berries. From such plants, botanists have been able to breed the much larger polypoid berries commonly sold in markets. Aside from their larger size, what other obvious differences can you see in the polyploid strawberries?

SUMMARY

Most present-day scientists believe that primates are all descended from a common ancestor, and that ultimately every mammal can be traced back to a single ancestral species. Darwin's theory suggests some clues as to how these many species evolved out of one.

In Darwin's day, a species was regarded as a group of organisms that looked alike and could produce offspring together. Even in the early twentieth century, scientists still felt that similar appearance and interbreeding went together. They believed that once a species became adapted to a particular environment it lost all alleles except those which were best suited to that environment. Later genetic findings disproved this theory. Scientists now define a species as a group of populations that potentially or actually interbreed and produce fertile offspring.

In practice it is often difficult to tell whether certain organisms are separate species in the reproductive sense. This may interfere with our understanding of the processes which bring about speciation. However, certain theories about the causes of speciation are now widely accepted.

If an original population has genetic potential for a number of variations, many of these may not be expressed. However, a condition of geographic isolation, with plentiful food and lack of competition, may allow the population to expand and these variations to be expressed in adaptive radiation. As the population grows and competition increases, the reproductive advantage will lie with those individuals possessing variations with the greatest survival value.

A number of other isolating mechanisms can split a radiated population into many separate species and then keep them separate. These include structural and behavioral differences, which would contribute to the formation of different breeding populations. Adaptation to different ecological niches is another such isolating mechanism, which tends to increase the percentage of variations that reduce competition. Seasonal isolation may be created by different times of breeding. Mechanical isolating mechanisms include structural differences which make mating unlikely. All these are known as premating isolating mechanisms.

Postmating mechanisms occur when the genetic makeups of the two parent species are incompatible. Hybrid sterility, such as is seen in mules, may prevent the offspring from reproducing. If they do reproduce, hybrid breakdown may occur when genetic flaws appear in later generations. Once a postmating isolating mechanism exists, the two species will remain permanently separate.

Polyploidy is a special type of postmating isolating mechanism. It is the possession of extra haploid sets of chromosomes, and probably occurs when meiosis is disrupted in one of the parent organisms. In animals, the polyploid zygote usually dies. But in plants it may result in a vigorous offspring which is fertile only with other similar polyploids.

Allopatric speciation occurs when the events that will ultimately prevent species from interbreeding take place while the populations are geographically separated. Sympatric speciation may occur when competition for a single ecological niche favors specialization which leads to separate breeding groups.

Subspecies, or races, are populations that appear different and occupy different geographical regions but will interbreed if brought together. In some cases they may represent stages in the evolution of separate species. Artificial selection practiced by humans results in breeds or varieties, many of which would not remain distinct under natural conditions.

Review questions

1. What was the nineteenth-century defin-

ition of "species"? Give a modern definition.

2. What is speciation?

3. Explain how the Cocos Island finches might have evolved into their present form.

4. What is adaptive radiation?

5. Name some of the isolating mechanisms that may have influenced the development of the Galápagos finches.

6. What is an environmental niche? What happens when two populations compete for the same niche?

7. What is seasonal isolation? Give one or more examples.

8. Distinguish between premating and postmating isolating mechanisms. Name two varieties of each.

9. Give one or more examples of hybrid sterility.

10. How does hybrid breakdown occur?

11. What is the long-term significance of postmating isolating mechanisms?

12. What is polyploidy? How does it occur? Does it have any adaptive significance?

13. Distinguish between allopatric and sympatric speciation.

14. Construct a hypothetical set of situations that might result in sympatric speciation.

15. What is a subspecies? Does every subspecies represent a stage in the evolution of separate species? Why?

16. Distinguish between a breed and a subspecies. Under what circumstances might a breed remain distinct under natural conditions? Which one is likely to have the greatest long-term survival advantage?

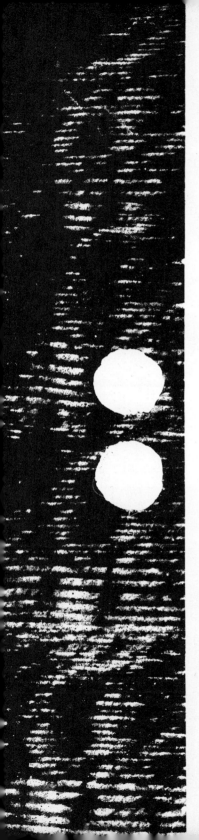

Order out of Chaos

"The world is so full of a number of things," wrote the nineteenth-century author Lewis Carroll. Probably no one is more aware of this than the biologist. It has been estimated that well over a million animal species, and half a million plant species, have so far been discovered and classified. Living species yet to be described may number in the millions. And some half-billion other species, now extinct, are thought to have existed in the past.

For various reasons, all of these organisms must be named and classified. First, biologists must be able to compare different life forms with one another, in order to make generalizations and to understand possible relationships. Also, they must be able to communicate with one another about these life forms. The common names of species vary widely: the same flower may be called chicory or cornflower, the same animal a skunk or a polecat. Thus, a commonly accepted scientific name must be established. The biological sub-discipline that names and classifies organisms is known as **taxonomy.**

PRINCIPLES OF CLASSIFICATION

The modern science of taxonomy began early in the eighteenth century with the work of the Swedish scientist Carolus Linnaeus. Linnaeus proposed dividing the living world into two large kingdoms, the plants and the animals. The basis of his system was simple. Organisms that were structurally similar were classified in the same category.

Linnaeus' great contribution to taxonomy was simplification of the names. Before his work, naturalists could describe organisms only by long descriptive phrases.

A Samoyed dog, for example, would have had to be described as *Canis albus, oculis obscuris, pilus longus, cauda curvata* —the white dog with dark eyes, long hair, and curly tail. Linnaeus devised a shorter method, still used today, known as **binomial nomenclature.** In this system, each kind of organism is given two Latin names. The first name indicates its **genus,** the second its **species.** Thus, human beings belong to the genus *Homo* (man) and the species *sapiens* (wise). By convention, both genus and species names are italicized; the genus name is capitalized, but not the species name.

Linnaeus' system contained a hierarchy of seven levels, or **taxa.** From highest (most inclusive) to lowest (least inclusive), these are: **kingdom, phylum, class, order, family, genus, species.** All species that appear to be structurally related to one another are grouped in the same genus, all related genera in the same family, and so on. As knowledge of the diversity of life grew, other categories, such as subphyla and superclasses, were inserted between the major groups.

Modern taxonomists see the structural similarities among organisms as indicating probable **phylogenetic,** or evolutionary, relationships. Most scientists believe that each group has evolved from a single ancestral species. The more similar one group's ancestor was to another group's ancestor, the more nearly related the present-day groups are thought to be.

Scientists have reached these conclusions by studying a variety of evidence. For one thing, there are the structural homologies and embryological evidence that we described in chapter 18. Further similarities can be observed at the cellular and molecular levels. Thus, cells in many different organisms—but not all—have organelles of the same kinds. Such similarities, when carefully evaluated, help to build up the picture of overall taxonomic relationships.

How many kingdoms?

Only the lower taxonomic categories—

Figure 20-1. This student of taxonomy is grouping ducks according to their types of beak and feathers. What other obvious categories for classification are visible here?

Figure 20-2. Linnaeus proposed to divide the living world into plant and animal kingdoms. There can be no doubt that these pine trees are plants.

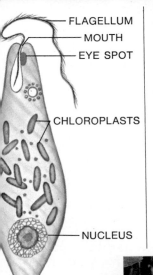

— FLAGELLUM
— MOUTH
— EYE SPOT

CHLOROPLASTS

— NUCLEUS

uglena viridis

Figure 20-3. This red-spotted newt is obviously an animal. So far, Linnaeus' system continues to be applicable.

Figure 20-4. Here the two-kingdom system ceases to be helpful. This single-celled *Euglena* has characteristics of both plants and animals. It is a member of the kingdom Protista.

Figure 20-5. These edible morels belong to the kingdom Fungi.

family, genus, and species—represent anything like truly natural groupings. All taxa have been, in a sense, created by the human mind. It is not surprising, then, that there are still some conflicting ideas about which organisms belong in which group (even at the species level, as we saw in chapter 19). There is even controversy about the highest taxon, the kingdom.

For Linnaeus, the living world consisted of two kingdoms—the plants and the animals. The plants were rooted in place and manufactured their own food. The animals, by and large, could move about and obtained their food from other organisms. But it later became apparent that this is not the whole story. For example, there are the single-celled organisms. Some of these seem more like plants, others more like animals, while others combine characteristics of both plants and animals. For this group, a third kingdom, the Protista, was proposed.

The three-kingdom scheme ran into difficulty when it was found that some single-celled organisms differ from the rest in a key respect. Bacteria and blue-green algae are procaryotic cells; they lack a nucleus with a membrane, and many of their other organelles are structurally different from those in other single-celled creatures. And the viruses present still another taxonomic problem. They are parasites, and reproduce by injecting their genetic material into the cells of plants and animals. There is some doubt whether they should even be considered living organisms.

Some biologists, therefore, divide the living world into four kingdoms, excluding the viruses. The kingdoms are the Monera (bacteria and blue-green algae), Protista (other single-celled organisms and all fungi), Metaphyta (multicellular plants) and Metazoa (multicellular animals).

However, there is some question as to whether the fungi should be grouped with the Protista. After all, many fungi are multicellular. Yet they are not like most plants, for they do not make their own food. On the other hand, they do not appear to be ani-

401

mals: they do not move, nor do they ingest food as animals do. Rather, the fungi absorb food through the walls of their cells.

In view of this difficulty, the biologist R. H. Whittaker, in the 1950s, proposed a five-kingdom system that places the fungi in a kingdom of their own. Whittaker bases his taxonomy partly on the way in which organisms obtain their nutrients: photosynthesis, absorption, or ingestion. The procaryotic **Monera** and the eucaryotic, mainly single-celled **Protista** utilize all three methods. Above these are the three mainly multicellular kingdoms: **Plantae** (photosynthesis), **Fungi** (absorption), and **Animalia** (ingestion).

The present book follows the Whittaker system. This is not to say that the Whittaker system is perfect, and all other systems are wrong. Rather, in the light of present knowledge, the Whittaker system seems to fit the facts best. As more is learned about the diversity of life, this system too may be replaced by another.

MONERA

The monerans are the most numerous organisms on earth. They are also the simplest in structure and the smallest, which explains why we seldom notice them around us, on us, and in us. All monerans are procaryotic cells, lacking a well-defined nucleus. Instead, they have a nuclear area that lacks a membrane, but contains a single large, circular chromosome. The moneran also lacks an endoplasmic reticulum, mitochondria, lysosomes, plastids, and a Golgi apparatus—organelles found in eucaryotic cells.

The kingdom Monera is generally considered to contain two large phyla, the blue-green algae (**Cyanophyta**—about 2,500 species) and the bacteria (**Schizomycetes** —about 1,500 species). However, some modern taxonomists feel that the blue-greens are really a type of bacteria, and

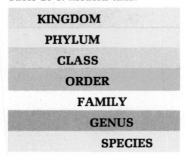

Table 20-1. Modern taxa.

| KINGDOM |
| PHYLUM |
| CLASS |
| ORDER |
| FAMILY |
| GENUS |
| SPECIES |

should be considered members of the same phylum. For one thing, the slimy outer layers of the blue-greens contain a substance known as a mucopeptide, which is found in no other algae. But it is found in the cell walls of bacteria. Second, the viruses associated with blue-green algae are very similar to those associated with bacteria.

Bacteria occur in three basic shapes. The **coccus** is round or oval; the **bacillus** is rod-shaped; the **spirillum** is like a spiral or corkscrew. Although bacteria are basically single-celled organisms, there are some that join together in clusters or filaments of various characteristic shapes. But even these multicellular forms contain only one kind of cell.

Bacteria may be classified by the ways in which they get their energy. They have more different means for this than any other group of organisms. Some are autotrophs, others are heterotrophs. (Refer back to chapter 3 if you have forgotten the meaning of these terms.) Furthermore, unlike plants, not all the autotrophic species are photosynthetic; and some of the heterotrophs do photosynthesize. Some bacteria cannot live without oxygen, others cannot live with it. Still others are facultative or "part-time" anaerobes, performing some reactions when oxygen is available and others when it is not.

The energy reactions of bacteria are basically similar to those of other organisms— photosynthesis, glycolysis, fermentation, and so on. However, bacteria differ in some of the materials they use for these reactions.

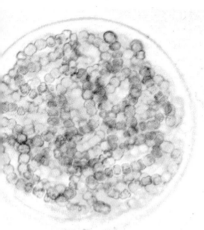

Figure 20-6. *Nostoc*, a blue-green alga, belongs to the kingdom Monera. Note that it lacks a well-defined nucleus.

Figure 20-7. Certain bacteria, as shown here, are enclosed within a tough covering which protects them against changes in their environment.

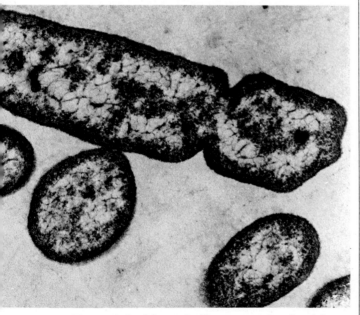

Bacterial chlorophyll, except in the blue-greens, is not the chlorophyll-*a* of all green plants. Perhaps more importantly, bacteria use many different substances as electron donors and acceptors for the energy reactions. For example, plants get hydrogen electrons for photosynthesis by oxidizing water. Many photosynthetic bacteria, however, get them by oxidizing hydrogen sulfide. In the process, the bacteria do a service to plants, for if hydrogen sulfide were left alone and allowed to build up to high concentrations in the ground, it would make the soil too acid for plants to grow. Similarly, we saw in chapter 4 that bacteria in the digestive tracts of cattle and some other animals utilize cellulose. In doing so they break down the cellulose into substances the animals can digest.

Bacteria in general have an undeserved bad reputation as agents of disease. While it is true that some bacteria do cause disease in plants and animals, most are harmless, and even useful to their hosts. *Escherichia coli*, which lives in the human digestive tract, probably outcompetes harmful bacteria and keeps them from getting a foothold in our systems. Then there are the bacterial saprophytes. They reduce decaying organic matter, allowing its components to be recycled into the soil and water where they can be used again by other organisms.

PROTISTA

The kingdom Protista contains mostly unicellular organisms. Although in some species the individual cells are grouped together in colonies, yet the cells are not specialized into tissues or organs. All protists are eucaryotic. They include slimy-feeling, plant-like "algae," animal-like "protozoa," and some groups that combine characteristics of both plants and animals.

Plant-like protists

There are five so-called algal phyla among the protists. The smallest group, with about 350 species, are the **Euglenophyta,** which exhibit both plant and animal characteristics. Many, such as *Euglena*, have chloroplasts and photosynthesize. Others lack chloroplasts and are heterotrophs. Unlike

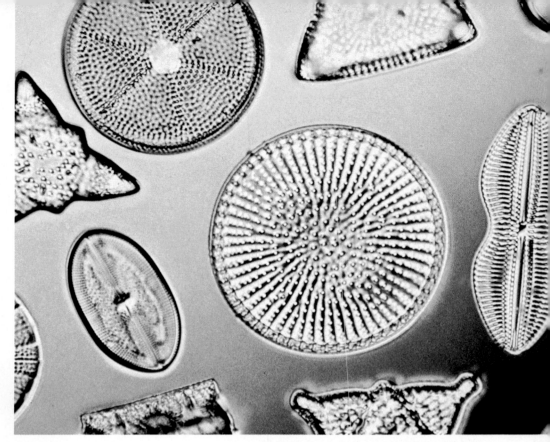

Figure 20-8. Diatoms make up a large part of the phytoplankton that are an important link in the oxygen cycle.

most algae, the euglenophytes lack a cell wall, having instead a membrane similar to that in animal cells. Nearly all euglenophytes have flagella, and are therefore motile, like animals.

The phylum **Chrysophyta** contains about 17,000 species. It includes the golden-brown and yellow-green algae and the diatoms. The phylum's name is derived from the yellowish pigments that color its members ("chrysos" is Greek for "gold").

Both the golden-brown and the yellow-green algae are found primarily in fresh water. Most of the golden-browns are unicellular or colonial, though some are multicellular. Some varieties have either one or two flagella, while others have none. The yellow-greens are usually more or less spherical or else filamentous. The filamentous species are **coenocytic:** that is, they contain many nuclei, without intervening cell walls. Both groups have hard cell walls, which may contain silica or calcium.

By far the most numerous chrysophytes are the diatoms. These organisms are found in both fresh and salt water. They make up a large part of the phytoplankton, the tiny ocean organisms that provide the basic food for much other marine life. The phytoplankton form an important link in the earth's oxygen cycle, for they produce vast amounts of oxygen during photosynthesis. This oxygen is released into the water, diffuses into the atmosphere, and is used by other organisms throughout the earth.

The diatom's cell wall is hard enough to be considered a shell. In some parts of the world, undecomposed shells of billions of diatoms form deposits known as diatomaceous earth. The organisms store energy in the form of oil as well as starch. Some scientists think that the oil synthesized by diatoms over millions of years may have created an important part of the earth's petroleum deposits.

A third algal phylum is the **Pyrrophyta,** or

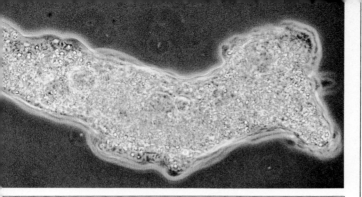

Figure 20-9. *Amoeba* is a protozoan, belonging to phylum Sarcodina.

fire algae, with about 1,000 species. They are named for their typical red color, or perhaps for the phosphorescent light that some of them give off at night. Most of the algae in this group are unicellular. One species, *Gonyaulax*, can be the cause of "red tides." They secrete nerve toxins that can be picked up by shellfish and are lethal to fish and humans. *Gonyaulax* belong to the class called **dinoflagellates** or "spinning flagellates," whose flagella spin the cell as it moves. Most dinoflagellates are photosynthetic. Their cell walls are composed of cellulose and pectin, and their characteristic red color is caused by a carotenoid pigment. Some pyrrophyte groups lack photosynthetic pigment. These obtain their nutrients by ingesting organic materials.

Also sometimes classified with the algae are the two phyla **Hypochytridiomycota** and **Plasmodiophoromycota.** These two phyla are difficult to place exactly. Both lack photosynthetic pigments, and some taxonomists regard them as fungi (hence the "-mycota" in their names). But both groups seem to have more in common with the protists. They look and behave much like the true slime molds, which we shall discuss with the fungi, Both phyla are heterotrophs. Some species of Hypochytridiomycota feed on dead and decaying plant and animal remains, while others are parasites on living organisms. All Plasmodiophoromycota are parasites, feeding on fresh-water algae and fungi, and also on some land plants. They do serious crop damage to plants of the cabbage family.

Other algal phyla are mainly multicellular and are classified in the kingdom Plantae.

Animal-like protists

The protozoans are the animal-like or "preanimal" protists. They are heterotrophic, ingesting algae, bacteria, other protozoans, and various organic particles. Most species reproduce asexually by dividing, but some can also reproduce sexually by fusion or by **conjugation.** In conjugation, the nucleus of each cell divides by meiosis, producing two haploid nuclei. The two cells join, and one nucleus of each cell migrates into the other cell, where it joins with the nucleus that is still there. Then the two cells separate again. Each now has a recombined nucleus containing genetic material from both the cells.

Protozoans are found in virtually all environments, including soil, water, and the bodies of plants and animals. They are variously classified, often into five main phyla. Three of these—Zoomastigina, Sarcodina, and Ciliophora—can move under their own power. The other two—Sporozoa and Cnidosporidia—cannot.

Members of phylum **Zoomastigina** move by flagella. Some, such as the genus *Trypanosoma*, are parasites. Certain trypanosomes, when transmitted to humans by the bite of the tsetse fly, cause the deadly African sleeping sickness. Another species, found in tropical and subtropical America, produce Chagas disease, which can severely damage the heart and other organs.

Individuals in phylum **Sarcodina** travel by means of a **pseudopodium,** or false foot. This is formed by a portion of the cytoplasm near the edge of the cell, which pushes outward, drawing the rest of the cell after it in a flowing motion. Probably the best-known member of Sarcodina is *Amoeba*, which under the microscope resembles a tiny blob of jelly.

Ciliophora, as the name suggests, are covered with cilia, which enable them to swim around in search of food. One ciliate, the

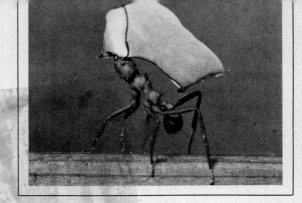

FUNGUS-GROWING ANTS

It is a hot tropical morning. The gardeners awake and set out to do their daily chores. Some go out and gather materials for enriching the soil. Others stay close to home and tend the crop. They are self-sufficient, and will eat only what they produce through long hours of hard work in the garden. The only thing unusual about this well-organized community is that the crop is a fungus and the gardeners are ants.

Fungus-growing ants belong to the tribe called Attini, and are found only in the Western hemisphere. Probably they originated in the tropics, but they are now found throughout South America and over much of the United States. The varieties of fungus they grow constitute their sole diet. These fungi have not been found anywhere else, and are believed to grow only in the carefully planted and tended ant gardens.

The fungus-growing ants are leaf-cutters, especially well adapted for their work. Many have long spindly legs which end in hooks that enable them to climb trees in search of leaves, and strong mandibles for cutting the leaves to a manageable size. The leaves, however, are never eaten, since they lack sufficient nutritional value to support these large and active insects. Instead, they serve as a substrate upon which the edible fungus is grown.

Following odor trails laid down by earlier explorers, the ants travel in long lines as they seek out leaves, stems, flowers, and insect excreta to carry back to their garden. The garden itself generally resembles a honeycomb of gathered plant and insect matter, held together by strands of growing fungus. It is built underground in a space cleared by the ants, usually supported by roots and surrounded by open space at the top and sides. Sometimes the ants will build a garden on stones from which the soil has been removed, creating an excellent drainage system.

Once an ant arrives at the nest with its portion of leaf, it chops the leaf into still smaller pieces, licking the pieces and often depositing an anal fluid on them. It then uses its forelegs and mandibles to push the leaf fragments into place. As the garden grows larger, the ants plant tufts of fungus at intervals along this carefully prepared substrate.

One of the mysteries of the Attini is why only a single variety of fungus grows in each garden despite the overwhelming likelihood of random contamination. It was once suggested that the ants actively weed out any alien growths. Now, however, scientists believe that a substance in the insects' saliva inhibits the development of foreign spores and at the same time promotes the growth of the right fungus.

The central figure in any colony of fungus-growing ants is the queen. Winged

and much larger than the others, the queen starts a new colony when she leaves her home nest with a small pellet of fungus in a pouch below her mouthparts. In a suitable location she then digs a hole and begins her own garden, using her excrement as the substrate. Next, she lays eggs of two kinds. Those that are larger and richer in yolk are eaten, providing the queen and her first brood with energy. The smaller eggs hatch into workers who will help to enlarge the fungus garden. As more ants are hatched, the garden grows larger, and the larger it grows, the more ants it can support.

An ant colony is a well-organized, cooperative society. Each of its members has a distinct social function, and the ants within a colony vary greatly in size and appearance, depending upon that function. Smaller, younger ants stay in the garden to cultivate the fungus and care for the eggs and larvae. Worker ants constantly lick the pupae to aid in the birth process, and groom the queen and each other throughout their lives. Larger workers add leaf-cutting to their daily labors. Soldier ants, the largest of all, remain near the queen and protect the nest. Their strong mandibles can deliver a nasty bite and are capable of cutting a neat, crescent-shaped hole in a piece of tough shoe leather.

Communication is a necessity for such a complex society. Ants can communicate in their underground chambers by means of vibrations that they perceive through the soil. Two ants of the same species will approach each other with wide-spread antennae, touching their antennae briefly as they meet before proceeding with their tasks. It is believed that ants use chemical signals to express such responses as alarm, attraction, recognition, and determination of social caste.

Humans are not always appreciative of the ants' labors. Leaf-cutting ants of one species present a threat to pine trees in the southern United States, starting at the top of a tree and neatly clipping off the pine needles as they work their way downward. Another species damages coffee and citrus crops in South America. Most species will consider a wide variety of materials that might be useful in growing their fungus crop. The ants observed by one experimenter, for example, were especially keen on cornflakes.

In the tropical rain forests where they originated, the leaf-cutting ants pose no threat to the ecology, since an abundant supply of leaves is always available. Unmolested by the fierce army ants with whom they share their habitat, the leaf-cutters tend to keep to themselves. In the long run, their introduction of organic matter into the soil of these tropic areas has great survival value to other creatures, long after the nest has been abandoned by the industrious fungus-growing ants.

Paramecium, possesses a "mouth," or oral groove, into which food particles are carried on water currents produced by the cilia. All ciliates have two nuclei, known as a **macronucleus** and a **micronucleus.** The macronucleus governs the cell's metabolic processes. The micronucleus produces the macronucleus during reproduction; it is also the nucleus that participates in conjugation.

All members of phylum **Sporozoa** are parasites, and nonmotile. A few species are dangerous to humans. Certain species of the genus *Plasmodium*, for instance, are responsible for malaria. They are carried in the bodies of *Anopheles* mosquitoes, and are injected into the human bloodstream when the mosquito bites a human.

Finally, the **Cnidosporidia** are also potentially dangerous to organisms economically important to humans. They establish themselves in species such as honeybees, fish, and silkworms. Occasionally, they may proliferate so rapidly that they cause epidemics among these animals. One species, *Nosema apis*, is particularly virulent and has been responsible for lethal epidemics among honeybees.

FUNGI

The kingdom Fungi is divided into two phyla. The **Eumycophyta,** or true fungi, contain an estimated 90,000 species. The **Myxomycophyta,** or true slime molds, are unusual organisms, generally considered to be more primitive in origin.

The fungi range in size from microscopic yeasts to giant puffballs, and are all saprophytes. They are unlike most plants in that they lack chlorophyll. Therefore they cannot photosynthesize and must live off other organisms. Their chief role is as decomposers.

Many fungi are important to humans. The truffle and the morel, for example, are sought after as food delicacies. Yeasts are

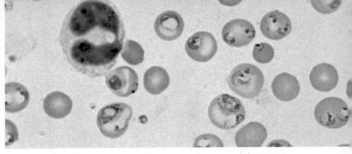

Figure 20-10. The members of genus *Plasmodium* are responsible for the disease malaria.

Figure 20-11. These mushrooms are typical members of the kingdom Fungi. They belong to phylum Eumycophyta.

Figure 20-12. The *Penicillium* mold is the original source of penicillin. Certain other blue molds are used to ripen cheeses such as Roquefort.

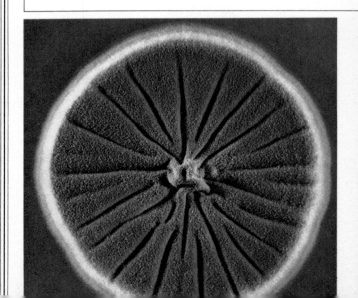

essential for making leavened bread and alcoholic beverages. Molds produce antibiotics that are used to control diseases. Molds, rusts, smuts, and mildews parasitize food plants, causing disease and crop loss.

The body of a multicellular fungus, during most of its life cycle, is a multinucleate mass known as a **mycelium.** This consists of a network of filaments called **hyphae.** The hyphae penetrate the dead or living substrate on which the fungus grows, secrete digestive enzymes, and absorb the liquefied nutrients. Reproduction in most fungi is rather complex, and may involve up to five cycles. Sexual reproduction is by spores, and some species reproduce asexually as well.

The true fungi can be divided into four classes, according to their method of spore production. The **Phycomycetes,** or algal fungi, are the simplest. They may reproduce either sexually or asexually. In either case, spores are produced in sporangia at the tips of the hyphae and are dispersed by the wind. Some phycomycetes are found in freshwater environments or in damp soil. Others, such as the common black bread mold *Rhizopus,* are terrestrial. *Rhizopus* will grow on bread, some fruits, and other substances. Other phycomycetes include water molds, downy mildews, and blights.

The **Ascomycetes,** or sac fungi, include the yeasts, molds, powdery mildews, truffles, and cup fungi. Most of these are terrestrial and are relatively more complex than the phycomycetes. They are called sac fungi because in sexual reproduction they form long sacs, known as **asci,** in which the spores—usually eight—are produced. They can also reproduce asexually. *Penicillium,* the original source of the antibiotic penicillin, is a member of this group.

The **Basidiomycetes,** or club fungi, include the smuts, rusts, mushrooms, toadstools, puffballs, bracket fungi, and stinkhorns. What we think of as mushrooms and toadstools are the temporary sexual **fruiting bodies,** or spore-bearing bodies, of these fungi. The fruiting bodies contain club-shaped cells called **basidia,** each of which produces four haploid **basidiospores.** Very few club fungi can reproduce asexually. However, their mycelia may continue to grow almost indefinitely, periodically putting up a new crop of fruiting bodies. Perhaps the best-known basidiomycetes are the mushrooms. Some of these are deliciously edible, others are deadly poison, and only an expert can tell which is which by sight.

The fourth class of true fungi are the **Fungi Imperfecti,** so-called because no sexual reproductive stages are known for them. Some taxonomists think that most of them will eventually turn out to be ascomycetes. They cause a number of diseases in plants and animals. One species is responsible for ringworm and athlete's foot in humans.

Myxomycophyta

The slime molds, or Myxomycophyta, are a curious group, unique enough to warrant a phylum of their own. They grow on rotting tree stumps, in moist soil, or on decaying organic matter in damp, woody environments. During its early life, the slime mold has no fixed shape but moves around in amoeba-like flowing fashion. At this stage, the body of one common type of slime mold is called a **plasmodium.** It is a mass of unspecialized cytoplasm that contains many nuclei and lacks cell walls. The fan-like plasmodium oozes along the ground like an amoeba, surrounding and engulfing bacteria and other substances. When food becomes scarce, the plasmodium stops moving, develops specialized sporangia, and produces spores. The spores are scattered by the wind, germinate, and give rise to zygotes that develop into new plasmodia.

Lichens

Another of nature's stranger life forms, to our eyes, is the lichen. This is a mutually beneficial combination of an alga and a fungus. Typically a lichen consists of an as-

Figure 20-13. Slime molds, such as the one shown here, are primitive fungi belonging to phylum Myxomycophyta.

comycete fungus sheltering a population of Chlorophyta, or green algae. The union allows the lichen to grow on bare rocks and in other places where neither partner, probably, could survive alone. The fungus lives on the food produced by the alga in photosynthesis, and the alga finds protection and a source of moisture among the hyphae of the fungus. Some lichens—notably *Cladonia,* or reindeer "moss"—grow in the barren arctic and sub-arctic regions, where they provide food for reindeer and other grazers. The lichens also serve as pioneer organisms, or first organisms, in their environment. As they grow on the rocks, they gradually break down the rock surface, providing the beginnings of soil where plants will later grow.

PLANTAE

There are about 300,000 multicellular plant species on earth. Most are found on land. The great majority of plants share two principal characteristics. The first is photosynthesis, by which they synthesize their own food. The second is the alternation of generations, which was described in chapter 12.

It is customary to divide kingdom Plantae into two very general subkingdoms: **Thallophyta,** which have relatively unspecialized tissues, and **Embryophyta,** which have more specialized tissues and also form embryos as part of sexual reproduction.

Thallophyta

The Thallophyta are the mainly multicellular algae. All of them possess photosynthetic pigments. Most possess other pigments as well, and they are classified on the basis of their pigmentation. They are found in both fresh and salt water, and vary in size from a single cell to the huge seaweeds that may grow to 50 meters (about 150 feet) or more in length. ~~All are nonmotile.~~

The **Chlorophyta,** or green algae, are believed to represent the group whose ancestors gave rise to terrestrial plants. The phylum contains about 6,000 species and is one of nature's major producers. Most species of green algae live in fresh water, but some are found in tropical seas or on land. Member species may be unicellular, filamentous, colonial, or coenocytic in form. Reproduction may be sexual or asexual. *Volvox* is one of the colonial varieties. Its cells cluster together in a hollow sphere, and a few of them are specialized for reproduction.

The **Phaeophyta,** or brown algae, are the large seaweeds. They get their color from phaeophytin, a carotenoid pigment. About 1,000 species are known. They are found in marine habitats, often along the coast.

PATTERNS OF CHANGE

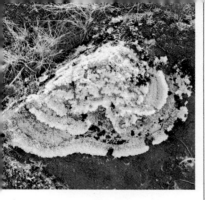

Figure 20-14. Lichens are a combination life form, composed of an alga and a fungus. They can live where neither partner would be able to survive alone.

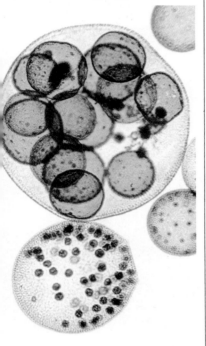

Figure 20-15. *Volvox* is a colonial variety of green alga. Some of its cells are specialized for reproduction.

Figure 20-16. In some parts of the tropical oceans red algae such as these may color the water red over a large area.

Fucus, or rockweed, with its air bladders that invite popping by beachcombers, reaches as much as three feet in length and is common on coastal rocks. The *Laminaria,* or kelps, are far larger, with crinkled, lettuce-like fronds. Brown algae are rich in potassium and nitrogen, which they absorb from the ocean water. Hence they are sometimes used as fertilizer, to replace these easily-depleted elements in the soil.

The **Rhodophyta,** or red algae, number about 2,500 species. They live mostly in the depths of clear tropical seas. Varying in length from an inch to two feet, they have numerous shapes. They contain pigments known as phycobilins, which produce colors ranging from deep pink to black. Some species—notably *Chondrus,* or Irish "moss" —are eaten by humans and animals.

The characteristic pigments of the brown and red algae are important for photosynthesis, though they do not take a direct part in it. These pigments absorb light at the wavelengths that penetrate to the depths where these algae live. Then they transfer the energy of that light to chlorophyll, which is also present in the algae. The chlorophyll performs the actual photosynthesis.

Embryophyta

With the Embryophyta, we come to the plants that are adapted to life on land. These plants differ from the Thallophyta in two principal ways. First, they all show alternation of generations. Second, their tissues are more specialized. The Embryophyta include two general groups: the **Bryophyta** and the **Tracheophyta.**

Bryophyta

The Bryophyta are simpler in structure than the Tracheophyta, though they are more complex than the algae. They include the liverworts, horned liverworts, and mosses. All of them are small. They lack true roots, stems, and leaves, with vascular tissues that would carry water, food, and minerals through the plant. Thus, substances move rather slowly from cell to cell—a method of transport that serves well enough for these low-growing plants but would not do for tall ones. Bryophytes are most common in the tropics, but many grow in temperate or even in arctic regions. All, however, require a damp environment—a bog, a swamp, a marsh, or some other moist, shaded place.

In chapter 12 we discussed the alternation of generations that is typical of land plants, and we noted that in mosses the gametophyte generation is dominant over the sporophyte generation. The same is true of most other bryophytes as well. This pattern is apparently one of the things that limit them to moist, sheltered environments.

The liverworts **(Hepaticae)** have a flat gametophyte **thallus,** or unspecialized plant body, which resembles a leaf. Root-like rhizoid cells grow from the lower surface, attaching the plant to the soil. In the genus *Marchantia,* the reproductive organs grow on stalks from the upper surface of the thallus. Fertilization takes place in the female organ, or archegonium. The sporophyte then grows out of the archegonium and remains attached to it while forming and shedding its spores. Like many other liverworts, *Marchantia* can also reproduce asexually by means of buds known as **gemmae.** The gemmae are formed in cup-like structures on the surface of the thallus.

The mosses **(Musci)** differ from the liverworts in appearance, but their reproductive organization is generally similar. We described reproduction of one moss in chapter 12. One of the more important moss varieties is the sphagnum, or peat moss. The decaying bodies of this moss make up the chief component of peat, which in some places is burned for fuel.

The horned liverworts **(Anthocerotae)** have a scalloped thallus with rhizoids. Each gametophyte cell has only one large chloroplast. The reproductive organs are sunk in the thallus, and the sporophyte consists of nothing more than a sunken foot and

Figure 20-17. Liverworts, such as *Marchantia,* require a damp, shady environment.

Figure 20-18. Club mosses are not true mosses. They are spore-bearing plants belonging to phylum Lycopsida.

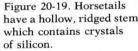

Figure 20-19. Horsetails have a hollow, ridged stem which contains crystals of silicon.

a tapering spore capsule that may range from a centimeter to two inches in length. The genus *Anthoceros*, which grows in boggy places, is the most widespread of this group.

Tracheophyta

Unlike the bryophytes, the tracheophytes possess specialized conductive tissue. There are generally considered to be four tracheophyte phyla. Apparently most primitive are those plants that reproduce by spores instead of seeds. Three phyla are entirely spore-bearing: the **Psilophyta**, the **Lycopsida** or club mosses, and the **Arthrophyta** or horsetails. Together, these three phyla contain about 900 species. The fourth phylum, the **Pteropsida**, includes by far the greater number of vascular plants now living on the earth. Altogether, there are some 260,000 species of Pteropsida. This phylum, in turn, can be divided into three main subgroups: the spore-bearing **Pterophyta** (ferns) and the seed-bearing **Gymnospermae** (cycads and conifers) and **Angiospermae** (flowering plants).

Psilophyta, Lycopsida, Arthrophyta

The Psilophyta, which probably evolved about 500 million years ago, have vascular tissue but lack true roots and leaves. Like the bryophytes, they have root-like underground rhizoids. Photosynthesis takes place in the green, branching stems, and round sporangia are produced at the tips of some of the branches. The psilophytes have all but vanished now. There are only two living genera, *Psilotum* and *Tmesipteris*. Both are found in tropical and subtropical environments.

The club mosses have true leaves and roots, and therefore slightly more extensive vascular systems than Psilophyta. The phylum gets its common name from the club-like shape of the cone, or **strobilus,** which actually consists of a compact spiral of modified leaves. The strobilus generally grows on the tips of shoots. The two living genera of club mosses are *Lycopodium* and *Selaginella*. *Lycopodium*, found in some temperate forests, is the "ground pine" often used in Christmas decorations. Most species are creeping plants, with erect branches arising from a prostrate stem. *Selaginella* are interesting in that, like seed plants, they produce both male and female spores. The gametophyte generation is very small and inconspicuous. In fact, the male gametophyte develops entirely within its microspore wall and never becomes independent at all.

The horsetails contain only one living genus, *Equisetum*, which has leaves, stems, and true roots. The hollow, ridged stem, which contains silicon crystals, sometimes ends in a strobilus. The plant has an overall jointed appearance, caused by the nodes, with whorls of branches, that occur at intervals along the main stem. The branches are often long and hair-like, giving the plant its common name. The high silicon content of the horsetail makes it an excellent pot-scourer.

Pterophyta

There are about 9,000 species of fern. Most live in tropical and subtropical habitats, but many are familiar denizens of temperate forests. Some, such as the bracken fern, have horizontal underground stems. Others, mostly in the tropics, have thick, erect stems and may grow as tall as trees. The leaves of the fern possess stomata, veins, and mesophyll with many chloroplasts.

The fern's reproductive pattern was described in chapter 12. The graceful, fuzzy "fiddleheads" that dot the woods in spring are actually the young fronds of fern sporophytes, their delicate leaflets still tightly rolled.

Gymnospermae

The gymnosperms are all trees or woody shrubs. They can flourish in a drier environment than the groups we have so far considered, and they are common in every continent except Antarctica. This wide distribution is due in part to their reproductive structures, which were described in chapter 12. As you may recall, their sperm do not need liquid water to enable them to reach and fertilize the female gamete. So, while we find gymnosperms in the humid tropical forests, we find them as well on rocky, windblown coasts and sunbaked sandhills.

most of the wood pulp for paper. Some conifers also have edible seeds (for example, pine "nuts") and leaves. However, the leaves and seeds of some conifers have been found to be poisonous.

The two other living gymnosperm classes are the **Ginkgoae** and the **Cycadae.** The Ginkgoae are represented by only a single species, the maidenhair tree or *Ginkgo biloba.* This "living fossil" with its two-

---

IS DIABETES TRIGGERED BY A VIRUS?

Diabetes takes thousands of lives annually in this country, ranking just behind heart disease and cancer. It comes in many varieties. One type, called acute onset juvenile diabetes, tends to begin suddenly in childhood or adolescence. Other types are associated with aging or overweight. All are directly caused by a deficiency or malfunctioning of a hormone, insulin.

Researchers have known for years that the tendency to diabetes is inherited. But what brings it on? In particular, why does it suddenly turn up in healthy children and teenagers? Current research suggests that the juvenile form of diabetes, at least, may be triggered by a virus.

In a recent study, two groups of mice were exposed to a virus known as coxsackie B. One group were genetically predisposed to diabetes; the other group were not. The first group developed diabetes; the second did not. This suggested that the virus alone could not cause diabetes, but that it could trigger the disease in animals that were already predisposed to it. In addition, in the diabetic mice, the virus could be seen to be attacking the pancreas. And the pancreas is the gland that manufactures insulin.

If further tests prove that viruses such as coxsackie B are indeed responsible for the onset of juvenile diabetes, then a vaccine could be manufactured. In families where a tendency to diabetes is known to exist, children could be routinely vaccinated against the virus. Juvenile diabetes could become as preventable as polio or smallpox.

Many of the approximately 1,000 species of gymnosperm are **conifers,** or cone-bearers, with thin, needle-like leaves. Common temperate-zone conifers are the pines, firs, spruces, cedars, and hemlocks. The giant California redwoods and the gnarled, ancient bristlecone pines also belong to this group.

The wood of conifers, known as soft wood, is structurally different from that of other trees. It supplies much of our lumber and

lobed, fan-shaped leaves is, somewhat surprisingly, one of the best trees for city planting, because of its high resistance to pollution.

The palm-like or fern-like cycads are mainly restricted to tropical and subtropical regions. The seeds of some of them can be eaten, but only after treatment to separate the edible starch from the poison that is also present. Many cycads are ecologically valuable, because they serve as hosts for

Figure 20-20. The air plant is an excellent example of an epiphyte. Most epiphytes grow in subtropical forest regions.

Figure 20-21. This illustration shows some of the more obvious differences between monocots and dicots.

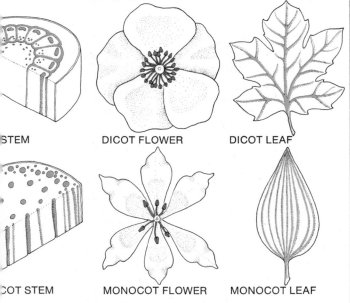

STEM DICOT FLOWER DICOT LEAF

COT STEM MONOCOT FLOWER MONOCOT LEAF

nitrogen-fixing bacteria that renew the depleted nitrogen supply in the soil.

Angiospermae

About 70 percent of all plant species are flowering plants, or angiosperms. They are the broad-leaved trees, shrubs, flowers, vegetables, and grasses that can be seen in nearly any natural environment. The flower is the reproductive organ of all members of this class. However, most angiosperms can also reproduce asexually.

There are few environments to which some flowering plant has not adapted. **Xerophytic** plants, such as cacti, have special structures that reduce water loss. **Halophytes,** or salt-marsh plants, are adapted to environments high in salt. **Hydrophytes,** or fresh-water plants, contain networks of intercellular air reservoirs which the submerged roots can draw on for oxygen and carbon dioxide. **Epiphytes** grow on other plants, usually on trees. Most of them are not parasites; they photosynthesize and produce their own food, receiving from their "hosts" only support and a high place from which they may reach the sunlight. Epiphytes are most common in the dark forests of warm-climate lands; they include orchids, Spanish "moss," and even some members of the cactus family.

The two subphyla of the angiosperms are the **Monocotyledoneae,** or monocots, and **Dicotyledoneae,** or dicots. We noted some of the differences between them in chapter 12. More obvious differences can be seen in the leaves and flowers. Monocot leaves are usually parallel-veined, and the petals and other organs of the flower are present in threes or multiples of three. Dicots, in contrast, usually have net-veined leaves, and the organs of the flower are in fours or fives or multiples of these numbers. Cattails, grasses, all cereal grains, and orchids are examples of monocots. Roses, sunflowers, and dandelions, and virtually all angiosperm trees are examples of dicots.

ANIMALIA

The animal kingdom contains more species than any other of the five kingdoms. In general, animals have developed more complex internal systems than plants or fungi. All animals are heterotrophs, and most move about, so they need sensory organs and means of locomotion. The organic food they ingest must usually be broken down before it can be used, and there are always unusable portions that must be gotten rid of. Coordination must be swifter in moving creatures than in stationary ones, so nervous systems are required. In addition, animals have transport, gas exchange, and hormonal systems, as plants do.

Most animals possess all these systems, though sometimes only in a very simple form. The systems differ from one species to another, depending on the environment and how the animal is adapted to it. Most animal phyla are best suited to a watery environment. Only in two, the arthropods and the chordates, have a substantial number of species become fully adapted to terrestrial life. Let us look at some of the largest phyla.

Porifera

The sponges, or **Porifera,** which number about 5,000 species, are probably the simplest animals. They seem to have first appeared about 500 million years ago, and they remain virtually unchanged today. Mature sponges are **sessile,** spending their lives attached to some rock or other object. They have no organs or organ systems, and their tissues are quite simple, being developed from only two basic germ layers, rather than three as in higher animals. Aside from the opening and closing of pores to admit or release water—or in reaction to some sort of danger—the sponge shows little movement. Individual cells may be highly specialized, but each acts independently—there is very little coordination.

Sponges can reproduce both sexually and asexually. Eggs and sperm are produced by amoeba-like undifferentiated cells in the central mesogleal layer of the sponge's body. These cells are known as **archeocytes,** a name that might be translated "first cells." Asexual reproduction, on the other hand, begins when **gemmules,** or small groups of archeocytes, are enclosed in a hard protective envelope, forming a kind of spore. The gemmule eventually develops into an em-

bryo, then into a young sponge. Sponges may also reproduce by regeneration. An internal skeleton is usually present, secreted by the animal itself. Bath sponges—if you can find a natural one—are the skeletons of the common *Spongia.*

Cnidaria

There are about 10,000 species of **Cnidaria.** The majority are marine organisms. The phylum includes both sessile and motile groups: jellyfish **(Scyphozoa),** sea anemones and coral **(Anthozoa),** and hydras **(Hydrozoa).** All cnidarians have radially symmetrical bodies (recall the discussion of radial and bilateral symmetry in chapter 10). The body may be either a sedentary polyp, standing upright with tentacles extended above, or a free-swimming medusa, like an overturned bowl with the tentacles hanging down below. Hydrozoans and jellyfish have both forms at different points in their life cycle. In hydrozoans, the polyp is the dominant stage; in jellyfish the medusa is dominant. The anthozoans apparently have only the polyp form.

Cnidarian tentacles are armed with stinging cells known as **cnidocysts,** with which the animal kills or paralyzes its prey. As we saw in descriptions of the hydra in earlier chapters, digestion takes place in a gastrovascular cavity. There is a nerve net, but no brain or central nervous system. Like sponges, the cnidarians can reproduce both sexually and asexually.

Platyhelminthes

The phylum **Platyhelminthes** consists of three classes: the free-living flatworms **(Turbellaria),** the **flukes,** and the **tapeworms.** Planarians are the most common free-living flatworms. They are normally found in fresh-water habitats, and are distinguished by two "eyespots" in the head region. The other two classes are parasitic. Flukes are usually tongue-like in shape and have an oral sucker with which they attach

Figure 20-22. Both sponges and corals can be seen here.

Figure 20-23. Tapeworms are long, segmented parasites. Only the scolex is shown here.

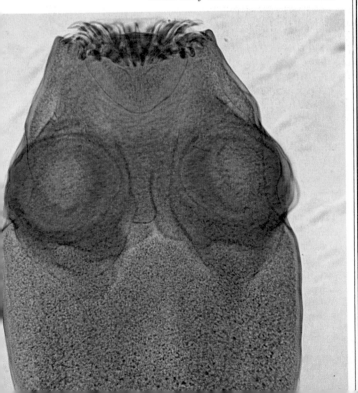

themselves to their host. Tapeworms are long and ribbon-like, with many segments or **proglottids,** and a small, grotesque "head" or **scolex** with hooks and suckers.

The flatworms are more complex than the sponges and cnidarians. Their bodies, and the bodies of all the remaining phyla we shall consider, develop from three embryonic layers rather than two. This additional layer, the mesoderm, allows for the formation of more complex tissues and organs. The respective roles of ectoderm, mesoderm, and endoderm were discussed in chapter 14.

Unlike the cnidarians, flatworms are bilaterally symmetrical. They possess a front end with some sort of sensory concentration—that is, the beginnings of a head. The turbellarians have a central nervous system, with a ganglion that serves as a simple brain. The eyespots, which are part of the nervous system, are sensitive to different intensities of light but do not form images. Specialized digestive, reproductive, and excretory systems are also present.

Nematoda

The phylum **Nematoda** includes some 12,000 known species. It includes **nematodes,** which are free-living worms, and **roundworms,** which are parasites. One of the parasites, *Ascaris lumbricoides,* lives in the human intestinal tract and usually causes only moderate problems. More dangerous to humans is the smaller hookworm that also lives in the intestine. This species of hookworm is a bloodsucker, and a serious infestation of them can produce anemia, hemorrhaging, and even death. Hookworms are often picked up from the soil by people walking barefoot.

Nematodes have a complete digestive system, with a mouth at the front end and an anus at the rear end. They also possess a **pseudocoelom,** a body cavity located between the outer body wall and the gut. This cavity contains muscles and various organs, including the reproductive organs.

The free-living nematodes are especially abundant in the top layer of fertile soil. Some of them are serious agricultural pests, causing major damage to crops such as potatoes.

Annelida

The **Annelida,** which number about 9,000 species, have segmented bodies and so are also called segmented worms. They include three main classes: the mostly marine **Polychaeta,** the **Hirudinea** or leeches, and the fresh-water or terrestrial **Oligochaeta,** including the common earthworm. We have already discussed many of the annelid body systems as they appear in the earthworm. A split in the mesoderm during embryonic development produces a fluid-filled body cavity, the **coelom.** The coelom provides the space necessary for the growth and elaboration of internal organs. It differs from the pseudocoelom of the Nematoda in that the latter is surrounded in part by mesodermal tissue, and in part by ectodermal tissue. The coelom is surrounded entirely by tissue formed out of the embryonic mesoderm layer.

Mollusca

The soft-bodied **Mollusca,** with 110,000 known species, constitute the second-largest phylum in the animal kingdom. They are highly adaptable and are found both on land and in the water. The phylum includes six classes, but we shall consider only three. These are **Pelecypoda,** the bivalves (including clams, oysters, and scallops), **Gastropoda** (snails), and **Cephalopoda** (squid, cuttlefish, and octopi). Although mollusks vary widely in appearance—who would imagine that a clam was a relative of a giant squid?—they do share a common body plan. The main elements in this plan are a **head,** a **foot,** a **visceral mass,** and a **mantle.** In many mollusks, the head has well-developed nervous tissue. The foot is a large muscle used chiefly for locomotion. In the cephalopods, the foot is subdivided and specialized into a set of sucker-covered tentacles that are used for catching prey. The mantle, a heavy membrane that covers the visceral mass, also secretes the exoskeleton, or shell.

Many mollusks have a distinctive feeding organ known as a **radula.** This is a sort of tongue with a chitinous surface, containing many small teeth. The radula is used to scrape algae and other food particles from rocks. Bivalves, however, lack a radula and feed in a different way. Water is taken in through a **siphon** between the shell halves, and passes through a **mantle cavity** under the mantle, flowing over the gills as it goes. The water also passes over a stream of mucus that flows toward the mouth. Tiny food particles in the water adhere to the mucus and are ingested with it.

Most mollusks have an open circulatory system, but the cephalopods, which are more active, have a closed system.

The gastropods are especially intriguing in one respect. During development the middle part of the body, containing the visceral mass, undergoes a 180-degree twist. The visceral mass ends up above the head in the front part of the body. This twisting or **torsion** occurs, apparently, because the internal organs have begun to develop asymmetrically—right side larger than left.

Mollusks reproduce sexually. In most cases, fertilization occurs outside the body, when eggs and sperm are released into the water and come together. However, in some mollusks, notably land-dwelling snails, fertilization is internal.

Arthropoda

The **Arthropoda,** which live in every conceivable environment, include more species than all other animal phyla together. Some 925,000 species are known, and there are perhaps thousands more still unclassified. Like annelids, the arthropods are segmented, but the segments are not internally separated by septae. The body is supported

Figure 20-24. Mollusks vary widely in appearance. Can you see any obvious similarities between this octopus and an oyster?

Figure 20-25. Fertilization takes place internally in land-dwelling snails such as the one shown here.

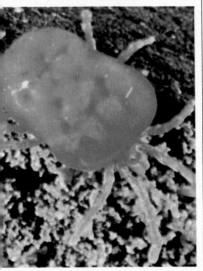

Figure 20-26. The red mite, a major agricultural pest, is an arachnid. Note the eight legs and lack of antennae.

Figure 20-27. Despite its familiar common name, the ladybug is really a beetle. Ladybugs are very helpful to gardeners for control of aphids and other insect pests.

and protected by a hard exoskeleton composed of the polysaccharide chitin. This exoskeleton might be expected to hamper movement, but it contains many joints, particularly along the appendages. (In fact, the name "arthropod" means "joint-footed.") The exoskeleton cannot enlarge as the animal grows; instead, it is periodically shed or molted. A new one is grown underneath the old, just before the latter is ready to be discarded. There are various appendages, which are used for locomotion, food procurement, and obtaining sensory information.

The three largest and most important arthropod classes are the arachnids, crustaceans, and insects. Class **Arachnida** includes about 60,000 species of scorpions, spiders, ticks, and mites, most of which are terrestrial. They have eight legs, but no antennae. Most of them are carnivores. The **Crustacea** number over 25,000 species, and are mostly aquatic. Lobsters, crabs, and shrimp are marine forms; crayfish and water fleas live in fresh water; sowbugs and wood lice are found on land. Crustaceans, unlike other living arthropods, have two sets of antennae. **Insecta** is the largest class, with about 750,000 known species. Adult insects have six legs, and most have two pairs of wings. A few insects are aquatic, but most live on land. The majority develop through metamorphosis from a larval or pupal stage, as was described in chapter 9.

Five of the twenty-nine orders of insects make up over two-thirds of all insect species. These are the **Coleoptera** or beetles and weevils (about 300,000 species), the **Lepidoptera** or butterflies and moths (about 125,000, the **Hymenoptera** or bees, wasps, and ants (about 110,000), the **Diptera** or flies and mosquitoes (about 100,000) and the **Hemiptera** or true bugs (about 40,000).

Echinodermata

Members of phylum **Echinodermata** ("spiny-skin") are all marine animals, and most of them live on the sea floor. The

419

phylum is interesting in a number of ways. For instance, the larvae are bilaterally symmetrical, but in adults this changes to radial symmetry on a basically five-sided plan. Again, echinoderms have an unusual water-vascular system, found in no other phylum. This circulates water inside the animal, and assists in locomotion and in the gripping of prey. The best-known echinoderms are starfish, sea lilies, sea cucumbers, sea urchins, and sand dollars.

As with mollusks, fertilization is external, and the larvae are free-swimming. A coelom is present. There are no true gills, but the water-vascular system probably supplies some oxygen. Bony plates called **ossicles,** embedded in the body wall, form an internal skeleton. However, the ossicles are not jointed, like a vertebrate skeleton; they either remain separate or else are fused rigidly together.

In regard to evolution, the echinoderms have attracted a good deal of interest. In some respects they seem quite primitive, yet in others they are similar to our own phylum, the chordates, which is considered the most advanced. This similarity is most pronounced in regard to embryonic development. Both the echinoderms and the chordates are **deuterostomes.** That is, the mouth is formed, not from the first opening in the early embryo (the blastopore), but from a second, later opening. All other animal phyla are **protostomes:** the blastopore forms the mouth. Other characteristic differences between protostomes and deuterostomes are in the ways the mesoderm and coelom are formed. Since the echinoderms are our only fellow deuterostomes, the starfish may be one of our closest nonvertebrate relatives.

Chordata

All members of the phylum **Chordata** share three important features, though most do not possess all of them throughout their life cycle. The first is a **notochord,** a cartilage-like rod extending the length of the body.

Figure 20-28. Echinoderms such as this starfish may be our closest non-vertebrate relatives.

Figure 20-29. Like the sharks and skates, rays such as this black sting ray have a skeleton composed entirely of cartilage.

Second is a hollow **dorsal nerve cord,** lying just above the notochord. Third is a pharynx with **pharyngeal pouches** (sometimes incorrectly called gill slits).

Most chordates are vertebrates, but there are two invertebrate subphyla, **Urochordata** and **Cephalochordata.** These subphyla bear little resemblance to other chordates. Urochordata, also called tunicates, acorn worms, or sea squirts, include some 2,000 marine species. The larvae are free-swimming and look rather like tadpoles. The adults, however, are sessile, and have lost the notochord and most of the nerve cord.

Subphylum Cephalochordata contains about 30 species, also marine. They grow to a length of about two inches and live in shallow water where there is plenty of sand for burrowing. *Amphioxus*, a much-studied species, has a permanent notochord and nerve cord, and resembles a headless fish with a flattened body.

Four classes of **fish**, along with **amphibians, reptiles, birds,** and **mammals,** make up the subphylum **Vertebrata.** The group takes its name from the backbones, consisting of a series of vertebrae, that are possessed by all members. The backbone serves either to support or to replace the notochord.

The most primitive class of fish are the **Agnatha,** or jawless fishes. The extinct members of this class, the **Ostracoderms,** appear to date back some 500 million years. Living Agnatha are the **cyclostomes,** which include only hagfish and lampreys. These have eel-shaped bodies, cartilaginous rather than bony skeletons, and smooth, scaleless skin. They are the only parasites among the vertebrates.

Class **Placodermi,** now long extinct, flourished about 200 million years ago. They had a hinged jaw and paired fins, which allowed them to leave the sea bottom and become actively swimming, full-fledged predators.

The modern **Chondrichthyes** and **Osteichthyes** show more similarity to the placoderms than to the Agnatha. The Chondrichthyes are the sharks, skates, and rays. They have a cartilaginous skeleton and leathery, scaleless skin. The Osteichthyes, or bony fish, include about 20,000 known species. Many are covered with scales, and most have air bladders. They are found in practically all fresh-water and marine environments, and many are important to humans as food.

Smallest in number of the five main groups of vertebrates is the class **Amphibia,** with about 2,400 species. They are the earliest land vertebrates to appear in the fossil record. Adult amphibians are air-breathers, but the larvae breathe by gills and must live in water. The most common amphibians are the newts, frogs, toads, and salamanders.

Reptilia, the next class, contains about 6,000 surviving species, most of them snakes or lizards. Turtles, alligators, and crocodiles are also reptiles, as were the great dinosaurs of the past. All reptiles are air-breathers and are primarily adapted to terrestrial life. Fertilization is internal, and the egg is enclosed in a membranous shell. Eggs can therefore be laid on land, and the reptile, unlike the amphibian, need not return to the water to breed. Turtles, in fact, though they live mainly in water, must come ashore to deposit their eggs.

Members of the class **Aves**—the birds—are masters of flight. There are about 8,600 bird species, and only a few, such as the ostrich and the penguin, are unable to fly. Birds are believed to have evolved from reptiles, and the oldest known fossil bird, *Archeopteryx*, probably looked like a reptile with feathers. The presence of feathers, though, is an important difference, for it implies that *Archeopteryx*, unlike reptiles, was endothermic and needed the heat-retaining insulation that feathers provide. Modern birds combine feathers with an extremely high metabolic rate. This keeps their body temperature high and supplies the large amount of energy needed for flight.

Finally, humans and their closest relatives are members of the class **Mammalia.** Members of this class, which includes some 4,300 species, live in virtually every habitat on earth. Typically, mammals have a body covering of hair, and many get rid of excess heat through sweat glands. All newborn mammals are nursed by their mothers, on milk secreted by special **mammary glands.** Like the birds, mammals are endothermic, maintaining a constant body temperature.

There are three large groupings of mammals, classified according to the ways they

Figure 20-30. Frogs are among the most familiar amphibians. This male spring peeper, calling to attract a mate, has expanded the skin of his throat to form an air-filled sac which allows the sound to resonate.

Figure 20-31. Courting the drabber-colored female, the male frigate bird at right has expanded its bright red, featherless neck pouch as a prelude to the mating ritual.

Figure 20-32. Many reptiles resemble survivors from the age of dinosaurs. The ferocious-looking Jackson's chameleon at left is really quite small and perfectly harmless except to the insects it preys on.

Figure 20-33. Awkward on land and entirely unable to fly, the penguin is a skilled and graceful swimmer as it pursues the fish which make up most of its diet.

Figure 20-34. This koala, one of the world's few varieties of marsupial, is as gentle and friendly as it looks.

Figure 20-35. Dolphins are sea-dwelling mammals despite their fish-like appearance. They are extremely intelligent, and scientists now suspect that they may use a very sophisticated form of vocal communication.

bear their young. The order **Monotremata** are egg-layers and have some other characteristics not usually associated with mammals. They include only the duckbilled platypus and the spiny anteater, both native to Australia.

Members of the order **Marsupialia** are also found mostly in Australia, though a few are native to America. As we noted in chapter 13, they do not form a placenta, and the young are therefore born very soon after conception. Development continues in a protected pouch on the mother's abdomen, where the embryo nurses and grows. Some

Figure 20-36. In spite of its forbidding expression this gorilla is really a shy and unaggressive primate who prefers a largely vegetarian diet.

marsupials are the kangaroo, the koala, the opossum, and the wombat.

Finally, there is the largest group, the **placental mammals.** Young of this group undergo far more extensive development in the mother's uterus before birth. Placental mammals include many orders, among them the **Insectivora** (shrews and moles), **Chiroptera** (bats), **Edentata** (sloths, anteaters, and armadillos), **Rodentia** (mice, squirrels, beavers, porcupines, and others), **Lagomorpha** (rabbits, hares, and others), **Perissodactyla** (horses, rhinoceroses, and others), **Artiodactyla** (cows, sheep, goats, deer, hippopotamuses, and others), **Proboscidea** (elephants), **Cetacea** (whales, dolphins, and porpoises), **Carnivora** (cats, dogs, bears, seals, and others), and **Primates** (prosimians, monkeys, apes, and humans).

SUMMARY

Taxonomy is the science that names and classifies organisms. It originated with Linnaeus, who divided organisms into plant and animal kingdoms. His system contained a hierarchy of seven levels—kingdom, phylum, class, order, family, genus, and species. The basis of his classification was structural similarity. Modern taxonomists regard such similarities as indicating probable evolutionary relationships. The Whittaker system of taxonomy is divided into five kingdoms: Monera, Protista, Plantae, Fungi, and Animalia.

Monerans are the smallest, simplest, and most plentiful organisms; all are procaryotic. They include the bacteria and the blue-green algae, which some taxonomists now consider to be bacteria also. Bacteria may be classified by the ways in which they obtain energy.

The kingdom Protista contains mostly unicellular organisms, all of which are eucaryotic. There are five plant-like phyla, including both autotrophic and heterotrophic forms. There are also five animal-like phyla. All are heterotrophic, and most species reproduce asexually. Many protozoans are able to cause disease in other organisms.

The kingdom Fungi is divided into the Eumycophyta, or true fungi, and the Myxomycophyta, or slime molds. There are four classes of true fungi, and most have a complex reproductive cycle. This phylum includes the yeasts, mushrooms, molds, and mildews. Lichens are a combination life form, made up of a fungus which shelters a population of green algae. Lichens can grow in places where neither partner could survive by itself.

The kingdom Plantae includes the Thallophyta, which are aquatic and have little or no specialized tissue, and the Embryophyta, which are mainly terrestrial, possess specialized tissues, and form embryos. The Thallophyta are the mainly multicellular algae, and are classified on the basis of their photosynthetic pigmentation.

The Embryophyta are divided into Bryophyta and Tracheophyta. All of the bryophytes require a moist environment. They include the liverworts, horned liverworts, and mosses. The tracheophytes have specialized conductive tissue. The largest phylum of tracheophytes, Pteropsida, includes three main subgroups containing the ferns, gymnosperms, and flowering plants.

The kingdom Animalia has the largest number of species. Most animal phyla are best suited to an aquatic environment. Only the arthropods and the chordates have a wide variety of terrestrial species.

Sponges, or Porifera, are the simplest animals, having no organs or organ systems and being developed from only two basic germ layers. They reproduce both sexually and asexually. Slightly more complex are the Cnidaria, including jellyfish, coral, and hydras. Both Porifera and Cnidaria are radially symmetrical.

The phylum Platyhelminthes includes flatworms, flukes, and tapeworms. They are bilaterally symmetrical and have simple nervous systems. Phylum Nematoda includes free-living nematodes and parasitic roundworms. The Annelida are segmented worms, including marine, fresh-water, and terrestrial forms.

The Mollusca are the second-largest animal phylum, found both on land and in water. Their common body plan includes a head, a foot, a visceral mass, and a mantle. The largest phylum is Arthropoda, which includes land and water species capable of living in every conceivable environment. All arthropods have segmented exoskeletons and three main body regions. The most important classes are the arachnids, crustaceans, and insects. Phylum Echinodermata appears quite primitive but bears some resemblance to the chordates in embryonic development.

All members of phylum Chordata possess a notochord, a dorsal nerve cord, and pharyngeal pouches. The subphylum Vertebrata includes the fish, amphibians, reptiles, birds, and mammals.

Review questions

1. What are some of the purposes for scientific classification of organisms?

2. What is binomial nomenclature? Who devised this system?

3. From lowest to highest, what are the seven levels of classification of organisms?

4. How do taxonomists determine relationships between organisms?

5. What is the basis of Whittaker's five-kingdom system of taxonomy?

6. Describe the general structure of a typical moneran.

7. List some of the ways in which bacteria are important to their environment.

8. Into what two general categories is the kingdom Protista divided? Name two phyla from each and describe their general characteristics.

9. What are the two phyla of the kingdom Fungi?

10. Name and describe at least two classes of Eumycophyta. How are they important to the environment?

11. What unusual feature do lichens possess? Describe a typical lichen.

12. What two principal characteristics are typical of the kingdom Plantae? What are its two subkingdoms and how do they differ?

13. How do thallophyte algae differ from the algal protists? List and describe at least two phyla of thallophyte algae.

14. What are the major characteristics of bryophytes? What sort of environment do they require?

15. What important characteristic is shared by all tracheophytes?

16. What are some of the adaptations that enable gymnosperms to live in a wide variety of climates?

17. What are some of the typical environmental adaptations of the flowering plants?

18. What is the simplest animal phylum? In what ways do its members resemble plants?

19. What important structural characteristic is seen in phylum Platyhelminthes?

20. Describe the body plan common to all mollusks.

21. What is the largest of the animal phyla? What are the three most important classes and what structural features do they have in common?

22. What important features are shared by all chordates?

23. List the five main vertebrate groups and the distinguishing features of each.

24. How are mammals classified? Describe each of the three main groups of mammals.

25. Why would we expect placental mammals to be the largest and most widespread mammal order?

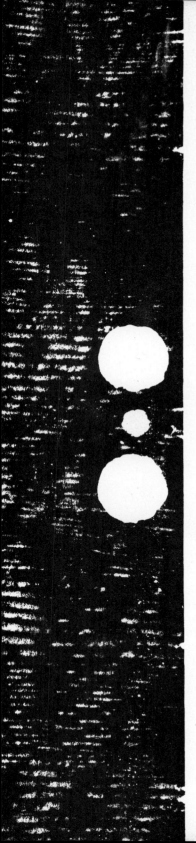

Receiving and Communicating Information

Communication is the simplest way in which individuals interact with other individuals. It implies an exchange of information, in which one individual signals or conveys a message and the other responds to it. The message may be hostile or friendly, warning or attractive, and the ways in which its receiver reacts are equally varied. But in order to react, the individual must first receive the information. That is, it must take the information from the environment to its own central nervous system.

Thus communication has two components: sending signals to individuals through the environment, and receiving messages from the environment. Not all signal and response sequences can be regarded as communication. For example, an animal may take in information about the nature and location of food—its prey animals, perhaps. But the food cannot be regarded as communicating just because it has inadvertently provided the information. The nature of the relationship between sending and receiving is an important part of communication.

SENSORY RECEPTION

Although animals send messages only to other animals, they receive information from their entire environment—from living as well as nonliving things. The process by which information is taken from the outside

427

Figure 21-1. The antennae of many insects can receive both chemical and vibration signals. The male luna moth uses his sensitive antennae to detect the scent of a female.

to the inside of the animal's body is an aspect of what is known as **sensory reception.**

Information from the environment takes the form of changes in the levels of energy, such as heat, light, or sound. These energy changes are picked up by sensory receptors, which are specialized according to the nature of the stimuli they pick up. Changes in vibration energy are detected by auditory or other mechanical receptors, changes in light energy by visual or photoreceptors, and changes in chemical concentration by chemical receptors. Higher animals generally have many receptors that pick up different stimuli. But even in single-celled organisms, parts of the cell are often specialized for receiving some kind of sensory information.

Each of the main receptor types includes many different receptors. Mechanical receptors respond to a mechanical force, which may be the movements of bending or stretching, the vibrations of sound waves, or the pressures of touch. Chemical receptors respond to molecules that are dispersed in gas or liquid; visual receptors respond in various ways to light.

428

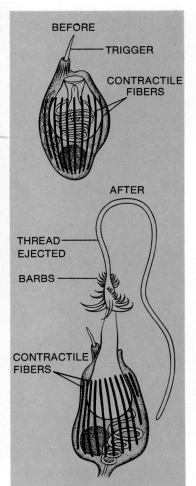

Figure 21-2. Specialized stinging cells, or cnidocysts, in their tentacles assist jellyfish, sea anemones, and hydras in locating and capturing food. The cnidocyst contains a pointed thread coiled inside a capsule. When a victim touches the trigger, the thread is ejected, often carrying a toxic chemical with it.

Mechanical receptors

Mechanical receptors, or **mechanoreceptors,** like all sensory receptors, consist of one or more sensory nerve endings, linked to specific regions of the central nervous system. Suppose you were blindfolded and someone pressed the point of a pencil against the tip of your index finger. If you were asked to name the place on your body that had been touched, you could easily do so.

The receptor does not usually interpret information; it is merely one end of a pathway that transports information. The interpretation is made by the region of the brain that receives the message. This means that the end of the pathway in the brain, not its beginning in the receptor, determines the nature of the sensation. In fact, sometimes the receptor need not even be there. Suppose that your leg has to be amputated. Afterward, you will almost certainly continue to feel occasional sensations—itching, pain, and so on—in the leg that is no longer there. This cannot be explained merely by supposing that impulses are carried from the severed nerve ends in the stump of the leg. When the leg was amputated, the cell bodies of its afferent neurons were removed (recall the discussion of afferent and efferent neurons in chapter 10). Therefore any part of these neurons that remained in the stump soon degenerated. Rather, the brain has stored the memories of past sensations, and can activate them in situations that it interprets as appropriate.

The sense of touch

Touch receptors deal not only with sensations of touch, but also with those of pressure, pain, heat, and cold. In humans and many other animals, many of these receptors are located in the skin.

The structure of all skin receptors is very similar, and the impulses they send to the brain are also very much alike. The impulse that registers heat, for example, is exactly the same as that for cold, or for touch. We experience them as different sensations because they go to different centers in the brain. If the pathways were altered, so that the cold receptors sent impulses to the heat center in the brain, you would probably feel a sensation of heat every time you touched a piece of ice. Actually, "heat" and "cold" are relative terms. The same room may feel hot to someone coming in from the ski slopes, and cold to someone coming out of a steamy kitchen.

Pain receptors are exposed nerve endings—that is, endings not covered by a myelin sheath. If the nerve ending is injured, it sends an impulse that the brain interprets as pain. Even if the nerve ending itself is not injured, it can pick up signals from those that are, and can transmit the same message. This causes a slow buildup of the pain sensation. Pain receptors are more numerous than receptors for heat or cold or touch, especially in humans. Moreover, the receptors that register heat, cold, and pressure can also register pain, simply by receiving too much stimulation.

Monitoring the body

Another kind of mechanoreceptor picks up information about the state of affairs inside the body. Receptors that respond to stretching and bending are of this kind. In vertebrates they are found in the muscles, tendons, and joints. Tension and relaxation, as well as position of the bones, activate these receptors in different ways, providing us with feedback about the results of muscular activity. Thus we can coordinate the force and direction of our muscle movements. Insects, too, although they have an external skeleton, have stretch receptors. These take the form of little pads of sensory hairs, located in the joints between segments of the insect's body. When the two sides of the joint move, the tiny hairs bend too, sending an impulse to the nervous system.

Touch receptors enable many animals to monitor their environments. For certain aquatic animals, such as the jellyfish, sea anemone, and hydra, touch receptors in the tentacles help in locating food. The feet of certain web-spinning spiders have clusters of touch receptors that monitor vibrations in the web. From these vibrations, set up by a trapped animal, a spider learns much about the nature of its catch. Weak vibrations indicate a small insect that can simply be killed with a bite. Too large an insect might destroy the web, and its strong vibrations may lead the spider to free it. Somewhat less violent vibrations may signal the spider to rush out and wrap the prey in silk,

Figure 21-3. The fennec fox, an inhibitant of the North African desert, has very acute hearing. Its large outer ears are very efficient in capturing sound waves. What other purpose might be served by these large ears in such a climate?

or give it a long bite that injects a large dose of venom. The spider also locates its victim through touch receptors. By lifting each strand of the web with its legs, it can detect the area of greatest resistance, and thus determine where the prey is trapped.

The reception of sound

Perhaps the most highly specialized of the mechanoreceptors are those that respond to vibration waves of air or water. These vibrations are perceived by special sense receptors as sound.

Humans can distinguish among sounds in terms of volume (loud to soft), pitch (high to low), and quality (harsh, sweet, and so on).

INTERACTING WITH
THE ENVIRONMENT

Figure 21-4. The lateral line can be clearly seen on this southern hake. It appears as a series of black dashes on the fish's side.

These three aspects are not of equal importance to all animals, even those with well-developed senses of hearing. Insects, for example, cannot pick up differences in pitch. But they can distinguish very small changes in volume and in sound quality. Consequently, they can recognize tiny differences in sound patterns. The mating song of a certain grasshopper has an abrupt, staccato rhythm which must be maintained exactly to attract the female grasshopper. So long as the male keeps the correct rhythm, he can "sing" in any pitch and win his mate.

The detection of low-frequency vibrations is very important to fish. Vibrations in the water serve as warnings, as navigational aids, and probably in many other ways. Such information is received largely by a special network of mechanoreceptors along the sides of the fish's body. This network, called the **lateral line system,** consists of specialized hair cells inside a canal-shaped organ. Currents of water bend the hairs. Moving things or stationary obstacles close by change the currents, and this affects the bending of the hairs and the impulse they transmit. Lateral line systems function most often to detect the presence of prey or predators nearby. They also enable the fish to keep properly oriented in the water and to stay with the school. Less often, they serve to locate prospective mates. In general, an object must be within one or two body lengths to be detected by the lateral line system.

High-frequency vibrations are usually received by more specialized mechanoreceptors, called **auditory receptors.** Animals with such receptors are usually described as having a sense of hearing.

The human ear, though not as sensitive as the ears of many other vertebrates, is an organ with auditory receptors. Structurally, each ear consists of three regions: outer, middle, and inner. The **outer ear** functions as a sort of funnel that traps high-frequency vibrations and channels them into the **auditory canal.** At the end of the auditory canal a thin membrane, the **tympanic membrane,** or eardrum, is set in motion by the vibrations. A series of three tiny bones transmits this motion through the **middle ear,** where the vibrations are made stronger. At the far side of the middle ear, the vibrations reach the small **oval window,** the gateway to the **inner ear.** The lower region of the inner ear is known as the **cochlea,** and contains three liquid-filled canals separated by membranes.

Inside the canals the vibrations are transmitted through the fluid to other membranes. These membranes vibrate against receptor hair cells in the **organ of Corti.** Sensory nerve endings associated with the cells are stimulated by the pressure, and transmit impulses to the **auditory nerve,** which connects to the brain.

The sense of balance

Just above the cochlea of the inner ear are three small **semicircular canals.** These function together as an organ of balance. Like the cochlea, they are filled with liquid. Any movement of the head—and, therefore, of the body—automatically causes some movement of the liquid. The canals are at right angles to each other, so the liquid moves differently in each. For instance, when it is moving lengthwise in one canal, it is moving crosswise in another. Hair cells in the canals are bent by the movement of the fluid, and the information is then transmitted to the brain. The brain coordinates messages from all three canals, in order to determine changes in speed or direction of movement.

Chemical receptors

Another large class of sense receptors is composed of the **chemoreceptors,** which are stimulated by chemicals of various kinds. The degree to which a chemoreceptor is sensitive to chemical stimulation varies.

Olfactory receptors are so sensitive that a few molecules of a gaseous chemical drifting through the air will stimulate them. Animals with such receptors are usually said to have a sense of smell. **Gustatory receptors** are less sensitive; a liquid or a dissolved chemical must come in contact with the receptor before stimulation can occur. Animals receiving information by this method are said to have a sense of taste.

Note that the olfactory receptors enable an animal to receive information from a distance. In this respect the olfactory receptors can be placed in a general category with the auditory receptors; both are considered to be "distance" receptors. On the other hand, gustatory and pressure receptors are not stimulated unless there is considerable contact with the stimulating agent. Both of these are conveniently described as "contact" receptors.

In most vertebrates, chemical receptors are located in specialized organs for taste or smell. In land vertebrates, as a rule, the olfactory receptors are highly developed in the nasal passages, particularly near the open-

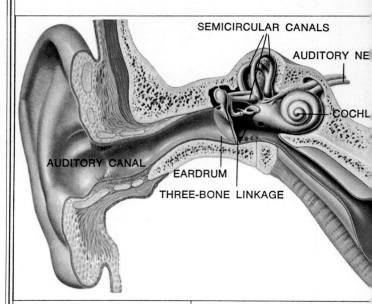

Figure 21-5. The structure of the human ear.

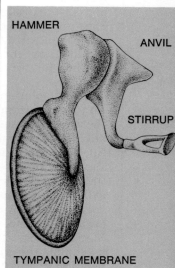

Figure 21-6. An enlarged view of the three-bone linkage within the inner ear. These three tiny bones transmit the vibrations of the tympanic membrane. The stirrup is about half as big as a grain of rice.

ings. Fish do not have such passages, yet there is no doubt that they can smell. Anyone who has fished in shark-infested waters knows that small amounts of blood in the water will quickly be detected by sharks over a wide area. Olfactory organs in the fish take the form of nostrils, paired openings just in front of the eyes. However, in most

INTERACTING WITH
THE ENVIRONMENT

Figure 21-7. Sharks have very sensitive olfactory receptors. Even a few drops of blood mixed with the sea water will attract sharks from great distances.

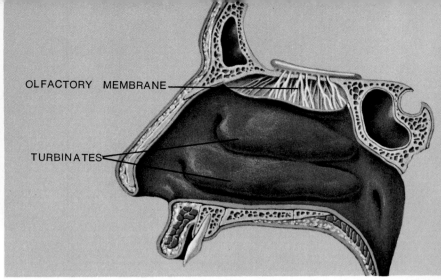

OLFACTORY MEMBRANE

TURBINATES

Figure 21-8. Two of the three turbinates, or bony ridges, are seen in this sectional view of the nasal area. The turbinates provide an expanded surface area which is covered with olfactory receptors.

fish these do not open into the respiratory tract or the fish's mouth. Olfactory receptors line the nostrils and pick up low concentrations of chemicals, as they do in land vertebrates.

Taste or gustatory receptors, known as taste buds, are concentrated in small clusters of **papillae.** In most land vertebrates, the papillae are located primarily on the tongue and much less thickly on the pharynx and larynx. Many fish, though, have taste buds all over their bodies, especially on the fins and tail.

Four basic qualities of taste—sweet, sour, salt, and bitter—can easily be detected by humans. At one time taste was thought to be localized in these terms, with each part of the tongue responding to a specific quality. But taste buds have proved to be more complex: for instance, receptors that detect salts also respond to acids and sugars. In addition, other specific aspects have been distinguished that cannot be considered mere combinations of the four. Frogs, for example, have specialized taste receptors that respond to distilled water.

Odors are even more difficult to pin down. Some investigators claim to have identified nine basic odors. Others count only seven, each with a characteristically shaped molecule. But various tests have cast doubt

on the value of any of these classifications, since a great many different odors appear to involve independent receptors. Moreover, most foods contain a vast number of olfactory chemicals. In coffee, for example, no fewer than 103 substances contribute to that delectable odor.

We have made a distinction here between the senses of taste and smell. In fact, though, the two are closely connected—as anyone knows who has tried to enjoy a meal while suffering from a cold. The food odors reaching the olfactory receptors in the nose usually stimulate the taste receptors in the mouth. When the olfactory receptors are blocked, as they are during colds, the odors do not stimulate the taste receptors.

In other animals, too, tasting and smelling are closely associated. In fact, the snake combines both senses in a single organ. This is why the snake flicks its tongue. By so doing it captures and dissolves molecules that are not detected in its nasal passages. The molecules are transported on the tongue to the roof of the mouth, where a special group of chemical receptors known as **Jacobson's organ** acts as a kind of "taster–smeller."

Insects have olfactory receptors in the antennae, as well as in other parts of the body. Some insects, particularly bees and ants,

THE KANGAROO RAT

Days are quiet in the dry deserts and plains of the western United States and northern Mexico. Here the noon temperature sometimes climbs to an unbearable 130°F. But as evening falls and the air grows cooler, the desert creatures emerge from their hiding places to search for food. During the twilight, snakes and lizards are abroad; as darkness falls, they are followed by the nocturnal foxes, bobcats, coyotes, owls, and bats. All are predators, and a favorite target of their predation is an unusual mouse-like rodent known as the kangaroo rat.

The kangaroo rat is neither a kangaroo nor a rat. It can be any of about twenty species of closely related mammals, ranging in size from the six-inch dwarf to the fourteen-inch banner-tailed kangaroo rat. But much like its Australian namesake, the kangaroo rat generally stands upright and gets around by hopping on its hind legs, holding its tiny forelimbs close to its chest. Its tufted tail, longer than the animal's head and body combined, serves to balance the unusually large head as the kangaroo rat leaps from place to place.

This appealing little animal is remarkably well adapted for survival in the inhospitable desert. The fur on its back is much darker than the belly fur, a color pattern which makes it less noticeable to a hungry owl approaching from the air. It can run as fast as 17 feet per second, leap a full two feet in the air, and execute sudden turns and zigzags with the help of its long tail, all tactics that help it to evade capture by its enemies. Like many other desert creatures, the kangaroo rat has sharp eyesight and a keen sense of smell.

But most important to the kangaroo rat's survival is the remarkable structure of its ears. The resonating cavity of the middle ear is extremely large, and sound waves which strike the enormous eardrum can be amplified nearly a hundred times. The kangaroo rat can thus detect certain very slight sounds that most other animals cannot hear. The soft rush of air as a snake strikes, or the gentle whirring of an owl's wings in flight, are enough to warn it of danger, and its unusually speedy reflexes often enable it to escape an attack.

The kangaroo rat avoids light; even bright moonlight is often enough to keep it underground. During the day it spends most of its time sleeping in its burrow. This underground home is a complex labyrinth on several levels, with many chambers connected by a system of ramps and hallways. Special areas of the burrow are designed for food storage, and a single kangaroo rat may hoard as much as 100 quarts of seeds and dried grasses in its den. Sometimes it even stashes small amounts of food in temporary refuges, constructed at strategic locations for emergency shelter from predators.

The door to the burrow is usually built in a large mound of excavated soil, seed hulls, spoiled food, and droppings which the kangaroo rat has removed from the burrow. By positioning the entrance holes above ground level in this way, the animal protects its home from being flooded out by a sudden desert cloudburst. Near the bottom of the burrow, the kangaroo rat builds a "bedroom" by lining a chamber with soft grasses and rootlets.

The kangaroo rat's preoccupation with food storage relates to the fact that it does not hibernate. In winter it becomes much less active and sleeps for longer periods, but will still wake up to eat several times a day. Thus a year-round food supply is absolutely essential, particularly since kangaroo rats often steal from each others' storehouses. If one is caught in the act, however, the penalty for thievery is almost invariably death.

When it is ready to emerge at night, the kangaroo rat stands upright in its doorway, keenly alert to the possibility of a hidden enemy. Once assured that it is safe to proceed, it begins its search for food, sometimes hopping, sometimes walking on all fours. With its strong incisor teeth and its front paws, the kangaroo rat gathers seeds and snips off bits of grasses. Sometimes it may vary this diet with an occasional fungus, insect, or moth. Like many rodents, the kangaroo rat has fur-lined pouches on either side of its head and neck. Most of the food it gathers is tucked into these built-in pockets and taken home to be stored.

Most of the kangaroo rat's den is covered with its droppings. Only its bed and food supply are kept free of contamination. This may sound like an unpleasant situation, but the droppings are very dry, and usually inoffensive when mixed with bits of grass.

The dryness of its feces is only one of the kangaroo rat's adaptations to the heat and dryness of its desert home. Although it may occasionally sip dew or drink from a rare puddle, the kangaroo rat never needs a drink of water. It gets all the moisture it requires from the water content of the seeds it eats and from the metabolic water that is produced by cellular respiration. It lacks sweat glands, and is equipped with highly efficient kidneys, which excrete an extremely concentrated and salty urine. Even the kangaroo rat's respiratory system conserves water: water vapor in the warm, moist air from its lungs condenses into liquid water inside the nasal passages, and is then reabsorbed.

Obviously, the kangaroo rat's behavioral pattern is important to its survival. By staying in its cool underground home during the day it avoids exposure to the scorching desert sun. Even very young kangaroo rats, after their single week of nursing is finished, will promptly proceed to build cool, protective burrows that are miniature versions of their parents' homes. The shyness of these little creatures is also an important factor in successful avoidance of predators. Nevertheless, kangaroo rats are as curious and intelligent as most other rodents. With patience, they can be tamed to the point where they will emerge from their burrows at the sound of a familiar voice and accept bits of food from the hand of a human friend. Fortunately, such unusual friendships do not interfere with the behavior patterns which help to protect the kangaroo rat from less trustworthy acquaintances!

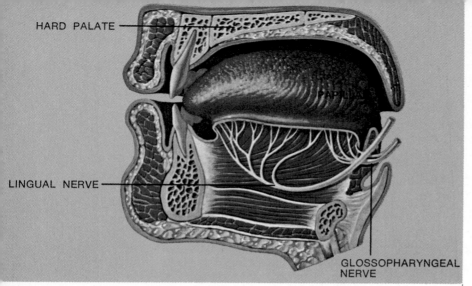

HARD PALATE

PAPILLA

LINGUAL NERVE

GLOSSOPHARYNGEAL NERVE

Figure 21-9. Dissolved substances stimulate nerve cell endings in the papillae, which are scattered over the upper surface of the tongue. The tongue connects with two nerves: the lingual nerve and the glossopharyngeal nerve

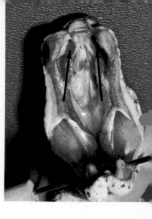

Figure 21-10. The Jacobson's organs of this yellow tree boa are in the long oval depressions on each side of the roof of the mouth.

have taste receptors in their antennae also. Thus equipped, the antennae can be used for both smelling and tasting food. In a number of insects, such as the fly, gustatory receptors are found in the same organ as touch receptors. It is not always the mouth parts that have such combinations. Sometimes taste is located in the feet, enabling the insect to taste any substance it may walk over.

Visual receptors

Receptors that transform light into nerve impulses are called visual receptors or **photoreceptors.** "Light" includes all the visible wavelengths of electromagnetic radiation. The ultraviolet and infrared regions of the spectrum, which are invisible to human eyes, are received by photoreceptors in some other organisms.

Almost all organisms pick up some form of information in the form of light. Light has two distinct advantages: it is fast, traveling more than 186,000 miles per second, and it travels in straight lines. With photoreceptors, organisms can receive information from their environments more rapidly and more accurately than with any other distance receptor. However, visual reception

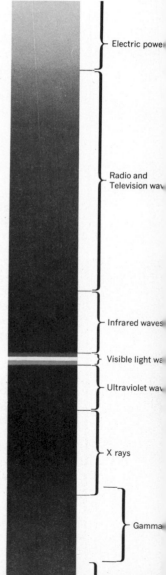

Electric power

Radio and Television waves

Infrared waves

Visible light waves

Ultraviolet waves

X rays

Gamma

Cosmic rays

Figure 21-11. Only a small portion of the electromagnetic spectrum can be detected by human visual receptors. Certain other organisms, however, can detect infrared and ultraviolet wavelengths.

would have disadvantages if it were an animal's only form of sensory reception—most notably the fact that it is of limited use in darkness.

Visual receptors vary widely in ability to receive patterns and images from the environment. Some organisms, such as planarians, have receptors capable only of telling the difference between shades of brightness or darkness. The eyes of the squid, the octopus, and all vertebrates, on the other hand, can form precise images. They can also discriminate between various frequencies of light, thereby detecting color.

The arrangement of visual receptors also varies among different animals. In some cases, light-sensitive cells are simply scattered over the surface of the animal. The earthworm responds to different degrees of light intensity by means of such cells. Other animals have one or more groups of specialized cells that form a visual organ. However, all photoreceptors are much alike in cellular and molecular organization.

In general, when photoreceptors are scattered over the body, they can detect only the presence of light and perhaps differences in intensity. For an organism to pick up the direction of the light source or to perceive an image, photoreceptors must be specialized and organized into a visual organ called an **eye.**

Simple and compound eyes

The visual organs of arthropods form an interesting contrast to those of vertebrates. In general, they might be called "intermediate" in complexity and "discriminatory" in ability. The arthropods' visual receptors are organized into two basic types of eye, simple and compound. Many insects have both simple and compound eyes.

The simple eyes, or **ocelli,** of insects and spiders are probably not concerned with image formation. Rather, they seem to respond to overall conditions of light—its intensity, its direction, its wavelength. This probably triggers activity appropriate to the time of day and the stage of the animal's life cycle.

The large, bulging eyes of insects are usually **compound eyes.** These eyes can form a multiple image. Structurally, the compound eye is made up of many cone-like structures known as **ommatidia.** Each ommatidium contains a lens, receptor cell, and neuron to transmit information to the brain.

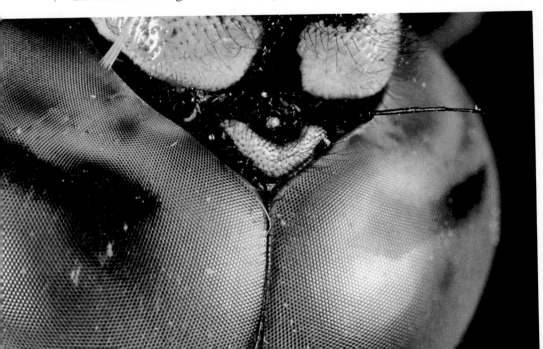

Figure 21-12. Thousands of individual ocelli can be observed in the compound eyes of a dragonfly.

The entire image is focused on each receptor cell, resulting in a visual field such as that in Figure 21-13.

Each lens of the compound eye receives information from a slightly different direction. Together the lenses provide a continuous image over a much greater area than is possible with the human eye. The compound eye is also very sensitive to flickering motions, or rapid shifts from dark to light. Thus it can detect movement very quickly. The maddening ability of houseflies to elude the swiftest slap is explained in part by this ability to detect motion.

The camera eye

Two unrelated groups of animals have remarkably similar organs of visual reception—the cephalopod mollusks and the vertebrates. Both organs are similar in structure and function to a camera. For this reason they are often called "**camera eyes.**"

The opening by which light enters the human eye is known as the **pupil.** Its diameter can be adjusted by a muscular structure called the **iris,** to let in different amounts of light. The iris also gives the eye its color. The action of the iris is involuntary, controlled by a reflex of the autonomic nervous system. Thus the pupil automatically contracts when exposed to bright light and slowly expands in dim light.

The smooth muscles of the iris also regulate the thickness of the **lens,** which controls the focus. The lens, made up of protein fibers, becomes thicker when focusing on nearby objects, and thinner for those at greater distances. Between the lens and the transparent **cornea** in front of it is a space, filled with a fluid called the **aqueous humor.** This fluid constantly washes the lens. A thicker substance, the **vitreous humor,** fills the cavity behind the lens and maintains the shape of the eyeball.

Together, the cornea and lens capture and bend the incoming light rays so that they focus on the **retina** at the back of the eyeball. The retina is made up of pigmented photo-

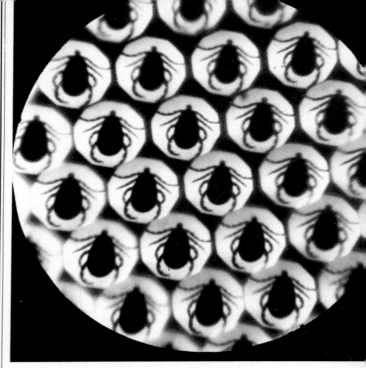

Figure 21-13. As the dragonfly prepares to capture a tick, this is approximately what it sees.

receptor cells—some 130 million in each human eye. Each receptor cell records only a small part of the image, instead of the whole image as in the arthropod ommatidium. The information from all of the cells is then integrated by the brain to create the full image.

The human retina, like the retinas of most vertebrates, contains receptor cells of two kinds. They are very similar in structure, but not at all similar in function. These are the **rods** and the **cones.** At one end of each is a light-sensitive pigment, and at the other end is a nerve-like fiber that transmits light energy to a nerve ending.

The cones, clustered together at the center of the retina, register very fine detail. They can do this because each cone connects with a different nerve ending, and thus has its own separate pathway to the brain. The rods do not have separate pathways and cannot register detail. In some cases many rods connect with a single neuron. This enables the organism to respond to very dim

INTERACTING WITH
THE ENVIRONMENT

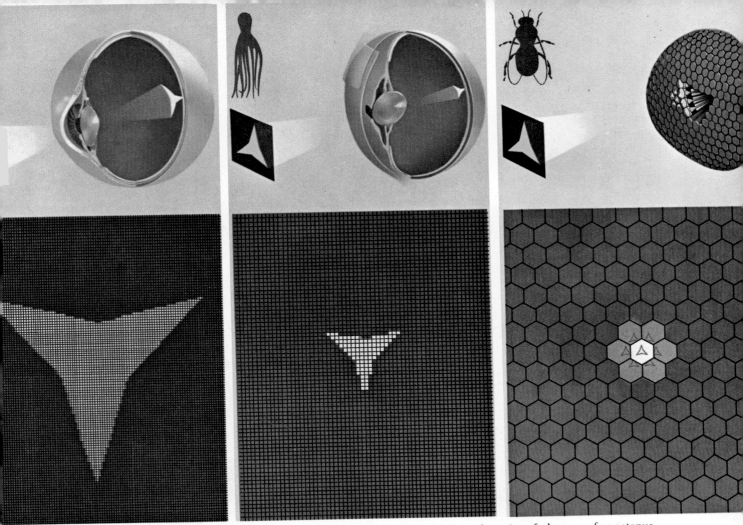

Figure 21-14. These diagrams show how the image of a three-pointed star falls on the retina of a human, of an octopus, and of an insect. Each unit of the compound insect eye views a different part of a scene. How does the octopus eye differ from the human eye?

light. The reaction of any single receptor to dim light is too slight to stimulate an impulse in the connecting neurons. But the many stimuli from a number of rods to a single neuron are enough to trigger an impulse. The rods are most numerous near the edges of the retina. The next time you want to see an object in dim light, you might try looking at it out of the corner of your eye, thus making the best use of the rods.

It is the cones that are mainly responsible for detecting color. Each cone contains a **photopigment** that responds to one of the three primary colors—red, yellow, and blue. Animals with eyes differ in their ability to see color. Many nonhuman vertebrates, including fish and birds and reptiles, can distinguish colors, whereas most mammals cannot. Some animals can pick up light beyond the range of human vision. Some vipers, for example, respond to infrared radiation; pits beneath the eye are stimulated by the presence of warmblooded prey animals, and in a sense the viper "sees" the prey.

The ways in which insects respond to

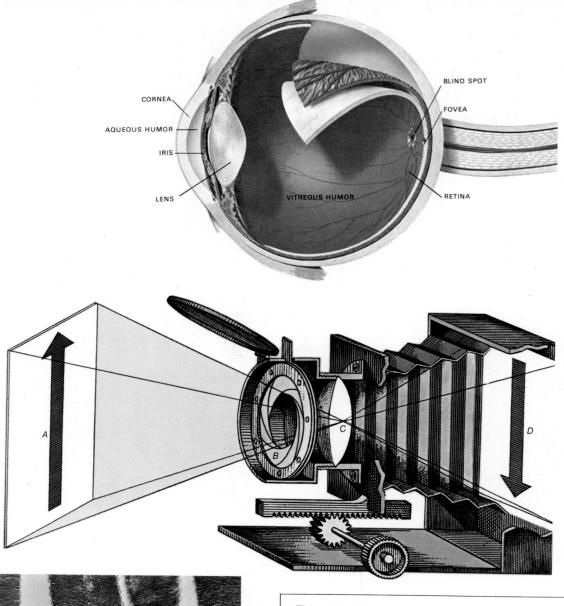

CORNEA

AQUEOUS HUMOR

IRIS

LENS

BLIND SPOT

FOVEA

VITREOUS HUMOR

RETINA

A   B   C   D

Figure 21-15. Compare the human eye with the old-fashioned camera. Each has an adjustable diaphragm to control the amount of light that enters. Each has a lens to focus those light rays to form an image at the rear. In the camera, the diaphragm is labeled *B*, and the lens is labeled *C*.

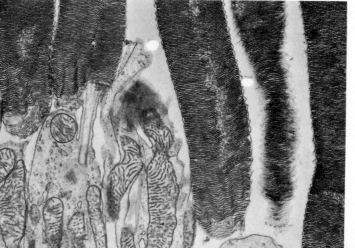

Figure 21-16. This electron micrograph shows a cross-section through the rods in the retina of a kangaroo rat.

color are various and subtle. Unlike humans, insects can see at the ultraviolet end of the spectrum. However, colors toward the other end, which we perceive as red, may appear to an insect as black. The ability to sense ultraviolet light apparently helps the insect orient itself in regard to the sun. Many insects perceive color in the middle range of the spectrum as well. These insects often choose among flowers of different kinds on the basis of their colors. In the honeybee, the ability to perceive color in the middle range also depends on sex. The females, who feed on the nectar of flowers, are sensitive to yellow, blue, and green, in addition to ultraviolet shades. The males, however, do not respond to these middle-range colors and—whether for this reason or not—cannot feed themselves.

THE SENDING OF MESSAGES

The sending, like the receiving, of messages is basic to all forms of animal behavior. By picking up messages, organisms receive needed information about their environment. By exchanging information with other organisms, animals learn more about their environment than any one of them could learn by itself. In this way they increase the survival chances of all members of the population.

Chemical messages
Humans are highly dependent on auditory and visual information. We tend to discount information transmitted by chemicals, especially those secreted by other humans, even though it may influence our behavior in subtle, possibly unconscious ways. Yet the most widespread type of message exchanged between animals is the chemical message.

Detected by means of smell or taste, chemical messages are probably used by all living organisms, and are quite diverse in function. Often they serve for defense. Some butterflies, as we saw earlier in this book, secrete substances that taste very unpleasant. These substances keep the population relatively safe from would-be predators—at least from those who have once tasted a butterfly. Many animals produce a warning odor, making even a single taste unlikely. Skunks are the most obvious example.

A special group of chemicals communicate information within a species. Chemicals that are secreted by one individual and stimulate behavior responses in other members of the species are known as **pheromones.** The information conveyed by pheromones is of all kinds. It includes, among other things, marking the boundaries of individual territories, attracting future mates, locating food sources, and conveying status distinctions, or positions in the group pecking order.

For instance, although we might have difficulty telling a superior bullhead catfish from an inferior one, the fish themselves have no such problem; it is impossible to conceal a losing battle record in such communities. Catfish are night hunters, with limited vision but extremely keen senses of smell and taste. Both females and males tend to occupy small territories within the larger pond or tank, and to fight off intruders. In experiments with a number of catfish in a single tank it was found that the dominant fish soon occupied the largest and most desirable area, and those of lower rank got the more exposed and smaller territories. The experimenters removed a dominant fish, and allowed it to be defeated in battle elsewhere. When it was replaced in the original tank, the others no longer respected it, or its territory. In another experiment, a male bullhead became excited and aggressive when water that had contained a fish he had previously battled with was introduced into his tank. Apparently the skin of these fish secretes different pheromones according to the fish's status in the group, and these are detected by smell.

One of the first to study the ways in which

pheromones function in animal communication was a nineteenth-century French schoolteacher, Jean-Henri Fabre. Fabre took a moth cocoon from a wooded area near his home and placed it in a cloth cage. Soon after the adult female moth emerged, Fabre left the cage near an open window one evening. Shortly, he discovered that sixty adult males had gathered on the outside of the cage. Through numerous experiments he learned that male moths as far away as a mile could detect a chemical excretion from the tip of the female's abdomen. They could not detect the substance when their antennae were removed, however. This suggested that they were attracted to the chemical by means of its odor. We now know that more than 10,000 sensory hairs at the tips of the antennae capture the odorous molecules, and a single molecule is enough to stimulate a receptor cell.

Sexual attraction may be the most widespread function of chemical communication. But another important use is in conveying information about food. Have you ever noticed that as soon as one fly discovers a piece of food, a great many others suddenly turn up? When a fly touches the food for the first time, it deposits a certain chemical on it. Other flies can smell this chemical from a distance. An elaborate version of this type of communication is performed by ant colonies, as shown in figure 21-19. Worker ants start out foraging independently for food. After locating a food source, such as a lump of sugar, the worker returns to the hill or nest, leaving a pheromone trail as it goes. It does this by touching its abdomen to the ground in a regular pattern (A). Soon many of the ants follow the well-marked trail to and from the food (B). Later, when the food is gone, the ants no longer secrete the pheromones. The chemical soon diffuses from the area, thus erasing the trail. As the trail vanishes, the movement of the ants becomes random (C), and eventually they leave the area (D).

This example illustrates some of the advantages as well as the disadvantages of

Figure 21-17. The female gypsy moth excretes a pheromone that is detectable by male gypsy moths as much as a mile away.

Figure 21-18. Simple traps such as this, with a one-way entrance and a synthetic attractant as bait, are used to attract and capture male gypsy moths for experimentation.

chemical communication. Chemical signals can be detected in the dark, are not blocked by obstacles, and can be perceived for a considerable distance: a small amount of chemical goes a long way. On the other hand, such signals travel very slowly and tend to fade fairly quickly. In addition, once sent, chemical messages are hard to change, or even modify. Changes in relative status during a conflict, for example, cannot be communicated by such signals.

Many animals have a number of different mechanisms of chemical communication. The deer, for instance, has glands in its hooves that secrete an odor warning of danger. Other deer, perceiving it, quickly

442

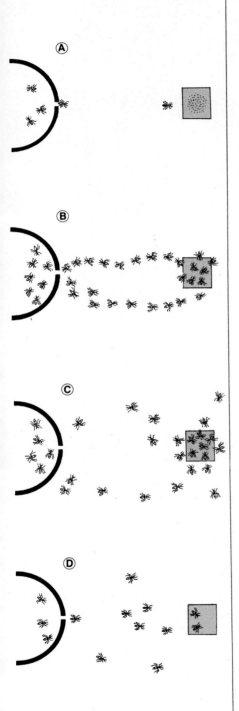

Figure 21-19. Ants following a pheromone trail to locate food.

flee. Other glands at the base of the antlers secrete a substance that indicates a male's territory when rubbed on the trunks of trees. This tells other males to stay clear, and invites the females to enter the territory and mate. Secretions in the urine and the feces convey still other messages.

Pheromones and hormones appear to work together. (In fact, pheromones are sometimes known as **ectohormones.**) Most female mammals, for example, secrete a chemical odor at one point in the hormone-controlled sexual cycle. This signals their period of sexual receptivity, or estrus. It has usually been thought that human females do not secrete such pheromones. However, a number of experiments with group-living human females, such as hospital nurses and college dormitory residents, have turned up some interesting information. Within a six-month period, all of the women's menstrual periods were found to have synchronized. This suggests that perhaps pheromones function among humans in ways we have only begun to discover. For that matter, it would be surprising if we did not use chemical communication in some way, as all other living things do.

The importance of chemical communication, and the likelihood that we ourselves use it, suggest a question for our "civilized" age. Are we, without meaning to, disrupting chemical communication systems? Chemical pollution of the air may be "jamming" pheromone messages. And our concern with getting rid of disagreeable odors may be causing trouble also. We have learned that insecticides kill both helpful and harmful insects. Similarly, deodorants and air fresheners may destroy needed pheromones along with unpleasant smells.

Sending messages by sound

Like chemicals, sound travels in darkness and around obstacles. It covers considerable distances, too: the call of the North American prairie chicken can be heard from a distance of three miles. Birds are the great callers, of course, but many other animals communicate by making different sounds, most of them remarkably precise and specialized according to the message they are meant to carry.

Like all messages, those that travel by sound waves are multifunctional. They serve to locate food, send alarms, attract a sexual partner, and coordinate group activity. A few of the many examples, some familiar, some less so, will give us a glimpse of how they work.

Alarm calls work in different ways. Some serve as warnings to possible predators that the signaler is well armed and should be avoided. The barking of a dog, the hissing of a cat, and the buzz of a rattlesnake's rattles are familiar examples. More social functions are performed by signals that alert members of the group to the presence of danger. Some send word to flee; most bird calls are of this kind. Others send a call for help, such as the howl of an injured wolf that summons the rest of the pack to its aid. The strategy set off by the alarm signal depends on how the group is organized for defense.

The great advantage that auditory signals have over chemical signals is that they can be modulated—in volume, duration, pitch, and quality. How sounds are varied depends on the purpose they are meant to serve, as well as on the ability of the organism to make and receive the sound.

Since insects cannot distinguish pitch, they vary the volume and pace of their sounds instead, creating different overall patterns. Some make clicking sounds with their jaws or whirring sounds with their wings. Katydids and crickets "fiddle" their songs by rubbing their wing covers together. The underside of each wing has a raised vein with ridges, much like a metal file. The upper side of the wing has a sharp ridge, like a scraper. When the file rubs against the scraper in different patterns, different "songs" are produced. The locust, or grasshopper, has similar equipment, with the "file" on the hind leg instead of the wing. The cicada, in contrast, produces vibrations

Figure 21-20. The male deer possesses glands at the base of the antlers. The secretion of these glands attracts female deer but repels other males.

within its body. Inside the abdomen is an air chamber, containing a set of powerful muscles attached to a membrane. When the muscles contract, they tighten the membrane; when they relax, they release the tension. The sound of this movement, resonating in the air chamber, produces the cicada's shrill song.

All of these signals communicate messages of sexual invitation, and most of them are made by the males only. Among mosquitoes, however, it is the females of each species that make a characteristic hum with their wings, which the males of that species are able to recognize and so locate a mate. Variations in pattern are thus essential to species identification among insects that have a sense of hearing. In this way they function as an important isolating mechanism, such as those we discussed in chapter 19.

Animals that have "voice-boxes," or larynxes, can vary their vocal signals in a number of ways. Howler monkeys, for example, use low-pitched roars to signal rival groups far away in the dense rain forests of South America. These low frequencies are particularly good at bypassing obstacles, such as trees. Tamarin monkeys, on the other hand, have a high-pitched call, which dies out faster and scatters quickly on the leaves and trunks of trees. This serves for

INTERACTING WITH
THE ENVIRONMENT

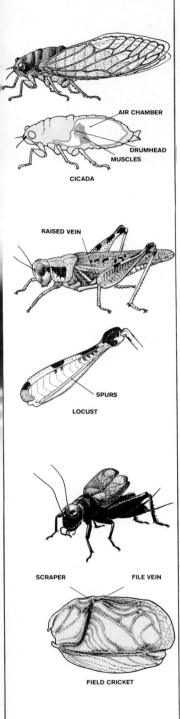

Figure 21-21. Inside the cicada's abdomen is a set of powerful muscles attached to a membrane. When the muscles contract, they tighten the membrane; when they relax, they release the tension. The sound of this movement, resonating in the large air chamber in the abdomen, produces the cicada's shrill song. The locust, or grasshopper, produces its song by rubbing its hind legs against its wings. The hind legs have spurs along the inside that vibrate as they are rubbed over a raised vein in the wing. The field cricket "fiddles" its song by rubbing its wings, one on top of the other. The underside of each wing has a raised vein with ridges, much like a metal file. The upper side of the wing has a sharp ridge, which acts as a scraper. When the file rubs against the scraper, the characteristic sound is produced.

AIR CHAMBER

DRUMHEAD
MUSCLES

CICADA

RAISED VEIN

SPURS

LOCUST

SCRAPER   FILE VEIN

FIELD CRICKET

short-range contact. Because it does not travel far, the high-pitched call does not expose the smaller tamarin in the way the low-pitched call would do.

The vocal sounds made by birds are produced by an organ called the **syrinx.** Birds also have a well-developed sense of hearing, and rely on auditory communication for a great many things. Both males and females send calls, not only for warnings, but also to signal the location of food sources. Males also employ song to attract their mates and establish a domain. Unlike the other calls, these songs have elaborate structures and are usually long. They convey the information that a sexually mature male of a certain species has found a territory he intends to defend and will share it with a suitable female.

Most of the auditory signals of both birds and mammals are produced by specialized vocal organs. But birds and mammals also make sounds in other ways, primarily in territorial displays. The North American ruffed grouse, for example, "drums" by beating its wings rapidly against the air, thereby warning an intruder not to cross its boundaries. And the rat-a-tat-tat of a woodpecker drilling into a tree does not always mean it is looking for insects. Sometimes the noise is part of a territorial display, and if no tree is at hand, a metal roof will do as well. The effectiveness of sound in dominance or leadership displays was discovered by one of the chimpanzees observed by Jane van Lawick-Goodall in Tanzania. Such displays usually involve waving large branches in a menacing fashion. But one contender discovered that empty five-gallon cans were much more effective. By clanging the cans together, he created a deafening roar that made his meaning very clear, and the other chimps soon showed proper respect.

Echolocation
Some animals depend on hearing as a sort of "second sight." These animals produce a series of regular sounds like small clicks which bounce off obstacles as echoes. By

picking up these echoes, the animals can determine the nature of an object and its location. This process is known as **echolocation,** and it is used by whales, dolphins, and some bats. Bats are most active at night, when vision is of little help in locating food and avoiding obstacles. They use sounds of very high frequencies—often too high to be heard by the human ear. These are apparently most effective in picking up detail, which is particularly important when locating the small insects on which many bats feed. Until recently it was assumed that insects were helpless victims of such a system. However, certain moths have been found to have sensitive auditory receptors that detect the bat's high-frequency sounds. Thus warned, the moth has a chance to get out of the way.

A similar system, using short clicks, is employed by whales and dolphins, especially at night. These animals use even higher frequencies than bats do, as these are the frequencies that travel best in the water. Clicks are produced in different places, including the larynx of dolphins and the blowholes of whales. Most recently it was found that a specialized bulbous fatty area on the heads of porpoises and small whales serves this purpose. Differences in the echoes produced enable the sea mammals to determine size, shape, and distance of fish.

This system is very similar to the sonar system used by ships to detect underwater submarines. Indeed, we first became aware of the existence of the animal signals during World War II, when some sonar receiving devices began picking up an alarming number of strange clicks and squeaks. These were later found to be coming from dolphins and other marine animals. Since that time, scientists have been trying to determine whether or not these marine mammals use the echolocation system to "talk" to each other as well as locate food and objects. Recent research indicates that a great many more sea mammals, including seals and sea lions, may employ echolocation.

"Listening in" on animals that communi-

Figure 21-22. Bats use echolocation to locate food and avoid obstacles.

cate by sound is not always easy, for as we become less directly dependent on nature, we also become less aware of sound. Naturalist Farley Mowat has recorded that certain groups of arctic Eskimos, however, whose survival depends on hunting caribou, can listen to the howling wolves and thereby learn when and from which direction the caribou herds will be coming.

Visual messages

It is usually easy to tell whether an animal utilizes visual information, by exposing the animal to light and observing its reaction. It is much more difficult to determine the exact manner in which the animal sends and receives visual information. Color, shape, and movement are all aspects of a visual image. And it is not always clear just which aspect provokes the response—or whether all three are involved.

Movement is perhaps the most basic type of visual message. Animals with low-sensitivity photoreceptors, such as the housefly, may detect movement only as a sudden change from light to dark. But this may be enough to trigger an escape reaction.

The form or shape of an animal is known to be a type of visual message. To young chicks, for example, it is the characteristic shape of a descending hawk that triggers a crouching response; the shape of a sparrow passes unnoticed. More flexible signals are conveyed by changes in posture. Many animals communicate threat by means of a rigid, often forward-thrusting stance. Cats and dogs are familiar examples, but it may be surprising to learn that crabs and lizards

INTERACTING WITH
THE ENVIRONMENT

ATTITUDE OF ALARM THREATENING AT A DISTANCE ALL-OUT ATTACK

STRONG CONFLICT BETWEEN AGGRESSION AND FEAR WEAK CONFLICT BETWEEN AGGRESSION AND FEAR DEFENSIVE

INFERIORITY TIMID SOCIAL APPROACH APPROACH TO PROSPECTIVE MATE

Figure 21-23. The overall position of the body can be a visual message. This is some of the visual "vocabulary" used by greylag geese.

do the same thing. Again, cats and dogs ruffle their fur, making themselves appear larger and more menacing. Lizards can raise their crests and get the same effect. A whole range of different moods is conveyed by the greylag goose, simply by altering its body posture.

Facial expression may be considered an aspect of shape. Often a distinct facial expression accompanies a given body posture. Rhesus monkeys are known to glare at invaders, their bodies rigid and muscles tense. And chimpanzees have a marvelous range of facial expressions.

Color and shading also convey information. Color signals often take the form of a "badge" or bright patch of feathers, fur, or skin. Most people are familiar with the robin's red breast. This, like most such color badges, functions both to indicate the species identity and to attract a mate. Among the birds, it is usually the males who initiate courtship, and they therefore have the colorful feathers. But in many species the females do the inviting. Most nonhuman primates display a "sexual skin," patches of color on the chest or genitals that indicate sexual receptivity.

The above examples all illustrate the highly variable nature of visual communication. This is the chief advantage of such systems. Quick changes of mood or temper can be indicated, making visual communication widely used in both aggressive and

But visual messages require light. Moreover, in most cases, the receiver must look directly at the sender, or the message will be lost. Perhaps for these reasons, visual displays are often combined with other signals, both chemical and auditory.

CHEMICAL SEDUCERS IN HUMAN FEMALES?

From ants to elephants, females of all animal species secrete chemicals that attract the males. Recently, scientists have been looking into the possibility that young women may also secrete such sex attractants, or pheromones.

Experiments have shown that a chemical known as aliphatic acid is produced in the vaginas of sexually mature female monkeys. Its odor, which resembles vinegar, acts as a chemical seducer on male monkeys. Now, aliphatic acid appears to have been isolated in human females by a team of Atlanta researchers. Its presence is most easily detectable during the woman's fertile period. The odor of the chemical is most powerful during the post-ovulatory and menstrual stages of her cycle.

The question of whether this human pheromone has any effect on males, as it does in lower animals, remains up in the air. At least one researcher believes that this chemical may "turn on" a small number of men. For the most part, though, the presence of the pheromone is probably masked by frequent bathing and the use of perfumes and other artificial scents.

There is also evidence that humans, like many other animals, may secrete pheromones that are not related to sexual attraction. In one experiment, performed at a medical center in San Francisco, it was found that by the age of six months, most nursing infants will respond to the smell of their mothers and can distinguish between the mother's odor and those of other nursing women. Another experiment by the same researchers involved a "sniff test" using T-shirts that had been worn for twenty-four hours. The results indicated that adults of both sexes can distinguish by smell, with a good deal of accuracy, whether a garment has been worn by a male or a female.

The significance of pheromones in humans has yet to be fully analyzed. The sex attractants, for example, play an important role in the sexual behavior of most animals but a lesser role in that of primates, and may have no real importance in humans. The ability to distinguish between individuals and between the sexes by smell may possibly play a role in the sexual orientation of infants and young children, whose sense of smell appears to be much more acute than that of adults.

courtship displays. The source of a visual message, moreover, is easy to pinpoint. It is simpler to pick out the one bird in a flock that is flapping its wings and displaying its colored breast than it is to determine which one is singing.

There is one type of visual message, however, that can be seen in the dark. This is sent by organisms that are capable of emitting light, a phenomenon called **bioluminescence.** Certain sponges, corals, jellyfish, insects, fish, and other animals can produce

INTERACTING WITH
THE ENVIRONMENT

FEAR   ATTENTION   JOY

ANGER   EXCITEMENT   SADNESS

Figure 21-24. The different facial expressions of chimpanzees can convey a considerable range of visual messages.

such signals. The most familiar example is probably the firefly, or lightning bug.

Like so many visual signals, the firefly's flashes are a part of courtship. On summer nights the male flies about, flashing light in a pattern characteristic of that species only. The female of the species, responding to the pattern, answers with a softer, steadier light. The male recognizes this and flies toward it. The light is produced by an oxygen-activated enzyme catalyst in the body of the firefly, and it ranges in color from bright green to bright yellow. The color and timing of the flashes differ for every species. Such differences help to prevent species mixups, which would be unlikely to produce fertile offspring.

The females of at least one species, however, profit from the difference in signal patterns. By imitating the pattern of another species, they attract mate-seeking males of that species—and then eat them when they arrive.

The dance of the honeybee

We have already noted that one of the primary functions of animal communication is to coordinate group activity. This is especially important in highly organized animal societies. If the methods of communication are not understood by its members, there can be no society.

Bees maintain such a highly organized society. As we might expect, the patterns of communication are varied. Most are employed by the workers—the nonreproducing females that make up the major portion of the hive population. The workers communicate by means of chemical, auditory, and visual messages—sometimes by means of all three.

The first major breakthrough in the study of honeybee "language" resulted from experiments conducted by an Austrian biologist, Karl von Frisch. Von Frisch placed several dishes of sugar water in the vicinity of a hive of bees. He found that it might take hours or even days before a dish of sugar water was discovered by a worker bee in her search for food. But within an hour of her discovery, hundreds of other workers had visited the dish. Marking with colored paint the bees that first found the sugar, he watched them when they returned to the hive. He soon noticed that they often performed what he called a "round dance," in which they whirled around in a small circle, first to the right, then to the left. Other workers gathered round the dancers and began to imitate the dance. Then they left the hive and flew directly to the dish of sugar water.

In other instances, returning workers performed what von Frisch called a "waggle dance," making a series of figure-eight patterns. In the middle of the figure eight, the bee ran a short distance in a straight line, wagging her abdomen back and forth. As with the round dance, excited workers first imitated the dance, then touched the worker with their antennae. Then they headed for the food. Von Frisch found that they began to look on the ground within 20 percent of the right distance. He later discovered that distance determined which dance the bee performed. When the food was placed within about 275 feet of the hive, she did the round dance; when it was further away, she did the waggle dance.

When von Frisch moved a dish even further away, say from a distance of 1,000 feet to 2,000 feet, he found that the tempo of the waggle dance decreased, and the length of the straight run increased. The complete waggle pattern was accomplished fifteen times in 30 seconds when the food was 1,000 feet away, and only eleven times when it was moved to 2,000 feet.

The other important information contained in the waggle dance is direction. When dancing outside the hive on a horizontal surface, the bees point directly at the food source. The others then fly in that direction. But the dance is usually performed inside a dark hive and on a vertical surface. Thus the straight-line portion of the dance cannot point directly to the source of food.

Figure 21-25. Honeybees are marked with a dab of red paint as they collect at a dish of sugar water.

Figure 21-26. The round dance is used when the nectar is less than 275 feet away. The returning worker, carrying the scent of the flower, does the round dance. The speed of the dance indicates the richness of the nectar source. The faster the dance, the more excited the workers become. The scent and the dance are enough information for the other workers, who then leave the hive to search for the nectar. The waggle dance is used when the nectar is more than 275 feet away. This dance also tells the workers in which direction to fly in order to locate the food.

ROUND DANCE

WAGGLE DANCE

INTERACTING WITH
THE ENVIRONMENT

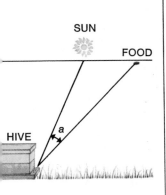

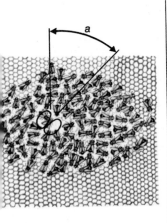

SUN

FOOD

HIVE

a

a

a

Figure 21-27. Von Frisch learned that the bee doing the waggle dance oriented itself at some angle from a vertical line inside the hive. By experimenting, he found that this angle always indicated the direction of the food source with respect to the position of the sun. In the upper diagram, the food is located at an angle to the right of the sun.

Inside the hive, the worker orients itself at this same angle from the vertical, saying, in effect, "Fly in this direction in relation to the sun."

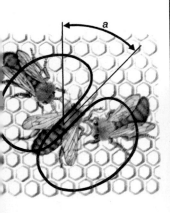

Figure 21-28. The electric eel is not a true eel but a relative of the sucker, minnow, and catfish. A native of South America, it sometimes reaches a length of 8 feet. The electric charge it generates is reputed to have killed horses and men.

Instead, this portion of the dance is performed at an angle from the vertical, as shown in figure 21-27. The others then reach the food by flying at this same angle in relation to the rays of the sun. Thus, when the food is on a direct line between the hive and the sun, the center run of the dance points straight up. When it is to one side of the line between hive and sun, the dancer orients the center run at a corresponding angle. Put another way, by running straight up during the waggle dance, the bee says, in effect, "Fly on a line with the sun." By running at an angle 40 degrees to the right of the vertical, she says, "Fly on a line 40 degrees to the right of the sun."

Several recent experiments indicate that bees may also use other clues in locating food. For one thing, the workers in the hive always touch the dancing bee with their antennae. This may communicate various sorts of information. In many cases there are flowers of different kinds at the indicated place. Which kind has the prized nectar? Experiments show that the bee usually heads straight for the right flower, suggesting that she has already had a clue. Each kind of pollen or nectar has a distinctive scent. Particles of pollen, carrying this odor, cling to the bee when she returns to the hive. Hence, other bees may use their antennae to smell or even taste the characteristic odor, thus identifying the flower.

But it has also been found that, while dancing, the bee produces a distinctive buzzing sound by vibrating her wings. This sound is made only upon discovery of food. It may signal another message which the others pick up through mechanoreceptors in their antennae. One particular buzzing pattern occurs as the worker runs through the straight-line portion of her dance, suggesting that the signal may communicate the direction of the food.

Still more messages

Most animals exchange information by means of chemical, auditory, or visual signals, or by a combination of two or more

451

kinds. But the more we learn about how animals communicate, the more kinds of message we discover. Two of the better known of these involve a special kind of mechanoreception. They are **surface-wave communication** and **electrical communication.**

Scientists have long been aware that a number of animals respond to waves or ripples in the water to locate potential prey or predators. Several species of fish do this; so do the whirligig beetle and the water spider. The whirligig beetle picks up ripples by resting its feet on the surface of the water. The water spider turns the process upside down. It hangs from the surface, detecting similar waves with its hairy legs. Both the spider and the beetle then go after struggling insects that have fallen into the water, or flee from the stronger waves made by fish or other large predators.

One species of water spider also sends and receives messages by means of surface waves. Both male and female spiders send patterned wave signals in courtship. The male starts by seizing a small object and using it to send waves toward a female. The female approaches, responding with her own waves.

Some organisms even respond to electricity. There is increasing evidence that all organisms generate a weak electric field around themselves. Some aquatic predators, such as sharks, rays, and catfish, appear to "home in" on this field.

Certain fish and fresh-water eels generate stronger electric fields, usually by muscles in their tails, producing a series of weak-voltage shocks. Objects within the field set up disturbances in the field, and are therefore detected. Electric fish give off a special electrical discharge pattern just before attacking their prey. These same signals are apparently used as threats to other members of their own species, whom they normally avoid. Although this method is effective over only a short distance, it seems to work well at night and in the murky waters where the fish live. Also, because electrical communication is used by so few animals, it has the great advantage of privacy—it is hard for other species to "tune in on."

SUMMARY

Communication is the way in which individuals exchange information; one conveys a message and the other responds to it. Animals send information only to other animals, but they receive information from all aspects of their environment. The process by which information is taken from the outside to the inside of their bodies is part of sensory reception. Specialized sensory receptors pick up environmental stimuli and transmit them to the brain. Mechanical, chemical, and visual receptors each receive different types of stimulus. The nature of the sensation provoked by each stimulus is determined by the brain.

All sensory receptors consist of one or more sensory nerve endings. Mechanoreceptors known as touch receptors are located in the skin, and are sensitive to touch, pressure, heat, cold, and pain. Stretch receptors in muscles, tendons, and joints respond to changes in muscle activity and the position of the bones. The most specialized mechanoreceptors are those that respond to air or water vibrations, which are perceived as sound. Sound can be interpreted in terms of volume, pitch, duration, and quality. In higher animals and some lower ones the specialized sound receptor is the ear, which may also monitor information about balance.

Chemoreceptors respond to chemical stimuli. Olfactory receptors can receive information from a distance, but gustatory receptors must come into direct contact with a liquid chemical stimulus in order to produce the sensation of taste. In many animals the senses of taste and smell are combined; some others also have combined chemical and touch receptors.

Photoreceptors translate light into sensory nerve impulses. Animals with low-sensitivity visual receptors respond only to the presence or absence of light; others have specialized organs of vision known as eyes. The simple eye transmits only a blurred image. The compound eye transmits a multiple image, and is sensitive to flicker or changes from dark to light. The camera eye can adjust to varying intensities of light and varying distances of an object, and can function in both light and darkness.

The sending of messages can also be broken down in terms of the way the message is received. Chemical signals are detected by smell and taste, and are used by all organisms. Pheromones are chemicals secreted by one individual of a species that stimulate behavior responses in other members of the species. They convey information concerning the location of food, facilitate courtship and mating, and coordinate group activities.

Auditory signals are more flexible than chemical signals, but they require a sense of hearing and usually a specialized organ for sound production. Echolocation is a special form of auditory communication. This process consists of sending a series of high-frequency clicking noises and picking up their echoes as they bounce off of obstacles. Different echoes convey information about the size, shape, and distance of objects.

Visual signals may involve changes in movement, shape, color, or combinations of these. Some organisms, such as the firefly, produce their own light signals by bioluminescence. Because visual signals can be quickly changed, they frequently serve in courtship and aggressive display. In complex animal societies, such as that of the honeybee, signalling may involve a combination of chemical, auditory, and visual methods.

Review questions

1. What are the two components of communication?

2. What is sensory reception?

3. Where are the touch receptors located? What sensations do they deal with?

4. Describe the way in which a pain receptor functions.

5. What aspects of sound can humans detect? Which of these would probably be least valuable to a lower animal?

6. What is the lateral line system? How does it function?

7. Describe the general structure of the human ear.

8. How are chemoreceptors stimulated? Describe two types of chemoreceptor and explain how their functions are related.

9. List some of the variations found in photoreceptors and the light patterns they can receive. Is the lack of specialized eyes necessarily a disadvantage?

10. Distinguish between the structure and function of simple and compound eyes.

11. Describe the structure of the human eye.

12. What are the functions of the rods and cones?

13. What is the commonest method by which animals exchange messages? Describe some examples.

14. What are pheromones? What sort of information can they convey? Give some examples.

15. Describe some of the ways in which animals communicate by sound.

16. What is echolocation? What animals are known to employ it?

17. Name some of the ways by which animals communicate visually. Is this sort of communication always under voluntary control?

18. Describe the round dance and the waggle dance of the honeybee. What information is conveyed by each dance?

19. What is surface-wave communication?

20. Describe an example of electrical communication.

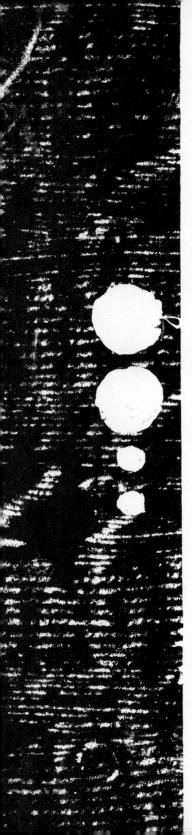

Animal Behavior

Wherever people have a chance to watch animals—at a zoo, park, pet store, or circus—it is evident that animal behavior is a source of fascination for most humans. As they watch animals at play and at rest, feeding or protecting themselves, and tending to their young, onlookers frequently marvel at the similarities between animal and human behavior. These similarities are, in fact, one important reason for studying the activities of animals: that is, their implications for the better understanding of human behavior.

The question of why animals behave the way they do has attracted the interest of scientists from many fields—psychologists, zoologists, ecologists, geneticists, endocrinologists—to name a few. Despite this broad interest, though, and despite major gains in recent years, knowledge in this field remains in its infancy.

WHAT IS BEHAVIOR?

Simply defined, **behavior** is activity in response to an internal or external stimulus. All animals make adjustments to information or stimuli, from their external and internal environments. These adjustments may be voluntary or involuntary, and may range from a simple, single act to a complex and elaborate sequence of activities.

Taxis, kinesis, reflex

A very important behavioral response in the lives of many invertebrates and some vertebrates is the **taxis.** This is a directional movement in response to a specific type of environmental stimulus. The taxis response is inborn, and need not be learned; but it is fixed, and cannot be altered to suit unusual conditions.

For example, a moth navigates in a straight line by keeping at a constant angle to the parallel rays of the sun (or more often the moon, since most moths are nocturnal). This taxis works well under natural conditions. However, it can cause trouble when the light source is so near that it produces diffused instead of parallel rays, as in the case of a candle or a light bulb. In this case, instead of a straight path, the constant angle may lead the moth into a spiral, so that it circles ever inward toward the light source and is eventually burned to death.

Another involuntary behavior pattern, best known in simple organisms, is **kinesis.** This is an increase or decrease in the movement of an animal in proportion to the intensity of a stimulus. Such movements are not directional, like the taxis. Instead, they consist of increases in the rate of turning from side to side, or in other body movements. Planarians, for instance, when placed in the light, do not swim directly back to the darker areas where they normally stay. Instead, they continue weaving from side to side, but they turn more strongly toward the side where they encounter less intense light. This turning eventually brings them back to the dark area.

A third behavior pattern involving relatively simple, innate responses to stimuli is the **reflex.** A reflex is the involuntary movement of some part of the animal's body in response to a stimulus. A familiar example is the kicking motion you make when the tendons below your kneecap are struck by a doctor's hammer. Unlike the taxis and kinesis, the reflex does not involve a complete body movement.

Biorhythms: circadian, lunar, annual

Many of the external stimuli that influence animal behavior are irregular or unpredictable. Floods, forest fires, and predator attacks do not happen on schedule. But animals are also strongly influenced by regular and predictable changes in their environments, such as the divisions of day and

Figure 22-1. A flock of water fowl take flight for the autumn migration. Migration is a pattern of animal behavior that is not yet fully understood.

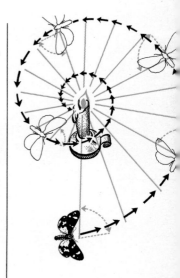

Figure 22-2. Why does a moth fly in a spiral around a candle flame, a path that eventually takes it to its doom? Moths use light from the sun or the moon for their navigation. These light sources are so far away that their rays reaching the earth are almost parallel; so the moth can fly in a straight line by using the rays as a reference point. But the rays from "point" light sources—candles, light bulbs, and so forth—spread out in all directions. The moth attempts to keep at the same angle to the candle's light that it would if it was navigating by the sun. Here the moth flies a path that forms a constant angle of 80° with the candle, a pathway to a fiery death.

456

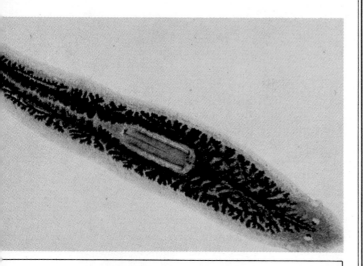

Figure 22-3. A planarian placed in the light will turn more strongly toward the direction from which the light is less intense. (Courtesy General Biological Supply House, Inc., Chicago.)

Figure 22-4. The color of a fiddler crab is influenced by tidal changes. It darkens as the tide comes in and becomes lighter when the tide is ebbing.

night, tidal variations, and the change of seasons. The cyclic behavior patterns by which animals adapt to these phenomena are called **biorhythms.** Plants, too, have biorhythms, though we shall not discuss them here. Like the simple responses of taxis, kinesis, and reflex, biorhythms are essentially involuntary.

Many of the biorhythms that we can observe in nature are based on a species' apparent preference for day or night activity. Thus we find small birds and squirrels busy during the warmer daylight hours, and owls, raccoons, and certain insects appearing only in the cooler, darker, more humid hours of night. Such cycles of activity, based on a schedule roughly twenty-four hours in length, are known as **circadian rhythms** (from the Latin words "circa:" "about," and "dies": "day").

Until recently, it was believed that circadian rhythms were dependent on environmental cues, such as light or temperature. Laboratory experiments have shown, however, that rhythmic behavior generally continues with amazing accuracy even after such indicators are removed.

For example, what happens to the fiddler crab when it is placed in an environment whose rhythms do not correspond to those of its natural habitat? Normally the fiddler crab, an inhabitant of ocean shorelines, becomes lighter in color as the tide goes out. When the tide comes in, it darkens again. If it is removed from the shore to a place where tides do not occur, the crab continues to show regular changes in body color. Furthermore, the changes are still timed to the tides, although the crab no longer encounters the tidal ebb and flow.

Experiments such as this demonstrate that there is something more at work than outside stimuli in these rhythmic responses. Some internal timing mechanism appears to be present as well. Referred to as a **biological clock,** this regulating mechanism within the organism will influence it to respond according to a settled pattern, even when the environmental stimuli are missing. The precise processes involved in the "clock" are as yet unknown.

People as well as other animals possess biorhythms. Most familiar, perhaps, would be a person's natural rhythms of hunger and sleepiness. Recent research has shown that humans also have rhythms associated with body temperature, pulse rate, blood pressure, hormone secretions, lung capacity, and a variety of other physiological events. All of these rhythms are associated with complex functions of many different internal organs.

Biological clocks can be reset. Experimenting further with the fiddler crab, scientists placed the crab in a situation where tides occurred on a new schedule. Over a period of time, the crab then adjusted its color changes to this schedule. However, the resetting does take time. Jet lag, the time-change adjustment faced by airplane travelers flying across several time zones, occurs because the times of dawn, dusk, and so on are suddenly changed, while inner bodily rhythms continue on the same schedule as before.

A second form of biorhythm is known as a **lunar rhythm,** and relates to a lunar or moon period of 29.5 days. This pattern is extremely important to the animals living in the intertidal zone, the area of a beach between high tide and low tide lines. As the tides rise and fall, this zone is alternately covered and uncovered by water. The moon's gravitational pull causes the tides to occur every 12 hours and 25 minutes. The moon's position in relation to the earth and sun also varies the height of the tides, over a cycle of about fourteen days.

One organism whose activities are based on lunar rhythms is the grunion, a small fish living in the waters off the California coast. From February to September, these fish appear on the beach at the uppermost tide line during the highest tide of the lunar cycle. Females dig holes in the sand and lay their eggs; males fertilize them. When this task is completed, the grunions return to the sea. The fertilized eggs develop in the warm sand

Figure 22-5. A female grunion has buried herself in the sand in order to lay her eggs. Only her head is exposed. At left another female is beginning to burrow into the sand tail first.

during the next two weeks, while the tides are lower. At the next extra-high tide, 14 days from the time the eggs were laid, the young grunions are covered with water and are carried down to the sea.

Yearly rhythms, referred to as **annual rhythms,** have also been identified. These are generally associated with activities that tie in with seasonal changes, such as reproduction, feeding, hibernation, and growth. Annual rhythms are probably widespread in the animal world. There is evidence that the human species follows annual rhythms in such matters as frequency of certain diseases, birth rates, and a variety of physiological states.

SPECIES-TYPICAL BEHAVIOR: INNATE AND LEARNED

A moth navigates by the rays of the sun, a

INTERACTING WITH
THE ENVIRONMENT

Figure 22-6. These wildebeests are migrating to their appropriate breeding area. Such animal migration is an example of instinctive behavior.

fiddler crab adjusts its body color to darkness, a grunion lays eggs at high tide—these forms of behavior are **species-typical.** That is, they are recognizable, predictable, and constant among all members of a given animal species. We may assume, then, that they have a genetic basis. Insofar as this is true, such behavior is termed **innate** or inborn.

Innate behavior may involve a very simple response, as in the case of a reflex, or it may be quite complex, as in the nest-building behavior of birds. When behavior is inherited, complex, and not dependent upon learning, it is referred to as **instinctive.** A spider spinning its web, a squirrel storing food, and an opossum playing dead are all engaged in instinctive behavior. Instinct is the basis of animal hygiene, social interaction, reproductive activities, food procurement, and defensive strategies.

The question of whether animal behavior is largely a matter of instinct or of learning was hotly debated in the early twentieth century. Once posed as either–or alternatives, learning and instinct are now seen to interact. Clearly an animal cannot be made to learn an activity for which its inherited set of muscles and nerve pathways is inappropriate. Inheritance, therefore, sets the limits within which learning can occur, but much instinctive behavior can be modified through experience. Whether or not a particular form of behavior can be modified by learning is determined by the capacity of each species to adapt to environmental change.

For example, walking through a vacant field on a summer day, you see a wasp alight on the back of a grasshopper. Deftly the wasp stings the grasshopper behind the head. In moments the grasshopper's legs give out, and the wasp, seizing its victim's antennae, drags off the paralyzed prey.

Curious to know the wasp's next move, you follow it, and see it deposit the insect in a carefully-prepared hole in the ground. Then the wasp lays an egg on the body, buries both egg and grasshopper, and flies away. The grasshopper will serve as fresh food for the young larva that will hatch from the egg.

This elaborate sequence of behavior was also of interest to Jean-Henri Fabre, whose studies of moth communication we noted in the last chapter. He noticed that this species of wasp would select only female grasshoppers, so he attempted to fool it by substituting a male grasshopper. The wasp rejected the substitute. Fabre also attempted to imitate the surgical skill of the wasp by probing for the nerve ganglion that controlled the grasshopper's legs. The wasp proved to be the better surgeon. Because of the seemingly intelligent and precise way the wasp behaved, Fabre termed this the "wisdom of instinct."

An almost contradictory finding was what Fabre called the "ignorance of instinct." Tampering further with the physical factors in the animal's sequence of behavior, Fabre cut off the antennae of a grasshopper. Instead of grasping the leg of its victim to compensate for the missing antennae, the wasp merely abandoned the insect.

Again, Fabre interfered in the sequence, this time removing the grasshopper before the wasp could seal the hole. As Fabre described this experiment:

I intervene in the middle of the work. Pushing the Sphex (the wasp) aside, I carefully clear the short gallery with the blade of a knife, take away the materials that close it and restore full communication between the cell and the outside. Then, with my forceps, without damaging the edifice, I take the Ephippiger (the grasshopper) from the cell. . . . The wasp's egg is on the victim's breast, at the usual place, the root of one of the hinder thighs: a proof that the Sphex was giving the finishing touch to the burrow, with the intention of never returning.

Having done this and put the stolen prey safely away in a box, I yield my place to the Sphex, who has been on the watch beside me while I was rifling her home. Finding the door open, she goes

Figure 22-7. A *Sphex* wasp, such as Fabre observed, is carrying a paralyzed katydid, a relative of the grasshopper. The sequence of activities it is following is an example of innate behavior.

in and stays for a few moments. Then she comes out and resumes her work where I interrupted it, that is to say, she starts conscientiously stopping the entrance to the cell by sweeping dust backwards and carrying grains of sand, which she continues to heap up with scrupulous care, as though she were doing useful work. When the door is once again thoroughly walled up, the insect brushes itself, seems to give a glance of satisfaction at the task accomplished and finally flies away.[1]

The wasp could carry out an elaborate sequence of behavior, but could not change it to adjust for the fact that the grasshopper and egg—the reason for the whole business—were no longer there.

Fabre summed up the seemingly contradictory "wisdom" and "ignorance" of insect behavior with the following observation:

To know everything and to know nothing, according as it acts under normal or exceptional conditions: that is the strange antithesis presented by the insect race.[2]

In the wasp, a complex behavior pattern was entirely innate. In some other animal species, a capacity for certain behavior is innate, but the behavior pattern itself must be learned from other members of the species. An extensively studied example is the chaffinch.

INTERACTING WITH
THE ENVIRONMENT

The intricate relationship of inheritance and learning in the ability of a chaffinch to sing its normal song was studied by isolating young birds from others of the species. The song produced by these laboratory-bred birds varied greatly from that of the wild chaffinch. However, when given an oppor-

which it was exposed. Both inheritance and learning, therefore, played a role in developing an appropriate species-typical behavior.

Experience is also important in modifying the innate behavior of brown rats. The nest-building activities of this rodent consist of gathering materials, heaping them up

CHATTING WITH CHIMPS

When Lana the chimpanzee is thirsty—or hungry or wants to see a movie—she tells her keeper by tapping a few buttons on a computer keyboard in her Plexiglas cage. The message flashes on a screen at the keeper's keyboard outside; he taps out a reply for Lana and does her bidding.

Such "conversations," at the Yerkes Regional Primate Center in Atlanta, exemplify language-learning research being carried out with primates in a handful of laboratories around the United States. Scientists are using a variety of techniques to determine whether chimps can learn to communicate in symbolic language of the sort used by humans. So far, it looks as if the answer is "yes."

Among the first techniques to be tried was sign language, because chimps lack the vocal apparatus needed for spoken human speech. The form chosen was American Sign Language, which is used by many deaf people. Some chimps learned as many as 165 words, and were able to string them together into meaningful sentences. Currently,

two young chimps are being raised from infancy by deaf people who use signs for ordinary communication among themselves. Predictably, these youngsters are learning faster than other chimps, who typically were not exposed to signs until well after their first birthday.

Similarly exciting is the success with the computer language being taught to Lana at Yerkes. The computer console in her see-through room contains 75 keys, each with a geometric symbol denoting a word. After learning the basic mechanics of computerese, Lana surprised her keepers by taking the initiative in asking questions, just like a human child. When presented with an object she had never seen before—a box or a cup, for example—the four-year-old chimp asked her keeper its name via the computer.

Such active learning is important, because it strengthens earlier findings that hinted at the possibility that chimps could handle abstractions. What is the next step in this intriguing research area? Once some chimps become fluent in language, perhaps they can teach others to communicate in the same way.

tunity to hear the normal song early in its life, the chaffinch was quickly able to reproduce it quite expertly. Thus, the bird seemed to have inherited the program for its song, but it could not draw on the inheritance until it had heard the song sung at least once. Interestingly, the chaffinch did not respond similarly to the songs of other birds to

in a circular pattern, and smoothing down the inside nest wall. An inexperienced rat will mix up the order of the activities, making heaping-up movements in the air, or neatly patting down a wall it has not yet built. Yet it performs each of the separate movements exactly right. After some experience, the rat learns to postpone the later steps of the sequence until the earlier steps are complete.

In the case of the wasp, we saw a complex and beautifully adapted sequence resistant to alteration. Strictly programmed to make a particular sequence of responses to particular internal stimuli and environmental clues, the wasp is unable to accommodate unpredictable events. This elaborate sequence, in which each step is the necessary **releasing stimulus** that impels the insect to perform the next step, will maintain a flourishing species population under appropriate conditions.

The chaffinch and brown rat, on the other hand, reveal a more modifiable behavior sequence. These animals are capable of dealing with a broader range of environmental conditions and unexpected events.

Homing and migration

Suppose you had been born in Pittsburgh and were taken as a baby to Rio de Janeiro. At the age of eighteen, imagine yourself put out on the street and told to go back to Pittsburgh—without maps, instructions, airline schedules, or money for the fare. You might be forgiven for feeling a bit nervous about your chances of getting there. But birds, fish, reptiles, insects, and mammals of many species make journeys just as impressive as this every year. The tiny ruby-throated hummingbird goes back and forth between nesting grounds in southern Canada and winter quarters in Panama. Fur seals gather on one small group of islands off Alaska—the Pribilofs—for the breeding season, then scatter to waters as much as 3,000 miles away, to return again the next year. Salmon are born in fresh water, swim down to the ocean, mature there, and return as adults to their native streams to spawn. These **migrations,** as such cyclical journeys are called, involve traveling thousands of miles, often under adverse conditions. They also involve ending up in a particular pond, a particular marsh, even a particular suburban backyard, at the end of the journey. How

do the animals manage it? Quite apart from the sheer stamina required for such a trip, how do they navigate?

The fullest studies of migratory behavior have dealt with birds. A variety of interesting explanations have been offered to account for the directional certainty of these feathered voyagers. Most of the theories involve the sun as a reference point by which the bird can calculate relative direction. It may do so by comparing the sun's present arc with the arc it makes in the latitude to which the bird is migrating. The fact that (in the Northern Hemisphere) the sun lies directly south when it is at the highest point of its arc may also help the bird to orient its flight by supplying a fixed directional standard. In either case these theories suggest an innate ability on the part of the bird to interpret stimuli from the environment and to adjust its flight direction accordingly.

Certainly the sun is involved somehow, at least for many birds. In some experiments, migratory birds have been placed in "orientation cages" in which the apparent angle of the sun could be varied. So long as they saw the sun in its true position, the birds would tend to flutter to the side of the cage that represented the direction in which they would normally be migrating at that time of year. But if the apparent angle of the sun was changed, so that its light seemed to come from a different direction, the birds would change their direction of flight accordingly.

Several other factors may also contribute to a bird's navigational ability. These include star patterns, the earth's magnetic attraction, wind characteristics, and stable cloud formations. Landmarks, including mountains, rivers, and visible vegetation, and climatic factors, including air temperature, may also serve as directional guides.

One thing seems to be clear about bird migration: the bird either knows where it is going or can interpret cues very swiftly, even in territory over which it has never flown before. For example, a Manx shearwater was taken by airplane from its home in Wales to Boston, Massachusetts, far beyond its nor-

462

Figure 22-8. Silhouetted against the full moon, these birds may be using star patterns as a guide for their night migration.

mal range. The bird was home again thirteen days later. Assuming it flew only in the daytime, it would have had to average at least 20 miles per hour for the whole journey. This hardly leaves much time for trial-and-error navigation. Somehow the shearwater sensed the proper direction and stayed with it, over a distance of more than 3,000 miles.

This **homing** power of migratory birds— the ability to find their way home when released in unfamiliar locations—was once of significant communications value to hu-

mans. Homing pigeons carried many an important message for rulers, military officers, and financiers before the telegraph was developed to provide quicker service.

For migratory fish, the navigational problems are similar and the theories equally abundant. Some answers may involve water currents, judging water temperature and turbulence, using such landmarks as river junctions, orienting by the sun, responding to chemical components of the water, utilizing their keen sense of smell, and relying on some form of sonar. Thus for fish as well as for birds, navigation appears to involve a combination of innate and learned aspects.

What stimulates the animals to begin their migration? Again, most of the studies so far have been of birds. Apparently there is an interaction of an internal annual rhythm with various environmental stimuli. Prior to migration, certain physiological changes occur. The bird eats more, and fat accumulates in the body tissues. These changes are governed by the pituitary gland, whose action appears to be triggered by factors such as changes in day length and in the strength of sunlight.

If these rhythmic changes were the only factors, the birds would begin their migrations at the same time every year, regardless of weather conditions, food availability, or other considerations. But these considerations are life-and-death matters. If a flock of geese, for instance, stay at their Arctic breeding grounds despite an unusually early frost, they may freeze or starve before their normal departure time. So in fact, once the birds are biologically ready to migrate, environmental cues seem to provide the signal that starts them off. Similar environmental factors seem to be important in the migration patterns of aquatic creatures and many land mammals.

LEARNING: THE MODIFICATION OF BEHAVIOR PATTERNS

Many animals, especially mammals, are

capable of learning an amazing variety of new behavior patterns, even some that are totally unrelated to patterns they may inherit or learn from their natural surroundings. The fundamental means by which this happens involves some form of **reinforcement.** This may be a "reward" for appropriate responses, or a "punishment" for inappropriate ones. Although animal learning has been studied mainly in the laboratory, the same basic forces govern it in natural situations.

Two factors that influence the effectiveness of reinforcement are **repetition** and **immediacy.** Repetition of a new behavior pattern helps it to become fixed in an animal's nervous system. If the reinforcement is presented immediately after the response, the animal is more likely to associate the two than if the reinforcement is delayed, and hence is more likely to learn the "correct" response.

Habituation

The simplest form of learning is **habituation.** This may be defined as the gradual extinction of an animal's response to stimuli that repeatedly bring no reinforcement. In this way animals eventually eliminate many unproductive responses to environmental stimuli that have no practical purpose in their lives.

An example of habituation is the crouching behavior of chicks when a moving object passes overhead. After several experiences, they become habituated to familiar and proven harmless shapes. They will not, however, become accustomed to hawks and other birds of prey, which appear infrequently, and whose shape is consequently unfamiliar. Learning therefore modifies the chick's innate alarm response by eliminating crouching at the sight of harmless stimuli.

Classical conditioning

The ability to modify innate behavior pat-

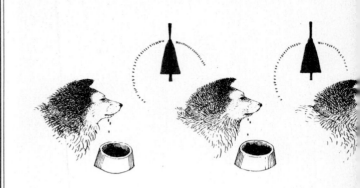

Figure 22-9. Pavlov's experiments with dogs illustrate the technique of classical conditioning. In this sequence of steps the dog has been conditioned to salivate in response to a bell rather than in response to the sight and smell of food.

Figure 22-10. B. F. Skinner, with a hungry brown rat in one of his Skinner boxes. This rat will soon learn to trip the lever in order to be rewarded with a food pellet. Later, it can learn that food is available only when a light goes on. The incentive for this learning is the immediate reward, or reinforcement—the food that the rat receives.

464

Figure 22-11. Mammals, such as these brown bears, are capable of learning an amazing variety of new behavior patterns.

terns through reinforcement was first demonstrated in the late nineteenth century by a Russian physiologist, Ivan Pavlov. Using a dog as his subject, Pavlov experimented with a simple reflex—the dog's increased flow of saliva when exposed to the sight or smell of food. In what is now considered a classic study, Pavlov harnessed a dog and blew meat powder into its mouth. He did this many times over a period of days, always ringing a bell at the same time. Eventually the sound of the bell alone was sufficient to cause the dog to salivate. The animal had apparently learned to associate the bell with the arrival of food.

Pavlov's concept, known as **classical conditioning,** was subsequently found to apply even to animals such as planarians, whose extremely simple nervous systems had previously seemed to be incapable of learning.

Trial-and-error learning

A rat enters an experimental maze for the first time, goes into a pathway, and encounters a blind alley. It retraces its path, tries another route, and after proceeding some distance again finds itself in a blind alley. Finally, after successive attempts, it finds the correct route. On the next occasion, it will find the route with fewer false starts, and eventually with none. The learning that has taken place is known as **trial and error.**

The ability of animals to associate their activities with the attainment of some reward has been best illustrated by the work of Harvard University behaviorist B. F. Skinner. Skinner restricted the diet of a rat until it had lost 15 percent of its normal weight and acted extremely hungry. Then he placed it in a closed metal box with a food slot and a food-releasing lever, which has come to be known as a Skinner box. The rat was allowed to poke around randomly until it accidentally tripped the lever and released a food pellet. The rat soon learned to trip the lever whenever it wanted food. This sort of learning is sometimes called **instrumental learning** or **operant conditioning.**

Skinner later found that some animals can learn to perform an intricate series of actions in order to secure a reward. The capacity for such varied behavior seems likely to be of value in natural settings. Here the ability to learn by trial-and-error behavior, and to associate effective responses with desired goals, would help the animal deal with changing conditions and unfamiliar experiences.

Problem-solving behavior

Insight is the ability of an animal to respond correctly the first time it encounters a new problem or situation. Whether animals other than humans are capable of such **problem-solving behavior** is a subject for debate. However, evidence indicates that at least some nonhuman primates probably have this capacity to some degree.

One significant experiment involved placing chimpanzees in a large room with walls that they could not scale. Suspended from the ceiling was a bunch of bananas that hung above their reach. The only other feature of the room was a number of boxes strewn around. At first the chimps attempted to reach the bananas by reaching and jumping for them. Frustrated in this effort, one chimp noticed the boxes, paused, then, as though realizing their potential, began stacking one box upon another until it was able to reach the fruit.

If we assume that such a behavior pattern is not instinctive, should we conclude that it was probably accidental? Experiments of this kind suggest that it was not. The proba-

bility of this same sequence of events occurring twice by accident is very low, yet other chimps readily solve similar problems. Can we then conclude that the chimp mentally considered the various trial-and-error possibilities until arriving at the correct response? No satisfactory answer has thus far been provided.

The role of play in learning
Play is a form of behavior in which animals engage in everyday activities but without the usual goals of those activities. One common form of play is mock fighting and fleeing. Here the attacker is not really intent on doing harm, and the fugitive is not really in danger, but they both behave as if they were. The fact that "only a game" is in progress is usually betrayed by two things: the players keep repeating the activities, and they are likely to exchange roles.

Play, which is engaged in mostly by

Figure 22-12. Human intelligence is characterized by imagination and creativity. But certain other primates share these capacities to some degree. This chimpanzee is quite capable of devising a solution to the problem with which he has been presented.

Figure 22-13. Baroness Jane van Lawick-Goodall has made an extensive study of the behavior of African chimpanzees. Here this curious 10-month-old chimp investigates with his lips, more sensitive than his fingers. The degree of curiosity displayed by a species is frequently an index of its general level of intelligence.

young animals, but also by mature members of certain species, offers many opportunities for learning. It may help the animal to develop new motor skills and new perceptions of the environment and of its own physical limitations and capabilities. This is not to say, however, that the animal is seeking such goals. Unlike other animal behavior, in play the activity itself serves as the reward.

Imprinting: a special form of early learning

About 40 years ago, an Austrian zoologist named Konrad Lorenz studied a behavior pattern that was considered to be genetically programmed in greylag geese. A gosling seemed to be born with an instinct for following its mother and with the capacity for doing so very soon after it hatched from the egg. There was obvious survival value in this behavior, since the mother was the natural provider of food, warmth, shelter, and protection. Yet as Lorenz studied this behavior further, he turned up an interesting finding—the gosling would not always follow its mother. Instead, it would follow the first moving object it saw.

In a remarkable series of experiments, Lorenz separated the eggs laid by one female goose into two groups: the first to be hatched by her, and the second to be hatched in an incubator. As predicted, the first group, upon hatching, set out after their mother. But the second group, which saw Lorenz when they hatched, followed him everywhere, as though he were their mother. When both groups were placed under a box and then released, each group returned to its respective "mother."

Lorenz used the word **imprinting** to describe this early modification of behavior. He and later workers noted some unusual characteristics of this form of learning. First, there is a critical time period during which a young animal will respond to an imprinting experience. This period appears to begin when the animal has sufficiently developed the physical capacity for following. For chicks and ducklings the critical

THE BLACK BEAR

Strolling down a scenic mountain path in one of America's national parks, you suddenly find yourself face to face with a great shaggy beast. Slowly, you reach into your knapsack and take out the sandwich you had planned to have for lunch. The animal obligingly takes the food, gobbles it down, then looks hopefully for more. Finally, after a few nerve-wracking moments, he gives up and saunters away. Later, you will boast to your friends about how you calmly shared your lunch with a black bear.

Ursus americanus is one of the commonest of all large North American mammals. Despite its wide range, which covers most of the continent, you may never see one in the wild, since black bears are notoriously shy and inclined to avoid people. For the most part, they are loners and have little to do even with each other except during the mating season.

The black bear is not always black, and not every black-colored bear is *Ursus americanus.* The long, shaggy fur may range in color from jet black to cinnamon brown or even a blue-grey shade. At first glance, the bear's large, bulky body seems almost too heavy for its short, stout legs. Its long snout, humpless shoulders and straight profile have been taken to indicate a close evolutionary link between bears and the various members of the dog and wolf family.

Much of the black bear's time is spent looking for food as it shuffles along at a leisurely pace. Although it is classed as a carnivore, it will eat practically anything. The bulk of its food comes from plants— nuts, berries, roots, fruits, and even the tender inner bark of trees. Bears are especially fond of honey, and will go to great lengths to get it. They will swallow up honey, honeycomb, and live bees at one indiscriminate gulp, seemingly unperturbed by the stings of the angry insects.

The animal portion of the bear's diet consists mainly of insects, rodents, reptiles, and small mammals, although a hungry bear will occasionally attack sheep or cattle. But bears are efficient scavengers, and find most of their animal food in the form of decomposing carcasses. Rotting garbage also has a particular appeal for the bear, and it is very common for him to raid garbage cans or invade camps in search of scraps.

For the most part, the bear is lazy and slow-moving. When it is frightened, however, it can run as fast as 25 miles per hour, jumping over, dodging, or knocking down any obstacles in its path. As a cub, one of the first lessons it learned was how to climb a tree. But this interest wanes as it matures, and older bears usually prefer to fight it out

on the ground rather than scurry up a tree to safety.

Bears mate during the early summer. For three or four months after mating, a pair will stay together and show each other great affection. During this brief period of intimacy, the male bear will fight fiercely to retain possession of his mate. But as cold weather approaches this temporary bond is broken, and male and female search for separate winter dens.

During autumn, the black bear prepares for its winter sleep by eating voraciously and acquiring a thick layer of fat beneath its warm fur. Finally it is ready to settle into its den, chosen for its protected position in a thicket, beneath a log, or on the side of a hill. The bear's winter sleep is deep, but is not true hibernation, since its body temperature remains normal and it can easily be awakened by any intruder who disturbs it. Pregnant females settle in early, and are usually quite fussy about their surroundings. Often they will line the den with layers of leaves and grasses to make a comfortable nest.

Black bear cubs are born in the den while their mother sleeps. Blind and hairless, they weigh only a half-pound at birth. The cubs begin to nurse immediately, feeding and sleeping in the warmth of their mother's fur. By the time they leave the den in spring, they are furry and weigh nearly five pounds. They will not be weaned until the end of the following summer.

The mother bear spends a great deal of time teaching her cubs how to survive on their own. She shows them how to hunt, dig, swim, and climb, protecting them with great ferocity and enforcing discipline with a quick and firm cuffing. One ever-present danger to the cubs is the male bear, hungry after its winter fast. It is not uncommon for an adult male to kill and devour a helpless cub that has wandered too far from its mother.

The mother bear continues to protect her cubs until they reach the age of one and a half years. At that time she is ready to mate again, and the cubs soon discover that their mother is less interested in taking care of them than in finding a compatible new partner. Gradually, her indifference and the hostility of her new mate force the reluctant yearlings to strike out on their own. They may stay together for a while, but eventually each takes up the hermit-like existence of the adult black bear.

Despite its fundamental shyness, the black bear has adjusted remarkably well to the presence of humans. Some black bears in the national parks have learned to clown and panhandle to get handouts from the tourists. Unfortunately, the "DON'T FEED THE BEARS" signs are often ignored, and people are injured by over-eager bears that are dissatisfied with the table scraps they receive. Occasionally, the more aggressive bears will break into cars or cabins, and the tourist is suddenly forced to recognize the cute, furry bear as the powerful wild animal that it really is.

Figure 22-14. These greylag goslings have been imprinted on Konrad Lorenz, and will follow wherever he goes. Later, when they reach maturity, their mating behavior will be directed at Lorenz rather than at their own species.

period lasts until the bird is about 36 hours old, with peak sensitivity occurring between 13 and 16 hours. It is during this peak period that the animal can most easily be imprinted on an object not its mother. After 36 hours, imprinting is no longer possible, even on the true mother. The bird may still be taught to follow another object, but the nature of this learning experience will be distinctly different from the imprinting experience.

A second interesting factor is that the general environment alters the tendency to imprint on nonspecies objects. Coots, for instance, are more likely to follow objects in a familiar environment, and less likely to do so if they are reared in shielded, isolated pens. Unlike other learning, imprinting seems to occur independently of reinforcement, unless a growing familiarity with the imprinted object itself provides a sort of reinforcement.

Imprinting is an ideal example of the interaction of inheritance and learning. The timing of the critical period, the rapidity and strength of the animal's response, and the durability of the attachment are all innate, yet it is only through learning that the imprinted object is adopted and internalized as a "parent figure."

SOCIAL BEHAVIOR

Social behavior is interaction between two or more animals for more or less constructive ends. It may involve relationships between animals of the same species or of different species, and these relationships are usually based on both cooperation and competition.

Among the most interesting elements of social behavior are those involving courtship, mating, and the care of offspring. Many animals' behavior patterns for these activities are so stylized that they are almost rituals. There are displays, often elaborate, whose sole function seems to be to attract or impress a potential mate. There are also more long-term sequences of action and interaction that turn out, on close examination, to have direct practical value for the producing and raising of young. Let us look at some typical patterns.

INTERACTING WITH
THE ENVIRONMENT

Figure 22-15. Many animals display a highly complex type of social behavior. These sea lions maintain a close family relationship, defending the family territory during breeding season and tending their young pups until the pups are old enough to care for themselves.

Reproductive behavior: sticklebacks and penguins

Display signals and a complex, innate sequence of mating behavior can be seen in the three-spined stickleback, which is a small, grayish-green fish, only an inch or two in length. At the start of the mating season, the male stickleback stakes out a territory and develops a bright red color on his throat and belly. If other males invade the territory, an aggressive display of the red belly may be enough to drive them away without a fight, but if not, the male will actively defend his chosen spot.

To build its nest, the fish first clears a shallow hole, fills it with loose vegetation, and then binds the vegetation together with bodily secretions. Next, it tunnels through the mass, providing a passageway. Once this is done, courtship can begin. A second color change turns the male's back a bluish-white color. At the sight of a female whose body is swollen with eggs, the male begins a zigzag "dance" that may succeed in attracting her. The female signals acceptance by a head-up movement and is led to the nest site, where the male turns on his side and points out the entrance with his snout. She enters the passageway, and her mate nudges the base of her tail, causing her to deposit her eggs. Then she departs, and the male fertilizes the eggs. Afterward he stays by the nest, fanning oxygen-laden water through it. In a week or more the eggs will have hatched, and the male, again garbed in his aggressive coloring, stands guard over his brood.

This complex behavior pattern forms a sequence known as a **behavioral chain.** Each step in the chain must be stimulated by the previous one. If one step is omitted, the whole process stops, and the male must begin courtship anew. This makes it unlikely that he will waste valuable sperm, or that the female will waste eggs, trying to mate with members of other species.

Both similarities and differences can be noted between the reproductive behavior of the stickleback and that of a creature more interesting to most humans—the penguin. On the jagged rocks of the Antarctic coast the Adélie penguins mate and raise their young. On nests of stone, in freezing weather, and in crowded rookeries, these birds pursue their display and mating rituals in apparent order and normalcy.

Arriving at the shore nearest their breeding ground or rookery, long lines of penguins plow inland through the ice and snow on their bellies, one "breaking trail" for those behind. The males usually reach the rookery first and reoccupy their previous year's territory, sometimes fighting a hard battle for it against new challengers. They then begin to gather stones for nest-building, pausing now and then for a display of bowing and flapping. The sound uttered during this ritual attracts a female. If she is a stranger, the two birds alternately stare and bow toward each other for a time. The male then lies down and rounds out the inside of his pile of stones with his feet. However, if his previous mate returns, she will usually drive off the new female and reunite with her former mate.

After mating, two eggs are laid. The female, who has fasted for about two weeks, then departs to the sea to seek food. The male stays behind and begins to incubate the eggs. Incubation requires more than a month, and the birds relieve each other on the nest at intervals, each time with a noisy display and a characteristic ceremony. Upon hatching, the chicks are covered and guarded by the parents for a period of five weeks. Then they are left unguarded while the parents seek out and return with food. When they have sufficient plumage, the young birds will swim northward to remain until they, too, are of breeding age.

Two very different species of animal, the stickleback and the Adélie nevertheless have much in common in their social behavior. Both engage in complex and ritualized display behavior to attract potential mates. One function of this display may be to demonstrate the male's fitness as a mate—his general good health and his ability to defend the nest, as evidenced by his brilliant color and/or vigorous movements.

A second common factor is the consistency of the sequence of events. The actions are performed in the same order each time, and each step triggers the next. While the sequence is more rigid and strictly programmed in the stickleback, penguins that are unable to complete their behavioral chain are likewise unsuccessful at mating, though the chain itself is more flexible than that of the fish.

There are also notable differences between the social behaviors of the two species. One is in the permanency of the pair bond between mates. The penguins mate with one individual—the previous year's mate if available—and the couple remains together till the chicks are old enough to live on their own. Sticklebacks demonstrate no preference for one mate over another; males, in fact, mate with several females during one season. Care of the offspring likewise differs. The male stickleback is solely responsible for the protection of his young, while this role is shared by both partners of the Adélie penguin pair. Again, the male penguin generally returns to his previous territory, while the stickleback seems unconcerned about prior associations. Both animals, however, defend their territory with great vigor. Without a territory, neither species will breed. This helps guarantee that they will have adequate space for breeding and for their young to develop. In the case of the stickleback, the territory also provides feeding grounds for the brood.

Year-round societies: bees, wolves, and primates
Virtually all animals engage in social behavior at some time in their lives. With solitary species, this may occur only during mating. But other animals are most often found in fairly permanent groups, such as herds, schools, or flocks, living in close proximity and often in cooperation with others of their kind.

In some animal societies there is an intricate and well-organized set of relationships. Specific tasks, such as food-gathering, caring for the young, reproduction, or defense, are performed by specific individuals or groups. In some cases, this division of labor is so fixed that individuals performing one task have body structures different from those in individuals performing other tasks. Soldier ants, for instance, may have huge pincer-like jaws that are quite lacking in worker ants of the same colony, born of the same queen.

INTERACTING WITH
THE ENVIRONMENT

With the exception of human society, some insect species have the most elaborate social structures among animals. Such insect societies often have enormous populations. A single colony of African driver ants, for example, may number as many as 22 million members.

Probably the best-known example of an insect society is the hive, or colony, of honeybees. In a honeybee colony, which contains about 40,000 members, there are three types or castes. The first is the queen, the only female in the colony who can reproduce. She is also by far the largest bee, with a long abdomen that contains ovaries. Her lifespan is from five to seven years.

A second caste comprises the workers—sterile females, which are small in size and are responsible for all the work in the colony. The youngest workers, sometimes called "nurse workers," remain in the colony tending the eggs laid by the queen and feeding the larvae. Somewhat older workers build the combs and guard the entrance to the hive. The oldest workers gather the pollen and nectar that feeds the colony. Workers communicate with one another via pheromones and dancing movements, such as we described in chapter 21. They have a short lifespan, about six to eight weeks.

The third caste in the colony is the drones, the only males. They are produced from unfertilized eggs, and their sole function is to provide sperm to fertilize the eggs laid by the queen. Being incapable even of feeding themselves, they are often driven out of the hive when they have served their reproductive purpose.

All members of a bee colony are descended from one queen and her mate, forming what is known as a **parental society.** In late winter the queen begins to lay her eggs, depositing them in separate wax cubicles. The larvae that develop are fed honey and pollen; future queens are fed royal jelly, a mixture of honey, pollen, and hormonal secretions that develop their sex organs. When the new queens mature, they fight among themselves till only one survives. She then challenges the old queen, and one of the two of them leaves the comb, accompanied by a swarm of workers, and settles in a new site. This reduces the hive population and prevents overcrowding. The new queen then embarks on her nuptial flight, pursued by drones, and returns with enough sperm to fertilize all the eggs she will ever produce.

The social order in the beehive is strictly defined by role, dictated by birth, and clearly evident in physical appearance. In the social order of wolves, on the other hand, roles are less rigidly defined, more subject to change, and structured in line with a variety of factors. Reproductive ability and size are important, but the social ranking of members of a wolf pack is determined also by such qualities as maturity, physical attributes, experience in combat, or possibly even some personality characteristic.

The clearest division of the wolf society is into dominant and subordinate members. There are a dominant male, called the alpha male, an alpha female, subordinate males and females, peripheral males and females, and offspring. The status of the alpha male is immediately apparent when conflict arises over food, partners, territory, or other disputes. The less dominant members defer to the ranking wolf with a display of begging and submissive behavior. The alpha male's leadership is also evident by the "greeting ceremonies" of howls and affectionate nuzzling that he receives upon returning from his patrol of the pack territory. A similar hierarchy exists among the females of the pack.

The social bonds of the pack appear to be very close. Inferior wolves are kept to the outskirts of the group, but the mischievous offspring are patiently tolerated within the closely woven inner circle. Overly aggressive pups, however—which might grow up to be troublemakers—are sometimes killed by their elders.

The social structure of the wolf pack is relatively stable. For the most part, inferiors do not challenge the alpha male and female to the point of actual fighting. Change in the hierarchy is most likely if the alpha male is killed, old, or disabled. It may occur during the reproductive season, when group rivalry is at its highest, and younger animals become more aggressive. In general, though, the alpha male and female rigidly control the mating activities of the rest of the pack, even violently attacking other pack members that attempt to mate. The need for leadership approval to carry on courtship, combined with the definite preferences of certain pack members toward others, severely limit the number of successful matings, and hence the size of the pack. This limitation of numbers is valuable for a large predator species that needs extensive territory to provide food for each animal.

Despite this strict hierarchy in the wolf society, there is a great deal of cooperative behavior. Mothers share supervision of their pups, and both parents are attentive to their offspring. All animals help in maintaining the hierarchy, largely by punishing less dominant animals who challenge the authority of the alpha leader. Securing food, defending pack members against outside attack, and a variety of other activities are group undertakings.

The social dominance pattern evident in wolf families is true of some primate species as well. Notable among them is the baboon. As with the wolf pack, sub-adult or less dominant male baboons are kept in subordinate groups or cliques that travel at the outer edge of the troop, and juveniles are welcomed inside. Although there is no single leadership animal, there is a central cooperating clique, dominated by two or three males who take the lead in keeping outsiders away. These leaders are replaced when they become old or weak enough to be successfully challenged by younger baboons. The troop cooperates largely through intensive grooming sessions, in which individuals remove parasites and foreign objects from each other's fur. Most adults mate and produce offspring, making this a **sexual society.** Parent–child and sexual bonds serve to reinforce the social structure.

Figure 22-16. The social structure of a troop of baboons is reinforced by the bonds between parent and child. Here a mother baboon holds her infant in a protective manner.

INTERACTING WITH
THE ENVIRONMENT

Figure 22-17. Male baboons take part in the parent–child dependency relationship, functioning as disciplinarians. Their role is shown in this series of pictures. To punish a youngster who has misbehaved, the male is biting him on the neck (top). The youngster drops to the ground squealing, while the male stands looking reproachfully at him (center). Finally the male walks away, while the still wailing youngster regains his feet (bottom). This young baboon has probably learned his lesson and will not repeat the behavior that occasioned the punishment.

Departing somewhat from this format is the chimpanzee troop. Although some males in a troop seem "more dominant" than others, there is no strict hierarchy. With the exception of occasional competition over a food source, quarrels among members are infrequent. Nor is the structure of the troop as permanent as it is among baboons. The individual family, not the large troop, is the most permanent social unit. However, chimps from one family mingle with and join others without conflict. Some chimps may choose to travel alone. This social organization allows the mobility necessary to utilize the changing seasonal food supplies in the forest. The chimps are nevertheless quite willing to share abundance by calling loudly, thus attracting others to plentiful food supplies.

The parent–offspring relationship in ape and monkey troops is extremely important for the socialization of the young primates. Closeness and nurturing between mother and infant monkeys has been shown to be essential for proper adaptation of the young monkeys to their peers. In an experiment by Harry and Margaret Harlow, in which infant monkeys were given a choice of two substitute mothers—a stiff wire model with a supply of milk and a soft terrycloth model without milk—the monkeys showed clear preference for the terrycloth "mother." If deprived completely of maternal contact, young monkeys develop poorly in their own social, sexual, and maternal behavior. In some monkey troops, adult males are also attentive parents, at times assuming full care of one youngster when its younger brothers or sisters arrive.

Play is of great importance in socializing young primates. It encourages inexperienced monkeys to test their agility and strength, their social and sexual skills, and their ability to communicate, to ward off potential challenges, and to relate to their peers. Monkeys raised in isolation show incompetence in monkey social behavior. They are inappropriately aggressive, are inadequate at sexual contact, and become poor, even hostile, parents. The fact that the inclination to play disappears in the adult monkey may indicate that its function is to educate and socialize.

In all the animal species we have examined, it is clear that social behavior is critical for maintaining the adaptations that enable the species to survive in its environment. To protect themselves, to deal with competitors and predators, to secure food and shelter, to procreate, to maintain warmth and security, most animals must work together. The societies we have examined demonstrate only a few of the myriad ways in which they do so.

SUMMARY

The activities of animals are studied both for their immediate interest and because they provide a better understanding of human behavior. Behavior is activity in response to a stimulus from the external or internal environment. It may range from a simple act to a complex sequence of activities.

Several involuntary behavior patterns are important to the lives of many animals. The taxis is a directional movement in response to a specific environmental stimulus. Kinesis is an increase or decrease in the animal's movement in proportion to the intensity of a stimulus. The reflex is an involuntary movement of a particular part of the body in response to a stimulus.

Biorhythms are the cyclic behavior patterns by which animals adapt to such predictable changes in their environment as the divisions of day and night, tidal variations, and seasonal change. They are essentially involuntary. Cycles of daytime or nocturnal activity based on a twenty-four-hour schedule are called circadian rhythms. They are not wholly dependent on environmental cues but are also controlled by an internal timing mechanism, the biological clock. Other biorhythms include lunar rhythms and annual rhythms.

Species-typical behavior is innate and constant among all members of a species. Instinctive behavior is inherited and not dependent upon learning, but much of it can be modified through experience. There exists a very delicate balance between inheritance and learning.

Migratory behavior in birds has been extensively studied. Their ability to navigate is apparently based on sun position, star patterns, the earth's magnetic attraction, wind characteristics, and cloud formation, as well as landmarks. Fish may use water currents, variations in water temperature and turbulence, and physical landmarks in their migrations. The stimulus seems to be a combination of internal annual rhythm and environmental factors.

The fundamental means by which animals can learn new behavior patterns involves some form of reinforcement. Its effectiveness is influenced by repetition and immediacy. Habituation is the simplest form of learning. Classical conditioning involves modification of behavior by reinforcement. Trial-and-error learning helps animals adapt to changing conditions and new experiences.

Insight is the ability of an animal to evaluate and respond correctly to a new situation. It appears that some nonhuman primates have the capacity for problem-solving behavior. Play is a type of behavior that has an important role in learning among young animals. In play, the activity itself serves as the reward. Imprinting has survival value because it forms a firm bond, almost at birth, between parent and offspring.

Social behavior is usually based on cooperation and competition. Animal behavior patterns for courtship, mating, and care of offspring can be amazingly complex. In some animals social behavior occurs only at mating time. Other animals live in permanent social groups in which specific tasks are performed by specific individuals or groups.

A parental society, such as that of bees, is formed of members all descended from a single queen and her mate. A sexual society is made up of members that are the offspring of many different pairs of parents. In societies such as that of the wolf, social ranking of members is determined by a variety of factors, including reproductive ability, size, maturity, and possibly even personality characteristics. Such societies include dominant and subordinate members. In all animal societies, social behavior is critical for maintaining the adaptations that enable a species to survive in its environment.

Review questions

1. Distinguish among taxis, kinesis, and reflex behavior. Which would be likely to have the greatest survival value?

2. What are biorhythms? Describe an example.

3. What is a biological clock?

4. What type of animal would be most likely to be strongly influenced by lunar rhythms?

5. List some examples of activities associated with annual rhythms.

6. What is instinctive behavior?

7. Give an example of how instinctive behavior can be modified by learning.

8. What is a releasing stimulus?

9. List several factors that may contribute to a bird's ability to navigate during migration.

10. In learning, what factors influence the effectiveness of reinforcement?

11. What is habituation? Give an example.

12. Describe Pavlov's classic conditioning experiment.

13. What is trial-and-error learning? How does it compare in survival value with problem-solving behavior? Give an example.

14. In terms of animal behavior, what is play? How does it differ from normal survival and maintenance activity?

15. What is imprinting? Considering the words of a popular nursery rhyme, can we say that imprinting is confined to birds?

16. What is a behavioral chain? What happens if it is interrupted?

17. Give some examples of cooperative social behavior among animals.

18. What is a parental society? What are its distinguishing characteristics?

19. Describe the social structure of a typical wolf pack. What is the survival value of such a structure?

20. What is a sexual society?

21. What is the importance of the parent–offspring relationship among primates?

22. In what type of animal might we expect to find no instances of social behavior?

The Web of Life

"Pick up anything and you will find it hitched to everything in the universe." So commented one of America's most famous naturalists, John Muir. Today we are more and more learning how right he was. Almost all living things depend on each other for food, for protection, even for their own reproduction. Darwin was one of the first moderns to recognize this. He helped to popularize the notion of the interdependence of organisms as an all-embracing "web of life." The delicate spider's web depends on many connecting strands. Likewise, the structure of any community depends on the links that bind together the individuals in that community.

Biological organisms also interact with their physical environment. An organism's environment thus has both **biotic** (living) and **abiotic** (nonliving) elements. The interdependent individuals in a community, and the abiotic environment with which they interact, make up the **ecosystem.**

Plants and animals in an ecosystem affect each other either directly or indirectly. They may feed on, compete for food with, shelter, clean, protect, transport, or otherwise interact with each other. They may do these things with an organism of the same or of a different species. Thus the basic elements of animal social behavior—cooperation and competition—are found in the relations among different species as well as within a single species. This chapter will deal with some of the ways in which individuals and populations are bound together in an ecosystem.

PATTERNS OF INTERDEPENDENCE

Organisms are linked together in a com-

Figure 23-1. The zebras and wildebeests shown here interact with one another and with their environment.

Figure 23-2. Every ecosystem is made up of biotic and abiotic elements.

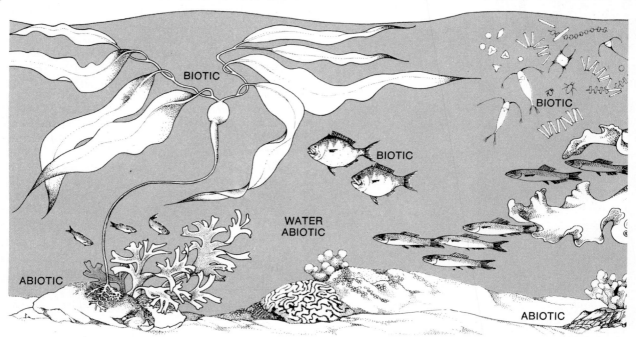

BIOTIC

BIOTIC

BIOTIC

WATER
ABIOTIC

ABIOTIC

ABIOTIC

Figure 23-3. A simple food chain.

munity by three basic needs. Clearly, each must have an adequate food supply in order to stay alive. Also, each must protect itself from enemies. For example, almost every species is preyed on, or eaten, by other species in the same ecosystem.

In addition, there are the ever-present hazards of the physical environment, such as wind, drought, heat, or cold. And even if an organism manages to find enough food and to survive the hazards of its environment, it is still a very temporary unit in a population. The lives of most individuals in an ecosystem are counted in hours, days, or weeks. Relatively few individuals survive for more than a year. Thus, the survival of populations depends on the fact that most organisms are active in reproduction.

Patterns of nutrition

The food-dependency relationships in any ecosystem form a kind of linked chain. In fact, biologists use the term **food chain** to describe it. A simple food chain in a desert ecosystem is shown in figure 23-3.

As pictured, the relationship is quite simple. The population of mice feeds on a population of grasses. The snake eats the mice, the roadrunner eats the snake, and finally the ring-tailed cat eats the roadrunner. We can picture each dependency relationship as a single link in the chain. Four such relationships exist in this example.

The concept of the food chain has advantages. It allows us to pinpoint the role of certain populations in an ecosystem, such as the basic function of grass in the desert food chain. Grass, though, is only one example. In all food chains, the basic role is played by green plants and other chlorophyll-containing organisms. These are the only ones that can capture energy from the sun and turn it into the chemical energy of food.

Because green plants produce the foods that keep the community running, they are called **producers.** All populations that depend on them are called consumers. Animals that eat producers are called **primary**

Figure 23-4. Identify the producer, the primary consumer, and the secondary consumer as seen in this series of pictures.

consumers. Those that eat primary consumers are called **secondary consumers,** and so on. The food chain, though, is more than a simple sequence of who eats whom. It is also an "energy chain." By identifying the producers and consumers it traces the flow of energy through the ecosystem. Each consumer in the food chain receives a certain amount of energy from the organisms it consumes. It uses some of this energy, and passes the rest on to whatever higher-level consumer eats it. Eventually most of the original energy is used up. There is not enough left to support very many consumers at the higher levels. For instance, it takes less than an acre of grassland to support a mouse, because the mouse gets most of the stored energy in the grass. But it takes many acres—perhaps several square miles—to support the ring-tailed cat, because so much

of the grass's energy is used up during the transfer from the mouse to the snake to the bird. This kind of energy relationship can be shown as an **energy pyramid,** with the producers forming the broad base and the highest consumer the point at the top.

But the term "chain" should not be taken literally. Almost always, there is more than one link at each step. Mice do not eat only one kind of grass, nor do snakes eat only mice. Each population of consumers nearly always depends on several other populations for its food supply. Thus a wide range of food links binds the populations of an ecosystem together. It is really more accurate to think of this complex, overlapping series of relationships as a **food web** rather than as a food chain.

We might think that because green plants are producers, they get their food without

INTERACTING WITH
THE ENVIRONMENT

ANIC
ERIAL

SECONDARY
CONSUMERS

PRIMARY
CONSUMERS

PRODUCERS

ORGANIC MATERIAL
RETURNED TO THE
SOIL
BACTERIA AND FUNGI
TURN ORGANIC MATERIAL
INTO USEABLE NUTRIENTS
FOR PRODUCERS

Figure 23-5. A food web is made up of an overlapping
series of relationships.

help from other organisms. However, to produce food, green plants must have carbon dioxide, water, and minerals, as well as sunlight. Such substances are partly furnished by populations of consumers that are called **decomposers.** These are bacteria and fungi which feed on dead plants and animals. In doing so, they break down the dead tissue into carbon dioxide, water, and mineral compounds that green plants can use. Thus, an unending cycle binds one population to another in each ecosystem.

Patterns of protection

Certain populations in an ecosystem depend on other populations for protection. Some of the most interesting protective relationships are very specific. The color of some moths, for example, is such that when resting on the black and white bark of a birch tree they are barely visible. This naturally tends to hide them from consumers that would prey on them. Such coloration, which protects an organism in a particular environment, is known as **concealing coloration.** Concealing coloration may also resemble some part of the physical environment. Figure 23-7 shows some Rocky Mountain ptarmigan in their summer plumage. The birds are almost invisible against the rocks on which they rest. In winter, the plumage turns white, giving concealment in the snow.

Another way in which organisms are concealed against their backgrounds is **disruptive coloration.** In this, the organism does not match the background. Instead, it is patterned in such a way that its outline is hard to pick out against its surroundings. The zebra is a good example. Its stripes break the outline of its body, and blend into the stripes of neighboring animals in the herd. Moreover, the stripes are confusing when the animal moves, especially when it is seen through the tall grass.

A fascinating instance of disruptive coloration is the larva in figure 23-8. The "eyes" are really large color spots on its rear end.

These may frighten away a would-be predator by presenting it with the appearance of an enormous head.

A different pattern of protection, **mimicry,** occurs when members of one species resemble members of another species. (The "mimicry," of course, is not conscious or even deliberate. It is simply a result of natural selection.) In some cases the species imitated is more dangerous or aggressive than the mimic. This type of relationship is called **Batesian mimicry,** after English naturalist Henry Bates. In figure 23-9, note the resemblance between the harmless bumblebee moth and the real bumblebee. The real bee is equipped with a stinger that causes pain or death. Experiments have shown that many predators, even those whose diet may consist entirely of insects, will leave both moth and bee alone, once they have sampled a bee.

A variation of this kind of false identity is **Müllerian mimicry.** Here, not-so-harmless animals mimic other well-defended species. German zoologist Franz Müller noted that several species of butterfly looked remarkably alike. All seemed to be distasteful to butterfly-eating predators. The benefit to the butterflies lay in the fact that a predator that tried any one of them soon learned to avoid them all. Thus not all of the butterfly species needed to make the original sacrifice.

Figure 23-6. The coloring of this noctuid moth blends in perfectly with the birch tree on which it is resting.

Carolina Biological Supply Co.

Figure 23-7. How many ptarmigan can you see in the larger photograph? During the winter, the plumage of this high-altitude bird is white and blends with a snowy background. In this picture the birds are shown in their summer plumage. You can see how successfully this coloration blends with the surroundings.

Figure 23-8. This larva is protected both by its coloration and by the fearful "face" that is actually its rear end.

Figure 23-9. The bumblebee moth (left) is harmless. The real bumblebee (right) is equipped with a sting that can cause birds and other predators pain or even death. The moth is the mimic. It is highly dependent upon the existence of the bumblebee for its own survival.

A third type of mimicry does not serve for defense. Rather, it provides a weapon in the competition for food. This is called **aggressive mimicry**, and is often seen in plants as well as animals. The sundew, for example (figure 23-10), secretes glistening drops of a sticky digestive fluid on tentacles at the end of its leaves. The fluid looks just like pollen. Insects land on it and are trapped. Then the digestive juice in the droplets dissolves them.

Patterns of reproductive interdependence
Some species cannot reproduce without assistance from others. Such dependency relationships link many plant species with animal species, mainly insects. For instance, the flowers of some plants can be fertilized only by pollen from a flower of another plant of the same species. In some species, pollen is blown from one plant to another by the wind—a factor in the abiotic environment. But in other species it is carried on the bodies of insects, mainly bees or certain flies. Insects thus fill an important role in many ecosystems. Without them, an important group of producer organisms would fail to reproduce.

A less harmonious case of reproductive dependence is that of the female mosquito. Unlike the male, which feeds on plant juices only, the females of some species require a good meal of animal blood before they can produce and lay their eggs. Thus, by letting a mosquito bite us, we not only feed the pest but help to populate the world with new mosquitoes.

ECOLOGICAL INTERACTIONS

Now that we have identified the general patterns of species interdependence, we can look more directly at cooperation and competition among species. Patterns of interaction are limitless. Some of them involve two species, some many. **Symbiosis**, which literally means "living together," is a relationship in which individuals from two species establish a more or less permanent physical relationship with one another. Each species thus becomes part of the permanent environment of the other. At least one of the species needs the other in order to survive or reproduce. Sometimes both do. If one species is destroyed, the other may not be able to set up the same relationship with a different species.

Other interactions allow more options. In **predation** and **competition,** the relationship is not limited to two species. Instead, it can involve a number of species, depending on what is available. Such patterns tend to stabilize the ecosystem as a whole. They link together the survival needs of a variety of species. Thus, these interrelationships in an ecosystem are not static but dynamic. That is, they do not remain the same, but are constantly changing.

Symbiosis

Biologists tend to classify symbiotic relationships in three broad patterns, depending on which of the participating species benefits. These patterns are mutualism, commensalism, and parasitism.

In **mutualism,** both individuals gain some benefit from the association. As we saw in chapter 20, a lichen is a community of certain algae and fungi that live together. Lichens have invaded such barren environments as boulders and rock outcroppings, where neither partner could live alone. The algae photosynthesize a sugar. Some of this diffuses into the fungus, which uses it as a source of energy and body-building material. The fungi may also obtain vitamins from the algae. Biologists are not sure of all the benefits to the algal population, but at least two are known. The fungi absorb water and minerals that are transferred to the algae. They also protect the algae, mainly from the intense sunlight that strikes the lichen's bare rock habitat.

Many mutualistic relationships can be

Figure 23-10. The drops of sticky digestive fluid on the tentacles of this carnivorous sundew are apparently mistaken for pollen by insects that land on it. (Courtesy Carolina Biological Supply Company).

Figure 23-11. The hummingbird and the hummingbird moth look remarkably alike as they hover over a nectar-filled honeysuckle flower. In what ways might this close resemblance be advantageous to either organism?

INTERACTING WITH
THE ENVIRONMENT

seen among marine species. The clownfish, for example, is able to hide among the sea anemone's waving tentacles without being stung. The anemone benefits because the brightly colored fish may lure other, larger fish within reach of the stinging tentacles. Again, a number of small fishes feed on the barnacles and algae that adhere to the sides of larger fish. At first, observers could see no benefit to the large fish. But then it was found that the removal of algae and barnacles was a valuable cleaning service, allowing the big fish to move more easily and rapidly.

Other mutualistic relationships are less visible. For instance, every animal with a well-developed digestive system normally houses several different populations of microorganisms. Most of these populations are in the intestine, where they find a ready supply of food. The host benefits because some microbes aid in the digestion of food. Others manufacture vitamins or other chemicals that the organism cannot manufacture. Vitamin K, for instance, is produced by intestinal bacteria. Even termites depend on the protozoans in their intestines. These microbes digest the wood the termites eat, and the insects use some of the resulting sugar as food. Neither termites nor protozoans can live without the other.

In the second type of symbiosis, called **commensalism,** only one species benefits from the association. The other is apparently not affected. One example can be seen in tropical and subtropical forests. Here the green plants called epiphytes live on the trunks and branches of trees. The epiphytes, being raised up from the ground, benefit from greater exposure to sunlight. However, they do not take water and nutrients from the interior of the tree. They get water from the humid air, and from the rain that collects on their leaves, which are often cup-shaped. They also absorb mineral salts from the dust in the rainwater. Thus, the tree is more or less unaffected by the relationship.

Many examples of commensalism in animals can be found in the ocean. The shark, for instance, may be the unaffected partner in two different symbiotic associations, as shown in figure 23-12.

As we learn more about the species involved, some relationships once thought to be commensal may turn out to be mutualistic. As we saw, this has already happened with the cleaner fish. It is even possible that mutualistic relationships may evolve from commensal ones. For example, the cattle egret associates with large mammals. This bird finds food sources all around the animal it lives with. It eats undigested particles in

Figure 23-12. Two remora fish are attached to the back of a lemon shark. A large sucker on the underside of the remora allows it to obtain this free ride. When the shark begins to feed, the remoras detach themselves and feed on some of the leftovers. This is a commensal relationship, since the smaller fish provide no known harm or benefit to the shark. The striped fish in front of the shark is a pilot fish, believed by early mariners to guide sharks toward their prey.

THE SNOW LEOPARD

Imagine yourself high up in the snowy Himalayas, more than 12,000 feet above sea level. Hiding behind a boulder, you watch in awed silence as a herd of wild goats skillfully threads its way upward. Suddenly, a ghostly flash of grey and white dives into the middle of the herd and seizes a young ewe by the throat. Before you can stand up for a better view, the attack is over; predator and prey have vanished.

What you have witnessed has been seen by very few people. You have witnessed the attack of the snow leopard.

The snow leopard, sometimes called the ounce, is unquestionably one of the most beautiful—and also one of the most dangerous—of all predators. It is not especially large, weighing only about 100 pounds and measuring about 6½ feet, including its long, black-tipped tail. Peaceful and unaggressive when left alone, the snow leopard is a deadly foe when provoked.

If you happen to be camping in the cold and treeless mountains of eastern Afghanistan, Kashmir, Tibet, western China, or southern Siberia, you might well want to watch for a large cat with thick, woolly fur. Its coat is milky white on the underparts and pale grey on top, spotted with large rosettes. This coloring allows the snow leopard to blend in with the snow-covered rocks of its native terrain—unnoticed by its unsuspecting prey until too late.

Like most carnivorous animals, this elusive cat adjusts its traveling schedule to the seasonal movements of the animals on which it preys—wild sheep, goats, deer, gazelles, birds, and small mammals. During the summer, it generally climbs to an elevation of more than 13,000 feet, but it prefers the warmer valley regions during the winter. When food is scarce in the winter, the snow leopard will sometimes attack domesticated animals, but only out of desperation; most often such an act means death at the hands of an angry herdsman.

Effectively camouflaged by its coloring, a snow leopard may either stalk its prey or lie in ambush for an unsuspecting creature to come along. Its attack is invariably deadly and lightning fast, for it can leap 30 feet forward and 12 feet in the air. Usually loners, these wily cats may occasionally hunt in pairs, one partner chasing the prey into the area where the other partner waits in ambush.

Snow leopard cubs are born in the spring, usually in litters of two or three. Within a few months they are able to travel and hunt with their mother throughout the winter. In the following spring, the young cats strike out on their own, each establishing its own den in a secluded and hard-to-reach cave or crevice. Left undisturbed, the cat may continue to use this shelter for many years.

Today the snow leopard is threatened with extinction. The source of the danger is its beautiful fur, which many people find more beautiful on humans. Some hunt the snow leopard just for the challenge of capturing such a powerful and beautiful animal. Efforts to protect it have been largely ineffective, and fewer than 500 snow leopards are believed to exist in the wild.

Zoos have been no more fortunate. Before the turn of the twentieth century, only two snow leopards were held in captivity. But as of 1970, 96 of these beautiful creatures were exhibited in 42 zoos around the world. Unfortunately, the attempt to protect the species by breeding it in captivity has proved largely unsuccessful. Only 20 cubs have so far been born in captivity.

In Mongolia, the snow leopard is treated like any other predator, and is fair game for hunters all year round. In Pakistan, it may be freely hunted without a license. Export of the skins is forbidden by law, but trade in articles manufactured from the skins is highly profitable. Thus far, the Pakistani government has not enacted any laws that would place the snow leopard under national protection.

The Soviet Union has shown the greatest concern for the snow leopard by affording it full legal protection and creating sanctuaries for it. In India, the species has been officially protected since 1952, but the sanctuaries established by the Indian government have been unsupervised and have provided very little real protection.

Few people have ever seen a snow leopard in the wild. Its native habitat is cold and remote, and only the most determined of humans have been able to seek out this elusive creature. Naturally reclusive, snow leopards are few in number and are distributed over a wide territory. What little is known of their behavior in the natural state is based on the reports of a handful of hardy mountaineers. Several of these bold observers have reported seeing snow leopards resting in vulture nests, while others have seen them exchanging playful blows while rearing up on their hind legs. Most people, however, will probably have to settle for watching this beautiful cat as it paces restlessly in its cage at the zoo, half a world away from its true home in the mountains of central Asia.

the feces, scraps from the beast's diet, or even cattle-loving insect pests. In this relationship, the bird seems to benefit most. But in others, the animals have come to depend more on their feathered partners. The crocodile, for instance, lets the crocodile bird pick parasites from its rough skin. The bird gets a meal, and the crocodile gets a cleaning. In addition, the cries of the bird serve to warn the less-alert crocodile of approaching danger.

The third type of symbiotic relationship is **parasitism.** In this, the parasite lives at the expense of the host and harms it. Such relationships are widespread. In fact, the majority of organisms in a natural community are hosts for one or more species of parasite. It has been estimated that nearly one-quarter of all known animal species are parasites at some stage of their development.

Parasitic plants are found in many ecosystems. Their host is often another plant, on which they grow and from which they draw food, water, and mineral salts. Some parasitic plants are capable of photosynthesis, and so take only part of their nourishment from the host plant.

Animal parasites are usually classified in two categories, according to whether they live on or inside the host. An **ectoparasite** lives on the outside of the host. The ectoparasite is usually the most independent of all parasites. Many are capable of walking, flying, or swimming from one host to another. Examples include leeches, fleas, lice, mites, and ticks. The other kind of animal parasite is the **endoparasite.** It lives inside the host and is usually much more dependent on it for all its needs. Human beings may be hosts for all sorts of endoparasitic bacteria, tapeworms, flukes, roundworms, and fungi.

Parasites are the most dependent populations in any ecosystem. They rely on their hosts for most, if not all, of their basic needs. The host is a source of food and protection, and quite often is a necessary link in the parasite's reproductive cycle. Even microbes that cause the death of their hosts

Figure 23-13. A shield bug is depositing its eggs in this living caterpillar. When the eggs hatch, the larvae will feed on the tissues of the caterpillar, eventually killing it.

Figure 23-14. The orange mite, pictured here just above the eye of the fly, is an ectoparasite that attaches itself to the host and remains until the host lays its eggs. Then the mite feeds on the eggs, after which it reproduces without further dependence on the host.

490

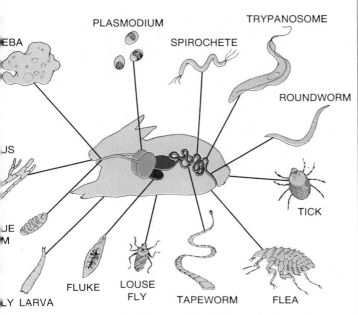

PLASMODIUM   TRYPANOSOME
EBA

SPIROCHETE

ROUNDWORM

JS

TICK

JE
M

FLUKE   LOUSE
LY LARVA   FLY   TAPEWORM   FLEA

Figure 23-15. A single rabbit may be host to many varieties of ectoparasites and endoparasites, at all the same time.

Figure 23-16. The lamprey is a parasitic fish that attaches itself to a host fish and drinks its blood, eventually causing the death of the host. In this picture the lamprey has been detached from the host to show the injury it caused. What is the difference between parasitism and predation? Why is the lamprey classified as a parasite rather than a predator?

require new hosts for their continued existence. The most persistent parasites are those that can flourish with only limited damage to the host. From the development of this kind of stable relationship it is possible to imagine the gradual development of a commensal relationship.

Predation

Generally speaking, **predation** is the feeding of one organism on another. Owls are predators; mice are their prey. Actually, we could also say that mice are predators and grass seeds are their prey. The principle is the same, whether the prey species is another animal or a plant. However, it is usual to discuss predation in terms of animal–animal relations.

In most cases, any predator species has more than one prey species. Likewise, a single prey species has many predators. For instance, the small subarctic rodents called lemmings are preyed on by foxes, lynx, snowy owls, and perhaps other predators as well. But these predators also hunt mice, rabbits, and other small animals. The value of this for the predators is obvious. When one type of prey is scarce, the predator usually need not go hungry. It can simply turn to catching more of the other types. Sometimes, of course, prey of all sorts may be scarce, and then some predators may starve. But this would be far more likely to happen if there were only one sort of prey the predator could eat.

Predation has definite benefits for the prey species as well. Perhaps the most important is that it helps regulate the number of individuals in a prey population. Without it, the population is likely to outgrow its food supply. Then large numbers may starve, or be so weakened that they fall victim to disease.

A good example is the case of moose and wolves on Isle Royale, an island national park in Lake Superior. Moose have lived on the island since early in this century. At first they had no predators, and their population varied enormously. Sometimes it may have been as high as 3,000 on the 210-square-mile island. Then it would "crash" to a hungry few hundred, and slowly build up again.

In the 1940s, a few wolves arrived, probably by crossing the ice from Canada. They began to prey on the moose, and in a few years the moose population stabilized. Today it varies only between about 600 and 900. This is below the **carrying capacity** of the environment—that is, below the number the island could adequately feed. Hence all the moose have food enough.

But why does predation not wipe out the prey species entirely? Why did the wolves not kill off all the Isle Royale moose? One reason is that large prey, such as moose and deer, are hard to capture. Even several wolves together have trouble bringing down a healthy adult moose. They would probably use up more energy in chasing and killing it than they would get back by feeding on it. Some of them might even be killed in the battle. So the predators are limited mostly to taking old, sick, or very young prey. This not only ensures that some prey animals will survive and reproduce. It also means that the ones that survive will probably be the strongest and healthiest. Thus predation not only keeps the prey population stable; it also keeps it healthy.

Another reason prey species survive is that as their numbers fall, they become harder to find. One or two rabbits in a field are harder for a prowling fox to locate than are a large population of rabbits. And if the fox fails to find rabbits in that field for a while, it may be attracted by some tender, juicy field mice instead. The few rabbits that are left will then have a better chance to survive, mate, and raise their young.

It has not always been recognized that a prey species needs its predators. Such ignorance has led to serious mistakes in attempts to protect endangered species. Sometimes the whole ecology of an area has been damaged. For instance, at the turn of the century the Kaibab Plateau in Arizona was made a game preserve. Federal officials especially wanted to protect the herd of about 4,000 mule deer on the plateau. So they destroyed all the predators of the deer—coyotes, wolves, mountain lions. The deer multiplied in a few years to nearly 100,000. Of course, the plateau simply could not support such numbers for very long. The hungry deer stripped away the vegetation and then began to starve by thousands. Without plants to hold the soil, erosion set in. As a result, much of the lost plant growth could not be replaced, and the plateau's carrying capacity was permanently reduced. The deer herd shrank to about 10,000, the most that could be supported by the diminished vegetation. If the predators had not been destroyed, the herd probably would never have grown that large. And the vegetation would have remained ample enough to provide the deer with much more abundant food.

Hunting is often justified as a means of population control. It is said that, since the natural enemies of deer and other species have been killed off, humans must take their place. This is true only to a certain extent. The problem is that human hunters with guns do not kill the old and sick animals first. Rather, they go after the best animals—the ones that are needed most for reproduction. Consequently, they may do much more harm to the herd than natural predators, even if they kill the same number of animals.

Competition

In **interspecies competition,** members of at least two different species are competing to use the same resources. The resource may be food, water, space, light, or anything that is needed for survival and available in limited supply. If two or more species in the same community are competing for all of such resources, only one species will survive. This was demonstrated in an experiment with different species of fruit fly. *Drosophila melanogaster*, a rapidly reproducing species, was introduced into a cage of slower-

INTERACTING WITH
THE ENVIRONMENT

reproducing *D. pseudoobscura*. The latter species was soon wiped out. As both were competing for limited food sources, the greater numbers of *D. melanogaster* simply took over.

Yet species that have similar resource requirements often do survive in the same community. They can do so because they are not in direct competition with one another.

two populations are not really competing for the same food supply. They have managed to exploit different aspects of the same habitat. That is, they have found different **ecological niches.**

We ordinarily think of a niche as a place. An ecological niche, however, is both more abstract and more complex. Each organism's ecological niche depends on all the

---

IS ORGANIC FARMING EFFICIENT?

Can a farm that uses only organic methods compete with one that uses synthetic chemical fertilizers and pesticides? Most agricultural experts would say no. But the results of a recent study by a group at Washington University indicate that the conventional wisdom may be wrong.

The group, headed by Barry Commoner, studied 16 organic and 16 nonorganic farms in five states in the nation's corn belt. All were large commercial enterprises, with an average size of 476 acres. All raised corn, wheat, soybeans, hay, oats, and livestock.

The study found that organic farms used roughly one-third as much fossil fuel energy as nonorganic farms to get a given crop yield. The organic farmers' total crops were worth roughly 8 percent less, in market value, than those of conventional farmers. But the organic farmers offset this loss by spending less on

fertilizer. In the end, the organic farmers made just as much money as their nonorganic rivals.

One farmer, for example, had been farming organically for 18 years. He had 700 acres, with 800 cattle and 500 hogs. He had stopped using synthetic fertilizers when a doctor attributed his skin rash to them. Instead, he had begun using animal wastes and commercial organic fertilizers, such as fish emulsion. To fight pests, he rotated his crops and relied on natural predators, such as ladybugs. By the time of the study, laboratory reports showed his corn to be higher in protein than corn grown on nonorganic farms. Moreover, he said that his livestock was healthier after he switched to organic methods. And a number of formerly skeptical neighbors were beginning to follow his lead.

The report suggested that more government-supported agricultural research on organic farming could lead to even higher yields by organic methods.

When *melanogaster* fruit flies are put into a cage of *D. funebris*, which also reproduce slowly, the latter are not wiped out. Instead, they are reduced in number till they form about 5 percent of the cage population. Then they remain at that level. This is due to their ability to survive on a rather dry area at the edge of the food source, leaving the larger moist areas to the invaders. In this case the

activities that define its role in the ecosystem. What does it eat, where does it eat, when does it eat? Does it thrive in wet or dry, hot or cold weather? Does it lay its eggs in water or on the ground under a rotting log? These and many more things are all parts of its ecological niche.

Each resource in an ecosystem may have many different aspects. This allows for numerous ecological niches in a single habitat. On the Serengeti Plains of Africa, herds of zebras, wildebeests, and Thomson's gazelles follow each other in succession during seasonal migrations across the plains. The largest of the three, the zebra, eats the top parts of the grasses and herbs, primarily the leaves. The smaller wildebeest favors the sheaths in the middle. And the smallest animal, the gazelle, prefers the lower stem areas. Each herd moves on when it has used up its favorite part, leaving the plains to the next animals.

Competition for resources does not involve food alone. Niche differentiation can develop around sleeping or nesting sites. Baboon and patas monkey groups overlap in areas of the Uganda plains where trees are scarce. But only the monkeys sleep in trees; the baboons prefer high cliffs. In the case of plants, the need for insect pollination can define niches. At least eight different species of flowering plants belonging to the phlox family manage to coexist, because their flower shapes accommodate different pollinators. The different flowers are favored by hummingbirds, beetles, butterflies, bees, flies, and even bats.

THE NATURE OF THE ECOSYSTEM

We see, then, that different ecological niches exist in every environment. This may suggest ways in which the biotic relationships in an ecosystem are influenced by the abiotic environment. This environment includes such things as climate, soil composition, geological makeup, and physical contours, such as mountains or rivers. Just as interrelationships in the biotic community are always changing, so too is the abiotic world in which they occur.

Ecological succession
Any change in the physical environment will sooner or later affect the plants and animals that live in it. The change may be drastic, as when a flood or a fire wipes out local vegetation and wild life. Or it may be more gradual, as when rocks or hillsides erode, or rivers fill up with silt. And, in turn, biotic changes can influence the abiotic environment. Growing tree roots can split boulders; beavers may dam a stream and create a pond. The physical and biological changes together result in an ongoing pattern known as **ecological succession.**

Ecological succession begins with an uncolonized territory, one that has never before supported plant life. An example is the succession that occurs in areas of barren rock. For long periods of time, lichen may be all that grows there. This first living population is known as a **primary community.** Then soil may be deposited in small crevices in the rock by wind or water. This soil may receive numerous kinds of windblown seeds, some of which eventually will develop into plants. Thus a foothold is gained. Soon the pressure of the plant roots may expand the cracks in the rocks. The roots will also trap more soil. When these pioneer plants die, they will add organic matter to the soil. As the quality and quantity of the soil increases, plants of other species will take over the area. The process of succession will continue until one or two plants become dominant. This stage is a period of equilibrium in the ecosystem called the **climax community.** If not disturbed by outside forces, it may last indefinitely.

Succession on a large scale, such as that from glacier bed or sandy beach to hardwood forest, is hard to see. But on a smaller scale, such as the successive occupations of a puddle or a fallen log, the process of change can be observed over a much shorter time.

Succession that begins with territory where no community existed before is known as **primary succession.** In contrast, the series of changes that takes place where humans have altered the natural community is known as **secondary succession.** An abandoned field shows this type of succes-

Figure 23-17. Successions may be drastically affected by disasters such as floods or forest fires. However, plants usually manage to regain a foothold after these setbacks.

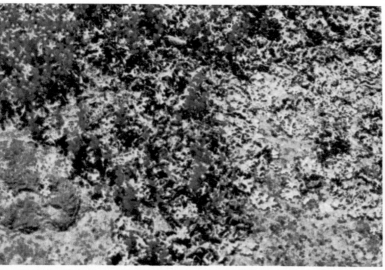

Figure 23-18. These pictures illustrate a type of primary succession. Lichens develop on barren rock and eventually give way to other plant life of increasing complexity.

Abandoned farm

Figure 23-19. The pictures on this page and the following page illustrate the stages of secondary succession.

Tufts of crabgrass

Broomsedge

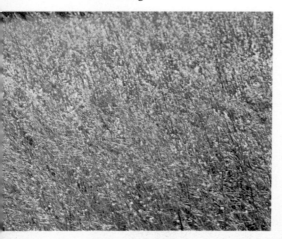

sion. The penetration of human populations has upset many stable communities. Often it has destroyed them, as when a field is bulldozed or a forest cut down for the expansion of agriculture.

We can watch the process of secondary succession in a vacant city lot. First come the weeds. These are gradually replaced by fast-growing "weed trees" that harbor various types of insect. The cynthia moth, for example, seems to thrive on the ailanthus tree. Other insects feed on garbage. And before the garbage is decomposed by soil bacteria, scavengers such as rats, cats, and dogs may vie for food scraps.

Usually such lots remain in a weedy state for a very long time, because the surrounding streets and buildings prevent the invasion of forest life. A community that remains for a long time at a stage before a climax is often called a **subclimax community.**

Biomes

Plants and animals in similar climatic areas tend to reach similar climax communities. Thus, ecosystems can be grouped together into a few major climax communities. These are called **biomes.**

INTERACTING WITH
THE ENVIRONMENT

Figure 23-20. Broomsedge with pine seedling

Deciduous saplings among maturing pines

The world has both land and water biomes. The major land biomes include rain forest, desert, grassland, deciduous forest, taiga, and tundra. The water biomes include both ocean and fresh-water environments. Because it is hard to make any general statements about water biomes, this section will look only at the more familiar land biomes.

The warmest and wettest land biome is the tropical **rain forest,** located near the equator. Africa, Asia, and South and Central America all have rain forests. The warmth and moisture in these areas support many different kinds of plant and animal life. Often it is hard to find two individuals of the same kind in an area. Because the trees grow very tall, with thick, interwoven branches, very little sun penetrates, and the forest floor is cool, dim, and moist. Without much

Pines at 20 years

Oak/hickory dominance

SHORT-TAILED SHREW

COTTONTAIL RABBIT

WHITE-TAILED DEER

RED SQUIRREL

RED FOX

WHITE-FOOTED MOUSE

RUFFED GROUSE

MEADOW MOUSE

TOWHEE

PURPLE FINCH

ROBIN

BLACK-THROATED GREEN WARBLER

VEERY

FIELD SPARROW

SONG SPARROW

JUNCO

NASHVILLE WARBLER

GRASSHOPPER SPARROW

MEADOWLARK

GRASS   LOW SHRUB   HIGH SHRUB   SHRUB-TREE   OPENING   LOW TREE   HIGH TREE

Figure 23-21. Animal communities change as plants follow a typical succession. The horizontal line under each animal or group of animals indicates which of the successive plant communities these animals inhabit.

sun, there is no dense undergrowth. This makes a rain forest easy to walk in, unlike a tropical jungle. Many epiphytes and parasites live in or below the treetops. Most of the colorful forms of life live up in the treetops, or canopy. Here the sunlight and moisture support a rich variety of vegetation. The many bird species are often as vivid as the flowers.

The driest biome is the **desert,** where average annual rainfall is not more than 10 inches. Although we may think of deserts as hot places, they are not always hot. Some, such as the Central Desert in Iceland, are frozen wastes. And when the sun goes down, even the hot ones cool off very quickly. These extremes in temperature, combined with the low rainfall, mean that the desert does not have much vegetation. Cacti and other desert plants are adapted to the dryness, since they can store water inside themselves. Animals often live underground, and

INTERACTING WITH THE ENVIRONMENT

Figure 23-22. Four different biomes: a grassland (top left); a deciduous forest (top right); a desert (bottom left); and a tundra (bottom right).

Figure 23-23. The coloration of this desert rattlesnake blends in nicely with its background.

only come out to eat at night. Then it is cooler and they cannot be seen so easily. Others, such as the numerous snakes, have colors that blend in with their pale, sandy background.

A more hospitable biome is the **grassland.** Here rainfall averages between 10 and 30 inches—enough for grasses, but not for trees. Many grasses have long or branching roots that can absorb water from deep in the ground. Herds of grazing animals cross this biome, feeding as they go. Their great speed protects most of them from the meat-eating predators. Smaller animals, such as prairie dogs and mice, dig burrows underground and so avoid capture. Because there are few trees, most birds build nests on the ground and have protective coloration. Some, such as the roadrunner in the western United States, and the ostrich in Africa, have long legs that enable them to make a quick escape. Large areas of grassland still exist in the midwestern and western United States, though many of the large grazers, such as the buffalo and the antelope, are almost gone.

The eastern United States, along with

Figure 23-24. Deciduous forests such as this one support a wide variety of animals, insects, and birds.

Figure 23-25. An artificial biome has been created in this marine aquarium. How are the autotrophs and the heterotrophs dependent on each other?

much of western Europe and central Asia, once formed a vast forest area. Although it has been greatly altered by human settlements, the temperate climate and generous rainfall make it naturally a **deciduous forest** biome. Deciduous trees and shrubs are those that lose all their leaves each autumn. Warm summers encourage the growth of broad-leaved deciduous trees, often beech and maple. As the fallen leaves decay they enrich the soil. The deciduous forest is not so dark as the rain forest: sunlight does reach the ground, encouraging small plants and shrubs. And an annual rainfall of 30 to 60 inches permits a great variety of life, even now. Birds such as owls, ravens, and eagles—now rare—once haunted the inner forests. But many more can still be seen and heard around the edges. Some large forest browsers—feeders on twigs, leaves, and young shoots—remain, mainly the deer. But the wolves that once hunted them have almost vanished from this biome.

The northernmost biomes are the taiga and the tundra. The **taiga** is the last forest biome before the northern timberline. It is cold and often snow-covered. In many places a single kind of evergreen, such as spruce or fir, covers vast uncut areas. Other, moister areas produce the willow, alder, and other broad-leaved trees favored by migrating browsers. Herds of caribou and moose come down to the taiga for food in winter. Hares and beavers may live in the forests all year. All of them are hunted by hungry predators, including wolves and foxes. Other migrants are the birds, which go south in winter.

Few animals stay year round on the **tundra,** an icy biome whose Russian name means "north of the timberline." Only the first one or two feet of soil freeze in winter and thaw in spring. Below this is a permanently frozen layer known as **permafrost,** into which roots cannot penetrate. Bitter cold and frozen landscape discourage all but the hardiest creatures from staying in winter. Those that do stay must keep warm. Many smaller animals burrow under the

snow. Others, such as the polar bear and the musk ox, depend on their large body mass and thick coats. In the spring thaw, the lengthening periods of daylight bring forth thick clusters of plants, herbs, and mosses, many of them covered with bright flowers. Because the permafrost inhibits drainage, the landscape is covered with bogs and ponds.

SUMMARY

The world of living things is one of interdependence. Plants and animals in a community, along with the physical environment with which they interact, make up an ecosystem. An ecosystem thus has both biotic (living) and abiotic (nonliving) components.

Major patterns of interdependence include nutrition, protection, and reproduction. Food-dependency relationships can take the form of sequential food chains. Autotrophic organisms that manufacture food by photosynthesis are called producers. Heterotrophic organisms that eat the producers are called primary consumers. Producers depend on consumers for the raw materials for photosynthesis. Decomposers feed on nonliving organic matter, breaking it down into CO_2, water, and mineral compounds. This relationship of consumers, producers, and decomposers is also an ongoing energy chain. But the concept of food web is more accurate than that of a food chain, since food dependency involves complex, overlapping relationships.

Patterns of protection include protective coloration and mimicry. Protective coloration either conceals an organism against its background or obscures its outline. Mimicry of a poisonous or harmful organism by a harmless one is called Batesian mimicry. Mimicry of one harmful organism by another is called Müllerian mimicry. A third form of mimicry is aggressive rather than defensive.

Plant and animal populations are often linked by reproductive interdependence. An example can be seen in flowering plants and their insect pollinators.

Symbiosis ("living together") is an intimate pattern of species interdependence. It is a more or less permanent relationship between two species. Mutualism is a symbiotic relationship in which both participants benefit. Commensalism is a relationship in which one member benefits and the other remains unaffected. In parasitism, one individual exists at the expense of the other, or host, individual.

Predation and competition are more comprehensive patterns of interdependence, which can involve many different species. Predation is the feeding of one organism on another. It serves the predator population more directly than it does the prey populations. But predation also regulates the numbers of a prey population, ensuring that they will not become too numerous for the resources that support them. In addition, predators usually manage to catch only the weakest or sickest of a prey population, and thereby help to keep that population healthy. Predation can thus be said to increase the survival potential of prey populations as well as of predators.

When two or more species in the same community compete for the same resources, only one will survive. Thus competition encourages the exploitation of different resources within the community. Species that utilize different resources in an ecosystem are said to be exploiting different ecological niches.

Changes in the abiotic environment influence the nature of the biotic community. Ecological succession is the replacement of one kind of plant or animal life by another. Succession on a previously uncolonized territory is called primary succession. It begins with a pioneer community and finally reaches equilibrium at a climax community. The climax community is both stable and complex. The changes that take place where a stable community has been destroyed are called secondary succession.

Ecosystems can be grouped into major climax communities called biomes. There are both land and water biomes. Six major land biomes are the rain forest, the desert, the grassland, the deciduous forest, the taiga, and the tundra.

Review questions

1. List some of the ways in which plants and animals in an ecosystem affect each other.

2. What are the three basic needs of organisms within a community?

3. Describe the roles of decomposers, producers, and consumers in a food chain.

4. Why are food-dependency relationships in an ecosystem more accurately described by the term "food web" than by "food chain"?

5. Describe an energy pyramid.

6. Distinguish between concealing coloration and disruptive coloration.

7. How is an organism with concealing coloration dependent upon another population within its ecosystem? Give an example.

8. Distinguish among three types of mimicry. Give an example of each type.

9. Name at least two examples of reproductive interdependence.

10. What is symbiosis?

11. What is the basis on which the three types of symbiosis are classified? Give an example of each.

12. Why are epiphytes most commonly found in the tropics and subtropics?

13. What is the difference between the two types of parasite? Which is the more independent?

14. Why is it advantageous for a predator to have a variety of prey species?

15. How does predation increase the survival potential of the two populations involved?

16. Give an example of how destroying the balance between predators and prey can upset the ecology of an area.

17. How might a new ecological niche be exploited as a result of competition?

18. What is ecological succession?

19. Describe an example of primary succession. Explain the effect of human interference upon ecological succession.

20. What is a biome?

21. What is most striking about life in the tropical rain forest?

22. Name and describe several other biomes.

23. Name some ways in which plants and animals have become adapted to the environment and so are able to survive on the tundra; on the grassland.

24. Seven shipwrecked sailors land on a barren arctic island with a case of cornflakes and seven hens. How can they make best use of the food energy in their small supply? (a) Eat the cornflakes, then the hens. (b) Eat the hens, then the cornflakes. (c) Feed the cornflakes to the hens, then eat the eggs. (d) Other.

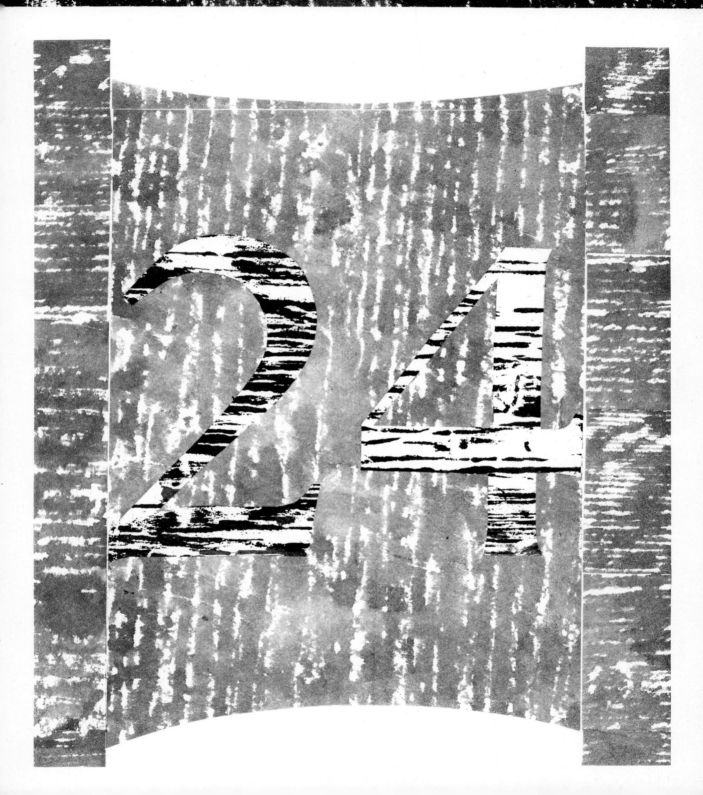

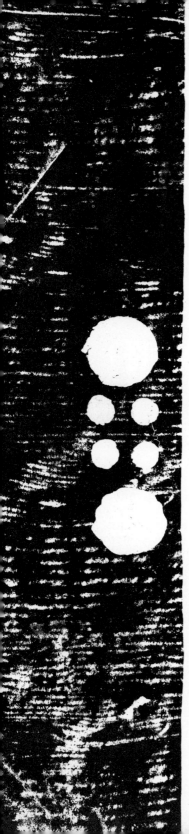

Resources and Pollution

Living things in an ecosystem form a tight web of interrelationships. If one thread is pulled out or changed, the whole web is affected. But the web could not exist at all without the support of the nonliving environment. At the beginning of all food chains and all energy cycles are autotrophic organisms. And these organisms need sunlight, water, and a variety of inorganic substances in order to live and grow.

Water, inorganic nutrients, and sunlight, or solar radiation, are abiotic (nonliving) factors in the ecosystem. So are some atmospheric gases. Without oxygen and carbon dioxide, both plant and animal life would very quickly cease. Then there is climate, which is really a combination of abiotic factors—moisture, temperature, and air movement (wind). We have seen that the climates of the different biomes have a profound effect on the life those biomes can support.

Organic and inorganic nutrients are found in soil and water. In aquatic habitats, they may be dissolved in the water, or they may be part of the sediment on the bottom of a lake or ocean. On land, nutrients are contained mostly in the upper layer, or topsoil. Here are partially decomposed organic material, inorganic minerals, and gases, including water vapor. Gases are also found, of course, in the atmosphere. Earth's atmosphere consists mostly of about 78 percent nitrogen, 21 percent oxygen, and a very small amount—.03 percent—of carbon dioxide. All of these are needed by living creatures. Surprisingly, though, the largest component of air—its nitrogen—cannot be used by plants and animals in its gaseous

505

form. We shall see later how it is made available.

As we saw in the last chapter, most nutrients follow a cyclical path through the ecosystem. When they reach the top of a food chain, they are recycled and start again at the bottom. But energy is another matter. It takes a one-way trip; that is, it cannot be recycled. At each stage of the journey, much of it is lost as heat and cannot be recovered. So the energy flow that begins with the plant producers and ends with the decomposers is not a cycle. It cannot begin again by itself. New energy must be supplied from outside the ecosystem. Hence the need for sunlight —solar radiant energy.

Actually, the earth receives far more solar energy than is used in photosynthesis. What happens to the rest? Much of it is absorbed by oceans and other bodies of water, heating them and causing evaporation. The evaporated water, or water vapor, collects in the atmosphere and eventually falls as snow or rain. But most solar energy strikes the earth and is radiated back to the atmosphere as heat. When warm air collides with colder air, winds result. Winds help to distribute the air's moisture, so that rain falls on the land as well as on the sea. Thus the amount of solar radiation reaching the earth affects heat and moisture, and through them the climates of all the biomes. The abiotic factors in the ecosystem, then, are affected by one another, just as living organisms are.

BIOGEOCHEMICAL CYCLES

The abiotic factors that can be recycled are said to follow a **biogeochemical cycle** through the ecosystem. As the name suggests, this is a pathway that leads through both living organisms and the non-living soil, water, and air of our planet. For example, when producer and consumer organisms die, decomposer organisms break down the organic substances in the dead bodies. Eventually, these substances are re-

Figure 24-1. Carbon, like other nutrients, follows a cyclic pathway through the ecosystem.

duced to their original inorganic molecules in the soil, air, or water. They can then be absorbed by new producer organisms, and used to form organic substances again.

Certain of the biogeochemical cycles are regarded as especially important. We shall consider several of these, namely the water, carbon, nitrogen, and phosphorus cycles.

The water cycle

The earth's supply of water is constant. It is recycled over and over again. Oceans, lakes, and rivers together constitute 98 percent of this supply. The remaining 2 percent is contained in living organisms, the soil, or the atmosphere, or else frozen into glaciers and polar ice.

Evaporation is essential to the water cycle. Evaporation, as we have seen, is driven

INTERACTING WITH
THE ENVIRONMENT

Figure 24-2. Most of the earth's water supply is contained in lakes and rivers like those shown here, as well as in the oceans. In what other parts of this community is water present?

by solar energy. It occurs not only from water environments—oceans, lakes, rivers, and streams—but also from moist soil and the bodies of plants and animals.

The evaporated water eventually falls back to earth as rain. Some of the rainwater evaporates quickly; some percolates down through the soil. Of the latter, some will later emerge in the form of springs and seepages in lakes, streams, and even the ocean floor. Some is stored in natural underground reservoirs. Rainwater travels through the biotic parts of the ecosystem, too. Some is absorbed by green plants and is either used in photosynthesis and other processes, or returned to the atmosphere through transpiration. Water remaining in plants enters the bodies of animals that eat the plants. There it joins other water that the animals drank from streams, ponds, or the kitchen tap, and water produced in cellular respiration. From the animal's tissues, the water may be returned to the atmosphere through evaporation. Or it may be excreted in urine or feces, returning to the soil or the nearest river. Or it may be released through decom-

position when the animal dies. Sooner or later, all of the water returns to the atmosphere and falls somewhere as snow or rain. The cycle begins again.

As can be seen, the water cycle is not a neat circle. A molecule of water may get around the cycle in very few steps—from air to rain and right back to the air through evaporation. Or it may take a little longer—air to rain to soil water to plant to air. Or it may follow a very long path—air to rain to soil water to plant to animal to urine to soil water to plant to animal to another animal to decomposer bacteria and back to air. But it will always get around eventually. The only way to lose it entirely would be to take it outside the earth's gravity altogether. If space travel ever becomes common, this could be a problem.

The constant circulation of water not only provides organisms with water for their own needs. The amount of vapor in the atmosphere helps to regulate temperatures on earth. And the movement of liquid water serves to carry dissolved nutrients through the ecosystem.

The carbon cycle

Carbon is a major building block in organisms. Carbohydrates, fats, proteins, ATP, and the nucleic acid components are all carbon compounds. The simplest carbon compound normally found in organisms is carbon dioxide (CO_2).

Like oxygen, carbon dioxide is a component of the atmosphere, but in a much smaller quantity. As we have said, 21 percent of the earth's atmosphere is composed of oxygen. However, carbon dioxide makes up only about .03 percent of the atmosphere.

During photosynthesis, carbon dioxide is removed from the atmosphere. Along with the hydrogen atoms from water molecules, the carbon dioxide is used in building carbon-containing (organic) molecules. Autotrophic organisms build all their own organic molecules, using carbon dioxide as a raw material. Heterotrophic organisms obtain necessary organic molecules directly from autotrophic organisms or indirectly from other heterotrophic organisms. An animal will eat a plant or another animal and utilize the carbon in that organism's molecules. Each time the carbon compounds are consumed during their passage through the food chain, they are broken down and resynthesized into new compounds.

The principal way in which carbon, in the form of carbon dioxide, is returned to the atmosphere is as a product of cellular respiration. As such, it is usually a waste product that is released from organisms. Plants give it off from their leaves; vertebrates usually release it through the gills or lungs. Equally important at this stage in the cycle are **decomposer organisms.** As we have said, the body of an organism is made up primarily of carbon compounds. When an organism dies, it is decomposed by various small organisms, such as bacteria and fungi. During the process of decomposition, some of the carbon from the dead organism is used by the decomposers themselves. But a great deal of it is released to the atmosphere in the form of carbon dioxide.

Figure 24-3. Water is the most important component of the bodies of both animals and plants. The water you drink today may have previously formed part of the Atlantic Ocean, a glacier in Antarctica, the sap of a palm tree, and the blood of a long-extinct dinosaur.

Like water, carbon may move through its biogeochemical cycle swiftly or slowly. Sometimes it gets "locked up" in the earth's crust. The lock-up may last for an indefinite time. An example is the carbon in the limestone shells of marine organisms. If that carbon remains in layers of limestone rock, it is likely to stay out of circulation for thousands or millions of years. But the limestone may gradually be eroded by wind and water —perhaps by ocean waves beating on a limestone cliff. In that case, slowly, the imprisoned carbon will be released. Another example is the fossilized carbon that is locked up in deposits of coal, oil, and natural gas. We can unlock this carbon by burning these deposits as fuel. When such fossil fuels are completely burned, much of the carbon is released in the form of carbon dioxide. The burning thus helps to renew the supply of atmospheric carbon. However, as we shall see later, it can have harmful ecological effects.

The nitrogen cycle

Every protein is made up of amino acids. Every amino acid has an amino group, made up of one atom of nitrogen and two atoms of hydrogen (NH_2). One use of nitrogen in the bodies of organisms, then, is in the amino acids. Other important molecules also contain nitrogen, such as ATP, DNA, and RNA.

As we noted above, the atmosphere (excluding water vapor and pollution) is

508

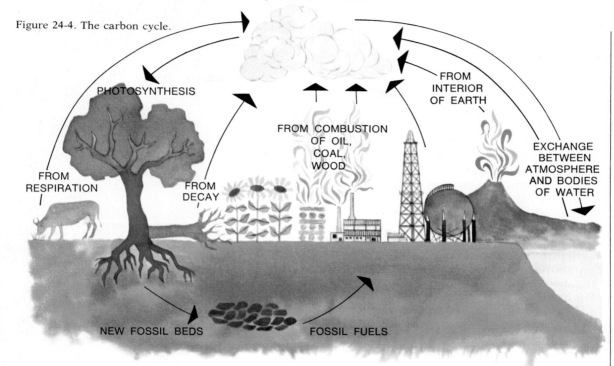

Figure 24-4. The carbon cycle.

CO₂ IN ATMOSPHERE

PHOTOSYNTHESIS

FROM
INTERIOR
OF EARTH

FROM COMBUSTION
OF OIL,
COAL,
WOOD

EXCHANGE
BETWEEN
ATMOSPHERE
AND BODIES
OF WATER

FROM
RESPIRATION

FROM
DECAY

NEW FOSSIL BEDS

FOSSIL FUELS

about 78 percent molecular nitrogen (N₂). Most organisms cannot use this molecular nitrogen. But those that can provide the basis for the nitrogen cycle. Let us see how.

Practically all organisms in the biosphere can use only "fixed" nitrogen. The term **fixed** means that the nitrogen is incorporated into a molecule that can be used by organisms. For example, most plants can best use nitrogen in the form of ammonium ions (NH₄) or nitrates (NO₃). When plants are supplied with such molecules, they can use them as raw materials in building amino acids and all other necessary nitrogen-containing molecules. Animals ultimately rely on plants for their nitrogen. They ingest the plant's nitrogen-containing molecules and reassemble them according to their own needs.

Nitrogen fixation occurs in nature in two basic ways. One method occurs in the atmosphere, as the result of lightning and perhaps meteor trails. These atmospheric phenomena provide bursts of high energy

that enable nitrogen in the atmosphere to combine with the hydrogen or oxygen of water. The resulting molecules are then washed out of the atmosphere by rainfall. The amount of nitrogen compounds added to the soil in this way is probably several pounds per acre per year, and may be far more in some places.

The second natural process of nitrogen fixation is carried out by certain organisms. Most of the nitrogen fixers are blue-green algae or bacteria. The blue-green algae probably have an important role in damp terrestrial environments. Certain species of bacteria, however, have the major responsibility for nitrogen fixation in terrestrial ecosystems.

There are two major kinds of **nitrogen-fixing bacteria.** Some are free-living; others are symbiotic. The symbiotic species probably do the bulk of the work in fixing atmospheric nitrogen. In particular, those that live in the roots of one plant family—the legumes—are the most important. (Legumes are members of the pea family, such as clover, beans, and alfalfa.) The bacteria penetrate the tiny root hairs of the legumes. Once inside, they multiply rapidly, causing the plant to form a swelling known as a nodule. Inside the nodule, the bacteria convert atmospheric nitrogen to ammonia. This ammonia then reacts with other substances in both the bacteria and the host plant, forming amino acids and other nitrogen compounds. When the plant dies or is eaten, the nitrogen compounds are passed on to consumers or decomposers.

In addition to legumes, many plants that thrive in poor soils are hosts to nitrogen-fixing bacteria. Alder trees are an example. These trees can grow on the tundra and in the poor soil high on mountain slopes. Another example is the common goldenrod.

Free-living nitrogen-fixing bacteria also convert gaseous nitrogen to ammonia. They then use it in synthesizing nitrogen compounds, or diffuse it into the soil or water in which they live.

The quantity of fixed nitrogen is the main nutrient factor limiting plant growth. Terrestrial and marine plants fix about 40 million tons per year. But modern agriculture requires more fixed nitrogen, to produce food for an ever-growing world population. In the United States alone, industry and agriculture use 7 million tons per year. Thus scientists have tried to discover ways of fixing nitrogen artificially. In 1914, German chemists learned how to fix atmospheric nitrogen in large quantities by means of electricity. Since then, the industrial fixing of nitrogen for fertilizer has become a major world industry. Today about 30 million metric tons are produced per year.

There are several pathways for nitrogen after it is fixed. One pathway is from the plant in which it was fixed to the animal that eats the plant. When the animal is decomposed, nitrogen compounds that can be reused by plants are released. In this pathway nitrogen does not return to the atmosphere.

A second pathway is a modification of the

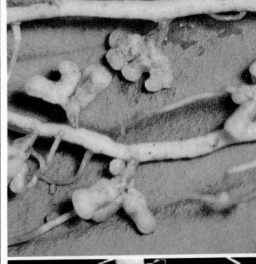
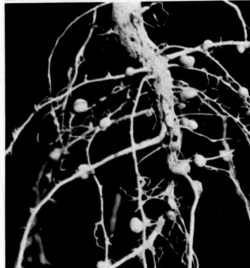

Figure 24-5. The roots of a clover plant (above) and a cowpea plant (below) show typical nodule formations due to the presence of nitrogen-fixing bacteria in the roots. (Courtesy Carolina Biological Supply Co.)

Figure 24-6. *Rhizobium* is one of the bacteria that have the ability to fix nitrogen.

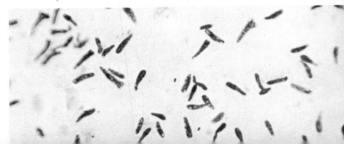

previous one. Some of the nitrogen released from animal (or plant) bodies by decomposers goes into the soil. But instead of being reused by a plant, it may wash out of the soil and become a part of the hydrosphere, which is the earth's water. There it may enter any number of different food webs in aquatic ecosystems.

A third pathway releases nitrogen back to the atmosphere. This occurs in a process called **denitrification.** It is an anaerobic process and therefore occurs in waterlogged soils that have a low oxygen content. In terrestrial ecosystems, it is accomplished by several different species of bacteria. However, we do not yet know how it occurs in marine habitats in which there is a high oxygen content.

Phosphorus: a mineral cycle

Carbon and nitrogen are only two of the elements needed by organisms. Many more are needed in smaller quantities, and these must also be recycled in the biosphere. Of these other elements, phosphorus is a typical example we can use to show a different type of cyclic pathway.

Phosphorus is like other essential mineral elements in that it is not a normal component of the atmosphere. In the cycles just discussed, the atmosphere served as a kind of "bank" from which carbon and nitrogen could be withdrawn and replaced. The pathway of phosphorus does not include the atmospheric storage bank. Phosphorus is stored as a mineral, released to the biosphere, and returned to mineral form.

Think of the role of adenosine triphosphate (ATP) as we described it in chapter 3, and you can appreciate the great importance of phosphorus in organisms. Every molecule of ATP has three phosphate atoms. Without phosphate, there would be no ATP

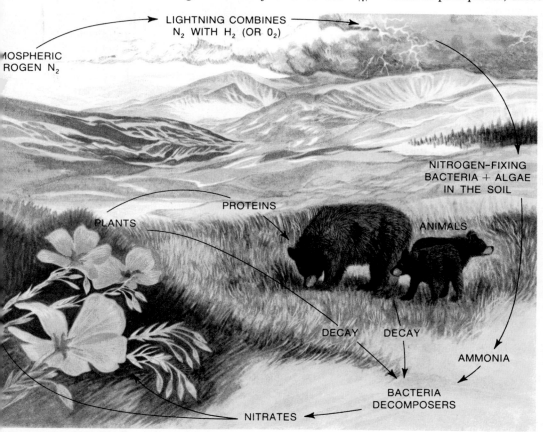

LIGHTNING COMBINES N_2 WITH H_2 (OR O_2)

ATMOSPHERIC NITROGEN N_2

NITROGEN-FIXING BACTERIA + ALGAE IN THE SOIL

PROTEINS

PLANTS

ANIMALS

DECAY

DECAY

AMMONIA

BACTERIA DECOMPOSERS

NITRATES

Figure 24-7. The nitrogen cycle.

and thus no means of transforming energy in any organism.

Phosphorus in the earth's crust is mainly present in the form of phosphate rocks. Throughout the years, these rocks are broken down by various forces of weathering and erosion. Some of the phosphorus will remain in terrestrial ecosystems and be used by plants. Some will be washed into streams and lakes and will eventually be carried into the oceans. In terrestrial ecosystems the phosphorus will be cycled from the bodies of plants to animals, and then to decomposers and back to plants.

For phosphorus that is carried from the land into oceans, the cycle is not equally perfect. As a matter of fact, there is a net loss of phosphorus in the ocean, because some of it settles to the bottom and forms phosphate rock. The major pathway of phosphorus in the biosphere seems to be from terrestrial phosphate rock to soluble phosphates in the soil, to organisms, then into sea water, and eventually into phosphate rock at the bottom of the sea. Thus it is normally a one-way path ending in the sea.

There is an interesting exception to this one-way path, which may be of some importance in returning phosphorus to the land. If the phosphate material is jarred a bit, and floats upward from the bottom, it may be taken up by marine algae. In some areas, the collison of warm and cold water currents produces vast upheavals of this sort. The grand banks of Newfoundland and some regions off the west coast of South America are examples. This is one reason why these regions are among the world's great fishing grounds, for the phosphate-rich algae resulting from these upheavals provide food for vast numbers of fish. Many of the fish, in turn, are eventually consumed by marine birds, such as gulls or terns, and some of the phosphate is later returned to the land in the birds' droppings. Certain coastal areas and islands of South America contain tons of phosphates that have been deposited over the years in the wastes of sea birds. This material, called guano, also contains nitrogen,

and for many years was a major source of fertilizer. Therefore, although most phosphate is lost in the sea, about 5 percent of it is returned to the land by these sea birds, thus completing the phosphorus cycle.

POLLUTION

The materials that circulate through biogeochemical cycles cannot be replaced. They can only be reused. Normally, the processes move fairly smoothly, making a steady supply available at each key point of the cycle. Once, therefore, there was no need to worry about the supply or quality of basic abiotic resources. In the last few centuries, though, we have developed a technology that can control many aspects of the environment. This has great benefits. Flood control and irrigation mean less suffering from floods and droughts. New techniques of food production can vastly increase the world food supply. But our power to change the physical environment is also a power to harm it. The new technology produces wastes that cannot be absorbed by the environment—water, land, air—without serious damage. Some of these wastes are biological poisons and cannot be absorbed at all. Others are man-made substances, such as plutonium, that do not occur under natural conditions. Eventually, such wastes may so alter the environment that it can no longer support life.

Pollution is a relative term. Generally it is defined as any process by which people reduce the quality of their environment. It is a relative term because deciding what does and does not harm the environment usually depends on many factors. For example, if I burn a pile of leaves in my back yard, am I polluting the environment? After all, the odor of burning leaves is pleasant, like the odor of a steak cooking over charcoal, or the fragrance of a favorite pipe. But if I burn the leaves in front of a large apartment building, so that the smoke fills all the rooms, I would

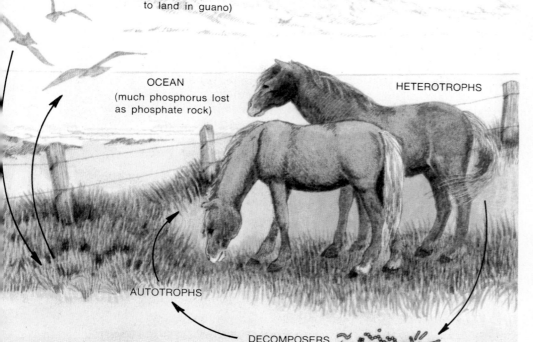

SEABIRDS (some phosphorus to land in guano)

OCEAN (much phosphorus lost as phosphate rock)

HETEROTROPHS

AUTOTROPHS

DECOMPOSERS

Figure 24-8. The phosphorus cycle.

probably be regarded as polluting the environment. Or how about a man smoking his pipe? If he smokes it on his breezy suburban patio, he will probably not be accused of polluting. But the reaction would be different if his environment were a crowded airplane. More and more, as people inhabit the earth in greater numbers, our situation is coming to resemble that of the crowded airplane.

For, in fact, many of our pollution problems stem from the classic problem of individuals exercising what have been their traditional freedoms—freedom to smoke, freedom to burn grass and leaves, freedom to dump wastes in rivers. When there were fewer people to do these things, the environment could absorb the effects of their activities with less harm. But more and more people mean more and more smoke, more and more wastes in the rivers, and so on. How long will it be before the environment is overloaded? And what will happen then?

Pests and pesticides

Technology and pollution are closely interrelated. For instance, in order to feed humans, we have tried to avoid feeding a large population of insects with the crops meant for human consumption. With some exceptions, the cheapest and most effective way to destroy these competitors has seemed to be the use of chemical poisons called **pesticides.** These, as we are now realizing, have caused numerous problems.

In part, the problems stem from the operation of natural selection. "If you want to eliminate pests, make it difficult for them to survive. Spray them or do anything else you can to make life hard for them." Sounds reasonable? Well, yes, it does seem logical to make life difficult for a competitor. Unfortunately, natural selection usually means that a harsh environment will favor tougher competitors. If an area is sprayed with a pesticide, most of the pests will probably be killed. But some will not. Some members of any pest population are likely to have

SEA SNAKES

Imagine the following scenario: It is a hot, bright day at Miami Beach, and the water is full of swimmers. Suddenly, close to shore, a boy yells and begins splashing madly. Fearing sharks, other swimmers make for land as a lifeguard dashes to the boy's aid. Presently boy and lifeguard emerge, apparently undamaged. Back on land, the boy explains, "It was a snake, just floating there. I never heard of snakes in the ocean. I guess I bumped it, and it bit me. Naw, the bite doesn't hurt. It's not swollen or anything. I reckon the critter wasn't poisonous, but it sure scared me!" Several hours later the boy becomes dizzy. His muscles ache; he has trouble breathing. His jaws lock. After three days, in spite of all the doctors can do, he dies. By now, other snakes have been sighted. . . .

All right, don't cancel your trip to Florida. The story is pure fiction—so far. There are no sea snakes anywhere near Miami Beach, or in the Atlantic Ocean. But they do exist in the Pacific and Indian Oceans, and they are among the most poisonous of all snakes—so poisonous that few other creatures dare to attack them. And they *could* turn up at Miami Beach under one condition. There have been proposals for building a sea-level canal across Panama between the Atlantic and Pacific Oceans. Unlike the present Panama Canal, which has a series of massive lock gates and a fresh-water lake in the middle, a sea-level canal would present no barrier to ocean creatures. They could swim freely between the two oceans, and eventually those poisonous sea snakes could turn up to menace swimmers off the coast of Florida.

So what are snakes doing in the water, anyway? Since they are air-breathers, don't they belong on land? And why should they be in some oceans and not in others?

Relatives of the highly venomous krait and cobra, the sea snakes are found mostly in tropical and subtropical waters. One species, the yellow-bellied sea snake, lives along the western American coast from Mexico to Ecuador. Sea snakes probably descended from land reptiles that returned to the sea. Their adaptations for marine living include a flat, oar-like tail and nostrils positioned at the top of the snout, with flaps that keep them closed under water. Most of them lack the broad belly plates needed for crawling, and are helpless on land. A few species come ashore to breed, but most mate at sea, bearing live young that can fend for themselves from the start.

Sea snakes are amazingly at home under water. After surfacing for a single deep breath, some can stay down for several

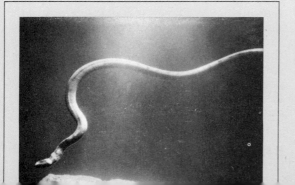

hours, searching for food as deep as 500 feet. Part of their secret is a very large lung with an air-storage sac at the end. They can also slow their heartbeat so that they use energy and oxygen more slowly. But even this hardly seems to explain the length of time they can remain submerged.

Despite their underwater skills, sea snakes are not very fast swimmers. Those that eat fish can easily be outdistanced by their prey. So the sea snakes must hunt by stealth, sneaking up on fish and trapping them with the coils of their bodies. A quick shot of venom, or just a snap of sharp-toothed jaws, and dinner is served. The surface-living yellow-bellied sea snake floats with the currents, looking for all the world like a dead stick, till a school of small fish approach and begin nosing at it. The snake strikes swiftly, and one of the fish finds out too late that the "stick" was not what it seemed.

Only by mistake would a fish be foolish enough to meddle with a sea snake. Even the most voracious Pacific fish avoid these creatures like the plague. They will refuse to eat sea snakes, living or dead, and with good reason. These fish swallow their prey whole, and a snake that is swallowed is quite capable of biting as it goes down. Result, one dead fish.

Given a chance at a sea snake (in ex-perimental studies), an Atlantic fish will eat it, and in perhaps one case out of twelve it will die. In dying, it may vomit up the still-living snake, which then has a chance to bite and kill another fish. If sea snakes got into the Caribbean, some important sport or commercial fish might be seriously reduced in numbers before they could develop forms that would avoid these deceptively attractive prey.

Just to complicate matters, a sea snake bite is not always fatal. These snakes can hold back their venom if they choose, and only about one bite in four is actually venomous. But when the venom is used, the victim has little chance of survival. Sea snake venom is anywhere from two to ten times as poisonous as that of cobras and death adders—and for many species, there is as yet no antivenom serum.

Sea snakes have not yet migrated into the Atlantic, mainly for reasons of temperature. Like most reptiles, they are warm-climate creatures. To reach the Atlantic, they would have to swim around the southern tips of Africa or South America, where the waters are too cold for them. So Miami Beach is safe, for the moment. But if that sea-level canal is built? Will we have swarms of yellow-bellied sea snakes floating ashore on all the beaches of the Caribbean? Brrrrr.

characteristics that enable them to survive the spraying. These survivors are left with the entire niche to themselves. So they eat and reproduce, and a higher percentage of their offspring survive, because there is plenty of food and little competition. And the offspring—or at least many of them—inherit their parents' pesticide resistance. With each year, the percentage of pesticide-resistant offspring will increase. So a more resistant pest population results. In a few years it will take more spray, or a different or stronger spray, to keep the pests under control.

What if a field is sprayed with a pesticide powerful enough to kill every animal in it? This has happened. What ecologists call a **vacant niche** has been created in this way. However, it is safe to assume that the niche will not stay vacant very long. Wherever there is a way of life—a niche—available,

Figure 24-9. Pollution not only reduces the quality of the environment but may waste valuable resources also.

Figure 24-10. Disposal of solid wastes is a rapidly growing problem in our society. What are some of the possible alternatives to the situation pictured here?

INTERACTING WITH THE ENVIRONMENT

Figure 24-11. It looks bad, smells bad, and may have damaging long-term effects on the human body. Many of the air-borne byproducts of combustion are known to produce cancer in laboratory animals.

some population will find and inhabit it. And the population that fills a vacant niche is likely to be more resistant to whatever destroyed the previous occupants. In order to kill the codling moth, for example, many apple orchards in the northeast United States were sprayed with DDT. The moth was practically eliminated. But then the red mite population increased. It has proved more difficult to control the red mite than the codling moth. This is partly because the insects that normally feed on the red mite were also killed by the spraying.

Another problem in using pesticides is that it is hard to limit the area affected. The pesticides may not stay where they were originally put. Also, many pesticides, such as DDT, do not break down for a long time after they are released in the environment. Such pesticides are called **persistent pesticides.** For example, a farmer may spray only a single field. But if it rains, the pesticide is washed into nearby streams. The streams empty into rivers, and the rivers empty into the ocean—carrying the pesticide with them. Along the way, the pesticide sets up its own biogeochemical cycle. DDT and related pesticides, as well as other

toxic chemicals such as mercury and lead, are picked up and stored in the bodies of animals. They cannot be used, as carbon and phosphorus are. And they can be excreted only very slowly. So the pesticides accumulate in the tissues, interfering with the normal functioning of the body cells. The first animals to pick them up are the primary consumers—those that feed on plants or on microscopic producer protists. Often the quantity of the chemical that the primary consumer stores in its body is not enough to do it any harm. But primary consumers, as we know, usually become a meal for secondary consumers. In fact, one secondary consumer may eat thousands of primary consumers. All the toxic chemicals from all these primary consumers are stored in the body of the secondary consumer. Therefore, this animal builds up a much greater percentage of chemicals in its body. And a consumer that eats secondary consumers will build up an even higher percentage. Animals near the top of a food chain accumulate very large concentrations of the toxic chemicals. This process is called **biological magnification.**

Because of biological magnification, organisms at the top of the food chain suffer the most from pesticide or other chemical poisoning. And people are at the top of many food chains. Much of the food they consume—meat and especially fish—comes from animals that are themselves very high on their respective chains. So humans are in particular danger of accumulating harmful quantities of toxic chemicals. In Japan, for instance, there have been many deaths from a type of nerve paralysis caused by mercury poisoning. The mercury came from fish. Industrial pollution had poured it into the lakes, and the fish had accumulated it from their contaminated food.

The birds at the end of food chains have been among the most tragic victims of pesticide use. Examples include the brown pelican and the golden eagle, both of which eat fairly good-sized animal prey. Usually the pesticide does not kill the birds directly.

Rather, it affects their eggshells, making them much thinner than normal. Then, when the mother bird sits on the eggs to hatch them, they are crushed under her. This has caused a serious decline in the populations of brown pelicans, golden eagles, and various hawks. In view of such consequences, pesticides might be more suitably called biocides—not pest-killers, but life-killers.

Air pollution

Of equal importance with soil pollution is pollution of the air. Air pollution causes changes in climate and weather, and in the major biogeochemical cycles. It therefore disrupts every ecosystem into which it intrudes. The air may be polluted by particles, which are often visible in the air—such as soot and smoke—and by organic and inorganic gases.

Air pollution is perhaps most obvious and annoying in the city, or around centers of heavy industry. But even in the country we can see its effects. The beautiful red color of the sun at twilight is the result of the presence of many dust, smoke, and soot particles in the air. These particles block the short light waves at the blue end of the spectrum, allowing only the longer red waves to get through and reach our eyes. Massive volcanic eruptions, which throw vast quantities of dust into the air, have been known to cause beautiful sunsets thousands of miles away.

Some years ago, scientists noted a sharp increase of carbon dioxide in the atmo-

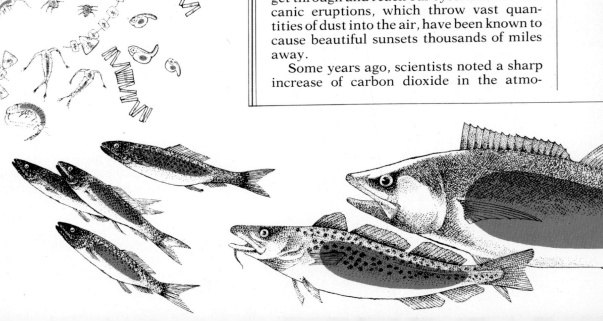

Figure 24-12. Elimination of the codling moth by spraying with pesticides left a vacant niche which allowed the red mite population, even more damaging to crops, to expand dramatically.

Figure 24-13. By spraying a crop with toxic chemicals, farmers almost guarantee that the pest they are trying to eliminate will evolve and become a hardier competitor.

Figure 24-14. In this illustration of biological magnification, the large tuna at right is not necessarily the end of the food chain. Often humans are the final consumers, and can be tragically affected by the concentrated amounts of poisonous chemicals stored in the bodies of animals they eat.

sphere. This has occurred mostly as a result of the ever-increasing burning of fossil fuels for heat and power. Some ecologists fear that carbon dioxide in the air may cause what is known as a "greenhouse effect." All sorts of tropical plants can be grown in a greenhouse, even in the coldest winter months. This is because the glass allows sunlight to get in, helping to warm the air inside, and then slows the escape of the warmed air. Carbon dioxide in the atmosphere is thought to work in the same way —allowing the sun to warm the surface of the earth but blocking the escape of the heat. The danger of increasing the average temperature of the earth, even by as little as one-half of one degree, is that it may increase the melting rate of the polar ice caps. The release of all that stored water would raise the level of all the earth's oceans by several feet, and flood many coastal cities and plains. And without the cooling effect of the ice, the earth would grow warmer and warmer, till many temperate and arctic species might be destroyed. Scientists believe that only a one-degree average increase was enough to cause the end of the great ice ages.

But the atmosphere itself may be compensating for the temperature increase. As the temperature rises, more water from the oceans may evaporate into the air, producing a heavier cloud layer. This would filter out the sun's rays, and so lower the temperature.

Chemical air pollutants, such as the gases given off by car engines and many industrial operations, do not just affect life indirectly, through climate. They are also directly poisonous to many organisms. Carbon monoxide is a case in point. It is rarely formed in nature, but it is abundantly produced by the internal combustion engines of our cars, buses, and trucks. These engines produce it because the carbon compounds in their fuel are incompletely burned. In vertebrate animals, carbon monoxide forms stable bonds with the hemoglobin in the blood, blocking the transport of oxygen and thus suffocating the cells.

The burning of fuels such as coal and oil produces not only carbon dioxide and carbon monoxide but other gases also—including sulfur dioxide, hydrogen sulfide, and nitrogen oxide. A study in Sweden found that these combine with moisture in the atmosphere, forming powerful sulfuric acid, which falls to earth and sea as a deadly rain. The acid rain has virtually wiped out salmon breeding grounds in Sweden, and has retarded forest growth. In addition, it is eat-

oceans made it seem as if they could absorb endless quantities of wastes without becoming wastes themselves. But in 1970 Thor Heyerdahl crossed the Atlantic on a boat made of papyrus reeds, which put him virtually at water level. He noted in his journal:

On June 16, one month after the start, the sea was so filthy that it was uncomfortable to wash in it. Big and small clots, from the size of a potato to a pea or a grain of rice, covered the water.

TURNING TRASH INTO FUEL

As the price of oil—and pollution—goes up, cities around the country are starting to consider recycling trash as a way of saving money and protecting the environment. Boston, St. Louis, New York, Baltimore, and other municipalities now have large-scale trash recycling systems on the drawing boards or in use.

A good example is the system planned for El Cajon, California, a town of 56,000 people. This $8-million plant, covering five acres, has been designed to handle 35 truckloads of garbage a day. Out of the garbage it will produce 200 barrels of liquid fuel, and reclaim some 25 tons of metals and glass. Experts put the value of the fuel at $1,700, and of

the metals and glass at about $750. Only about one-fourth of the original garbage will be left over to end up as landfill.

The recycling system will have several stages. All the wastes will be sent through a device that separates out the heavy materials. From these, the glass will be separated by a flotation bath, and the ferrous metals by a magnetic sorter. The lighter material—paper, textiles, and organic wastes—will be dried and shredded. It will then be placed in a so-called pyrolytic reactor, where extremely high temperatures will literally melt it into liquid fuel.

This method is expected to be much cleaner than other disposal systems which merely burn up the trash. And the recovered fuel, glass, and metals will save on resources and pay part of the cost of the operation.

---

ing away at metal and paint surfaces, and even stone structures, such as buildings and statues. Since that study, environmentalists have found similar effects in this country, most notably in the forests of the Adirondacks. And air pollution is said to be one of the chief dangers threatening the Parthenon and other magnificent stone relics of ancient Greece.

Water pollution
At one time the very vastness of the world's

Later on in the journey he wrote:

In the afternoon the smooth surface of the sea was covered with enormous quantities of brown and black clots of asphalt, floating in something that looked like soap suds, and here and there the surface shimmered in all colors as if covered with gasoline.[1]

The clots were oil. Oil pollution is one of the most serious problems facing the oceans. Oil spills out of great ocean-going tankers

INTERACTING WITH
THE ENVIRONMENT

Figure 24-15. Even in areas of the Atlantic Ocean hundreds of miles from the nearest coastline, members of Thor Heyerdahl's Ra II expedition found extensive pollution by oil and detergents.

and leaks from off-shore wells. Sometimes it is deliberately flushed out, as crews clean the sediment from emptied tanks. Sea birds swim or dive into great slicks of surface oil, coating their feathers with it. In consequence they cannot fly and may not be able to catch enough food to survive. Oil-soaked feathers are poor insulators from cold or wind, and the affected birds may die of exposure. The same thing happens to marine mammals such as sea otters and seals, which depend partly on their fur for warmth in the freezing arctic and antarctic seas.

Oil is not the only substance polluting the ocean. The soapy substance Heyerdahl noted illustrates the fact that oceans are the end of the line for many materials flushed into rivers and streams. Not only the oceans are affected. Lake Erie, one of the Great Lakes, is a prime example. For many years this lake was an excellent place to catch trout and whitefish. Less desirable fish, such as carp, were seldom caught and were present in relatively small numbers. The picture has drastically changed. Now, relatively few trout and whitefish are caught and the carp are very abundant. What happened?

A number of significant changes have occurred in the environment of Lake Erie over the past forty years. The major change occurred in the biotic environment. The human population surrounding the lake greatly increased. This in turn caused significant changes in the abiotic environment. Sewage wastes had always been dumped in the lake. Originally this was not a serious problem because the lake was large and the quantity of the wastes was small. However, the quantity of the wastes has increased many times, and the size of the lake has not. More recently, large quantities of phosphate from detergents have been deposited in the lake. The addition of nitrogen and phosphorus fertilizers to crops has added to the problem. The rivers and creeks that drain into the lake carry nitrate and phosphate washed from farmlands.

Every lake is a temporary body of water. Sooner or later it will fill up and disappear. Two major processes contribute to the aging of a lake. One of these processes is silting. Silt is fine soil that can be wind-blown or washed from the land by flowing water. Water that is moving rapidly, such as a river, can carry large quantities of silt. When the water slows down, as when a river enters a lake, the silt is deposited. The second process in aging is **eutrophication.** This is a gradual increase in dissolved nutrients, and if unchecked it ends by seriously depleting the lake's oxygen supply.

Normally eutrophication is a slow process. It is hardly noticeable in one person's lifetime. However, it can be greatly accelerated, thus causing the premature aging and death of a lake. That is what is happening to Lake Erie and to other important bodies of water throughout the world.

Increased nitrate and phosphate from sewage and fertilizers are probably involved in the problem. The effects of such contaminants have been studied closely in smaller lakes. The increased quantity of nitrate or phosphate causes a rapid multiplication of certain algae. Often the growth is so great that the algae either cover the water or color it. Such a condition is called an algal bloom.

An algal bloom greatly increases the

quantity of living material in a body of water. More important, the large bulk of living algae will eventually become dead matter. The increased dead matter from an algal bloom triggers population explosions of bacterial decomposers. As the decomposers do their work, they release nutrients from the dead algae. These nutrients return to the water and serve as a stimulant for more algal growth. This causes more dead algae and even larger populations of decomposers. The overall result is a "vicious cycle." However, the cycle does not continue forever. Decomposer organisms use oxygen—the oxygen that is dissolved in the water. This is the same oxygen that all the other animals in the lake use. Eventually the growing numbers of decomposers use so much of the oxygen that two things happen. The fish and other animals that need large quantities of oxygen die. The decomposer populations die and thus decline in numbers. The dead matter—algae, animals, and decomposers—accumulates on the bottom.

Trout and whitefish need considerably more dissolved oxygen than carp, so they die off while the carp are still healthy. With the trout and whitefish populations out of the way, populations of fish such as carp have less competition for food. Also, their young are not so likely to be preyed upon by the trout and whitefish.

Many other factors besides low concentration of dissolved oxygen could have caused the decline of the trout and whitefish populations in Lake Erie. Some of the chemicals dumped into the lake as industrial wastes were probably poisonous. Temperature could have had an effect, too. Both trout and whitefish need water that is relatively cold. Thus, the dumping of heated wastes in the lake could be a factor affecting population growth. Even natural biotic cycles may have contributed. But there is little doubt that human interference with the ecosystem has done the major harm.

PCBs

Sometimes the presence of harmful chemi-

Figure 24-16. Oil slicks washed ashore destroy the environment of many types of organism.

Figure 24-17. Lake Erie is dying prematurely, as a result of pollution by sewage wastes, nitrates and phosphates.

INTERACTING WITH
THE ENVIRONMENT

Figure 24-18. The Lake Erie trout is rapidly diminishing in numbers due to the pollution of its environment.

Figure 24-19. Aging is a normal process in the life cycle of a lake. But contamination may speed up the process of eutrophication.

Figure 24-20. The algal bloom pictured here will begin a vicious cycle as the algae die and become food for decomposers.

cals goes undetected amid efforts to clean up more obvious pollutants. This happened in the case of the Hudson River. Once a prime fishing ground, the Hudson eventually became so seriously polluted with sewage wastes that its fish were considered, by many, unsafe to eat. Some species, like the giant sturgeon, disappeared almost entirely. Eventually government and private groups undertook a cleanup campaign, and by the mid-1970s the river was getting measurably cleaner. Even the sturgeon—prized as sources of caviar—began to reappear. Then a new trouble developed. One of the ways in which chemical pollutants of water are detected is by measuring the levels of such chemicals in fish that are caught in those waters. Striped bass taken from the Hudson River turned out to contain high levels of a group of chemicals called polychlorinated biphenyls, or **PCBs.** PCBs are related to DDT, and until recently there was no test that could easily tell them apart. They are used in making electrical equipment, such as transformers, and in certain inks and paints. Like DDT, they tend to collect in the environment and in the bodies of fish that eat them. Only a few pounds of PCBs were being dumped into the Hudson each day, but this was enough to contaminate fish all the way down the river.

The effects of PCBs on humans are still being looked into. But people who have worked in places where they are used have complained of ailments such as dizziness and nausea, skin and eye irritation, and bronchitis. The fish may be returning to the Hudson, but levels of PCBs in these fish have led officials to warn against eating them.

POPULATION ECOLOGY

Populations, as we have seen, are ultimately dependent on their abiotic resources. The limits to which populations can expand are defined by the limits of the resource that is in

523

scarcest supply. At one time, human populations, like plant and nonhuman animal populations, were directly controlled by environmental factors. Disease, food shortage, or similar causes ensured that the rate at which people died was more or less equal to the rate at which they were born. But as people learned to control their environments, death no longer kept pace with birth, and populations began to increase dramatically. To understand the character of this expansion we can look at both a legend and a riddle.

The legend states that a clever man presented a Persian king with a beautiful new chessboard. "How can I repay you?" said the king. The clever man replied, "You can give me 1 grain of rice for the first square on the chessboard, 2 grains for the second square, 4 grains for the third, and so on, doubling the rice for each of the 64 squares." The king happily agreed to the bargain. He brought rice from his stores and his servants began counting out the grains. The fourth square required 8 grains, the tenth square required 512, and the fifteenth square required 16,384. The twenty-first square gave the clever man more than a million grains, and the fortieth square, a million million grains. Long before all the squares were used, the king had lost all the rice in Persia.

The riddle is of French origin. A man owns a pond on which a water lily is growing. The lily doubles in size every day. If it were allowed to grow at this rate, it would completely cover the pond in thirty days. The man does not want this to happen. However, for a long time the lily does not appear to grow very rapidly. Therefore, the man decides not to cut the lily back until it covers half the pond. On what day will the man have to cut the lily?

The legend of the rice grains and the riddle of the lily are given to illustrate a type of growth called **exponential growth.** Exponential growth proceeds at a constant percentage of the whole over a constant period of time. A bank account that is growing at 7 percent a year is growing exponentially.

Figure 24-21. Dumping hot liquid wastes into a frozen river will melt the ice, of course. But the sudden rise in temperature is also extremely detrimental to the organisms living in the river.

From percentages to people

The world's human population is growing at 2.1 percent. The United States population is growing at 1.1 percent. These percentages may not seem large. But a population growing at 2 percent per year will double itself in less than 50 years. Some countries are growing at 3 percent per year, or more. And the world already contains a great many people. It is like the fortieth square of the chessboard.

The world's population has been growing exponentially for thousands of years. But it was not until 1650 that the population reached one-half billion. The growth rate up to that time is estimated to have been 0.3 percent. Until 1650 the actual growth had been slow—like the rice on the first four squares of the chessboard. By 1850, only two hundred years later, the population had grown to one billion. By 1920, only 80 years later, the population had doubled to two billion. This was a growth rate just under 1 percent. From 1930 to 1960 another billion people were added. This was a growth rate of just over 2 percent, which is the present approximate rate of growth. By the end of 1975 the world population had grown to four billion. By the year 2000, it will probably be almost double that. Right now the world population is increasing by almost 200,000 people every day.

What about the United States? In 1900

Figure 24-22. The riddle of the water lily illustrates the principle of exponential growth.

Figure 24-23. This graph explains the nature of exponential growth. For example, if a man hides $10 each year under his mattress, his saving will grow arithmetically, at the rate shown by the lower curve. If, after twenty years, he invests his $200 at 7 percent interest, that $200 will grow exponentially, doubling itself every ten years.

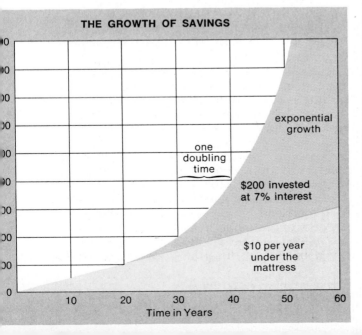

there were 76 million Americans. Seventy-two years later, in 1972, there were 210 million. Now, at our present 1.1 percent growth rate, we are adding about 2.25 million people per year. In other words, we are filling a city about the size of Philadelphia each year.

Most projections take into account that the growth rate will probably decline. Some people think there is a chance that families may limit themselves to two children. If this happens, and if there is no more immigration of people from other countries, what would be the result? Even under these conditions, our population would still continue to grow for 70 more years. We would have 322 million people by the year 2000. That is almost 100 million more people than we have right now.

Populations and pollution

The fact that pollution—which is, after all, the inadequate recycling of resources—results from expanding production to meet the needs of an expanding human population, has led some people to conclude that population growth is responsible for pollution. If we can control the rate of growth, they reason, the pollution will take care of itself. This is an oversimplification. The populations that are increasing most rapidly are not the greatest consumers of resources. For example, the United States, which has little more than 5 percent of the world's population, uses 33 percent of its energy sources each year. The Industrial Revolution, which promised the end of grueling labor and hardship for the people of the world, may have been a mixed blessing. That revolution represented a happy marriage of economic growth (and higher profits) with greatly expanded production of goods. Nineteenth-century philosophy held that this would create a paradise on earth. Few understood the biological effects that the new technology would produce. This lack of understanding has led directly to our present problems.

525

On the other hand, the less industrialized countries that are expanding most rapidly cannot always feed their people. At the very simplest level, the worldwide growth of populations requires more productive cultivation of land for food crops. This is usually interpreted as calling for fertilizers and insecticides. These factors alone, when introduced on a grand scale, present serious pollution dangers. In addition, modern farming is nearly always mechanized. This makes it inconvenient to have many small, separate fields. Huge tracts of land are planted to a single crop. Diseases and pests can easily spread through the entire field. Recent studies suggest that a number of smaller fields, separated by strips of trees or brush, may actually produce a higher yield. The strips of unfarmed ground serve as barriers, slowing the spread of pests. They also provide shelter for birds and other natural enemies of many pests.

The oceans and atmosphere can absorb the toxic output of a large number of people, but only with proper treatment. We have almost never provided such treatment. Pollution problems are tied to population problems because increased population has increased the concentration of untreated wastes. To put it another way, because few people asked what would happen if some insignificant waste product were dumped into the environment all over the world at an ever-increasing rate, the problem of pollution was not realized until the problem of population growth had become a crisis.

It is unrealistic to think that a pollution problem of such magnitude can be solved by telling people to stop littering, or to recycle their Coke bottles. The truth is that our social and economic system encourages waste. It is a sign of status to consume more than we need. It is more profitable to sell products in throwaway containers than to collect the containers for recycling. It is more profitable to dump wastes in the river than to clean them up. Building sewage treatment plants takes tax money, and is not nearly as exciting as developing a new pro-

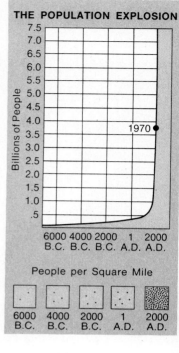

Figure 24-24. This graph, and the squares beneath it, dramatically illustrate the upward trend of human population growth during the past three hundred years. The line is continued upward to show the trend if this rate of growth continues.

duct. It is interesting to note that since the energy crisis began a few years ago, there is far more interest than before in developing new sources of energy. Plants are being built to process garbage into fuel, and houses are being built to get their heat from solar energy. The argument against these things was always that they cost too much money. They still cost money, but the other sources of energy are becoming expensive too. Now it begins to look as if there might be some profit in solar energy and recycled waste. Perhaps when the harm done by pesticides, chemical fertilizers, and PCBs becomes economically obvious, there will be more enthusiasm for finding safe replacements.

The same thing is true in regard to population. As long as families find it economically necessary to have many children, population growth is unlikely to stop. An interesting study of a village in India found that the economics of the Indian peasant society is such that fewer children mean less food for a poor family, not more. On farms too poor to buy modern machinery, children are needed to farm the land. And if parents are poor in land, they hope to send their

INTERACTING WITH
THE ENVIRONMENT

Carolina Biological Supply Co.

Figure 24-25. Proper management of resources becomes more essential as human population continues to grow. At the right of the fence, careless land management has led to overgrazing and erosion. The area at left has remained a useful pasture because the number of animals allowed on it was limited.

children away from the village to earn money so that more land can be bought. Moreover, children provide support in old age for their parents and grandparents—the only "social security" in some places. For these and many other such reasons, the economics of poverty in rural India means that peasants must have large families if they are to survive.

This illustrates the fallacy of relying on technology to solve the problems of the environment. Many such problems are rooted in social and cultural organization. Moreover, technology almost always creates problems that may not be solvable by technology. A case in point is the Green Revolution.

The Green Revolution is a name for a new type of agriculture introduced in many developing countries. The principle is to use new high-yielding plant varieties, fertilizers, and pesticides to increase the yield of each acre. In the hope of eliminating poverty and hunger, technology was here applied to a problem of the environment. And it solved the original problem; it did produce large harvests.

However, a new problem arose. For example, one place where the new technology was tried was the Punjab of India, an area of small farms and much poverty. Here the new practices worked amazingly well. But they required new equipment, so it was only the wealthier farmers who were able to change over to the new style of farming. These farmers were so successful that they were able to buy power machinery and cut down on hand labor. This put some of the landless laborers out of work. With their additional wealth, the successful farmers were also able to buy more land from their poorer neighbors. The unemployed laborers and dispossessed small farmers were left with no food and no income to buy it. So they began to drift toward the cities. There they found crowds of others in a similar situation, and too few jobs to go around. Poverty and

Figure 24-26. Overcrowded living conditions have been shown to produce startling effects in laboratory animals. Among rats, overcrowding results in sterility, a high abortion rate, and cannibalism. More than a thousand people can be seen here. If each person here has two children during his or her reproductive years, how many new individuals will be added to the world population at the end of one generation? At the end of two generations? What are some possible solutions to the growing problem of overpopulation?

hunger were evils they had always known, but now they had to face unemployment as well. The new technology had brought problems that technology could not solve. Only a re-directing of cultural attitudes can hope to solve the problems that arise from technological change.

We have raised these issues to show that the way in which "people cause pollution" is more complicated than direct cause and effect. People do not cause pollution; production to satisfy the so-called needs of the people does. Thus although recycling newspapers and Coke bottles is useful, it does very little to make the pollution picture brighter. Both people and corporations must seriously reassess their consumption and production goals if the environment is to have a chance. Just as families in India will not have fewer children until they believe that by doing so they will be better off instead of worse off, people in industrialized countries will not stop buying disposable bottles and cans so long as it seems cheapest and easiest to do so. And industry will not stop dumping wastes such as PCBs into the waterways until it becomes more expensive to get caught than to stop.

SUMMARY

At the beginning of all food chains and energy cycles are autotrophic organisms. These need sunlight, water, and inorganic nutrients, all abiotic factors in the ecosystem. They also require oxygen and carbon dioxide.

Nutrients follow a cyclical path through the ecosystem. But energy takes a one-way trip; much of it is lost as heat, and must be replaced by solar radiation. The solar energy reaching the earth affects the climates of all the biomes.

Some abiotic factors can be recycled. They follow a biogeochemical cycle through the ecosystem which leads through living organisms and the nonliving environment.

Among the most important biogeochemical cycles are the water, carbon, nitrogen, and phosphorus cycles. The phosphorus cycle differs from the others because phosphorus, a mineral, is not present in the atmosphere.

The materials that circulate through biogeochemical cycles cannot be replaced, but only reused. New technology produces wastes which cause serious damage when absorbed by the environment. Pollution, then, can be defined as any process by which people reduce the quality of their environment. Many pollution problems stem from the exercise of traditional individual freedoms. But the population has grown, and the environment can no longer absorb the effects of their activities.

Technology has produced a variety of pesticides, some of which are causing numerous problems. Some pests develop pesticide resistance. In other cases the pesticide may wipe out every animal population in an area, creating a vacant niche which may be filled by a new, pesticide-resistant population. The pesticide may also spread beyond the area it was intended to affect, damaging harmless or helpful animal populations.

Persistent pesticides remain active in the environment for a long time, setting up their own biogeochemical cycles. Some of these, such as mercury and lead, are stored in the bodies of primary consumers and are biologically magnified as they proceed up the food chain. Humans, at the top of the chain, thus receive the greatest damage, caused by high concentration of these substances in their food.

Air pollution changes climate, weather, and the major biogeochemical cycles. CO_2 and certain poisonous gases have increased in the atmosphere as the result of burning of fossil fuels. Eventually the "greenhouse effect" of carbon dioxide may raise temperature levels on earth, and even a slight temperature rise could increase the amount of water released by melting of polar ice. Chemical air pollutants, such as carbon monoxide, are directly poisonous to many organisms.

Water pollution by oil is one of the serious problems affecting the oceans. Pollution of water by detergents, chemical fertilizers containing phosphate and nitrate, and untreated sewage has speeded up the process of eutrophication in many lakes. PCBs dumped into rivers from manufacturing plants have contaminated some fish so that they are no longer safe to eat.

Exponential growth of populations is outstripping the ability of natural resources to support them. The birth rate is no longer balanced by the death rate, which has declined due to the application of modern medical technology. Increase in the population has increased the concentration of untreated wastes that are not being disposed of properly. More and more energy and food are required by these growing populations. Present social and economic systems encourage waste of resources as a symbol of status.

Technology usually creates problems that technology cannot solve. A good example is the Green Revolution, which produced more food but created cultural and social problems that have not yet been solved. In the end, much pollution is caused by production of things to satisfy the desires rather than the needs of people.

Review questions

1. List some of the abiotic factors which affect an ecosystem.

2. Why must new energy be constantly supplied from outside an ecosystem? What is its source?

3. List several ways in which solar energy affects the ecosystem.

4. What is a biogeochemical cycle? Give at least two examples.

5. In what ways is carbon returned to the atmosphere?

6. How is nitrogen important to the bodies of organisms?

7. Describe two methods of nitrogen fixation.

8. What is denitrification? How is it accomplished in a terrestrial ecosystem?

9. What is the importance of phosphorus? How is it stored and released?

10. Explain why pollution is a relative term. Give an example of how the growth of technology has turned nonpolluting acts into polluting ones.

11. Describe some of the ways in which indiscriminate use of pesticides can do long-term damage to the ecology.

12. What is a persistent pesticide? Give an example and describe its cycle which results in biological magnification.

13. What is a "greenhouse effect"?

14. Name some pollutants produced by the burning of fossil fuels. How can they affect the environment?

15. Describe some of the ways in which oil pollution affects the marine biotic community.

16. What problems are created by dumping of detergents into lakes and rivers? How does the use of chemical fertilizers add to the problem?

17. What are the two major processes which contribute to aging of a lake?

18. What is an algal bloom? What are its eventual effects?

19. Give an example of exponential growth.

20. How did the Industrial Revolution contribute to present problems of pollution and overpopulation?

21. What are some of the ecological problems caused by modern agricultural technology?

22. In what ways do social attitudes contribute to growing problems of pollution?

23. What unexpected social problems were directly caused by the Green Revolution?

Glossary

abiogenesis: theory that life arose from nonliving matter.

abortion: termination of pregnancy before the fetus is viable.

abscissic acid: plant hormone that promotes falling of leaves and winter dormancy.

absolute refractory period: period during which no more sodium ions can enter an area of neuron membrane.

acetylcholine: a neurotransmitter chemical.

acid: an ionic compound that increases the number of hydrogen ions (H^+) in a solution.

actin: one of the two proteins which make up the myofilaments.

action potential curve: changes in polarization of a neuron membrane as recorded by an oscilloscope.

active site: a particular site on an enzyme molecule into which a reactant fits.

active transport: movement of materials in an organism which requires expenditure of energy.

adaptation: any inherited characteristic that gives an organism or its population an advantage in the environment.

adaptive radiation: change of a single species into several species through adaptation to different aspects of the environment.

adenine: nitrogen base present in the DNA and RNA molecule.

adhesion: attraction between molecules of two different substances.

adjustor neuron: see **intermediate neuron.**

ADP (adenosine diphosphate): an organic compound having two phosphate groups; adding a third phosphate group forms ATP.

adrenal gland: a composite gland made up of cortex and medulla. One adrenal gland lies atop each kidney.

aerobic respiration: a respiratory pathway within the mitochondria; requires oxygen.

afferent neuron: see **sensory neuron.**

all-or-none law: law that states that any stimulus that can stimulate a neuron will produce an impulse of the same strength.

allele: any of the different possible forms of a single gene.

alternation of generations: reproductive pattern in which gametophyte and sporophyte generations alternate.

alveoli: thin-membraned air sacs in the lungs through which diffusion of gases takes place.

amino acids: organic acids that contain an amino group and a carboxyl group; the building blocks of protein.

amnion: inner membrane of the sac in which an embryo develops.

anaerobic respiration: the early steps in respiration, which take place in the cytoplasm and do not require oxygen. *See* **glycolysis.**

anaphase: stage of mitosis and meiosis during which the chromosomes move to opposite poles of the cell.

androgens: the male sex hormones.

angiosperms: the flowering plants.

animal hemisphere: section of early embryo in which cells divide quickly.

antenna: sensory organ of many invertebrates, especially arthropods.

anther: sac-like pollen container at the top of a stamen.

antheridium: male reproductive organ in plants, which produces sperm.

antibiotic: organic substance that inhibits growth of pathogenic bacteria.

antibody: protein produced by an organism in response to a foreign substance (antigen).

anti-codon: a tRNA triplet that pairs with a codon of mRNA.

antigen: a substance that stimulates production of a particular antibody.

anus: opening at the end of the digestive tract through which solid wastes are expelled.

aorta: main artery of the circulatory system.

apical dominance: inhibition of the growth of lateral branches by auxin produced in the terminal bud of a plant.

archegonium: female reproductive organ in plants, which produces ova.

archenteron: cavity in a gastrula that replaces the blastocoel.

arteries, arterioles: blood vessels that carry blood away from the heart.

asexual reproduction: reproduction that does not involve the fusion of gametes.

associative neuron: *see* **intermediate neuron.**

atherosclerosis: clogging of the arteries by an accumulation of fat deposits.

atom: the fundamental unit of all matter.

ATP (adenosine triphosphate): an energy-storing compound containing three phosphate groups.

atrium: either of the two upper chambers of the mammalian heart. Also known as an **auricle.**

autoimmune reaction: condition in which an individual produces antibodies against some of his own body tissues.

autonomic nervous system: system of nerves controlling involuntary body activity. Includes sympathetic and parasympathetic nerves.

autosomes: all chromosomes other than the sex chromosomes.

autotroph: organism capable of synthesizing nutrients from inorganic substances.

auxin: hormone that controls a variety of plant movements.

A-V (atrio-ventricular) node: one of two electrically sensitive tissue masses within the heart, which regulate the pace of heart action.

axil: the angle between a leaf and the stem to which it is attached.

axon: nerve process that conducts impulses away from the cell body.

balanced polymorphism: existence of a balance between two or more phenotypes in a population.

basal body: a centriole that attaches a cilium or flagellum to a cell.

base: any ionic compound that decreases the number of hydrogen ions (H^+) in a solution.

base-pairing rule: the rule that, in a DNA molecule, adenine pairs only with thymine and guanine pairs only with cytosine. In RNA, adenine pairs with uracil.

behavioral chain: sequence of behavior in which each step is stimulated by the previous step.

bilateral symmetry: body structure in which the two body halves are mirror images of each other, and having a posterior and an anterior end.

binding site: point at which an mRNA molecule attaches to a ribosome.

biogenesis: theory that all life originates from other life.

biogeochemical cycle: pathway that leads through both the biotic and abiotic elements of the environment.

biological clock: internal timing mechanism of an organism.

biological magnification: the increasing concentration of a toxic substance as it moves upward through a food chain.

bioluminescence: the ability, possessed by some organisms, to emit light.

biomes: the major climax communities.

biorhythms: cyclic behavior patterns by which animals adapt to regular changes in their environment.

birth canal: passageway formed by dilation of the cervix and vagina.

blastocoel: cavity in the animal hemisphere of the embryo.

blastocyst: in mammals, the hollow sphere of embryonic cells formed by the first stages of cell division.

blastopore: opening from the archenteron to the outside of a gastrula.

blastula: embryo in which a blastocoel has developed.

blood pressure: level of pressure within the blood vessels during contraction and relaxation of the heart, usually stated in terms of the height of a column of mercury.

Bowman's capsule: in a nephron, cup-like structure that surrounds the glomerulus.

brain stem: pathway between the brain and spinal cord, composed of the pons and the medulla oblongata.

breed: subdivision within a species, brought about by artificial selection.

bronchi, bronchioles: progressively smaller branching passageways leading from the trachea to the alveoli of the lungs.

bryophytes: non-vascular land plants, including the mosses and liverworts.

Caesarian section: surgical delivery of an infant through an abdominal incision.

calyx: *see* **sepals.**

camera eye: type of eye found in vertebrates and cephalopod mollusks.

capillaries: smallest blood vessels, through whose walls gases and nutrients are exchanged with the surrounding cells.

capillary action: the tendency of water to flow through very small tubes or pores, even upward against gravitational pull.

carbohydrates: organic compounds composed of carbon, hydrogen, and oxygen, used in energy reactions.

cardiac muscle: muscle of the heart.

carnivore: organism whose diet consists principally of the flesh of other organisms.

catalyst: substance that speeds up or regulates a chemical reaction without entering into or being changed by the reaction.

cell: the basic structural unit in most organisms.

cell membrane: envelope that separates the cell from its environment while allowing selective contact with the environment.

cell wall: stiffening wall around plant cells, composed largely of cellulose and lignin fibers.

cellular respiration: process that releases energy by breakdown of organic molecules.

central nervous system: (1) nervous system in which a concentrated mass of nerves, usually at the anterior end, forms a controlling center; (2) the brain and spinal cord.

centriole: rod-like structure in ani-mal cells, composed mainly of microtubules.

centromere: area on a chromosome to which a spindle fiber attaches during mitosis or meiosis.

cerebellum: round structure in the hindbrain that coordinates movement of skeletal muscles.

cerebral cortex: largest portion of primate brain, which contains sensory and control centers and is probably the seat of thought and intelligence.

chemical bond: connection formed between atoms when they transfer or share electrons.

chitin: noncellular material that makes up the exoskeleton of arthropods.

chlorophyll: light-sensitive green pigment in autotrophic cells, important to photosynthesis.

chloroplast: plant organelle that can trap and store solar energy.

cholesterol: lipid essential to digestion and hormone synthesis, but also capable of clogging arteries. *See* **atherosclerosis.**

chordate: any animal that possesses a notochord at some time in its life.

chorion: outer layer of the sac in which an embryo develops.

chromatids: a pair of replicated chromosomes that have not yet separated from each other.

chromatin: thread-like fibers within the nucleus of a cell, that appear as chromosomes during cell division.

chromoplast: plant organelle containing yellow, orange, or red pigment.

chromosome: body in cell nucleus that contains genetic material.

cilia: short, hair-like appendages of cells, used to move cell or move substances past cell.

circadian rhythms: biorhythms based on an approximate 24-hour schedule.

circulatory system: interrelated group of organs that perform the transport of blood.

class: a taxonomic group that includes one or more families.

climax community: period of equilibrium in an ecosystem.

clitoris: in female primates, a knob of sexually sensitive erectile tissue corresponding to the male penis.

cloaca: in lower animals, a single passage to the exterior serving both excretory and reproductive functions.

cnidocysts: specialized cells possessed by coelenterates, used in capture or paralysis of prey.

coacervate droplets: aggregations of complex macromolecules.

cochlea: lower region of inner ear, concerned with the sense of balance.

co-dominance: a situation in which two alleles are dominant and both are expressed in the phenotype.

codon: an mRNA triplet that is part of the genetic code.

coelenterate: radially symmetrical invertebrate composed of only two layers of cells; cnidarian.

coelom: cavity in the mesoderm of some animals.

coenzyme: substance which enables an enzyme to catalyze a reaction.

cohesion: attraction between molecules of the same substance.

coleoptile: in grasses, the sheath that encloses the stem of young plants.

collar cells: flagellated digestive cells found in Porifera.

colon: the large intestine.

commensalism: symbiotic relationship in which only one species benefits.

compound: substance formed by bonding between atoms of two or more elements; called organic if it contains one or more carbon chains.

compound eyes: large insect eyes that form a multiple image.

concentration gradient: the difference between the concentrations of molecules on either side of a semipermeable membrane.

conditioning: modification of behavior through repeated exposure to a stimulus.

cones: one of the two types of receptor cell found in the retina.

conifers: *see* **gymnosperms.**

connector neuron: *see* **intermediate neuron.**

cornea: transparent eye structure concerned with focus of light rays.

corolla: *see* **petals.**

corpus luteum: follicle from which

an egg has been released.

cortex: (1) storage layer in woody stems, just beneath the bark; (2) outer layer of tissue in certain animal organs, such as the brain and the adrenal glands.

cotyledons: the "seed leaves" of a plant.

covalent bond: chemical bond formed when two atoms share electrons.

cristae: shelf-like folds of the inner membrane in mitochondria.

crossing-over: exchange of sections of the inner chromatids during prophase of meiosis.

cross-pollination: pollination of a flower by pollen from another flower.

cuticle: waxy layer on the outer surface of a plant.

cytochrome: iron-containing pigment that serves as an electron carrier in the light reactions.

cytokinesis: division of the cytoplasm during mitosis and meiosis.

cytokinins: plant hormones necessary for cell division.

cytoplasm: all cellular material except the nucleus.

cytoplasmic streaming: pattern of flow that transports materials within certain individual cells.

cytosine: nitrogen base present in the DNA and RNA molecule.

dark reactions: series of reactions in photosynthesis that use ATP and NADPH in the formation of glucose.

decomposers: bacteria and fungi that feed on dead organisms.

dendrite: nerve process that receives incoming stimuli.

density: weight per unit volume.

development: sequence of programmed changes that take place during the lifetime of an organism.

diaphragm: (1) thin muscular partition that separates the thoracic cavity from the abdominal cavity; (2) rubber cervical cap that prevents sperm from entering the uterus.

diastole: period of relaxation following contraction of the ventricles of the heart.

dicotyledon (dicot): plant whose seeds have two cotyledons.

differential reproduction: the difference in reproductive rate between well-adapted and poorly-adapted members of a species.

diffusion: movement of molecules from one place to another.

digestion: breaking down of large nutrient molecules, which allows them to be used inside the individual cells.

dihybrid: an individual that is heterozygous for two traits.

diploid cell: a cell with two sets of chromosomes, one set contributed by the gamete of each parent.

DNA (deoxyribonucleic acid): nucleic acid present in the cell nucleus, believed to be the chemical constituent of the gene.

dominant trait: a trait that is phenotypically expressed in an F_1 hybrid.

dorsal lip: mound of dividing cells formed by cells spreading from animal to vegetal hemisphere of an embryo.

duct: passageway between one organ and another.

ecological succession: the process by which the species in a community gradually give way to other species, eventually forming a different kind of community.

ecosystem: an interacting unit composed of the individuals in a community and their environment.

ectoderm: outer cell layer of the gastrula.

ectohormones: *see* **pheromones.**

ectotherm: a "cold-blooded" animal.

effector: a muscle or gland that responds to a stimulus.

efferent neuron: *see* **motor neuron.**

egg: the gamete produced by the female parent.

ejaculatory duct: tube which conveys semen to the urethra.

electroencephalogram (EEG): a record of brain wave patterns.

electron: negatively-charged atomic particle that orbits the nucleus of an atom.

electron acceptor: an atom which receives an electron from another atom.

electron carrier: molecule that passes "excited" electrons along during the reactions of photosynthesis.

electron shell: the average distance at which a particular group of electrons orbits the nucleus of an atom.

element: a type of matter that cannot be further broken down by normal chemical means.

embryo: early stage of development in a plant or animal.

embryonic induction: the influence of one embryonic area on the development of another embryonic area.

endocrine glands: ductless glands that secrete hormones.

endoderm: inner layers of cells lining the archenteron of a gastrula.

endometrium: spongy lining of the uterus.

endoplasmic reticulum (ER): a network of membrane-bound canals in the cytoplasm of cells.

endoskeleton: an internal skeleton made up of bone and cartilage.

endosperm: tissue that provides food for the developing plant embryo.

endotherm: a "warm-blooded" animal.

energy-transfer reaction: a reaction in which one compound loses energy while another compound gains energy.

environmental niche: the functions of a species in relation to the other species present in its environment.

enzyme: a protein that catalyzes chemical reactions in the cells.

epidermis: outer layer of an animal's skin.

epididymis: tube above the testis in which sperm are stored.

epiphyte: a plant that exists commensally with another plant.

erectile tissue: spongy tissue that swells and becomes stiff when engorged with blood.

erythroblast: nucleated precursor cell that gives rise to an erythrocyte.

erythrocyte: a red blood cell, possessing no nucleus and containing hemoglobin.

esophagus: portion of the digestive tract that lies between the pharynx and the stomach.

estivation: dormant period of some animals during hot, dry weather.

estrogen: female hormone that stimulates the pituitary to produce luteinizing hormone.

ethylene: hydrocarbon gas that promotes ripening and may inhibit growth in plants.

eucaryotic cell: a cell possessing one or more well-defined nuclei.

eutrophication: the aging of a body of water.

evolution: changes in the genetic composition of a population over a period of time.

exocrine gland: gland that possesses ducts.

exoskeleton: external skeleton composed of chitin.

exponential growth: growth that proceeds at a constant percentage of the whole over a constant period of time.

extensor: a muscle that contracts to pull a joint back to its original position.

Fallopian tubes: the human oviducts.

family: in taxonomy, a group of related genera.

fermentation: pathway in anaerobic respiration by which pyruvic acid is converted to lactic acid or ethyl alcohol.

fertilization membrane: modified form of the cell membrane after fertilization of an ovum, which prevents further penetration by sperm.

fetus: a mammalian embryo past the first third of gestation, showing recognizable species characteristics.

filter feeder: animal that strains its food out of water passing through specialized body structures.

flagella: hair-like appendages, possessed by some cells, that assist in locomotion.

flexor: a muscle that contracts to move a joint away from its rest position.

florigen: plant hormone believed to stimulate flowering.

flow: the mass movement of liquids or gases.

follicle: fluid-filled sac on the ovary in which the oöcyte matures.

food chain: a series of food-dependency relationships.

food web: an overlapping series of food-dependency relationships.

foramen magnum: opening through which the brain stem enters the skull.

forebrain: front portion of brain, containing the olfactory bulbs, cerebrum, thalamus, and hypothalamus.

fossil: the preserved remains of an organism from an earlier geological period.

fossil record: the sequence of fossils as they appear over a given period of time.

founder effect: a change in gene frequencies resulting from the presence of only particular alleles at the time a population is begun.

fruit: the matured ovary of a flowering plant.

functional group: a group of atoms that reacts or functions as though it were a single atom.

gamete: a reproductive cell in sexually reproducing organisms.

gametophyte generation: gamete-producing generation in a plant's life cycle.

ganglion: compact mass of neurons that makes up a primitive brain or local controlling center.

gastrovascular cavity: digestive cavity with a single opening for the passage of both food and wastes.

gastrula: embryonic stage during which three well-defined cell layers develop.

gene: the basic unit of heredity, consisting of a nitrogen base sequence in DNA that codes for a single polypeptide chain.

gene frequency: in a population, the percentages of different alleles of a given gene.

gene pool: the sum of all genes present within a given population.

genotype: the genetic make-up of an individual.

genus: a taxonomic group that includes one or more species.

geotropism: a plant's response to gravity.

germ layers: the ectoderm, endoderm, and mesoderm of a gastrula.

germination: in pollen, the point at which the covering of the pollen grain ruptures. In seeds, the point at which the seed coat ruptures.

gestation: the period of embryonic development from fertilization to birth.

gibberellin: plant hormone that stimulates growth.

gills: respiratory structures that allow contact between the capillaries and the environmental water.

gizzard: thick-walled grinding organ found in digestive systems of birds and some lower animals.

glomerulus: tiny coil of capillaries within a nephron.

glycolysis: series of anaerobic reactions that begins with glucose and ends with pyruvic acid.

Golgi apparatus: organelle that contains and transports enzymes and other materials manufactured by the ER.

gonads: the reproductive organs in animals that produce gametes.

grana: stacks of pigment-containing thylakoids within chloroplasts.

grey matter: matter in the central nervous system which is composed of the cell bodies of modulator neurons.

guanine: nitrogen base present in the DNA and RNA molecule.

guard cells: cells that regulate the opening and closing of a stoma.

gymnosperms: group of woody plants whose seeds are usually produced in cones.

haploid cell: a gamete containing a single set of chromosomes.

Hardy–Weinberg principle: a mathematical theorem that determines the frequency of a given allele within a population.

Haversian canal: tiny central canal within a Haversian system.

Haversian system: small, cylindrical unit of bone.

hemoglobin: iron-containing red pigment in erythrocytes that functions in oxygen transport.

herbivore: organism whose diet is made up principally of vegetable matter.

hermaphrodite: an individual possessing reproductive organs of both sexes.

heterosis: *see* **heterozygote superiority.**

heterotroph: organism that obtains its energy by breaking down complex compounds.

heterozygote superiority: situation in which a heterozygous individual has adaptive advantages over either homozygote.

heterozygous individual: one whose alleles for a given trait are not the same.

hibernation: dormant period of some animals during very cold weather.

hindbrain: rear portion of the brain, containing the cerebellum and the medulla oblongata.

homeostasis: a steady state that preserves the stability of an organism's internal environment.

homozygous individual: one whose alleles for a given trait are the same.

hormone: regulator substance secreted by endocrine glands or tissues.

host: the organism on or in which a parasite lives.

hybrid: a heterozygous individual.

hydrogen bond: bond formed between a positive hydrogen atom and a small, highly negative atom.

hydrostatic skeleton: a skeleton made up of body fluids contained within expandable body cavities.

hyperventilation: deliberate reduction of the blood CO_2 level by deep, rapid breathing.

hypophysis: *see* **pituitary.**

hypothalamus: a portion of the forebrain that also has an endocrine function, stimulating production of hormones by the anterior pituitary.

immunity: possession of antibodies against an antigen.

imprinting: permanent behavior modification in newborn animals, based on a tendency of the animal to follow the first moving object it sees.

independent assortment, principle of: the concept that one pair of alleles can be assorted independently of another pair.

inheritance of acquired characteristics: Lamarck's theory that characteristics acquired by the parents could be transmitted to their offspring.

inhibitory neuron: one that interferes with transmission of a nerve impulse.

inorganic compound: a compound that does not contain a carbon chain.

instinctive behavior: inherited, complex behavior not dependent upon learning.

intermediate neuron: neuron that acts as a connection between a sensory neuron and a motor neuron.

interphase: stage of mitosis during which the chromosomes are duplicated.

inversion: situation in which a portion of a chromosome is turned upside down.

ion: an atom having an electrical charge.

ion pump: *see* **sodium pump.**

ionic bond: bond formed between two atoms when they transfer electrons.

ionization: separation of the ions in a compound by water molecules.

iris: muscular structure that controls dilation and contraction of the pupil of the eye.

islets of Langerhans: clusters of specialized pancreatic cells that secrete hormones.

isolating mechanism: any situation that prevents members of different populations from interbreeding.

isomers: compounds whose molecules contain the same number of each kind of atom but have different shapes.

Jacobson's organ: in snakes, a group of chemoreceptors in the roof of the mouth, concerned with both taste and smell.

joint: the point of connection between two bones.

kidneys: the primary organs of excretion in vertebrates.

kinetic energy: energy released by breaking of a phosphate bond.

kingdom: in taxonomy, the highest category in a hierarchy that includes all organisms.

Krebs cycle: reaction pathway in aerobic respiration that takes place in the mitochondria and results in the formation of ATP molecules.

labia: fleshy tissues covering the female genitals.

labor: the contractions of the uterus and abdominal muscles that expel the infant.

lamellae: straight intracellular membranes within the thylakoids, containing chlorophyll molecules.

larva: the second-stage body form in complete metamorphosis.

larynx: voice organ of the human respiratory system, located between the pharynx and the trachea.

lateral line system: a network of mechanoreceptors along the sides of a fish's body.

lens: structure that controls the focus of the camera eye.

lenticel: small pore in a plant stem through which gas exchange can take place.

leucocyte: a white blood cell.

leucoplast: plant organelle that stores food.

light reactions: the reactions of photosynthesis that use light energy to produce ATP.

lipids: organic group that includes the fats.

locus: the regular, fixed point at which a gene is located on a chromosome.

loop of Henle: hairpin-shaped loop in mammalian nephron, important in forming a concentrated urine.

lungs: spongy, paired respiratory organs in higher vertebrates.

lymph: body fluid containing lymphocytes but no blood cells nor platelets.

lymph node: structure that filters lymph before it empties back into bloodstream.

lymphocyte: white blood cell important in production of antibodies.

lysosome: intracellular sac of digestive enzymes.

macrophage: phagocytic lymph cell that attacks invading microorganisms.

mammary glands: milk-secreting glands in female mammals.

matrix: noncellular connective material secreted by cells of cartilage and bone.

medulla oblongata: structure in the hindbrain that transmits impulses between the brain and spinal cord and also controls certain involuntary functions.

meiosis: the process of cell division that results in the formation of haploid gametes.

meninges: the three membrane layers that enclose the brain and spinal cord.

menopause: in women, the end of ovulation and therefore of fertility.

menstrual cycle: regular sequence of changes that occur in the adult female reproductive system when fertilization does not take place.

meristem: region of a plant where cell division takes place.

mesoderm: middle layer of cells in a gastrula.

metabolism: the chemical reactions within a cell or an organism that create a balance between breakdown of wastes and damaged material and synthesis of new material.

metamorphosis: change of form, especially in arthropods; may be gradual or complete.

metaphase: in mitosis, stage in which the chromosomes align along the equator of the cell and the chromatids separate. In meiosis, the stage during which crossing-over of portions of homologous pairs of chromosomes is completed.

microtubule: tube-like structure found in bundles in the cytoplasm, apparently adding strength to cell walls.

microvillus: hair-like projection from an intestinal villus, adding surface area to the small intestine.

midbrain: middle part of brain, containing the optic lobes.

mimicry: type of protective relationship that occurs when members of one species resemble members of a more dangerous or more aggressive species.

miscarriage: an abortion that is not artificially induced.

mitochondrion: organelle active in production of ATP.

mitosis: process by which the nucleus duplicates prior to cell division.

modulator neuron: see **intermediate neuron.**

molecule: the smallest identifiable unit of a compound, formed by bonding between two or more atoms.

molt: to shed the skin or exoskeleton.

monocotyledon (monocot): a plant whose seeds have a single cotyledon.

morphogenesis: see **supracellular differentiation.**

motor neuron: neuron that carries an impulse from a sensory neuron to an effector.

mutation: a change in genetic material, either (1) by rearrangement of portions of a chromosome or (2) by change in the sequence of nitrogen bases in DNA.

mutualism: symbiotic relationship in which both individuals benefit.

myelin sheath: fatty insulating sheath around some axons, formed by the cell membranes of Schwann cells.

myocardial infarction: the com-

monest type of heart attack, involving death of a portion of the cardiac myocardium.

myocardium: middle muscle layer of the heart.

myofibrils: small fibers which together make up a single muscle fiber, and which are themselves made up of sarcomeres.

myofilaments: the small filaments composed of actin and myosin which make up a sarcomere.

myosin: one of the two proteins of which myofilaments are composed.

NAD (nicotinamide adenine dinucleotide): compound that functions as a hydrogen receptor in anaerobic respiration.

NADH: NAD to which a hydrogen ion has been donated.

NADP (nicotinamide adenine dinucleotide phosphate): an electron acceptor in noncyclic photophosphorylation.

NADPH: compound formed by addition of a hydrogen ion (H^+) to NADP.

natural selection: the mechanism in natural populations that allows only the best-adapted to survive and reproduce.

negative feedback: regulatory process in which the end product of a reaction cancels the stimulus and halts the reaction.

negative-pressure breathing: type of breathing that involves the active process of inspiration and the passive process of expiration.

nephron: the basic excretory unit of the kidney.

nerve net: simple nervous system in cnidarians, in which the nerve impulse travels in all directions.

nerve ring: primitive control center linked to part of nerve net in some cnidarians.

neural tube: structure in the embryo that will develop into the brain and spinal cord.

neuroglial cells: cells that form the myelin sheath of axons in the spinal cord and brain.

neuron: a nerve cell.

neurotransmitter chemical: chemical that transfers nerve impulses across the synaptic cleft.

neurulation: process that forms the beginnings of a nervous system in the embryo.

neutron: electrically neutral atomic particle found in the nucleus of an atom.

nitrogen bases: the units that form the rungs of the DNA molecule.

nitrogen fixation: incorporation of gaseous nitrogen into a molecule that can be used by organisms.

nodes of Ranvier: tiny gaps between the individual Schwann cells covering an axon.

nondisjunction: failure of a pair of chromatids to separate during meiosis.

nuclear pore: thin spot in nuclear membrane that allows movement of materials out of the nucleus.

nucleic acids: the main components of the hereditary units of the cell.

nucleolus: small, round body within the nucleus of a cell, composed largely of RNA.

nucleotide: a subunit of the nucleic acids, consisting of a phosphate, a sugar, and a nitrogen base all bonded together as a unit.

nucleus: organelle that contains the genetic information for eucaryotic cells.

nutrient: any material that supplies energy for metabolism in organisms.

nymph: immature form in gradual metamorphosis.

ocelli: simple eyes found in insects and spiders.

ommatidia: cone-like structures of which the compound eye is composed.

omnivore: organism whose diet includes both plant and animal matter.

one-gene–one-enzyme hypothesis: the theory that each gene is responsible for production of a specific enzyme.

oöcyte: an immature ovum.

operator gene: one that controls the operation of one or more structural genes.

operculum: protective gill covering.

operon: unit consisting of an operator gene and the structural genes it controls.

order: in taxonomy, a subdivision of a class.

organ: a group of tissues that form a functional unit.

organ of Corti: inner ear structure possessing receptor hair cells.

organ system: a group of organs that work together to perform a particular function.

organelles: the internal structures within a cell.

osmosis: the diffusion of any solvent, but especially water, across a semi-permeable membrane.

osmotic pressure: the amount of pressure needed to produce equilibrium between a solution on one side of a semi-permeable membrane and a pure solvent on the other side of the membrane.

ostia: slit-like openings on either side of the aorta in an arthropod open circulatory system.

oval window: the gateway to the inner ear.

ovary: in plants and animals, the egg-producing organ.

oviducts: in animals, the coiled abdominal tubes through which the maturing eggs pass.

ovulation: release of eggs from the ovaries.

ovules: sporangia inside the ovary of a flowering plant.

ovum: *see* **egg.**

oxidation: energy-releasing reaction involving the removal of an electron from a compound.

oxidation–reduction reaction: a reaction in which an electron donor gives up an electron to an electron acceptor.

oxidative phosphorylation: aerobic respiratory pathway in which hydrogen atoms are passed along a respiratory chain, losing energy which is used to manufacture ATP.

oxygen debt: situation incurred when muscles exhaust the available supply of oxygen and so must switch to anaerobic respiration.

pancreas: endocrine gland which is a part of the digestive system. In addition to the enzymes lipase and amylase, it manufactures the hormones insulin, glucagon, and pancreatic gastrin.

papillae: clusters of taste buds.

parasite: a plant or animal that draws its nutrients from another living organism; ectoparasites live on the host, endoparasites within the host.

parasitism: symbiotic relationship in which one species harms the other.

parasympathetic nerves: *see* **autonomic nervous system.**

parathyroid glands: small endocrine glands (usually four in humans) located in or on the thyroid, that secrete calcium-regulating parathormone.

parthenogenesis: a process in which an unfertilized egg develops into a new individual.

passive absorption: passage of materials across a semi-permeable membrane without expenditure of energy.

pathogen: a microorganism that causes disease.

pectoral girdle: division of the appendicular skeleton that includes the scapula and clavicle.

pelvic girdle: division of the appendicular skeleton that includes the hipbone, sacrum, and coccyx.

penis: the male copulatory organ.

peripheral nervous system: the branches that connect the central nervous system to all parts of the body.

peristalsis: wave-like contractions that propel food along the digestive tract.

pesticide: poisonous chemical used to destroy pests; called permanent if it remains in the environment and sets up its own biogeochemical cycle.

petals: brightly colored structures located just inside the sepals of a flower.

pH scale: a system that measures the acidity or alkalinity of a solution.

phagocyte: a cell that feeds on invading microorganisms.

pharynx: passageway between the mouth and the esophagus that is part of both the digestive tract and the respiratory system.

phenotype: the expression of genotype in an individual.

pheromones: chemicals secreted by one member of a species that stimulate behavior responses in other members of the species.

phloem: in vascular plants, a specialized conducting tissue that transports nutrients in both directions.

phospholipid: lipid in which a phosphoric acid group replaces a fatty acid chain.

photoperiod: period of light a plant must receive in order to flower.

photophosphorylation: light reactions of photosynthesis; may be cyclic or noncyclic, depending on whether or not the excited electrons are returned to the chlorophyll of photosystem I.

photosynthesis: process by which autotrophs convert solar energy to chemical bond energy.

photosystem I: cyclic pathway in photophosphorylation.

photosystem II: noncyclic pathway in photophosphorylation.

phototropism: tendency for plant structures to bend toward or away from the light.

phylum: in taxonomy, a division just below a kingdom, including one or more classes.

phytochrome: pigment involved in plant flowering that is believed to stimulate production of florigen.

pineal: lobe in the forebrain that secretes the hormone melatonin.

pistil: the female reproductive organ in flowering plants.

pituitary: so-called "master gland" located in the brain. Divided into anterior, intermediate and posterior sections, the pituitary is known to secrete at least 15 hormones.

placenta: structure that allows exchange of materials between the mammalian embryo and its mother.

plasma: the liquid component of blood.

plastid: plant organelle that contains pigments or stores food.

platelet: one of the formed elements of the blood; takes part in the clotting mechanism.

polar body: one of the two cells produced by the first meiotic division of an oöcyte.

polar covalent bond: hydrogen bond in which there is unequal sharing of atoms.

polar molecule: a molecule that has a positive pole and a negative pole.

polar nuclei: the two haploid nuclei produced by a plant ovule, which are joined in a single cell before fertilization.

pollen grain: the male gametophyte in flowering plants.

pollen tube: an extension of the pollen cell.

pollination: falling of pollen on the sticky stigma of a flower.

polyploidy: possession of extra haploid sets of chromosomes, probably caused by disruption of meiosis in one of the parent organisms.

polysaccharide: complex sugar formed by chaining together of several simple sugar molecules.

pons: bulging area above the medulla that coordinates facial movements and transfers information between the forebrain and cerebellum.

population: a group of individuals that do or can sexually interbreed with one another.

positive-pressure breathing: system of breathing in which both inspiration and expiration are active processes.

potential: difference in electrical charge between the inside of a neuron and the liquid surrounding it.

potential energy: energy locked in a chemical bond and unable to do work until released.

predation: the feeding of one organism on another.

primary community: the first living population in a previously uncolonized territory.

primary consumers: animals that eat producers.

primary growth: growth of tissues produced by the apical meristems.

procaryotic cell: a cell that has no well-defined nucleus. Procaryotic cells include the bacteria and blue-green algae.

producers: the green plants in a community.

progesterone: hormone that inhibits production of LH and stimulates the uterine lining.

prophase: stage in mitosis during which chromosomes thicken and disentangle, the spindle forms, and the nuclear membrane and nucleolus disappear.

prostaglandins: chemical control substances resembling hormones but apparently synthesized in most body tissues.

prostate gland: male reproductive gland surrounding the urethra, which contributes fluid to the semen.

protein: a chain of amino acids.

proton: atomic particle found in the nucleus, possessing a positive charge of +1.

protoplasm: any living cellular material.

puberty: the time at which sexual maturation occurs.

pulmonary: pertaining to the lungs.

pupa: third-stage form in complete metamorphosis, during which larval tissues are broken down and reorganized into the adult form.

pupil: opening through which light enters the camera eye.

race: *see* **subspecies.**

radial symmetry: body structure in which body parts are arranged around a central point.

radicle: part of the plant embryo that develops into the root system.

reactant: reacting substance which fits into an active site on an enzyme molecule.

receptor: a sensory organ or nerve ending.

recessive trait: a trait that is not phenotypically expressed in an F_1 hybrid.

reduction: energy-gaining process that occurs when a compound takes up an electron.

reflex: involuntary movement in response to a stimulus.

reflex action: automatic and involuntary response to stimulation of a specific nerve.

reflex arc: the simplest nerve pathway, often involving only two neurons.

regulator gene: one that synthesizes repressor substances that block the action of an operator gene.

relative refractory period: period during which the membrane of a stimulated neuron is returning to its resting state.

releasing stimulus: a step in a behavioral sequence that stimulates performance of the next step.

respiratory chain: electron-transport chain involved in aerobic respiration.

respiratory unit: a cluster of cytochromes and enzymes in a mitochondrion, which take part in the Krebs cycle.

resting potential: potential normally carried by an inactive neuron.

reticular formation: neuron network running from hindbrain to forebrain, which classifies stimuli according to their importance.

retina: group of pigmented photo-receptor cells at the back of the eyeball.

ribosome: small organelle that appears to function in protein synthesis.

RNA (ribonucleic acid): nucleic acid similar to DNA, present in both the nucleus and the cytoplasm of a cell. Assists in protein formation.

rods: one of two kinds of receptor cell found in the retina.

root cap: region at root tip covered with cells that protect the root from injury.

root hairs: projections from the epidermal cells of a root, which provide increased surface area for absorption.

S-A (sino-atrial) node: one of two tissue masses in the heart, serving as a pacemaker.

saprophyte: heterotrophic plant that gets its nutrients from dead organic matter.

sarcomere: unit which shortens during muscle contraction; made up of myofilaments.

saturated fat: a fat in which the fatty acid molecules contain as many hydrogen atoms as can possibly bond to all the carbon atoms.

Schwann cells: fatty cells that cover axons except for those in the brain and spinal cord.

sclerenchyma fiber: hard fiber, contained in phloem tissue, that provides structural support.

scrotum: external sac of skin that contains the testes.

secondary consumers: animals that eat primary consumers.

secondary growth: production of new xylem and phloem by plants that have a vascular cambium.

seed: the matured ovule of a flowering plant.

seed dormancy: a state of reduced activity that precedes seed germination.

segregation, principle of: Mendel's assumption that pairs of hereditary factors are separated in the parents, with factors from both parents being recombined in the offspring.

self-pollination: pollination of a perfect flower by its own pollen.

semen: the combination of sperm and seminal fluid.

semicircular canals: liquid-filled tubes just above the cochlea, concerned with the sense of balance.

seminal fluid: liquid that contains the sperm in higher animals.

seminiferous tubules: coiled system of tubes within the testes, in which sperm formation takes place.

semi-permeable membrane: a membrane that is permeable to some substances but not to others.

sensory neuron: neuron that receives a stimulus from a receptor.

sepals: protective outer structures of a flower.

septum: a wall that divides or separates body cavities.

sex chromosomes: the X and Y chromosomes whose combination determines the sex of an individual.

sex-linked genes: genes present on the sex chromosomes.

sieve cell: conducting cell in the phloem of vascular plants.

sieve plate: perforated cell wall separating sieve cells.

sieve tube: tube formed by long sieve cells connected end to end.

sinus: a body cavity or cavity within an organ.

skeletal muscle: striated muscle used in voluntary movement.

small intestine: portion of the digestive tract where chemical digestion is completed.

smooth muscle: nonstriated involuntary muscle.

social behavior: interaction between two or more animals for constructive ends.

sodium pump: system of active transport that pumps sodium ions out of a neuron membrane as the neuron returns to resting potential.

somatic nerves: nerves that control voluntary body activities.

speciation: the process by which separate species are formed.

species: a group of organisms that freely interbreed and produce fertile offspring in their natural environment.

species-typical behavior: behavior that is constant among all members of a given species.

sperm: the gamete produced by the male parent.

sperm nuclei: in plants, the male gametes produced by division of the generative nucleus.

spermatids: haploid cells produced by meiosis of spermatocytes.

spermatocytes: diploid cells produced by the lining of the seminiferous tubules.

spermatogenesis: sperm formation.

spermatozoa: mature sperm.

sphincter: a ring-shaped muscle around a body opening, which can constrict to close the opening.

spinal cord: a dorsal nerve cord protected by the vertebrae and connecting with the brain. Part of the vertebrate central nervous system.

spindle: the delicate mass of filaments, radiating from the two poles of a cell, that appears during prophase.

spiracle: valve which opens or closes the tracheal openings in arthropods.

spleen: ductless organ that destroys aging red blood cells and produces lymphocytes.

spontaneous generation: the theory that nonliving material can generate living organisms.

sporangium: plant organ that produces, stores, and releases spores.

spore: in plants, the asexual reproductive cell of the gametophyte generation.

sporophyte: in plants, the spore-producing generation.

stamen: male reproductive organ of the flower.

steroid: a class of lipid possessing four interlocking carbon rings, with a variety of attached side groups.

stigma: enlarged area above the style of a pistil.

stimulus: an agent that is capable of causing the transmission of a nerve impulse.

stoma: leaf opening that functions in gas exchange; its size is regulated by two guard cells.

stroma: protein solution surrounding a chloroplast.

structural gene: one that codes for structurally important polypeptides.

subspecies: populations with recognizable differences, but which will interbreed if given the opportunity.

supracellular differentiation: developmental stage during which cells become organized into tissues, organs, and systems.

surface tension: tension created by cohesive attraction among the molecules of a liquid.

surface-to-volume ratio: the relationship between the volume of a cell and the cell's surface area.

swim bladder: gas-containing organ that enables a fish to remain at any level in the water.

symbiosis: a permanent physical relationship between individuals of two different species.

sympathetic nerves: *see* **autonomic nervous system.**

sympatric speciation: speciation based on specialization rather than on geographical separation.

synapse: point at which axon filaments of one neuron lie close to the dendrites of another neuron.

synapsis: pairing of homologous chromosomes during meiosis.

synovial fluid: lubricating fluid within a joint.

synovial membrane: protective membrane lining the capsule of a joint.

systole: the contraction of the heart.

taxis: a directional response to a specific kind of external stimulus.

telophase: the final stage in mitosis and meiosis, during which cell division is completed.

tension–cohesion pull: osmotic tension between water molecules that is capable of pulling adjacent molecules up a column.

testes: the primary male reproductive organs, in which sperm are formed.

thalamus: structure in the forebrain which registers pain sensation and acts as a clearing-house for other sensory information.

threshold intensity: minimum strength of stimulus needed to begin a nerve impulse.

thrombocyte: *see* **platelet.**

thylakoid: pigment-containing structure within the chloroplast.

thymine: nitrogen base present in the DNA molecule.

thymus: double-lobed gland behind the sternum that assists in production of antibodies.

thyroid: paired endocrine gland located in the front of the neck. It secretes thyroxin, triiodothyronine, and calcitonin.

tissue: a group of cells of the same general sort, engaged in the same function.

trachea: passage from the larynx to the bronchi; the windpipe.

tracheae: in insects, hollow tubes that allow air to reach all parts of the body.

tracheid: xylem cell in gymnosperms.

tracheophytes: one of the two main groups of land plants, including all the vascular plants.

transcription: formation of a molecule of RNA using one strand of DNA as a template.

translation: synthesis of a polypeptide from the coded information in an mRNA molecule.

translocation: (1) the exchange of pieces between two nonhomologous chromosomes; (2) the movement of water and nutrients within a plant.

transpiration: evaporation of water from the interior of a leaf through the stomata.

trisomy: the presence of an extra chromosome along with a normal pair.

trophic hormone: a hormone that regulates the action of other endocrine glands.

trophoblast: outer cells of the blastocyst that are responsible for implantation of the embryo in the uterine lining.

turgor: the swollen condition of a cell that is inflated with water.

turgor pressure: the pressure of the inner contents of a cell against its outer cell membrane.

tympanic membrane: the eardrum.

umbilical cord: cord that connects the mammalian embryo to the mother's placenta.

uracil: nitrogen base present in the RNA molecule.

ureter: tube through which urine from the kidneys moves to the bladder.

urine: fluid that is the end product of excretion by the kidneys.

vacant niche: a "hole" in the food web of a community, caused by extermination of an entire species.

vacuole: membrane-enclosed pocket of fluid in the cytoplasm.

vagina: the genital opening of the female mammal.

valence electrons: electrons in an atom's outer shell that can be transferred or shared with other atoms.

vas deferens: tube leading from the epididymis to the ejaculatory duct.

vascular cambium: layer of tissue that produces new xylem and phloem cells.

vascular plant: any plant with a system of well-developed conducting vessels.

vegetal hemisphere: section of early embryo in which cells divide slowly.

vegetative reproduction: growth of a new organism from nonreproductive tissue of an existing organism.

veins, venules: blood vessels that carry blood toward the heart.

vena cava: either of two large collecting veins that empty into the right atrium of the heart.

venereal disease: a disease transmitted by sexual contact.

ventricle: either of the two lower chambers of the heart.

vessel cell: xylem cell in angiosperms.

villus: a finger-like projection of the lining of the small intestine.

Virchow's principle: the principle that every cell must come from another cell.

vitamin: chemical compound necessary to the health and/or growth of an organism.

vulva: the external female genitalia.

wax: a type of lipid composed of fatty acid chains linked to a molecule of alcohol.

white matter: matter in the central nervous system largely made up of myelin-sheathed axons.

xylem: specialized tissue that conducts nutrients upward in a vascular plant.

yolk: a source of food for the developing animal embryo; contained in the egg.

zygote: fertilized cell resulting from fusion of a male and a female gamete.

Suggested Readings

Patterns of Structure and Function

Cells, chemistry and energy

Arehart-Treichel, J., "Exploiting Synthetic Membranes," *Science News*, *107*:155, March 8, 1975.

A brief account of the use of artificial membranes in biological and medical practice.

Asimov, I., *Life and Energy*. Bantam, 1962.

A discussion for the layman, using some simple physics, math, and chemistry.

Bloom, W., and D. W. Fawcett, *A Textbook of Histology*. Tenth Edition, Philadelphia, Saunders, 1975.

A detailed work on the structure and function of human tissues.

Bretscher, M. S., "Membrane Structure: Some General Principles," *Science*, *181*:622, 1973.

A brief introduction to the subject of membrane function, control, and structure.

Dobell, C., *Antony van Leeuwenhoek and His "Little Animals."* Dover, 1962.

The life and work of the discoverer of microorganisms.

Erlander, S. R. "The Structure of Water," *Science Journal*, *60*, May 1969.

An excellent treatment of aqueous solutions in biological systems.

Frieden, E., "The Chemical Elements of Life," *Scientific American*, *227*:52 July, 1972.

An analysis of the inorganic ions and organic molecules essential to all living systems.

Kleinsmith, L. J., "Molecular Mechanisms for the Regulation of Cell Function," *Bioscience*, *22(6)*:343–348, June 1972.

A good account of the discoveries in recent years in the field of molecular biology of cellular control mechanisms.

Levine, R. P. "The Mechanism of Photosynthesis," *Scientific American*, *222*:58, December 1969.

A readable and well-illustrated account of photosynthesis.

The Living Cell: Readings from Scientific American. W. H. Freeman and Co., 1974.

A collection of articles about specific structures and functions of the cell.

Toporek, M. *Basic Chemistry of Life*, 2nd Ed., New York, Appleton-Century Crofts, 1975.

One of the best treatments of the chemistry of living systems.

Weisskopf, V. F., "The Significance of Science," *Science 76*:138–145, April 14, 1972.

The author identifies the aspects of human society that have been influenced by science.

Patterns of Maintenance and Regulation

General

Anthony, C. P. and N. J. Kolthoff, *Textbook of Anatomy and Physiology*. C. V. Mosby, St. Louis, 1975.

A technical but readable treatment of human systems.

Hoar, W. S. *General and Comparative Physiology*, 2nd Ed., Englewood Cliffs, New Jersey, Prentice-Hall, 1975.

Deals with the structure, function, and regulation of physiological mechanisms in vertebrate and invertebrate animals.

Digestion

Jones, Shainberg, and Byer, *Foods, Diet, Nutrition*. Canfield, 1970.

A quick look at the whole range of nutrition—food and energy, digestion, nutritional needs, diet and weight control, food processing and selection, misconceptions about food.

Wilson, C., "Vitamin C Makes Colds Less Complex," *New Scientist*, March 29, 1973.

Some verifiable properties of this controversial vitamin and its possible benefits to health.

Circulation

Diggs, L. W., *et al., The Morphology of Blood Cells*. Abbott Laboratories, North Chicago, 1954.

SUGGESTED
READINGS

A detailed narrative and pictorial account of the structure and function of red blood cells and white blood cells.

Maugh, T. H. II, "Coffee and Heart Disease: Is There a Link?" *Science*, August 10, 1973.

Some of the evidence for a relationship between coffee-drinking and heart disease.

Mayerson, H. S., "The Lymphatic System," *Scientific American, 208*:80, June, 1963.

The nature and role of the human lymphatic system.

Respiration

Comroe, J. H., Jr., *Physiology of Respiration: An Introductory Text*, Second Edition. Year Book Medical Pubs., Chicago, 1974.

A detailed treatment of the process of human respiration and control mechanisms.

Naeye, R. L., "Hypoxemia and the Sudden Infant Death Syndrome," *Science, 186*:837, Nov. 29, 1974.

A current hypothesis for the "crib death" syndrome in babies.

U.S. Dept. of Health, Education, and Welfare, "The Health Consequences of Smoking," 1974. (Stock #1723-00087).

A popular and readable account of the hazards of smoking.

Muscle

Eccles, J. C., "The Synapse," *Scientific American, 212*:56, Jan. 1965.

A popular work on the role of the synapse in nerve impulse transmission and muscular activity.

Hoyle, G. "How Is Muscle Turned On and Off?" *Scientific American, 222*:84, April, 1970.

A good account of the nervous, hormonal, and ionic control mechanisms involved in muscle movement.

Huxley, H. E., "The Mechanism of Muscular Contraction," *Scientific American, 213*:18, Dec., 1965.

A popular account of muscular movement by one of the original authors of the sliding filament theory.

Merton, P. A. "How We Control the Contraction of Our Muscles," *Scientific American 226*:30, May, 1972.

A discussion of voluntary control mechanisms involved in skeletal muscle control.

Science News, "Multiple Sclerosis: Two New

Approaches," *105*:383, June 15, 1974.

A brief description of the muscular disorder multiple sclerosis, along with two new techniques for its maintenance.

Homeostasis

Cannon, W. B., *The Wisdom of the Body*. W. W. Norton, 1967.

A beautifully written survey of the body's homeostatic mechanisms.

McQuade, W., "What Stress Can Do to You," *Fortune*, January 1972.

The role of stress in disease, and what makes a situation stressful for the individual.

Fluid balance and regulation

Hardy, J. D., *et al.*, *Physiological and Behavioral Temperature Regulation*. Charles C. Thomas, Springfield, Ill., 1970.

A detailed medical account of the role of the skin in temperature regulation, along with intrinsic and extrinsic control mechanisms.

Pitts, R. F., *Physiology of Kidney and Body Fluids*. Year Book Medical Publishers, Chicago, 1966.

An old but readable account of the composition of normal urine and the function of the kidney in maintaining the composition of normal body fluids.

Immunity

Arehart-Triechel, J., "Organ Transplants: What Hope for Patients?" *Science News, 106*:314, 1974.

A current account of the state of organ transplant types available.

Culliton, B. J., "Restoring Immunity: Marrow and Thymus Transplants May Do It," *Science, 180*:168, April 13, 1973.

Several transplantation methods which would allow a transplant patient to resume normal immunity responses.

Jerne, N. K., "The Immune System," *Scientific American, 229*:52, July 1973.

A popular and readable account of the various mechanisms that operate during the immune response.

Kleiger, M. J., *et al.*, "Fever and Survival," *Science, 188*:259, April 18, 1975.

The functions of the hypothalamus, nervous, and circulatory systems in fever production.

Porter, R. R., "The Structure of Antibodies," *Sci-*

*entific American, 217:*81, Oct. 1967.

The structure and function of antibodies. The nature and role of antibodies are discussed in detail.

Ross, Russell, "Wound Healing," *Scientific American,* 220:40, June 1969.

Detailed but readable.

Hormonal regulation

Beroza, M., and E. F. Knipling, "Gypsy Moth Control with the Sex Attractant Pheromone," *Science,* 177:19–27, July 7, 1972.

The author deals with the containment of the gypsy moth within its present geographical range by the use of synthetic pheromones and sterile male moths.

Cuthbert, M. F. (ed.), *The Prostaglandins.* Philadelphia, J. B. Lippincott, 1973.

The role that prostaglandins play in cellular metabolism and as a control mechanism.

Galston, A. W., and P. J. Davies, *Control Mechanisms in Plant Development.* Englewood Cliffs, N.J.: Prentice-Hall, 1970.

The role of hormones, light, and other factors in plant development.

LeBaron, R., *Hormones: A Delicate Balance.* New York, Pegasus, 1972.

A general and very readable description of the structure and role of hormones in living systems.

Levine, S., *Hormones and Behavior.* New York, Academic Press, 1972.

This text deals with genetic, hormonal, and nervous interactions as one mechanism in the complex aspects of behavior.

Trotter, R. J., "Stress, Confusion, and Controversy," *Science News,* 107:356, May 31, 1975.

An excellent treatment of the role that hormones play in stress situations.

Nervous system

Arganoff, B. W., "Memory and Protein Synthesis," *Scientific American,* 216:115, June 1967.

A well-illustrated and descriptive account of a popular theory concerning the mechanism of memory in man.

DiCara, L. V., "Learning in the Autonomic Nervous System," *Scientific American,* 222:30, Jan., 1970.

A detailed but readable presentation of the functional process of learning in man and animals.

Eccles, J. C., *The Understanding of the Brain.* New York, McGraw-Hill, 1972.

A Nobel prize winner describes in technical but readable fashion the variety of nervous system functions.

Lauria, A. R., "The Functional Organization of the Brain," *Scientific American,* 222:66, March, 1970.

A well-illustrated treatment of the regional functions of the human brain. Emphasis is nontechnical.

"Light for the Blind," *Newsweek,* Feb. 11, 1974.

Research involving electrical stimulation of the brain, allowing the blind to perceive spots of light.

"The Two Brains," *Newsweek,* August 6, 1973.

The differences in function and specialization between the right and left halves of the brain.

Reproduction and Development

Origin of life

Bernal, J. D., *The Origin of Life.* New York, World Publishing Company. 1967.

A readable posing of the philosophical and scientific questions regarding the origin of living systems.

Fox, W. W., and K. Dose, *Molecular Evolution and the Origin of Life.* San Francisco, W. H. Freeman, 1972.

A detailed treatment of the current experimental evidence on the origin of the universe and biological molecules.

Oparin, A. I., *The Origin of Life on Earth.* New York, Academic Press, 1957.

The author presents in a readable fashion his own theories regarding the origin of life and protocellular evolution.

Animal and plant reproduction and development

Arehart-Treichel, J. "Birth Control in the Brave New World," *Science News,* 102:93. Feb. 10, 1973.

An interesting presentation of birth control methods for the 1970s.

Arehart-Treichel, J., "Mother's Diet and Child's Health," *Science News,* 106:108, Aug. 17, 1974.

An excellent discussion of the influence that maternal nutrition plays in the normal development of the fetus.

Balinsky, B. I., *An Introduction to Embryology.* 3rd Ed., Philadelphia, W. B. Saunders, 1975.

A classic and readable text in human and animal embryology.

Bold, H. C., *Morphology of Plants.* 3rd Ed., New York, Harper & Row, 1973.

A readable text in the field of botany with excellent coverage of plant reproduction.

Etzioni, A., "Life, Dying, Death: Ethics and Open Decisions," *Science News, 106:*106, August 16, 1974.

The author discusses philosophical questions and arguments on the subject.

Gilbert, M., *Biography of the Unborn.* Hafner, New York, 1962.

A nontechnical account of human development from zygote to birth.

Hancock, J. L., "The Sperm Cell," *Science Journal,* June, 1970.

The significance of sperm in fertilization, semen fertilization capacity, and artificial insemination.

Jaffe, F. S., "Public Policy on Fertility Control." *Scientific American, 229:*17, July 1973.

A timely and readable article dealing with governmental and special interest group positions on the subject.

Marx, J. L., "Birth Control: Current Technology, Future Prospects," *Science, 179:*1222, March 23, 1973.

A succinct treatment on current human sterilization techniques along with future possibilities.

Masters, W. H., and V. E. Johnson, *Human Sexual Response.* Boston: Little, Brown, 1966.

A classic text on the subject. Intense clinical treatment of most topics.

Nathanson, B. N., "Deeper Into Abortion," *New England Journal of Medicine, 291:*1189, Nov. 28, 1974.

A statement by the medical profession on the legal, social, and philosophical questions of abortion.

"Your Smoking Affects Two Lives," Dept. of Health, Education and Welfare, 1974.

The effects of smoking on fetal development.

Patterns of Change

Genes and heredity

Bajema, C. J. "The Genetic Implications of Population Control," *Bioscience, 21*(2):71–75, 15 January 1971.

The probable genetic effects of three different population policies which would result in zero population growth.

Clark, B. F. C., and K. A. Marcker, "How Proteins Start," *Scientific American, 218:*36, Jan. 1968.

A classic and well-illustrated article on protein synthesis.

Cohen, S. N. "The Manipulation of Genes," *Scientific American, 233:*24, July 1975.

A few of the latest experiments in gene manipulation. The author raises questions on the future use of these techniques.

Gardner, E. J. *Principles of Genetics.* 5th Ed., New York, John Wiley & Sons, 1975.

A classic introductory text on the subject of animal and human genetics.

Gordon, E. "Molecular Genetics—A Survey of Highlights," *Bioscience, 22*(2):77–81, February 1972.

This article deals with some of the major breakthroughs in the field of molecular biology.

Lerner and Libby, *Heredity, Evolution, and Society.* San Francisco, W. H. Freeman, 1976.

Genetic processes and their human implications. One chapter even deals with genetics and politics.

McKusick, V. A., "The Mapping of Human Chromosomes," *Scientific American, 224:*104, April, 1971.

A readable discussion of the technique of determining human chromosomal traits and patterns.

Stern, C., and E. R. Sherwood (eds.), *The Origin of Genetics: A Mendel Source Book.* San Francisco, W. H. Freeman, 1966.

A translation of Mendel's original papers.

Watson, J. D., *The Double Helix.* Boston, Atheneum, 1968.

The story of the discovery of DNA, told in a way that throws light on the nature of biological research.

Watson, J. D., *The Molecular Biology of the Gene.* 2nd Ed., Philadelphia, W. A. Benjamin, 1970.

A Nobel prize winner gives a readable explanation of the structure and function of the gene.

Populations and speciation

Berrill, N. J., *Man's Emerging Mind.* Fawcett, 1955.

The origin and development of the human mind.

Calder, N., *The Life Game.* New York, Viking Press, 1974.

An enjoyable account of current research problems in evolutionary biology.

Cavalli-Sforza, L. L., "The Genetics of Human Populations," *Scientific American, 231:*80–89, September, 1974.

A well-illustrated article on human population genetics.

Crow, J. F. and M. Kimura, *An Introduction to Population Genetics.* New York, Harper & Row, 1970.

A basic primer for the serious student.

Hanson, E. D., *Animal Diversity.* 3rd ed., Englewood Cliffs, New Jersey, Prentice-Hall, 1972.

A clear and basic presentation of the subject of animal populations.

Howells, W., *Evolution of the Genus Homo.* Reading, Mass., Addison-Wesley, 1973.

A well-written survey of the fossil record of man's evolution.

Malthus, Thomas R., *Population: The First Essay.* Ann Arbor Paperbacks, The University of Michigan Press, 1959.

Malthus deals with the critical question: What is the ultimate limit on the growth of populations?

Moorehead, A., *Darwin and the Beagle.* New York, Harper & Row, 1969.

A lucid and revealing look at the classic work of Darwin.

Wessells, N. (ed.), *Vertebrate Adaptations: Readings from Scientific American.* San Francisco, W. H. Freeman, 1968.

A fine collection of readings which will give the beginning student a more comprehensive understanding of animals and man.

Wynne-Edwards, V. C., "Population Control in Animals." *Scientific American 211:*68–74, August 1964.

The author presents views on various artificial control mechanisms of natural animal populations.

Classification

Bold, H. C., *The Plant Kingdom.* 3rd ed., Englewood Cliffs, New Jersey, Prentice-Hall, 1970.

A well illustrated taxonomic survey of the plant kingdom.

Buchsbaum, R., *Animals Without Backbones.* 2nd ed., Chicago, University of Chicago Press, 1948.

A photographic survey of invertebrate animal forms.

Buchsbaum, R., and L. J. Milne, *The Lower Animals: Living Invertebrates of the World.* New York, Doubleday, 1960.

A photographic survey of aquatic and land invertebrate forms.

Herald, E. S., *Living Fishes of the World.* New York, Doubleday, 1961.

A photographic survey of freshwater and marine fishes.

Klots, A. B., and E. B. Klots, *Living Insects of the World.* New York, Doubleday, 1959.

A photographic survey of insect populations.

Porter, C. L., *Taxonomy of Flowering Plants.* 2nd ed., San Francisco, W. H. Freeman, 1967.

A well-organized and illustrated primer covering higher plant taxonomy.

Volk, W. A., and M. F. Wheeler, *Basic Microbiology.* 3rd ed., Philadelphia, J. B. Lippincott, 1973.

An introductory text that provides a readable survey of the microbial world.

Interacting with the Environment

Communication

Bower, T. G. R., "The Object in the World of the Infant," *Scientific American 225:*30–38, April, 1971.

Explores in detail the function of the brain, eye, and motor coordination of infants during the period of early infancy.

Droscher, V. B. *The Magic of the Senses: New Discoveries in Animal Perception.* New York, Harper & Row, 1971.

A well-illustrated and readable guide to research in animal perception.

Evans, W., *Communication in the Animal World.* Crowell, 1968.

An outstanding introduction to communication among animals and the techniques of studying it.

Gordon, M. S., *et al., Animal Function: Principles and Adaptation.* New York, Macmillan, 1968.

A classic work in the study of animal perception and communication.

Haber, R. N., "How We Remember What We See," *Scientific American, 222:*104, May 1970.

Masterfully outlines with vivid illustrations the process of visual memory and imprinting.

Neisser, V., "The Process of Vision," *Scientific American, 219:*204, September, 1968.

The mechanism of human vision.

Von Frisch, K., *Bees: Their Vision, Chemical Senses and Language.* Ithaca, New York, Cornell University Press, 1956.

A well-known worker shows in an intriguing manner the structure and function of vision and communication techniques in bees.

Animal behavior

Ardrey, R., *The Territorial Imperative*. New York, Dell, 1966.

A popular and authoritative account of instinctive and acquired behavioral patterns in various animal populations.

Armstrong, E. A., *Bird Display and Behavior*. New York, Dover, 1965.

A well-illustrated discussion of ritualistic display patterns and habits among birds.

Cousteau, J., and P. Cousteau, *The Shark: Splendid Savage of the Sea*. New York, Doubleday, 1970.

Two noted oceanographers share their observations and insights on the behavior of sharks.

Goodall, J., *In the Shadow of Man*. Boston, Houghton Mifflin, 1971.

A world-renowned researcher's fascinating account of the life of chimpanzees.

Hall, E. T., *The Hidden Dimension*. New York, Doubleday, 1966.

Human territoriality, and how personal space is affected by overcrowding, human interaction, and physiological stress.

Levine, S., "Stress and Behavior," *Scientific American*, 224:26–31, January 1971.

An authoritative examination of the nature of stress and those elements which influence successive behavioral patterns.

Lorenz, K., *King Solomon's Ring*. New York, Crowell, 1972.

A well-illustrated and engaging account of the author's field observations on behavior.

Wilson, E. O., *The Insect Societies*. Cambridge, Mass., Harvard University Press, 1972.

A comprehensive discussion of the world of insects. Behavioral patterns of selected insects are presented.

Ecology, environment and pollution

Commoner, B., *Global Effects of Environmental Pollution*. New York, Springer-Verlag, 1970.

The author discuss vividly the threats of various pollutants to our environment.

Commoner, B., *Science and Survival*. New York, The Viking Press, 1966.

A noted authority discusses how man disrupts his natural environment and analyzes the role that science plays in this destruction.

Ehrlich, P., *The Population Bomb*. New York, Ballantine, 1968.

An early and classic "alarm bell" about the population explosion and its effects.

Ehrlich, P. R., and A. H. Ehrlich, *Population, Resources, Environment: Issues in Human Ecology*. San Francisco, W. H. Freeman, 1970.

A contemporary text dealing with such world problems as overpopulation and pollution.

Hutchinson, G. E., *The Biosphere*. San Francisco, W. H. Freeman, 1970.

A readable and well-illustrated account of the field of ecology as it relates to the total environment.

Moore, R. J., (intro.), *Oceanography: Readings from Scientific American*. San Francisco, W. H. Freeman, 1971.

A collection of 41 illustrated articles presenting the philosophy of multiple use of the ocean and its resources.

Odum, E. P., *Fundamentals of Ecology*. 3rd ed., Philadelphia, W. B. Saunders, 1971.

An authoritative text on the principles of ecology.

Pyke, M., *Man and Food*. New York, McGraw-Hill, 1970.

A world-renowned authority discusses the food we eat in terms of nutrition and malnutrition.

Whittaker, R. H., *Communities and Ecosystems*. New York, Macmillan, 1970.

A basic text describing the relationships between the environment and species and energy flow in ecosystems.

Wilson, E. O., *Ecology, Evolution and Population Biology: Readings from Scientific American*. San Francisco, W. H. Freeman, 1974.

The 34 articles discuss the adaption of organisms to their natural environment, major topics of evolutionary theory, and biogeography.

Young, G., "Dry Lands and Desalted Water," *Science 167*:339–49, 1970.

The author presents an optimistic and realistic assessment of the problem of desalinization.

Zwick, D., and M. Benstock, *Water Wasteland*. New York, Grossman Publishers, 1971.

The role that industry has played in effectively blocking regulatory legislation of water pollution.

Credits

Chapter 1. 3T: Derek Bayes, courtesy Science Museum, London. 3M: Ward's Natural Science Establishment, Inc. 5T: Cliche Institute Pasteur, Musée Pasteur. 5B: Dr. Landrum B. Shettles. 7: Allan Roberts. 9–10: Jack J. Kunz. 11: Oscar W. Richards, Research Department, American Optical Company. 13T: Bernard Tandler, Sloan-Kettering Institute for Cancer Research. 13M: Faust Scientific Supply Company, Inc. 13B: Dr. Fritz Miller. 15T: Dr. H. Fernandez-Moran. 15M: Eva Cellini. 15B: Dr. Sam L. Clark Jr. 16–17: New York Zoological Society Photo. 18: Manfred Kage from Peter Arnold. 20: Eva Cellini. *Quotation:* 1, 2: *Great Experiments in Biology*, Mordecai L. Gabriel and Seymour Fogel, eds., pp. 2, 187. Prentice-Hall, © 1955. 3: *A History of Biology*, by Charles Singer, p. 344. Henry Schuman, © 1950.

Chapter 2. 29B: Eva Cellini. 31B: Mike Godfrey. 35: E. R. Degginger. 38–39: American Museum of Natural History. 42: John D. Firestone Associates, Inc. 43: NASA.

Chapter 3. 48B: John D. Firestone Associates, Inc. 52-a: Sol Mednick. 52-b: Ward's Natural Science Establishment, Inc. 52-c–f: Mell Hunter. 52B: Dr. J. Louis Martens. 53: Mike Godfrey. 55B: Leonard Lee Rue. 56–57: Donald G. Huttleston. 61: UPI.

Chapter 4. 68: Nickolas Fasciano. 69: Eric Grave. 70: Eva Cellini. 71: Roy Hyrkin; models by Louis D. Valentin. 72: Jean Helmer. 73: Eva Cellini. 74: Jean Helmer. 78–79: Donald G. Huttleston. 80T: PIP-ZFA Photo. 81T: Dr. E. R. Hutchins. 81B: E. R. Degginger.

Chapter 5. 86–87: Marg Moran. 88–90: Eva Cellini. 91T: Tom McHugh from Photo Researchers. 91B–93: Eva Cellini. 94–95: New York Zoological Society Photo. 97: Harwyn Medical Photographers. 99B: Eva Cellini. 101: Eva Cellini. 103: Jean Helmer. 105T: Eva Cellini. 105M: Ward's Natural Science Establishment, Inc. 106: Jack J. Kunz. 107: Eva Cellini.

Chapter 6. 113T: Ward's Natural Science Establishment, Inc. 113B: Eva Cellini. 114T: Eva Cellini. 114B: E. R. Degginger. 115: Peg Estey. 116–117: Vernon E. Ogilvie. 118: Faust Scientific Supply Co. 119: Eva Cellini. 121: Laboratory of Molecular Biology, Medical Research Council, Cambridge, England. 122T: Dr. Oscar Auerbach. 122B: Eva Cellini. 124T: Faust Scientific Supply Co. 124B: Marg Moran. 125B: Hoppock Associates.

Chapter 7. 131: E. R. Degginger. 134: Elliot Herman and Paul Calle. 135–136: Helen Erlik Speiden. 137T: Color by Fritz Kredel of Vesalius Drawing, courtesy University of Padua Library. 138: Manfred Kage from Peter Arnold. 139: Helen Erlik Speiden. 140–141: New York Zoological Society Photo.

Chapter 8. 149T: A Cosmos from Bruce Coleman. 149B: Eva Cellini. 151T: Leonard Lee Rue. 151B: Mike Godfrey. 152: E. R. Degginger. 154T: Jean Helmer.

154B: Eva Cellini. 155: Bob West from Photo Trends. 156: Eva Cellini. 157: Dr. Jerome Gross. 158–159: New York Zoological Society Photo. 160T: Manfred Kage from Peter Arnold. 160B: Franklin from Omikron. 161: Nicholas Fasciano, courtesy Charles Pfizer and Co. 163: United Nations.

Chapter 9. 169: Jean Helmer. 170T: Phil Brodatz. 170B: From "The Pituitary Body and Its Disorders" by Harvey Cushing, published by J. B. Lippincott. 171T, B: Russ Kinne from Photo Researchers. 172: Hermann Kacher. 173T: Eva Cellini. 173B: Leonard Lee Rue. 175T: Paul Almasy for WHO. 175B: Dr. Roberts F. Escamilla from Lisser and Escamilla: *Atlas of Clinical Endocrinology*, Second Edition, St. Louis, The C. V. Mosby Co., 1962. 177–179: Eva Cellini. 180–181: Robert Neulieb Photos. 182: Edmund B. Gerard. 183–185T: USDA. 185B: Mike Godfrey.

Chapter 10. 190: Manfred Kage from Peter Arnold. 191: Jean Helmer. 192T: L. V. Bergman and Associates. 192B: Eva Cellini. 196T: Eva Cellini. 196B: Allan Roberts. 197: Eva Cellini. 198: M. Woodbridge Williams from Photo Classics. 199T, M: Eva Cellini. 199B: Rudolph Freund. 200–201: New York Zoological Society Photo. 202: Jean Helmer. 203T: Manfred Kage from Peter Arnold. 203M, B: George Schwenk. 204: Eva Cellini. 206: Mike Godfrey.

Chapter 11. 213T: Dr. Landrum B. Shettles. 213M: Culver Pictures. 213B: Otto van Eersel. 214–215: American Museum of Natural History. 217T: Otto van Eersel. 217B: Anthony Saris. 218: J. R. Eyerman, courtesy Ames Research Center, NASA. 219T: Dr. Sidney W. Fox. 219B: Janet Stone from National Audubon Society. 220: Marg Moran. 224T: Dr. F. C. Steward. 225T: Rene Martin. 225B: Eva Cellini. 226T: Lennart Nilsson. 226B: Allan Roberts. 227: Marg Moran.

Chapter 12. 232T: Dale Marsh. 232B: E. R. Degginger. 233: Jeff Himmelstein. 234: Eva Cellini. 235: Mike Godfrey. 236: Eva Cellini. 237: Ward's Natural Science Establishment, Inc. 238T: Eva Cellini. 238B: Allan Roberts. 239: Milton J. Heiberg. 240R: Eva Cellini. 240L: Jean Helmer. 241T: Alfred Eisenstaedt for *Life*. 241M, B: Allan Roberts. 244: Mike Godfrey. 245: Eva Cellini. 246–247: Laboratory of Tree-Ring Research, Univ. of Arizona. 248T: Matt Greene. 248B: Eva Cellini. 249: Manfred Kage from Peter Arnold.

Chapter 13. 254T: Marg Moran. 254B: Manfred Kage from Peter Arnold. 256: Grant Heilman. 257T: Marg Moran. 257B–258: Eva Cellini. 259: Lynwood M. Chace from National Audubon Society. 260L: Douglas Baglin from National Audubon Society. 260TR: Eva Cellini. 260B: Allan Roberts. 261: Eva Cellini. 262T: Marg Moran. 262B: Lennart Nilsson. 264: Eva Cellini. 268–269: Robert Neulieb Photos. 271: Manfred Kage from Peter Arnold.

Chapter 14. 276T: Marg Moran. 279–281: Eva Cellini. 284–287: Lennart Nilsson. 290–291: New York Zoological Society Photo. 292: Reproduced with permission from the "Birth Atlas". Published by Maternity Center Association, New York.

Chapter 15. 298: Jack J. Kunz. 299–305: Eva Cellini. 307T: Fritz Goro for *Life*. 307B: Henry H. James. 308–312: Eva Cellini. 314–315: New York Zoological Society Photo. 316: Eva Cellini. 319: Jean Helmer. 321: Professor Shinobu Ishihara, courtesy Casper Krueger Drug Co.

Chapter 16. 326: The Ealing Corporation. 327: Robert Austrian from "Journal of Experimental Medicine." 328–329: Marg Moran. 330: E. R. Degginger. 331–333: Marg Moran. 333T: E. R. Degginger. 336–337: © National Geographic Society. 338: Marg Moran. 340: David Linton. *Quotation:* 1: "Molecular Structure of Nucleic Acids," by F. H. C. Crick, Dr. J. D. Watson, and Dr. M. H. F. Wilkins. *Nature, 171,* no. 4356 (April 25, 1953), p. 737.

Chapter 17. 346T: Bob Hines from the U.S. Fish and Wildlife Service. 346B: Kenneth W. Fink from National Audubon Society. 348: Hal H. Harrison from Grant Heilman. 350: E. R. Degginger. 352–353: New York Zoological Society Photo. 354: Gordon Tenney.

Chapter 18. 360L: Mike Godfrey. 360R: S. Samelius from Carl Ostman. 361: E. R. Degginger. 362TR: Grant Heilman. 362TL,BL,BR: E. R. Degginger. 364BR: Dr. H. B. D. Kettlewell, University of Oxford. 364TR: Dr. Paul C. Manglesdorf. 364MR: N.H.P.A. from Carl Ostman. 365: Carroll Weiss from Camera M.D. Studios, Inc. 366: Eva Cellini. 369: Richard Weiss from Peter Arnold. 370T: Historical Picture Service, Chicago. 370B: E. R. Degginger. 372–373: Hope Ryden. 374: Adolph E. Brotman. 375: Yale Joel for *Life*. 375BR: E. R. Degginger. 376: USDA. 377: E. R. Degginger. *Quotation:* 1: *Charles Darwin,* by Sir Gavin deBeer, p. 98. Doubleday and Co., © 1963.

Chapter 19. 382: George Roos, Courtesy of Michael Zappalorti. 384T: Eva Cellini. 384B: Robert Bowman. 385T: Douglas Faulkner. 385B: Alfred Eisenstaedt for *Life*. 386: Jean Helmer. 387: Jean Zallinger. 390–391: American Museum of Natural History. 393T: Courtesy Brookhaven National Laboratory. 393B: Aloe Scientific Company. 395: Grant Heilman.

Chapter 20. 400T: David Ellis for Silver Burdett. 400B: Grant Heilman. 401T: E. R. Degginger. 401M: Eva Cellini. 401B: W. H. Hodge from Peter Arnold. 403T: Winton Patnode from Photo Researchers. 403B: OMIKRON. 404–405: Manfred Kage from Peter Arnold. 406–407: New York Zoological Society Photo. 408T: Manfred Kage from Peter Arnold. 408M: William Smallwood. 408B: Walter Dawn, courtesy Charles Pfizer and Co. 410: R. L. Carlton from Photo Researchers. 411T: Fritz Goro for *Life*. 411B: Walter Dawn. 412T,M: Walter Dawn. 412B: Charles R. Wyttenbach. 415T: E. R. Degginger. 415B: Marg Moran. 417T: Bahamas News Bureau. 417B: Runk/Schoenberger from Grant Heilman. 419T: Robert Evans/Sea Library. 419MT: Jane Burton from Bruce Coleman. 419MB: E. R. Degginger. 419B: Grant Heilman. 420T: Z. Leszczynski. 420B: Allan Power from National Audubon Society. 422T: Allan Roberts. 422BL: Bucky and Avis Reeves from National Audubon Society. 422BR: E. R. Deggin-

ger. 423TL: Michael C. T. Smith from National Audubon Society. 423BL: Anthony Mercieca from National Audubon Society. 423TR: Norman Myers from Bruce Coleman. 423BR: Bucky Reeves from National Audubon Society.

Chapter 21. 428: Andreas Feininger for *Life*. 429: Eva Cellini. 430: San Diego Zoo. 431: Marine Studios, Marineland, Florida. 432T: Jack J. Kunz. 432B: Eva Cellini. 433L: Norman Tomalin from Bruce Coleman. 433R: Carroll Jones. 434–435: New York Zoological Society Photo. 436L: Carroll Jones. 436TR: Allan Roberts. 436BR: Matt Greene. 437: E. R. Degginger. 438: Roy J. Pence. 439: George V. Kelvin. 440T: Jack J. Kunz. 440M: Lowell Hess. 440B: Dr. K. R. Porter. 442T: E. R. Degginger. 442B: N. J. Dept. of Agriculture. 443: Eva Cellini. 444: S. J. Krasemann from Peter Arnold. 445: Frances W. Zweifel. 446: William L. Smallwood. 447: Hermann Kacher. 449: Rudolf Freund and Margaret Estey. 450T: Dr. Max Renner, Zoological Institute, University of Munich. 450B: Eva Cellini. 451L: Eva Cellini. 451B: Allan Roberts.

Chapter 22. 456T: C. G. Hampson from Annan Photo Feature. 456B: Matt Greene. 457B: Mike Godfrey. 458: Tom McHugh from Photo Researchers. 459: E. R. Degginger. 460: Dr. Howard E. Evans. 463: William D. Griffin. 464T: Jean Helmer. 464B: Nina Leen. 465: Ben Mancuso, Impact Photos, Inc. 466: Lilo Hess. 467: Photo by Baron Hugo van Lawick © National Geographic Society. 468–469: New York Zoological Society Photo. 470: Nina Leen. 471: Harald Sund. 474–475: Irven DeVore. *Quotations:* 1, 2: *The Insect World of J. Henri Fabre,* Edwin Way Teale, ed., pp. 60, 62. Dodd, Mead, & Co., © 1949.

Chapter 23. 480T: E. R. Degginger. 480B: Jean Helmer. 481: Eva Cellini. 482: Ernst G. Hofmann. 483: Jean Helmer. 484T: A. B. Klots. 484M: Caru Studios. 484B: Dr. Donald J. Obee. 485T: Mike Godfrey. 485B: Lilo Hess. 486B: Eva Cellini. 487: Ernest L. Libby. 488–489: New York Zoological Society Photo. 490T: Carl E. Ostman. 490B: C. P. Warner. 491T: Jean Helmer. 491B: Great Lakes Fishery Commission. 495–497: Mike Godfrey. 498: Jean Helmer. 499TL: U.S. National Park Service. 499TR: David Muench. 499ML: White Sands National Monument. 499MR: Fritz Goro for *Life*. 499B: Z. Leszczynski. 500T: Karales from Peter Arnold. 500B: Grant Heilman.

Chapter 24. 506: Joe Rychetnik from Photo Researchers. 507: Andreas Feininger for *Life*. 508: Mike Godfrey. 509: Eva Cellini. 510B: USDA. 511–513: Jean Helmer. 514–515: New York Zoological Society Photo. 516L: Milton J. Heiberg. 516R: Burk Uzzle from Magnum. 517: Ewing Galloway. 518: Jean Helmer. 519T: Grant Heilman. 519M: Frederick Ayer III from Photo Researchers. 521: H. LeCampion from Gamma. 522T: Karl Weidman from Carl Ostman. 522B: Tom McHugh from Photo Researchers. 523T: Tom McHugh from Photo Researchers. 523M: Anne E. Hubbard from Photo Researchers. 523B: Javier Palaus Soloer from Carl Ostman. 524: Charles Rotkin/PFI. 525: Grant Heilman. 527B: Joe Bilbao from Photo Researchers. *Quotation:* 1: *The Ra Expeditions,* by Thor Heyerdahl, tr. Patricia Crompton, pp. 336–337. George Allen & Unwin, © 1971.

Index

pharyngeal pouches, 420
pharynx, 120, 420
phenotype, 303, 307, 309, 310, 311, 312, 313, 317, 341
  population, 351
phenotypic ratio, 303, 304, 305, 312
pheromones, 441, 442, 443, 448, 473
phloem, 104ff, 185, 248ff
phosphate 49, 53, 59, 98
phosphate bonds, 47, 58
phosphate group, 48, 51, 53, 58, 143
phospholipids, 18, 19, 36–37
phosphorus, 25, 33, 43, 66, 81, 133, 175
  cycle, see biogeochemical cycle
phosphorylation, 48
  see also cellular respiration; photosynthesis
photoperiod, 184
photophosphorylation, 52–55
photopigment, 439
photoreceptors, 428, 436, 437, 446
  see also camera eye
photosynthesis, 14, 29, 34, 49, 50, 51–55, 59, 81, 124, 212, 218, 233, 234, 235, 245, 402, 403, 404, 413, 506, 508
photosynthetic units, 53
photosystems I and II, 53, 54
phototropism, 183
pH scale, 28
phycobilins, see pigment
Phycomycetes, see Fungi
phylogenetic relationships, 400
phylum, 400
phytochrome, 185
phytoplankton, 404
pia mater, see brain
pigment, 405, 410, 411
  cells, 172
pine
  bristlecone, 246–247
  reproduction in, 237
pineal, 178
pistil, 238, 239
pitch, see sound
pitcher plant, 78–79
pith, 105, 106, 249
pituitary, 169, 171–173, 174, 207, 264, 265, 289
placenta, 176, 259, 283, 288, 289, 423
placental mammals, 424
Placodermi, 421
Planaria, 197–198, 224, 437
plankton, 73
Plantae, 405, 410–415
plants, 87, 111, 401, 410–415
  cells, 9, 87–88
  digestion in, 81–82

gas exchange, 123–125
  hormonal regulation, 182–184
  land, 232, 235, 236, 410, 412
  marine, 232
  Mendel's research with, 297–306
  photoperiodism, 184–185
  photosynthesis, see photosynthesis
  polyploid, 392
  reproduction and development, 223–224, 232–250
  transport in, 104–107, 233
  vascular, see vascular plants
  waste disposal, 153
plasma, 97, 98, 103, 121, 122, 150, 152, 153, 155, 156, 316
plasmids, 349
Plasmodiophoromycota, 405
Plasmodium, 408
plasmodium, 409
plasmolysis, 88
plastids, 14, 402
platelets, 98, 104, 156
Platyhelminthes, 416–417, 456
platypus, 259
play, see behavior
pleura, 123
pleurisy, 123
pneumococcus, 326
pneumonia, 326
poison, see toxins
polar body, 263
polar compound, 54
polar covalent bond, see chemical bonds
polar molecule, 30, 36
polar nuclei, 239, 240
pollen, 237, 238, 240, 299
  scent of, 451
pollen tube, 239, 240
pollination, 238ff, 299, 303
pollution, 443, 512–523, 525, 526
Polychaeta, 418
polychlorinated biphenyls, 523, 526, 528
polypeptide, 218, 219, 334, 335, 338, 349
polyploidy, 392
polyps, 416
polysaccharide, see sugar
pons, see brain
population, 346, 381
  ecology and control, 492, 523–528
pore cells, 70
portal circuit, 102
portal vein, see veins
potassium, 32, 66, 81, 98, 154, 173, 192, 193, 411
praying mantis, 199, 268–269

predation, 491, 492
predator, 258, 277, 293, 441
pregnancy, 265, 266, 282–291, 319
  vaccine against, 176
pressure receptors, 431, 432
Priestley, J., 119
primary community, 494
primary growth, 249, 250
primates, 176, 204, 207, 424
primitive streak, 283, 286
Proboscidea, 424
procaryotic cells, 8, 11, 340, 401, 402
progesterone, 176, 264ff, 293
proglottids, 417
progressionism, 366
prophase, 222, 223, 227–228
prostaglandins, 178
prostate gland, 261, 272
protein, 18, 19, 20, 25, 31, 40–43, 58, 65ff, 87, 143, 155–157, 161–162
  digestion, 75, 76
  in plants, 81, 242
  structure, 41–42
  synthesis, 334–335
proteinoids, 219
prothallus, 235, 237
prothrombin, 155, 156
Protista, 401, 402, 403–408
proton, see atom
protoplasm, 8, 69
protostomes, 420
protozoa, 69, 153, 161, 223, 403, 405
pseudocoelom, 417, 418
pseudopods, 69, 71, 405
Psilophyta, 413
Pterophyta, 413
Pteropsida, 413
puberty, 262
pubic joint, 134
pulmonary circulation, 102
pulmonary edema, 120
Punnett square, 302, 309, 347
pupa, 179, 182, 419
pupil, see eye
pus, 161, 271
pyloric sphincter, 76
Pyrrophyta, 404–405
pyruvic acid, 59, 61, 62

R
R group, 40, 41
rabbits, 147, 212, 254–255, 312, 424
races, 393
radial symmetry, 197, 416, 420
radiation, 132, 217, 286, 288, 293

U

ulna, 134
umbilical cord, 282, 283, 289
unconsciousness, 123, 139, 195
unicellular organisms, 3, 5, 8, 11, 12, 14, 15
   see also specific organisms and processes
uniformitarianism, 366, 368
uracil, 334
urea, 98, 153
ureter, 154
urethra, 261
Urey, H., 217
uric acid, 98, 153
urination, 271
urine, 153, 154, 177, 178, 261, 263, 265, 287
Urochordata, 420
uterine lining, see endometrium
uterus, 137, 173, 176, 260, 262, 263, 265, 267, 282, 283, 286, 288, 289, 424

V

vacuoles, 15, 18, 69, 71, 87
vagina, 262, 263, 266, 267, 271, 289
valence, 27, 28
valine, see amino acids
van Lawick-Goodall, J., 445
vanadium, 66
variation, population, 345–355, 359, 387
varieties, see breeds
vas deferens, 261, 270
vascular plants, 104, 123–125, 233, 234, 411, 413
vascular rays, 106
vascular tissue, plant, see phloem; xylem
vasectomy, see sterilization
vasopressin, 172
vegetal hemisphere, 277, 282
veins, 97, 99, 102, 103, 104, 133, 155
vena cava, 99
venereal disease, 162, 267, 270–272
ventral blood vessels, 93
ventral root, see nerves, spinal
ventricles, 99, 100
venules, 102
vertebrae, 202
Vertebrata, 421, 438
vertebrates, 66, 93, 121, 178, 292, 420, 432, 437, 439
   circulatory systems, 93, 96–104
   muscles, 136–145
   nervous system, 194, 195, 199–207
   reproduction, 254, 256–258
   skeleton, 131–135
vesicles, 12
vessel cells, 104, 106
vibrations, see sound
Virchow's principle, 5
virus, 161, 162, 342, 401, 402
visceral mass, 418
visceral smooth muscle, see smooth muscle
visual messages, 446–451
visual receptors, see photoreceptors
vitamin A, 75
vitamin B, see B vitamins
vitamin C, 66, 67, 75
vitamin D, 75
vitamin E, 75
vitamin K, 157, 487
vitamins, 37, 65, 66–67, 75, 155, 157, 167, 168
vitreous humor, 438
viviparous animals, 259
vocal chords, 120
Volvox, 410
Von Frisch, C. 449–450
von Helmont, J. B., 213
von Siebold, K., 3
vulva, 263, 286

W

Wallace, A. R., 376
wasp, 148, 255, 419
Wasserman test, 271
water, 25, 65, 68, 81, 217, 452
   in cellular respiration, see cellular respiration
   cycle, see biogeochemical cycles
   diffusion and osmosis, 86–89
   in digestion, 65, 68
   in gas exchange, 112, 114–118, 121
   in homeostasis, 150–153
   in photosynthesis, see photosynthesis
   in plant reproduction, 234, 235, 244
   plant transport of, 104–105, 107, 124
   structure, 29–31
   in transport, 81, 90
water vapor, 216, 217, 506, 508
Watson, J., 329, 339
waxes, 31, 37
weed killer, 184
Weinberg, W., 347
Weiner, A. S., 318
whale, 73, 424, 446
   sperm, 390–391
white blood cells, see leucocytes
Whittaker, R. H., 402
windpipe, see trachea
withdrawal, see contraception
Wolff, C. F., 2
wolves, 394, 446, 473
wood, 105–106, 250

XYZ

X chromosome, 308, 309, 320
X-linked gene, see sex-linked gene
X-ray, 21, 325
xerophytes, 415
xylem, 104ff, 153, 248ff
Y chromosome, 308, 320
yeast, 59, 62, 408
yolk, 259, 276, 277
zinc, 66
zirconium, 120
Zoomastigina, 405
zygote, 225, 231, 234, 235, 236, 237, 240, 241, 243, 254, 256, 262, 275, 276, 277, 282, 308, 313, 382, 392